Handbook of Research on Public Information Technology

Volume II

G. David Garson
North Carolina State University, USA

Mehdi Khosrow-Pour
Information Resources Management Association, USA

INFORMATION SCIENCE REFERENCE
Hershey · New York

Acquisitions Editor:	Kristin Klinger
Development Editor:	Kristin Roth
Senior Managing Editor:	Jennifer Neidig
Managing Editor:	Sara Reed
Copy Editor:	Katie Smalley, Shanelle Ramelb
Typesetter:	Michael Brehm, Larissa Vinci
Cover Design:	Lisa Tosheff
Printed at:	Yurchak Printing Inc.

Published in the United States of America by
Information Science Reference (an imprint of IGI Global)
701 E. Chocolate Avenue, Suite 200
Hershey PA 17033
Tel: 717-533-8845
Fax: 717-533-8661
E-mail: cust@igi-global.com
Web site: http://www.igi-global.com

and in the United Kingdom by
Information Science Reference (an imprint of IGI Global)
3 Henrietta Street
Covent Garden
London WC2E 8LU
Tel: 44 20 7240 0856
Fax: 44 20 7379 0609
Web site: http://www.eurospanonline.com

Library of Congress Cataloging-in-Publication Data

Handbook of research on public information technology / David G. Garson and Mehdi Khosrow-Pour, editor.

p. cm.

Summary: "This book compiles estimable research on the global trend toward the rapidly increasing use of information technology in the public sector, discussing such issues as e-government and e-commerce; project management and information technology evaluation; system design and data processing; security and protection; and privacy, access, and ethics of public information technology"--Provided by publisher.

ISBN-13: 978-1-59904-857-4 (hbk.)

ISBN-13: 978-1-59904-858-1 (e-book)

1. Internet in public administration. I. Garson, David G. II. Khosrowpour, Mehdi, 1951-

JF1525.A8H363 2008

352.3'802854678--dc22

British Cataloguing in Publication Data
A Cataloguing in Publication record for this book is available from the British Library.

All work contributed to this book set is original material. The views expressed in this book are those of the authors, but not necessarily of the publisher.

If a library purchased a print copy of this publication, please go to http://www.igi-global.com/reference/assets/IGR-eAccess-agreement.pdf for information on activating the library's complimentary electronic access to this publication.

Editorial Advisory Board

Table of Contents

Volume II

Section IV
System Design and Data Processing

Section VI
Selected Readings

Detailed Table of Contents

There exists a growing controversy over whether government should be in the business of providing wireless broadband Internet. Public sector entities, particularly counties and cities, are developing the physical and intellectual infrastructure designed to provide wireless broadband Internet to their residents. Opponents of government entry into the wireless broadband market argue that existing private broadband vendors are fully capable of providing wireless Internet in an efficient manner. Supporters argue that government is uniquely capable of building and supporting, at least initially, wireless broadband at a lower cost and in a more pluralistic and efficient manner than private vendors have done thus far.

In this chapter, the authors use the term "e-participation" initiatives to refer to government's use of ICT to engage citizens in democratic processes. The term "e-participation" is chosen because it is sufficiently general to encompass all such efforts by governments. Instances of e-participation initiatives can be found globally, such as Denmark's Nordpol.dk, the United States's Regulations.gov, and Singapore's Government Consultation Portal. The past decade has witnessed an increasing trend of information and communication technologies (ICT) exploitation by governments around the world to enhance citizen participation. This is reflected in the emergence of a plethora of terms associated with the phenomenon, such as e-consultation or online consultation, online rule-making, online deliberation online public engagement, and e-participation.

This chapter focuses on applications in blogging. A blog can be simply defined in the following manner: "A blog is an easy-to-use content management tool. When you 'blog,' you are instantly adding new content to your site via a Web interface. No technical or programming skills are necessary" (Weil, 2004, n.p.). In a nutshell, a blog is a "do-it-yourself" Web site. Gone are the days (of say 2003) when one would have to be knowledgeable in html or xml programming or make use of complex, and often expensive, Web creation software to create or update a Web site. With a blog, your Web site can be constantly added to and updated, without having to do anything more than typing (or cutting and pasting) into a text box. Through posting links, you can link your blog to any other site on the Web. You can even add audio and visual material to your blog site by uploading them, much as you would add an attachment to an e-mail. Others who find your site of interest can use RSS (really simple syndication) or sign-up for e-mail alerts to be notified when you post or add material to your blog.

This chapter looks at a particular focus of e-government, that of support for business in general and SMEs (small and medium-sized enterprises) in particular. While this is only one segment of PIT (public

as international best practices and experiences. Moreover, it will demonstrate the arising opportunities and the key challenges.

World-wide governments are investing in initiatives to open access to information, resources, communication and services via channels typically used for electronic commerce. Government agencies are usually the leaders in communication technology commonly developed primarily for military use and later adopted by the general public. Since its inception, the Internet has gained widespread usage, prompting governments to provide online services to the public. The broad category for this type of information and services provision is called "e-government;" it is the general description of a way to provide better access to government information and services. This chapter presents New Zealand's e-government strategy in which the Internet will be used to improve the quality of the services and provide greater opportunities to participate in the democratic process for the citizens.

This chapter explores the use of e-census technologies in New Zealand. In New Zealand, the census is held every five years. A snapshot is taken on the chosen day and from that the number of people and housing units (houses, flats, apartments) are counted. Everyone in the country on that day is asked to fill in census forms. For the 2006 census an option was introduced to complete the forms on the Internet. Other initiatives included sending text messages about this process, amongst other things to the enumerators (collectors) whose job it is to collate the information in the field. The use of information technology, primarily with the Internet, offers the opportunity to distribute the information and deliver services on a very large scale.

This chapter examines the objectives and challenges of the Italian plan of e-government, within which the Italian job workfair is conceived. Public administrations, during the last few years, activated modernizations in public service delivery. In particular, this arrangement relates to the service digitalization and automation, thanks to the massive inclusion of information and communication technologies in public offices. This paved the way for internal and external organizational and technological changes, in that a new approach is required to leverage the new technologies. Moreover, the Internet technologies began to play an important role in public services delivery, and many transactions are Web-based nowadays. Eventually, several governments in Europe, and others all over the world, started their own plans of e-government with the goal of increasing the amount and the quality of the service offered via the Internet to their customers (citizens, enterprises, profit and no-profit organizations).

M-commerce possesses two distinctive characteristics that distinguish it from traditional e-commerce: the mobile setting and the small form factor of mobile devices. Of these, the size of a mobile device will remain largely unchanged due to the tradeoff between size and portability. Small screen size and limited input capabilities pose a great challenge for developers to conceptualize user interfaces that have good usability while working within the size constraints of the device. In response to the limited screen size of mobile devices, there has been unspoken consensus that certain tools must be made available to aid users in coping with the relatively large volume of information. Recommender systems have been proposed to narrow down choices before presenting them to the user (Feldman, 2000). The authors propose a product catalogue where browsing is directed by an integrated recommender system.

In time, due to the increase of human-computer interaction, trust has become one of the most challenging topics in computer science. Today, trust based e-commerce decisions are becoming more valuable as Internet services are increasingly being used in business to consumer e-commerce applications. E-commerce provides a new way of shopping for the customers by offering more choices and transforming economic activity into a digital media. It also provides an opportunity for the businesses to extend their sales to a larger community. However, the success of getting higher profits and improved services are based on better communication. As in the real world, critical understanding of users' behavior in cyberspace cannot be achieved without the analysis of the factors affecting the purchase decisions (Limayem, Khalifa, & Frini, 2000). Having lots of options in an environment that is missing face-to-face interaction enforce users to make trust-aware decisions to better protect their privacy and satisfy their expectations such as quality of services.

This chapter examines how to use partial least squares (PLS) and argues that this could help to incorporate more realistic assumptions and better measurements into digital government research. It does it through a commented example of a digital government research study (Gil-García, 2005b). It is important to clarify that the intention is not to suggest that every research project should use PLS, but to encourage scholars and practitioners to seriously consider this technique as an alternative when designing and carrying out their research. PLS is a structural equation modeling (SEM) technique similar to covariance-based SEM as implemented in LISREL, EQS, or AMOS. Therefore, PLS can simultaneously test the measurement model (relationships between indicators and their corresponding constructs) and the structural model (relationships between constructs).

Section II
Privacy, Access, Ethics, and Theory

The purpose of this chapter is to explain how digital convergence is affecting the public sector and the need for a cyber security policy that includes the active involvement of both the public and private sectors. Digital convergence constitutes the full realization of the information age and provides the foundation to link cultural, personal, business, governmental, and economic affairs into a rapidly expanding global digital world called cyberspace. However, this linking of people around the globe is challenging the government to actively work with private industry to ensure its critical infrastructures and associated information is adequately protected.

This chapter examines how public health information technology (IT) can aid public health preparedness in terms of bioterrorism preparedness and associated emergency response. Most analyses of possible future bioterrorism events predict they may be similar to the anthrax events of 2001, specifically a limited population of individuals may experience morbidity or mortality, but the concern, panic, and worry stirred up by the threat will catch the attention of the entire nation. If public health IT is to help with bioterrorism preparedness, it needs to not only address mitigation of civilian illnesses and deaths, but also help to manage individual and societal fears springing from the real or threatened occurrence of such an event.

All branches of federal government are required to migrate their business practices to a paperless operation. Privacy and information security (InfoSec) are critical for protection of information shared over networks internally between the US Government agencies and externally with non-federal organizations (businesses; state, local, and foreign governments; academia; etc.) or individuals. This chapter will examine public key infrastructure (PKI), which is the simplest, most widely used architecture for secure data exchange over not-secure networks. It integrates computer hardware and software, cryptography, information and network security, policies and procedures to facilitate trust in distributed electronic transactions and mitigate the associated risks.

We are in the midst of what may become one of the true technological transformations of our time. RFID (radio frequency identification) is by no means new a "new" technology. This chapter examines several dimensions of RFID, which is fundamentally based on the study of electromagnetic waves and radio, pioneered in the nineteenth century work of Faraday, Maxwell, and Marconi. The idea of using radio frequencies to reflect waves from objects dates back as far as 1886 to experiments conducted by Hertz. Radar was invented in 1922, and its practical applications date back to World War II, when the British used the IFF (identify friend or foe) system to identify enemy aircraft (Landt, 2001). Stockman (1948) laid-out the basic concepts for RFID. However, it would take decades of development before RFID technology would become a reality. Since 2000, significant improvements in functionality, decreases in both size and costs, and agreements on communication standards have combined to make RFID technology viable for commercial and governmental purposes. Today, RFID is positioned as an alternative way to identify objects to the ubiquitous bar code.

There has been a lot of research done on the area of intelligent agents. Unfortunately, there is no standardization in the various proposals, resulting in vastly different agent systems. Efforts are made to standardize some aspects of agent systems so that different systems can interoperate with each other. This chapter will examine some of the leading standards in agent representation including KQML and agent TCL, their security vulnerabilities and the application of safety protocols. This chapter will examine these standards in the context of e-commerce and m-commerce and efforts to protect transactions through SAFE (secure roaming agent for e-commerce) and offer a look at interoperability in roaming systems.

This chapter discusses security and integrity issues facing agent technology. Various frameworks are discussed including SAFER, or secure agent fabrication, evolution and roaming, which is a mobile agent framework that is specially designed for the purpose of electronic commerce (Guan & Hua, 2003, Guan et al., 2004; Zhu et al., 2000). By building strong and efficient security mechanisms, SAFER aims to provide a trustworthy framework for mobile agents to assist users in conducting mobile or electronic commerce transactions. Agent integrity is another area crucial to the success of agent technology (Wang et al., 2002). Despite the various attempts in the literature, there is no satisfactory solution to the problem of data integrity so far. Some of the common weaknesses of the current schemes are vulnerabilities to revisit attack when an agent visits two or more collaborating malicious hosts during one roaming session and illegal modification (deletion/insertion) of agent data. Agent monitoring protocol (AMP) (Chionh et al., 2001) is examined, which is an earlier proposal under SAFER to address agent data integrity, does address some of the weaknesses in the current literature.

Volume II

This chapter examines the several important contributions and improvements data mining has introduced to the field of IDS (intrusion detection system) technology. Over the past few years, the Internet has

this chapter, the author, recognizing the importance of e-government and KM to devolve into the public administration sector, continues his previous research related to the application of KM in e-government (Metaxiotis & Psarras, 2005), discusses key issues and presents a framework for the application of KM in e-government as a basis for future research.

This chapter examines the three layers of Web applications: conceptual, presentation, and navigation; and its two perspectives: designer and viewer. Software evolution is "the dynamic behavior of programming systems as they are maintained and enhanced over their life times" (Belady & Lehman, 1976). Web application evolution is of increasing importance as more Web systems are in production. Many companies use the Web to communicate with the external world as well as within their organizations and to carry out their business processes more effectively. Web technologies have been adopted by organizations in the public sector. Many state agencies provide their services via the Web. This study investigates the management of e-government applications at a U.S. state technology agency (STA).

A review of the development of information systems can help in understanding the potential significance of Web services and service oriented architecture (SOA) in the public sector. SOA involves the convergent design of information systems and organizational workflows at the level of services. The purpose of this chapter is to suggest a strategy for mapping the design of service oriented architectures on to the complex patterns of governance including combinations of federalism, regionalism and outsourcing of functions from government agencies to nonprofit organizations. This involves the modeling of workflows and the identification of opportunities for the sharing of services among agencies and nonprofits.

The goal of the research presented in this chapter is to analyze the strategic determinants influencing the decision-making for using and implementing shared services. The structure of this chapter is as follows. In the following section we discuss the historical and theoretical background of shared services. In the section thereafter we provide an overview of the strategic determinants influencing the shared services decision. Next, both future trends and future research directions are presented and finally, in section six, conclusions are drawn.

This chapter examines the application of data mining within public organizations. In general, data mining is a data analytical technique that assists businesses in learning and understanding their customers so that decisions and strategies can be implemented most accurately and effectively to maximize profitability. Data mining is not general data analysis, but a comprehensive technique that requires analytical skills, information construction, and professional knowledge. Businesses are now facing global competition, and are being forced to deal with an enormous amount of data. The vast amounts of data and the increasing technological ability to store it also facilitated data mining. In order to gain a certain level of competitive advantage, a data analytical technology called data mining is now commonly adopted among businesses. Organizations use data mining as a tool to forecast customer behavior, reduce fraud and waste, and assist in medical research.

This chapter examines data clustering, a discovery process that partitions a data set into groups (clusters) such that data points within the same group have high similarity while being very dissimilar to points in other groups (Han, 2001). The ultimate goal of data clustering is to discover "natural" groupings in a set of patterns, points, or objects, without prior knowledge of any class labels. In fact, in the machine learning literature, data clustering is typically regarded as a form of unsupervised learning as opposed to supervised learning. In unsupervised learning or clustering, there is no training function as in the supervised learning. There are many applications for data clustering including, but not limited to, pattern recognition, data analysis, data compression, image processing, understanding genomic data, and market-basket research.

This chapter reviews the main concepts at the basis of multidimensional (data warehouse) modeling and navigation. We also illustrate some peculiarities of statistical data that make the implementation of a statistical data warehouse that is a statistical dissemination system enabling the user to perform a multidimensional navigation, a challenging issue in many aspects. Finally, we analyze the main characteristics of some of the most important systems for the dissemination of statistical data on the Web, distinguishing two main approaches, the former based on a free navigation on specific subcubes, the latter on a constrained navigation on a single data cube.

Massive quantities of information continue accumulating at about 1.5 billion gigabytes per year in numerous repositories held at news agencies, libraries, corporate intranets, PCs, and the Web. A large portion of all available information exists in the form of texts. Researchers, analysts, editors, venture capitalists, lawyers, help desk specialists, and even students are faced by text analysis challenges. This chapter explores text mining tools which aim at discovering knowledge from textual databases by isolating key bits of information from large amounts of text, identifying relationships among documents. Text mining technology is used for plagiarism and authorship attribution, text summarization and retrieval,

Section V
Project Management and IT Evaluation

Information technology affects organization and society itself, as it redefines work content, reorganizes leadership styles and cultures, reshuffles power hierarchies and spawns a series of both man-designed and spontaneous adaptations. Information technology oftentimes necessitates a new division of labor that creates policy problems and loss of accountability. Organizational leadership, especially in the public sector, urgently requires a theoretical as well as a practical revaluation to cope with the structural and functional changes within work and administrative organizations. This chapter seeks to elucidate three leadership models in the context of IT-induced changes in organizational forms and processes, networked leadership, organic leadership, and gatekeeper leadership models.

This chapter examines the realm of human factors design for public information technology in the rapidly evolving post-modern "knowledge age" of the 21st century, with special focus on how new research and development into human cognition, perception and performance capabilities is changing the design function for IT systems and products. Many "one size fits all" IT designs are neither adaptive nor adaptable—promulgating a top-down technological imperialism penetrating every aspect of their use. The communication, collaboration, and interaction infrastructure of IT organizations thus remains acutely challenged with enduring problems of usability, learnability, accessibility, and adaptability. As the function and form of products undergoes increasingly rigorous scrutiny, one important design goal is emerging as a paramount priority: improving the usability of products, tools and systems for all stakeholders across the enterprise. It is therefore important to briefly describe emerging human factor design knowledge and practices applicable to organizations that invent, incubate, innovate, prototype, and drive the creation and application of public IT. The findings here suggest the most effective strategies to manage and augment user-centered design endeavors across a wide array of public IT products and organizations.

This chapter examines the outsourcing of services by governments as the result of public sector reforms. Outsourcing has been argued to lead to cost savings; "improved discipline"; better services; access to scarce skills; and the capacity for managers to focus more time on the "core business" of their organizations (Domberger, 1998). Government outsourcing initiatives have encompassed a range of services, but given the large sums of money invested in IT assets, outsourcing of IT services (IT outsourcing, or ITO) has been a major initiative for many agencies. Case studies have reported ITO successes and failures (e.g., Currie & Willcocks, 1998; Rouse & Corbitt, 2003a; Willcocks & Kern, 1998; Willcocks & Lacity,

2001; Willcocks & Currie, 1997), but much of the evidence presented to public sector decision makers to justify this reform is anecdotal and unsystematic, and when investigated in depth does not necessarily support widespread conclusions.

The purpose of this chapter is to undertake a critical examination of the emergence of e-health in the Canadian province of Ontario. More than solely a technological challenge, the emergence and pursuit of e-health denote a complex governance transformation both within the province's public sector and in terms of public-private partnering. The Ontario challenge here is complicated by the absence of formal regional mechanisms devoted to health care, a deficiency that has precipitated the creation of local health integration networks to foster e-health strategies on a sub-provincial basis, as well as ongoing difficulties in managing public information technologies. With respect to public-private partnering, a greater regionalization of decision-making and spending authorities, within transparent and locally accountable governance forums, could provide incentives for the private sector to work more directly sub-provincially, enjoying greater degrees of freedom for collaboration via more manageable contracting arrangements.

This chapter sheds light on the needed policy guidelines and standards for safeguarding an agency's information resources. The evolving nature of information security threats such as cyber crime, as well as the need to ensure confidentiality and privacy of citizen information and to protect critical infrastructure call for effective information security management in the public sector. E-government applications have made it easier for citizens to conduct business online with government agencies, although their trust in the ability of governments to keep that information private is low. Considering the amount of citizen information held by governments at all levels, and the steps needed to address potential homeland security and information technology (IT)-related threats to critical infrastructure, the need for effective means of safeguarding public agency data has become an issue of paramount importance. In addition, the need to ensure integrity and availability of public information resource is crucial to many government operations.

The intent of this chapter is to provide an overview of different approaches to Web site evaluation in order to suggest further application and development of evaluation instruments. In recent times, the popularity of the Internet has led to e-government practices being widely recognized as an important option for service to the general public. In response, various tiers of government from national to local level have sought opportunities to engage the public through Web sites. Many governments now provide some level of access to government through Web interfaces, for example through access to resources such as publications and government data. In some cases there are services provided that may be executed online. For example users may provide personal information for licensing or to undertake payments. There continues to be a diversity of implementation quality and levels for such services.

of applications, how may we assess, categorize, classify, compare, and discuss the e-government efforts of various government administrations? In answering this question the authors propose a generic e-government framework that will allow for the identification of e-government strategic agendas and key application initiatives that transcend country specific requirements. In developing the framework a number of requirements are first outlined. The framework is proposed and described. It is then illustrated using brief case studies from three countries. Findings and limitations are discussed.

Originally published in the International Journal of Electronic Government Research, Vol. 1, No. 2, this article describes a Web-based query system for semantically heterogeneous government-produced data. Geospatial Web-based information systems and portals are currently being developed by various levels of government along with the GIS community. Typically, these sites provide data discovery and download capabilities but do not include the ability to pose DBMS type queries. The authors extend work in schema integration by focusing on resolving semantics at the value level in addition to the schema or attribute level. They illustrate their method using land use data, but the method can be used to query across other heterogeneous sets of values. Their work starts from an XML Web-based DBMS and adds functionality to accommodate heterogeneous data between jurisdictions. Their ontology and query rewrite systems use mappings to enable querying across distributed heterogeneous data.

Originally published in the *International Journal of Electronic Government Research, Vol. 1, No. 1,* this article evaluates the current practice of digital government in large municipalities worldwide. The study assesses 84 cities from around the world using a five-stage e-government framework. The authors' research and methodology goes beyond previous research by utilizing 92 measures that were translated into the native language of each city, and the assessment of each municipal Web site was conducted by a native speaker of the municipality's language between June and October of 2003. They review relevant e-government literature for evaluating Web sites in the United States and internationally, discuss our sample selection, methodology, theoretical framework, findings, and recommendations. Their results indicate that Seoul, Hong Kong, Singapore, New York, and Shanghai are the top five large cities in the providing digital government opportunities to citizens online. In addition, the authors' research suggests a difference in the digital government capabilities between the 30 developed nations belonging to the Organization for Economic Co-operation and Development (OECD) and lesser-developed (non-OECD) nations.

Originally published in the Journal of Cases on Information Technology, Vol. 7, No. 1, this case describes issues in IT adoption at two large public sector organizations in India. Along with illustrating the significance of top management drive and end-user buy in, it particularly highlights the role of middle management in managing the IT adoption process at different levels in these large organizations.

Foreword

The breadth and speed of information technology in the public sector is breathtaking. Every day new software and hardware technologies are developed. Each of these new technologies has significant consequences for society and governments. For example, as online databases grow in their numbers, size, and accessibility over the Internet, the need to provide for robust security becomes more important. Likewise, new ethical questions and dilemmas arise as a result of these developments such as what balance should exist between rights of access and privacy. Different governments treat this balance in different ways.

Thus, there is a close interconnection between technical and social developments in information technology. The Internet, especially with respect to governmental e-commerce, depends on the development of trust between citizens and governments. Without that trust, participation in governmental e-commerce would be low and its impact muted. Similarly, e-government technologies are aimed at providing governments with increased capacity for more effective service but this increased effectiveness can only be achieved if organizations undertake changes in their processes and these changes also depend upon the actions of public managers, not just the technology. Thus, there is a need to keep up on research concerning technical, social, and managerial impacts of technologies.

All governmental organizations have been affected by these new technologies, ranging from small local governments to the largest nation-states. To what extent are the transformations due to technological change similar across organizations that differ in size and culture? These are questions that researchers are beginning to address.

In short, the sheer size and speed of change in public information technology is so broad and complex that it is extremely difficult even for those who have specialized in this area to keep abreast of these developments. There is a need for works that bring together these diverse strands of research on digital government. This volume provides a service to researchers in the field. It covers a broad range of research including hardware, software, social, managerial, ethical, and political issues of public information technology. Its coverage is international in scope, including the United States, Europe, and emerging countries. The breadth of coverage ensures that the book contains material relevant to a wide variety of researchers. The diversity of research is striking. For example, it includes chapters on radio frequency identification technology, service-oriented architecture, the bridging of the digital divide in Africa, and blogging. To summarize, this book will provide readers with an excellent perspective concerning the state of research on digital government.

Bruce Rocheleau
Northern Illinois University, USA

Bruce Rocheleau is a professor of political science in the Department of Public Administration at Northern Illinois University in DeKalb, Illinois. In the area of information management in the public sector, he is currently pursuing empirical research concerning the use of computers and related information technologies in the public sector. His research includes the study of information management, geographic information systems, impacts of networks, and organizational problems involved in sharing information and resources. In the area of policy analysis and evaluation, his research includes the study of welfare, mental health, and aging policies. His research has included studies of the implementation and impact of programs in these areas. He is the author of numerous publications about governmental information management. He recently published the book Public Management Information Systems *(Idea Group Inc., 2006) and edited the book* Case Studies in Digital Government *(IGI Global, 2007).*

Preface

This volume brings together a wide range of research on the past, present, and future of the international trend toward greater and greater use of information technology in the public sector. Rather than survey the content of these research contributions, which are adequately described in their respective abstracts, it seems better to devote this preface to considering the broad context of public sector information systems. Toward that end, what follows discusses three over-arching questions which arise time and again in this literature: (1) How and whether the vast international investments in e-government now occurring are justified in terms of the economic development and related advances for which e-government is purportedly a critical part of the infrastructure; (2) How and whether information technology will be a force for centralizing government, for decentralization, or for some synergistic new combination of trends affecting the powers that be; and (3) How and whether the unprecedented levels of participation potentially enabled by the Internet age will translate into political participation and social capital, energizing social development on a global scale.

E-GOVERNMENT AS INVESTMENT IN ECONOMIC DEVELOPMENT

Investment in information technology in the private sector and in e-government in the public sector is often seen as the path to economic expansion. From promotion of federal e-government by the National Performance Review in the 1990s to promote community-wide area networks at the local level in the 2000s, the e-government business model has been promoted as a critical economic development policy in the United States.

The argument that economic development would be promoted has led a number of communities to find ways to establish wide-area networks for their downtowns or even for their entire jurisdictions, sometimes free for citizens. Cities with WiFi initiatives in 2006 included: Anaheim, CA; Arlington, VA; Minneapolis, MN; Pasadena, CA; Philadelphia; Portland, OR; San Francisco; and Tempe, AZ. This was just one aspect of the worldwide movement toward "smart communities," which integrate information technology throughout civic infrastructure.

The same economic development logic has been promoted on a state basis also. In December 2006, Virginia Governor Timothy M. Kaine announced he would submit a $1.6 million budget amendment to extend broadband capacity on the state's eastern shore, additional to the $1.4 million already appropriated. Kaine said, "Providing access to reliable, high speed broadband is an essential public investment, attracting high tech industries and strengthening economic development."

In this context it is something of a contrast to note that in the first five years of existence of the Bush administration's e-government agenda, Congress funded only $13 million of the original $100 million goal. Over the same period, Congress became increasingly skeptical of the value of e-government fund

This volume brings together a wide range of research on the past, present, and future of the international trend toward greater and greater use of information technology in the public sector. Rather than survey the content of these research contributions, which are adequately described in their respective abstracts, it seems better to devote this preface to considering the broad context of public sector information systems. Toward that end, what follows discusses three over-arching questions which arise time and again in this literature: (1) How and whether the vast international investments in e-government now occurring are justified in terms of the economic development and related advances for which e-government is purportedly a critical part of the infrastructure; (2) How and whether information technology will be a force for centralizing government, for decentralization, or for some synergistic new combination of trends affecting the powers that be; and (3) How and whether the unprecedented levels of participation potentially enabled by the Internet age will translate into political participation and social capital, energizing social development on a global scale.

E-GOVERNMENT AS INVESTMENT IN ECONOMIC DEVELOPMENT

Investment in information technology in the private sector and in e-government in the public sector is often seen as the path to economic expansion. From promotion of federal e-government by the National Performance Review in the 1990s to promote community-wide area networks at the local level in the 2000s, the e-government business model has been promoted as a critical economic development policy in the United States.

The argument that economic development would be promoted has led a number of communities to find ways to establish wide-area networks for their downtowns or even for their entire jurisdictions, sometimes free for citizens. Cities with WiFi initiatives in 2006 included: Anaheim, CA; Arlington, VA; Minneapolis, MN; Pasadena, CA; Philadelphia; Portland, OR; San Francisco; and Tempe, AZ. This was just one aspect of the worldwide movement toward "smart communities," which integrate information technology throughout civic infrastructure.

The same economic development logic has been promoted on a state basis also. In December 2006, Virginia Governor Timothy M. Kaine announced he would submit a $1.6 million budget amendment to extend broadband capacity on the state's eastern shore, additional to the $1.4 million already appropriated. Kaine said, "Providing access to reliable, high speed broadband is an essential public investment, attracting high tech industries and strengthening economic development."

In this context it is something of a contrast to note that in the first five years of existence of the Bush administration's e-government agenda, Congress funded only $13 million of the original $100 million goal. Over the same period, Congress became increasingly skeptical of the value of e-government funding. The Congressional appropriations committees instituted some of the most restrictive language to date in their FY 2007 appropriations. As a result, almost all of the 25 showcase "Quicksilver" e-government initiatives announced by the Bush administration in 2001 have been delayed or affected by the low level of budgeting, forcing the devotion of the FY 2008 budget not to new initiatives but to trying to finish ones started long ago.

While the Office of Management and Budget (OMB) looks at the problem as one of educating ignorant members of Congress to get them "on board," Congress tends to see the problem as one of OMB's seeming inability to document the value of e-government investments. The American e-government funding model of pass-the-hat agency self-funding combined with user fees is rationalized as one which creates federal departmental "ownership" of e-goverment projects, but while few if any departments speak against the OMB/Bush administration strategy, it is clearly a strategy which has not forged the sort of strong political alliances among stakeholders which underpin Congressional funding of other programs which get higher priority.

Congress has never fully bought into the e-government program and support for it is weak on the hill. In the FY 2006, appropriations bill for transportation, treasury, housing and urban development, judiciary and other related agencies, Congress required that the OMB justify e-government expenditures and request renewal funds. As a result, in January 2006, the Office of Management and Budget submitted the mandated report to Congress, justifying the cost of the 25 e-government and five line of business consolidation projects—all of which would cost over $192 million in FY 2006—squeezed from existing agency budgets. In essence, in lean budgetary times, the OMB was forcing agencies to spend on non-priority items which Congress had not specifically appropriated money for, such as forcing the National Park Service to spend $1.5 million on e-government when the NPS was scrimping for basic park operations. OMB's contrary view was that its e-government guidance was simply helping agencies be efficient in getting the biggest bang for the buck.

All of this is to suggest one thing: public investment in information technology is controversial. It is at once a great hope, perhaps the great hope, for economic and governmental transformation, and it is an endeavor where cost over-runs, delayed implementation, and outright failure are commonplace. If the nature of public information systems was better understood, success would be more likely and political support more forthcoming. The purpose of this handbook of research on the nature of public information systems seeks to make a small contribution to that much-needed understanding.

INFORMATION TECHNOLOGY, CENTRALIZATION, AND DECENTRALIZATION

While advocates of the virtual state have often cited the advantages of networks over hierarchy in flexibly adapting to change, assembling and re-assembling to meet one or another ad hoc challenge, studies of actual organizational response to emergencies, such as the World Trade Tower bombing of 2001, strongly suggest that network effectiveness depends on pre-existing social capital and trust expressed through pre-existing strong networks. Organizational hierarchies play a critical role both in building an organizational culture oriented toward use of networks for coordinated response, and in building the networks themselves prior to and in the absence of emergency demands. That is, the hierarchy vs. networks dichotomy is false. Rather, the two exist in synergy in effective organizations.

Perhaps the leading example of centralization in recent years has been the push of the OMB to replace departmental IT systems with enterprise-wide lines of business systems in financial management, human resource management, and many other areas. For FY 2008, the OMB instructed departments that their budget proposals would have to demonstrate implementation of the administration's lines of business consolidation initiative. At the state level, consolidation and centralization is approached with almost religious zeal. Major recent IT consolidation efforts have occurred in California, Michigan, and New York, for example.

Some IT analysts and leaders have argued that centralization trends amount to over-centralization and urge a pendulum swing in the opposite direction. A chief executive of the Gartner Group, a leading IT consulting firm, for instance, recently argued that CIOs needed to relinquish some control and responsibilities to end users, that the centralized concentration of IT funding ironically leaves little for the original goal of business transformation or for needed investment in human aspects of IT. With re-centralization, end users again face the frustration of dealing with rigid central IT departments and turn to alternatives such as new consumer Internet, communications, and database technologies outside CIO control.

An interesting illustration occurred when the U.S. military implemented MCS2 (electronically networked maneuver control systems) in the Gulf War. An expected result was centralization of information in the hands of top-ranking officers. What was less expected was an increase in micromanagement, with many commanders unwilling to use new information systems to unleash the abilities of lower-level staff to make decisions. The desire not to relinquish decision-making power made available by centralization arising from information systems implementation, reinforced and enhanced existing bureaucratic structures in spite of the vision of some that these systems would allow flexible, informed, decentralized decision-making in the field.

Control systems can be programmed to reflect the political priorities of those in power. As systems design is not normally covered in the press, this comes to light only occasionally, but the practice is routine. A recent example was the attempt of the Bush administration to embed anti-union features in both the proposed merit-based personnel system of the Defense Department's National Security Personnel System (NSPS), and in a similar human resources system of the Department of Homeland Security. Anti-labor aspects of both were ruled illegal in federal court decisions in 2006 and 2005 respectively. The NSPS software system was found, for instance, to fail to ensure that employees could bargain collectively, did not provide for congressionally-required third-party review of labor relations decisions, and did not provide a fair appeals process for employees. Normally, however, embedding political controls in ostensibly neutral software goes unchallenged and unnoticed by the public at large. Even in the NSPS case, the Department of Defense did not accept the court ruling, but continued development of the system even as it was contested in the courts.

THE HOPE THAT INFORMATION TECHNOLOGY WILL BUILD SOCIAL CAPITAL

There is evidence that Internet access does indeed improve the ability of citizens to interact with their government, though most use at that time is information-seeking rather than undertaking actual participatory transactions. Empirical analysis of the 2000 presidential elections has revealed that the Internet did show promise of bringing new individuals into the political process. Numerous writers have speculated that the age of the Internet would lead to a more participatory citizenry, whose experiences in electronic participation would build social capital and energize social, political, and economic development of all types.

In traditional forms of political participation, community participation in politics has been found to correlate with socio-economic status, being older, and having lived in the community longer. Data do not show this to be the case for online political participants. Contrary to the predictions of social capital theory, recent findings show that engagement in non-political, social groups in the community is not correlated with online political participation.

We may well ask if online communities destined to play a major political role in the future. Again, empirical case studies related to this question lead to the conclusion that although public administration literature has cited the importance of online communities as a vehicle for the delivery of public goods, actual experiences suggests cybercommunities tend to have weak governance structures, undermining accountability and legitimacy.

This two-volume set is separated into six sections: (1) e-government and e-commerce, (2) privacy, access, ethics, and theory, (3) security and protection, (4) system design and data processing, (5) project management and IT evaluation, and (6) selected readings. Each chapter within these sections is separated into seven segments: (1) an introduction providing the historical perspective of the subject matter, (2) a background providing discussions supporting the author's view as well as the views of others, (3) a segment devoted to the primary information regarding the subject matter, (4) a future trends segment providing future and emerging trends in the field of research and insight into the future of the topic from the perspective of published research as well as future research opportunities within the domain of the topic, (5) a conclusion, providing discussion for the overall coverage of the topic, (6) as well as a future research directions segment that acts as a supplement, discussing the managerial and more technical aspects of the subject matter, (7) a references and further reading section , and (8) concluding is a complete list of terms and definitions for readers to familiarize themselves with the subject matter's terminology.

The first section, titled "E-Government and E-Commerce," covers the rise of e-government and its series of stages, from one way information dissemination to two-way interactions to two-way transactions, culminating in cross-agency integration of e-services. The transition from the first to second stage has not proved a difficult obstacle for most jurisdictions, which implement interactions such as feed back forms and e-mail. However, the transition to stage 3, the interaction stage, has proved more difficult. Although many examples of e-transactions exist (e,g., paying taxes online), mass adoption of e-transactions by the public has proved illusive. Even more difficult has been overcoming department-centric business of government models and replacing them with integrated cross-agency models. The chapters within this section examine these issues as well as others that exemplify the progressive movement toward electronic government which while problematic, still is in the process of fulfilling its potential.

The second section, titled "Privacy, Access, Ethics, and Theory," covers the potential of Internet technology to bring about democratic transparency in the way government conducts its business. However, even a transparent government must support individual privacy rights. Privacy is a growing issue because people have good reason to believe that data collected on them for one purpose may be appropriated and used for altogether difference purposes than the original ones about which they were informed. In theoretical terms, some seeking to understand these issues have turned to structuration theory, which is a variant of institutional theory growing out of the work of Anthony Giddens. Gidden held that individual actions both shape and are constrained by social structures. In addition to the structuration theory, the institutional theorist perspective, more specifically, Fountain's theory of technology enactment, is discussed throughout the section.

The third section, titled "Security and Protection," covers several security threats including massive data theft, cyber-terrorism, and the use of malware. In the United States, information technology security rose to first place in budget priority after the bombing of the World Trade Center and has remained a top priority to the present day. Although there are currently over 217,000 various known threats including identity theft, imposter Web sites, file sharing, this section will cover some of the most prevalent in the public sector.

The fourth section, titled "System Design and Data Processing," delves into topics such as service oriented architectures, enterprise resource planning systems, statistical data and statistical dissemination systems, and data cube technologies, amongst many others. Enterprise resource planning systems in particular has often been the result of systems architecture planning in the U.S. and worldwide. After a checkered start in the private sector in the late 1980s and early 1990s, such systems were widely adopted in the public sector in the late 1990s and by the 2000s transition from agency-specific to enterprise-wide software was the primary reform thrust of the U.S. Office of Management and Budget as well as many states and localities. Efforts were made to unify financial, human resources, payroll, procurement and other departmental software systems into single jurisdiction-wide systems.

The fifth section, titled "Project Management and IT Evaluation," examines the relationship between information technology and project management. Information technology frequently succeeds or fails on the strength or weakness of project management. The United States is seeing an increase in project management due to its emphasis in the Bush administration's FY 2007 budget. Project management is often tied to enforcing IT enterprise architecture, which reflects the IT policies at the national level and of state chief information officers at the state level. Evaluation is another topic covered within this section which is coequal in importance to project management. Project management may be more critical for short-term IT success, but in the long run the success of IT initiatives requires that they be proven to work in a cost-effective manner, hence the critical importance of evaluation.

Concluding the *Handbook of Research on Public Information Technology* is a "Selected Reading" section of 10 refereed journal articles for additional insight into the realm of information technology in the public sector. These articles come highly recommended and introduce innovative applications, trends and technologies within this fast growing area of information science and technology.

SUMMARY

A work much more famous than this volume could dream to be started with the phrase, "it was the best of times, it was the worst of time," and went on to contrast two cities, one cloaked in tradition and one in revolutionary upheaval. It is interesting to note that the vision of digital cities and global communities draws on such contrasts, comparing often-hierarchical traditional patterns of work and governance with the revolutionary potential of information technology as a liberating force, perhaps not for "liberty, equality, fraternity," but at least for participation, transparency, and empowerment. In this preface your editor has tried to suggest that empirical research can throw much-needed light on traditional and revolutionary perspectives alike. There are so many important issues attached to this subject, many explored by scholarly contributions in this volume, dealing both with pragmatic implementation and with conceptual design, that they cannot be enumerated here. What is certain, however, is something close to the heart of and bringing a smile to the lips of every academic: more research is needed! Toward this end, this volume seeks to make a small contribution.

G. David Garson
North Carolina State University, USA

Volume II

Chapter XLIV
The Role of Data Mining in Intrusion Detection Technology

Amalia Agathou
University of the Aegean, Greece

Theodoros Tzouramanis
University of the Aegean, Greece

INTRODUCTION

Over the past few years, the Internet has changed computing as we know it. The more possibilities and opportunities develop, the more systems are subject to attack by intruders. Thus, the big question is about how to recognize and handle subversion attempts. One answer is to undertake the prevention of subversion itself by building a completely secure system. However, the complete prevention of breaches of security does not yet appear to be possible to achieve. Therefore these intrusion attempts need to be detected as soon as possible (preferably in real time) so that appropriate action might be taken to repair the damage. This is what an intrusion detection system (IDS) does.

IDSs monitor and analyze the events occurring in a computer system in order to detect signs of security problems. However, intrusion detection technology has not yet reached perfection. This fact has provided data mining with the opportunity to make several important contributions and improvements to the field of IDS technology (Julisch, 2002).

BACKGROUND

IDSs are systems that aim at the detection of subversion and the prevention of similar attacks in the future (Sundaram, 1996). Therefore, an IDS identifies evidence of intrusions, either while they are in progress or after the fact. The most popular way to detect intrusions has been the use of the audit data generated by the operating system. An audit trail is a record of activities on a system that are logged to a file in chronologically sorted order. These data may be collected in many ways, but their sources are usually network activity and/or host-based logs.

Since almost all activities are logged on a system, a manual inspection of these logs may detect intrusions. However, too much data are collected, making manual analysis impossible to be usefully analyzed for intrusions. What IDSs achieve is the automation of the data analysis process. It is thus possible to establish the guilt of the intruders and to detect unauthorized and subversive user activity.

Postmortem analysis of the audit data is significant as it helps to determine the extent of the damage and to identify intruders so that steps may be taken to overcome system weakness.

Kemmer and Vigna (2002) describe an IDS as composed of several components: sensors for the capture of events and for their storage as audit data; an engine for the production of alarm signals upon detection of a potential intrusion, detected from the processing of the audit data captured; and a site security officer (SSO) for the reception of the alarms and for appropriate response.

Data Collection Issues

Achieving reliable and complete data collection about the target system's activities is a complex issue. As Kemmer and Vigna (2002) state, most operating systems offer some form of auditing that provides an operations log for different users.

These data might be collected at the lowest possible level, resulting in the collection of rather large quantities of system activity information to be analyzed for intrusions. To alleviate this problem, the use of random sampling has been suggested; however, this could mean that certain types of attacks may stay undetected. The problem is further complicated by the need to allow for differences in the data as a result of special circumstances such as holidays and other factors.

Finally, depending on a specific IDS solution and its correlation engine, a storage period for current audit files should be appropriately set. For retrieval analysis purposes, archive files should be stored as copies.

Detection Techniques

Traditionally, there are two basic categories of intrusion detection techniques: anomaly detection and misuse detection. Most current intrusion detection systems use one or both of these two approaches.

According to Lee and Stolfo (1998), the anomaly detection model devises a set of statistical metrics that model the behavior of an entity, usually a user, a group of users, or a host computer, interpreting deviations from this behavior profile as a problem. The profile of a user entity, for instance, may include information such as the CPU (central processing unit) usage and the frequency of system commands during a user log-in session. The IDS monitors the operation of a computer system and constantly compares the profile of, say, a current user session with the one stored in its database. If it detects a high deviation from the normal behavior, it signals an alarm to the system security officer. Deviation from a profile can be computed as the weighted sum of the deviations of the constituent statistical measures. Stored profiles are constantly being updated so that shifts of normal behavior are accounted for.

The misuse detection model, on the other hand, uses specifically known patterns of unauthorized behavior to predict and detect subsequent similar attempts. They contain attack descriptions (or signatures; Lee et al., 2000) and match them against the audit data stream, looking for evidence of known attacks. Depending on the robustness and seriousness of a signature that is triggered, some form of alarm, either a response or notification, should be sent to the proper authorities. An obvious difficulty in this architecture is the need for the constant updating of the rule base as new attack methods become known (Julisch, 2002).

Public Domain for Intrusion Detection

The fast development of information and communication technology over the past few years has led to the interconnection of corporations, small to medium companies, organizations, government bodies, and private citizens. Networks have many applications in the public domain such as e-government services that allow the user to submit her or his income declaration, view the tax position, request certificates, conduct estate checks, and so forth. As stated in the European Commission (2002) article, the Internet offers enormous opportunities to any person who knows how to use a computer and can take part in social life by clicking with a mouse. E-Europe and its programs (e-learning, e-health, e-government, and e-business) aim at fully exploiting this potential in favor of social development.

Official communications and medical and financial transactions require a higher level of authentication, integrity, and confidentiality. The public wants information systems to be secure as well as trustworthy. For instance, people need to trust these systems to ensure the privacy of their data, especially when it comes to sensitive information like medical or economic data.

Federal agencies are using data mining for the analysis and detection of terrorist patterns of activity. The *New York Times* in 2003 reported that U.S. intelligence officials believed that a recent rise in electronic attacks against government and military computer networks in the United States may be the work of terrorist hackers and could signal a potential crisis in national security (Lichtblau, 2003). Also, in April 2002, the *Los Angeles Times* reported that U.S. intelligence officials feared similar attacks by China (Lichtblau, 2002).

Common ways of protection against unauthorized access are the installation of a password and/or a firewall. However, these methods alone cannot provide extensive protection and must be integrated with other security devices such as devices for attack recognition and application intrusion detection systems. It is essential to reach a balance between the protection and availability of the data (Battelli et al., 2005).

The U.S. National Science Foundation (U.S. NSF, 2006) supports research concerning the integration of data mining and IDS. Novel data-mining-based anomaly detection techniques developed under NSF support have been incorporated in the Minnesota Intrusion Detection System (MINDS; Ertoz et al., 2004) that can help cybersecurity analysts to analyze vast amounts of network traffic and detect novel intrusions, insider abuse, and policy violations by evaluating the most anomalous connections identified by the system.

MINDS is currently being used at the U.S. Army Research Laboratory's Center for Intrusion Monitoring and Protection (ARL-CIMP) and at the University of Minnesota where it monitors over 40,000 computers. Data mining for rare events becomes critical as new technologies allow more and more data to be collected. The underlying techniques used by the Minnesota team can be applied in many areas beyond detecting computer intrusions, such as financial and health care fraud detection.

DATA MINING MEETS INTRUSION DETECTION

Data mining is, at its core, the process of analyzing data from different perspectives and summarizing it into useful information (Mannila, Smyth, & Hand, 2001). Data mining software finds regularities in large data sets. It allows data miners to analyze data and summarize the relationships identified. It can also present the data in a useful format, such as a graph or a table. Technically, data mining is the process of finding correlations or patterns in large data sets.

These tasks are accomplished with the following data mining techniques: classification, which enables the categorization of records into classes; clustering, which is a method used to discover the segmentation of the data into natural categories; and association rules for the definition

Table 1. The techniques used in data mining (Elite Analytics LLC, 2006)

Classification:	Enables the categorization of records into two or more pre-defined classes by the use of classification algorithms and a set of pre-classified examples.
Clustering:	Exploratory method used to discover natural groupings within records or entities. Clustering approaches are commonly used for segmentation.
Association Rules:	Basic types of patterns or regularities that are found in transactional-type data.
Sequential Pattern Detection:	Sequential patterns involve mining frequently occurring patterns of activity over a period of time.
Change & Deviation Detection:	A method useful for identifying significant changes in a data set from previously measured or normative values.

of normal activity and, hence, the discovery of anomalies (Phung, 2000). There are also techniques for identifying significant changes in a data set from normative values, as well as for visualization of the data through graphs or tables. Table 1 presents briefly the methods used in data mining whereas Table 2 lists the different tools used in its process.

Traditional statistical methods are also usually used to complement the data mining methods (Brugger et al., 2001). The distinction between data mining and applied statistics is not always clear. The main difference is that data mining enables data exploration and analysis without any specific hypothesis in mind. Also, data mining tends to be more application oriented and looks for useful patterns in a data set, whereas traditional statistical methods are more concerned with modeling. Furthermore, in contrast to statistical methods, data mining can handle massive data sets with many variables. The traditional statistical techniques include exploratory statistics, hypothesis testing, regression (linear, nonlinear, logistic), forecasting, and experimental design (Elite Analytics LLC, 2006).

How Data Mining Meets the Shortfalls with Current IDSs

Phung (2000) argues that while the misuse detection model is a useful and viable approach, there are shortfalls to using only this approach. As stated previously, signatures are developed in response to known vulnerabilities or exploitations that have been posted or released. However, developing unique signatures is a difficult task and often

Table 2. Data mining tools (Brugger, Kelley, Sumikawa, & Wakumoto, 2001; Thearling, 2006)

Neural Networks:	Are non-linear predictive models that learn through training and resemble biological neural networks in structure.
Decision trees:	Are tree-shaped structures that represent sets of decisions. These decisions generate rules for the classification of a dataset. Specific decision tree methods include Classification and Regression Trees (CART) and Chi Square Automatic Interaction Detection (CHAID).
Statistical Methods:	There are five statistical measures: the operational model, the mean and standard deviation model, the multivariate model, the Markov process model and the time series model.
Genetic Algorithms:	Optimization techniques that use processes such as genetic combination, mutation, and natural selection in a design based on the concepts of evolution.
Nearest Neighbour Method:	Classifies each record in a dataset based on a combination of the classes of the k most similar records to it in a historical dataset (where $k \geq 1$). It is also called the k-nearest neighbour technique.
Rule Induction:	It is related to the extraction of useful if-then rules from data based on statistical significance.

the IDSs fail in the sense that they produce many false positives, that is, by alerting too often rather than not enough. Another difficult problem is the detection of exploitations for which there are no known signatures. This leads to the concept of false negatives, where an IDS does not generate an alert when an intrusion is actually taking place. Finally, another aspect that does not relate directly to intrusion detection but that is of vital importance is the amount of data that an analyst can effectively and efficiently analyze. Depending on the intrusion detection tools employed by a company and its size, there is the possibility for logs to reach millions of records per day.

On the other side, data mining methods excel at processing large system logs of audit data. Therefore, data mining methods can contribute to an IDS by helping to integrate anomaly detection and misuse detection (Lippmann et al., 2000). A typical data mining method is correlated with finding association rules. Thus, it may identify data mining patterns for normal and abnormal activity and may help the IDS to generate an alert when an attack for which signatures have not been developed takes place (Bass, 2000). With data mining it is easy to correlate data related to alarms with mined audit data, thereby considerably reducing the rate of false alarms (Manganaris, Christensen, Zerkle, & Hermiz, 2000). For example, with regard to false positives, data mining can be used to identify valid network activity that can be filtered out by identifying false-alarm generators.

Fan, Miller, Stolfo, Lee, and Chan (2001) propose one of the fundamental data mining techniques used in intrusion detection technology that implements decision trees to detect network intrusions. Lee et al. (2000) present another data mining technique that refers to segmentation, allowing pattern extraction from unknown attacks. This is done by matching patterns extracted from a simple audit set with those referred to stored, warehoused unknown attacks.

Data mining is also sure to provide a solution to the issue of data reduction. As the amount of data an analyst needs to look at seems to be growing rapidly, data mining algorithms can help the identification of the most relevant data and aid a more efficient analysis.

Current Research Efforts

In the past years, a growing number of research projects have begun to explore the use of data mining to address data overload in intrusion detection. In the following, a broad overview of the work that has been done at the intersection between intrusion detection and data mining is presented.

Lee and Stolfo (1998) and Lee, Stolfo, and Mok (1999) propose the MADAM ID (mining audit data for automated models for intrusion detection), a software tool that uses data mining techniques to build better models for intrusion detection by analyzing audit data using associations and frequent episodes. The original idea behind this pioneering and awarded research activity[1] was to generate classifiers using a rule-learning program on training data sets of system usage. The output from the classifier, a set of classification rules, is used to recognize anomalies and detect known intrusions. The ADAM (Audit Data and Mining) test bed was proposed by Barbará, Couto, Jajodia, Popyack, and Wu (2001). It is a tool that employs data mining techniques to detect intrusions. It uses a combination of association rules, mining, and classification to provide a flexible representation of the network traffic pattern, uncover some unknown patterns of attacks that cannot be detected by other techniques, and accommodate the large amount of network audit data that keeps growing in size. In the first step, ADAM builds a repository of profiles for normal frequent item sets that hold during attack-free periods. It does so by mining data that is known to be free of attacks. In the second step, ADAM runs a sliding-window online algorithm that finds frequent item sets in the last N connections and compares them to a normal profile, discarding those that are deemed normal. With the rest, ADAM uses a classifier that has been previously trained to classify the suspicious connections as a known type of attack, an unknown type, or a false alarm.

The limitation of ADAM, as well as the limitation of most of the anomaly detection models, is that it cannot detect stealthy attacks as it raises an alarm only when the support of an unexpected rule, that is, an association of event attributes, exceeds a threshold. In other words, ADAM can detect an attack only when it involves a relatively large number of events during a short period of time.

In Abraham (2001), the IDDM (intrusion detection using data mining) is proposed, which aims toward the potential use of the data mining paradigm in near-real-time intrusion detection in order to extend intrusion detection capabilities. The research over IDDM focuses on the reuse and expansion of previous works as required, some of which are evaluated as part of the research. Rather than concentrating on the use of a particular technique in a certain application instance, IDDM explores multiple uses for any given data mining principle in a variety of ways by producing descriptions of network data and by using this information for deviation analysis.

IDDM makes feasible the characterization of network data and the detection of variations in these characteristics over time. Therefore, IDDM in combination with tools that recognize existing attack patterns or operate in a similar manner facilitates the recognition and potential reaction to unwanted violations to network operations.

In Ertoz et al. (2004), the MINDS is presented, which uses a suite of data mining techniques to automatically detect unusual network behavior and emerging cyber threats. It is a highly successful tool in automatically detecting several novel intrusions that could not be identified using popular signature-based tools. It includes miscellaneous modules for gathering and analyzing large amounts of network traffic. Typical analyses include behavioral anomaly detection, summarization, and profiling. In addition, the system has a module based on an association-pattern analysis that summarizes the highly anomalous ranked network connections that have been recorded by the anomaly detection module. Furthermore, given the huge number of connections observed per time unit, association-pattern-based summarization of novel attacks is quite valuable in allowing a security analyst to comprehend and distinguish emerging threats. According to Long (2004), MINDS is part of the Interrogator architecture at the ARL-CIMP, where network traffic from dozens of Department of Defense sites is analyzed.

As a consequence of the high cost of merging huge amounts of data and running analysis on one site, bringing the data collected at these different sites to one place and then analyzing it is not feasible. Therefore, future work is focused on a distributed framework in which these different sites can independently analyze their data and then share high-level patterns and results. That way, issues concerning the individual sites' data privacy will not arise. The provision of functions like handling distributed data, addressing privacy issues, and using data mining tools by a middleware would make the implementation of such a system a lot easier. The University of Minnesota, the University of Florida, and the University of Illinois at Chicago are developing and implementing such a system as a part of an NSF-funded collaborative project called Data Mining Middleware for the Grid (Kumar, 2005).

FUTURE TRENDS

Although there have been successful applications of data mining techniques in the field of intrusion detection, it is clear that there is room for the further improvement of this technology. One of the improvements that should be made is adjusting more precisely data mining algorithms and processes to fit intrusion detection. It is an integral part of identifying and obtaining better pictures of the data in order to provide accurate and effective results.

Another obstacle in developing an effective solution is the complexity of the dramatically increasing amount of data to be analyzed, which makes data mining quite computationally expensive.

CONCLUSION

The chapter overviews the research activity regarding the application of data mining techniques in the field of intrusion detection technology so that systems can achieve higher accuracy toward the recognition of the signatures of known forms of attack and higher adaptability in unknown forms of attack.

Some of the best known research efforts in the area of anomaly and misuse detection using data mining techniques were presented, and the main drawbacks and limitations of the existing systems that leave margins for further progress in the area were reported.

FUTURE RESEARCH DIRECTIONS

Most research in the area today focuses on the operational aspect of the IDSs rather than on the nature of attacks and false positives. On the other hand, more attention needs to be devoted to knowledge discovery in databases (KDD) and not to data mining alone.

Further research should also address the automatic (or semiautomatic) generation of high-quality labeled training data, or the existence of such data should no longer be assumed. Future work should also explore novel applications of data mining that do not fall into the categories of feature selection and anomaly detection. Also, to deal with some of the general challenges in data mining, it might be best to develop special-purpose solutions that are tailored to intrusion detection.

Up to now there has also been a lack of data visualization tools for computer network applications. The development of data visualization tools providing multiple perspectives is thus an urgent task.

Finally, a great concern of the research community is the lack of realistic data sets for experimentation purposes. However, experimentation studies based on synthetic data sets may not be similar to real data sets; on the other hand, methods that are not efficient on synthetic data sets may turn out to be effective on real data. Therefore, there is an immediate need for tools and computer network infrastructures that will collect real data sets for the research community while maintaining privacy policies and standards.

REFERENCES

Abraham, T. (2001). *IDDM: Intrusion detection using data mining techniques* (Tech. Rep. No. DSTO-GD-0286). Australia: Department of Defense, Defense Science and Technology Organisation.

Barbará, D., Couto, J., Jajodia, S., Popyack, L., & Wu, N. (2001). ADAM: Detecting intrusions by data mining. *Proceedings of the IEEE Workshop on Information Assurance and Security.*

Barbará, D., & Jajodia, S. (Eds.). (2002). *Applications of data mining in computer security.* Kluwer Academic Publishers.

Bass, T. (2000). Intrusion detection systems multisensor data fusion: Creating cyberspace situational awareness. *Communications of the ACM, 43*(1), 99-105.

Battelli, D., Bruschi, et al. (2005). *Network security: From risk analysis to protection strategies.* Istituto Superiore delle Comunicazioni e delle Tecnologie dell' Informazione. Retrieved from http://www.comunicazioni.it/it/Files/4/33/pub_002_eng.pdf

Brugger, S. T., Kelley, M., Sumikawa, K., & Wakumoto, S. (2001). *Data mining for security information: A survey* (Tech. Rep. No. UCRL-JC-143464). Retrieved from http://www.osti.gov/bridge/servlets/purl/15005288-EzHIww/native/15005288.pdf

Elite Analytics LLC. (2006). *Data mining & applied statistics.* Retrieved from http://www.eliteanalytics.com.

Ertoz, L., Eilertson, E., Lazarevic, A., Tan, P.-N., Kumar, V., Srivastava, J., et al. (2004). MINDS: Minnesota Intrusion Detection System. In H. Kargupta, A. Joshi, K. Sivakumar, & Y. Yesha (Eds.), *Data mining: Next generation challenges and future directions* (chap. 11). MIT/AAAI Press.

European Commission. (2002). *Towards a knowledge-based Europe: The European Union and the information society.* Directorate General Press and Communication Publications. Retrieved from http://ec.europa.eu/publications/booklets/move/36/en.pdf

Fan, W., Miller, M., Stolfo, S., Lee, W., & Chan, P. (2001). *Using artificial anomalies to detect unknown and known network intrusions.* Proceedings of the First IEEE International Conference on Data Mining, San Jose, CA.

Hu, Y., & Panda, B. (2004). *A data mining approach for database intrusion detection.* Proceedings of the ACM SAC, Cyprus.

Julisch, K. (2002). Data mining for intrusion detection: A critical review. In D. Barbará & S. Jajodia (Eds.), *Applications of data mining in computer security* (chap. 1). Boston: Kluwer Academic Publishers.

Kemmer, R. A., & Vigna, G. (2002). Intrusion detection: A brief history and overview. *Security and Privacy*, pp. 27-30.

Kumar, V. (2005). Parallel and distributed computing for cybersecurity. *IEEE Distributed Systems Online, 6*(10).

Lee, W., Nimbalkar, R. A., Yee, K. K., Patil, S. B., Desai, P. H., Tran, T. T., et al. (2000). A data mining and CIDF based approach for detecting novel and distributed intrusions. In *Lecture notes in computer science: Vol. 1907. Proceedings of the Third International Workshop on Recent Advances in Intrusion Detection (RAID 2000)* (pp.49-65). Springer.

Lee, W., & Stolfo, S. J. (1998). *Data mining approaches for intrusion detection.* Proceedings of the 7th USENIX Security Symposium, San Antonio, TX.

Lee, W., Stolfo, S. J., & Mok, K. W. (1999). Mining in a dataflow environment: Experience in network intrusion detection. *Proceedings of the 5th ACM SIGKDD International Conference on Knowledge Discovery and Data Mining (KDD'99)* (pp. 114-124).

Lee, W., Stolfo, S. J., & Mok, K. W. (2000). Adaptive intrusion detection: A data mining approach. *Artificial Intelligence Review, 14*(6), 533-567.

Lichtblau, E. (2002, April 24). CIA: China planning cyber-attacks on U.S., Taiwan. *Los Angeles Times.* Retrieved from http://www.siliconvalley.com/mld/siliconvalley/3132466.htm

Lichtblau, E. (2003, January 16). Warning on Iraqi hackers and US safety. *New York Times.* Retrieved from http://www.nytimes.com/2003/01/17/technology/17HACK.html

Lippmann, R. P., Fried, D. J., Graf, I., Haines, J. W., Kendall, K. R., McClung, D., et al. (2000). Evaluating intrusion detection systems: The 1998 DARPA off-line intrusion detection evaluation. *Proceedings of the 2000 DARPA Information Survivability Conference and Exposition* (pp. 12-26).

Long, K. (2004). Catching the cyber spy: ARL's interrogator. *Proceedings of the 24th Army Science Conference*.

Manganaris, S., Christensen, M., Zerkle, D., & Hermiz, K. (2000). A data mining analysis of RTID alarms. *Computer Networks, 34*, 571-577.

Mannila, H., Smyth, P., & Hand, D. J. (2001). *Principles of data mining*. MIT Press.

Phung, M. (2000). *Intrusion detection FAQ* (Tech. Rep.). SANS Technology Institute. Retrieved from http://www.sans.org/resources/idfaq/index.php

Sundaram, A. (1996). *An introduction to intrusion detection* (Tech. Rep.). Retrieved from http://www.acm.org/crossroads/xrds2-4/intrus.html

Thearling, K. (2006). *Information about data mining and analytic technologies*. Retrieved from http://www.thearling.com

U.S. National Science Foundation (NSF). (2006). *National Science Foundation: Where the discoveries begin*. Retrieved from http://www.nsf.gov

FURTHER READING

Network intrusion detection based on data mining techniques has been an ongoing research area for the last decade. The reader is directed to the references below for further study.

Axelsson, S. (2000). *Intrusion detection systems: A survey and taxonomy* (Tech. Rep.). Chalmers University.

Barbará, D., Couto, J., Jajodia, S., & Wu, N. (2001). ADAM: A testbed for exploring the use of data mining in intrusion detection. *SIGMOD Record, 30*, 15-24.

Campos, M. M., & Milenova, B. L. (2005). Creation and deployment of data mining-based intrusion detection systems in Oracle Database 10g. *Proceedings of the Fourth International Conference on Machine Learning and Applications (ICMLA'05)* (pp. 117-124).

Chan, P. K., Fan, W., Prodromidis, A., & Stolfo, S. J. (1999). Distributed data mining in credit card fraud detection. *IEEE Intelligent Systems, 14*(6), 67-74.

Chittur, A. (2001). *Model generation for an intrusion detection system using genetic algorithms*. Unpublished high school honors thesis, Ossining High School (in cooperation with Columbia University).

Clifton, C., & Gengo, G. (2000). *Developing custom intrusion detection filters using data mining*. Proceedings of the 2000 Military Communications International, Los Angeles, CA.

Dasgupta, S., & Gonzalez, F. A. (2001). An intelligent decision support system for intrusion detection and response. *Proceedings of International Workshop on Mathematical Methods, Models and Architectures for Computer Networks Security (MMM-ACNS)*.

Dickerson, J. E., & Dickerson, J. A. (2000). Fuzzy network profiling for intrusion detection. *Proceedings of NAFIPS 19th International Conference of the North American Fuzzy Information Processing Society* (pp. 301-306).

Domingos, P., & Hulten, G. (2000). Mining high speed data streams. *Proceedings of the Sixth ACM SIGKDD Conference on Knowledge Discovery and Data Mining* (pp. 71-80).

Endler, D. (1998). Intrusion detection applying machine learning to Solaris audit data. *Proceedings of the 1998 Annual Computer Security Applications Conference (ACSAC98)* (pp. 268-279).

Florez, G., Bridges, S. M., & Vaughn, R. B. (2002). An improved algorithm for fuzzy data mining for intrusion detection. *Annual Meeting of the North American Fuzzy Information Processing Society*.

Gabrielson, B. (1999). *Security using intelligent agents and data mining.* Proceedings of the National Security Space Architect MIM Technology Forum, Chantilly, VA.

Han, H., Lu, X. L., Lu, J., Bo, C., & Yong, R. L. (2002). Data mining aided signature discovery in network-based intrusion detection system. *ACM SIGOPS Operating Systems Review, 36*(4), 7-13.

Helmer, G., Wong, J., Honavar, V., & Miller, L. (1999). *Automated discovery of concise predictive rules for intrusion detection* (Tech. Rep. No. 99-01). Ames, IA: Iowa State University.

Julisch, C. (2003). Clustering intrusion detection alarms to support root cause analysis. *ACM Transactions on Information and System Security, 6*(4), 443-471.

Julisch, K., & Dacier, M. (2002). Mining intrusion detection alarms for actionable knowledge. *Proceedings of the Eighth ACM SIGKDD International Conference on Knowledge Discovery and Data Mining* (pp. 366-375).

Kumar, S. (1995). *Classification and detection of computer intrusion.* Unpublished doctoral dissertation, Purdue University, West Lafayette, IN.

Kuok, C. M., Fu, A. W.-C., & Wong, M. H. (1998). Mining fuzzy association rules in databases. *SIGMOD Record, 27*(1), 41-46.

Lane, T. D. (2000). *Machine learning techniques for the computer security domain of anomaly detection.* Unpublished doctoral dissertation, Purdue University, West Lafayette, IN.

Lee, W. (1999). A data mining framework for building intrusion detection models. *IEEE Symposium on Security and Privacy* (pp. 120-132).

Lee, W., Stolfo, S. J., Chan, P. K., Eskin, E., Fan, W., Miller, M., et al. (2001). Real time data mining-based intrusion detection. *Proceedings of DISCEX II.*

Lee, W., & Xiang, D. (2001). Information-theoretic measures for anomaly detection. *Proceedings of the 2001 IEEE Symposium on Security and Privacy* (pp. 130-143).

Leung, K., & Leckie, C. (2005). Unsupervised anomaly detection in network intrusion detection using clusters. *Proceedings of Twenty-Eighth Australasian Computer Science Conference (ACSC2005)* (pp. 333-342).

Luo, J. (1999). *Integrating fuzzy logic with data mining methods for intrusion detection.* Unpublished master's thesis, Mississippi State University, MS.

Me, L., & Michel, C. (2001). *Intrusion detection: A bibliography* (Tech. Rep. No. SSIR-2001-01). Rennes, France: Supelec.

Mohan, S. R., Park, E. K., & Han, Y. (2005). *An adaptive intrusion detection system using a data mining approach.* Proceedings of the IEEE ICDM 2005 workshop on Computational Intelligence in Data Mining, Houston, TX.

Neri, F. (2000). Mining TCP/IP traffic for network intrusion detection. In *Lecture notes in computer science: Vol. 1810. Proceedings of 11th European Conference on Machine Learning* (pp. 313-322). Barcelona, Spain: Springer.

Noel, S., Wijesekera, D., & Youman, C. (2002). Modern intrusion detection, data mining, and degrees of attack guilt. In *Applications of data mining in computer security.* Kluwer.

Petrovskiy, M. I. (2003). Outlier detection algorithms in data mining systems. *Programming and Computing Software, 29*(4), 228-237.

Portnoy, L., Eskin, E., & Stolfo, S. J. (2001). Intrusion detection with unlabeled data using clustering. *Proceedings of ACM-CSS Workshop on Data Mining Applied to Security (DMSA-2001).*

Sequeira, K., & Zaki, M. (2002). Admit: Anomaly-based data mining for intrusions. *Proceedings of the 8th ACM SIGKDD International Conference on Knowledge Discovery and Data Mining* (pp. 386-395).

Skorupka, C., Tivel, J., Talbot, L., Debarr, D., Hill, W., Bloedorn, E., et al. (2001). *Surf the flood: Reducing high-volume intrusion detection data by automated record aggregation.* Proceedings of the SANS 2001 Technical Conference, Baltimore.

Thuraisingham, B. (2002). Data mining, national security, privacy and civil liberties. *ACM SIGKDD Explorations Newsletter, 4*(2), 1-5.

Wagner, D., & Soto, P. (2002). Mimicry attacks on host-based intrusion detection systems. *Proceedings of the 9th ACM Conference on Computer and Communications Security* (pp. 255-264).

Zhang, J., & Zulkernine, M. (2006). Anomaly based network intrusion detection with unsupervised outlier detection. *Symposium on Network Security and Information Assurance, Proceedings of the IEEE International Conference on Communications (ICC).*

TERMS AND DEFINITIONS

Anomaly Detection: It detects activity that deviates from normal activity. Profile-based anomaly detection depends on the statistical definition of what is normal and can be prone to a large number of false positives.

Auditing: Auditing is the gathering and analysis of the information of assets to ensure such things as policy compliance and security from vulnerabilities.

Classification: It refers to the data mining problem of attempting to predict the category of data by building a model based on some predictor variables.

Data Mining: This is the process of automatically searching large volumes of data to uncover previously undetected relationships among data items. Data mining is also known as knowledge discovery in databases (KDD).

False Negative: This occurs when there is an attack and the product does not raise an alarm. Obviously, this case is problematic because the intruder's action can go completely unnoticed.

False Positive: This occurs when there is no attack and the product raises an alarm. This case can be problematic because administrators, facing a false positive, might take unnecessary actions.

Intrusion Detection Systems: They detect inappropriate, incorrect, or anomalous activity. ID systems that operate on a host to detect malicious activity on that host are called host-based ID systems. ID systems that operate on network data flows are called network-based ID systems.

Misuse Detection: It detects a pattern that matches closely activity that is typical of a network intrusion. Misuse detection is also known as signature-based detection.

Signature: A signature is a distinct pattern in network traffic that can be identified to a specific tool or exploit.

ENDNOTE

1. The research proposed one of the best performing systems in the DARPA 1998 Off-Line Intrusion Detection Evaluation and was awarded as a Best Paper in Applied Research at the Knowledge Discovery and Data Mining Tools Competition, which was held in conjunction with the Fifth International Conference on Knowledge Discovery and Data Mining (KDD-99).

Section IV
System Design and Data Processing

Starting in 2000, U.S. federal-level agencies were required to prepare documentation of their conformity with federal enterprise architecture policy. The objective of the enterprise architecture initiative was to make interdepartmental information transfer more compatible and efficient, to encourage multiple reuse of IT data and application resources, and to improve security levels. It was also expected that IT under enterprise architecture policy would become more scalable and thus new systems might be integrated more economically.

In the United States and worldwide, systems architecture planning has often led to promotion of enterprise resource planning (ERP) systems. After a checkered start in the private sector in the late 1980s and early 1990s, such systems were widely adopted in the public sector in the late 1990s, and by the 2000s transition from agency-specific to enterprise-wide software was the primary reform thrust of the U.S. Office of Management and Budget (OMB) as well as of many states and localities. Efforts were made to unify financial, human resources, payroll, procurement, and other departmental software systems into single jurisdiction-wide systems.

Enterprise software offered three central promises.

1. Enterprise-wide software systems would be less expensive than multiple departmental systems.
2. The consolidation of databases would improve management decision making.
3. Reliance on large ERP software vendors would assure critical systems remained state of the art, never obsolete.

Where ERP was sometimes seen as a relative failure when first introduced, by the mid-2000s, it had grown into a \$100 billion industry with many public-sector jurisdictions at all levels reliant upon it.

In March 2006, the U.S. Government Accountability Office (GAO) issued a report, "Financial Management Systems: Additional Efforts Needed to Address Key Causes of Modernization Failures." Evaluating ERP efforts in the Internal Revenue Service, defense department, and elsewhere, the GAO found continuing problems in ERP requirements management, testing, data conversion, system interfaces, and risk and project management. The report came after widespread publicity about over-budget, behind-schedule ERP projects from vendors such as CGI AMS, Oracle Corporation, and SAP America Inc.

Because of the high risk, frequent failures, and high price of ERP developed under agency control, the OMB moved to promote development of ERP systems through shared service providers, also called "centers of excellence," rather than through agencies on their own. The OMB became increasingly hostile toward customization of ERP software because customization was seen as a failure factor. Career-oriented agency CIOs (chief information officers), for their part, found pleasing their constituents through customization was not worth the career-busting price of being tagged with an ERP failure.

Just as after the 1980s, the contradiction between centralized mainframe computing and stand-alone desktop computing was partially resolved by the new synthesis found in networked distributed computing, so by 2007 many believed the contradiction between centralized one-size-fits-all ERP systems and decentralized, customized "stovepipe" systems at the departmental level might be at least partially resolved by the synthesis represented by service-oriented architecture (SOA). SOA is a model under which ERP or other system functions may be modularized and delivered as Web services. In the summer of 2006, the Organization for the Advancement of Structured Information Standards formally adopted the SOA Reference Model for organizing distributed capabilities in a way that different capabilities could be controlled by different ownership domains, transcending any one vendor. As with information technology in general, the effect of SOA will rest in human hands. It is perfectly possible to administer it in a centralized manner, with the CIO retaining all the resources for and control over the possible customization that SOA modularization might otherwise allow. Only if decentralized departments have the approval, budget resources, and technical staff to take advantage of SOA will the SOA model lead to the synthesis between centralization and decentralization for which it could be designed. Without these supports, SOA becomes simply a modular approach to ERP software with most of its problems.

G. David Garson, September 2007

Chapter XLV
System Dynamics to Understand Public Information Technology

Luis Felipe Luna-Reyes
Universidad de las Américas-Puebla, Mexico

INTRODUCTION

Information technology development and implementation have been recognized as forms of organizational change (Doherty & King, 2003; Orlikowski, 2000). Public-sector organizations are interested in this process of change because of the expected benefits of using IT, such as cost savings, improved service quality, increased accountability, and public participation (Gil-Garcia & Helbig, 2006). However, IT fails to deliver the anticipated payback in many projects (Jackson, 1997; Keil, Cule, Lyytinen, & Schmidt, 1998). Some of such failures are the result of our lack of understanding about the relationships among IT components and organizational factors involved in the implementation process, producing mismatches or unintended consequences in the process: "[t]he computer hardware may perform correctly, and the software may satisfy its specification; but the results are not what was intended, and may be disastrous" (Jackson, 1997, p. 5).

This chapter presents system dynamics as a method to get a better understanding of such mismatches in public information technologies. The method has already been used successfully in the planning and evaluation of both public and private IT applications (Abdel-Hamid & Madnick, 1991; Madachy & Tarbet, 2000; Wolstenholme, 2003; Wolstenholme, Henderson, & Gavine, 1993). The method allows us to understand the interactions among technologies and organizations as a continuous process of organizational change (March, 1981), in which it is possible to find brief periods of rapid change. However, even those periods of rapid change are conceptualized as the result of endogenous and continuous local adaptations (Hutchins, 1991), where technology enables, not causes change (Orlikowski, 2000).

The chapter presents the basic principles and tools of system dynamics and continues with an example of its application in the analysis of an IT project in the public sector. The chapter ends with a brief description of future trends in modeling and simulation as well as a brief conclusion.

BACKGROUND

System dynamics is a method for studying and managing complex feedback systems (Forrester, 1961; Richardson & Pugh, 1981; Roberts, Andersen, Deal, Grant, & Shaffer, 1981; Sterman, 2000). One of the basic principles of system dynamics is that a system's performance over time is closely linked to an underlying structure of endogenous feedback processes. That is to say, patterns of behavior in the system are explained mainly by endogenous processes, not by exogenous factors. The processes of modeling and simulation are mainly intended to learn about how the world works, helping policy makers to improve their way of thinking (Senge, 1990). Usually, a computer model is needed because of human limitations to predict and manage the behavior of these complex structures (Forrester, 1971). In this way, the modeling process becomes a formal way of developing and testing hypotheses about the impact of feedback processes on specific problematic behaviors in a system.

The Modeling Process

System-dynamics practitioners have described the modeling process as a series of steps going from problem understanding to model validation and use (Randers, 1980; Richardson & Pugh, 1981; Roberts et al., 1981; Sterman, 2000). The modeling process involves the analysis of problem dynamics (expressed on graphs of behavior over time) and problem structure (expressed graphically in causal-loop diagrams or stock-and-flow diagrams, and mathematically in systems of differential equations). In this way, a system-dynamics computer model is the result of an iterative process of comparing and contrasting a set of assumptions about the system structure and the known behaviors of it.

In this way, defining problems in terms of behavior over time (graphs over time), and developing feedback-rich diagrams (causal-loop and stock-and-flow diagrams) are two basic skills to model problems.[1]

Defining Problems in Terms of Behavior Over Time

In system dynamics, defining problems means to express them in terms of their dynamic behavior (Richardson & Pugh, 1981), moving from static pictures of symptoms of a problem to a dynamic definition of it (Mashayekhi, 1992; Senge, 1990).

The term *reference mode* refers to patterns of behavior over time. These patterns represent the dynamic behavior of important problem-related variables. The reference mode is an abstract concept to guide the modeling process, which is built by using multiple sources of historical evidence, such as verbal descriptions, time series, or key events (Saeed, 1998). In terms of the data available, a modeler can draw graphs of either historical data series (information available from records in the organization) or idealized reference modes (information available from actors' judgments and mental models). In terms of the project scope, modelers create sketches of historical data, forecasted dynamics (what we can expect to happen), or preferred dynamics (what we desire to happen).

Historical data series are complex patterns that represent the effects on system behavior of multiple problem components (Saeed, 1992). Therefore, historical data series can be used as the starting point to create a reference mode, but using that pattern as the reference mode itself can be misleading to the modeling effort. Although historical data series can show many different behaviors, most of those rich behaviors

Figure 1. Common patterns of problem behavior

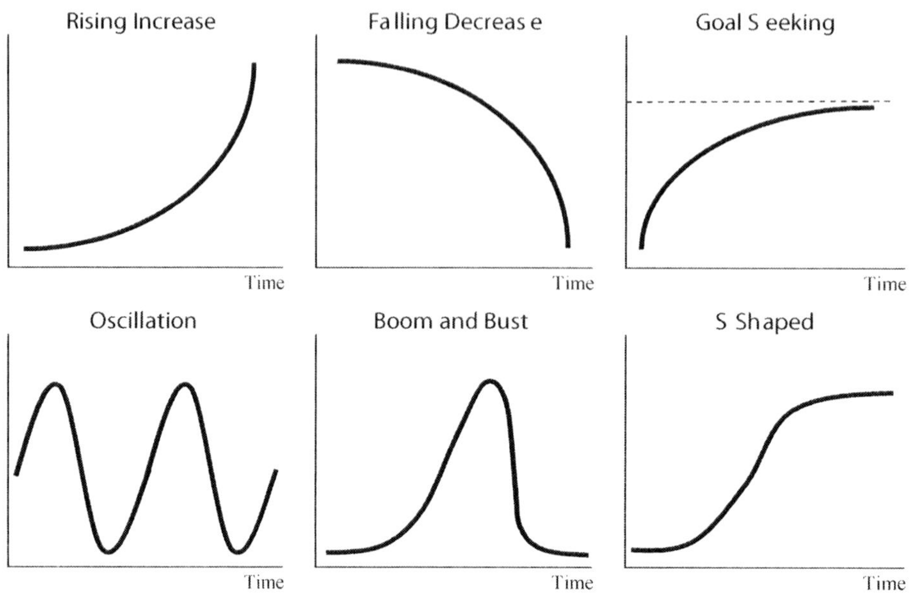

are combinations or instances of a limited set of behavioral patterns like the ones shown in Figure 1. Moreover, it is common to find out in public-sector applications that relevant variables are not recorded in any information system. Thus, many reference modes are based upon actors' judgments and mental models.

In fact, system dynamics is best suited for problems that show dynamic behaviors like the ones presented in Figure 1, particularly when the

Table 1. Definition of causal links

Graphic Representation	Conceptual Definition	Math Definition
X —(+)→ Y	X adds to Y, or changes in X lead to changes in Y in the same direction	$Y = \int_{t_0}^{t} (X + ...)ds + Y_{t_0}$ or $\frac{\partial Y}{\partial X} > 0$
X —(-)→ Y	X subtracts from Y, or changes in X lead to changes in Y in the opposite direction	$Y = \int_{t_0}^{t} (-X + ...)ds + Y_{t_0}$ or $\frac{\partial Y}{\partial X} < 0$

Table 2. Examples of feedback loops and ways to represent them

Examples of Feedback Loops	Common Representations
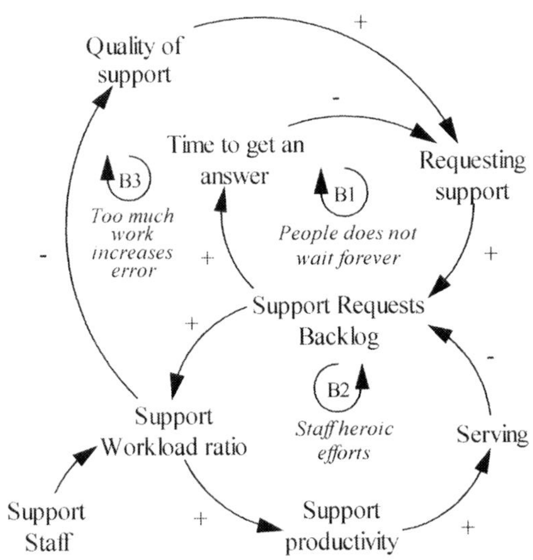	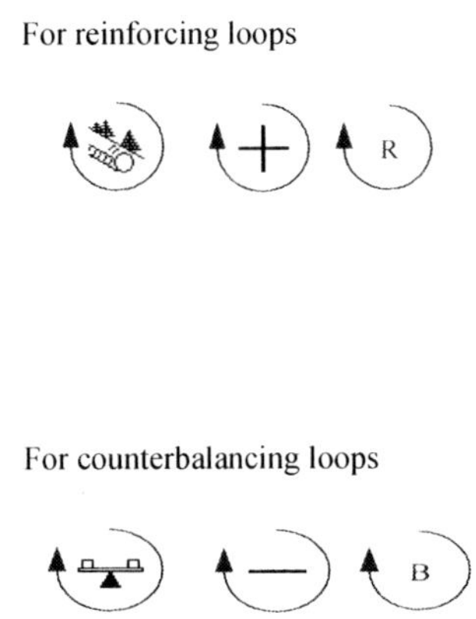

pattern can be explained by actors' decisions and actions (endogenous explanation).

Feedback-Rich Diagrams

Researchers in the field have developed a series of mapping tools to represent endogenous explanations of observed problematic behaviors (Morecroft, 1982). A study of best practices in the field suggested that the preferred mapping tools by a group of highly recognized experts are the stock-and-flow and causal-loop diagrams (Martinez-Moyano & Richardson, 2001).[2]

Causal-Loop Diagrams

The building blocks of causal-loop diagrams are variable names and causal links, which can be either positive or negative. Table 1 shows the conceptual and mathematical definition of the direction of causal relationships.

A closed path of causal links constitutes a feedback loop: "A feedback loop exists when decisions change the state of the system, changing the conditions and information that influence future decisions" (Richardson, 2000). A reinforcing loop (or positive loop) represents a changing process where the characteristic is growing, decaying, destabilizing, or accelerating. A reinforcing loop contains only positive links or an even number of negative links. A counterbalancing loop (negative or balancing) represents a process implying resistance to change, goal seeking, or stabilizing behavior. A balancing loop contains an odd number of negative links.

Table 2 shows three balancing loops representing processes associated with technical-support requests to a help desk that were used to represent problems with migrating a system to a client-server architecture in a state agency (the example will be described in the next section). As it is shown in the table, it is common to name the loops with words describing the main dynamic process.

Stock-and-Flow Diagrams

Other common structural representations are stock-and-flow diagrams. Stocks (or state variables) represent accumulations in the system and are increased or decreased only by inflows

Figure 2. Stock-and-flow diagram

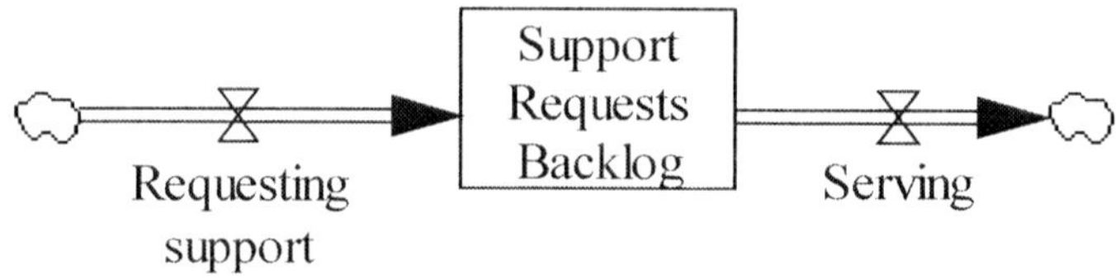

or outflows, which represent activities in the system. We can identify one accumulation and two activities in the feedback loops in Table 2 (See Figure 2). The "clouds" at the origin of the inflow and the end of the outflow represent conceptual boundaries of the system. That is to say, things flow from and to somewhere outside the representation of the problem. Challenging these conceptual boundaries is an important activity during the modeling process.

Stocks and flows are analogous to a bathtub. Inflows and outflows represent the pipes (faucets and drains), and the stock is analogous to the bathtub itself. Actors' decisions and actions in the system are influenced by accumulations in it. Figure 3 shows the same feedback loops from Table 2 associated with the accumulation and activities presented in Figure 2.

Causal-loop diagrams are considered better tools to communicate feedback processes to people while stock-and-flow diagrams are more suited to helping people think about a problem for simulation purposes. One caveat of causal-loop diagrams is that there are subtraction or addition links that can be misinterpreted as proportional links (Richardson, 1997). These links are clearer in the stock-and-flow representation because they are associated with inflows and outflows such as requesting support and serving.

This view has been successfully applied in the public sector. Many examples can be drawn particularly from the System Dynamics Group at

Figure 3. Feedback loops in a stock-and-flow diagram

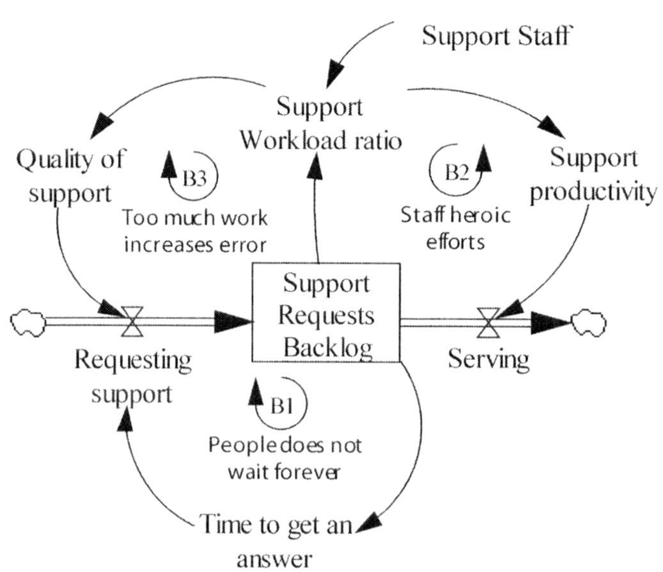

the University at Albany, which has been applying system dynamics to understand public policy problems with groups of managers since 1987 (Richardson, Andersen, & Luna-Reyes, 2004).

The very first application consisted of a group analysis of a crisis in the New York (NY) medical malpractice system, involving hikes in doctors' premiums, complex legal and technical arguments, and the interests of competing powerful stakeholders, such as hospital associations, medical associations, trial-lawyer associations, and insurance carriers (Reagan-Cirincione, Schuman, Richardson, & Dorf, 1991). Other examples include analyzing the impact of the 1996 welfare reform of NY state and county welfare systems (Zagonel, Rohrbaugh, Richardson, & Andersen, 2004), understanding foster care caseload dynamics (Wulczyn, Andersen, Richardson, & Wuestman, 1991), understanding rises in Vermont Medicaid costs (Andersen, Richardson, & Ratanawijitrasin, 1992), studying failed efforts to integrate vocational services for mental health clients (Huz, Andersen, Richardson, & Boothroyd, 1997; Richardson & Andersen, 1995), transforming the role of the NY State Office of Real Property Services into a consulting model with localities (Griffen, Andersen, Richardson, & Finn, 2000), understanding the dynamics of tobacco prevalence and control (Trochim, 2004), and understanding collaboration processes in public information technology implementations (Black et al., 2003; Luna-Reyes et al., 2004). The following section includes an application of system dynamics to analyze public information technology problems.

AN APPLICATION OF SYSTEM DYNAMICS TO PUBLIC IT: REAL PROPERTY ADMINISTRATION

This section starts with a description of the problem context, continuing with a description of the model purpose and the data sources used in the process. The section ends describing the system-dynamics model, important behaviors, and the main lessons from the process.

Problem Context

The nature of Ecuate State[3] real property demands that a diverse group of actors share information in the pursuit of efficient property assessment, tax administration, and equalization. Equitable taxation requires the consideration of issues surrounding information technologies, business and technical support, and organizational relationships.

In recent years, the Real Property Administration (RPA) has made considerable efforts to determine the role it should play in the pursuit of real-property tax equity. In its most recent efforts to implement an upgraded multifunction software system (RPSV4) to local governments, RPA has encountered several stumbling blocks.

RPSV4 was designed to be user-friendly software to share information among all the actors involved in real property in the state of Ecuate. From the RPA point of view, an important requirement of the new system was to reduce the development burden (programming) caused by continuous changes to the real-property laws and regulations, and by the diversity of computer platforms existent among users. After careful analysis, RPA decided to make RPSV4 a point-and-click Windows-like client-server application. However, putting processing power at the desktop of the assessor changed the distribution of user-support burden.

Model Purpose and Data Sources

The purpose of the simulation analysis was to gain a comprehensive understanding about pressures impacting the RPS conversion process. Particularly, the project team was interested in the dynamics of the conversion from one generation of real property software (RPSV3) to the next (RSPV4) and its impact upon development

Figure 4. The conversion process from RPSV3 to RPSV4

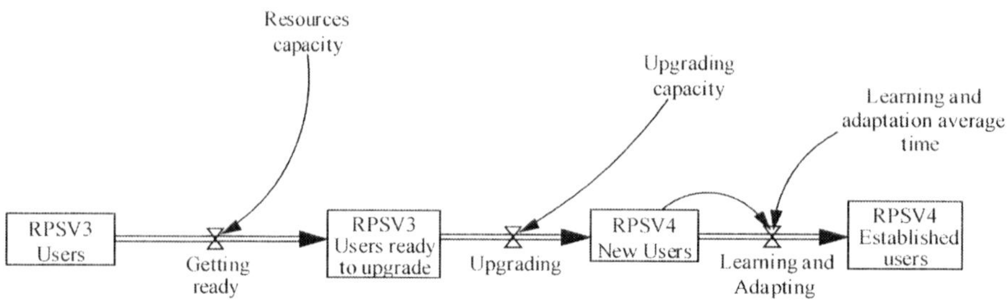

and support burdens in the system. Although the development burden was expected to decrease, RPA technical-support staff in central and regional offices were being overwhelmed trying to manage the support burden.

A system-dynamics model was built using information from several sources: working sessions with RPA staff, telephone interviews with assessors, county directors of real property and IT offices, staff from RPA regional offices, and document analysis.

Initial conversations were used to develop a reference mode, and a preliminary model was introduced to RPA staff to facilitate a conversation about the support and development issues associated with the conversion process. Model assumptions and formulations were enriched with the comments and suggestions of RPA staff.

Model Description

The model represents the transition of users converting from RPSV3 to RPSV4 (Figure 4). Two intermediate steps were identified during this transition: the preparation for the upgrading process, and the learning curve associated with upgrading. Getting users ready to upgrade depended mainly on the availability of resources to adjust business processes or hardware investments. Upgrading depended mainly on the RPA staff's capacity to install the system. Some time is needed to learn and adapt to the new system to become an established user of RPSV4.

The flow of users during the conversion process determined the developing and supporting burdens in the system (Figure 5). New developing tasks depended on adjustments needed in the program, the number of different versions of the program (four RPSV3 versions [one for each existing system platform] and one RPSV4 version), and the installed base of users of RPSV3 and RPSV4. System modifications responded both to periodical changes in regulations and to enhancements suggested by the users. These requests accumulate in the developing backlog, which declines when developing staff works on making the necessary coding.

On the support side, support requests are generated in a very similar way. Users generate requests, which accumulate in the support backlog, while support staff solves each incident.

Staff productivity is driven by the actual workload of both programmers and support staff (see Figure 3). Having more workload increases staff productivity. Additionally, increases in workload erode the quality of these two activities, raising errors and rework. In the case of the support requests, higher quality of work attracts more users to request support. Finally, long response time from the support system discourages people from following the official channels to ask for support (lower side of Figure 3). The average number

Figure 5. The conversion process and its impact on the burdens of support and development

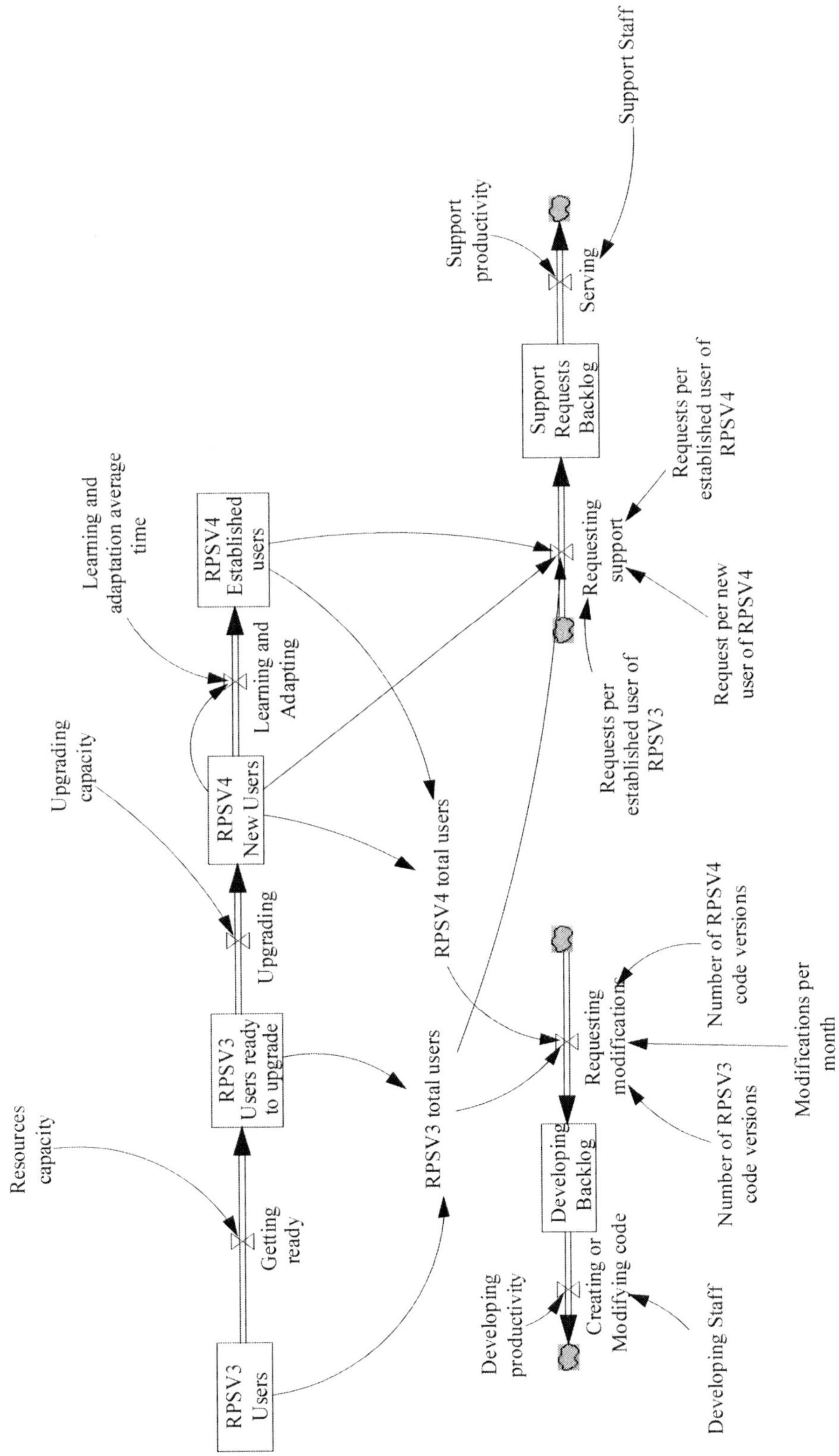

of support requests increases periodically as a response to new software releases.

Dynamics of the Conversion Process

Figure 6 shows the conversion process dynamics. The conversion process starts at Month 12 and extends for about 5 years. The vertical axis represents the number of users running any version of RPS. Line 1 shows how RPSV3 users discontinue the use of this software during the conversion process, while Line 2 represents RPSV4 adoption. The other two curves (3 and 4) describe the behavior of users either waiting for RPSV4 installation or who are in the learning and adaptation stage.

It is possible to identify three different stages in the conversion process. The first stage represents the initial equilibrium when all users are using RPSV3. The second stage depicts the conversion itself. The third stage represents the new equilibrium when all users are converted to the new version.

These three stages are also present in the behaviors of the burdens of developing and support (Figures 7a and 7b). The scenario of a conversion from RPSV3 to RPSV4 changes the initial equilibrium of these burdens to a different level after an adaptation process characterized by a temporary increase in both the burden of development and support.

The development burden behavior shows periodic peaks representing increases to the development burden due to adjustments to the real-property tax legal framework (Figure 7a). The size of each peak responds to the number of RPS versions that needed maintenance. Pressure generated by these peaks was one motivating factor for developing RPSV4. The impact of the legal adjustments declines over time given that the number of supported versions declines as a result of the conversion process. However, the initial addition of RPSV4 places an additional burden on system development. As RPSV4 becomes a more stable product, the requests for enhancements decrease as does the coding burden.

In the case of support burden (Figure 7b), support requests are expected to increase due to the technical capacity of the average user. With RPSV3, the average user was most likely a well-qualified mainframe operator, whereas with RPSV4, the average user may be an assessor with only cursory knowledge of Windows, let alone database-driven applications. Under this assumption, the number of technical problems is

Figure 6. Conversion from RPSV3 to RPSV4

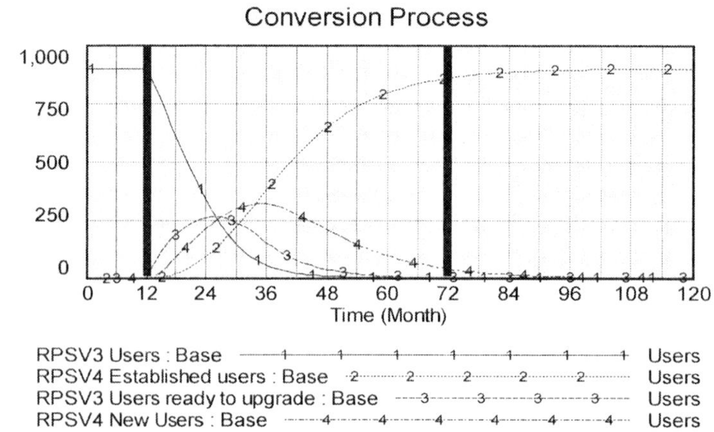

Figure 7. Typical behavior of development (a) and support (b) burdens during the conversion process

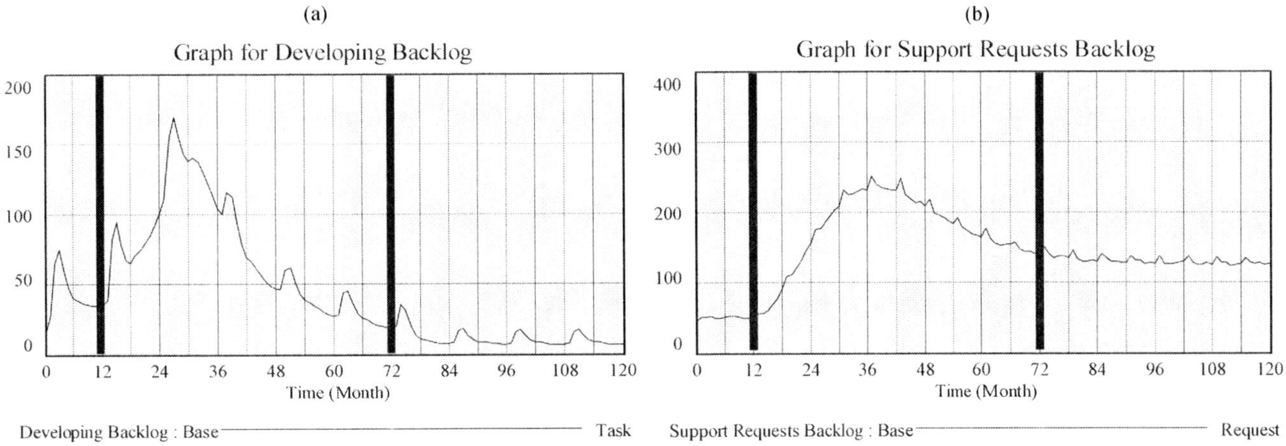

potentially larger with RPSV4 than with RPSV3. The small peaks on the support burden represent a small disturbance promoted by new controlled biannual software releases.

Lessons Learned

The increase in the burden of support during the conversion process is explained mainly by requests caused by the technical capacity of the average user (assessors) and learning curves associated with new functionalities in the system. According to this model, modest increases in the quantity of staff or increases to their productivity have almost no impact on the behavior of the support burden. Only significant changes on those variables improve the outcome. The lack of sensitivity to changes in these factors is related to the feedback structure inside the system. In general, having more staff or more productive staff will improve the response time and the quality of the service, attracting and accommodating more support requests from other users who did not utilize the service before. This characteristic of the system led to the conclusion that a fee structure for support or a partnership with other stakeholders such as county real-property offices, county IT shops, or external vendors is a key element in managing this burden.

In addition to the quantitative differences between both equilibrium stages, there is a qualitative difference in the mix of support requests. Given that assessors are more involved with RPSV4 functions, there will be a mix of different types of problems that should be tracked during the conversion process. Some technical incidents could be related to how to use the tool during the assessment of business processes, some other incidents could lead to software enhancements, and some incidents will be related to the actual network and hardware configuration of the users. Defining and understanding these qualitative differences is also an important factor to manage the burden.

The model indicated a shifting burden of support that in many ways is the result of the nature of the new product. Using the insights gained from the modeling process, the team identified potential measurable goals for RPSV4 and suggested building a technical support model.

FUTURE TRENDS

Challenges imposed by dealing with a group of clients (or group model building) are an important catalyst in the creation of conversational and visual tools to model dynamic problems (Andersen & Richardson, 1997; Andersen, Richardson, & Vennix, 1997; Lane, 1993; Luna-Reyes, Martinez-Moyano, Pardo, Cresswell, Andersen, & Richardson, 2005; Richardson & Andersen, 1995; Vennix, 1996; Vennix, Andersen, Richardson, & Rohrbaugh, 1994). Important advances in system dynamics come from researchers in this area, which offers important potential to understand the implementation of public information technologies. Although the number of documented client-group modeling exercises has increased over time, future research needs to focus on experimental evaluations of these interventions and the creation of frameworks to facilitate the evaluations (Andersen et al., 1997; Rouwette, 2003; Rouwette, Vennix, & Van Mullekom, 2002).

Another trend consists of the use of system-dynamics models combined with other modeling techniques. Interesting examples include the use of system assumptions surfacing and testing (SAST) and multiattribute utility models (Reagan-Cirincione et al., 1991), soft systems methodology (Lane & Oliva, 1998), event maps (Howick, Ackermann, & Andersen, 2006), spatial modeling and geographic information systems (BenDor & Metcalf, 2006), and agent-based or econometric models (Ortiz, Sarriegi, & Santos, 2006).

CONCLUSION

System-dynamics modeling and simulation provides effective means to deal with complex problems. Moreover, the method provides public managers with tools to surface and test assumptions and mental models related to planning, development, implementation, and evaluation of information technology. The endogenous point of view is empowering because performance is guided mainly by managerial decisions. From my personal point of view, the method is best suited to promote individual or team understanding about the implications of information technology applications in the public sector, and consequently, improving managerial planning and decision-making capabilities. One of the main criticisms to the method is related to the process of model validation. Model validation in system dynamics consists of a series of semiformal processes involving a "social conversation, rather than objective confrontation [with reality]" (Barlas & Carpenter, 1990). Although this view has promoted multiple debates about the formality of the method, it adheres to practices of theory confirmation from the contemporary relativist philosophy of science, promoting conversations about the adequacy of the model as a policy tool with a specific purpose.

FUTURE RESEARCH DIRECTIONS

Information technologies are perceived as powerful tools to reduce costs, promote efficiencies and synergies, increase public programs' impact, increase the quality of public services, and promote democratic values. Unfortunately, many IT initiatives in government fail to deliver the expected results. This kind of result is in fact observed in many other attempts to improve organizational performance. Such phenomena has been characterized as an improvement paradox that results from unintended consequences from the initial improvement effort (Repenning, 2002; Sterman, Repenning, & Kofman, 1997).

The system-dynamics approach has been used successfully to get a better understanding of the unintended consequences, modeling them in form of feedback-rich stories, which help in identifying either reinforcing or balancing processes that prevent change (Abdel-Hamid & Madnick, 1990; Repenning, 2002; Sterman, Repenning, & Kofman, 1997; Wolstenholme, 2003). Future research in public information technologies should focus on applying system dynamics to understand the improvement paradox in IT implementation processes (D. F. Andersen, personal communication, May 2004). Given that many IT initiatives in government involve the collaboration of several agencies, such a research program should include the analysis of interagency collaboration dynamics.

ACKNOWLEDGMENT

This chapter is based on earlier work contributed to by Liz Fairwether, Chris Pagano, and Bill Shinn.

REFERENCES

Abdel-Hamid, T. K., & Madnick, S. E. (1990). The elusive silver lining: How we fail to learn from software development failures. *Sloan Management Review*, pp. 39-48.

Abdel-Hamid, T. K., & Madnick, S. E. (1991). *Software project dynamics: An integrated approach.* Englewood Cliffs, NJ: Prentice Hall.

Andersen, D. F., & Richardson, G. P. (1997). Scripts for group model building. *System Dynamics Review, 13*(2), 107-129.

Andersen, D. F., Richardson, G. P., & Ratanawijitrasin. (1992). *Vermont Medicaid interim report.* Albany, New York: Rockefeller College of Public Affairs and Policy.

Andersen, D. F., Richardson, G. P., & Vennix, J. A. M. (1997). Group model building: Adding more science to the craft. *System Dynamics Review, 13*(2), 187-201.

Barlas, Y., & Carpenter, S. (1990). Philosophical roots of model validation: Two paradigms. *System Dynamics Review, 6*(2), 148-166.

BenDor, T. K., & Metcalf, S. S. (2006). The spatial dynamics of invasive species spread. *System Dynamics Review, 22*(1), 27-50.

Black, L. J., Cresswell, A. M., Pardo, T. A., Thompson, F., Canestraro, D. S., Cook, M., et al. (2003, January). *A dynamic theory of collaboration: A structural approach to facilitating intergovernmental use of information technology.* Paper presented at the Hawaiian International Conference on System Sciences, HI.

Doherty, N. F., & King, M. (2003). From technical change to socio-technical change: Towards a proactive approach to the treatment of organisational issues. In S. Clarke, E. Coakes, M. G. Hunter, & A. Wenn (Eds.), *Socio-technical and human cognition elements of information systems* (pp. 22-40). Hershey, PA: Information Science Publishing.

Forrester, J. W. (1961). *Industrial dynamics.* Waltham, MA: Pegasus Communications.

Forrester, J. W. (1971). Counterintuitive behavior of social systems. *Technology Review, 73*(3), 52-68.

Gil-Garcia, J. R., & Helbig, N. (2006). Exploring e-government benefits and success factors. In A.-V. Anttiroiko & M. Malkia (Eds.), *Encyclopedia of digital government* (pp. 803-811). Hershey, PA: Idea Group Reference.

Griffen, T., Andersen, D. F., Richardson, G. P., & Finn, C. (2000). *Using group model building to support strategic reform of the real property tax system in New York state: A case study.* Paper presented at the 18th International Conference of the System Dynamics Society, Bergen, Norway.

Howick, S., Ackermann, F., & Andersen, D. F. (2006). Linking event thinking with structural thinking: Methods to improve client value in projects. *System Dynamics Review, 22*(2), 113-140.

Hutchins, E. (1991). Organizing work by adaptation. *Organization Science, 2*(1), 14-39.

Huz, S., Andersen, D. F., Richardson, G. P., & Boothroyd, R. (1997). A framework for evaluating systems thinking interventions: An experimental approach to mental health system change. *System Dynamics Review, 13*(2), 149-169.

Jackson, M. (1997). The meaning of requirements. *Annals of Software Engineering, 3*, 5-21.

Keil, M., Cule, P. E., Lyytinen, K., & Schmidt, R. (1998). A framework for identifying software project risks. *Communications of the ACM, 41*(11), 76-82.

Lane, D. C. (1993). The road not taken: Observing a process of issue selection and model conceptualization. *System Dynamics Review, 9*(3), 239-264.

Lane, D. C., & Oliva, R. (1998). The greater whole: Towards a synthesis of SD and SSM. *European Journal of Operational Research, 107*(1), 214-235.

Luna-Reyes, L. F., Martinez-Moyano, I. J., Pardo, T. A., Cresswell, A. M., Andersen, D. F., & Richardson, G. P. (2005). *Group modeling of IT-based innovations in the public sector.* Paper presented at the 23rd International Conference of the System Dynamics Society, Boston.

Luna-Reyes, L. F., Mojtahedzadeh, M., Andersen, D. F., Richardson, G. P., Bodor, T., Burke, B., et al. (2004). *Emergence of the governance structure for information integration across governmental agencies: A system dynamics approach.* Paper presented at the 22nd International Conference of the System Dynamics Society, Oxford, England.

Madachy, R. J., & Tarbet, D. (2000). Case studies in software process modeling with system dynamics. *Software Process Improvement and Practice, 5*(2-3), 133-146.

March, J. (1981). Footnotes to organizational change. *Administrative Science Quarterly, 26*(4), 563-577.

Martinez-Moyano, I., & Richardson, G. P. (2001). *Best practices in system dynamics modeling.* Paper presented at the 19th International Conference of the System Dynamics Society, Atlanta, GA.

Mashayekhi, A. N. (1992). *From a static picture to a dynamic problem definition.* Paper presented at the 1992 International System Dynamics Conference of the System Dynamics Society, Utrecht, the Netherlands.

Morecroft, J. D. W. (1982). A critical review of diagraming tools for conceptualizing feedback system models. *Dynamica, 8*(1), 20-29.

Orlikowski, W. (2000). Using technology and constituting structures: A practice lens for studying technology in organizations. *Organization Science, 11*(4), 404-428.

Ortiz, A., Sarriegi, J. M., & Santos, J. (2006). *Applying modelling paradigms to analyse organisational problems.* Paper presented at the the 2006 International Conference of the System Dynamics Society, Nijmegen, the Netherlands.

Randers, J. (1980). Guidelines for model conceptualization. In J. Randers (Ed.), *Elements of the system dynamics method* (pp. 117-138). Cambridge, MA: Productivity Press.

Reagan-Cirincione, P., Schuman, S., Richardson, G. P., & Dorf, S. A. (1991). Decision modeling: Tools for strategic thinking. *Interfaces, 21*(6), 52-65.

Repenning, N. P. (2002). A simulation-based approach to understanding the dynamics of innovation implementation. *Organization Science, 13*(2), 109-127.

Richardson, G. P. (1997). Problems in causal loop diagrams revisited. *System Dynamics Review, 13*(3), 247-252.

Richardson, G. P. (2000). *Tools for systems thinking and modeling.* Retrieved from http://www.albany.edu/faculty/gpr/PAD624/Conceptualization.pdf

Richardson, G. P., & Andersen, D. F. (1995). Teamwork in group model building. *System Dynamics Review, 11*(2), 113-137.

Richardson, G. P., Andersen, D. F., & Luna-Reyes, L. F. (2004, October). *Joining minds: Group modeling to link people, process, analysis, and policy design.* Paper presented at the 26th Annual APPAM Research Conference, Atlanta, GA.

Richardson, G. P., & Pugh, A. L., III. (1981). *Introduction to system dynamics modeling with dynamo.* Cambridge, MA: Productivity Press.

Roberts, N. H., Andersen, D. F., Deal, R. M., Grant, M. S., & Shaffer, W. A. (1981). *Introduction to computer simulation.* Waltham, MA: Pegasus Communications.

Rouwette, E. A. J. A. (2003). *Group model building as mutual persuasion.* Nijmegen, the Netherlands: Wolf Legal Publishers.

Rouwette, E. A. J. A., Vennix, J. A. M., & Van Mullekom, T. (2002). Group model building effectiveness: A review of assessment studies. *System Dynamics Review, 18*(1), 5-45.

Saeed, K. (1992). Slicing a complex problem for system dynamics modeling. *System Dynamics Review, 8*(3), 251-262.

Saeed, K. (1998). *Defining a problem or constructing a reference mode.* Paper presented at the 16th International Conference of the System Dynamics Society, Quebec, Canada.

Scholl, G. J. (1995). Benchmarking the system dynamics community: Research results. *System Dynamics Review, 11*(2), 139-155.

Senge, P. (1990). *The fifth discipline.* New York: Currency.

Sterman, J. D. (2000). *Business dynamics: Systems thinking and modeling for a complex world.* Boston: Irwin/McGraw-Hill.

Sterman, J. D., Repenning, N. P., & Kofman, F. (1997). Unanticipated side effects of successful quality programs: Exploring a paradox of organizational improvement. *Management Science, 43*(4), 503-521.

Trochim, W. e. a. (2004). *Isis report.*

Vennix, J. A. M. (1996). *Group model building: Facilitating team learning using system dynamics.* Chichester, England: Wiley.

Vennix, J. A. M., Andersen, D. F., Richardson, G. P., & Rohrbaugh, J. (1994). Model building for group decision support: Issues and alternatives in knowledge elicitation. In J. D. W. Morecroft & J. D. Sterman (Eds.), *Modeling for learning organizations* (pp. 29-49). Portland, OR: Productivity Press.

Wolstenholme, E. F. (2003). The use of system dynamics as a tool for intermediate level technology evaluation: Three case studies. *Journal of Engineering and Technology Management, 20*(3), 193-204.

Wolstenholme, E. F., Henderson, S., & Gavine, A. (1993). *The evaluation of management information systems: A dynamic and holistic approach.* John Wiley & Sons.

Wulczyn, F. H., Andersen, D. F., Richardson, G. P., & Wuestman, E. A. (1991). *Caseload and fiscal implications of the foster care baby boom: Executive summary report to Joseph Semidei, deputy commissioner, and James Purcell, associate commissioner, of the New York State Department of Social Services.* Albany, New York: New York State Department of Social Services.

Zagonel, A. A., Rohrbaugh, J., Richardson, G. P., & Andersen, D. F. (2004). Using simulation models to address "what if" questions about welfare reform. *Journal of Policy Analysis and Management, 23*(4), 890-901.

FURTHER READING

Abdel-Hamid, T. K., & Madnick, S. E. (1990). The elusive silver lining: How we fail to learn from software development failures. *Sloan Management Review*, pp. 39-48.

Abdel-Hamid, T. K., & Madnick, S. E. (1991). *Software project dynamics: An integrated approach.* Englewood Cliffs, NJ: Prentice Hall.

Andersen, D. F. (1980a). How differences in analytic paradigms can lead to differences in policy conclusions. In J. Randers (Ed.), *Elements of the system dynamics method* (pp. 61-74). Cambridge, MA: Productivity Press.

Andersen, D. F. (1980b). Using feedback simulation to test educational finance policies. *Policy Sciences, 12*(3), 315-331.

Andersen, D. F., Bryson, J. M., Richardson, G. P., Ackermann, F., Eden, C., & Finn, C. B. (2006). *Integrating modes of systems thinking into public strategic management education and practice: The TPI approach.* Paper presented at the Academy of Management.

Black, L. J., Carlile, P. R., & Repenning, N. P. (2004). A dynamic theory of expertise and occupational boundaries in new technology implementation: Building on Barley's study of CT scanning. *Administrative Science Quarterly, 49*(4), 572-607.

Bryson, J. M. (2004). *Strategic planning for public and nonprofit organizations: A guide to strengthening and sustaining organizational achievement* (3rd ed.). San Francisco: Jossey-Bass.

Bryson, J. M., Ackermann, F., Eden, C., & Finn, C. B. (2004). *Visible thinking: Unlocking causal mapping for practical business results.* Chichester, England: John Wiley & Sons.

Huz, S., Andersen, D. F., Richardson, G. P., & Boothroyd, R. (1997). A framework for evaluating systems thinking interventions: An experimental approach to mental health system change. *System Dynamics Review, 13*(2), 149-169.

Luna-Reyes, L. F., & Andersen, D. L. (2003). Collecting and analyzing qualitative data for system dynamics: Methods and models. *System Dynamics Review, 19*(4), 271-296.

Luna-Reyes, L. F., Martinez-Moyano, I. J., Pardo, T. A., Cresswell, A. M., Andersen, D. F., & Richardson, G. P. (2006). Anatomy of a group model-building intervention: Building dynamic theory from case study research. *System Dynamics Review, 22*(4), 291-320.

Martinez-Moyano, I. J., & Gil-Garcia, J. R. (2004). Rules, norms, and individual preferences for action: An institutional framework to understand the dynamics of e-government evolution. In R. Traunmüller (Ed.), *Electronic government* (pp. 194-199). Berlin, Germany: Springer Berlin/Heidelberg.

Randers, J. (1980). Guidelines for model conceptualization. In J. Randers (Ed.), *Elements of the system dynamics method* (pp. 117-138). Cambridge, MA: Productivity Press.

Richardson, G. P. (Ed.). (1996). *Modelling for management: Simulation in support of systems thinking.* Aldershot, United Kingdom: Dartmouth Publishing Company.

Richardson, G. P., & Pugh, A. L., III. (1981). *Introduction to system dynamics modeling with dynamo.* Cambridge, MA: Productivity Press.

Rohrbaugh, J. (2000). The use of system dynamics in decision conferencing. In D. Garson (Ed.), *Handbook of public information systems* (pp. 521-533). New York: Marcel Dekker.

Rouwette, E. A. J. A., & Vennix, J. A. M. (2003). Using groupware to gather and analyze intelligence in a public setting: Development of integral safety plans in an electronic meeting. In D. Vriens

(Ed.), *Information and communication technology for competitive intelligence* (pp. 114-128). Hershey, PA: Idea Group Publishing.

Rouwette, E. A. J. A., Vennix, J. A. M., & Thijssen, C. M. (2000). Group model building: A decision room approach. *Simulation & Gaming, 31*(3), 359-379.

Rouwette, E. A. J. A., Vennix, J. A. M., & Van Mullekom, T. (2002). Group model building effectiveness: A review of assessment studies. *System Dynamics Review, 18*(1), 5-45.

Senge, P. M. (1990). *The fifth discipline: The art and practice of the learning organization.* New York: Doubleday.

Stallinger, F., & Grünbacher, P. (2001). System dynamics modelling and simulation of collaborative requirements engineering. *The Journal of Systems and Software, 59*(3), 311-321.

Sterman, J. D. (2000). *Business dynamics: Systems thinking and modeling for a complex world.* Boston: Irwin/McGraw-Hill.

Vennix, J. A. M. (1999). Group model-building: Tackling messy problems. *System Dynamics Review, 15*(4), 379-401.

Wolstenholme, E. F. (1990). *System enquiry: A system dynamics approach.* John Wiley.

Wolstenholme, E. F. (2003). The use of system dynamics as a tool for intermediate level technology evaluation: Three case studies. *Journal of Engineering and Technology Management, 20*(3), 193-204.

Zagonel, A. A. (2002, July-August). *Model conceptualization in group model building: A review of the literature exploring the tension between representing reality and negotiating a social order.* Paper presented at the Proceedings of the 20th International Conference of the System Dynamics Society, Palermo, Italy.

Zagonel, A. A., Rohrbaugh, J., Richardson, G. P., & Andersen, D. F. (2004). Using simulation models to address "what if" questions about welfare reform. *Journal of Policy Analysis and Management, 23*(4), 890-901.

TERMS AND DEFINITIONS

Feedback Loop: A feedback loop is a closed path of causal relations among variables. Feedback loops usually represent the process of monitoring the state of the system, the effects of decisions in the system state, and future decisions.

Mental Model: Mental models are representations of reality built in people's minds. These models are based on arrangements of assumptions, judgments, and values. A main weakness of mental models is that people's assumptions and judgments change over time and are applied in inconsistent ways when building explanations of the world.

Model Formulation: This is the stage in the modeling process where the modeler creates a mathematical representation of a conceptual model.

Model Validation: This consists of a series of activities to build confidence in a system-dynamics model as a useful policy tool in a specific context.

Problem Conceptualization: This is the stage in the modeling process where the modeler focuses on understanding the problematic behavior over time and the important feedback processes associated with it.

Reference Mode: The reference mode is a historical or hypothesized dynamic characterization of a problem. These behaviors are the guiding principle for the system-dynamics modeling process.

Simulation Model: Simulation models are formal representations of a portion of reality. Simulation models allow managers to share and test assumptions about problem causes and solutions.

ENDNOTES

1. There are other skills related to formulating, analyzing, and validating simulation models that go beyond the scope of this short chapter. Interested readers can refer to Sterman (2000) for further information on developing simulation models.
2. Alternative diagramming tools described by Morecroft (1982) are sector diagrams, used for a high-level representation of a model, and policy-structure diagrams, used to represent decisions and structures from the manager's point of view. As found by Scholl (1995), the four mapping tools are frequently combined in system-dynamics projects. From his sample, 82% of the projects utilized causal-loop diagrams, 70% of them used stock-and-flow diagrams, 41% included sector diagrams, and 19% employed policy structure diagrams.
3. The data and models presented here are based upon a real case in a state government office. The agency and state names are disguised to keep their identities confidential.

Chapter XLVI
Government Innovation Through Knowledge Management

Luis Felipe Luna-Reyes
Universidad de las Américas-Puebla, Mexico

INTRODUCTION

Contemporary organizations face the challenge of growing and advancing in a complex and changing environment (Johannessen, Olaisen, & Olsen, 2001; Malhotra, 2000). In order to accomplish this objective, private organizations continuously innovate to attract customers (Johannessen et al.). Competition has been accelerated by information technology, which allows the appearance of new business models, introducing new competitors in the business arena (Rayport, 2001). Under these circumstances, it appears that innovation is one of the most valuable activities for any organization (Nonaka, 1996). Furthermore, the management of intangible assets such as knowledge is one of the critical factors to promote innovation and sustainable competitive advantage (Davenport, 2001; De Long & Fahey, 2000; Malhotra; Nonaka).

The need for innovation in government does not respond directly to competition, but to several intertwined factors, such as the complexity of the problems being faced by government, the emergence of new organizational forms such as networks, the pressure to improve service to the citizens, and the need to learn about new information technology.

Government faces complex social problems that require collaboration from different levels of government, private organizations, and nonprofits (Snyder & de Souza Briggs, 2003; Snyder, Wenger, & de Souza Briggs, 2004). These new collaboration patterns challenge the traditional hierarchical government organization, deriving on the need to innovate in the structure of institutions (Gascó, 2004) and the creation of networks of public and/or private organizations needing to share what they know about a specific problem domain (Fountain, 2001a; Snyder & de Souza Briggs; Zhang, Cresswell, & Thompson, 2005). Innovation is also needed to respond to citizens demanding from government levels of service similar to the ones they are used to getting from private companies (Kannabiran, Xavier, & Anantharaaj, 2004). Additionally, movements such as the New Public Management or the Reinvention of Government are also adding pressure to improve these levels of service (Fountain, 2001b).

IT is being used to respond to these challenges, and public-sector organizations are using IT to promote better relationships between government and citizens (Gil-García & Helbig, 2006; Heeks, 2006; Lee, Tan, & Trimi, 2005; Rocheleau, 2006). However, introducing IT in government poses the challenge of continuous learning and education of government employees, promoting also the need for sharing knowledge (Heeks, 2006). In several countries, additional pressures promoting knowledge management (KM) come from personnel turnover from retirements (Bontis, 2007).

In this way, promoting innovation and managing knowledge is becoming increasingly important for public agencies. As with many other public information technologies, knowledge management and knowledge management systems require the integration of technical design in a series of social processes and interactions among government, citizens, and private organizations, where knowledge is continuously created or transformed (Awad & Ghaziri, 2003; Barrett, Cappleman, Shoib, & Walsham, 2004; Fountain, 2001a).

The purpose of the present chapter is to discuss the process involved in managing knowledge and innovation in government, considering some critical factors in the process. To accomplish this objective, the chapter is organized in four different but conceptually interrelated sections. In the first of them, I describe some of the main concepts of knowledge management. The second section is a description of the knowledge management process, and the next one is a brief discussion about the impact of the four critical factors identified by Arthur Andersen and Company on the main stages in the KM process. The last sections of the chapter constitute a description of future trends and conclusions.

BACKGROUND: THE CONCEPT OF KNOWLEDGE AND KNOWLEDGE MANAGEMENT

Knowledge management is the activity of administering knowledge. De Long and Fahey (2000) consider that the purpose of knowledge management "is to enhance organizational performance by explicitly designing and implementing tools, processes, systems, structures, and cultures to improve the creation, sharing and use of all types of knowledge that are critical for decision making."

Although knowledge is an abstract concept difficult to define, there are two common ways of conceptualizing knowledge. Some experts consider knowledge as an accumulation of actionable information (Davenport, de Long, & Beers, 1998; Nonaka, 1994) or intellectual capital (Becerra-Fernandez, Gonzalez, & Sabherwal, 2004; Bontis, 2007). Some others consider knowledge as a dimension of practice (Black, Carlile, & Repenning, 2004; Levina & Vaast, 2005; Walsham, 2005).

In this way, knowledge management projects take two different forms, characterized as person to person and person to document, responding to each of these views (Dennis & Vessey, 2005). Although both perspectives recognize that knowledge resides in people, person-to-document projects consider knowledge as a codifiable asset to manage. Examples of person-to-document projects include knowledge repositories, decision support systems, expert systems, data warehouses, or executive information systems. The federal Mexican government, for instance, maintains a public repository of government procedures known as Tramitanet (http://www.tramitanet.gob.mx). The e-Mexico program, on the other hand, has invested part of its resources to create knowledge portals in areas such as education, health, economy, and government (Luna-Reyes, Gil-García, & Cruz, 2006).

Person-to-person projects assume that knowledge is embedded in practice, and they look to promote innovation and knowledge sharing by establishing means to connect people. Knowledge directories, groupware, customer relationship management (CRM), workflow management tools, and communities of practice are examples of this kind of projects. In Argentina, for instance,

CIOs (chief information officers) have created an interorganizational network to share knowledge and solve IT-related problems in government (Kaufman, 2004). Similarly, the New York State Office of the State Comptroller (NYS-OSC) has developed and consolidated a workflow management and CRM tool known as Multi-Purpose Access for Customer Relations and Operational Support (MACROS; Luna-Reyes, Zhang, Gil-García, & Cresswell, 2005). In the next two sections, I will discuss some basic ideas associated with these two perspectives, linked in an interesting way on a matrix (Belardo, 2001).

THE KNOWLEDGE MANAGEMENT PROCESS

Although there are different ways of conceptualizing the knowledge management process (Awad & Ghaziri, 2003), this section follows a four-activity approach in which managing knowledge involves its identification, elicitation, dissemination, and utilization.

Identification

Knowledge identification involves the activities associated with answering the questions of who knows what, where the knowledge is, and what type of knowledge it is (Awad & Ghaziri, 2003). The intelligence quadrant is a tool to help during the identification process (Hall, 2000). The quadrant has four cells (Table 1). The first cell contains the items we know that we know, and the second cell has the items we know that we do not know. The third and fourth cells contain knowledge we do not know that we know and we do not know that we do not know, respectively. The first two cells in the quadrant contain knowledge that is possible to identify through knowledge fairs, networks, communities of practice, decision conferences, talk rooms (Gray, 2001), and interactions with clients and providers (Davenport, 2001). For instance, e-Mexico participants identified knowledge categories to include in the portals in the context of face-to-face meetings. Similarly, NYS-OSC has continuously defined and redefined the main characteristics of MACROS on the basis of input from users and managers. In both cases, a critical factor to succeed is getting involved with the main stakeholders and domain experts.

The third and fourth cells, on the other hand, constitute places to use tools developed to build business intelligence, such as data warehousing, data mining, customer relationship management, and so forth. For example, the e-health group from the e-Mexico initiative is mining electronic

Table 1. Intelligence quadrant (Adapted from Hall, 2000)

	...That We Know	... That We Don't Know
We Know...		
We Don't Know...		

Figure 1. Example of a concept map based on Dennis and Vessey (2005)

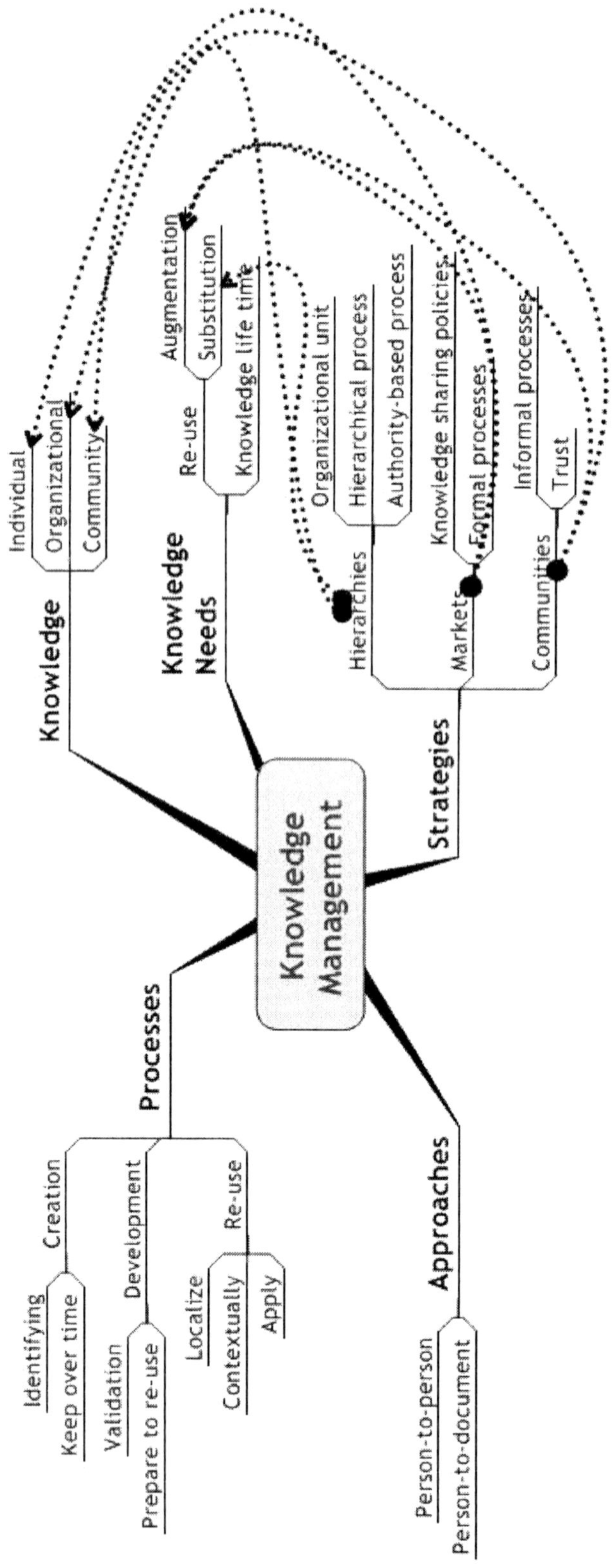

health records to identify health trends and risks in some pilot communities.

Elicitation

Knowledge elicitation is associated with protocols and tools used to acquire and codify knowledge (Byrd, Cossick, & Zmud, 1992; Eriksson, 1992). From a problem-solving point of view, knowledge is acquired during the process of problem solving, particularly the new or unique kind of problems (Gray, 2001).

From the accumulation view of knowledge, the purpose of knowledge elicitation is to obtain and codify knowledge from domain experts. From the practice point of view, the processes associated with acquiring or creating knowledge can also be conceptualized as the result of the interaction of the knowledge that resides in our heads, the one associated with the context of our physical and social context and the proper act of knowing (Cook, 1999): "The source of new knowledge and knowing lies in the use of knowledge as a tool of knowing within situated interaction with the social and physical world" (p. 383).

The acquisition and codification of knowledge are difficult tasks. Even when companies have access to a rich set of tools such as surveys, interviews, decision conferences, teaching, counseling, repertory grids, or talk rooms, the characteristics of practice-embedded knowledge poses several challenges for the process (Black et al., 2004). These kinds of knowledge are context related, embedded in a tacit level of understanding difficult to make explicit and charged with power, having the potential of create conflict during the acquisition of knowledge across organizational or departmental boundaries (Bechky, 2003; Black et al.; Carlile, 2002). In such cases, the use of objects to facilitate knowledge sharing at the boundary is recommended. For instance, concept maps are becoming a standard to represent specific problems or content domains in group sessions. In fact, the e-Mexico group has intensively used concept maps to define knowledge domains associated with each of the e-Mexico portals (see Figure 1 for an example of a concept map).

Dissemination

The process of dissemination involves the creation of knowledge representations that allow the processing and storage of knowledge. Additionally, the main concerns for managers are related to the problem of making knowledge available to the right people at the right time (Belardo, 2001). Depending on the project, dissemination of knowledge is related to one of two main purposes: knowledge augmentation or knowledge substitution (Dennis & Vessey, 2005).

Knowledge augmentation projects look to incrementally build over existing knowledge and innovation. These projects usually involve the creation of repositories and making more accessible the knowledge kept in these repositories. Repositories keep internal, external, and informal knowledge (Davenport et al., 1998). Improving-access projects have as their most common purpose the creation of a catalog or other artifact intended to find the person who knows how to deal with specific problems (expert networks).

The MACROS system at the NYS-OSC is an example of a knowledge augmentation system. The purpose of MACROS is to help several divisions of the Office of the State Comptroller to manage their relationships with customers by keeping a record of the interactions with them, and to give advice and technical support. Knowledge substitution systems have the purpose of substituting expert knowledge such as in expert systems.

Knowledge transfer and dissemination is also a difficult task. The problems associated with this process have led some researchers to characterize it as a "sticky" process (Szulanski, 1999). There is a conflict between the knowledge created by a community of practice and the knowledge needed to promote collaboration between communities

(Carlile, 2002). From this point of view, knowledge is a barrier and a source of innovation and collaboration.

Utilization

Knowledge utilization involves not only the actual internalization processes (Nonaka, 1994, 1996), but also an assessment of the benefits that the organization is obtaining through the use of this knowledge. Under these assumptions, knowledge utilization is related to both knowledge internalization and evaluation processes.

The internalization process has aroused the interest of researchers who conclude that knowing what to do is not enough (Pfeffer & Sutton, 2000). Actually, it is possible to identify several knowing-doing barriers such as the tendency to substitute action with talking or the substitution of thinking with memory (Pfeffer & Sutton, 2000).

A MODEL TO INTEGRATE KNOWLEDGE MANAGEMENT APPROACHES

Interpretations of the knowledge management process can be integrated with descriptive models involving critical success factors as shown in Table 2 (Belardo, 2001). The purpose of this part of the chapter is to make some comments and to stress the role of each of the four factors during the different stages in the KM process. Instead of discussing the role of the critical factors across all the stages in the process, I will focus on the shaded cells in Table 2. That is to say, I will discuss the role of technology in the dissemination process, the role of measurement on the identification process, and so on.

Technology

Technology is an important factor that can influence positively the dissemination of knowledge, as well as the other stages in the process. It is important to point out that technologies, broadly defined, include not only computer hardware and software, but a rich set of hard and soft technologies that can be used in the process of dissemination of knowledge. Examples of hard technologies are whiteboards, bulletin boards, overhead projectors, and computers. On the other hand, soft technologies include Post-its, overhead transparencies, and software used with hardware, but also the technologies developed to design and manage this series of artifacts.

From this point of view, "[k]nowledge management tools are technologies, broadly defined, which enhance and enable knowledge generation, codification and transfer" (Ruggles, 1997), and they include among others data warehouses, search engines, and visualization tools.

An interesting set of technologies for the dissemination process are the tools associated with the development of knowledge repositories or knowledge bases. They are different from databases or information bases in the sense that they contain interrelationships, history, and past usage

Table 2. A matrix approach to knowledge management (Adapted from Belardo, 2001)

	Identification	Elicitation	Dissemination	Utilization
Technology				
Measurement				
Leadership				
Culture				

of the knowledge inside them. Three technologies are changing the way in which this kind of repositories can be organized and accessed. First, the extensible markup language (XML) offers the possibility to create a meaningful syntax for a community of practice, and to embed this syntax inside documents, making possible to have the contents of these documents self-describing (Bosak & Bray, 1999). On the other hand, there is the resource description framework (RDF), which encodes meaning in sets of triplets with each triple being like the subject, verb, and object of an elementary sentence (Berners-Lee, Hendler, & Lassila, 2001). Finally, recent developments in ontology engineering add to these basic technologies the capability to develop documents that formally define the relation among terms (or ontologies). This triplet of technologies makes possible the development of software to help people find information and services called agents. From my personal point of view, this powerful combination of technologies will revolutionize the way in which knowledge repositories are used nowadays.

Some other technologies used in the dissemination of knowledge are portals, component- or modular-based products (integration of knowledge tools, legacy systems, enterprise resource planning [ERP], and CRM systems), e-mail based solutions, expert systems, and collaborative working environment servers (Silver, 2000). All these technology-based solutions have the potential of increasing the ways in which knowledge is transferred and communities of practice acquire new knowledge.

However, it is important to be aware that technological solutions are not enough, and the extensive use of them without taking into account a set of soft technologies has the potential to overemphasize person-to-document over person-to-person initiatives (Johannessen et al., 2001).

Measurement

Measurement is another critical factor along the knowledge management process, and projects involving the development of better ways to measure intangible assets are very common across organizations (Davenport et al., 1998). Moreover, there exist several systems to measure the impact of knowledge and knowledge management programs (Martin, 1999). Some of these approaches focus on accounting methods (market-to-book ratios or Sveiby invisible balance sheets), some of them focus on the output of the system (peer-reviewed performance or customer appraisal), and some of them involve a more integral approach (balance scorecard or intangible assets monitor).

However, some problems have been identified in measurement practices in organizations (Martin, 1999). The first one is that organizations do not measure what they perceive as important. For example, 76% of the organizations included in a survey rated morale as important, but only 37% measure it. The second problem is that even when organizations collected relevant data, most of them did not use it for anything.

Interesting approaches to identify and measure what we think is actually relevant can be found in the education literature. Core-competencies identification to identify e-learning and training initiatives can be guided, for example, by Bloom's taxonomy of learning objectives (Belardo, 2001). This statement makes a lot of sense if we think that Bloom developed this taxonomy to help educators think about what was really important to teach as an aid to setting objectives and as the basis of the creation of learning measurement instruments.

Bloom's taxonomy (Bloom, Messia, & Krathwohl, 1964) involves three domains of knowledge: cognitive, affective, and psychomotor. For each domain, he developed a hierarchy of levels of skill (see Table 3). Both tacit and explicit dimensions of knowledge are present in the taxonomy. The tacit dimension is present particularly in the levels of skill that imply knowledge embedded in practice (particularly in the affective and psychomotor domains).

In this way, we can use this framework to think about the kinds of knowledge and core competen-

Table 3. Bloom's taxonomy of learning objectives

COGNITIVE DOMAIN	AFFECTIVE DOMAIN	PSYCHOMOTOR DOMAIN
Knowledge	Receiving phenomena	Perception
Comprehension	Responding to phenomena	Readiness to act
Application	Valuing	Guided response
Analysis	Organization	Mechanism
Synthesis	Characterization	Complex overt response
Evaluation		Adaptation

cies that we really want to promote and leverage, as well as key skills and attitudes.

Finally, it is important to stress the importance of taking care of the reliability and validity of our measurement systems, thinking of reliability as the consistency of an assessment device and validity as the extent to which the instrument measures what it was designed to measure (Aiken, 1994).

Leadership

The role of the leader is important in knowledge management, particularly in the world of public administration where complex problems need to be solved by networks of public and private organizations in which power is shared (Crosby & Bryson, 2005; Frederickson, 2005).

The leader in this environment has new roles to play. First, the leader is a designer of vision, policies, and learning processes that enable knowledge utilization. Additionally, the leader is a teacher who helps people get more insightful views of a current problem. Finally, the leader is a steward of the people's needs and the broader mission (Bertucci, 2006; Senge, 1996).

Building a shared vision is particularly important in network environments where no actor has full control or jurisdiction over a problem or resources for potential solutions (Crosby & Bryson, 2005; Frederickson, 2005). Encouraging people to have a personal vision, to communicate and ask for support when needed, and to bring the external views to blend them with internal practices and activities constitutes an important activity for the leader.

Crosby & Bryson (2005) propose the Leadership for the Common Good framework for public-sector leaders. The framework includes four components: attention to the dynamics of a shared-power world, the wise design and use of forums, effective navigation of the policy change cycle, and the exercise of leadership capabilities.

Complex public-sector problems require from leaders to understand that collaboration is needed to solve problems. The main challenge is to get together key stakeholders with different and complementary expertise in the problem domain. A wise design of forums involves the leader's capabilities to design a place to share meanings and knowledge about the problem and its solutions. Leader activities should rest on the principle of creative tension, that is, "from seeing clearly where we want to be and telling the truth about where we are" (Senge, 1996). This principle promotes actions to close the gap between what we know and what we do. Navigating the policy change cycle involves project management activities needed to push the shared vision of a solution forward, from problem identification to implementation and evaluation. Leadership, in fact, has played a key role in several projects that I have observed in Mexico and the United States such as the e-Mexico program or specific projects like MACROS.

Culture

Organizational culture is a major barrier (or facilitator) to knowledge management projects (De Long, 1997; De Long & Fahey, 2000), and it is critical in the acquisition and creation of knowledge involved in the elicitation stage.

First of all, it is important to state that culture is reflected in values (tacit preferences about objectives and relevant issues), norms (informal rules inside the organization), practices (individual and collective behaviors), and artifacts shared by the people across an organization (Beer & Eisenstat, 2000; De Long, 1997; De Long & Fahey, 2000). Values and assumptions are commonly referred to as the ideational components of culture, while norms, practices, and artifacts constitute the material components of culture (Leidner & Kayworth, 2006). Establishing these values, norms, and common understandings are recognized as important components in a KM program (Snowden, 1999). Although values are difficult to observe directly, they are linked to observable practices and artifacts. That is to say, values shape norms, which in turn determine specific practices. De Long (1997) found four different ways in which organizational culture shapes knowledge management initiatives. First, culture mediates how knowledge is to be distributed between the organization and the individual, and what is to be shared. Norms about status and trust among individuals are crucial for knowledge acquisition given that it is very difficult to acquire knowledge from a distant or distrusted source (Szulanski, 1999). In this way, although government agencies encourage the transfer of knowledge and best practices to reduce the costs of innovation, differences in norms or shared meanings about how work must be done between government agencies represent a barrier to facilitate knowledge sharing. On the other hand, culture creates the rules and practices of communication (vertical vs. horizontal, and opened vs. closed) and social interaction, both critical in the creation of knowledge. In the e-Mexico project, for example, differences between the centralized Ministry of Transportation and Communications and the highly decentralized Ministry of Education or the professional-oriented Ministry of Health have been important challenges to facilitate knowledge sharing. Finally, culture determines how we gather information from the environment or internal sources, shaping directly the creation and adoption of new knowledge. Public-sector organizations are, for instance, much more cautious and risk averse in their decisions about IT investments than private firms (Rocheleau, 2006).

FUTURE TRENDS

Most of the existing research favors an epistemology of possession (knowledge as an asset) over an epistemology of practice (knowledge as practice). In this way, current and future research trends call for developing such epistemology of practice that differentiates knowledge from the act of knowing, and recognizes the differences between knowledge that is part of practice and knowledge that resides or is possessed in the heads of the members of a group (Cook, 1999; Walsham, 2005). This practice approach is particularly important in understanding interorganizational networks like the ones emerging in the public sector to innovate and solve complex problems.

Associated with this practice approach to knowledge, knowledge transfer across boundaries is an area future research should try to better understand (Bechky, 2003; Black et al., 2004; Carlile & Rebentisch, 2003; Levina, 2005; Levina & Vaast, 2005). Carlile (2002), for example, identifies three approaches to analyze knowledge transfer: syntactic (common syntax to communicate), semantic (shared meanings), and pragmatic approaches (communities are reluctant to change their own knowledge through interaction across boundaries). To solve the problem, boundary objects can be used to clarify meaning and specify dependencies (Carlile, 2002). Boundary objects are "objects that are shared and shareable across different problem solving contexts" (p. 451). Moreover, boundary objects will play an important role in identifying and eliciting knowledge from groups of stakeholders playing the role of domain experts analyzing public problems and policies.

Finally, another important trend is associated with the use of social network analysis to better understand the social relations among members of an organization to develop better strategies and channels to share knowledge (Borgatti & Cross, 2003), and to better understand relationships in communities of practice (Wenger & Snyder, 2000).

CONCLUSION

I want to finish this chapter by remarking again that all efforts in identifying, eliciting, disseminating, and using knowledge are closely related to increasing individual and collective capabilities to innovate. Innovation is without a doubt one of the core competencies of public organizations in order to improve governance and create public value. Although it is possible to create new ideas by contemplation or by encouraging serendipity, most of the creative efforts came from reorganizing, challenging, or taking different points of view about the things that we actually know. In the face of complex problems, innovation also involves bringing together a diversity of stakeholders in a creative way to build and negotiate shared meanings about the problem and its solutions. This very nature of the innovative process pinpoints the importance of identifying, acquiring, sharing, and using the knowledge that we already have.

FUTURE RESEARCH DIRECTIONS

There are a lot of knowledge-related phenomena that are yet to be explored. We need to understand and find better ways to share knowledge that forms part of practice. It is important also to get a better understanding of the act of knowing, and the ways in which the act of knowing interacts with our actual knowledge in the creation or innovative process.

Although information technologies have a great potential to facilitate both the administration of knowledge and the innovation processes, understanding the social relationships of networks of individuals and looking for better organizational designs need attention to truly improve the way of doing government. Leaders in this process are the architects of the technological and organizational designs that will increase the innovative processes.

ACKNOWLEDGMENT

The research reported here is supported by the Consejo Nacional de Ciencia y Tecnología (CONACYT-Mexico) Grant No. SEP-2004-C01-46507. The views and conclusions expressed in this chapter are those of the authors alone and do not necessarily reflect the views or policies of CONACYT.

REFERENCES

Aiken, L. (1994). *Psychological testing and assessment* (8th ed.). Boston: Allyn & Bacon.

Awad, E. M., & Ghaziri, H. M. (2003). *Knowledge management.* Upper Saddle River, NJ: Prentice Hall.

Barrett, M., Cappleman, S., Shoib, G., & Walsham, G. (2004). Learning in knowledge communities: Managing technology and context. *European Management Journal, 22*(1), 1-11.

Becerra-Fernandez, I., Gonzalez, A., & Sabherwal, R. (2004). *Knowledge management: Challenges, solutions, and technologies.* Upper Saddle River, NJ: Pearson Prentice Hall.

Bechky, B. (2003). Sharing meaning across occupational communities: The transformation of understanding on a production floor. *Organization Science, 14*(3), 312-330.

Beer, M., & Eisenstat, R. (2000). The silent killers of strategy implementation and learning. *Sloan Management Review, 41*(4), 29-40.

Belardo, S. (2001). *Learning organizations and knowledge management: A conventional view and an alternative view.*

Berners-Lee, T., Hendler, J., & Lassila, O. (2001). The semantic Web. *Scientific American.*

Bertucci, G. (2006). Unlocking the human potential for public sector performance. *Public Personnel Management, 35*(3), 175-179.

Black, L. J., Carlile, P. R., & Repenning, N. P. (2004). A dynamic theory of expertise and occupational boundaries in new technology implementation: Building on Barley's study of CT scanning. *Administrative Science Quarterly, 49*(4), 572-607.

Bloom, B., Messia, B., & Krathwohl, D. (1964). *Taxonomy of educational objectives.* New York: David McKay.

Bontis, N. (2007). Mining the nation's intellectual capital: Knowledge management in government. In S. Borins, K. Kernaghan, D. Brown, N. Bontis, P. 6, & F. Thompson (Eds.), *Digital state at the leading edge* (pp. 155-182). Toronto, Canada: University of Toronto Press.

Borgatti, S. P., & Cross, R. (2003). A relational view of information seeking and learning in social networks. *Management Science, 49*(4), 432-445.

Bosak, J., & Bray, T. (1999). XML and the second-generation Web. *Scientific American.*

Byrd, T. A., Cossick, K. L., & Zmud, R. W. (1992). A synthesis of research on requirements analysis and knowledge acquisition techniques. *MIS Quarterly, 16*(1), 117-138.

Carlile, P. (2002). A pragmatic view of knowledge and boundaries: Boundary objects in new product development. *Organization Science, 13*(4), 442-455.

Carlile, P., & Rebentisch, E. (2003). Into the black box: The knowledge transformation cycle. *Management Science, 49*(9), 1180-1195.

Cook, S. J. B. (1999). Bridging epistemologies: The generative dance between organizational knowledge and organizational knowing. *Organization Science, 10*(4), 381-400.

Crosby, B., & Bryson, J. (2005). A leadership framework for cross-sector collaboration. *Public Management Review, 7*(2), 177-201.

Davenport, T. (2001). How do they know their customers so well? *Sloan Management Review, 42*(2), 63-73.

Davenport, T., de Long, D., & Beers, M. (1998). Successful knowledge management projects. *Sloan Management Review, 39*(2), 43-57.

De Long, D. (1997). *Building the knowledge-based organization: How culture drives knowledge behaviors.* Unpublished manuscript.

De Long, D., & Fahey, L. (2000). Diagnosing cultural barriers to knowledge management. *The Academy of Management Executive, 14*(4), 113-127.

Dennis, A. R., & Vessey, I. (2005). Three knowledge management strategies: Knowledge hierarchies, knowledge markets and knowledge communities. *MIS Quarterly Executive, 4*(4), 399-412.

Eriksson, H. (1992). A survey of knowledge acquisition techniques and tools and their relationship to software engineering. *The Journal of Systems and Software, 19*, 97-107.

Fountain, J. E. (2001a). *Building the virtual state.* Washington, DC: The Brookings Institution.

Fountain, J. E. (2001b). Paradoxes of public sector customer service. *Governance: An International Journal of Policy and Administration, 14*(1), 55-73.

Frederickson, H. G. (2005). Transcending the community: Local leadership in a world of shared power. *Public Management, 87*(10), 8-15.

Gascó, M. (2004). E-gobierno en Bolivia y Paraguay. In R. Araya Dujisin & M. A. Porrúa Vigon (Eds.), *América Latina puntogob: Casos y tendencias en gobierno electrónico* (pp. 125-150). Santiago, Chile: FLACSO-Chile/AICD-OEA.

Gil-García, J. R., & Helbig, N. (2006). Exploring e-government benefits and success factors. In A.-V. Anttiroiko & M. Malkia (Eds.), *Encyclopedia of digital government* (pp. 803-811). Hershey, PA: Idea Group Reference.

Gray, P. (2001). A problem-solving perspective on knowledge management practices. *Decision Support Systems, 31*, 87-102.

Hall, H. (2000). Online information sources: Tools of business intelligence? *Journal of Information Science, 26*(3), 139-143.

Heeks, R. (2006). *Implementing and managing egovernment: An international text.* London: Sage Publications.

Johannessen, J., Olaisen, J., & Olsen, B. (2001). Management of tacit knowledge: The importance of tacit knowledge, the danger of information technology, and what to do about it. *International Journal of Information Management, 21*, 3-20.

Kannabiran, G., Xavier, M. J., & Anantharaaj, A. (2004). Enabling e-governance through citizen relationship management: Concept, model and applications. *Journal of Services Research, 4*(2), 223-240.

Kaufman, E. (2004). E-gobierno en Argentina: Crisis, burocracia y redes. In R. Araya Dujisin & M. A. Porrúa Vigon (Eds.), *América Latina puntogob: Casos y tendencias en gobierno electrónico* (pp. 151-188). Santiago, Chile: FLACSO-Chile/AICD-OEA.

Lee, S. M., Tan, X., & Trimi, S. (2005). Current practices of leading e-government countries. *Communications of the ACM, 49*(10), 99-104.

Leidner, D. E., & Kayworth, T. (2006). A review of culture in information systems research: Toward a theory of information technology culture conflict. *MIS Quarterly, 30*(2), 357-399.

Levina, N. (2005). Collaborating on multiparty information systems development projects: A collective reflection-in-action view. *Information Systems Research, 16*(2), 109-130.

Levina, N., & Vaast, E. (2005). Competence in practice: Implications for implementation and use of information systems. *MIS Quarterly, 29*(2), 335-363.

Luna-Reyes, L. F., Gil-García, J. R., & Cruz, C. B. (2006, August). *Collaborative digital government in Mexico: Some lessons from federal Web-based inter-organizational information integration initiatives.* Paper presented at the 12th Americas Conference on Information Systems, Acapulco, Mexico.

Luna-Reyes, L. F., Zhang, J., Gil-García, J. R., & Cresswell, A. M. (2005). Information systems development as emergent socio-technical change: A practice approach. *European Journal of Information Systems, 14*(1), 93-105.

Malhotra, Y. (2000). Knowledge management for e-business performance: Advancing information strategy to "Internet time." *Information Strategy, The Executive's Journal, 16*(4), 5-16.

Martin, W. (1999). Approaches to the measurement of the impact of knowledge management programs. *Journal of Information Science, 26*(1), 21-27.

Nonaka, I. (1994). A dynamic theory of organizational knowledge creation. *Organization Science, 5*(1), 14-37.

Nonaka, I. (1996). The knowledge-creating company. In K. Starkey (Ed.), *How organizations learn* (pp. 18-31). London: International Thompson Business Press.

Pfeffer, J., & Sutton, R. (2000). *The knowing-doing gap* (1st ed.). Harvard Business School.

Rayport, J. B. J. (2001). *E-commerce* (1st ed.). New York: McGraw-Hill.

Rocheleau, B. (2006). *Public management information systems.* Hershey, PA: Idea Group Publishing.

Ruggles, R. (1997). *Using technology to manage knowledge better.* Unpublished manuscript.

Senge, P. (1996). The leader's new work: Building learning organizations. In K. Starkey (Ed.), *How organizations learn* (pp. 288-315). London: International Thompson Business Press.

Silver, C. (2000). Where technology and knowledge meet. *The Journal of Business Strategy, 21*(6), 28-33.

Snowden, D. (1999). Three metaphors, two stories and a picture. *Knowledge Management Review, 7*, 30-33.

Snyder, W. M., & de Souza Briggs, X. (2003). *Communities of practice: A new tool for government managers.* Retrieved March 20, 2007, from http://www.businessofgovernment.org/pdfs/Snyder_report.pdf

Snyder, W. M., Wenger, E., & de Souza Briggs, X. (2004). Communities of practice in government: The case for sponsorship. *The Public Manager, 32*(4), 17-21.

Szulanski, G. (1999). The process of knowledge transfer: A diachronic analysis of stickiness. *OBHDP.*

Walsham, G. (2005). Knowledge management systems: Representation and communication in context. *Systems, Signs & Actions, 1*(1), 6-18.

Wenger, E., & Snyder, W. (2000). Communities of practice: The organizational frontier. *Harvard Business Review, 78*(1), 139-145.

Zhang, J., Cresswell, A. M., & Thompson, F. (2005). Participants' expectations and the success of knowledge networking in the public sector. In W. Huang, K. Siau, & K. K. Wei (Eds.), *Digital government: Strategies and implementation from developing and developed countries* (pp. 260-281). Hershey, PA: Idea Group Inc.

FURTHER READING

Andersen, D., & Dawes, S. (1991). *Government information management: A primer and casebook.* Englewood Cliffs, NJ: Prentice Hall.

Argote, L., McEvily, B., & Reagans, R. (2003). Managing knowledge in organizations: An integrative framework and review of emerging themes. *Management Science, 49*(4), 571-582.

Bechky, B. (2003). Sharing meaning across occupational communities: The transformation of understanding on a production floor. *Organization Science, 14*(3), 312-330.

Black, L. J., Carlile, P. R., & Repenning, N. P. (2004). A dynamic theory of expertise and occupational boundaries in new technology implementation: Building on Barley's study of CT scanning. *Administrative Science Quarterly, 49*(4), 572-607.

Bontis, N. (2007). Mining the nation's intellectual capital: Knowledge management in government. In S. Borins, K. Kernaghan, D. Brown, N. Bontis,

P. 6, & F. Thompson (Eds.), *Digital state at the leading edge* (pp. 155-182). Toronto, Canada: University of Toronto Press.

Carlile, P. (2002). A pragmatic view of knowledge and boundaries: Boundary objects in new product development. *Organization Science, 13*(4), 442-455.

Carlile, P., & Rebentisch, E. (2003). Into the black box: The knowledge transformation cycle. *Management Science, 49*(9), 1180-1195.

Dawes, S. S. (1996). Interagency information sharing: Expected benefits, manageable risks. *Journal of Policy Analysis and Management, 15*(3), 377-394.

Dawes, S. S., Pardo, T. A., Simon, S., Cresswell, A. M., LaVigne, M. F., Andersen, D. F., et al. (2004). *Making smart IT choices: Understanding value and risk in government IT investments.* Retrieved March 20, 2007, from http://www.ctg.albany.edu/publications/guides/smartit2

Fountain, J. E. (2001). *Building the virtual state.* Washington, DC: The Brookings Institution.

Gascó, M. (2004). E-gobierno en Bolivia y Paraguay. In R. Araya Dujisin & M. A. Porrúa Vigon (Eds.), *América Latina puntogob: Casos y tendencias en gobierno electrónico* (pp. 125-150). Santiago, Chile: FLACSO-Chile/AICD-OEA.

Gherardi, S. (2001). From organizational learning to practice-based knowing. *Human Relations, 54*(1), 131-139.

Gil-García, J. R., & Helbig, N. (2006). Exploring e-government benefits and success factors. In A.-V. Anttiroiko & M. Malkia (Eds.), *Encyclopedia of digital government* (pp. 803-811). Hershey, PA: Idea Group Reference.

Heeks, R. (2006). *Implementing and managing egovernment: An international text.* London: Sage Publications.

Levin, D., Cross, R., & Abrams, L. (2002). *Why should I trust you? Antecedents of trust in a knowledge transfer context.* Unpublished manuscript.

Levina, N. (2005). Collaborating on multiparty information systems development projects: A collective reflection-in-action view. *Information Systems Research, 16*(2), 109-130.

Levina, N., & Vaast, E. (2005). Competence in practice: Implications for implementation and use of information systems. *MIS Quarterly, 29*(2), 335-363.

Luna-Reyes, L. F., Cresswell, A. M., & Richardson, G. P. (2004). *Knowledge and the development of interpersonal trust: A dynamic model.* Paper presented at the Hawaiian International Conference on System Sciences, HI.

Luna-Reyes, L. F., Zhang, J., Gil-García, J. R., & Cresswell, A. M. (2005). Information systems development as emergent socio-technical change: A practice approach. *European Journal of Information Systems, 14*(1), 93-105.

Orlikowski, W. (2002). Knowing in practice: Enacting a collective capability in distributed organizing. *Organization Science, 13*(3), 249-273.

Pardo, T. A., Cresswell, A. M., Thompson, F., & Zhang, J. (2006). Knowledge sharing in cross-boundary information system development in the public sector. *Information Technology and Management, 7*(4), 293-313.

Polanyi, M. (1966). *The tacit dimension.* Garden City: Doubleday & Company.

Rocheleau, B. (2006). *Public management information systems.* Hershey, PA: Idea Group Publishing.

Snyder, W. M., & de Souza Briggs, X. (2003). *Communities of practice: A new tool for government managers.* Retrieved March 20, 2007, from http://www.businessofgovernment.org/pdfs/Snyder_report.pdf

Snyder, W. M., Wenger, E., & de Souza Briggs, X. (2004). Communities of practice in government: The case for sponsorship. *The Public Manager, 32*(4), 17-21.

Walsham, G. (2005). Knowledge management systems: Representation and communication in context. *Systems, Signs & Actions, 1*(1), 6-18.

Zhang, J., Cresswell, A. M., & Thompson, F. (2005). Participants' expectations and the success of knowledge networking in the public sector. In W. Huang, K. Siau, & K. K. Wei (Eds.), *Digital government: Strategies and implementation from developing and developed countries* (pp. 260-281). Hershey, PA: Idea Group Inc.

TERMS AND DEFINITIONS

Customer Relationship Management (CRM): CRM is an IT-supported process that has as its objective to increase value to customers or citizens. There are two common ways in which public organizations are approaching CRM. The first of them involves improving customer support and service through one-step shopping through the Internet, toll-free numbers, or in some countries through service kiosks. The second approach consists of mining data to better understand citizens' needs in areas such as health or education.

Decision Conferences: These are computer-supported meetings where a group negotiates a shared meaning about a policy problem and alternative solutions to it.

E-Learning: E-learning is a process to improve knowledge dissemination and sharing through the application of information technologies to learning programs such as mentoring or on-the-job training. The concept is also used to refer to formal distance education programs offered through the Internet or other electronic means.

Expert Systems: These are computer programs that codify expert knowledge associated with a specific problem domain. An expert system is formed by a set of rules and an inference engine with the capability to reach a conclusion by combining and applying the rules to a set of facts or statements.

Groupware: Groupware is a computer program that offers services to support group collaboration such as e-mail, meeting scheduling, shared libraries, forums, and chat rooms.

Knowledge Management (KM): KM is a professional field committed to innovation and improved organizational performance by identifying, eliciting, disseminating, and using knowledge and other intangible assets within an organization.

Knowledge Portal: A knowledge portal is an Internet-based computer program that constitutes a single point of access to organizational knowledge, integrating knowledge repositories, expert directories, collaboration tools, and other knowledge-intensive applications.

Chapter XLVII
A Framework for Knowledge Management in E-Government

Kostas Metaxiotis
National Technical University of Athens, Greece

INTRODUCTION

E-government, driven by an ever-increasing and pervasive use of information and communication technologies, is affecting the public sector more and more (Bannister, 2005; Eyob, 2004; Metaxiotis & Psarras, 2004). Many governments across the globe have resorted to instituting e-government initiatives as a way of better positioning themselves in the Information Age (Information for Development Programme [InfoDev], 2004), or seem at least to be showing commitments in redressing the imbalances resulting from the low utilization of knowledge resources and ICT in the economy and governance (Joi, 2004). E-government is enabling government organizations to provide better services to their constituents. The ability to improve citizens' access to services has made e-government an attractive investment for government organizations, fueling worldwide implementation of such applications (Amaravadi, 2005; Scherlis & Eisenberg, 2003). As an emerging practice, e-government seeks to realize processes and structures for harnessing the potentialities of information and communication technologies at various levels of government and the public sector for the purpose of enhancing good governance. The key issues in transformation are the adoption and uptake of interoperable standards, the development of appropriate business models, the legal and policy frameworks that will facilitate integration, and governance arrangements that support both enterprise responsibilities and cross-agency approaches and responsibilities.

On the other hand, in order to gain competitive advantage for their survival, most of the large companies in the private sector have been actively taking initiatives to adopt new management tools, techniques, and philosophies. Governments always follow suit. History shows that most of the management philosophies were first practiced in large companies; once they gained foot in the field, they became adopted in other sectors. Enterprise resource planning (ERP), business process reengineering (BPR), and total quality management (TQM) are indicative examples. Now comes the turn of knowledge management (KM). Governments are now realizing the importance of KM to their policy making and service delivery to the public, and some of the government departments are beginning to put KM high on their agenda.

Public administrations are knowledge-intensive organizations. They host a particularly high percentage of professionals and specialized staff who command important domains of knowledge. This is particularly the case in ministerial departments and in the judiciary and regulatory agencies. Many public organizations are chiefly "intelligence organizations" where human actors cooperate in order to store and process information and to produce information output for further use. If we ask the question, "How does the public administration know what it knows?" it becomes immediately evident that even though there is indeed a lot of knowledge in the organizations, it is not necessarily available anywhere, anytime for anybody. Not all parts of a public organization or even citizens can necessarily benefit from that knowledge. This means that a lot of "wheel reinventing" is going on in public administration.

Not only does the trend toward the knowledge society call for KM solutions (Davenport & Prusak, 1998; Metaxiotis, Ergazakis, & Psarras, 2005; Wiig, 1993) but also current e-government developments significantly influence the public sector. E-government implies fundamental knowledge redistribution and requires a careful rethinking of the management of information resources and knowledge bases.

Implementing a framework for the application of KM in e-government is a very challenging task as it requires many agencies, departments, and policy makers to coordinate their efforts in addition to preparing the technology and supporting the infrastructure—the soft infrastructure, meaning the laws, rules, and regulations that must be changed—in order to facilitate the development of both the new infrastructure and information and knowledge services. While most of the prior research studies have investigated the possible application of KM in the public sector, none have focused on the application of KM in e-government; this is done in this chapter. In this chapter, the author, recognizing the importance of e-government and KM to devolve into the public administration sector, continues his previous research related to the application of KM in e-government (Metaxiotis & Psarras, 2005), discusses key issues, and presents a framework for the application of KM in e-government as a basis for future research.

KNOWLEDGE MANAGEMENT IN E-GOVERNMENT: BACKGROUND

While literature on KM has been addressing issues, challenges, and opportunities for the private sector, little has been discussed for the public sector, and even less in e-government. Frank (2002) reported that several e-government initiatives in USA are using knowledge management principles as the way to knock down the stovepipes that keep government from operating as efficiently as it could....The idea of "collect once, use many" is a common theme in several of the 24 e-government initiatives led by the Office of Management and Budget...

Lenk (2003) presented typical situations in order to stress the specific significance of KM for the public sector.

- Clerical and professional work concerning individual cases to be decided upon
- Individual services to citizens
- Pursuit, by citizens or enterprises, of business or personal affairs involving public bodies
- Management of administrative work and organizations
- Policy formulation by ministerial departments and other public bodies
- Parliamentary work

Other researchers (Stracke, 2002; Bresciani, Donzelli, & Forte, 2003; Palkovits, Woitsch, & Karagiannis, 2003) recognized that in order to efficiently manage e-government evolution, it is fundamental to transform the public administration into a learning organization, characterized by a high level of sharing, reuse, and strategic application of the acquired knowledge and lessons learned. A learning organization is an organization that facilitates the learning of all its members and continuously transforms itself. The basic idea behind it is to create a knowledge chain (collection, production, customization, and delivery) suitable to support and improve the whole organization functioning.

Bruecher (2003) presented the development of a requirement analysis for a KM system in the field of e-government; the objective of the analysis was to figure out the various requirements of the heterogeneous user group and to provide the basis for a more detailed blueprint of the system. Key issues, challenges, and opportunities of KM in the public sector were addressed by Cong and Pandya (2003).

According to Liebowitz (2004), KM in an e-government environment can be a powerful tool for reformers, inside and outside government. Recently, Metaxiotis and Psarras (2005) discussed the application of knowledge management in e-government initiatives and described a knowledge model as a basis for future research in the field.

THE PROPOSED FRAMEWORK FOR KNOWLEDGE MANAGEMENT IN E-GOVERNMENT

The Positioning of Knowledge Management in E-Government

Nowadays, it is quite clear that the traditional bureaucratic model of government is no longer functional. E-government can contribute to better functioning of democracy by online provision of reports and other government information (open government) that would otherwise be difficult to obtain or be unavailable, and through online debates and plebiscites. It can bring efficiency through providing citizens with relatively inexpensive, real-time access to consistent, up-to-date information and transaction facilities, and in parallel can enable governments to disseminate information at lower costs than ever before. Simultaneously, modernization and reorganization of governmental work and responsibilities imply significant changes to knowledge resources. KM concepts and tools can really provide great support to exploit the huge knowledge and information resources, and assist e-government introduction to a modern public administration in an effective way. The positioning of a KM system in an e-government environment is presented in Figure 1, adopted by Manuel (2005).

Figure 1. The positioning of knowledge management in e-government

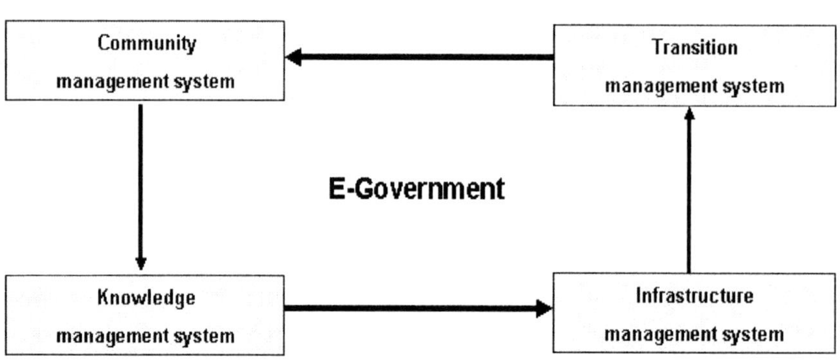

A good e-government model provides a platform where various communities and special-interest groups represent themselves; it builds an environment with specialized expertise that can help answer questions and guide people to find solutions. This is called the community management system of e-government. E-government is a transition process from a conventional to a people-oriented proactive electronic system. To accept this transition process, the communities need to be trained and educated, and in addition the model should be accessible by different communities including the disabled and the underprivileged. This is called the transition management system of e-government. A knowledge management system provides an environment where knowledge flows from a source with knowledge to a destination that needs knowledge and/or captures knowledge and creates new knowledge. Finally, a good e-government environment needs to maintain a powerful integrated hardware and software network so that several billions of information and knowledge pieces can be found in this system by users. This is called the infrastructure management system of e-government.

The Proposed Framework

As e-government implementations progress, the focus shifts from simply providing access to services in electronic form to actively engaging citizens or empowering various stakeholders to create an electronic, knowledge-based democracy. Increasingly knowledgeable citizens require governments to be on top of newly created knowledge as it is increasingly rapidly produced by more differentiated actors. Malhotra (2000) has stressed that a new perspective of KM is to be effectively deployed in the world of e-business.

Due to the fact that public administrations and their organizational environments are characterized by the presence of very diverse kinds of actors (e.g., citizens, employees, businesses, politicians, and decision makers), the critical point for applying a KM concept to e-government is principally to build a suitable knowledge model (Metaxiotis & Psarras, 2005) and then to create an appropriate framework for the application of KM in e-government environments, having in mind the positioning of KM in e-government (Figure 2).

We used the following main principles for deriving our framework.

Universal access. Every citizen has the right to access basic and relevant knowledge of all aspects of society; therefore, the framework should offer knowledge-sharing services that can be accessed through multichannels and multidevices.

Public education and training. Every citizen should be equipped with skills to be independently involved in the knowledge-based society.

Infrastructure development. An affordable, secure, and reliable information, knowledge, and communication infrastructure should be developed on a local, regional, and national level with an efficient connectivity to global networks. The hard infrastructure will create a broadband system linking every home, school, and public institution within the community.

Unified KM portal. Portal technologies should integrate content, applications, and processes together. Hence, the portal can deliver better communications and collaboration between citizens, businesses, suppliers, public institutions, and so forth, providing real-time access to knowledge stored in various systems and knowledge bases to push citizens to store, apply, or create new knowledge.

Customer-centric communication and knowledge sharing. Is knowledge provided based on customer-perceived preferences, needs, and desires? Does the definition mention customer focus or customer preferences? Is there an avenue for customers to address their preferences, needs, and desires?

Based on the above-mentioned principles, we have conceptualized our framework for the application of KM in e-government, which is presented in Figure 2.

Figure 2. The proposed framework

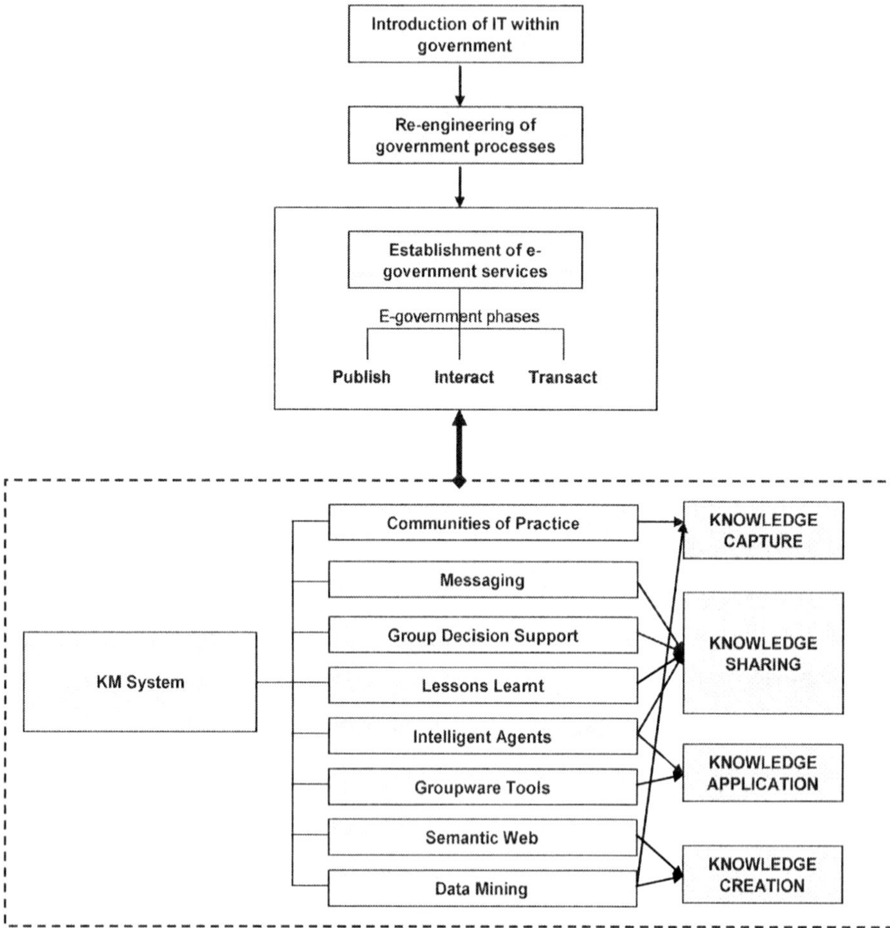

The proposed framework points that the gradual development of e-government environments in public-sector organizations is similar to the one in private-sector organizations. "If you automate inefficient processes, they will become more inefficient" is a well-known adage in the IT community. Reengineering is in many instances necessary to align an agency's internal processes with those of other agencies or governments and thus facilitate cooperation. Without this, e-government will remain only partial and therefore is likely to be an unsuccessful exercise.

In the phase of the establishment of e-government services, we follow the World Bank's (Center for Democracy and Technology [CDT], 2002) model, which defines three stages.

- **Publish:** Broadening access to government information
- **Interact:** Increasing public participation in government decision making
- **Transact:** Making government services more readily available to the public

Due to the high complexity in e-government applications and sometimes the "fuzziness" in public administration procedures, the application of KM principles is a difficult task that should be combined with traditional business process management actions. The development of a KM system in an e-government environment can touch each of the above-mentioned stages and can be related to any of the KM processes: knowledge capture, knowledge sharing, knowledge application, and knowledge creation. Knowledge identification and capture refer to identifying the critical competencies, types of knowledge, and the right individuals (civil servants) who have the necessary expertise that should be captured. Then, this captured knowledge is shared between individuals, departments, and the like. The knowledge application involves applying, which includes retrieving and using, knowledge in support of decisions, actions, and problem solving, and which ultimately can create new knowledge. As new knowledge is created, it needs to be captured, shared, and applied, and the cycle continues.

Depending on which KM process or function we want to apply to an e-government phase, we can use the appropriate technology, as shown in Figure 2. It is obvious that the application of KM in e-government, based on the proposed framework, should be necessarily characterized by the "divide and conquer" rule; due to the high risk involved, the government organizations need to modularize the KM initiative efforts and implement them one piece at a time.

It is important to be stressed that the supply side of such a framework requires a range of legislative changes, which is a key issue. Legislative changes could include the recognition of electronic documents in courts of law, electronic signatures, data matching, knowledge protection, the certification of knowledge, and intellectual property rights legislation. Regulatory changes are also required for a host of activities from knowledge capture to knowledge creation and knowledge-based service delivery. On the other hand, the demand side of the framework gives customers access to online knowledge-based services through multiple channels and systems. This framework includes developing a critical mass of manpower and knowledge sufficient to support an e-governance strategy. Unless citizens are trained and have requisite skills to participate in e-governance, citizens' participation and engagement would be a difficult task for evolving electronic, knowledge-based democracy.

Applying the Proposed Framework in a Greek Municipality

The application of the proposed framework to the Greek municipality is, according to our best knowledge, the first attempt to bring KM into e-government in real practice.

The municipality of Maroussi is located in the north suburbs of Athens, about 11 km from Athens' center, at the foot of Penteli Mountain. About 70,000 inhabitants live in the municipality and its area is 16.2 m^2. In economical terms, it is one of the most important municipalities in Greece. It is the center of financial and cultural development. The city's infrastructure is well developed and a series of quality services are offered to the citizens. Some of the city's most important assets are the following.

- In its premises lies the main complex in which the majority of the Olympic Games 2004 activities have taken place, such as the opening and closing ceremony and a series of important field sports. This was a major event for the local region, as well as the whole country. Due to the Olympic Games, many of the city's infrastructures (e.g., road axes, public transportation, and sports installations) have been significantly improved. Many other positive interventions have also taken place.
- Due to the Olympic Games, the whole region gained publicity and reputation outside the country, something that created new ways of cooperation with other cities.
- Maroussi is the heart of the modern economic life in Athens since it hosts the offices of many innovative and hi-tech enterprises. There are more than 1,800 medium and large

companies that are based in the city representing the following sectors: telecommunications, IT, financial services, insurance, construction, and so forth. More than 33,000 people are working in these companies.

- It is one of the largest commercial centers in Greece, with many stores and shopping malls.
- The municipality offers to all of its citizens, through a series of innovative (compared to other municipalities in Greece) lifelong learning initiatives, the possibility to acquire a high level of skills and knowledge so as to remain competitive in the contemporary, competitive environment.
- The local government is very active in various sectors. It tries to implement new and modern methods of organization and to improve the municipality's infrastructure so as to attract businesses and offer a high quality of life.

It is true that not every city in the world can pursue strategies and undertake initiatives so as to be transformed successfully into a KM-based e-governed city. In other words, these strategies will not eventuate into the desired results for every city, at least to the extent in which they would permit one to characterize their use as a successful case. A city should have the necessary level of development, on the basis of which the proposed framework will be applied, so the whole effort will bring successful results. Although all urban regions contain knowledge activities, not all cities can be knowledge centers.

The application of the proposed framework to Maroussi started in early 2006 and is still ongoing. The results until now show that the proposed framework is being successfully applied and put into practice in spite of the given constraints (e.g., limited funding, political will, public bureaucracy, and so forth). The pilot project began with a period of familiarization of the municipality's local government with the concepts of KM and knowledge-based development (KBD), and continued with the diagnosis of its current status as an e-governed city. This diagnosis constituted the main input for the next stage: the definition of the implementation strategy. An analytical action plan was prepared, incorporating a detailed description of needed actions or projects (for each year). The results, outcomes, and lessons learned at the end of this pilot project will be used in order to assess the applicability of the framework and fine-tune the implementation methodology.

MEASURING KNOWLEDGE MANAGEMENT IN E-GOVERNMENT

Measuring KM is a difficult task. During the E-Gov Institute Knowledge Management 2004 Conference, the American Productivity & Quality Center (APQC) focused on how some government organizations implement KM initiatives, mobilize resources, and measure and evolve their KM programs (APQC, 2004) by stressing that "[j]ust because knowledge is intangible does not mean that its impact is."

Some of the very important measurement points from the APQC study include the following.

- Cost reduction
- Quality improvement
- Increase in services provided
- Citizen satisfaction
- Time saved
- Quick problem resolution

Detailed discussion on the above measurement points and proposed models for the measurement of knowledge are not in the scope of this chapter.

FUTURE TRENDS

The above described framework is quite comprehensive and is helpful in identifying measures to assess knowledge-based e-government implementation for e-participation and e-democracy. Future research should focus on examining the effectiveness of the proposed framework. Detailed questionnaires and other survey instruments could be developed from this framework to assess citizens' participation and engagement.

Finally, a major future challenge is the application of the framework to a big city, which will incorporate structures missing from our case (e.g., hospitals, universities) and at the same time, it will be able to make available larger amounts of funds from the beginning of the initiative. Concluding, we can say that the application of knowledge management in e-government is clearly an area that needs to be more fully addressed.

CONCLUSION

E-government is the latest buzzword for governments trying to involve people in administration, address transparency in their bureaucracies, and make themselves more responsive to their citizens. It has become an everyday reality, but still needs to be shaped with vision and long-term planning. E-government success requires changing how government works, how it deals with information and knowledge, and how officials view their jobs and interact with the public.

Knowledge management is the mental, behavioral, and cultural shift from the old adage "Knowledge is power" to the new mindset "Sharing knowledge is power." It is important to note that acting and decision making in the public sector is not a prerogative of management. Complex decisions are made at the operational level, and it is precisely here that most knowledge demands originate. In general, knowledge management is not only required to know which rules and regulations to apply, but also to be able to reconstruct afterward whether the right procedures were followed.

This chapter has attempted to integrate the two fields of KM and e-government into one singular focus to foster new strategic thinking in KM-based e-government. A framework for the application of KM in e-government was presented and discussed. Since most products of public administration and governance work are delivered in the shape of information and knowledge themselves, KM concepts and tools can really provide great support to the introduction of e-government into a modern public administration. In addition, the retirement of civil servants and frequent transfer of civil servants across government departments also create new challenges for the application of KM in the public sector. Knowledge management is a promising way to enlarge the scope of e-government and improve the modernization and reorganization of governmental work.

FUTURE RESEARCH DIRECTIONS

Visions of knowledge-based e-government or a global-knowledge government are being discussed in the scientific community. There is a common agreement that KM can offer many advantages in e-government. However, as it also happened in the early stages of the evolution of KM, there is neither a coherent framework nor a unified methodology for the design and implementation of successful KM applications in e-government. Consequently, a major stream of future research is to propose coherent frameworks and methodologies for the design, development, and operation of successful KM applications in e-government.

Undoubtedly, there is need for concerted efforts toward the direction of formulating a generally accepted, comprehensive framework for KM in e-government. However, the role of technology in this effort should not be underestimated. This is reflected by the fact that according to recent studies, the technologies used to support KM initiatives are evolving rapidly. Consequently, another stream of future research is to use advanced KM technologies and tools for the proper development of successful KM applications in e-government. In what follows, there is a classification of KM tools that is available in the market and could be used.

- Knowledge Mapping
- Data Mining
- Information Retrieval
- Knowledge Discovery
- Document Management
- Organizational Memory

On the other hand, any KM initiative that is driven purely by technology, without a corresponding change in the culture of the organization, is certain to eventually fail. Too often, organizations implement state-of-the-art technology and then discover that culture and behavior are slow to change. The success of KM initiatives in many fields (including e-government) depends equally to the active involvement of everyone throughout the organization as well as to their consistency with the organization's broader business strategy and culture. Technologies and social systems are equally important in KM. Organizations that follow the KM program with clear objectives and approaches and that manage to coordinate their social relations and technologies tend to be more successful, whereas some other organizations that implement a KM initiative with focus on IT in order to reap some quick benefits without having focus on the human side and a long-term strategy fail. This is the case for KM initiatives in e-government, and consequently more research should be directed in this specific subfield.

REFERENCES

Amaravadi, C. (2005). Digital repositories for e-government. *Electronic Government: An International Journal, 2*(2), 205-218.

American Productivity & Quality Center (APQC). (2004, April). *Measuring the impact of knowledge management.* Proceedings of the E-Gov Institute Knowledge Management 2004 Conference.

Bannister, F. (2005). E-government and administrative power: The one-stop-shop meets the turf war. *Electronic Government: An International Journal, 2*(2), 160-176.

Bresciani, P., Donzelli, P., & Forte, A. (2003). *Requirements engineering for knowledge management in egovernment.* Proceedings of the Fourth Working Conference on Knowledge Management in Electronic Government, Rhodes Island, Greece.

Bruecher, H. (2003). *Requirement analysis for a knowledge management system in egovernment.* Proceedings of the Fourth Working Conference on Knowledge Management in Electronic Government, Rhodes Island, Greece.

Center for Democracy and Technology. (2002). *2002 digital state survey.* Retrieved from http://centerdigitalgov.com

Cong, X., & Pandya, K. (2003). Issues of knowledge management in the public sector. *Electronic Journal of Knowledge Management, 1*(2), 25-33.

Davenport, T., & Prusak, L. (1998). *Working knowledge: Managing what your organisation knows.* Boston: Harvard Business School Press.

Eyob, E. (2004). E-government: Breaking the frontiers of inefficiencies in the public sector. *Electronic Government: An International Journal, 1*(1), 107-114.

Frank, D. (2002). *E-gov theme: "Collect once, use many."* Retrieved from http://www.fcw.com/fcw/articles

Information for Development Programme (InfoDev). (2004). *E-government handbook for developing countries.* Retrieved from http://www.infodev.org

Joi, L. (2004). Bridging the digital divide: Some initiatives in Brazil. *Electronic Government: An International Journal, 1*(3), 300-315.

Lenk, K. (2003). *Relating knowledge management in the public sector to decision-making and administrative action.* Proceedings of the Fourth Working Conference on Knowledge Management in Electronic Government, Rhodes Island, Greece.

Liebowitz, J. (2004). Will knowledge management work in the government? *Electronic Government: An International Journal, 1*(1), 1-7.

Malhotra, Y. (2000). Knowledge management for e-business performance. *Information Strategy: The Executives Journal, 16*(4), 5-16.

Manuel, P. (2005). A model of e-governance based on knowledge management. *Journal of Knowledge Management Practice*, pp. 1-10.

Metaxiotis, K., Ergazakis, K., & Psarras, J. (2005). Exploring the world of knowledge management: Agreements & disagreements in the research community. *Journal of Knowledge Management, 9*(2), 6-18.

Metaxiotis, K., & Psarras, J. (2004). E-government: New concept, big challenge, success stories. *Electronic Government: An International Journal, 1*(2), 141-151.

Metaxiotis, K., & Psarras, J. (2005). A conceptual analysis of knowledge management in e-government. *Electronic Government: An International Journal, 2*(1), 77-86.

Palkovits, S., Woitsch, R., & Karagiannis, D. (2003). *Process-based knowledge management and modelling in e-government: An inevitable combination.* Proceedings of the Fourth Working Conference on Knowledge Management in Electronic Government, Rhodes Island, Greece.

Scherlis, W., & Eisenberg, J. (2003). IT research, innovation and e-government. *Communications of the ACM, 46*(1), 67-68.

Stracke, J. (2002). *E-government: Supporting knowledge and information flows with supply chain management.* Proceedings of the Third Working Conference on Knowledge Management in Electronic Government, Copenhagen, Denmark.

Wiig, K. (1993). *Knowledge management foundations: Thinking about thinking. How people and organizations create, represent and use knowledge.* Arlington, TX: Schema Press.

FURTHER READING

Amidon, D. M. (2004). *In the knowledge-zone: Architecting a blueprint for the World Trade of Ideas.* Retrieved from http://www.inthekzone.com

Amin, A., & Thrift, N. (1995). The globalisation of the economy: An erosion of regional networks? In G. Grabher (Ed.), *The embedded firm.* London: Routledge.

Arbonies, A. L., & Moso, M. (2002). Basque Country: The knowledge cluster. *Journal of Knowledge Management, 6*(4), 347-355.

Asheim, B. T. (1996). Industrial districts as learning regions: A condition for prosperity. *European Planning Studies, 4*, 379-400.

Bailey, C., & Clarke, M. (2000). How do managers use knowledge about knowledge management? *Journal of Knowledge Management, 4*(3), 235-243.

Baqir, M. N., & Kathawala, Y. (2004). "Ba for knowledge cities: A futuristic technology model. *Journal of Knowledge Management, 8*(5), 83-95.

Carrillo, F. (1999). *The knowledge management movement: Current drives and future scenarios.* Paper presented at the Third International Conference on Technology, Policy and Innovation: Global Knowledge Partnerships. Creating Value for the 21st Century, Austin, TX. Retrieved from http://www.knowledgesystems.org

Carrillo, F. J. (2002). Capital systems: Implications for a global knowledge agenda. *Journal of Knowledge Management, 6*(4), 379-399.

Carrillo, F. J. (2004). Capital cities: A taxonomy of capital accounts for knowledge cities. *Journal of Knowledge Management, 8*(5), 28-46.

Chatzkel, J. (2004). Greater Phoenix as a knowledge capital. *Journal of Knowledge Management, 8*(5), 61-72.

Davenport, T., & Prusak, L. (1998). *Working knowledge: Managing what your organisation knows.* Boston: Harvard Business School Press.

DeLong. (1996). *Endogenous growth: Economic theory and faster growth.* Retrieved from http://econ161.berkeley.edu/OpEd/endo

Drucker, P. (1998). From capitalism to knowledge society. In D. Neef (Ed.), *The knowledge economy* (p. 15). Woburn, MA: Butterworth.

Ergazakis, K., Karnezis, K., Metaxiotis, K., & Psarras, J. (2005). Knowledge management in enterprises: A research agenda. *Intelligent Systems in Accounting, Finance and Management, 13*, 17-26.

Ergazakis, K., Metaxiotis, K., & Psarras, J. (2004). Towards knowledge cities: Conceptual analysis and success stories. *Journal of Knowledge Management, 8*(5), 5-15.

Ergazakis, K., Metaxiotis, K., & Psarras, J. (2005). An emerging pattern of successful knowledge cities' main features. In J. Carrillo (Ed.), *Knowledge cities: Approaches, experiences and perspectives.* Academic Press, Butterworth-Heinemann/Elsevier.

European Commission. (2000). *Innovation policy in a knowledge-based economy.* Brussels, Belgium: Office for Official Publications of the European Communities.

Gibbons, J. H., & Malone, T. F. (2001). Intergenerational ethics. *New Ethical Challenges in Science and Technology: Proceedings of a Sigma Xi Forum in Albuquerque NM, 9-10 November 2000* (pp. 149-161, 180).

Komninos, N. (2002). *Intelligent cities: Innovation, knowledge systems and digital spaces.* Routledge.

Laszlo, K. C., & Laszlo, A. (2002). Evolving knowledge for development: The role of knowledge management in a changing world. *Journal of Knowledge Management, 6*(4), 400-412.

Laszlo, K. C., Laszlo, A., Campos, M., & Romero, C. (2002). Evolutionary development: An evolutionary perspective on development for an interconnected world. *World Futures.*

Maier, R., & Remus, U. (2003). Implementing process-oriented knowledge management strategies. *Journal of Knowledge Management, 7*(4), 62-74.

Malone, T. F. (1995). Reflections on the human prospect. In R. H. Socolow (Ed.), *Annual review of energy and the environment* (pp.1-19). Palo Alto, CA: Annual Reviews.

Malone, T. F. (1998). A new agenda for science and technology for the twenty-first century. *Proceedings of the KOSEF's 20th Anniversary Symposium on Issues of Science and Technology in the 21st Century* (pp. 67-90).

Malone, T. F., & Yohe, G. W. (2002). Knowledge partnerships for a sustainable, equitable and stable society Journal of Knowledge Management, *6*(4), 368-378.

Mansell, R. (2002a). Constructing the knowledge base for knowledge-driven development. *Journal of Knowledge Management, 6*(4), 317-329.

Mansell, R. (Ed.). (2002b). *Inside the communication revolution: Evolving patterns of social and technical interaction.* Oxford: Oxford University Press.

Mansell, R., & Steinmueller, W. E. (2002). *Mobilising the information society: Strategies for growth and opportunity.* Oxford: Oxford University Press.

Metaxiotis, K., Ergazakis, K., & Psarras, J. (2005). Exploring the world of knowledge management: Agreements and disagreements in the academic/practitioner community. *Journal of Knowledge Management, 9*(2), 6-18.

Milton, N., Shadbolt, N., Cottman, H., & Hammersley, M. (1999). Towards a knowledge technology for knowledge management. *International Journal of Human-Computer Studies, 51*, 615-641.

Rubenstein-Montano, B., Liebowitz, J., Buchwalter, J., McGaw, D., Newman, B., & Rebeck, K. (2001). SMARTVision: A knowledge-management methodology. *Journal of Knowledge Management, 5*(4), 300-310.

TERMS AND DEFINITIONS

Collaborative Tools: Collaborative tools are electronic tools that support communication and collaboration: people working together; essentially they take the form of networked computer software.

Community Management System: This is a platform where various communities and special-interest groups with specialized expertise represent themselves and try to find solutions to specific problems.

Data Mining: Data mining is a process of automatically searching large volumes of data for patterns such as association rules. It is also called knowledge discovery in databases (KDD).

Distributed Knowledge Management Model: This is the model that combines the interdependence of one partial product state model to others with the idea of knowledge acquisition rather than just an operational exchange relationship.

Groupware Tools: These are specific software tools that allow groups of people to share information and to coordinate their activities over a computer network.

Intelligent Agents: This is a software agent that exhibits some form of artificial intelligence that assists the user and will act on his or her behalf in performing repetitive computer-related tasks.

Semantic Web: The Semantic Web is a new technology that intends to create a universal medium for information and knowledge exchange by putting documents with computer-processable meaning (semantics) on the World Wide Web.

Chapter XLVIII
Web Application Classification: A Maintenance/Evolution Perspective

Hsiang-Jui Kung
Georgia Southern University, USA

Hui-Lien Tung
Paine College, USA

INTRODUCTION

Many companies use the Web to communicate with the external world as well as within their organizations and to carry out their business processes more effectively. A survey on Web application development shows that 84% of development projects do not meet business needs, 56% do not have the required functionality, 79% are behind schedule, and 63% are over budget (Standish Group, 2002). García-Cabrera, Rodríguez-Fórtiz, and Parets-Llorca (2002) report that the development of a Web application is never finished, and the nature of Web applications is evolutionary. The architecture of Web applications has three layers: conceptual, presentation, and navigation. It also has two perspectives: designer and viewer. Software evolution is "the dynamic behavior of programming systems as they are maintained and enhanced over their life times" (Belady & Lehman, 1976). Web application evolution is of increasing importance as more Web systems are in production.

Taylor, McWilliam, Sheehan, and Mulhaney (2002) indicate issues of Web application maintenance activities. Those issues are the impacts of dynamic Web application, Web system structure, coding for specific Web browsers, documentation, and development standards. They classify Web application into two categories in terms of data: static and dynamic. Dynamic Web systems require more maintenance considerations than do static systems.

Web technologies have been adopted by organizations in the public sector. Many state agencies provide their services via the Web. This study investigates the management of e-government applications at a U.S. state technology agency (STA).

BACKGROUND

Web applications are the glue joining IT infrastructure with the business processes that deliver e-government services to the state constituents. Reviewing Web applications over the last 10 years, we can clearly see that they offer more features every year, and they are better structured with the advance of Web design methods and technologies. The factors contributing to the evolution of Web applications are the demand for new features and new Web technologies (Jazayeri, 2005). This section introduces the e-government application evolution from three perspectives: evolution stages and applications, processes, and services.

E-government is the use of information and communication technology in general and e-commerce in particular to carry out government operations such as providing citizens and organizations with more convenient access to government information and services, and the delivering of public services to citizens, business partners and suppliers, and other government agencies (United Nations [UN] & ASPA, 2002). E-government evolves from one stage to the other: from developing a Web page to integrating government systems behind the Web interface (Schelin, 2003). Each of the e-government evolution stages represents a different level of technological sophistication, citizen orientation, and administrative change (Holden, Norris, & Fletcher, 2003; Moon, 2002).

There are different stage models for e-government evolution stages (Hiller & Bélanger, 2001; Ho, 2002; Layne & Lee, 2001; Melitski, 2003; Moon, 2002; Sandoval & Gil-García, 2005; UN & ASPA, 2002; West, 2004). At the aggregate level, technological sophistication has been continuously added to e-government applications. Four different stages for e-government evolution emerge from the aggregation of the different stage models: publishing, interaction, transaction, and integration. The growth stages of this approach are determined by the service provision or functionality (sophistication) of the e-government applications.

- **Publishing:** This refers to providing access to services, applications, or data through the same user interface (e.g., Web site or portal) with static information about agencies and some of the services they provide to citizens and private organizations. Content in this stage is generally limited to HTML (hypertext markup language), images, PDF files (Portable Document Format), and Office files (such as word processing documents, spreadsheets, presentations).
- **Interaction:** This refers to the increasing interaction between citizens and different government agencies. Citizens and businesses can access information according to their different interests. The government portal provides both static and dynamic or interactive content. At this level, users interact with information in the form of a survey, an account, or another means of personalizing the Web experience.
- **Transaction:** This refers to customizing the government portal for citizens and businesses. The government portal communicates either synchronously or asynchronously with various enterprise application (back-end) environments. This portal provides secure electronic payment services to facilitate transactions such as taxes, fines, and service payments.
- **Integration:** This refers to the full integration (vertical and horizontal) of government services. Governments must undertake institutional and administrative reforms to

reach this stage. This stage is considered interactive democracy with public outreach and a range of accountability measures.

WEB APPLICATION CLASSIFICATION

The context for this chapter is a state government in the United States. On May 24, 2001, the governor of the state signed an executive order, effective July 1, 2001, officially transferring information technology and telecommunications services from the state's Department of Administrative Services (DOAS) to the State Technology Authority. The STA was created to bring state agencies together to achieve the vision of a digital government, and its creation formally represented a major shift in how the executive branch of the state government viewed IT. Approving the transfer of IT and telecommunications services from the DOAS effectively placed the STA on equal footing with other major state agencies and formally signaled the governor's recognition of the importance of IT to the evolution of state government. This is reflected in a statement featured on the agency's Web site that the STA works to bring the state "the benefits of technology: greater efficiency, security safeguards, expanded access to information and services, and economic development throughout the state."

The individual who engineered the creation of the STA gained credibility and the governor's ear by virtue of a successful career in the private sector. Before being hired as the state's first de facto chief technology officer (CTO), his employer had been involved in several statewide IT-oriented economic development initiatives. Numerous IT executives in the private sector were surprised by the state's ability to hire such an accomplished IT professional. His hiring indicated that the state was serious about using IT to enhance government services and to elevate the perception of the state's IT services from playing little more than a support role to being a strategic enabler.

One of the first challenges that he faced was how to structure the STA and position it to provide technological leadership for state government. Prior to his arrival, the state's IT infrastructure could be best described as a mixture of centralized and decentralized elements. For most agencies, the IT infrastructure consisted primarily of systems and applications that were chosen to best support the operations. Most agencies were responsible for funding IT solutions and support personnel from their own budgets, and when acquiring solutions, little thought (or concern) had been given to whether or not the chosen solutions would interoperate with systems in other state agencies. Uneven funding for IT across agencies meant that the IT infrastructure was more sophisticated in some agencies than in others. Some agencies' systems were designed and implemented with DOAS assistance, but only a subset of the systems that were in place when the architect of the STA was hired took advantage of the statewide telecommunications infrastructure that the DOAS had developed and managed during the previous two decades.

It did not take long before the STA started to receive its first accolades. In 2002, the state portal received the Sustained Leadership Award (Digital State Survey Sustained Leadership Award, 1997-2002). The remarkable changes that the portal underwent in 2001 and 2002 positioned the state to receive this award. Since its inception, the STA's e-government portal has been consistently ranked among the top 25 state portals.

The STA case provides an opportunity to critically evaluate the procedures used by a state technology authority to manage the evolution of its e-government applications. E-government applications have the potential for improving governance and the quality of life of citizens, but their ability to do so requires them to evolve over time. In many states, including this one, e-

Table 1. Static Web application maintenance requirement

Functional Requirement		Resource Cluster	# FTEs
Traffic	=>	Project Manager I (PM I)	0.25
Graphic Artist	=>	Creative Services (CRE)	0.25
Technical Designer	=>	Prog/Coding/Dev I (PCD I)	1.00
Baseline			1.50

government applications that began as relatively simple, static HTML documents have progressed through a series of phases to become much more complex.

STA classifies Web application systems within the state Web portal into four categories: static, Web-enabled forms, custom, and enterprise application integration (EAI). The units involved with the Web application maintenance are Traffic, which records user requests and monitors requests, Creative Services, which delivers graphical design work to accommodate the look and feel of Web applications, and E-Development, which is responsible for the state web portal development and maintenance. STA uses full-time equivalent (FTE) to determine the number of full-time positions to maintain the state Web portal.

Static Web Applications

Static Web sites, sometimes called "brochureware" sites, provide a snapshot of information about an organization or activity. Such sites consist primarily of content files that require no run-time compilation, interpretation, or execution. Content in these sites is generally limited to HTML, images, PDF files, and Office files. This content is statically presented to users when requested and changes only when files are manually replaced or updated. Dynamic content and interactive forms on static Web sites are limited to common, across-the-board simplistic functionality (e.g., an online e-mail form).

The static Web application maintenance requirement is listed in Table 1. The Traffic unit provides initial triage to static Web site change requests. Technical designers do the majority of maintenance performed on static Web sites. Graphic artists may be required to update images. For a negligible percentage of the time, developers may be required to provide minor updates to the limited number of interactive forms.

Web-Enabled Forms Application

Web-enabled forms provide limited interactivity by automating simple paper-based business processes. An example of a Web-enabled form would be a Web-based survey that generates either e-mail or a flat-file extract to the business owner.

Table 2. Web-enabled form application maintenance requirement

Functional Requirement		Resource Cluster	# FTEs
Traffic	=>	Project Manager I (PM I)	0.25
Graphic Artist	=>	Creative Services (CRE)	0.25
Technical Designer	=>	Prog/Coding/Dev I (PCD I)	0.50
Developer	=>	Prog/Coding/Dev I (PCD I)	1.25
Baseline			2.25

Table 3. Custom Web application maintenance requirement

Functional Requirement		Resource Cluster	# FTEs
Traffic	=>	Project Manager I (PM I)	0.50
Project Manager (or Supervision/Mgt)	=>	Project Manager II (PM II)	0.75
Requirements Engineer (or Senior Developer or Supervision/Mgt)	=>	Requirement & Testing Engineer (RTE)	0.75
Graphic Artist	=>	Creative Services (CRE)	0.25
Technical Designer	=>	Prog/Coding/Dev I (PCD I)	0.75
Developer		Prog/Coding/Dev I (PCD I)	1.25
Test Engineer (or Senior Developer or Project Manager or Supervision/Mgt)	=>	Req. & Testing Engineer (RTE)	0.50
Baseline			4.75

Common modules provide limited dynamic Web content by reusing (copy and paste) existing software modules. An example of a common module is the press-release application. Both static content and a modest amount of interactive and dynamic content (that requires run-time compilation, interpretation, or execution) typically comprise development at this level. Dynamic content or interactive forms at this level usually contain minor customizations.

The Web-enabled forms application maintenance requirement is listed in Table 2. Traffic provides initial triage for maintenance requests for Web-enabled forms and common modules. Technical designers may be able to perform minor modifications. Graphic artists may be required to update images. For a large percentage of the time, developers will need to make the requested modifications.

Table 4. EAI application maintenance requirement

Functional Requirement		Resource Cluster	# FTEs
Traffic	=>	Project Manager I (PM I)	0.50
Project Manager (or Supervision/Mgt)	=>	Project Manager II (PM II)	0.75
Requirements Engineer (or Senior Developer or Supervision/Mgt)	=>	Req. & Testing Engineer (RTE)	0.75
Graphic Artist	=>	Creative Services (CRE)	0.25
Technical Designer	=>	Prog/Coding/Dev I (PCD I)	0.75
Developer	=>	Prog/Coding/Dev I (PCD I)	1.25
EAI Developer	=>	Prog/Coding/Dev I (PCD I)	1.25
Test Engineer (or Senior Developer or Project Manager or Supervision/Mgt)	=>	Req. & Testing Engineer (RTE)	0.50
Baseline			6.00

Custom Web Applications

Custom Web applications generally provide both static and dynamic or interactive content. Such applications may augment a static Web site or may constitute a Web site on its own. Custom Web applications may include simple Web-enabled forms or common software modules, but provide additional business-level processing. Examples of such additional business-level processing could include automated workflows such as scheduling and calendaring, custom search applications, or online reporting. Dynamic content and interactive forms at this level usually contain significant customizations.

The custom Web application maintenance requirement is listed in Table 3. Traffic provides initial triage and requirements discovery for maintenance requests on custom Web applications. Changes in the underlying business process may require formal project management by a project manager or team supervisor, as well as detailed requirements gathering by a requirements engineer, developer, or team supervisor. Graphic artists may be required to update images. Technical designers may resolve user interface (UI) design issues. Developers must make program changes to accommodate new business requirements. A test engineer may be required for user acceptance testing.

EAI Web Applications

EAI Web applications exhibit the same characteristics as custom Web applications but add an additional level of complexity because they communicate either synchronously or asynchronously with various enterprise application environments that are autonomous of STA's Web application environment. Examples of existing enterprise application environments include mainframe-based systems (such as GRATIS and CJIS), COTS (commercial off the shelf; such as LicenseEase and Systems Automation), or agency data stores (such as SoS SQLServer and OSR SQLServer). Dynamic content and interactive forms at this level usually contain significant customizations.

The EAI application maintenance requirement is listed in Table 4. Traffic provides initial triage and requirements discovery for maintenance requests on EAI Web applications. Changes in the underlying business process may require formal project management lead by a project manager or team supervisor, as well as detailed requirements gathering by a requirements engineer, developer, or team supervisor. Graphic artists may be required to update images. Technical designers may resolve UI design issues. Developers must make program changes to accommodate new business requirements. A test engineer may be required for user acceptance testing.

STA has been classifying a Web application portfolio on the state portal since 2001. In 2005, STA had 26 static applications, 10 Web-enabled forms, 57 custom Web applications, and 55 EAI Web applications in its Web application portfolio. STA indicates that the application portfolio management is an ongoing project. The Web applications may change or evolve from one type to another over time. The number of different types of applications varies from time to time. In 2001, the number of static Web applications was greater than that of 2005. STA has a dedicated e-development staff managing the outsourced application portfolio management project.

FUTURE TRENDS

Web application evolution is the result of important dynamics regarding the fact that Web applications interact with actions in organizational settings, technology, and the external environment. The e-government application evolution is a never-ending process that delivers services and enhances or improves products (Web applications themselves). The application classification can be seen as a starting point, but not as an end, to evolution management. STA manages Web application evolution from three perspectives: establishing processes, delivering services, and enhancing products.

Web-based application development becomes more complicated and thus increasingly risky; the state must take steps to mitigate this risk. STA believes that standardizing common application development platforms for the creation of new Web-based applications will have the effect of creating an overall expertise in the chosen application development environment and related technologies. This allows professionals throughout the state to support and advise each other in the course of developing Web-based applications.

With limited funds and staffing and growing responsibilities, agencies must prioritize IT projects and practice proper project management techniques to ensure that the projects are completed on time and under budget. According to a 10-year study of major industries conducted by the Standish Group (2001), only 28% of application software development projects are successful, meaning they are completed within budget and on time, and they meet business needs. Ensuring that IT dollars yield business results requires increased competency in project management. The state's critical project review process links IT expenditure requests with budget and program priorities to enhance the success of projects of strategic interest to state government. Having solid requirements also puts the state on firmer footing to assess vendor performance.

STA and other state agencies sign the Inter-Agency Agreement (IAA) to define, measure, monitor, and deliver services. The IAA documents the characteristics of services that are required by agencies as they are mutually understood and agreed to by the agencies and STA. The IAA ensures that the proper elements and commitment are in place to provide optimal support of content and applications being developed and managed by the agencies for inclusion on the state portal that is managed by STA. The IAA uses ServiceCenter (SC) to classify and monitor all maintenance requests for the four Web application categories. The ServiceCenter also provides historical data to fine-tune the maintenance requirements for the four Web application categories.

CONCLUSION

Much of the existing literature in Web applications attempts to describe and understand the Web application development processes. Web application maintenance and evolution gets its attention when more Web applications are in production. Insights of the properties and maintenance requirements of Web application will make planning, control, and execution of maintenance and evolution process improvements more systematic and effective. The Web application category will indicate the types of activities, methods, and tools required; when and how they should be used; and how they relate to one another.

FUTURE RESEARCH DIRECTIONS

Three directions for future research have emerged from this study. They include (a) a survey of Web application classifications, (b) a longitudinal study of Web application evolution, and (c) the development of an effort estimation model.

Survey of Web Application Classification

In the current study, we investigate the STA Web application classification process. This study has shown the STA's classification method, but other organizations may use different classification schemes to categorize its Web applications. The e-government evolution stage is correlated to its Web applications. It is natural to extend the study by using surveys to investigate multiple organizations. The survey will answer the following questions. Do organizations classify their Web applications? How do organizations classify their Web applications? What are the benefits of their classification schemes? Which evolution stage is the organization in? What is the organization's Web application portfolio, and what is the relationship between Web application portfolio and evolution stage.

Longitudinal Study of Web Application Evolution

In this study, we took a snapshot of a Web application portfolio at STA. This study did not investigate the evolution of Web applications. Since Web applications evolve from simple brochureware to more complicated applications, it is natural to extend the study by taking multiple snapshots at different time periods and comparing the changes of the Web application portfolio. The future study will collect Web application classification data every 6 months for 2 to 3 years. The longitudinal study will track a few Web applications that go through the changes from one category to another. The longitudinal study will answer the following questions. How many Web applications evolve over the study period? What is the frequency of a Web application evolution? What is the intensity of the evolution and what factors enable or trigger the evolution?

Development of Effort Estimation Model

The current study shows the resources required for different types of Web applications in terms of FTE throughout the applications' life cycles. The FTE is only a rough estimation. In the next phase of the study, estimation models will be developed to predict the effort in terms of man-month (or man-hour) for the evolution of Web applications from one category to the next.

REFERENCES

Belady, R. A., & Lehman, M. M. (1976). A model of large program development. *IBM Systems Journal, 15*(1), 225-252.

Bennett, K. H., & Rajlich, V. T. (2000). Software maintenance and evolution: A roadmap. *Proceedings for International Conference on the Future of Software Engineering* (pp. 73-87).

Digital State Survey Sustained Leadership Award. (1997-2002). Retrieved May 30, 2006, from http://www.centerdigitalgov.com/center/02sustained.php

García-Cabrera, L., Rodríguez-Fórtiz, M. J., & Parets-Llorca, J. (2002). Evolving hypermedia systems: A layered software architecture. *Journal of Software Maintenance and Evolution: Research and Practice, 14*(5), 389-405.

Hiller, J. S., & Bélanger, F. (2001). Privacy strategies for electronic government. In *EGovernment 2001.* Lanham, MD: Rowman & Littlefield Publishers.

Ho, A. (2002). Reinventing local governments and the e-government initiative. *Public Administration Review, 62*(4), 434-444.

Holden, S. H., Norris, D. F., & Fletcher, P. D. (2003). Electronic government at the local level: Progress to date and future issues. *Public Performance and Management Review, 26*(3), 1-20.

Jazayeri, M. (2005). Species evolves, individuals age. *International Workshop on Principles of Software Evolution* (pp. 3-9).

Layne, K., & Lee, J. (2001). Developing fully functional e-government: A four stage model. *Government Information Quarterly, 18*(2), 122-136.

Melitski, J. (2003). Capacity and e-government performance: An analysis based on early adopters of Internet technologies in New Jersey. *Public*

Performance and Management Review, 26(4), 376-390.

Moon, M. J. (2002). The evolution of e-government among municipalities: Rhetoric or reality? *Public Administration Review, 62*(4), 424-433.

Sandoval, R., & Gil-García, J. R. (2005). Assessing e-government evolution in Mexico: A preliminary analysis of the state portals. *Information Resources Management Association International Conference Proceedings.*

Schelin, S. H. (2003). E-government: An overview. In *Public information technology: Policy and management issues.* Hershey, PA: Idea Group Publishing.

Standish Group. (2001). *Extreme chaos.* Retrieved May 30, 2006, from http://www.standishgroup.com/sample_research/PDFpages/extreme_chaos.pdf

Taylor, M., McWilliam, J., Sheehan, J., & Mulhaney, A. (2002). Maintenance issues in the Web site development process. *Journal of Software Maintenance and Evolution: Research and Practice, 14*(2), 109-122.

United Nations (UN) & ASPA. (2002). *Benchmarking e-government: A global perspective.* Retrieved May 30, 2006, from http://unpan1.un.org/intradoc/groups/public/documents/UN/UNPAN021547.pdf

West, D. M. (2004). E-government and the transformation of service delivery and citizen attitudes. *Public Administration Review, 64*(1), 15-27.

FURTHER READING

Anderson, K. V., & Henriksen, H. Z. (2005). The first leg of e-government research: Domains and application areas 1998-2003. *International Journal of Electronic Government Research, 1*(4), 26-44.

Bruno, V., Tam, A., & Thom, J. (2005). Characteristics of Web applications that affect usability: A review. *Proceedings of the 19th Conference of the Computer-Human Interaction Special Interest Group (CHISIG).*

Cardellini, V., Casalicchio, E., Colajanni, M., & Yu, P. S. (2002). *The state of the art in locally distributed Web-server systems. ACM Computing Surveys, 34*(2), 263-311.

Chen, Y. N., Chen, H. M., Huang, W., & Ching, R. K. H. (2006). E-government strategies in developed and developing countries: An implementation framework and case study. *Journal of Global Information Management, 14*(1), 23-46.

Costagliola, G., Di Martino, S., Ferrucci, F., Gravino, C., Tortora, G., & Vitiello, G. (2006). Effort estimation modeling techniques: A case study for Web applications. *Proceedings of the Sixth International Conference on Web Engineering.*

Eirinaki, M., Vazirgiannis, M., & Varlamis, I. (2003). SEWeP: Using site semantics and a taxonomy to enhance the Web personalization process. *Proceedings of the Ninth ACM SIGKDD International Conference on Knowledge Discovery and Data Mining.*

Elbaum, S., Chilakamarri, K., Fisher, M., & Rothermel, G. (2006). Web application characterization through directed requests. *Proceedings of the International Workshop on Dynamic Systems Analysis.*

Gates, S. C., Teiken, W., & Cheng, K. F. (2005). Taxonomies by the numbers: Building high-performance taxonomies. *Proceedings of the 14th ACM International Conference on Information and Knowledge Management.*

Grant, G., & Chau, D. (2005). Developing a generic framework for e-government. *Journal of Global Information Management, 13*(1), 1-30.

Heller, R. S., Martin, C. D., Haneef, N., & Gievska-Krliu, S. (2001). Using a theoretical multimedia taxonomy framework. *Journal on Educational Resources in Computing, 1*(1), 1-22.

Ho, K. K. W. (2007). The e-government development, IT strategies, and portals of the Hong Kong SAR government. *International Journal of Cases on Electronic Commerce, 3*(2), 71-89.

Kraemer, K., & King, J. L. (2006). Information technology and administrative reform: Will e-government be different? *International Journal of Electronic Government Research, 2*(1), 1-20.

Kung, H. J., Tung, H. L., & Case, T. (2007). Managing e-government application evolution: A state government case. *International Journal of Cases on Electronic Commerce, 3*(2), 36-53.

Lee, J., & Kim, J. (2007). Grounded theory analysis of e-government initiatives: Exploring perceptions of government authorities. *Government Information Quarterly, 24*(1), 135-147.

Lee, J. K., Kang, H., Lee, H. K., & Lee, H. S. (2002). Evolutionary stages of e-tailors and retailers: Firm value determinants model. *Journal of Global Information Management, 10*(3), 15-35.

Lee-Kelley, L., & James, T. (2003). E-government and social exclusion: An empirical study. *Journal of Electronic Commerce in Organizations, 1*(4), 16-32.

Mahler, J., & Regan, P. M. (2006). The evolution of Web governance in the federal government. *International Journal of Electronic Government Research, 2*(1), 21-35.

Melitski, J., Holzer, M., Kim, S. T., Kim, C. G., & Rho, S. Y. (2005). Digital government worldwide: A e-government assessment of municipal Web sites. *International Journal of Electronic Government Research, 1*(1), 1-18.

Nahrstedt, K., & Balke, W. (2004). A taxonomy for multimedia service composition. *Proceedings of the 12th Annual ACM International Conference on Multimedia.*

Norris, D. F., & Lloyd, B. A. (2006). The scholarly literature on e-government: Characterizing a nascent field. *International Journal of Electronic Government Research, 2*(4), 40-56.

Scholl, H. J. (2005). E-government-induced business process change (BPC): An empirical study of current practices. *International Journal of Electronic Government Research, 1*(2), 27-49.

Sharma, S. K., & Gupta, J. N. D. (2003). Building blocks of an e-government: A framework. *Journal of Electronic Commerce in Organizations, 1*(4), 1-15.

Tan, C. W., Pan, S. L., & Lim, E. T. K. (2005). Managing stakeholder interests in e-government implementation: Lessons learned from a Singapore e-government project. *Journal of Global Information Management, 13*(1), 31-53.

Titah, R., & Barki, H. (2006). E-government adoption and acceptance: A literature review. *International Journal of Electronic Government Research, 2*(3), 23-57.

Weerakkody, V., Janssen, M., & Hjort-Madsen, K. (2007). Integration and enterprise architecture challenges in e-government: A European perspective. *International Journal of Cases on Electronic Commerce, 3*(2), 13-35.

TERMS AND DEFINITIONS

Application Evolution: This concerns any change that is being made to the entire set of programs, procedures, and related documentation associated with a computer system that makes up an application software system. Application evolution contains two parts: evolution processes and the evolution of their products.

Brochureware: This refers to Web sites or pages that are produced by taking an organization's printed brochure and translating it directly to the Web without regard for the possibilities of the new medium. The result will almost always be static.

E-Government: This is the use of information and communication technology in general to provide citizens and organizations with more convenient access to government information and services. It is an efficient way of conducting business transactions with citizens and business and within the governments themselves.

Enterprise Application Integration (EAI): This is a process that helps to integrate applications inside an organization (e.g., an ordering system with an inventory on hand) or applications of different organizations in a seamless fashion. It is done by EAI vendors with special software tools.

Organization/Government Portal: This is a personalized, single point of access through a Web browser to critical business information located inside and outside of an organization. Portals provide gateways to organization data, information, and knowledge.

Stage of E-Government Development: The stages are a method for quantifying progress. They are representative of the government's level of development based primarily on the content and deliverable services available through official Web sites.

Web Application System: This is computer software using a Web browser as the interface to support organizational functions or processes. The system is the integration of computer hardware, software, databases, networks, procedures, and people to collect, process, store, and distribute information for specific business purposes.

Chapter XLIX
Web Services and Service-Oriented Architectures

Bruce J. Neubauer
University of South Florida, USA

INTRODUCTION

A review of the development of information systems can help in understanding the potential significance of Web services and service-oriented architecture (SOA) in the public sector. SOA involves the convergent design of information systems and organizational workflows at the level of services. The purpose of this chapter is to suggest a strategy for mapping the design of service-oriented architectures onto the complex patterns of governance including combinations of federalism, regionalism, and the outsourcing of functions from government agencies to nonprofit organizations. This involves the modeling of workflows and the identification of opportunities for the sharing of services among agencies and nonprofits.

The structures of government agencies reflect political jurisdictions, legislative committee structures, areas of public policy, and geographical locations. Federalism creates situations in which multiple agencies (often at different levels of government) have similar responsibilities in the same geographic areas. Metropolitan areas are complex mosaics of local governments and special districts. In addition, nonprofit organizations are also involved in strategic alliances with government agencies to provide services to citizens. The coordination of efforts among multiple organizations has been one of the major functions of public administrators acting through formal or informal networks of relationships within and across organizational boundaries. Web services and SOA can be used to help integrate the often costly and fragmented delivery of government services.

BACKGROUND

Information systems were historically centralized. It is still common for departments within an organization to each have their own computer applications used to support accounting, payroll, or other specific responsibilities. Such applications and systems are sometimes referred to as "stovepipe" applications, suggesting the fact that they stand alone. While such applications may well optimize specific functions, they may not be designed to support business process workflows that cut across departments. As a consequence, common business processes often require manually entering data multiple times and making adjustments for the different ways the same data are stored in multiple databases.

Modern systems of applications are sometimes called enterprise systems or ERPs. The acronym ERP stands for enterprise resource planning. Examples of ERP solutions include SAP and Oracle applications. Such systems are designed at the scale of an entire organization. ERPs are modular in nature. An organization can purchase the modules it needs from the same vender and be assured that they are compatible with one another. The benefit of systems of computer applications designed at the enterprise level is an improved ability of the applications to support entire business processes. Many enterprise systems share one enterprise database. It should not be necessary to enter data into multiple stovepipe applications. The underlying database should provide top managers with one version of the truth rather than a collection of summaries gleaned from multiple databases within the organization. Electronic data interchange (EDI) is a similar technology for creating data communications between organizations. EDI solutions tend to be point-to-point connections between specific organizations for specific purposes.

Government agencies can more easily coordinate their efforts and outsource responsibilities when they have modern information systems. ERP and EDI technologies are valuable and widely used. However, ERP solutions tend to be inflexible and EDI solutions may not support agile relationships among multiple organizations in networks of strategic alliances. Web services is a modern aspect of computer programming that facilitates the linking together of disparate legacy computer resources. SOA is an application of design principles to both computer resources and organizational units that can facilitate the creation of agile relationships between departments within large organizations and among organizations working together.

Early computer programmers worked in procedural programming languages such as FORTRAN and COBOL. The entire program usually ran on one machine and data were often managed by the software application itself rather than by the use of a separate database management system. Later, when programmers wrote procedural applications to run on networked computers, they sometimes used remote procedure calls to make use of subprocedures of code physically residing on another machine. The application would send a request across the network and wait for the subprocedure to run on the other machine and send data back to the application. This way of thinking evolved into object-oriented programming. A major benefit of this approach is reuse of the work required to create the subprocedure. Another benefit relates to loose coupling, meaning that the task of building a very large and complex application can be assigned to many individuals who can each build his or her own part of it without a detailed knowledge of what other programmers are doing (Kaye, 2003). As long as the interface between the part of the system and the rest of the system is agreed upon, how the part does what it does is not especially important to other programmers.

To an object-oriented programmer, a use of a Web service is the invocation (calling) of structured code residing across a network on a Web server. To a business analyst, a Web service is an opportunity to reuse not just code but entire services provided by organizations. Service-oriented architecture involves the orchestration or choreography of multiple services. An orchestration involves one focal application calling one or more services as needed within the same organization. A choreography is a coordination of services between or among organizations. Having been asked to make the transition from procedural programming to object-oriented programming, computer programmers are now facing the challenge of working at the level of the design of services. The design of Web-based information systems can be very challenging (Andrew et al., 2006; Terrasse, Becker, & Savonnet, 2003). Modeling such systems in terms of services can help address that complexity while helping to bridge the traditional divide between organization design and the design of business processes.

Some books on Web services and SOA are intended primarily for managers and executives (Barry, 2003; Bloomfield, Coombs, Knights, & Littler, 2000; Linthicum, 2004; Manes, 2003). Other sources not specifically written for managers are certainly approachable by people without technical backgrounds (Erl, 2004, 2005). Ties between workflow design and service-oriented architecture are addressed by Marks and Bell (2006) and Allen (2006).

O'Toole (1997) has written that governments often seek to execute their efforts via structures of interagency collaboration, that the role of not-for-profit organizations is large and growing, and that the frequency and variety of links with for-profit firms is impressive. There are many situations that present possibilities for managers to add or remove actors from the array of their activities involving networks with others (Brudney, O'Toole, & Rainey, 2000). With human oversight, Web services can be used to facilitate the assembly and reassembly of agile strategic alliances. Strategic alliances are held together by networks of human trust rather than by the compatibility of computer network protocols.

IMPLEMENTING GOVERNMENT WEB SERVICES AND SERVICE-ORIENTED ARCHITECTURES

Some Web services are relatively small units of functionality that can be accessed by software applications of various kinds. For example, currency exchange rates change frequently. It is inefficient to expect employees to find current rates of exchange each time the need for this information arises. This kind of activity can be automated and then either consumed or made available to others via a Web service (see Figure 1, where Activity B can be to apply a currency conversion to an amount of money). By using Web services, it is entirely feasible for one organization (almost anywhere in the world) to continually update a database with currency exchange rates and expose that information as a service to the computer applications of other organizations using the Internet. The organization maintaining the data can expose a Web service by providing the necessary WSDL (Web Service Description Language) file at a Web address, and by publishing the availability of the service using UDDI (Universal Description, Discovery and Integration). In computer jargon, such a relationship between two entities is called client-server, meaning that the client entity always asks for something, and the server entity always acts in the role of a provider (please see "Key Terms" below for brief explanations of WSDL, UDDI, and other technical acronyms).

What makes a service a Web service is its implementation across the Internet using XML (extensible markup language) and SOAP (Simple Object Access Protocol) standards. Humans may or may not be directly involved in the maintenance of the database containing exchange rates in the example above. When the request from a computer application comes in, the service hits the database and returns the needed information to the application across the Internet. The arrival of the request is not synchronized with the work required to keep the database updated. The work required to be done is not a factor of the number of requests received. Although it may be costly to continually update the database, there is little or no cost associated with making the information available to additional organizations. The major constraints on scaling up to serve large numbers of requests are bandwidth to and from the server providing the Web service, and the speed of the processor(s) on the server. Of course, if the Web

Figure 1. Simple Business Process Invoking a Web service

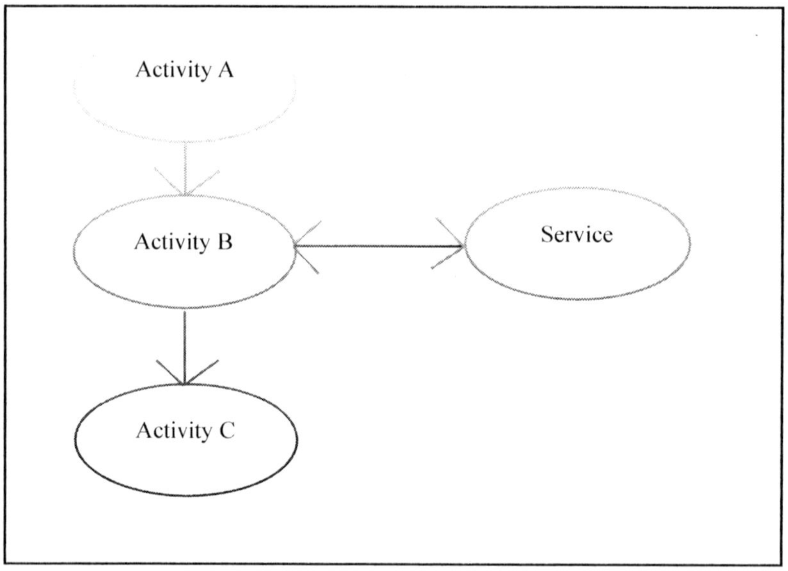

server or the database fails or is taken off line for maintenance, the business processes of many organizations may be affected. One idea behind UDDI is that the failure of a Web service could trigger an automated substitution of another Web service to assure the continuity-dependent processes.

As a slightly more complex example, consider the business process of a city government responding to a request to renew a business license. Several activities may be required to make the decision regarding whether or not to renew the license. It may be necessary to verify the physical integrity of the building in which the business is housed. It may also be necessary to verify that property taxes have been paid and that there is no evidence that the business is being used for criminal purposes. In the past, each of these three activities may have been performed manually and in sequential order. As a result, it might have taken a month or more to issue each renewal. There is often no reason why multiple related activities cannot be initiated in parallel. For example, checking for taxes and crime reports can probably be automated and performed almost instantly. Within the organization, automated activities can be implemented using Web services or other means. If the city government has an intranet, it uses the same technologies as the Internet and it makes sense to automate selected services using Web services. As previously indicated, the design of Web services exposed only within one organization is called orchestration. The orchestration of Web services is a step toward the choreography of Web services involved in the business processes of multiple organizations. Figure 2 is a model of a business process that includes the parallel performance of activities and the outsourcing of two activities via Web services.

Web services can be simple or very complex. An entire business process involving many activities and business rules can be nested inside a Web service and made available to others as a subprocess in a larger context. If real-time human intervention is required for the process triggered by the call to the Web service to be completed, the calling process may have to wait until the secondary process is completed before going forward.

Leymann, Roller, and Schmidt (2002) make a distinction between hierarchical patterns and peer-to-peer structures, noting that in many cases a

Figure 2. More complex business process invoking multiple Web services

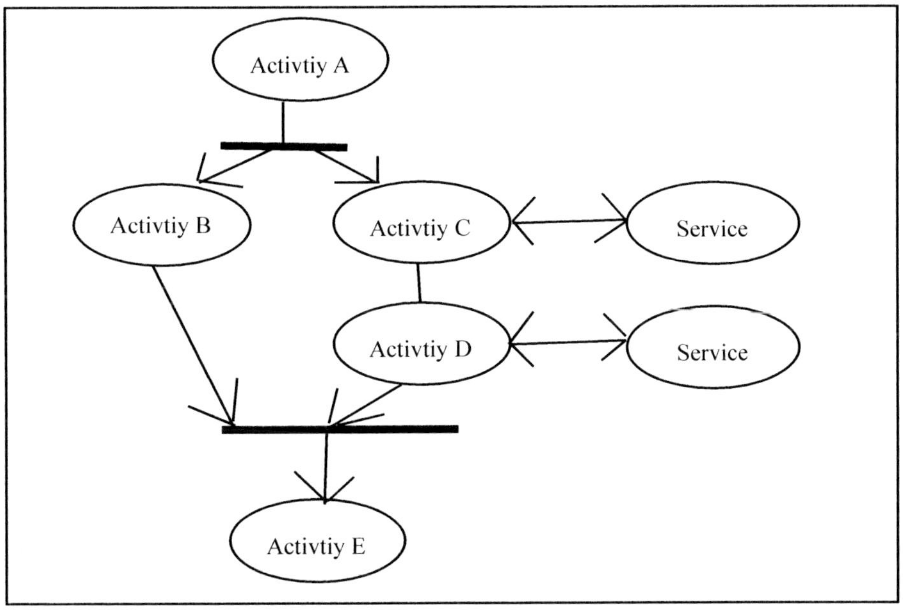

mixture of hierarchical and peer-to-peer structures is used to realize complex multipartner business processes. In a hierarchical structure, the ultimate process transcends any of the organizations supporting its activities. The supporting organizations are each likely to have internal workflows independent of one another and choreographed at the level of the transcendent process. This arrangement can allow each organization to keep its secrets regarding how it performs its work internally and to protect contents of databases from unintended uses by others. In a peer-to-peer relationship between organizations (or between departments in one organization), each partner is both providing services and consuming services provided by others (see Figure 3). Each partner

Figure 3. Peer-to-peer relationship between organizations or departments exposing and consuming each other's Web services

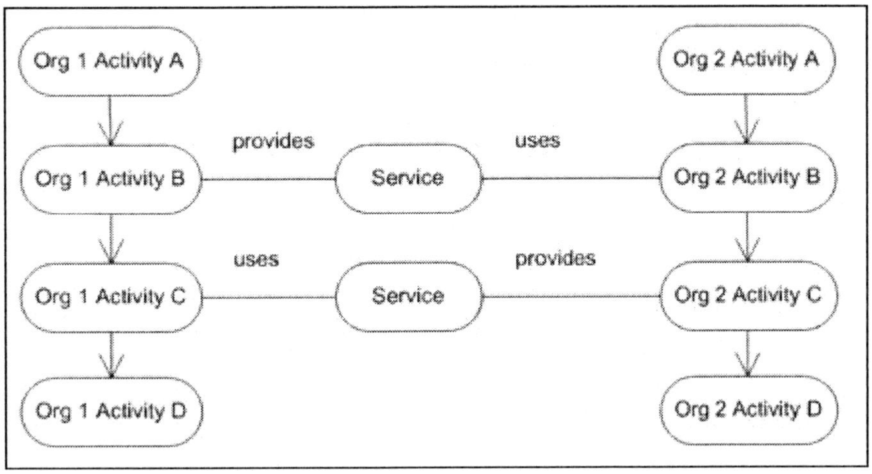

outsources what it is less well equipped to do and provides to its partners services it performs well.

In a hierarchical architecture, each Web service supports a transcendent process, represented in Figure 4. A hierarchical architecture begs the question regarding who or what is responsible for the transcendent process. In the private sector, a transcendent process may be a supply chain that includes multiple companies such as a manufacturer, warehouse, shipper, and retailer. No one company owns the entire supply chain and yet all participate in it. Examples of transcendent processes in the public sector are not as obvious. Federalism tends to ensure that large processes are managed by state or national governments. Regional governance (as in a metropolitan area with many overlapping jurisdictions) provides opportunities for peer-to-peer service architectures and for hybrid architectures. State agencies can manage large processes, and city and county agencies (and special districts) may provide Web services to each other and in support of the larger processes managed by state governments. The same pattern exists at the next larger scale, meaning that there may be opportunities for state governments to share services as peers while also supporting larger processes managed at the national level. The notion of transcendent processes may suggest an interpretation of the virtual state (Fountain, 2001).

Relationships among organizations via Web services are negotiated by humans and should include service-level agreements that spell out the responsibilities of partners to one another. Agility does not suggest that working relationships among agencies and nonprofits should be brief encounters. Technical agility helps assume that technology will not impede substitution of strategic partners or make changes in alliances difficult and costly. In a time of crisis, such as a natural disaster or terrorist event, the ability to quickly reassemble sets of strategic relationships among agencies may be very important (Harrald, 2006). In such circumstances, the possible automated substitution of Web services supported by UDDI may become valuable.

The following is a list of suggestions and guidelines intended to help generalist managers steer their organizations toward acceptance and adoption of information technologies that include Web services and SOA.

- Encourage employees to think about the organization in terms of sequences of activities that cut across functional areas (departments).

Figure 4. Hierarchal relationship between a transcendant process and Web services provided by organizations

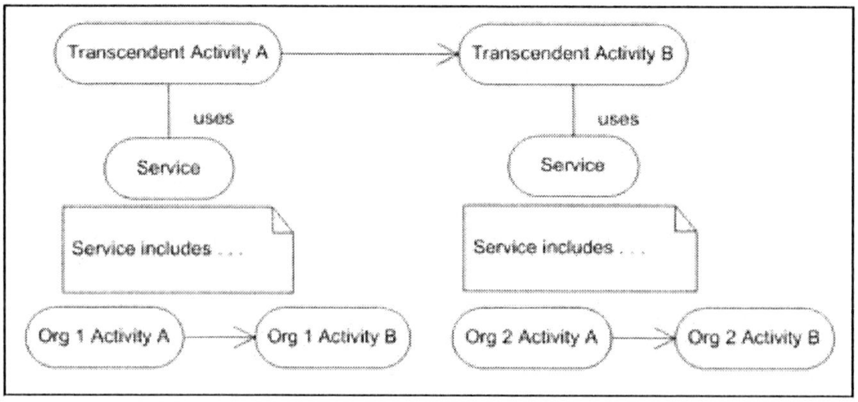

Identify major business processes that the organization performs frequently, either to create value for citizens or for the organization's own internal needs.

- Encourage IT professionals and other employees to begin thinking of activities and the computer software that support them as services.
- Encourage programmers and other IT employees to better understand what the organization does and the business processes that it performs, including business rules that affect the flow of work through activities within business processes. Help them realize that this is similar to ways they manage the flow of execution within computer applications.
- Try to create an organizational culture in which nontechnical employees do not blame IT professionals for their technical problems and in which IT professionals recognize and appreciate the knowledge and skills of end users.
- Create incentive systems that encourage employees to optimize processes rather than to maximize the interests of their own departments.
- Encourage programmers and other IT professionals to continue their educations by attending training in object-oriented analysis and design, modern programming languages, and emerging Web-based technologies.
- Accept the fact that there are limits to the ability of programmers to jump paradigms. Most large organizations need some programmers with legacy skills and others with more cutting-edge skills. Legacy specialists can help "wrap" older applications for inclusion in modern systems. Programmers who are experts in object-oriented programming are likely to be unable and unwilling to maintain legacy applications written in COBOL, for example.

The most difficult aspects of implementing government Web services and service-oriented architectures are likely to be political and administrative issues. There are close relationships between the possession of information, political power, and administrative discretion. Employees are likely to resist change even if change does not threaten their employment. For budgetary reasons, political and administrative resistance to the introduction of Web services is likely to become greater at the level of the extension of workflows across organizational boundaries. Agencies may become smaller and more specialized as redundant activities are identified in multiple agencies. Government agencies have legal and ethical responsibilities for the protection of data about citizens. Administrators may rightly feel that their ability to assure proper handling of confidential data is compromised when data become accessible to other organizations via Web services. Other major issues involve relationships among agencies regarding federalism, relationships among agencies regarding regional governance, and relationships between sectors involving privatization and outsourcing. Almost any major e-government initiative today is likely to be implemented using Web services. Citizens and employees as users are not likely to see or realize that the resources of multiple departments and/or organizations are involved in making the system functional. The following are brief descriptions of several government projects in Europe and the United States, involving BEA and its partners, available on the Web in the fall of 2006. What is common to each of the following examples is the need to tap into multiple disparate IT systems in order to support either a business process or a complex visualization needed for monitoring or decision-making purposes. The National Institute for Agricultural Research (INRA) is a French public research body responsible for producing and distributing innovations relevant to agriculture, food, and the environment. INRA needed to transform its purchasing management system, rationalize its global ordering process, and analyze its expenses. INRA deployed an intranet purchasing program. As a result, INRA is able to more effectively manage its €100 million of annual purchases. Process automation has streamlined and enhanced many of INRA's day-to-day processes. INRA has also benefited from a significant increase in productivity, largely due to the automation of complex tasks. Its managers now have a unified view of expenditures and purchasing decisions.

Oslo is the capital of Norway and has a parliamentary model of government. Each city district has its own district administration, which administers multiple social and health services. In addition, there are approximately 40 departments and agencies with specific areas of responsibilities. In total, up to 55 operations offer more than 250 different services to the citizens of Oslo. The local government's vision and strategic plan is to provide all relevant services online. More than 200 services were made available interactively in less than 1 year. Citizens can now apply online for a wide range of public-sector services, including building-construction permits, child care, and the payment of parking tickets.

A United States Department of Agriculture (USDA) mainframe-based system known as STARS (Store Tracking and Redemption System) was the primary tool used by the agency to manage the Food Stamp Program. Technicians were unable to automate many key processes and the legacy system had become difficult to maintain. Systems integrator Ventera Corporation designed a new system named STARS II involving Web services and SOA. As indicated by the USDA's Privacy Impact Assessment Form available on the Web at the USDA site, the new system draws upon data from the treasury department and the Social Security Administration, and also from state agencies and third-party providers.

The City of Chicago Public Housing Commission needed to link multiple legacy systems and provide a consistent view into project information for city executives, project managers, contractors, architects, and other personnel. The goal was to improve planning, expedite problem resolution, and reduce expenditures triggered by contract provisions regarding project deadlines missed. A company named Enterpulse designed and implemented a project management portal using a BEA portal. The resulting application enables improved project tracking and substantial cost savings by visually displaying data that enable administrators to prioritize project work efforts and avoid contract penalties.

FUTURE TRENDS

Interest in the use of Web services in the public sector will increase as they become more widely used in corporations. The focus of governmental budgetary deliberations may shift toward business processes in continuing efforts to constrain costs and increase performance. Because Web services do not expose actual databases and other resources on legacy systems, it is possible to share services while also addressing concerns of agency administrators regarding the responsibilities of agencies for information security and the privacy of citizens and others.

Over time, service orientation may gradually change our primary way of perceiving organizations. Information systems then become the mediator of what employees do, and Web services become a means by which activities and entire processes can be shared among organizations. Because different kinds of organizations have similar processes, distinctions between organizational sectors (government, nonprofit, and for profit) may become less apparent. Organizations may tend to become smaller and more specialized.

CONCLUSION

The essential questions in designing processes based upon services are the following. How should activities be defined? When should an activity be made available to others and when should an activity be outsourced to others? Organizations (and departments within organizations) that are closest to the data should be responsible for capturing and managing that data. Organizations (and departments within organizations) whose employees have a specialized expertise should make that expertise available to others. These guidelines still leave a number of high-level design decisions open for discussion.

The essential assertion of this chapter is that hierarchical SOA patterns can be used to support relationships among agencies at different levels of government (federalism) and that peer-to-peer SOA patterns can be used to support relationships based upon regional governance and the outsourcing of functions from agencies to nonprofit organizations. In terms of hierarchical relationships, parent entities (i.e., states vis-à-vis local governments) may be more likely to share business processes with child entities, and child entities may be more likely to share access to data with parent entities using Web services. In other words, the states might share business processes with their political subdivisions as Web services. The federal government might share business services with state governments as Web services. Local governments might make data available to both state agencies and federal agencies using Web services. Also, the states might make data available to the federal government using the same technology. The sharing of Web services among local governments and special districts could become very complex given the variety of relationships involving overlapping jurisdictions and different policies.

This chapter has proposed the application of modeling and design principles to the challenge of using service orientation to help government agencies and nonprofit organizations become more cost effective. Reports of implementation experiences with actual details of patterns of design including administrative, political, and technological implications are needed. In the design sciences, an evidence of maturity within a domain is the emergence of commonly observed patterns that become the building blocks for complex systems. SOA is a young and promising design science with the potential to significantly reshape the delivery of real services by government agencies and nonprofit organizations.

FUTURE RESEARCH DIRECTIONS

Opportunities for future research regarding SOA can be categorized into technical questions, political questions, and administrative questions. Regarding technical questions, because they depend upon Internet protocols, calls to Web services are relatively slow when compared to dedicated connectivity such as EDI. Attempts to address other technical challenges tend to lead to solutions that add additional overhead to making calls to Web services. Application performance may become an issue because the communications are based on SOAP, XML, and other Internet standards. Assuring that calls to Web services are chunky helps minimize the number of calls across networks. Nevertheless, Web applications may not scale well (i.e., serve increasing numbers of simultaneous users) because Web protocols and standards tend to be slow. Security, of course, is always important and a direction for future research.

The encryption required to secure XML-based communications adds to the technical overhead that degrades the performance of Web services. Web services are usually stateless, meaning that the computer providing the service to other applications does not remember previous communications that may be part of the same transaction. That being the case, additional information regarding past events must often be included in subsequent calls to the same Web service. The management of transactions involving multiple Web services is especially problematic. Two-phase and three-phase commit protocols that can be implemented when one organization owns or controls all parts of a distributed application cannot easily be implemented using Web services that are usually stateless. Web services are not likely to be widely reused unless they can easily be found. Automated discovery of available Web services may not satisfy the concerns of managers regarding security, privacy, and service-level agreements. The technical vision of distributed applications that can swap out Web services on the fly (perhaps to achieve load balancing) will not actually be fully implemented until managers of organizations can feel confident that they can safely delegate to software agents a variety of human concerns regarding who their partners are. Although these are essentially political and/or administrative concerns, any actual implementation of solutions will become technical concerns that may well call for technical research.

Regarding political implications and the need for future research, Web services have the potential to substantially change the ways that organizations perform their work. The long-term implications involve the very design of organizations, including government agencies and nonprofits. While Web services are usually cast at the grain of activities rather than at the grain of the tasks of entire departments or missions of entire agencies, it is possible that Web services could lead to major changes in the ways agencies and nonprofits perform their work. The budgetary processes of governments often involve incremental adjustments from the previous fiscal year without regard for the possibility that technology may facilitate major changes in workflows that might dramatically reduce costs. Even administrators who have positive attitudes toward the adoption of new information technologies may have political reasons to resist the adoption of distributed information systems that may make possible substantial reductions in necessary funding. SOA may also tend to compromise the ability of agency administrators to control information available to others. Research to better understand how agency and nonprofit administrators perceive Web services and SOA (as both threats and opportunities) might help assure that their organizations will not be unnecessarily penalized by the adoption of these technologies in budgetary and other political processes.

It follows that a future research direction regarding administration is to better understand how Web services and SOA tend to affect existing business processes and relationships among organizations. There are opportunities to model and simulate knowledge-based workflows involving combinations of computer networks and human operators. Software like Arena and TechSmith's Morae could be used to study not only the usability of computer-facilitated workflows, but also the identification of bottlenecks in selected workflow designs. As activities become broken out of the context of specific workflows and reused in multiple workflows, humans may lose their sense of understanding the meaning of their efforts in a larger context. This may tend to make work less satisfying. It may also lead to errors in judgment because the programmers who design distributed applications (including services provided by humans using technology) may not anticipate humans' need to exercise judgment within meaningful contexts.

A Web service involving human participation that one moment is used to select a good location for a new gas station and 10 minutes later is used to target a warhead may fail to provide human participants with necessary contexts required for the true exercise of judgment. Web services and SOA might be the next big step toward alienation of employees (life in the cubicles) and at worse a cruel exploitation of human minds harnessed to exercise judgments in the absence of knowing the consequences of related decisions. In light of globalization, Web services and SOA could be for knowledge work what outsourcing of production has been to industrial employment. The prospect that the mind might be reduced to a commodity is not attractive. Research regarding how employees regard their work experiences and their need for the context that provides meaning to their employment could inform the humanistic implementation of systems involving SOA. Research into the administrative implications of SOA can help assure that organizations and societies reap the benefits of this new technology while avoiding its use in ways that alienate employees and make inappropriate delegations of discretion to software systems.

REFERENCES

Allen, P. (2006). *Service orientation: Winning strategies and best practices.* Cambridge: Cambridge University Press.

Andrew, P., Conard, J., Woodgate, S., Flanders, J., Hatoun, G., Hilerio, I., et al. (2006). *Presenting Windows Workflow Foundation, beta edition.* Indianapolis, IN: SAMS.

Barry, D. K. (2003). *Web services and service-oriented architectures.* San Francisco: Morgan Kaufmann Publishers.

Bloomfield, B. P., Coombs, R., Knights, D., & Littler, D. (Eds.). (2000). *Information technology and organizations: Strategies, networks, and integration.* New York: Oxford University Press.

Brudney, J. L., O'Toole, L. J., Jr., & Rainey, H. G. (2000). *Advancing public management: New developments in theory, methods, and practice.* Washington, DC: Georgetown University Press.

Erl, E. (2004). *Service-oriented architecture: A field guide to integrating XML and Web services.* Upper Saddle River, NJ: Prentice Hall.

Erl, E. (2005). *Service-oriented architecture (SOA): Concepts, technology, and design.* Upper Saddle River, NJ: Prentice Hall.

Fountain, J. E. (2001). *Building the virtual state: Information technology and institutional change.* Washington, DC: Brookings Institution Press.

Harrald, J. R. (2006). Agility and discipline: Critical success factors for disaster response. *The Annals of the American Academy of Political and Social Science, 614*(1), 256-272.

Kaye, D. (2003). *Loosely coupled: The missing pieces of Web services.* Marin County, CA: RDS Press.

Leymann, F., Roller, D., & Schmidt, M.-T. (2002). Web services and business process management. *IBM Systems Journal, 41*(2), 198-211.

Linthicum, D. S. (2004). *Next generation application integration: From simple information to Web services.* Boston: Addison-Wesley.

Manes, A. T. (2003). *Web services: A manager's guide.* Boston: Addison-Wesley.

Marks, E. A., & Bell, M. (2006). *Service-oriented architecture (SOA): A planning and implementation guide for business and technology.* Hoboken, NJ: Wiley Press.

O'Toole, L. J., Jr. (1997). Treating networks seriously: Practical and research-based agendas in public administration. *Public Administration Review, 57*(1), 45-52.

Terrasse, M.-N., Becker, G., & Savonnet, M. (2003). Metamodeling architectures and interoperability of Web-enabled information systems. In A. Dahanayake & W. Gerhardt (Eds.), *Web-enabled systems integration: Practices and challenges* (pp. 1-18). Hershey, PA: Idea Group Publishing.

FURTHER READING

Agrawal, R., Bayardo, R., Jr., Gruhl, D., & Papadimitiour, S. (2002). Vinci: A service-oriented architecture for rapid development of Web applications. *Computer Networks, 39*(5), 523-539.

Bieberstein, N., Sanjay, B., Fiammante, M., Jones, K., & Shah, R. (2006). *Service-oriented architecture compass: Business value, planning and enterprise roadmap.* Upper Saddle River, NJ: Pearson.

Buschman, F., Meunier, R., Rohnert, H., & Sommerlad, M. (1996). *Pattern-oriented software architecture: A system of patterns.* New York: John Wiley & Sons.

Cox, D. E., & Kreger, H. (2005). Management of the service-oriented-architecture life cycle. *IBM Systems Journal, 44*(4), 709-726.

Datz, T. (2004, January 15). What you need to know about service-oriented architecture. *CIO Magazine.* Retrieved February 23, 2007, from http://www.cio.com/archive/011504/soa.html

Debevoise, T. (2005). *Business process management with a business rules approach: Implementing the service oriented architecture.* New York: Business Knowledge Architects.

Ferguson, D. F., & Stockton, M. L. (2005). Service-oriented architecture: Programming model and product architecture. *IBM Systems Journal, 44*(4), 753-780.

Foster, I. (2005). Service-oriented science. *Science, 308*(6723), 814-817.

He, H. (2003, September 30). What is service-oriented architecture? *O'ReillyXML.COM.* Retrieved February 23, 2007, from http://webservices.xml.com/pub/a/ws/2003/09/30/soa.html

IBM Business Consulting Services. (2004). *IBM service-oriented architecture and modeling.* Retrieved February 23, 2007, from http://www-935.ibm.com/services/us/gbs/bus/pdf/g510-5060-ibm-service-oriented-modeling-arch.pdf

IBM Redbooks. (2004). *Patterns: Service-oriented architectures and Web services.* White Plains, New York: IBM Corporation.

Kragzig, D., Banke, K., & Slama, D. (2004). *Enterprise SOA: Service-oriented architecture best practices.* Upper Saddle River, NJ: Prentice Hall.

Marks, E. A., & Bell, M. (2006). *Service-oriented architecture (SOA): A planning and implementation guide for business and technology.* Hoboken, NJ: Wiley Press.

Marks, E. A., & Werrell, M. J. (2003). *Executive's guide to Web services (SOA, service-oriented architecture).* Hoboken, NJ: Wiley Press.

McGovern, J., Sims, O., & Jain, A. (2006). *Enterprise service oriented architectures: Concepts, challenges, recommendations.* New York: Springer.

McKendrick, J. (2006, January 3). Ten examples of SOA at work, right now. *ZD Net.* Retrieved February 23, 2007, from http://blogs.zdnet.com/service-oriented/?p=508

Nagaratnam, N., Nadalin, A., Hondo, M., McIntosh, M., & Austel, P. (2005). Business-driven application security: From modeling to managing secure applications. *IBM Systems Journal, 44*(4), 847-868.

Newcomer, E., & Lomow, G. (2004). *Understanding SOA with Web services.* Reading, MA: Addison-Wesley Professional.

Papazoglou, M. P., & Georgakopoulos, D. (2003). Service-oriented computing. *Communications of the ACM, 46*(10), 25-28.

Pulier, E., & Hugh, T. (2005). *Understanding enterprise SOA.* Greenwich: Manning Publications.

Schmidt, M. T., Hutchison, B., Lambros, P., & Phippen, R. (2005). The enterprise service bus: Making service-oriented architecture real. *IBM Systems Journal, 44*(4), 781-798.

Walend, D. (2006, April 4). *Understanding service oriented architecture.* Retrieved February

23, 2007, from http://today.java.net/pub/a/today/2006/04/04/understanding-service-oriented-architecture.html

Woods, D., & Mattern, T. (2006). *Enterprise SOA: Designing IT for business innovation.* Cambridge, MA: O'Reilly Media.

Zimmermann, O., Krogdahl, P., & Gee, C. (2004). *Elements of service-oriented analysis and design: An interdisciplinary modeling approach for SOA projects.* Retrieved February 23, 2007, from http://www-128.ibm.com/developerworks/webservices/library/ws-soad1/

TERMS AND DEFINITIONS

Business Process: A business process is a sequence of purposeful activities frequently performed within an organization or by multiple organizations in a coordinated way. It creates value for citizens or customers, or fulfills an internal need of an organization. Workflow designs are models of business processes.

Electronic Data Interchange (EDI): EDI is a commercial way to create and use an electronic connection between two computers or networks geographically distant from one another and often owned by different organizations. These connections can be secure and may be relatively costly and inflexible as compared to solutions based upon Web services.

Extensible Markup Language (XML): XML is a way to mark up text-based content into a structure that can be interpreted by a computer application that has the schema necessary for interpretation.

Object-Oriented Programming: Most modern computer programming languages are object oriented, meaning that conceptually the programming code consists of units (objects) that include both a data structure and an ability to do things. Some kinds of objects correspond to things that exist in the real world, such as citizens. Web services are an extension of this modular way of structuring programming code and designing programs that are distributed across computer networks.

Service-Oriented Architecture (SOA): An SOA is a design by which multiple services are called in sequence or in parallel so as to implement the activities that compose a business process.

Simple Object Access Protocol (SOAP): SOAP refers to an XML protocol used to provide a container in code for communications with Web services. The expression "SOAP envelope" is often used to describe the function of this technology.

Strategic Alliance: A strategic alliance is a working association between two or more organizations, such as between a government agency and a nonprofit organization.

Universal Description, Discovery and Integration (UDDI): A UDDI is a Web-based directory that lets organizations publish the availability of Web services they provide that are available to be used by software applications used by other organizations. UDDI is often compared to a telephone book or yellow pages.

Web Service: A Web service is a service made available within an organization or between organizations at the level of computers connected by in intranet or across the Internet using specialized standards including WSDL, SOAP, and UDDI.

Web Service Description Language (WSDL): A WSDL is a file on a Web server that is associated with a Web service that contains information about how a software application can talk to the Web service and what services the Web service is prepared to provide. WSDL files are intended to be read by computers. Because they are text files, they can be opened and read with Microsoft Notepad and other ASCII editors.

Chapter L
The Strategic Determinants of Shared Services

Anton Joha
Delft University of Technology, The Netherlands

Marijn Janssen
Delft University of Technology, The Netherlands

INTRODUCTION

Stimulated by recent advances in information and communication technology, and in their continuous pursuit for ways to reduce costs while at the same time improving customer orientation, public agencies have started to share services. By unbundling services of multiple public agencies, standardizing these services, and concentrating them in a separate organization, the basic premise of shared services seems to be that services provided by one local department or agency can be provided to others with relatively few efforts, potentially resulting in both cost savings and service quality improvements (Bergeron, 2003). Public agencies share their role as service provider by joint development, operation, control, and governance of services. As such, the sharing of services can be viewed as a particular type of sourcing arrangement. Services remain within public administration, and public agencies control and govern the shared-service arrangement.

In many countries the promising benefits of sharing services resulted in the establishment of a new type of electronic intermediary (e-intermediary) named shared-service centers (SSCs). E-intermediaries are autonomous organizations supporting organizations to improve the coordination of their activities. The basic premise of SSCs is that services operated by the intermediary organization can be used by the other organizations with relatively few efforts. The SSC provides services to many users. A number of U.S., Canadian, and Australian states, as well as Ireland and the Netherlands, have adopted shared services to support and hasten e-government developments (e.g., Accenture, 2005). The choice for sharing services is a major decision having a long-term and strategic impact, which often competes with outsourcing arrangements (Janssen & Joha, 2006b).

Just like in outsourcing arrangements (Baldwin, Irani, & Love, 2001; Fowler & Jeffs, 1998), the intended benefits are often not met and there are many strategic determinants affecting decision making concerning the use and implementation of shared services.

The goal of the research presented in this chapter is to analyze the strategic determinants influencing the decision making for using and implementing shared services. The structure of the chapter is as follows. In the following section we discuss the historical and theoretical background of shared services. In the section thereafter, we provide an overview of the strategic determinants influencing the shared-services decision. Next, future trends are presented, and finally, conclusions are drawn.

BACKGROUND

History shows various cycles of the centralization and decentralization of computing power, functionality, and organization structure. The mainframe area has resulted in the centralization of large systems in so-called data centers, whereas the introduction of personal computers resulted in a major decentralization of computing power, functionality, and control. With the advent of the Internet, it has become possible to combine aspects of centralized and decentralized models. These kinds of mixed models are often aimed at capturing the best elements of centralized and decentralized models. A SSC is an example of such a mixed model. The selected government services supporting the business processes of local, decentralized agencies are unbundled and concentrated into a shared-service center, whereas service provisioning of the service remains the responsibility of the local agencies.

SSCs are a particular type of sourcing arrangement, where resources and services are retained in-house. A SSC differs from outsourcing arrangements as the SSC is a complete internal arrangement that is founded and governed by the initiators, who are often also the users; outsourcing is externally oriented as it is about the relationship with external parties. In an SSC arrangement, there are relationships between many users and one provider, whereas outsourcing generally addresses the relationship between one user and one or more providers. Janssen and Joha (2006b) pointed out that these specific differences also have consequences for the decision-making processes and risks involved.

There are many theories underpinning sourcing theory and its decision-making process. Lee, Huynh, Kwok, and Pi (2003) and Jayatilaka, Schwarz, and Hirschheim (2003) provide an overview of sourcing theories and the strategic determinants influencing these decisions. We adopt their process-driven decision approach and use four major decision categories for implementing shared services: (a) make-or-buy decision, (b) scope and type of shared-service arrangement, (c) cost benefits and risks assessment, and (d) implementation choice and change management strategy. These categories are shown in the left column of Table 1. In general, the process starts when politicians and/or public managers decide whether to develop services in-house, share them with others, or buy them on the market. Next, the scope and type of the shared-service arrangement should be decided on, which will result in the identification of various options available to share services. Thereafter, the cost benefits and risks of the identified options should be assessed and the decision to implement one arrangement should be taken. Finally, the shared-service arrangement should be implemented using a change management strategy. In the following paragraphs, we discuss these four categories in detail.

The make-or-buy decision for sourcing is largely determined by resource-based theory and core competency theory, which explain that organizations should retain core capabilities in-house and that noncore capabilities do not have to be owned.

Table 1. Decision categories for shared services and their driving theories and motto

Decision Categories	Driving Theories	Driving Motto
1. Make-or-buy decision	- Core competencies theory - Resource-based theory	Performing activities either in-house or by external suppliers
2. Scope and type of shared-service arrangement	- Coordination theory - Resource dependency theory - Transaction cost theory	Determining the potential scope and options for sharing services, including the objectives that should be met
3. Cost benefits and risks assessment	- Power-political theory - Principal-agent theory - Transaction cost theory	Assessing the financial feasibility of the shared-service options, also taking into account the risks involved
4. Implementation choice and change management strategy	- Power-political theory - Organizational theories	Defining the optimal way to implement the shared-services concept within the organization

Choices about the scope of services and the type of shared-service arrangement are driven by coordination, transaction costs, and resource dependency theory. Coordination theory is about the management of interdependencies between organizational business processes (Malone & Crowston, 1994). The basic view in resource dependency theory is that organizations are dependent on external resources to function (Pfeffer & Salancik, 2003). The problem that resource dependency theory emphasizes is that the environment changes and resources become more or less scarce, resulting in power differences between organizations and providing an explanation of how independent organizations come to depend on and dominate each other.

Cost benefits and risks assessment of the selected sourcing options are often based on the power-political, principal-agent, and transaction cost theories. The basic idea of outsourcing is based on the transaction cost theory (Coase, 1937). Transaction costs result from the transfer of property rights between parties and exist because of friction in economic systems. An organization will tend to expand until the cost of organizing an extra transaction internally becomes equal to the costs of carrying out the same transaction on the open market. The use of a communication network and integration technology will decrease the transaction costs, enabling organizations to source functions and to focus on their core competencies. Principal-agent theory deals with the relationship between the principal and agent based on the division of labor, information asymmetry and environment, and partner behavior (Jensen & Meckling, 1976). Both the transaction cost and principal-agent theories are based on rationality, an efficiency criterion used for explaining outsourcing structures. Political organizational theories are used for explaining organizational arrangements and include social, coordination, risk, and strategic management theories. These view actors as political entities having different degrees of power.

The way shared services will be implemented and how changes are managed depend on power-political and organizational theories, which are interdisciplinary and based on knowledge from the fields of psychology, political science, economics, anthropology, and sociology. They seek to explain behavior and dynamics in both individual and group contexts.

Now we have discussed the historical and theoretical foundation, we will further explore the strategic determinants of shared services in the following section. We will do this using the four decision categories that were presented in this section.

DETERMINANTS OF SHARED-SERVICES DECISIONS

Make-or-Buy Decision

The make-or-buy decision requires the creation of an overview of services that might be sourced and their potential sourcing options. Quinn and Hilmer (1994) argue that profit organizations ideally concentrate on those activities where they can add value to customers and strategically outsource other services for which the organization has neither a critical strategic need nor special capabilities. When translating this to public organizations, services can be categorized along two dimensions: (a) the degree of public interest in the service and (b) the potential vulnerability that could arise from market failure if the service is outsourced. Figure 1 shows schematically the two axes and the relationship with sourcing arrangements.

When there is a high degree of public interest and vulnerability, the agency would generally like to have a high degree of control, usually selecting an insourcing option, which could be a shared-service center. When the degree of public interest in a service is low and there is a low degree of vulnerability, activities can be outsourced. In between, there is a continuous range of activities requiring different degrees of control. Assessing the make-or-buy decision will result in a high-level categorization of core activities that need to be executed internally and noncore activities that can potentially be outsourced to an external supplier.

Scope and Type of Shared-Service Arrangement

Those services that are identified as potentially sharable need further analysis to determine the scope and type of arrangement. There are two key ways in which the scope can be expanded, namely, through functional integration of corporate services within one agency or through sharing along functional lines with other government departments or agencies. Figure 2 highlights the scope choice by showing four quadrants of

Figure 1. Make-or-buy decision for public organizations (based on Quinn & Hilmer, 1994)

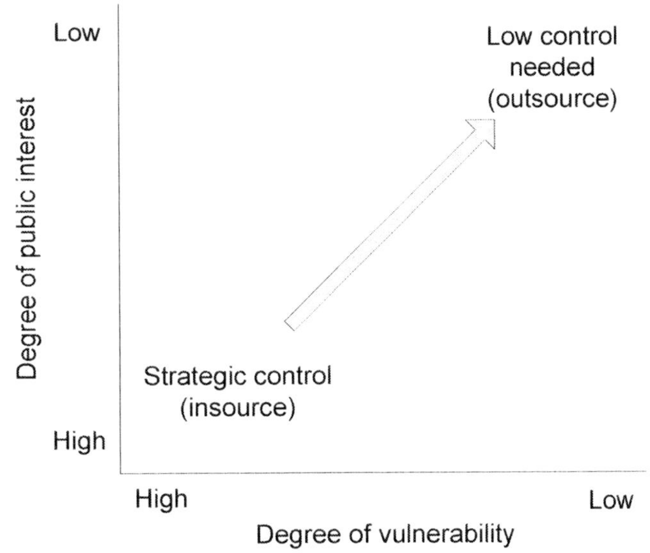

Figure 2. Determining the potential scope of shared services

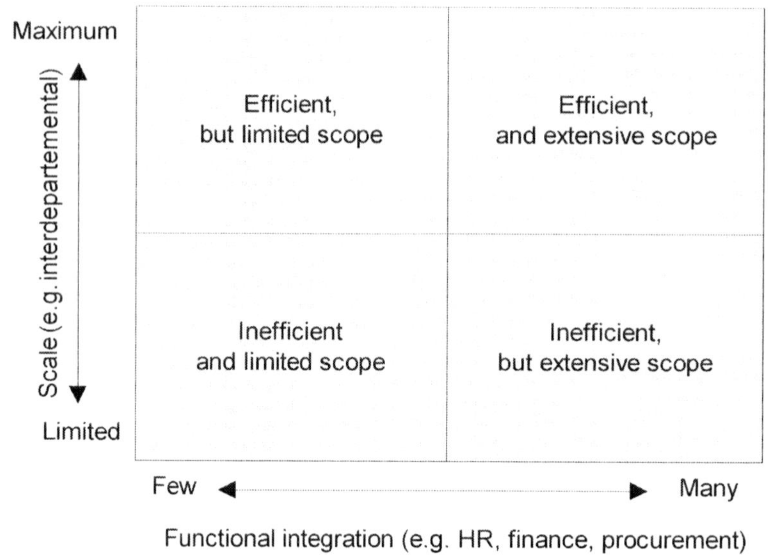

sharing options. The top-right quadrant, efficient and extensive scope, might be viewed as the total shared-service arrangement option; however, a long-lasting implementation process involving many kinds of risks might be necessary to accomplish this. Janssen and Joha (2006b) investigated a case study were the accomplishment of a mature shared-service center took almost two decades.

Various types of arrangements can be chosen, including joint ventures with other public agencies, the creation of a new semiautonomous agency, the concentration of existing services in one of the existing agencies, or other models. The type of arrangement influences the way the SSC will need to be operationalized and designed in terms of its service and financial model, organizational structure, and IT governance mechanisms. IT governance mechanisms determine how communication, responsibilities, and decision-making structures are formalized (Weill & Ross, 2005).

The choice for the type of arrangement and its organizational design are affected by the objectives that the shared-service arrangement should meet and vice versa. Sharing might be risky or even impossible if agencies have opposing objectives; for example, one might focus on improving the cost efficiency of existing services, whereas another agency might want to share resources to gain access to services that would be out of reach if it had to invest in these services individually. Moreover, each service might have (slightly) different objectives. Janssen and Joha (2006b) provided an overview of the objectives of shared-service centers by categorizing them into four categories, namely, (a) strategic and organizational, (b) political, (c) technical, and (d) economical objectives. This phase should result in a detailed overview of the available options to share services, thereby also identifying the accompanying objectives for each type of service.

Cost Benefits and Risks Assessment

The different combinations of options that are identified in the former step need to be translated to a number of preferred scenarios that need to be assessed on their merits, disadvantages, and risks. This step requires gathering accurate details of the current IT, people costs, and head count for the individual processes in order to accurately model the potential savings. The specific cost benefits of the sharing of services should be assessed taking into account the potential for cost reduction, service improvement, better control, gaining access to expertise or services out of reach for the organization, and so on. Also the risks involved with the defined scenarios need to be addressed. Following Charette (1991) and Willcocks and Margetts (1994), risk can be defined as an undesired outcome that has a known or estimated probability of occurrence and impact based on experience or some theory. In Table 2, an overview of risks is presented based on Earl (1996), ISPL (1999), and Willcocks, Lacity, and Kern (1999). This table can help decision makers to assess the probability and impact of the potential risks, resulting in appropriate risk measures necessary for risk mitigation.

Table 2. Potential risks of shared services

Risks (based on Earl, 1996; ISPL, 1999; Willcocks et al., 1999)	Risk Definition (based on ISPL, 1999)
Unclear service requirements	The requirements of the services are not clear or not available.
Unstable service requirements	The requirements of the services are not stable and they are changing and evolving.
Uncertain interfaces	Interfaces may be with other services, processes, or systems within the internal organization or with other (local) agencies.
Lack of stakeholder participation	The involved stakeholders (e.g., users) have insufficient participation in the service development or execution.
Shortfalls in subcontracted tasks	Tasks that are subcontracted are not performed to the required quality.
Loss of control of the services	The management loses control of the services.
Delays in the deliveries	Some deliverables, being either intermediate deliverables in projects or management deliverables for services in general, are delivered late.
Poor quality of deliverables	Some deliverables, being either intermediate deliverables in projects or management deliverables for services in general, are not delivered to the required quality.
Increased service costs	The costs of the services increase.
Discouragement of the service actors	Some actors responsible for delivering the services lose their motivation and commitment for various reasons.
Poor quality of the services	The delivered services do not have the required quality; this may mean that it is not working, not adapted to the needs and requirements, or that there are shortfalls in some quality properties (functionality, efficiency, reliability, etc.).
Services not accepted by (local) agencies	The services are not accepted by the (local) agencies involved; the reason may be poor quality but may also encompass sociological or human issues (e.g., due to unrealistic expectations).
Unpredictable costs for the (local) agencies	The delivered services generate unpredictable costs for the (local) agencies; these costs may relate to usage, operation, maintenance, and so forth, and be due to bad quality or other reasons.
No attainment of the objectives	The delivered services do not contribute to the predefined objectives. The reasons may be bad quality, unpredictable costs, or some complex combinations of factors.
No formal governance mechanisms	Communication and decision-making structures are not (effectively) implemented and/or roles and responsibilities are not fomalized.

Unstable and unclear requirements form a major risk in the development of an SSC, particularly in defining the future service delivery. Risk mitigation can be achieved by involving users and organizational representatives in the design process and sign off at all stages, and by executing strong change and requirements management. Also, dividing the project into manageable phases with a gating process at the end of each phase before proceeding to the next might well reduce these risks.

A lack of upfront commitment and participation from the majority of the involved stakeholders will restrict the potential range of solutions and potentially its feasibility. Related to this is that the initial resistance to change and poor planning will cause procrastination and slow the project implementation timescales. Risk measures include developing and implementing a communication program to focus on reasons for change, involving staff in the process of redesign and training, and mentoring managers in working in the new environment.

Not attaining the objectives might be the result of not clearly defining, monitoring, and tracking the potential benefits. A project board will need to agree on benefits milestones, measurement architecture, and the used monitoring process. Other important risks are loss of control of the service and poor service quality due to an undefined or unclear IT governance structure. Clear roles and responsibilities under the new structure need to be defined.

Based on the results of this and the former steps, all predefined scenarios can be compared and a choice will have to be made out of the potential sourcing scenarios. The scenarios can be evaluated from three key perspectives.

1. Functionality and quality, which is about the ability of the service to support the agencies in meeting future challenges and changes
2. Risks, taking into account the factors that could cause an option to fail to deliver all of the required outcomes and/or benefits
3. Business case, which deals with the financial investment that is required, also including a comparison with the market best practice in case the service would be outsourced

Implementation Choice and Change Management Strategy

When a decision is made about which services will be shared and the architecture has been determined, an implementation strategy can be developed. A big-bang strategy, an incremental strategy, or a combination of these strategies can be used (Bruijn, Heuvelhof, & Veld, 2002). In essence, the issues around implementation are whether to concentrate all shared services for all involved agencies in one organization at once or to gradually implement processes and technology solutions among all involved agencies before trying to move to a shared-services concept.

The choice of a change management strategy might be determined by political and technical issues. Political issues include the initial resistance that might be present or expected within local departments not willing to give up some of their autonomy, and individuals who are afraid that their carrier options might be affected. Change management strategies can try to deal with political issues by, for example, defining such extremely high performance levels that local departments need to cooperate to accomplish these levels. Another example is that a service is so expensive that the local departments are very much willing to share the costs with others.

Technical issues are related to the technical constraints and limitations of an organization's ICT infrastructure as this is a necessary condition for establishing shared services. This not only includes the technical platform, but also software and interfaces. Shared services should also be able to technically cope with changes and therefore require an adaptive architecture. Failure of service provisioning can result in a shut down of critical operations and result in a major loss of productivity and complaints from constituents. The management of the SSC should mitigate these risks by having duplicate versions of systems and an emergency communication network to avoid the single-point-of-failure problems. The design of the necessary ICT infrastructure is therefore an essential factor in the implementation strategy.

FUTURE TRENDS

The sharing of services is a strategic decision having a long-term impact. We expect that sharing services will be less and less focused on technology aspects and more and more on organizational matters. The focus on the design of effective IT governance mechanisms and the introduction of risk mitigation mechanisms are especially emerging trends. The IT governance of shared services is a complicated endeavor as it often involves multiple agencies having different objectives and resources; also, the number of shared services used varies among agencies, technology sophistication differs, and unshared resources of the public agencies are interwoven with shared services (Janssen & Joha, 2006a).

The use of shared services has initially been limited to easy-to-standardize services. In the future, the scope might be expanded and public agencies might share complete back-office functions and processes. Even seemingly different services might be shared, such as finance and accounting and parts of procurement and human resources services. Moreover, a trend is that these services are customized to the local situation of public agencies. In this way, the advantages of economies of scale, by means of sharing services, and the ability to customize services to the local situation are combined.

CONCLUSION

There are many strategic determinants affecting decision making concerning the implementation and operation of an e-intermediary like a shared-service center. To obtain the promised benefits of shared services and avoid the risks, the right design trade-offs and decisions have to be made influencing the performance and success of the shared-service arrangements. As a result, the sharing of services requires the design of a conscious decision-making process influenced by a variety of strategic determinants. In this chapter, we presented four major decision categories: (a) make-or-buy decision, (b) scope and type of shared-service arrangement, (c) cost benefits and risks assessment, and (d) implementation choice and change management strategy. We gave an overview of the decision categories, and discussed the strategic determinants associated with the decision-making process and implementation of shared services in public administration.

A decision-making process regarding shared services starts with identifying viable sourcing options; assessing these on functionality, quality, risks, and financial implications; and developing a carefully crafted change management strategy. An important strategic determinant is risk, not only as a necessary input variable for the decision process, but also in order to be able to mitigate risks once the decision for implementing a shared-service arrangement has been made. Furthermore, there are a variety of strategic determinants that affect the decision-making processes of public agencies and might result in different arrangements to share services. Therefore, it is of prime importance that the strategic determinants are taken into account in a systematic and structured way when deciding whether to make use of shared services.

FUTURE RESEARCH DIRECTIONS

There are many potential research directions in this field and these are clustered according to our previous categorization.

Make-or-Buy Decision. An important question is whether activities can be outsourced or need to be kept in-house. There still is a need for a framework that provides all the different dimensions that need to be taken into account to determine which services are suitable for outsourcing and which are not. Besides the degree of vulnerability and public interest, other factors might well play a role, including the competency of the organization in executing the service and in managing external suppliers, the complexity of the service, and the market maturity.

Scope and Type of Shared-Service Arrangement. The way the SSC supports an organization does have major consequences for the way it should be embedded in the organization. It has to be determined what the specific objective of the SSC should be such as service improvement, cost reduction, or innovation. It is still not evident whether all advantages can be combined and achieved and which factors are of importance to meet a specific objective (Janssen & Joha, 2006b).

The configuration of the right SSC business model to ensure a good and effective service delivery is an important research direction (Janssen & Joha, 2007). There is no theory addressing which business model the best choice is given certain circumstances. The specific model that is chosen has consequences for policy making and accountability, making it clear to whom the SSC reports and what its specific responsibilities are. The way the organization needs to be structured in terms of roles and responsibilities is also a topic for further research. Moreover, it is not yet clear which pricing structures can be adopted and what governance model fits best for the different models.

Cost benefits and risks assessment. From a macro organizational economic perspective, it has to be determined whether the SSC is feasible. Such a feasibility study should include different analyses, for example, costs of technology adaptations, costs of changing or modifying facilities, and customer satisfaction with current services or potential shared services. Yet, the major cost factors are not well understood. From an economic perspective, it is of interest to analyze whether the nature of an SSC changes over time in terms of economies of scale, efficiency, and governance, and in what way it evolves. Finally, the difference in efficiency and effectiveness between SSC and outsourcing arrangements is a fruitful research direction.

Implementation choice and change management strategy. The dependency on the internal resources and people within SSC arrangements is extremely high. Research is necessary to identify the different strategies to cope with initial resistance and to analyze which specific strategies are most appropriate and effective given the specific circumstances (Janssen & Joha, 2007).

A well-functioning ICT infrastructure is a necessary condition for establishing an SSC. This not only includes the technical platform, but also software and interfaces. The SSC should also be able to technically cope with contingencies, such as mergers and acquisitions, and therefore requires an adaptive architecture. Research issues include the following questions. What ICT is at least necessary for SSCs? What technology is suitable for sharing services? The design of the ICT infrastructure not only determines whether an SSC is possible and viable, but also how it should be implemented.

REFERENCES

Accenture. (2005). Shared services: Government shared services model for high performance. Retrieved June 23, 2006, from http://www.accenture.com/Global/Services/By_Industry/Government/R_and_I/DrivingServices.htm

Baldwin, L. P., Irani, Z., & Love, P. E. D. (2001). Outsourcing information systems: Drawing lessons from a banking case study. *European Journal of Information Systems, 10*(1), 15-24.

Bergeron, B. (2003). *Essentials of shared services.* John Wiley & Sons.

Bruijn, H. de, Heuvelhof, E. ten, & Veld, R. in 't. (2002). *Process management: Why project management fails in complex decision making processes.* Dordrecht, the Netherlands: Kluwer Academic Publishers.

Charette, R. (1991). *Application strategies for risk analysis.* New York: McGraw Hill.

Coase, R. (1937). The nature of the firm. *Economica, 4*, 386-405.

Earl, M. J. (1996). The risks of outsourcing IT. *Sloan Management Review, 37*(3), 26-32.

Fowler, A., & Jeffs, B. (1998). Examining information systems outsourcing: A case study from the United Kingdom. *Journal of Information Technology, 13*, 111-126.

ISPL. (1999). Introduction to ISPL. *ISPL Consortium.*

Janssen, M., & Joha, A. (2006a). *Governance of shared services centers in public administration.* Paper presented at the 12th Americas Conference on Information Systems, Acapulco, Mexico.

Janssen, M., & Joha, A. (2006b). Motives for establishing shared service centers in public administrations. *International Journal of Information Management, 26*(2), 102-116.

Janssen, M. & Joha, A. (2007). Governance and design issues of shared service centers. In Anttiroiko, A. and Mälkiä, M. (Eds.) *Encyclopedia of digital government, Vol. II.*

Jayatilaka, B., Schwarz, A., & Hirschheim, R. (2003). Determinants of ASP choice: An integrated perspective. *European Journal of Information Systems, 12*(3), 210-224.

Jensen, M., & Meckling, W. (1976). Theory of the firm: Managerial behavior, agency costs, and capital structure. *Journal of Financial Economics, 5*, 305-360.

Lee, J. N., Huynh, M. Q., Kwok, R. C. W., & Pi, S. M. (2003). IT outsourcing evolution: Past, present and future. *Communications of the ACM, 46*(5), 84-89.

Malone, T. W., & Crowston, K. (1994). The interdisciplinary study of coordination. *ACM Computing Surveys, 26*, 87-119.

Pfeffer, J., & Salancik, G. R. (2003). *The external control of organisations.* Stanford, CA: Stanford Business Classics.

Quinn, J. B., & Hilmer, F. G. (1994). Make versus buy: Strategic outsourcing. *Sloan Management Review, 35*(4), 43-55.

Weill, P., & Ross, J. (2005). A matrixed approach to designing IT governance. *MIT Sloan Management Review, 46*(2) 26-34.

Willcocks, L., & Margetts, H. (1994). Risk assessment in information systems. *European Journal of Information Systems, 4*(1), 1-12.

Willcocks, L. P., Lacity, M. C., & Kern, T. (1999). Risk mitigation in IT outsourcing strategy revisited: Longitudinal case research at LISA. *Strategic Information Systems, 8*(3), 285-314.

FURTHER READING

Beynon-Davies, P., & Williams, M. D. (2003). Evaluating electronic local government in the UK. *Journal of Information Technology, 18*(2), 137-149.

Duivenboden & Thaens, M. (2006). Information and communication technology and public innovation. In *Assessing the ICT-driven modernization of public administration* (pp. 141-158). Amsterdam: IOS Press.

Eisenhardt, K., & Martin, J. A. (2000). Dynamic capabilities: What are they? *Strategic Management Journal, 21*(10-11), 1105-1121.

Grant, G., McKnight, S., Uruthirapathy, & Brown, A. (in press). Designing governance for shared services organizations in the public service. *Government Information Quarterly.*

Grant, R. M. (1991). The resource-based theory of competitive advantage. *California Management Review, 33*(3), 114-135.

Grembergen, W. van, & Haes, S. De. (2004). IT governance and its mechanisms. *Information Systems Control Journal, 6*, 32-35.

Hirschheim, R., & Lacity, M. (2000). The myths and realities of information technology insourcing. *Communications of the ACM, 43*(2), 99-107.

Hodgkinson, S. L. (1996). The role of the corporate IT function in the federal IT organization. In M. J. Earl (Ed.), *Information management: The organizational dimension* (pp. 247-269). Oxford: Oxford University Press.

Janssen, M., & Joha, A. (2004). Issues in relationship management for obtaining the benefits of a shared service center. *Sixth International Conference on Electronic Commerce* (pp. 219-228).

Janssen, M., & Joha, A. (2007). Understanding IT governance for the operation of shared services in public service networks. *International Journal of Networking and Virtual Organizations, 4*(1), 20-34.

Janssen, M., & Wagenaar, R. W. (2004). *An analysis of a shared services center in e-government.* Paper presented at the Hawaii International Conference on System Sciences, HI.

Kern, T., & Willcocks, L. (2000). Exploring information technology outsourcing relationships: Theory and practice. *Journal of Strategic Information Systems, 9*(4), 321-350.

Kern, T., & Willcocks, L. (2002). Exploring relationships in information technology outsourcing: The interaction approach. *European Journal of Information Systems, 11*(1), 3-19.

Kern, T., & Willcocks, L. P. (2001). *The relationship advantage: Information technologies, management and sourcing.* Oxford: Oxford University Press.

Lacity, M. C., & Hirscheim, R. (1995). *The information systems outsourcing: Myths, metaphors and realities.* Chichester, United Kingdom: Wiley.

Lacity, M. C., & Willcocks, L. P. (1998). An empirical investigation of information technology sourcing practices: Lessons from experience. *MIS Quarterly, 22*(3), 363-308.

Lacity, M. C., & Willcocks, L. P. (2002). *Global IT outsourcing: In search of business advantages.* Chichester, United Kingdom: Wiley.

Ray, G., Muhanna, W. A., & Barney, J. B. (2005). Information technology and the performance of the customer service process: A resources-based analysis. *MIS Quarterly, 29*(4), 625-652.

Reich, B. H., & Benbasat, I. (2000). Factors that influence the social dimension of alignment between business and information technology objectives. *MIS Quarterly, 24*(1), 81-111.

Roy, V., & Aubert, B. A. (2002). Research contributions: A resource-based analysis of IT sourcing. *ACM SIGMIS Database, 33*(2), 29-40.

Strikwerda, J. (2005). Shared service centers. In *Van kostenbesparing naar waardecreatie.* Assen, the Netherlands: Van Gorcum.

Teece, D., Pisano, G., & Shuen, A. (1997). Dynamic capabilities and strategic management. *Strategic Management Journal, 18*(7), 509-533.

Ulbrich, F. (2005). Improving shared service implementation: Adopting lessons from the BPR movement. *Business Process Management Journal, 12*(2), 191-205.

Wagenaar, R. W., Bruijn, J. A. de, Voort, H. van der, & Wendel de Joode, R. van. (2006). *Implementation of shared service centers in public administration: Dilemma's and trade-offs*. Amsterdam, the Netherlands: IOS Press.

Weill, P. (2004). Don't just lead, govern: How best performing organisations govern IT. *MIS Quarterly Executive, 3*(1), 1-17.

Willcocks, L. P., & Kern, T. (1998). IT outsourcing as strategic partnering: The case of the UK inland revenue. *European Journal of Information Systems, 7*(1), 29-45.

Yang, C., & Huang, F. B. (2000). A decision model for IS outsourcing. *International Journal of Information Management, 20*(3), 225-239.

TERMS AND DEFINITIONS

Business Process: A business process is a sequence of tasks initiated by an event and aimed at providing products or services.

Change Management Strategy: A change management strategy is the plan for the development of a program and procedure for ensuring the fulfillment of intended functions or services.

E-Intermediary: An electronic intermediary is a (semi)autonomous organization that supports other organizations in coordinating their activities.

IT Governance: IT governance is the system and structure for defining policy and monitoring and controlling the policy implementation, and managing and coordinating the procedures and resources aimed at ensuring the efficient and effective execution of services.

Risk: Risk is an undesired outcome that has a known or estimated probability of occurrence and impact based on experience or some theory.

Shared Service: Shared services are services that are shared by multiple users and provided by one service provider.

Shared-Service Center (SSC): The SSC is a type of business model in which selected services are unbundled and concentrated into an accountable, semiautonomous unit or organization that provides the predefined services to all local, decentralized agencies on the basis of agreed conditions.

Sourcing: Sourcing is the decision process of identifying and selecting potential internal or external suppliers of specified services.

Strategic Determinant: A strategic determinant is an influencing or determining element or factor in a decision choice.

Chapter LI
Data Mining in Public Administration

John Wang
Montclair State University, USA

Xiaohua Hu
Drexel University, USA

Dan Zhu
Iowa State University, USA

INTRODUCTION

Data mining involves searching through databases for potentially useful information such as knowledge rules, patterns, regularities, and other trends hidden in the data. In order to complete these tasks, the contemporary data mining packages offer techniques such as neural networks, inductive learning decision trees, cluster analysis, link analysis, genetic algorithms, visualization, and so forth (Hand, Mannila, & Smyth, 2001; Wang, 2006). In general, data mining is a data analytical technique that assists businesses in learning and understanding their customers so that decisions and strategies can be implemented most accurately and effectively to maximize profitability. Data mining is not general data analysis, but a comprehensive technique that requires analytical skills, information construction, and professional knowledge.

Businesses are now facing globalized competition and are being forced to deal with an enormous amount of data. The vast amounts of data and the increasing technological ability to store them also facilitated data mining. In order to gain a certain level of competitive advantage, businesses now commonly adopt a data analytical technology called data mining. Nowadays, data mining is more widely used than ever before, not only by businesses who seek profits, but also by nonprofit organizations, government agencies, private groups, and other institutions in the public sector. Organizations use data mining as a tool to forecast customer behavior, reduce fraud and waste, and assist in medical research.

BACKGROUND

Data mining uses statistical analysis, artificial intelligence, and machine-learning technologies to identify patterns that cannot be found by manual analysis alone. The primary function of data mining has already amazed many people and is now considered one of the most critical issues toward a business's success. However, data mining was not born all of a sudden. The earliest usage of data mining can be traced back to the World War II years. Data analytical methods such as model prediction, database segmentation, link analysis, and deviation detection were used for military affairs and demographic purposes by the U.S. government, but data mining had not been seriously promoted until the 1990s.

Gramatikov (2006) compares statistical methods to data mining, differentiating them by the ultimate focus of these two tools. Statistical methods use data that are collected with a predefined set of questions. Statisticians are either looking for describing parameters of data or making inferences through statistics within intervals. With data mining, knowledge is generated from hidden relations, rules, trends, and patterns that emerge as the data are mined.

The reason that data mining has been developed enormously again in the last few years is that a huge amount of information was demanded by modern enterprises due to globalization. Important information regarding markets, customers, competitors, and future opportunities were collected in the form of data to be put in databases, and businesses needed data mining to unearth useful information and knowledge. Otherwise, a huge, overloaded, and unstructured database could just make it very difficult for companies to utilize it, and it would in turn mislead the database users.

Public administration is, broadly speaking, the study and implementation of policy. The term may apply to government, private-sector organizations and groups, and individuals. The adjective *public* often denotes government at federal, state, and local levels, though it increasingly encompasses nonprofit organizations such as those of civil society or any not specifically acting in self-interest. Then, a long list exists, including colleges and universities, health care organizations, and charities, as well as postal offices, libraries, prisons, and so forth.

In the public sector, data mining initially was used as a means to detect fraud and waste, but has since grown for purposes such as measuring and improving program performance. Data mining has been increasingly cited as an important tool for homeland security efforts, crime prevention, and medical and educational applications to increase efficiency, reduce costs, and enhance research.

BENEFITS OF DATA MINING IN PUBLIC ADMINISTRATION

Data mining techniques offer public-sector opportunities to optimize decisions based on general trends extracted from historical data. With the knowledge that can be extracted from the data, public organizations can level up its knowledge accumulation strategies and steps. The knowledge that can be derived with the data mining could serve first as a tool for better governance and second as a means for sustaining the organizational knowledge. Data mining technology is applied in different aspects of public administration such as health care, immigration, law enforcement, and other public sectors to solve specific business or research problems. Examples of application areas follow.

Improving Service or Performance

The purpose of SBA's (Small Business Administration) lender and loan monitoring system is to improve service and performance. The system was developed by Dun and Bradstreet. SBA uses the system to identify, measure, and manage risk in its business loan programs. Its outputs include reports that identify the total amount of loans outstanding for a particular lender and estimate the likelihood of loans becoming delinquent in the future based on predefined patterns (U.S. Government Accounting Office [GAO], 2005).

Hospitals are currently using data mining to save money in the long run by reducing medication errors and the cost of transcribing doctors' dictation. For example, a family practitioner at UW Health's Meadowood clinic uses the Epic System to order a drug; the computer automatically checks a database of potential cross-reactions with other medications that the patient is currently taking. This system makes it easier for doctors to do their job very well, and at the same time, this system makes it easier for patients to see their information and interact with doctors. Also, with the growing rate of infections in hospitals in the United States, some hospitals are adopting data mining techniques to inform doctors of problems they might miss. MedMined of Birmingham is a company that has sold its data analysis services to hospitals to help detect infection in its early stage. Hospitals transmit encrypted data from patients' records to MedMined, which then uses its data mining algorithms to detect unusual patterns and correlations. At first only a few hospitals used this system, but now it is becoming a necessity in hospitals (Lok, 2004).

Cahlink (2000) reported that data mining techniques are used by health organizations and hospitals to improve upon work processes. The Center for Disease Control and Prevention National Immunization Program in Atlanta implemented data mining software to allow better tracking of reactions to vaccine. The program has a huge database of adverse reactions to vaccines reported by physicians, clinics, hospitals, patients, and pharmaceutical companies across the nation. Statisticians and federal researchers monitor the data regularly to find problems caused by a single vaccine or vaccine combinations.

Through a cooperative agreement, the FDA's (Food and Drug Administration) Division of Drug Risk Evaluation in the Office of Drug Safety has been working for almost 2 years to implement a desktop data mining software system. This data mining tool will help to evaluate the hundreds of thousands of reports submitted annually to the Adverse Events Reporting System (AERS), a system that has become more widely available to the public (Anonymous, 2005).

Delavari, Shirazi, and Beikzadeh (2004) showed that higher educational institutes use data mining models to identify which part of their processes can be improved by data mining technology and how they can achieve their goals. Data mining is used in the educational system to allocate resources and staff more efficiently, manage student relations, and enhance the performance of the institution and its students and faculty. Databases include information on students and teachers, course schedules, academic performance, test scores, extracurricular activities, postgraduation activities, and so forth, all of which can guide an institution on how to improve.

Helping Customer Relations Management

Studying consumer behavior is the primary purpose of data mining. Data mining has enabled businesses to provide better customer service through the use of CRM (customer relations management) technology. Most federal agencies have different customers such as citizens, businesses, other government agencies, and even offices within agencies, and each customer interaction provides extensive data that are used to develop new channels of service for customers. CRM is a conglomeration of technologies and management strategies that is used by organizations to control the operational side of their businesses. CRM is implemented in every department that deals with customers, be it in sales, technical support, customer service, or marketing. CRM combines all customer data derived from these departments into one place such that the information can be accessed anywhere. This will enable the company to see the snapshot of a customer's history whenever a customer is contacted.

According to Dean (2001), the government's use of CRM technologies is very different from the private sector's benefits. Businesses use CRM to weed out customers that are costly to serve while the government uses CRM as a tool to help them acquire customers. All the same agencies use CRM to learn about customer habits to create efficiency and cost-savings solutions. The Internal Revenue Service (IRS) uses CRM as a federal tax payment system; it uses this system to facilitate the collection of tax payments from corporations. Also, this system is incorporated in the IRS's call center and helps customer service representatives to have access to taxpayers' data to help resolve any issues they may have with their tax payments. This system has been said to help reduce the time it takes taxpayers to phone in payments by more than 40%, and the number of taxpayer requests have dropped by 90%. The average payment now takes just 2 minutes and 20 seconds, and it happens 100,000 times a day.

CRM has helped governments and businesses to take an inventory of their customers, identify the products and services provided to customers, identify the methods of providing the products and services, and measure the effectiveness of communications with the customers through service channels.

Analyzing Scientific and Research Information

The increasing amount of data accumulated in the health care industry creates databases that can serve as the basis for data mining. As the health care industry continues its work to enhance the quality of care, promote services, and reduce cost, undiscovered patterns of care will become increasingly transparent, first for physicians, nurses and other clinicians, and ultimately for all consumers of health care. Providers are now beginning to recognize the value of data mining as a tool to analyze patient care and clinical outcomes. As providers deploy advanced clinical data systems, more granular, primary data are becoming available for analysis.

In health care, increased access to data and information has facilitated the development of new drugs that seem to be produced at ever-increasing speeds, as Boire (2005) claims. By being able to quickly analyze volumes of data from all kinds of different tests and during different time periods, data mining represents a critical cog within the drug development process. What was once a few years ago almost considered impossible entered the realm of the possible through access to these newfound capabilities due in large part to data mining. According to scientists, the breakthrough discovery of being able to map the DNA genome offers limitless possibilities in the development of new drugs now that specific genes can be isolated.

Data mining gives an opportunity to analyze the actual impact of one variable on another. The analysis of data mining results enables the health care industry to discover new approaches in care delivery that consider a multitude of data points. A big step forward was achieved in medical research with the help of data mining. Children's Memorial Research Center, a leading U.S. pediatric hospital and research institute, has gained unique insights into tumor classification and treatment strategies with the help of SPSS predictive analysis. The automated extraction of information from biomedical literature promises to play an increasingly important role in text-based knowledge discovery processes ("SPSS Predictive Analytics Accelerating Cancer Research at Children's Memorial Research Center," 2005).

Managing Human Resources

According to Ashbaugh and Miranda (2002), the human resource management system (HRMS) is an integral part of the digital government that streamlines government processes in accounting, payroll, and personnel administration. The underlying architecture for digital government is the Internet and integrated administrative systems commonly known as enterprise resource planning (ERP) systems. ERP systems are built on software that integrates information from different applications into a common database. The ERP system and HRM system are the linkage between financial and human resources applications through a single database in a software application that is both rigid and flexible. The rigidity comes from the need to standardize processes and deter customers from modifying the underlying software source code. Flexibility refers to the customer's ability to configure the software to collect specific data and other business goals. Business intelligence is a new concept in the public sector that uses advanced analytical tools such as data mining to provide insights into organizations' trends and patterns, and helps organizations to improve their decision-making skills. HRMS and business intelligence can be used to support personnel management decisions, including turnover analysis, recruitment, training analysis, and salary and workforce planning.

The U.S. Air Force uses data mining to manage its human resources. It has signed an $88.5 million multiyear contract with the Oracle Corp., which includes a closely watched deal to build a new logistics system for the organization. The Air Force's Expeditionary Combat Support System (ECSS) is intended to replace more than 500 legacy IT systems with one integrated commercial supply chain management system. Oracle was competing against other enterprise resource planning vendors for the ECSS contract. Oracle uses data mining to provide information on promotions, pay grades, clearances, and other information relevant to human resources planning (Cowley, 2005).

Detecting Fraud, Waste, and Abuse

In the government, data mining was initially used to detect financial fraud, waste, and abuse. The Department of Agriculture's Risk Management Agency (RMA) uses data mining methods to identify potential abusers, improve program policies and guidance, and improve program performance and data quality. RMA uses information collected from insurance applicants as well as from insurance agents and claims adjusters. The department produces several types of output, including lists of names of individuals whose behavior matches patterns of anomalous behavior, which are provided to program investigators and sometimes insurance agencies. In addition, it also produces programmatic information, such as how a procedural change in the federal crop insurance program's policy manual would impact the overall effectiveness of the program, and information on data quality and program performance, both of which are used by program managers (U.S. GAO, 2005).

Fraud in health care is controlled by the use of data mining by federal agencies. The agency can compare costs charged for medical services and find health care providers overcharging their patients. Data mining is used to compare treatments for different medical conditions to determine if a patient is receiving inadequate or excessive care. Researchers are currently using data mining to review records of infants stored in the database to compare the effectiveness and safety of the narcotics morphine and fentanyl in easing pain. The need to mine existing data is very important in newborn intensive care units, where different treatments cannot always be studied in large-scale randomized clinical trials (Landro, 2006).

Instead of insurance companies continuing to rely on the medical expertise of physicians as well as other trained clinicians, to manually review insurance claims to detect health care fraud and abuse, companies can now use a data mining framework that assesses clinical pathways to construct an adaptable and extensible detection model. Clinical pathways are driven by physician orders as well as industry and local standards of clinical care. Pathways provide the medical community with algorithms of the decisions to be made and the care to be provided to a particular patient population. The use of clinical pathways in detecting insurance fraud and abuse by service providers shows significant promise. A care activity is highly likely to be fraudulent if it orders suspiciously. For example, a typical pattern of physicians is that of ordering noninvasive tests before ordering more invasive ones. Therefore, there is a high probability that the same set of medical activities ordered in a different order is fraudulent or abusive (Yang & Hwang, 2006).

Detecting Criminal Activities

Data mining is also used by federal and state agencies to identify criminal activities, fraudulent misuse of governmental credit cards, and Medicaid and Medicare abuse. The SPSS predictive analytics software is used for crime prevention. This software's ability to detect unusual activity patterns has aided in the detection of credit card and Medicare fraud. In Richmond, Virginia, police use data mining to help them predict where to put patrols for crime prevention. An arm of the U.S. Army's homeland security uses the SPSS software to fight cybercrime. The Army aims at protecting the databases of utility companies from hackers bent on shutting down these systems (Van, 2005).

The IRS uses the system to identify financial crime, including individual and corporate tax fraud. Its outputs include reports containing names, social security numbers, addresses, and other personal information of individuals suspected of financial crime. Reports are shared with IRS field office personnel, who conduct investigations based on the report's results (U.S. GAO, 2005).

In line with Boire (2005), the murder rate in New York City was reduced from 2,200 in the late 1970s to between 600 to 700 murders a year over time under Mayor Giuliani's leadership. Some other factors like Bill Clinton's bill to increase the number of police officers and the zero-tolerance policy, initiated by Giuliani, resulted in the full prosecution of even minor crimes such as the illegal placement of graffiti on public property. Giuliani used technology and data mining to analyze data concerning crimes in all sectors of his city. Data mining made it possible to analyze massive amounts of data that allowed uncovering trends and patterns concerning future crime behavior within high-risk areas.

Detecting Terrorist Activities

Following the terrorist attacks of September 11, 2001, data mining has been used increasingly as a tool to help detect terrorist threats through the collection and analysis of public- and private-sector data. Data mining has become one of the key features of many homeland security initiatives and its use has also expanded to other purposes.

In the context of homeland security, data mining can be a potential means to identify terrorist activities, such as money transfers and communications, and to identify and track individual terrorists themselves, such as through travel and immigration records. Some of the homeland security data mining applications represent a significant expansion in the quantity and scope of data to be analyzed. Some efforts that have attracted a higher level of congressional interest include the Terrorism Information Awareness (TIA) project (now discontinued) and the Computer-Assisted Passenger Prescreening System II (CAPPS II) project (now canceled and replaced by Secure Flight; Seifert, 2006). Other initiatives that have been the subject of recent congressional interest include the Multi-State Anti-Terrorism Information Exchange (MATRIX), the Able Danger program, and data collection and analysis projects being conducted by the National Security Agency (NSA; "MATRIX Pilot Project Concludes," 2005).

Other government data mining projects include Talon, a program run by the Pentagon's Counterintelligence Field Activity, which collects reports on demonstrators outside U.S. military bases. Thousands of such reports are stored in a database called Cornerstone and are shared with other intelligence agencies. The Pentagon's Advanced Research and Development Activity based at Fort Meade, Maryland, runs a research program whose goal is to develop better ways to mine huge databases to help the nation avoid strategic surprises such as those of September 11, 2001 (Boyd, 2006).

BARRIERS OF DATA MINING IN PUBLIC ADMINISTRATION

Two precursors are necessary for a successful data mining expedition: a clear formulation of the problem to be solved, and access to relevant data. Complicating the formulations of the problems to be solved and inherent in the public sectors are constraints raised by political opposition, privacy considerations, and concerns arising from the inherent limitations of the technology itself and the competency and hidden agendas of those who would implement the data mining projects and interpret its outputs. The most potent threat to privacy interests created by data mining technology arises from efforts to prevent terrorism in this country and overseas. As a result of anguished inquiries into the failure of the Unites States military and intelligence branches to detect the risk, and to intercept at least one previously identified terrorist before he boarded the airplane at Newark Airport and participated in the attacks, it became more politically acceptable for politicians and public servants to procure and develop more effective and potentially intrusive data mining techniques in the interest of public safety.

Building on the U.S. Patriot Act was the Total Information Awareness Project (TIA) developed by the Department of Defense. TIA was designed to collect information on individuals' financial transactions, travel records, medical records, and other activities from a wide variety of public and private databases. The data mined from these sources were to be used to prevent terrorism. Unlike the Patriot Act, which passed through Congress with little opposition, two bills were introduced in Congress to prevent TIA from moving forward. TIA was much broader in scope than the Patriot Act and focused on collecting information about ordinary Americans rather than terror suspects. Because TIA was seen as a greater threat to with less return in security, Congress was widely against it. The TIA project has since been scrapped (Bagner, Evansburg, Watson, & Welch, 2003).

FUTURE TRENDS

The world is fast becoming a global village and with this comes the urgent need for a new generation of computational tools to assist humans in extracting useful information from the rapidly growing volumes of digital data. The future of data mining lies in predictive analysis or one-click data mining, accomplished through the simplification and automation of the entire data mining process.

Despite the limitations, data mining will have a tremendous impact on how business is done in the future. As a technology, data mining will become more embedded in a growing number of business applications, making it more readily available to a wider market segment. The developers of data mining applications therefore need to develop it into something that most users can work with and that can provide and add value to our every day lives. Easier interfaces will allow end user analysts with limited technical skills to achieve good results.

CONCLUSION

Data mining has become an indispensable technology for businesses and researchers in many fields including public administration. Since public-sector organizations and decision makers are dealing with a large amount of information from the public, a systematic way of collecting and reading data is necessary. This solution would not only find the similarities in one case to another, but also would identify unique cases and extreme values. Decision makers, service providers, and researchers would then be able to launch the next action based on the knowledge discovered from the database, and this increases their chances of being right. When the target market is the entire human population in the universe instead of a specific business market, data mining means more than making money for one's self. Exercising data mining in public administration is done to help the public, improve people's lives, and hence benefit the public as a whole.

FUTURE RESEARCH DIRECTIONS

Predictive Analysis

Augusta (2004) suggested that predictive analysis is one of the major future trends for data mining. Rather than being just about mining large amounts of data, predictive analytics looks to actually understand the data content. They forecast based on the contents of the data. However, this requires complex programming and a great amount of business acumen. They do more than simply archive data, which is what data mining is currently known for. Organizations aim not just to process data, but understand them more clearly, which will in turn allow them to make better predictions about future behavior. With predictive analytics you have the program scour the data and try to form, or help form, a new hypothesis. This shows great promise and would be a boon for public administration everywhere.

Diversity of Application Domains

In data mining and the "X" phenomenon, as Tuzhilin (2005) coined it, X constitutes a broad range of fields in which data mining is used for analyzing the data. This has resulted in a process of the cross-fertilization of ideas generated within this diverse population of researchers interacting across the traditional boundaries of their disciplines. The next generation of data mining applications covers a large number of different fields from traditional businesses to advanced scientific research. Kantardzic and Zurada (2005) observed that with new tools, methodologies, and infrastructure, this trend of diversification will continue each year.

REFERENCES

Anonymous. (2005). FDA drug safety reviewers to use data mining tool. *Washington Drug Letter, 37*(5).

Ashbaugh, S., & Miranda, R. (2002). Technology for human resources management: Seven questions and answers. *Public Personnel Management, 31*(1), 7-19.

Augusta, L. (2004). The future of data mining: Predictive analytics. *DM Review, 14*(8), 16-20, 37.

Bagner, J., Evansburg, A., Watson, V. K., & Welch, J. B. (2003). Senators seek limits on DoD mining of personal data. *Intellectual Property & Technology Law Journal, 15*(5), 19-20.

Boire, R. (2005, October). Future of data mining in marketing: Part 1. *Direct Marketing News.*

Boyd, R. S. (2006, February 2). Data mining tells government and business a lot about you. *Knight Ridder Washington Bureau.*

Cahlink, G. (2000). Data mining taps trends. *Government Executive, 32*(12), 85-87.

Cowley, S. (2005, October 24). Oracle wins $88.5 million Air Force contract. *IDG News Service.*

Dean, J. (2001). Better business through customers. *Government Executive, 33*(1), 58-60.

Delavari, N., Shirazi, M. R. A., & Beikzadeh, M. R. (2004). A new model for using data mining technology in higher educational systems. *5th International Conference on Information Technology Based Higher Education and Training* (pp. 319-324).

Gramatikov, M. (2006). *Data mining techniques and the decision making process in the Bulgarian public administration*. Retrieved March 8, 2007, from http://unpan1.un.org/intradoc/groups/public/documents/nispacee/unpan009209.pdf

Hand, D. J., Mannila, H., & Smyth, P. (2001). *Principles of data mining*. Cambridge, MA: MIT Press.

Kantardzic, M. M., & Zurada, J. (Eds.). (2005). *Next generation of data-mining applications*. IEEE Press, Wiley-Interscience.

Landro, L. (2006, January 26). The informed patient: Infant monitors yield new clues. Studies of digital records are used to identify problems with medications: Practices. *Wall Street Journal*, p. D5.

Lok, C. (2004, October). Fighting infections with data. *Technology Review*, p. 24.

MATRIX pilot project concludes. (2005). Retrieved March 8, 2007, from http://www.fdle.state.fl.us/press_releases/expired/2005/20050415_matrix_project.html

SPSS predictive analytics accelerating cancer research at Children's Memorial Research Center, Chicago. (2005, March 7). *Business Wire*.

Tuzhilin, A. (2005). Foreword. In J. Wang (Ed.), *Encyclopedia of data warehousing and mining* (1st ed.). Hershey, PA: Idea Group Reference.

U.S. Government Accounting Office (GAO). (2005). *Data mining: Agencies have taken key steps to protect privacy in selected efforts, but significant compliance issues remain* (GAO-05-866). Author.

Van, J. (2005, October 17). Cybercrime being fought in new ways. *Knight Ridder Tribune Business News*, p. 1.

Wang, J. (Ed.). (2006). *Encyclopedia of data warehousing and mining* (1st ed.). Hershey, PA: Idea Group Reference.

Yang, W. S., & Hwang, S. Y. (2006). A process-mining framework for the detection of healthcare fraud and abuse. *Expert Systems with Applications, 31*(1), 56-68.

FURTHER READING

Agard, B., & Kusiak, A. (2004). Data-mining-based methodology for the design of product families. *International Journal of Production Research, 42*(15), 2955-2969.

Álvarez-Macilas, J. L., Mata-Vázquez, J., & Riquelme-Santos, J. C. (2004). Data mining for the management of software development process. *International Journal of Software Engineering & Knowledge Engineering, 14*(6), 665-695.

Berberidis, C., & Vlahavas, I. (2005). Mining for weak periodic signals in time series databases. *Intelligent Data Analysis, 9*(1), 29-42.

Besson, J., Robardet, C., Boulicaut, J. F., & Rome, S. (2005). Constraint-based concept mining and its application to microarray data analysis. *Intelligent Data Analysis, 9*(1), 59-82.

Brito, P., & Malerba, D. (2003). Mining official data. *Intelligent Data Analysis, 7*(6), 497-500.

Calders, T., Lakshmanan, L. V. S., Ng, R. T., & Paredaens, J. (2006). Expressive power of an algebra for data mining. *ACM Transactions on Database Systems, 31*(4), 1169-1214.

Ceglar, A., & Roddick, J. F. (2006). Association mining. *ACM Computing Surveys, 38*(2), 1-42.

Cheng, B.W., Chang, C. L., & Liu, I. S. (2005). Enhancing care services quality of nursing homes using data mining. *Total Quality Management & Business Excellence, 16*(5), 575-596.

Cheng, D., Kannan, R., Vempala, S., & Wang, G. (2006). A divide-and-merge methodology for clustering. *ACM Transactions on Database Systems, 31*(4), 1499-1525.

Cho, S. B., & Won, H. H. (2003). Data mining for gene expression profiles from DNA microarray. *International Journal of Software Engineering & Knowledge Engineering, 13*(6), 593-608.

Churilov, L., Bagirov, A., Schwartz, D., Smith, K., & Dally, M. (2005). Data mining with combined use of optimization techniques and self-organizing maps for improving risk grouping rules: Application to prostate cancer patients. *Journal of Management Information Systems, 21*(4), 85-100.

Chye, K. H., Chin, T. W., & Peng, G. C. (2004). Credit scoring using data mining techniques. *Singapore Management Review, 26*(2), 25-47.

Czerwinski, M., Gage, D. W., Gemmell, J., Marshall, C. C., Pérez-Quiñonesis, M. A., Skeels, M. M., et al. (2006). Digital memories in an era of ubiquitous computing and abundant storage. *Communications of the ACM, 49*(1), 44-50.

Dumouchel, B., & Demaine, J. (2006). Knowledge discovery in the digital library: Access tools for mining science. *Information Services & Use, 26*(1), 39-44.

Fan, W., Wallace, L., Rich, S., & Zhang, Z. (2006). Tapping the power of text mining. *Communications of the ACM, 49*(9), 77-82.

Fatemieh, S. O. (2006). A review of "Discovering knowledge in data: An introduction to data mining." *Journal of Biopharmaceutical Statistics, 16*(1), 127-130.

Feng, C. X. J., & Wang, X. F. (2004). Data mining techniques applied to predictive modeling of the knurling process. *IIE Transactions, 36*(3), 253-263.

Firestone, J. M. (2005). Mining for information gold. *Information Management Journal, 39*(5), 47-52.

Ford, J. M. (2005). Data and text mining: A business applications approach. *Personnel Psychology, 58*(1), 267-271.

Gama, J., Fernandes, R., & Rocha, R. (2006). Decision trees for mining data streams. *Intelligent Data Analysis, 10*(1), 23-45.

Garatti, S., Savaresi, S. M., Bittanti, S., & Brocca, L. L. (2004). On the relationships between user profiles and navigation sessions in virtual communities: A data-mining approach. *Intelligent Data Analysis, 8*(6), 579-600.

Gibert, K., Sànchez-Marrè, M., & Flores, X. (2005). Cluster discovery in environmental databases using GESCONDA: The added value of comparisons. *AI Communications, 18*(4), 319-331.

Guo, G., & Neagu, D. (2005). Fuzzy knnmodel applied to predictive toxicology data mining. *International Journal of Computational Intelligence & Application, 5*(3), 321-333.

He, B., Chang, C. C., & Kevin. (2006). Automatic complex schema matching across Web query interfaces: A correlation mining approach. *ACM Transactions on Database Systems, 31*(1), 346-395.

Holzman, L. E., Fisher, T. A., Galitsky, L. M., Kontostathis, A., & Pottenger, W. M. (2004). A software infrastructure for research in textual data mining. *International Journal on Artificial Intelligence Tools, 13*(4), 829-849.

Hormozi, A. M., & Giles, S. (2004). Data mining: A competitive weapon for banking and retail industries. *Information Systems Management, 21*(2), 62-71.

Hou, J. L., Yu, F. J., & Lin, R. K. (2006). A knowledge component analysis model based on term frequency and correlation analysis. *Journal of Computer Information Systems, 46*(4), 64-77.

Hu, Y. C. (2005). Finding simplified fuzzy if-then rules for function approximation problems using a fuzzy data mining approach. *Applied Artificial Intelligence, 19*(6), 601-619.

Jones, K. (2006). Knowledge management as a foundation for decision support systems. *Journal of Computer Information Systems, 46*(4), 116-124.

Kajko-Mattsson, M., & Chapin, N. (2004). Data mining for validation in software engineering: An example. *International Journal of Software Engineering & Knowledge Engineering, 14*(4), 407-427.

Kersten, G. E., & Zhang, G. (2003). Mining inspire data for the determinants of successful Internet negotiations. *Central European Journal of Operations Research, 11*(3), 297-316.

Last, M., Friedman, M., & Kandel, A. (2004). Using data mining for automated software testing. *International Journal of Software Engineering & Knowledge Engineering, 14*(4), 369-393.

Macdonell, C. (2005). Easy data mining for school libraries. *Library Media Connection, 24*(1), 38-39.

Morbitzer, C., Strachan, P., & Simpson, C. (2004). Data mining analysis of building simulation performance data. *Building Services Engineering Research & Technology, 25*(3), 253-267.

Nayak, R., & Qiu, T. (2005). A data mining application: Analysis of problems occurring during a software project development process. *International Journal of Software Engineering & Knowledge Engineering, 15*(4), 647-663.

Neaga, E. I., & Harding, J. A. (2005). An enterprise modeling and integration framework based on knowledge discovery and data mining. *International Journal of Production Research, 43*(6), 1089-1108.

Padmanabhan, B., & Tuzhilin, A. (2003). On the use of optimization for data mining: Theoretical interactions and eCRM opportunities. *Management Science, 49*(10), 1327-1343.

Perng, Y. H., & Chang, C. L. (2004). Data mining for government construction procurement. *Building Research & Information, 32*(4), 329-338.

Qian, G., Zhu, Q., Xue, Q., & Pramanik, S. (2006). Dynamic indexing for multidimensional non-ordered discrete data spaces using a data-partitioning approach. *ACM Transactions on Database Systems, 31*(2), 439-484.

Ren, Y., Ding, Y., & Zhou, S. (2006). A data mining approach to study the significance of nonlinearity in multistation assembly processes. *IIE Transactions, 38*(12), 1069-1083.

Riquelme, J. C., Polo, M., Aguilar-Ruiz, J. S., Piattini, M., Ferrer-Troyano, F. J., & Ruiz, F. (2006). A comparison of effort estimation methods for 4 GL programs: Experiences with statistics and data mining. *International Journal of Software Engineering & Knowledge Engineering, 16*(1), 127-140.

Šef, T., & Gams, M. (2004). Data mining for creating accentuation rules. *Applied Artificial Intelligence, 18*(5), 395-410.

Sinha, A. P., & May, J. H. (2005). Evaluating and timing predictive data mining models using receiver operating characteristic curves. *Journal of Management Information Systems, 21*(3), 249-280.

Spangler, W. E., Gal-Or, M., & May, J. H. (2003). Using data mining to profile TV viewers. *Communications of the ACM, 46*(12), 66-72.

Spangler, W. S., Kreulen, J. T., & Newswanger, J. F. (2006). Machines in the conversation: Detecting themes and trends in informal communication streams. *IBM Systems Journal, 45*(4), 785-799.

Subramanyam, R. B. V., & Goswami, A. (2005). A fuzzy data mining algorithm for incremental mining of quantitative sequential patterns. *International Journal of Uncertainty, 13*(6), 633-652.

Toussaint, G. (2005). Geometric proximity graphs for improving nearest neighbor methods in instance-based learning and data mining. *International Journal of Computational Geometry & Applications, 15*(2), 101-150.

Vason, B. J. (2004). Mine data to discover infection control trends. *Nursing Management, 35*(6), 46-47.

Wang, S., Chung, K. F. L., & Shen, H. (2005). Fuzzy taxonomy, quantitative database and mining generalized association rules. *Intelligent Data Analysis, 9*(2), 207-217.

Wood, C. A., & Ow, T. T. (2005). Corporate data to data derived from the Web. *Communications of the ACM, 48*(9), 99-104.

Wu, R. C., Chen, R. S., & Chian, S. S. (2006). Design of a product quality control system based on the use of data mining techniques. *IIE Transactions, 38*(1), 39-51.

Xing, Z., & Stroulia, E. (2006). Understanding the evolution and co-evolution of classes in object-oriented systems. *International Journal of Software Engineering & Knowledge Engineering, 16*(1), 23-51.

Zhong, N., Hu, J., Motomura, S., Wu, J. L., & Liu, C. (2005). Building a data-mining grid for multiple human brain data analysis. *Computational Intelligence, 21*(2), 177-196.

Zurada, J., Karwowski, W., & Marras, W. (2004). Classification of jobs with risk of low back disorders by applying data mining techniques. *Occupational Ergonomics, 4*(4), 291-305.

TERMS AND DEFINITIONS

Business Intelligence: Business intelligence is a new concept in the public sector that uses advanced analytical tools such as data mining to provide insights into organization trends, patterns, and decision making.

Customer Relations Management (CRM): CRM is a conglomeration of technologies and management strategies used by organizations to control the operational side of the business, and this is the domain for human resources and financial systems.

Data Mining: This is a process of sifting through the mass of organizational data to identify patterns critical for decision support.

Data Quality: This refers to the accuracy and completeness of data.

Enterprise Resource Planning Systems (ERPS): This is a system built on software that integrates information from different applications into a common database.

Interoperability: This is the ability of a computer system and/or data to work with other systems using common standards.

Public Administration: The term may apply to government, private-sector organizations and groups, or individuals.

Chapter LII
Categorization of Data Clustering Techniques

Baoying Wang
Waynesburg University, USA

Imad Rahal
College of Saint Benedict, Saint John's University, USA

Richard Leipold
Waynesburg University, USA

INTRODUCTION

Data clustering is a discovery process that partitions a data set into groups (clusters) such that data points within the same group have high similarity while being very dissimilar to points in other groups (Han & Kamber, 2001). The ultimate goal of data clustering is to discover natural groupings in a set of patterns, points, or objects without prior knowledge of any class labels. In fact, in the machine-learning literature, data clustering is typically regarded as a form of unsupervised learning as opposed to supervised learning. In unsupervised learning or clustering, there is no training function as in supervised learning. There are many applications for data clustering including, but not limited to, pattern recognition, data analysis, data compression, image processing, understanding genomic data, and market-basket research.

BACKGROUND

Data clustering is an important human activity. As humans, we can easily perform mental tasks such as distinguishing between cats and dogs, or between animals and plants. A more concrete example of clustering is given in Figure 1, which demonstrates the clustering of padlocks. In this example, there are 10 padlocks with different colors and shapes that we would like to cluster into three different groups.

Figure 1. A simple example of clustering

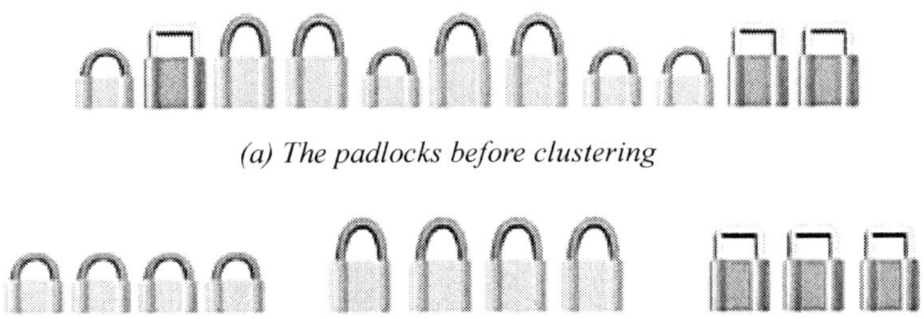

(a) The padlocks before clustering

(b) The padlocks after clustering

Clustering has its roots in a number of fields including data mining, statistics, biology, and machine learning. The importance and interdisciplinary nature of clustering is evident in its rich and diverse literature. Besides the phrase data clustering, a number of other terms and phrases have been coined to describe the same process, namely, cluster analysis, automatic classification, numerical taxonomy, botryology, and typological analysis (Jain & Dubes, 1988).

Representing data by fewer clusters necessarily introduces a loss of certain fine details such as specific properties pertaining to individual data objects, but achieves the more important goal of simplification—a highly desirable characteristic in an age of inexorable abundance of data. Clustering represents many data objects using a few clusters; hence, it models the data by these clusters. From a machine-learning perspective, the clusters correspond to hidden patterns where the search for clusters can be viewed as a form of unsupervised learning and the resulting system as a representation of a data concept. Consequently, clustering is the unsupervised learning of a hidden data concept.

Data mining focuses primarily on large databases that impose additional severe computational requirements on data clustering as a process. These challenges led to the emergence of numerous powerful and broadly applicable clustering approaches (Berkhin, 2002).

DATA CLUSTERING TECHNIQUES

Categorization of Data Clustering Techniques

Generally speaking, data clustering techniques can be categorized in a number of distinct ways (Berkhin, 2002; Han & Kamber, 2001; Jain & Dubes, 1988), one of which, based on the structure of the produced clusters, is shown in Figure 2.

As depicted, clustering can be subdivided into partitioning clustering, hierarchical clustering, and hybrid clustering. Hierarchical clustering produces a nested sequence of partitions, whereas partitioning clustering results in a single partition. Hierarchical clustering approaches can be further categorized into agglomerative (bottom-up) and divisive (top-down) hierarchical clustering depending on whether the hierarchical decomposition is carried in a bottom-up or a top-down fashion. Partitioning clustering consists of two subcategories, distance based and density based, depending on the similarity measure utilized by the clustering process. A recent trend has been to combine features of hierarchical and partitioning

Figure 2. Categorization of data clustering approaches

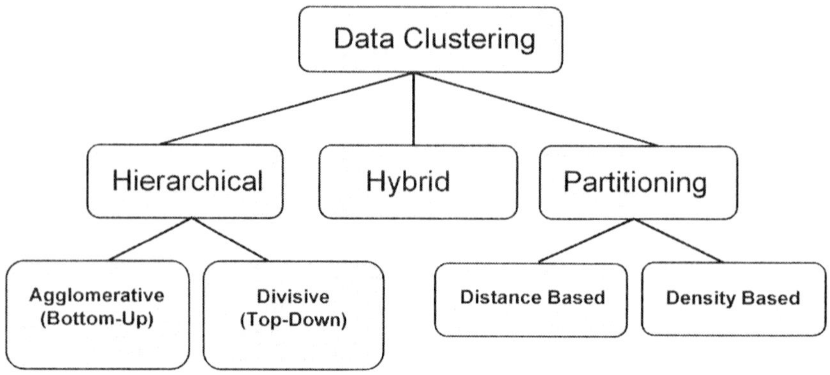

clustering in an attempt to reap benefits from both categories; approaches that follow this trend are usually identified as hybrid clustering.

Partitioning Methods

Partitioning clustering methods generate a partition of a data set in order to recover any natural groupings present in the data. Figure 3 shows a data set partitioned into three clusters. As aforementioned, partitioning clustering can be further subdivided into distance-based partitioning and density-based partitioning.

A distance-based partitioning approach breaks a data set into k subsets or clusters such that data points in the same cluster are closer to each other than to data points in other clusters. By and large, the most classical distance-based partitioning methods are k-means (Hartigan & Wong, 1979) and k-medoids, where each cluster is organized around a gravity center, either the mean or the mode of the points in the cluster, respectively.

In general, distance-based partitioning approaches suffer from several problems: (a) They require an input parameter k, the number of resulting clusters, which needs to be predetermined by the user, (b) they are only suitable for clusters with isotropic shapes, (c) they are not good for clusters with different sizes, and (d) they are sensitive to the choice of the initial cluster centers and may converge to local minima of the criteria function values if the initial partitions are not properly chosen.

Figure 4 shows two different partitions produced by the same k-means algorithm with different initial partitions (Jain, Murty, & Flynn,

Figure 3. Data set partitioned into three clusters

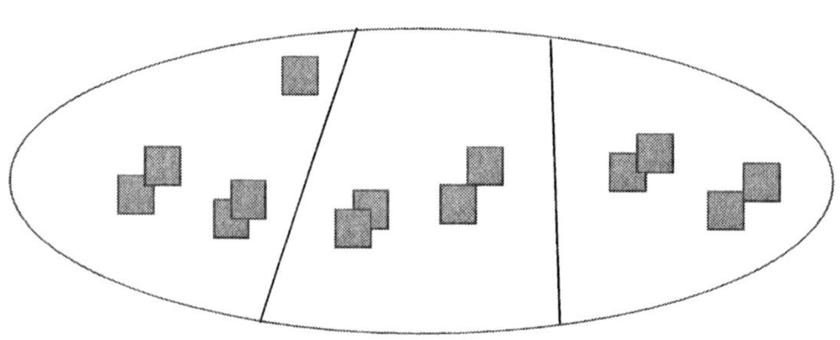

Figure 4. K-means is sensitive to the initial partition

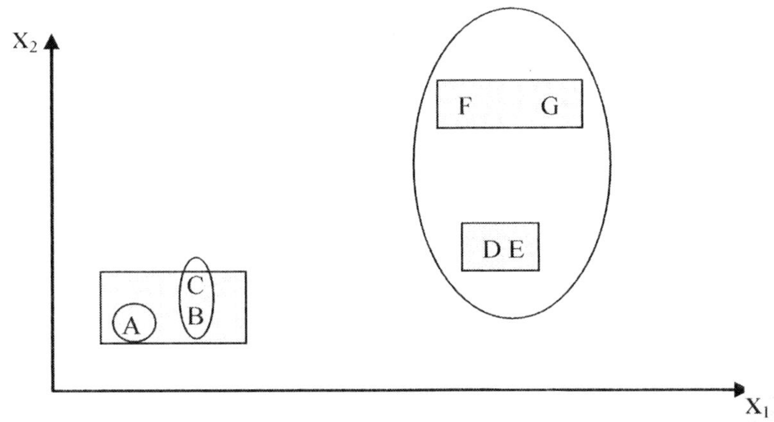

1999). When *k*-means starts with patterns A, B, and C as the initial cluster means, it ends up with the partition {{A}, {B, C}, {D, E, F, G}} shown by ellipses. However, a better three-cluster partition can be obtained by choosing A, D, and F as the initial cluster means as depicted in the rectangular partition {{A, B, C}, {D, E}, {F, G}}. The rectangular partition is better because data points in the same cluster are closer to each other than to data points in other clusters.

In density-based clustering, clusters are dense areas of points in the data space separated by areas of low density (usually referred to as noise). A cluster is regarded as a connected dense area of data points that can grow in any direction to which the density leads. Density-based clustering can usually discover clusters with arbitrary shapes without predetermining the number of clusters. However, like partitioning clustering, density-based clustering is also very sensitive to input parameters such as the density threshold, as illustrated in Figure 5 (Hinneburg & Keim, 1998). Usually, higher density thresholds result in fewer points falling inside clusters and more points labeled as noise or outliers.

One of the most typical density-based clustering algorithms is DBSCAN (Ester, Kriegel, Sander, & Xu, 1996). DBSCAN views each cluster as a maximal set of density-connected points. Points are connected if they are reachable, which means that they fall within a core neighborhood with each other. The core neighborhood is determined by the input parameters, the neighborhood radius, and the minimum number of neighbors.

Hierarchical Clustering

Hierarchical algorithms create a hierarchical decomposition of a data set X. The hierarchical decomposition is represented by a dendrogram,

Figure 5. Sensitivity of density-based clustering

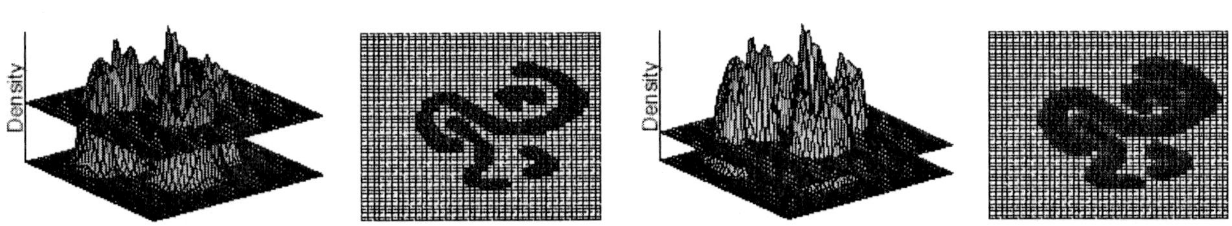

Figure 6. Hierarchical decomposition and the resulting dendrogram

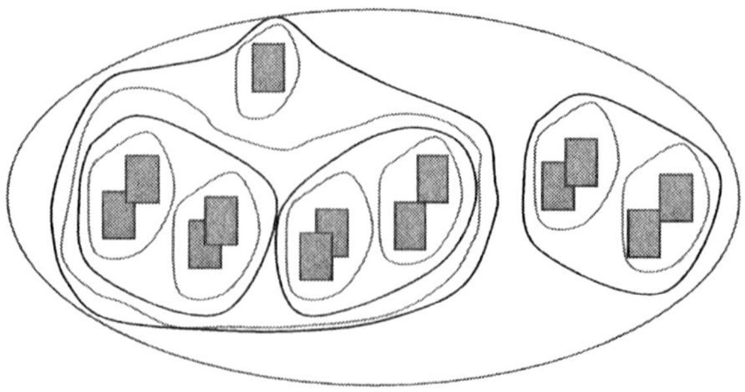

(a) Hierarchical decomposition

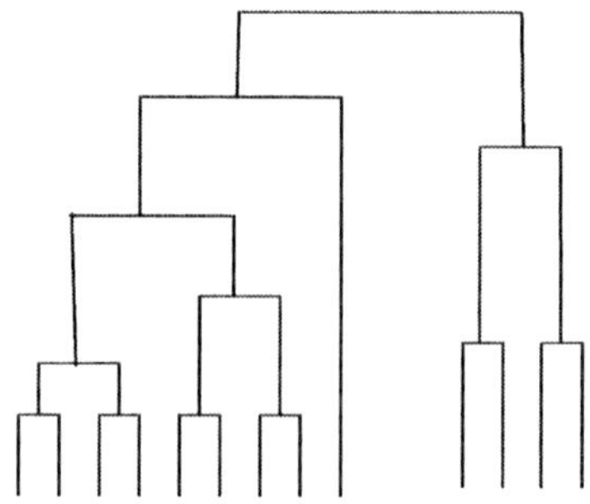

(b) Dendrogram

a tree that iteratively splits X into smaller subsets until each subset consists of only one object. In such a hierarchy, each level of the tree represents a clustering of the data points in X. Figure 6 shows the hierarchical decomposition process and the corresponding dendrogram of the hierarchical clustering.

Hierarchical clustering approaches are subdivided into agglomerative (bottom-up) and divisive (top-down) approaches (Han & Kamber, 2001). Agglomerative approaches start with each point residing in its own distinct cluster; then they successively merge clusters together until a stopping criterion is satisfied. Divisive approaches operate in the opposite direction by starting with all points in a single cluster, which is then split recursively until a stopping criterion is met. Figure 7 shows a hierarchical clustering of five data points performed agglomeratively (upper part of the figure) and divisively (lower part of the figure).

Agglomerative clustering algorithms are greedy by nature. At each step, the two most similar clusters are determined and merged into a new cluster. The algorithm stops when a certain stopping criterion is met. Usually, it proceeds until one large cluster containing all data objects is

Figure 7. Agglomerative vs. divisive hierarchical clustering

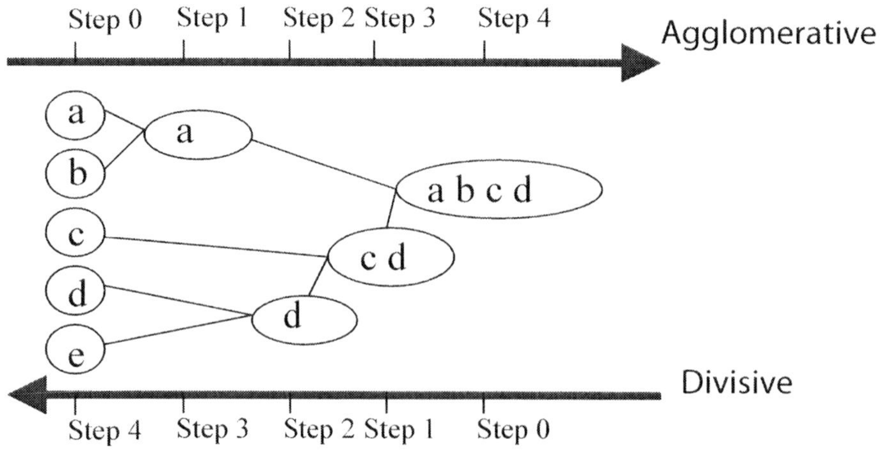

formed. Divisive clustering is very similar except that it splits the most dissimilar clusters instead of merging the most similar ones.

There are several ways to define cluster similarity. Most hierarchical clustering algorithms utilize either the single-link or the complete-link method. In the single-link method, the distance between two clusters is defined as the minimum distance between all pairs of points from the two clusters; in the complete-link method, the distance between two clusters is defined as the maximum of all pair-wise distances between all points in the two clusters. In either case, two clusters are merged to form a larger cluster (or a single cluster is split to form two smaller clusters) based on the minimum distance (or maximum similarity) criteria.

Complete-link-based algorithms produce tightly bound or compact clusters while the single-link-based ones suffer when there is a chain of noise between two given clusters. In general, it has been noted in the literature that algorithms based on complete-link clustering produce better results than their single-link counterparts, which usually produce skewed results (Jain & Dubes, 1988).

In summary, hierarchical clustering algorithms are considered more flexible than their partitioning counterparts largely because they do not require input parameters from users. However, their computational complexities are typically higher than those of the partitioning algorithms. The time complexities of single-link-based and complete-link-based clustering algorithms are $O(n^2)$ and $O(n^3)$, respectively, while *k*-means requires only $O(n)$. This observation spurred the development of many hybrid algorithms aimed at exploiting the benefits of both hierarchical clustering and partitioning clustering.

Hybrid Clustering

Several hybrid clustering algorithms have been proposed in the literature to reap the benefits of both hierarchical and partitioning clustering. In general, these algorithms first partition the data set into preliminary clusters and then construct a hierarchical structure on top of these subclusters. Figure 8 shows a data set partitioned into 15 subclusters that are then merged into two clusters (Lin & Chen, 2005).

One of the earliest hybrid algorithms was developed by combining *k*-means and hierarchical clustering (Murty & Krishna, 1981). This algorithm first partitions the data set into several groups and then performs *k*-means clustering on each partition to obtain several subclusters. Then, hierarchical clustering is used to build up levels using the centers of the subclusters from the previous level. This process continues until exactly *k* clusters are formed. In a final step, the algorithm reassigns all points of each subcluster to the cluster of their corresponding center.

Another hybrid approach, BIRCH, is considered as one of the most efficient clustering algorithms (Zhang, Ramakrisshnan, & Livny, 1996). BIRCH performs a linear scan of all data points to create cluster summaries that are then stored in a memory-resident data structure called a CF-tree (clustering-feature tree). In a CF-tree, a nonleaf node represents a cluster consisting of all the subclusters. BIRCH first partitions the data set into many small subclusters and then applies a global clustering algorithm on those subclusters to achieve the final results. The main strength of BIRCH derives from its highly efficient data preprocessing of large input data sets, making the global clustering algorithm execute more efficiently.

A third popular hybrid approach called CHAMELEON operates on a *k*-nearest-neighbor graph (Karypis, Han, & Kumar, 1999). The underlying algorithm consists of three basic steps: (a) constructing a *k*-nearest-neighbor graph, (b) partitioning the *k*-nearest-neighbor graph into many small subclusters, and (c) merging those subclusters to get the final clustering results.

CAMP is a fourth efficient hybrid clustering approach that utilizes density attractor trees

Figure 8. Hybrid clustering process

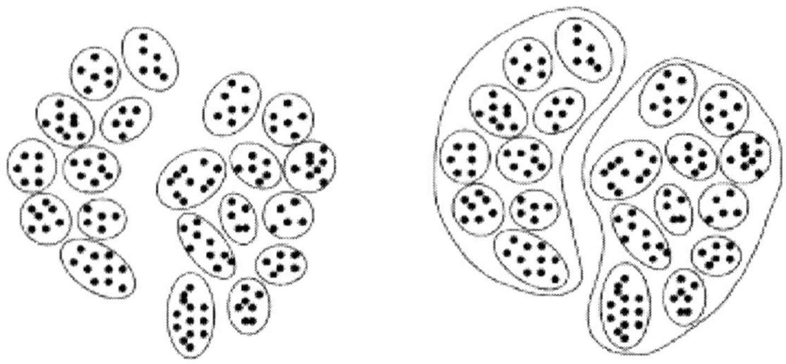

(a) Obtain subclusters *(b) Merge subclusters into larger clusters*

(Wang & Perrizo, 2005). CAMP consists of two processes: (a) clustering using local density attractor trees and (b) merging clusters based on similarity. The data set is first grouped into local attractor trees via density-based clustering. Each resulting local attractor tree represents a preliminary cluster. In a subsequent step, the small clusters are then merged level by level based on their cluster similarity.

An Alternative Clustering Categorization

Clustering techniques can alternatively be categorized into prototype-based, density-based, and graph-based approaches according to the type of the resulting clusters (Tan, Steinbach, & Kumar, 2006). Each such category can be further subdivided into partitioning, hierarchical, and hybrid clustering (see Figure 9).

In prototype-based clustering, a cluster is a set of data points in which any point is closer to the prototype than to the prototype of any other cluster. For example, *k*-means is a simple prototype-based clustering algorithm where the prototype is the cluster mean. Other prototype-based approaches include fuzzy clustering and the SOM (self-organizing maps) algorithm (Kohonen 1997). Density-based clustering can be expanded to include grid-based clustering and subspace clustering, which are more efficient than the traditional density-based clustering techniques discussed above. In graph-based clustering, data objects are represented by nodes and the distance or similarity between two data objects is represented by the weight of the edge between the corresponding nodes. The graph is often made sparser by keeping only the edges among the nearest neighbors. The similarity between two objects is based on the number of the nearest neighbors they share (Tan et al., 2006). A typical graph-based clustering is the minimum spanning tree (MST) clustering (Xu, Olman, & Xu, 2001). Another more recent graph-based clustering approach is CHAMELEON.

FUTURE TRENDS

With the inexorable growth of volumes of data collected in various application areas, a number of new data clustering techniques are being developed to meet the following challenges in one way or another (Han & Kamber, 2001).

- **The curse of scalability:** Many clustering algorithms work well on small data sets. However, it is currently common for databases to contain millions or even billions of data records. Thus, highly scalable clustering algorithms are in great demand.

- **Nonparametric clustering:** Many clustering algorithms require users to provide certain parameters for the clustering process (such as k, the number of desired clusters, in k-means). As a result, clustering results can be quite sensitive to such input parameters.
- **Ability to deal with noisy data:** Most real-world data sets and databases contain erroneous or missing data. Consequently, clustering techniques sensitive to noise tend to produce clusters of poor quality.
- **The curse of high dimensionality:** Many databases store objects in high-dimensional spaces. This may complicate the clustering process due to the required time expense, especially when the data are sparse and highly skewed.

CONCLUSION

Clustering is an interesting, useful, and challenging process. Currently, there are many clustering techniques already available and many more are still under development. Different clustering techniques may have completely different focal objectives. Some techniques consider clustering accuracy as the primary concern while other techniques focus mostly on computational efficiency and scalability. A number of techniques aim mostly on relieving the user from the burden of predetermining input parameters without sacrificing the overall quality of the resulting clusters. Thus, selecting a good clustering technique can be quite challenging. For some applications, such as creating a biological taxonomy, a hierarchical clustering is preferred. In the case of clustering for summarization, a partitioning clustering is appropriate. In some other applications, the hybrid approach may prove more efficient.

FUTURE RESEARCH DIRECTIONS

Data clustering has gained more and more popularity as volumes of data increase in many different areas. Data clustering can be used in agriculture to provide farmers with information on irrigating and fertilizing based on the image from the previous year. USDA (U.S. Department of Agriculture) has grants on such a project. Data clustering is also widely used in medical image analysis, stock markets, and bioinformatics. Many research foundations such as NSF (National Science Foundation), GSA, NIH, and so forth provide large grants for research on data clustering and mining. The International Data Corporation has recently projected that market demand for data mining tools will grow dramatically.

REFERENCES

Berkhin, P. (2002). *Survey of clustering data mining techniques* (Tech. Rep.). Accrue Software.

Clatworthy, J., Buick, D., Hankins, M., Weinman, J., & Horne, R. (2005). The use and reporting of cluster analysis in health psychology: A review. *British Journal of Health Psychology, 10*, 329-358.

Ester, M., Kriegel, H.-P., Sander, J., & Xu, X. (1996). A density-based algorithm for discovering clusters in large spatial databases with noise. *Proceedings of the 2nd ACM SIGKDD* (pp. 226-231).

Han, J., & Kamber, M. (2001). *Data mining, concepts and techniques.* Morgan Kaufmann.

Hartigan, J. A., & Wong, M. A. (1979). A k-means clustering algorithm. *Applied Statistics, 28*, 100-108.

Hinneburg, A., & Keim, D. A. (1998). An efficient approach to clustering in large multimedia databases with noise. *4th International Conference on Knowledge Discovery and Data Mining* (pp. 315-326).

Jain, A. K., & Dubes, R. C. (1988). *Algorithms for clustering data.* Prentice-Hall, Inc.

Jain, A. K., Murty, M. N., & Flynn, P. J. (1999). Data clustering: A review. *ACM Computing Surveys, 31*(3), 264-323.

Karypis, G., Han, E. H., & Kumar, V. (1999). CHAMELEON: A hierarchical clustering algorithm using dynamic modeling. *IEEE Computer, 32*(8), 68-75.

Kohonen, T. (1997). *Self-organizing maps.* New York: Springer-Verlag.

Lin, C., & Chen, M. (2005). Combining partitional and hierarchical algorithms for robust and efficient data clustering with cohesion self-merging. *IEEE Transactions on Knowledge and Data Engineering, 17*(2), 145-159.

Murty, N. M., & Krishna, G. (1981). A hybrid clustering procedure for concentric and chain-like clusters. *International Journal of Computer and Information Sciences, 10*(6), 397-412.

Tan, P., Steinbach, M., & Kumar, V. (2006). *Introduction to data mining.* Pearson Education, Inc.

Wang, B., & Perrizo, W. (2005). Tree-based clustering for gene expression data. *20th ACM Symposium on Applied Computing* (pp. 204-205).

Xu, Y., Olman, V., & Xu, D. (2001). Minimum spanning trees for gene expression data clustering. *Genome Informatics, 12*, 24-33.

Zhang, T., Ramakrisshnan, R., & Livny, M. (1996). BIRCH: An efficient data clustering method for very large databases. *International Conference on Management of Data, ACM SIGMOD* (pp. 87-94).

FURTHER READING

There is a vast amount of research in the data-clustering area. In order to have a solid understanding of clustering, the reader should read at least two data mining books, and keep updated with a few research journals and the proceedings of some prestigious international conferences. The following is a suggested reading list.

- Han, J., & Kamber, M. (2001). *Data mining, concepts and techniques.* Morgan Kaufmann.
- Jain, A. K., Murty, M. N., & Flynn, P. J. (1999). Data clustering: A review. *ACM Computing Surveys, 31*(3), 264-323.
- Tan, P., Steinbach, M., & Kumar, V. (2006). *Introduction to data mining.* Pearson Education, Inc.
- *IEEE Transactions on Knowledge and Data Engineering*
- *International Journal of Computer and Information Sciences*
- *Data Mining and Knowledge Discovery*
- *International Conference on Management of Data, ACM SIGMOD*
- *International Conference on Knowledge Discovery and Data Mining*
- *IEEE International Conference on Data Mining*

TERMS AND DEFINITIONS

Cluster: A cluster is a group of objects having some common natural characteristics.

Data Clustering: Data clustering is a discovery process that partitions a data set into groups such that data points within a group have high similarity in comparison to one another but are very dissimilar to points in other groups.

Data Mining: Data mining is a knowledge discovery process that focuses on extracting previously unknown, actionable information from very large databases.

Distance Measure: This measure is a metric that is used to compute the distance between two data objects. The most commonly used distance measures are Manhattan distance and Euclidean distance.

Hierarchical Clustering: Hierarchical clustering is the process of creating a hierarchical decomposition of a data set.

Hybrid Clustering: Hybrid clustering is a clustering process that partitions a data set into preliminary clusters and then constructs a hierarchical structure upon these subclusters based on a given similarity measure.

Partitioning Clustering: Partitioning clustering is the process of generating a single partition of the data in an attempt to recover any natural groupings hidden in the data.

Unsupervised Learning: This is a machine-learning approach in which a model is fit to a given set of observations. It is distinguished from supervised learning by the fact that there is no a priori output.

Chapter LIII
Statistical Dissemination Systems and the Web

Sindoni Giuseppe
Eurostat, Luxembourg

Tininini Leonardo
CNR - Istituto di Analisi dei Sistemi ed Informatica "A. Ruberti", Italy

INTRODUCTION

The Web is increasingly used as a preferred medium for A2C (administration to citizens) and A2B (administration to business) service delivery. An increasing number of government initiatives are aimed at making access to electronic records easier for the general public. For example, the Electronic Record Archives program of the U.S. National Archives and Records Administration is aimed at preserving virtually any kind of electronic record, free from dependence on any specific hardware or software, and at enabling customers to find records they want and to deliver those records in formats suited to customers' needs (Lake, 2006). This in particular will include records coming from the 2010 U.S. census. International professional associations are increasingly paying attention to public availability of statistical data. For example, the last meeting of the International Association for Social Science Information Services & Technology (IASSIST, 2006) dedicated entire sessions to problems like knowledge and resource discovery, innovative data dissemination systems, and data-intensive Web site design.

In this context, the world of public statistics has the opportunity to exploit many efficient, flexible new technologies and standards to deliver better quality statistics in a more timely and accessible way. First, Web technologies can greatly reduce the gap between data producers and users as published data can be made available immediately after their production to a worldwide community of users. Second, as published statistical data are multidimensional, it would seem that the consolidated methodologies and techniques for data warehouse (DWH) modeling and navigation could be easily applied to support user navigation among the available data. However, this methodological and technological scenario cannot be implemented straightforwardly due to some specific features of statistical data in contrast with conventional business data, which require the introduction of specifically designed models and techniques.

In this chapter we review the main concepts at the basis of multidimensional (data warehouse) modeling and navigation. We also illustrate some peculiarities of statistical data that make the implementation of a statistical data warehouse, that is, a statistical dissemination system enabling the user to perform a multidimensional navigation, a challenging issue in many aspects. Finally, we analyze the main characteristics of some of the most important systems for the dissemination of statistical data on the Web, distinguishing two main approaches, the former based on a free navigation of specific subcubes, and the latter on a constrained navigation of a single data cube.

BACKGROUND

In this section we review the main terms and concepts related to data warehousing and statistical databases (SDBs). A key concept common to both contexts is that of (statistical) aggregate data. These are obtained by applying simple aggregation functions (Cabibbo & Torlone, 1999; Klug, 1982), like the standard count, sum, min, max, and avg, or more complex statistical analysis functions to groups of elementary data (usually called microdata in statistical terminology). In statistical surveys, microdata are commonly obtained from questionnaires, but data extracted from public registries are also becoming increasingly important.

Microdata are rarely processed in their original form, but are instead transformed by specifically designed tools for extraction, transformation, and loading (ETL), performing a general reconciliation of the source data and a reclassification of some attributes, as well as some preaggregations. The resulting data are stored in the so-called fact tables (see Figure 1), comprising both dimension codes, used to classify the data, and measures, on which the aggregation and statistical functions are applied (Cabibbo & Torlone, 1997; Kimball, 1996). Each fact table is typically linked to a collection of dimension tables to form the so-called star and snowflake schemas (see Figure 2). Dimension tables are used to both decode the dimension codes and define groups of codes, which represent the levels of detail of the classifying dimensions and consequently also of the aggregate data. These levels are commonly known as dimension levels and are organized in dimension hierarchies (Jagadish, Lakshmanan, & Srivastava, 1999). For example, if D_i is an area dimension, $D_{i,1}$, $D_{i,2}$, and $D_{i,3}$ may correspond to the national, regional, and municipality levels, and may also have a temporal evolution that affects the corresponding aggregate data (Tininini, Paolucci, Sindoni, & De Francisci, 2002). Figure 2 shows an example of star schema with three dimension tables, one of which (the area dimension) has three dimension levels.

Figure 1. From microdata to aggregate data

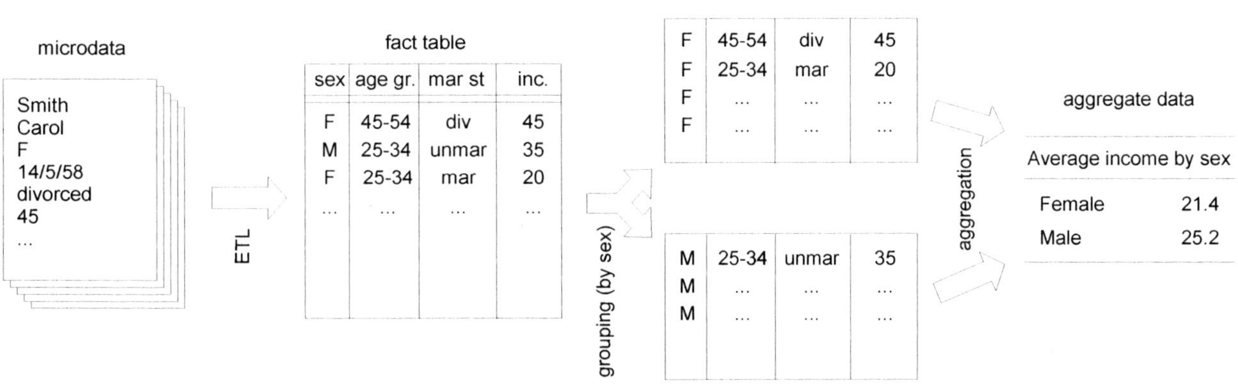

Figure 2. A star schema with one fact table and three dimension tables

sex	description
F	female
M	male

mar st	description
unmar	unmarried
mar	married
div	divorced
…	…

sex	area	mar st	inc.
F	2345	div	45
M	2345	unmar	35
F	2376	mar	20
…	…	…	…

area	municip	region	nation
2345	Florence	Tuscany	Italy
2364	Pisa	Tuscany	Italy
2376	Perugia	Umbria	Italy
…	…	…	…

As mentioned above, dimensions are used to classify data, defining the data groups to which aggregation functions are applied. Consequently, aggregate values are associated with specific combinations of dimension values and the mapping between them is commonly represented by the multidimensional data cube metaphor (Gray, Bosworth, Layman, & Pirahesh, 1996): For each of the n dimensions used to classify the data, a dimension of an n-dimensional space is considered. Single dimension values are mapped to distinct points on the dimension axis and their combination in this n-dimensional space defines a multidimensional hypercube. Each cell of the hypercube is identified by a specific combination of dimension values and is associated with the corresponding aggregate value, namely, the value obtained by applying the aggregation function on the data group defined by that dimensional combination (see Figure 3).

Figure 3. The mapping from the combination of dimension values (female, married, Florence) to the corresponding aggregate value (resident population) in a three-dimensional hypercube

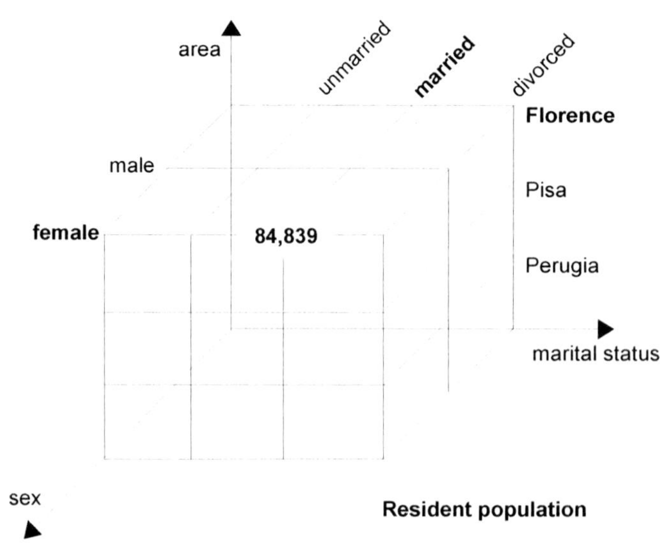

Figure 4. Roll-up and drill-down on the area dimension

Resident population (x1000)
by nation and sex

	Female	Male
France	31,298	29,555
Germany	42,093	40,166
Italy	29,409	27,587
...	...	...

roll-up ←

drill-down →

Resident population (x1000)
by region and sex

	Female	Male
Sicily	2,567	2,402
Tuscany	1,817	1,681
Umbria	427	399
...	...	...

The presence of dimension levels may further complicate the structure of the hypercube, enabling the user to perform a multidimensional navigation, for example, to decrease or increase the level of detail by performing the well-known operations of roll-up and drill-down (Agrawal, Gupta, & Sarawagi, 1997; Li & Wang, 1996). For instance, the user may have accessed some data on the resident population by region and sex, and use the DWH user interface to drill down on the area dimension, thus obtaining data classified by municipality and sex, or conversely to roll up on the same dimension, visualizing population data by nation and sex (see Figure 4).

STATISTICAL DISSEMINATION SYSTEMS

The strict correspondence between SDBs, that is, systems specifically designed to disseminate statistical data, and DWHs, also known as online analytical processing (OLAP) systems, was pointed out a few years ago by Shoshani (1997). Consequently, as DWHs have well-established methodologies and techniques, as well as powerful and user-friendly tools supporting the design, storage, and multidimensional navigation of data, one may think to straightforwardly extend their use to the interactive dissemination of statistical data. However, despite the evident similarities, SDBs have several peculiarities that require conventional DWH techniques to be extended with more specific models and structures. In the following, we briefly analyze the most relevant of these peculiarities, the impact they have on the multidimensional navigation paradigm, and how the most well-known Web SDBs have dealt with the related issues, trying to achieve a good trade-off between the characteristic freedom and flexibility of DWH multidimensional navigation and the constraints arising in the statistical-dissemination context.

Statistical Dissemination vs. Multidimensional Navigation

In this section we show the reasons why conventional DWHs cannot be used straightforwardly to disseminate statistical data. Several features of such data will be analyzed as well as the impact that they have on the well-known data warehouse multidimensional interaction paradigm.

Sample surveys. The first peculiarity regards sample surveys. Unlike conventional DWHs, statistical surveys can only rarely observe the entire target population. Observations are instead often limited to fairly small subpopulations, commonly known as samples. Sample selection is driven by sophisticated methods in order to limit bias problems and make the sample representative of the entire population, at least for the specific context of interest (Hansen, Hurwitz, & Madow, 1993; Thompson, 1997). However, the representativeness of any sample decreases with increased classificatory detail, and beyond a certain level the inferred results can produce a distorted or completely incorrect view of the phenomenon under consideration. For example, each individual in a sample survey on working conditions may be representative of 5,000 individuals of the actual population. As a consequence, in any aggregation operation each record will have a weight corresponding to 5,000 units. This assumption is certainly reasonable at the national level and for a moderate level of classificatory detail, but it will certainly produce distorted distributions for generic dimension combinations at the municipality level. In a multidimensional navigation perspective, this implies that drill-down operations should be significantly limited when dealing with sample data.

Data quality. The problem of data quality is very relevant in any information system, but in conventional DWHs, fact tables are usually supplied with data extracted from transactional (electronic) information systems whose quality is usually much higher than that of data collected using paper forms compiled by nonexperts, as is the case in census surveys (Statistics Canada, 2003). This issue is closely related to the previous one as samples unavoidably introduce statistical approximations that negatively affect the quality of aggregate data, especially in cases of fine-grained classifications.

Preserving privacy. A further issue regards privacy and secondary disclosure. Most published statistical data are subject to national and international laws protecting the privacy of citizens. For example, a simple table publishing the number of companies classified by country, economic activity, and revenue class may disclose sensitive information even if it publishes data at the national level: If in a given country there is only one active company in a specific economic sector (e.g., car manufacturing), it is possible to deduce the name of the (only) company from the published table and consequently also its revenue. In general, the data production process should prevent this kind of problem through specifically designed techniques of secondary disclosure control (Kleinberg, Papadimitriou, & Raghavan, 2000; Malvestuto & Moscarini, 2003), providing a reasonable certainty that no sensitive information can be disclosed from the published data. This control is typically based on complex algorithmic techniques that are incompatible with online processing times and therefore with typical data warehouse and Web interactions.

Microdata unavailability. All DWHs are based on the classification and aggregation of microdata in fact tables. Aggregate data are precomputed, stored in materialized views, and later used to speed up the computation of cube elements, but if the result cannot be obtained by using the materialized views alone, the microdata can be accessed and aggregated online. In SDBs it is often the case that microdata are not available and only statistical tables (i.e., a collection of already aggregated data) are available for dissemination. This is particularly true in international statistical organizations, whose mission is to collect aggregated data from their member states and publish them in a harmonized way. Even when microdata are available, data in some selected statistical tables represent the only data that the survey manager wants to be made accessible to users (United Nations [UN] Statistics Division, 2006).

Filter questions and heterogeneous hierarchies. Statistical questionnaires have quite complex structures and cannot be easily mapped to data warehouse dimensions. This is due to filter questions used to drive the flow of responses through the questionnaire. For example, a respondent could be asked if she is employed. If the answer is yes, then the type of job and starting year are asked for, otherwise the questionnaire flow jumps to the next question. These questions cause several modeling problems as they require complex generalization hierarchies and a consequent proliferation of fact tables, or alternatively a flat structure with null-value issues to be tackled. This problem is analogous to that of heterogeneous hierarchies described by Lehner (1998).

The differences between multidimensional navigation in a conventional DWH and an SDB are depicted in Figure 5, where the dimension levels are represented with an increasing level of detail on the dimension axes (e.g., if D_2 is an area dimension, $D_{2,1}$, $D_{2,2}$, and $D_{2,3}$ may correspond to the national, regional, and municipality level) and the grey areas represent the dimension-level combinations that can be accessed by users. In conventional DWHs, the user is free to drill down and roll up along any dimensional hierarchy, independently of the detail level of the other dimensions. In contrast, drill-down on a dimension in an SDB can only be performed starting from certain combinations of the other dimensions and, conversely, rolling up on a dimension increases the number of possible explorations (drill-down) on other dimensions.

Dealing with Inaccessible Dimensional Combinations

There are many online Web-enabled data warehouse systems that try to fulfill statistical dissemination requirements. They are either modules developed as part of a complete commercial statistical analysis suite or general-purpose statistical dissemination systems developed by public statistics agencies. The former are based on commercial statistical analysis systems, for example, SAS, SPSS, and business objects, which usually include a module for the Web-enabled publishing of statistical reports in their software suites. These modules normally rely on the system's storage facilities and often provide several system-specific APIs to implement limitations and constraints required by the application domain. Examples of systems of the latter category are Beyond2020 from the Canadian Statistical Office; Data Explorer from Eurostat, the European Commission Statistical Office; StatLine from the Dutch Statistical Office; American FactFinder

Figure 5. Combinations of dimensional levels accessible in

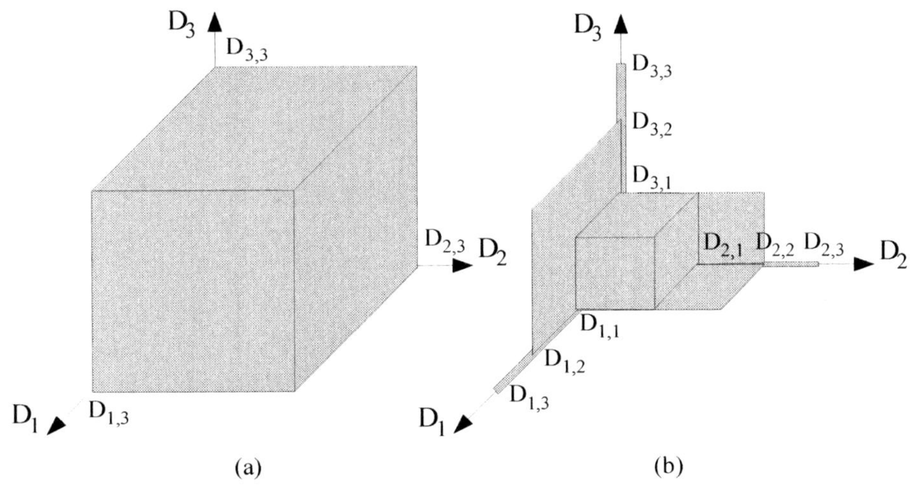

(a) a conventional data warehouse and (b) a statistical dissemination system

from the U.S. Census Bureau; and DaWinciMD from Istat, the Italian National Office of Statistics, which were originally developed to meet the dissemination requirements of their stakeholders but resulted in generic solutions suitable for any statistical domain and organization.

All these systems aim at providing a good trade-off between the constraints arising in the statistical dissemination context and the characteristic freedom and flexibility of data-warehouse multidimensional navigation. Broadly speaking, there are two main approaches to the multidimensional navigation in SDBs and they are both based on the idea of splitting the entire cube into several subcubes, where free multidimensional navigation is safe. In the former approach, the user first selects the subcube of interest and then performs a conventional (completely free) multidimensional navigation on the selected subcube. We call this the free subcube navigation paradigm. In the latter approach, no preliminary subcube selection is required, although the navigation is constrained by the defined subcubes. In other words, the user can navigate on (the permitted subsections of) the entire cube, and the interface continuously adapts to the current selection, thus enabling the user to only reach permitted dimension combinations. We call this the constrained cube navigation paradigm.

The main advantage of the free subcube navigation approach is that it enables the use of commercial data warehouse systems and conventional multidimensional interaction paradigms. Its main drawback lies in the subcube selection step: Due to the proliferation of subcubes, selecting the right one (i.e., the one corresponding to the desired combination of measure and dimension levels) from a collection of hundreds or even thousands of possible subcubes can be quite complex for the end user and may well lead to failure.

The constrained cube navigation approach is harder to achieve as it requires a specifically designed interaction paradigm and can be implemented on commercial data warehouse systems only by a substantial effort of customization using the proprietary APIs. However, it has the advantage of enabling the user to navigate across different subcubes, thus facilitating the construction of the desired measure-dimension combination. It is also more consistent with the typical exploratory spirit of multidimensional navigation. In the following we illustrate the approach adopted by some of the most important Web SDBs, as well as their support for the basic multidimensional navigation functions.

Systems Based on Free Subcube Navigation

Beyond2020 (http://www.beyond2020.com) is a statistical report dissemination system initially developed by Statistics Canada to produce reports for the 1991 census and later turned into commercial software due to the strong domain independence of the achieved solution. The system allows users to select the subcube of interest from a hierarchy of statistical domains, then to select the measure and dimensions from among those available for the selected subcube, and finally to perform a fully multidimensional navigation on the chosen dimensions. As noted above, its main weak point is in the initial subcube selection, which can be cumbersome and error prone, particularly if the global cube (i.e., the one from which the several subcubes are extracted) has a high number of available dimensions. Once the cube is visualized as a statistical table, many functions are available to modify its appearance and structure, for example, to drill down along one dimension and to remove one or more dimensions.

StatLine (http://statline.cbs.nl) is a system developed by the Dutch Statistical Office, also available to other statistical public organizations under a specific licensing agreement. The subcube selection functions are similar to those in Beyond2020, so the desired measure and dimension combination must be chosen as the first step, which normally entails a complex navigation among tens of subcubes. Hierarchical code lists are not managed, so drill-down and roll-up are not allowed.

Eurostat's Data Explorer (http://ec.europa.eu/eurostat) is a system to disseminate European statistics through the Web. Though its general features are similar to StatLine, two types of OLAP interaction are possible. Users can select predefined tables, on which only partial slicing and dicing operations can be performed, or customizable tables on which fine-tuned selections can be made through a flexible query interface. The main drawback is once again in subcube selection, which can be very difficult, especially when the global cube has a high number of dimensions. Subcube selection is based on a hierarchical classification of measures; this can be misleading for nonexpert users with no knowledge of this classification who may have to proceed by trial and error in order to find the desired subcube.

The American FactFinder (http://factfinder.census.gov) is the Web-enabled data warehouse of the United States Census Bureau. Subcubes are selected through a sequential process by which a file must first be chosen, corresponding to a set of subcubes referring to a given statistical domain. In the second step, the reference area is chosen and finally the user can select the subcube to be visualized from a flat list of predefined cubes. This hierarchical information structure offers very flexible area-oriented data selection features. A drawback of this approach is that the nature of specific subcubes can be revealed only after the area selection has been made. In addition, selections can lead to meaningless combinations of areas and tables, where cube data are available only for a subset of the chosen areas.

Constrained Cube Navigation and DaWinciMD

The only currently available system implementing constrained cube navigation is DaWinciMD (Sindoni & Tininini, 2006), originally developed to disseminate aggregate data from the 2001 Italian Population and Housing Census (http://dawinci.istat.it/MD) and more recently used to disseminate data from the household budget survey of the Bosnia and Herzegovina Agency of Statistics (http://dawinci.istat.it/dawincibosnia). The system is based on the definition of the maximum-detail dimensional combinations of each global cube, basically corresponding to all permitted subcubes (e.g., the gray zones in Figure 1a). The user can start by displaying the data corresponding to a certain combination of measure and dimension levels and then navigate to other subcubes through roll-up and drill-down without ever violating the dissemination constraints or returning to the data cube selection page. It is the system itself that proposes, on each navigation page, only the dimension levels compatible with the measure and dimension levels already selected, thereby always leading the user to a permitted dimensional combination.

Preliminary cube selection is based on the interdependent selection of the object and classifications of interest. The concept of object in the system basically corresponds to that of measure in a conventional data warehouse, although an object may also incorporate some slicing operations on the data cube. In order to guide the user in selecting the required cube, objects are organized into hierarchies, mainly based on generalization relationships, and the user can choose generic objects, that is, those located in the higher levels of the hierarchy. The system is able to combine the generic user choices and map them to the actual object-classification combinations specified by the metadata. DaWinciMD classifications basically correspond to specific dimension levels of the data cubes, although a classification's structure can be more complex than usual flat dimension levels. Classifications can be shared by several cubes, enabling a user to perform classification-based navigations; the user can select a combination of classifications and ask the system to show all available statistical aggregates (cubes) classified in that way, independently of the measure. As with objects, classifications are organized into hierarchies to enable the user to express generic queries and consequently facilitate access to data.

FUTURE TRENDS

Statistical software producers are continuously improving their systems to provide ever more sophisticated functions. Improvements are mainly focused on dashboard features, that is, an integrated set of tools to perform complex business performance analysis, starting from sales, customer behavior, and personnel data. These instruments can be very useful in the private sector, but their usefulness to public statistics is still far from proven.

Statistical organizations are also trying to improve their systems to offer more usable interfaces to access and download statistical data. In addition, there has recently been a certain emphasis on proposals for data sharing standards. For example, the Statistical Data and Metadata Exchange (SDMX) initiative proposes a set of XML- (extensible markup language) based formats and architectural standards to improve the exchange of statistical aggregates among national and international organizations (see http://www.sdmx.org). In this perspective, statistical data dissemination is likely to become a joint exercise where many organizations agree on standard structures and content in specific domains and set up a network of Web services to present users with a single interface to all their published data, avoiding redundancy and inconsistencies.

CONCLUSION

In this chapter we illustrated the main issues related to the dissemination of statistical aggregate data on the Web. We have shown that, despite the multidimensional nature of this kind of data, the well-known, consolidated methodologies and techniques for data warehousing cannot be applied straightforwardly due to some specific features of statistical data with respect to conventional business data. Finally, we have analyzed the main features of some of the most important systems for the dissemination of statistical data on the Web, aiming at achieving a good trade-off between the flexibility of multidimensional navigation, the efficiency and usability requirements of any Web application, and the specific requirements related to the statistical context, such as the protection of sensitive data, significance of published aggregates, and compliance with the statistical production process.

FUTURE RESEARCH DIRECTIONS

The statistical dissemination field is a relatively unexplored one by academic researchers, probably because it is highly interdisciplinary, involving competencies in statistics, data warehousing, Web technologies, and so forth. Nevertheless, many related problems deserve to be carefully explored and could be interesting research subjects, also suitable for doctoral programs. In this section, two areas are presented that are what the authors believe to be the most promising ones.

Online Secondary Disclosure Control

As stated above, secondary disclosure control is typically based on complex algorithmic techniques that are incompatible with online processing times and therefore with typical data warehouse and Web interactions provided by current technologies. In this respect, it could be very interesting to explore possible solutions to this problem aimed at enabling the development of statistical Web dissemination systems that provide users with the ability of directly and efficiently querying a data warehouse while preserving data privacy.

This could involve topics like materialized views, query decidability, query optimization, dynamic data scrambling, and assuring anonymousness.

The achievement of important results in this research field could have a big impact on the data warehouse system market because it would substantially increase the amount of information that could be safely provided to the public, while at the same time reducing the needed effort, since there would be no more need for defining and producing predefined hypercubes.

Languages for Web-Based Statistical Exchange

The use of Internet and Web technologies in the statistical production chain is ever increasing the level of process automation. Paper-based data collection is more and more being substituted by electronic processes, DBMSs (database management systems) and sophisticated data analysis tools are available for statistical production, and, as presented in this chapter, data-warehouse and Web technologies bring statistics closer to users. As pointed out in the section "Future Trends," this new scenario is also enforcing new ways of implementing collaboration efforts between organizations at both the national and international level. Now, what is disseminated via the Web by an organization can be directly used as input for further elaboration by another organization, or many organizations can decide to set up data sharing systems, where each one contributes to a portion of the data available to the public. This high degree of system interoperability is made possible mainly by the use of Web and XML technologies. Specific XML standards have been proposed by the statistical communities and by their data providers. For example, the SDMX and XBRL (extensible business reporting language, http://www.xbrl.org) standards have been proposed to provide models, schemes, and query languages for efficient data exchange between statistical information systems.

Unfortunately, since these proposals came mainly from the business world and were developed according to mostly operational requirements and without the involvement of computer scientists, they lack robust and sound formal specifications. So, aspects like expressive power, decidability, and equivalence, which are theoretical but have important consequences on the efficient use of these languages, cannot be assessed. This leaves room for some interesting theoretical research.

REFERENCES

Agrawal, R., Gupta, A., & Sarawagi, S. (1997). Modeling multidimensional databases. *International Conference on Data Engineering (ICDE'97)* (pp. 232-243).

Cabibbo, L., & Torlone, R. (1997). Querying multidimensional databases. *International Workshop on Database Programming Languages (DBPL'97)* (pp. 319-335).

Cabibbo, L., & Torlone, R. (1999). A framework for the investigation of aggregate functions in database queries. *International Conference on Database Theory (ICDT'99)* (pp. 383-397).

Gray, J., Bosworth, A., Layman, A., & Pirahesh, H. (1996). Data cube: A relational aggregation operator generalizing group-by, cross-tab, and sub-total. *International Conference on Data Engineering (ICDE'96)* (pp. 152-159).

Hansen, M. H., Hurwitz, W. N., & Madow, W. G. (1993). *Sample survey methods and theory.* John Wiley.

International Association for Social Science Information Services & Technology (IASSIST). (2006). *Program of the International Association for Social Science Information Services & Technology 2006 meeting.* Retrieved September

2006 from http://www.icpsr.umich.edu/iassist/index.html

Jagadish, H. V., Lakshmanan, L. V. S., & Srivastava, D. (1999). What can hierarchies do for data warehouses? *International Conference on Very Large Data Bases (VLDB'99)* (pp. 530-541).

Kimball, R. (1996). *The data warehouse toolkit.* John Wiley & Sons.

Kleinberg, J. M., Papadimitriou, C. H., & Raghavan, P. (2000). Auditing Boolean attributes. *ACM Symposium on Principles of Database Systems (PODS 2000)* (pp. 86-91).

Klug, A. (1982). Equivalence of relational algebra and relational calculus query languages having aggregate functions. *Journal of ACM, 29(3)*, 699-717.

Lake, D. (2006). *The Electronic Records Archives (ERA).* Retrieved September 2006 from http://www.archives.gov/era/pdf/2006-saa-lake.pdf

Lehner, W. (1998). Modelling large scale OLAP scenarios. *International Conference on Extending Database Technology (EDBT'98)* (pp. 153-167).

Li, C., & Wang, X. S. (1996). A data model for supporting on-line analytical processing. *Conference on Information and Knowledge Management (CIKM'96)* (pp. 81-88).

Malvestuto, F. M., & Moscarini, M. (2003). Privacy in multidimensional databases. In M. Rafanelli (Ed.), *Multidimensional databases* (pp. 310-360). Idea Group Publishing.

Shoshani, A. (1997). OLAP and statistical databases: Similarities and differences. *ACM Symposium on Principles of Database Systems (PODS 97)* (pp. 185-196).

Sindoni, G., & Tininini, L. (2006). Statistical warehousing on the Web: Navigating troubled waters. *International Conference on Internet and Web Applications and Services (ICIW'06).*

Statistics Canada. (2003). *Quality guidelines.* Retrieved from http://www.statcan.ca/english/freepub/12-539-XIE/12-539-XIE03001.pdf

Thompson, M. E. (1997). *Theory of sample surveys.* Chapman & Hall.

Tininini, L., Paolucci, M., Sindoni, G., & De Francisci, S. (2002). Spatio-temporal information systems in a statistical context. *International Conference on Extending Database Technology (EDBT'02)* (pp. 307-316).

United Nations Statistics Division. (2006). *Fundamental principles of official statistics.* Retrieved June 2006 from http://unstats.un.org/unsd/methods/statorg/FP-English.htm

FURTHER READING

Bimonte, S., Tchounikine, A., & Miquel, M. (2005). Towards a spatial multidimensional model. *International Workshop on Data Warehousing and OLAP (DOLAP 2005)* (pp. 39-46).

Cabibbo, L., & Torlone, R. (2001). An architecture for data warehousing supporting data independence and interoperability. *International Journal of Cooperative Information Systems, 10*(3), 377-397.

Cabibbo, L., & Torlone, R. (2004). On the integration of autonomous data marts. *International Conference on Scientific and Statistical Database Management (SSDBM 2004)* (pp. 223-231).

Cabibbo, L., & Torlone, R. (2005). Integrating heterogeneous multidimensional databases. *International Conference on Scientific and Statistical Database Management (SSDBM 2005)* (pp. 205-214).

Calvanese, D., De Giacomo, G., Lenzerini, M., Nardi, D., & Rosati, R. (2001). Data integration in data warehousing. *International Journal of Cooperative Information Systems, 10*(3), 237-271.

Cuzzocrea, A. (2005). Providing probabilistically-bounded approximate answers to non-holistic aggregate range queries in OLAP. *International Workshop on Data Warehousing and OLAP (DOLAP 2005)* (pp. 97-106).

Cuzzocrea, A. (2006). Accuracy control in compressed multidimensional data cubes for quality of answer-based OLAP tools. *International Conference on Scientific and Statistical Database Management (SSDBM 2006)* (pp. 301-310).

Duncan, G. T., & Mukherjee, S. (2000). Optimal disclosure limitation strategy in statistical databases: Deterring tracker attacks through additive noise. *Journal of the American Statistical Association, 95*(451), 720-729.

Fan, H., & Poulovassilis, A. (2003). Using AutoMed metadata in data warehousing environments. *International Workshop on Data Warehousing and OLAP (DOLAP 2003)* (pp. 86-93).

Fayyoumi, E., & Oommen, B. J. (2006). A fixed structure learning automaton micro-aggregation technique for secure statistical databases. *International Conference on Privacy in Statistical Databases (PSD 2006)* (pp. 114-128).

Fidalgo, R. d. N., Times, V. C., & de Souza, F. d. F. (2002). Providing OLAP interoperability with OLAPWare. *International Conference of the Chilean Computer Science Society (SCCC 2002)* (pp. 167-176).

Ge, R., Ester, M., Jin, W., & Hu, Z. (2006). A disc-based approach to data summarization and privacy preservation. *International Conference on Scientific and Statistical Database Management (SSDBM 2006)* (pp. 321-332).

Gingras, F., & Lakshmanan, L. V. S. (1998). nD-SQL: A multi-dimensional language for interoperability and OLAP. *International Conference on Very Large Data Bases (VLDB'98)* (pp. 134-145).

Grumbach, S., & Tininini, L. (2000). Automatic aggregation using explicit metadata. *International Conference on Scientific and Statistical Database Management (SSDBM 2000)* (pp. 85-94).

Hua, M., Zhang, S., Wang, W., Zhou, H., & Shi, B. (2005). FMC: An approach for privacy preserving OLAP. *International Conference on Data Warehousing and Knowledge Discovery (DaWaK 2005)* (pp. 408-417).

Hurtado, C. A., & Mendelzon, A. O. (2001). Reasoning about summarizability in heterogeneous multidimensional schemas. *International Conference on Database Theory (ICDT 2001)* (pp. 375-389).

Jarke, M., & Vassiliou, Y. (1997). Data warehouse quality: A review of the DWQ project. *2nd Conference on Information Quality (IQ 1997)* (pp. 299-313).

Malvestuto, F. M., & Mezzini, M. (2004). Privacy preserving and data mining in an on-line statistical database of additive type. *International Workshop on Privacy in Statistical Databases (PSD 2004)* (pp. 353-365).

Malvestuto, F. M., & Pourabbas, E. (2004). Customized answers to summary queries via aggregate views. *International Conference on Scientific and Statistical Database Management (SSDBM 2004)* (pp. 193-202).

Maniatis, A. S., Vassiliadis, P., Skiadopoulos, S., & Vassiliou, Y. (2003). Advanced visualization for OLAP. *International Workshop on Data Warehousing and OLAP (DOLAP 2003)* (pp. 9-16).

Mansmann, S., & Scholl, M. H. (2006). Extending visual OLAP for handling irregular dimensional hierarchies. *International Conference on Data Warehousing and Knowledge Discovery (DaWaK 2005)* (pp. 95-105).

Pourabbas, E., & Shoshani, A. (2006). The composite OLAP-object data model: Removing an unnecessary barrier. *International Conference on*

Scientific and Statistical Database Management (SSDBM 2006) (pp. 291-300).

Priebe, T., & Pernul, G. (2003). Ontology-based integration of OLAP and information retrieval. *International Workshop on Database and Expert Systems Applications (DEXA'03)* (pp. 610-614).

Sampaio, M. C., de Sousa, A. G., & Baptista, C. d. S. (2006). Towards a logical multidimensional model for spatial data warehousing and OLAP. *International Workshop on Data Warehousing and OLAP (DOLAP 2006)* (pp. 83-90).

Scotney, B., Dunne, J., & McClean, S. (2002). Statistical database modelling and compatibility for processing and publication in a distributed environment. *Research in Official Statistics, 5*(1), 5-18.

Sung, S. Y., Liu, Y., Xiong, H., & Ng, P. A. (2006). Privacy preservation for data cubes. *Knowledge and Information Systems, 9*(1), 38-61.

Timko, I., Dyreson, C. E., & Pedersen, T. B. (2006). Pre-aggregation with probability distributions. *International Workshop on Data Warehousing and OLAP (DOLAP 2006)* (pp. 35-42).

Torlone, R., & Panella, I. (2005). Design and development of a tool for integrating heterogeneous data warehouses. *International Conference on Data Warehousing and Knowledge Discovery (DaWaK 2005)* (pp. 105-114).

Trottini, M., Franconi, L., & Polettini, S. (2006). Italian household expenditure survey: A proposal for data dissemination. *International Conference on Privacy in Statistical Databases (PSD 2006)* (pp. 318-333).

Westlake, A. (2006). Provenance and reliability: Managing metadata for statistical models. *International Conference on Scientific and Statistical Database Management (SSDBM 2006)* (pp. 204-216).

TERMS AND DEFINITIONS

Data Cube: A data cube is a collection of aggregate values classified according to several properties of interest (dimensions). Combinations of dimension values are used to identify the single aggregate values in the cube.

Data Sharing: This is a data exchange process where open, freely available data formats and process patterns are known and standard. Thus, any organization or individual can use any counterparty's data and metadata (assuming they are permitted access to it).

Data Warehouse: A data warehouse is a repository of an organization's data, specifically designed to support activities of analysis and decision making.

Dimension: It is a property of data used to classify them and navigate the corresponding data cube. In data warehouses, dimensions are often organized into several hierarchical levels, for example, a time dimension can be organized into days, months, and years.

Drill-Down (Roll-Up): Drill-down is typical data warehouse operation by which aggregate data are visualized at a finer (or coarser for roll-up) level of detail along one or more analysis dimensions.

Fact Table: This is a table of reconciled elementary data (microdata in statistical terminology) to be grouped and aggregated in the process of data-cube construction.

Measure: The measure is a numeric value obtained by applying an aggregate function (such as count, sum, min, max, or average) to groups of data in a fact table.

Metadata: According to the ISO (International Organization for Standardization) standard, it is defined as data that define and describe other data and processes.

Statistical (Dissemination) Database: A statistical database is a database whose structure is specifically designed for the dissemination of statistical data (usually, but not necessarily, on the Web).

Chapter LIV
Text Mining

Antonina Durfee
Appalachian State University, USA

ABSTRACT

Massive quantities of information continue accumulating at about 1.5 billion gigabytes per year in numerous repositories held at news agencies, at libraries, on corporate intranets, on personal computers, and on the Web. A large portion of all available information exists in the form of text. Researchers, analysts, editors, venture capitalists, lawyers, help desk specialists, and even students are faced with text analysis challenges. Text mining tools aim at discovering knowledge from textual databases by isolating key bits of information from large amounts of text, identifying relationships among documents. Text mining technology is used for plagiarism and authorship attribution, text summarization and retrieval, and deception detection.

INTRODUCTION

The proliferation of computers, storage devices, and the World Wide Web makes access to various data sources very convenient. The availability and accessibility of many up-to-date data sources offer an extensive support for ordinary people and decision makers in the dynamic, complex, and demanding environment of today. With technological advances, our technological abilities to collect, generate, distribute, and store data have outgrown our ability to process and understand them. Business and governmental units, collecting and storing information by the click of a mouse button, now want to understand the trends lying behind this information quickly. Understanding those trends allows optimizing the processes of decision making and reaching customers more effectively. Although technology devices can deliver vital data for decision-making purposes anywhere, anytime, the utilization of these advances is mediocre. Technological devices such as computers, Internet-enabled mobile phones, laptops, and personal digital assistants contribute to data multiplication, leading to information overload. Information overload creates data tombs resulting in unavoidable losses and missed opportunities. This environment dictates the strong need for intelligent solutions for data analysis and exploration.

A substantial portion of the available information is stored in text or document databases. This information resides in a company's internal and external documents, technical and financial reports, customer feedback on products, market analyses and overviews, electronic mail and notice-board messages, advertisements, managerial notes, business-related publications, business plans, correspondence with partners and creditors, competitor releases, news articles, research papers, books, digital libraries, and various company-related Web pages. Compounding the problem is that text, by its very nature, can have multiple meanings and interpretations. The structure of text is not only complex, but also not always directly obvious. Even the author of a text might not know the extent of what might be interpreted from the text. These features of text make it a very rich medium for conveying a wide range of meanings, but also very difficult to manage, analyze, and mine using computers (Nasukawa & Nagano, 2001). Therein lies the conundrum: There is too much internal and external text to analyze manually, but it is problematic for computer software to correctly interpret, let alone create, knowledge from text.

Text mining (TM) looks for a remedy for that problem. TM seeks to extract high-level knowledge and useful patterns from textual data. Text mining tools seek to analyze and learn the meaning of implicitly structured information automatically (Dörre, Gerstl, & Seiffert, 1999). TM or data mining (DM) from textual databases is an essential part of discovering previously unknown patterns useful for particular purposes from textual databases (Dörre et al.; Hearst, 1999). While users of numeric data can explore a new, previously unknown pattern in numeric data stored in a database, the users of natural-language text can only associate the discovery of previously unknown patterns in textual data with rediscovery or with a new interpretation of what the author of a text had already written. It is very argumentative to state that an author of a text might not know himself or herself what is stated in a text. A new interpretation of all the facts stated in the text can only appear because different readers understand the same text differently based on their backgrounds. Witten, Bray, Mahoui, and Teahan (1998) argue that TM has potential because one does not have to understand the text in order to extract useful information from it.

BACKGROUND

TM has its roots in computational linguistics, natural-language processing, text analysis, cognitive psychology, information retrieval (IR), machine learning, statistics, and information and library sciences. The confluence of multiple disciplines in the area of TM is presented in Figure 1. Some of the parental disciplines, for instance, statistics, artificial intelligence, and information science, are the same for TM and DM. TM can be seen as a subpart of DM that deals with one specific format of data, namely, text.

Working with Textual Data

Since text is the most popular and convenient way of transferring meaning from authors to readers, the amount of digitally available text is mounting. A recent study indicates that 80% of a company's information is contained in text documents (Tan, 1999). Managers and knowledge workers spend a lot of time dealing with textual-information overload looking for useful points in it. For instance, a Gartner Group survey reveals that 75% of managers spend more than an hour per day sorting out and answering their e-mails (Marino, 2001). The dynamic business environment does not allow managers the luxury to devote enough time to read and analyze all available documents that might contain information that might impact managerial decisions.

Being the most common vehicle for written communication, text has a complicated and am-

Figure 1. TM as a confluence of multiple disciplines

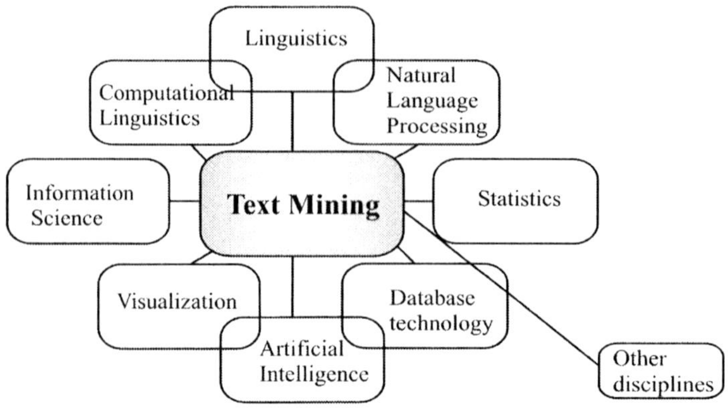

biguous multilevel structure. Structural principles exist in the formation of words (morphology of language), creation of grammatical sentences (syntax), and representation of meaning (semantics). The three components of text—word usage, grammatical construction, and content—vary very much within every individual language. Furthermore, the authors and readers of the text often represent the same semantics using different words (synonymy) or describe different meanings using words that have various meanings (polysemy). For instance, in human-system communication, Furnas, Landauer, Gomez, and Dumais (1987) discovered that two people favored the same term in one out of five cases, which consequently resulted in 80 to 90% failure rates in communication. This feature of NL words as the basic units of text confuses TM technologies such as document management systems, automatic thesauruses, and search engines. These technologies are based on keywords, indexes, or text properties, such as author, subject, type, word count, printed-page count, and time last updated. Those approaches are less effective in working with NL text because of the ambiguity, polysemy, synonymy, complexity of syntactic construction, and multivariance of interpretations discussed above. TM technologies aim to increase the productivity of managers, decision makers, and knowledge workers and reduce textual-information overload by retrieving "golden nuggets" or insights from textual databases. The user of TM technology should be able to categorize, prioritize, compare documents, and understand and utilize the meaning of any particular document without browsing, reading, and analyzing an entire document collection.

Information Needs

The fulfillment of TM tasks, such as clustering, categorization, feature extraction, thematic indexing, and information retrieval by content, is associated with satisfying the primary information needs of text users, such as searching, browsing, and visualization.

In searching, the user specifies an information request in terms of a finely defined query, and asks the system to locate individual documents that correspond to that query. Search engines, such as Google, AltaVista, and Overture, are the most successful Web applications that try to satisfy the needs of searching and information access.

In browsing, a person navigates the text collection with the help of links between individual documents that are provided by the system. Hypertext technology can link Web pages, creating a hierarchical structure of a document collection such as the one of Yahoo. Summaries and semantic maps can be created for navigating and browsing large textual databases. A summary represents the content of the document in a more compact form than the original, such as keywords or key sentences (Neto, Santos, & Kaestner, 2000). A semantic map graphically represents concepts and relations that compose a concept. It assumes multiple relations between a concept and the knowledge that is associated with the concept. Searching is used to obtain a suitable starting point of browsing (Lagus, 2000). Visualization, like a map, displays categories or associations. Learning and memorizing of that map can improve users' searching and browsing abilities (Lin, 1995).

Searching and browsing systems require an explicit description of the information needed by the user in the form of queries. However, while searching and browsing text collections for relevant information, users face problems in constructing smart queries. It is easy to imagine situations where the user might not be fully acquainted with established terminology in a field, or not fully sure about the content of the documents he or she needs to retrieve. Most users, as was noticed in Anick and Vaithyanathan (1997), prefer to answer questions about the relevance of information already presented to them by the system rather than describe explicitly what they are looking for. Additionally, the vocabulary problem that is studied in human-system communication negatively influences users' ability to construct efficient queries.

For the visualization of any type of information, something familiar, such as a hierarchy or map, is used as a means of illustrating something more complex or unfamiliar. Under text visualization, researchers consider the illustration of similarities, differences, overlaps, and other relationships existing in documents and document collections. Text visualization contributes to faster and more intuitive understanding of the entire document collection by filtering out uninteresting items. Graphical interpretation of the relationships in mailing lists and semantic maps is an example of text visualization, for example, WebSOM (Kohonen, 1999).

Text Mining Tasks

The most general and common task of textual data analysis is exploring patterns in text. This general task can be divided into finer, more specific tasks: categorization, clustering, feature extraction, thematic indexing, and, according to Hand, Mannila, and Smyth (2001), information retrieval by content.

Categorization assigns documents to preexisting categories, called topics or themes. Applications of text categorization include indexing text to support document retrieval and extracting data from the text. According to Hidalgo (2002), the classes are usually content based and can be labeled, for example, as topics, keywords, or subject headings, but can also reflect genres or authors. Automatic document categorization for knowledge-sharing purposes, document indexing in libraries, Web page classification into Internet directories, and some other tasks can be accomplished by implementing categorization algorithms.

Clustering in TM is the process of partitioning a given collection into a number of previously unknown groups of documents with similar content. Clustering allows for the discovery of unknown or previously unnoticed links in the subset of documents or terms in any particular document collection. Document clustering has been extensively explored for TM since researchers historically have perceived clustering techniques as discovery tools. Clustering does not require any predefined categories for grouping the documents (Jain, Murty, & Flynn, 1999) as opposed to categorization. Clustering is considered to be exploratory in nature. Document clustering not only allows the classification of text domains and improved document search and retrieval (Willett, 1988), but also provides more information about text collections by finding similarities among documents.

Feature extraction refers to the extraction of linguistic items from the documents to provide a representative sample of their content. Distinctive vocabulary items found in a document are assigned to the different categories by measuring the importance of those items to the document content.

Thematic indexing or topic tracking refers to the identification of the significant terms for a particular document collection. Indexing identifies a given document or a query text by a set of weighted or unweighted terms obtained from a document or a query text. Those terms are often referred to as index terms or keywords.

According to van Rijsbergen (1979), IR is the process of locating the subset of the documents that is deemed to be relevant to a posed query. IR by content is the process of inferring parts of a document that are semantically similar to a query pattern. IR is the oldest and most established field in text processing that, according to Hand et al. (2001), can be regarded as a subtask of TM. IR deals with "the representation, storage, organization, and access of information items" (Durfee Baeza-Yates & Ribeiro-Neto, 1999). To perform IR, the user is supposed to have an idea in mind about what question should be answered by retrieving information. An IR system does not directly provide an answer, but rather points a user to an appropriate document. It is assumed that the user has a classification system in mind that separates the relevant documents from irrelevant ones. Successful IR systems aim to discover and characterize this dichotomy to assist users in achieving their information needs in a search process. Traditionally, IR systems are query based, and it is assumed that users can describe their information needs explicitly and adequately in the form of a query. The IR system aims at satisfying the searching and browsing needs of a user by performing text indexing and using a particular searching strategy.

General Model of TM

TM solutions tend to automatically provide an overview of the documents in order to grant a user overall understanding of what the text documents are about without the need to read them. Visually, the TM framework consists of three parts and can be represented as a sequence of the following processes.

1. Text representation and distillation transforms and represents free-form text in a chosen format and/or consolidates documents from various sources. Text from a string of symbols has to be encoded in some numeric format within a document or through document collections; that is, words are represented as numeric vectors or ranges. Encoded text from every individual document is transformed further into a lower dimensional format that is more appropriate for computers. This transformation is achievable via different procedures, such as word stemming, meaning only using the canonical form of a word; word disambiguation, to determine which of the senses of an ambiguous word are invoked in a particular use of the word in order to fight both word polysemy and synonymy by constructing a dictionary of word senses; and word removal, excluding words that do not contribute to document meaning.
2. Knowledge sophistication deduces concepts (tokens or meaningful concepts) and patterns from the distilled text by utilization of knowledge discovery algorithms. A document or entire document collection can be clustered, categorized, or visualized to reveal interdocument or interterm relationships. The extracted features from a document or collection can be summarized to present new knowledge to a user.
3. Knowledge (relationship) representation delivers and presents the deduced knowl-

edge to a user. The discovered relationships from the previous part are presented in some graphical or other visual form that a user can easily interpret (i.e., lists and tags, hierarchies, hypertext diagrams, semantic maps, tables or matrixes).

A general TM framework is presented in Figure 2, where the text distillation step consolidates documents into a subbase, filtering and converting them from various formats into one acceptable by the TM method, such as conceptual graph representations or vectors. The knowledge sophistication step identifies and extracts concepts and patterns from the distilled documents, which supposedly capture the main meaning of text in the form of tokens and consolidate discovered patterns into evocative knowledge. The former can be achieved via clustering, categorization, or associative discovery methods. In most of the available TM programs, tokens are picked out by calculating word frequencies and co-occurrences. Tokens are chosen according to Zipf's law and collocations. Collocations are frequently used phrases, such as fixed expressions accompanied by certain connotations (Hearst, 1997). The knowledge representation step retrieves the documents that have notable tokens or patterns in them. This part visualizes documents with tokens and patterns and/or interrelationships among them by building semantic maps, hierarchies, summaries, or hypertexts with highlighted links.

Text Mining Applications

Text mining is extensively used in business and competitive intelligence. Zanasi (2000) defines competitive intelligence as timely and fact-based data on which management may rely in decision making and strategy development. TM helps in information extraction, topic tracking, summarization, document comparison, categorization, clustering, and concept linkage and information visualization. By performing all those tasks, TM can help in detecting deceptive messages in financial reports or in insurance claims, attribute authorship or a source of a copyrighted material, find similar concepts and link them together in medical or scientific reports trying to find a cure or an answer to a problem, create summaries of a lengthy document, compare stories on the same subject from different sources, build thesauruses of new information domains, or visualize content of a document or a set of documents in an easy to understand form of concept maps or topics.

TM software can determine that a main topic

Figure 2. General TM framework

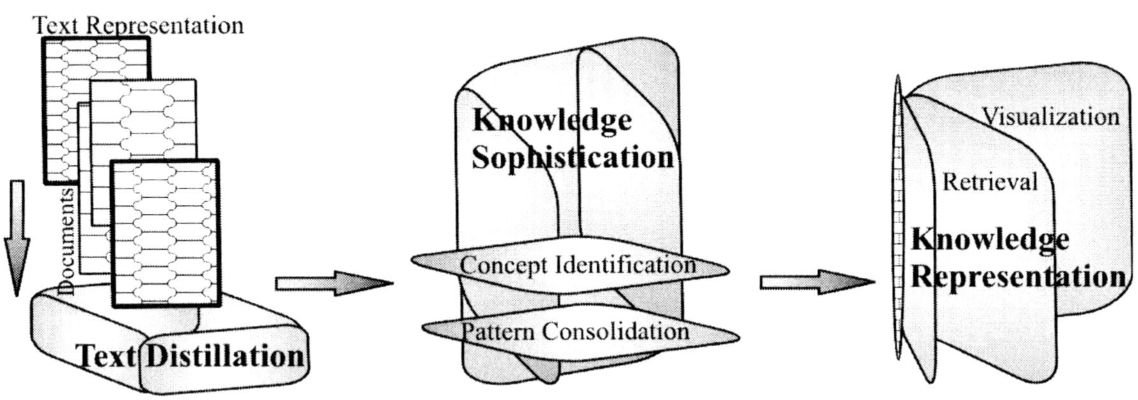

in the document A is X, and link this topic to a topic Y in a document B, which in terms is commonly related to a well-known topic Z. As a result, the relationship is built between topics X, Y, and Z. Dan Swanson's research in the '80s identified a relationship between migraines and the deficiency of magnesium by looking up medical articles that contain the keyword migraine linking it to "spreading depression" and finally arriving to a key term "magnesium deficiency" (Fan, Wallace, Rich, & Zhang, 2005). Although Swanson's work was done manually, modern TM products are capable of deploying the same method automatically.

Deception detection is a growing concern for information quality. Plagiarism detection and authorship attribution pose a lot of concerns in the easy-to-copy-and-paste environment of today. TM software can pick up distinctive linguistic cues and check the validity or integrity of the entire document or set of documents. Every author has his or her own unique writing style, which includes sentence and clause length, the order and use of particular words, parts of speech, and tenses. Lying is considered to be a cognitively more consuming process. When a person lies, his or her style becomes less elaborate, more simplistic, and direct (there is no time to come up with a lot of details and comments on a fly). This cognitive human peculiarity can help in retrieving faulty insurance claims. TM software can cluster a claim written by a person and determine how truthful all parts of this claim are.

FUTURE TRENDS

As a future development, TM systems should offer an easy-to-use graphical interface, the ability to discover knowledge, and the ability to process relevant data in different languages and formats automatically. Many currently available tools are generic tools from machine learning or statistical communities. The tools operate separately from the data source and require significant preprocessing. At the same time, a realistic knowledge discovery process is iterative and interactive. Intelligent TM tools should include tight integration with database management systems for data selection, preprocessing, and result validation. The capability to directly access different data sources from online as well as offline will greatly reduce the data transformation task. In the light of increasing numbers of proposed algorithms and mathematical models for text mining, it is important to provide architecture for easy synthesis and adaptation of new methods for experienced users as well as novice ones.

CONCLUSION

Knowledge workers and decision makers are intuitive thinkers who observe reality, collect and analyze the facts about it, and react upon the produced information. A good knowledge and deep understanding of reality, and observations and predictions about the business environment constitute a basic premise for success. With huge amounts of information available on the Internet and in internal databases, efficient and effective discovery of knowledge has become an imminent issue. Despite the availability and potential benefits of analyzing existing digital information, its usefulness is limited by IT. Data and text mining methods attempt to resolve information overload by finding and delivering valuable nuggets to knowledge workers and decision makers automatically. Modern information technology aspires to offer its users built-in data and text mining capabilities to discover those value-adding nuggets.

Text mining is becoming an integral part of predictive analytics or so-called decision automation systems. The intelligence in all of those systems comes from humans who have a deep understanding of the business and know where to point the tools, how to prepare the data, and how to interpret the results (Eckerson, 2007).

FUTURE RESEARCH DIRECTIONS

Several directions are emerging based on domain types of an unstructured text: Web applications, medicine, biology, science, finance, and marketing. Regardless of the domain, the types of text-related tasks remain the same: visualization; security monitoring, such as detection or intrusion detection; authorship attribution; summarization and thematic hierarchy building; and clustering and categorization.

One of the most prominent application domains for text mining becomes the Internet with its abundance of digital text and challenges in creating the semantic web, authenticity detection, and activity monitoring. Pons-Porrata, Berlanga-Llavori, et al. (2007) present a topic discovery system aimed to reveal the implicit knowledge present in news streams to create a hierarchy of topic or subtopics, where each topic contains the set of documents that are related to it and a summary extracted from these documents. Their methodology consists of a new incremental hierarchical clustering algorithm that combines both partition and agglomerative approaches and a new summarization method based on the Testor Theory. Adeva, José, et al. (2007) investigated a use of text mining for intrusion detection, such as detecting attempts of either gaining unauthorized access or misusing a Web application. Their intrusion detection software uses *text* categorization: It is capable of learning the characteristics of both normal and malicious user behavior from the log entries generated by the Web application server. The Web-based telemedicine domain was used for testing the robustness of the text mining approach to intrusion detection. It used the text categorization capability to learning the characteristics of both normal and malicious user behavior from the regular, high-level log entries generated by the Web application through its application server. Another online challenge is the multilingual nature of the Internet. Lam, Chan, et al. (2007) introduced a named entity matching model that makes use of both semantic and phonetic patterns in text. A *mining* system based on the entity matching model was developed for discovering new named entity translations from daily Web news outside of a bilingual dictionary. Köhler, Philippi, et al. (2006) tried to shorten the gap between the HTML- (hypertext markup language) based Internet and the RDF-based vision of the semantic Web by linking words in *texts* to concepts of ontologies as opposed to using indexes. The authors developed fully automated methods for mapping equivalent concepts of imported RDF ontologies. The method's seamless integration of domain-specific ontologies for concept-based information retrieval was tested on a set of Web pages that contain synonyms and homonyms.

Text mining has great potential in medicine and biology domains (Karamanis, 2007). By adding meaning to *text*, text mining techniques produce a more structured analysis of textual knowledge than simple word searches, and can provide powerful tools for the production and analysis of systems biology models (Ananiadou, Kell, et al., 2006). Currently, literature in system biology studies is integrated in three ways: handpicking models, concepts represented by the Medical Subject Headings and Gene Ontologies, or functional relationships captured in protein databases. M*ining text* directly for specific types of information is on the rise as *text* analytics methods become more accurate and accessible. Roberts (2006) states that uses of text mining for manual curing of related literature and deriving concepts captured in ontologies and databases are a very beneficial, direct application of *text mining for the development of* systems biology. Van Driel, Bruggeman, et al. (2006) systematically classified the relationships between genes and proteins in various species at the phenotype level. The researchers have used *text mining* to classify over 5,000 human phenotypes contained in the Online Mendelian Inheritance in Man database. We find that similarity between phenotypes reflects biological modules of interacting functionally related genes.

REFERENCES

Adeva, G., José, J., et al. (2007). Intrusion detection in Web applications using text mining. *Engineering Applications of Artificial Intelligence, 20*(4), 555-566.

Ananiadou, S., Kell, D., et al. (2006). Text mining and its potential applications in systems biology. *Trends in Biotechnology, 24*(12), 571-579.

Dörre, J., Gerstl, P., & Seiffert, R. (1999). *Text mining: Finding nuggets in mountains of textual data.* Proceedings of KDD-99, Fifth ACM SIGKDD International Conference on Knowledge Discovery and Data Mining, San Diego, CA.

Durfee Baeza-Yates, R., & Ribeiro-Neto, B. (1999). *Modern information retrieval.* New York: ACM Press.

Eckerson, W. (2007). *Predictive analytics: Extending the value of your data warehousing investment (TDWI best practices report).* Renton, WA.

Fan ,W., Wallace, L., Rich, S., & Zhang, Z. (2005). Tapping into the power of text mining. *Communications of ACM.*

Fayyad, U., & Uthurusamy, R. (2002). Evolving data mining into solutions for insights. *Communications of the ACM, 45*(8), 28-31.

Furnas, G. W., Landauer, T. K., Gomez, L. M., & Dumais, S. T. (1987). The vocabulary problem in human-system communication. *Communications of the ACM, 30*(11), 964-971.

Hand, D., Mannila, H., & Smyth, P. (2001). *Principles of data mining.* Boston: MIT Press.

Hearst, M. (1999). *Untangling text data mining.* Proceedings of the 37th Annual Meeting of the Association for Computational Linguistics (ACL'99), MD.

Hidalgo, J.-M.-G. (2002). *Text mining and Internet content filtering.* Proceedings of ECML/PKDD-2002, Helsinki, Finland.

Jain, A., Murty, M., & Flynn, P. (1999). Data clustering: A review. *ACM Computing Surveys, 31*(3), 265-323.

Karamanis, N. (2007). Text mining for biology and biomedicine. *Computational Linguistics, 33*(1), 135-140.

Köhler, J., Philippi, S., et al. (2006). Ontology based text indexing and querying for the semantic web. *Knowledge-Based Systems, 1.*

Kohonen, T. (1999). *WEBSOM.* Helsinki, Finland: Helsinki Technological University.

Lagus, K. (2000). *Text mining with WEBSOM.* Espoo, Finland: Department of Computer Science and Engineering, Helsinki University of Technology.

Lam, W., Chan, S., et al. (2007). Named entity translation matching and learning: With application for mining unseen translations. *ACM Transactions on Information Systems, 25*(1), 1-32.

Lin, X. (1995). *Searching and browsing on map displays.* Proceedings of American Society for Information Science (ASIS-95), Chicago, IL.

Marino, G. (2001). Workers mired in e-mail wasteland. *CNET.* Retrieved from http://www.news.com.

Nasukawa, T., & Nagano, T. (2001). Text analysis and knowledge mining system. *IBM Systems Journal, 40*(4).

Neto, J. L., Santos, C., & Kaestner, A. (2000). *Document clustering and text summarization.* Proceedings of the Fourth International Conference on Practical Applications of Knowledge Discovery and Data Mining (PADD-2000): The Practical Application Company, London.

Pons-Porrata, A., Berlanga-Llavori, R., et al. (2007). Topic discovery based on text mining techniques. *Information Processing & Management, 43*(3), 752.

Roberts, P. (2006). Mining literature for systems biology. *Briefings in Bioinformatics, 7*(4), 399-406.

Tan, A. (1999). *Text mining: The state of the art and the challenges.* Proceedings of PAKDD-99, Workshop on Knowledge Discovery from Advanced Databases (KDAD'99), Beijing, China.

van Driel, M., Bruggeman, J., et al. (2006). A text-mining analysis of the human phenome. *European Journal of Human Genetics, 14*(5), 535-542.

van Rijsbergen, C. (1979). *Information retrieval* (2nd ed.). London: Butterworths.

Willett, P. (1988). Recent trends in hierarchic document clustering: A critical review. *Information Processing and Management, 24*(5), 577-597.

Witten, I., Bray, Z., Mahoui, M., & Teahan, B. (1998). *Text mining: A new frontier for lossless compression.* Proceedings of the Data Compression Conference '98.

Zanasi, A. (2000). Web mining through the online analyst. In N. F. F. Ebecken & C. Brebbia (Eds.), *Data mining II* (pp. 3-14). WIT Press.

FURTHER READING

Adeva, G., Jose, J., et al. (2006). Web misuse detection through text categorization of application server logs. *International Journal on Artificial Intelligence Tools, 15*(5), 849-854.

Adeva, G., José, J., et al. (2007). Intrusion detection in Web applications using text mining. *Engineering Applications of Artificial Intelligence, 20*(4), 555-566.

Ananiadou, S., Kell, D., et al. (2006). Text mining and its potential applications in systems biology. *Trends in Biotechnology, 24*(12), 571-579.

Berry, M. (2004). *Survey of text mining: Clustering, classification, and retrieval.* Springer.

Byrne, T. (2005). Text mining's next step. *KM World, 14*(9), 1-3.

Chen, Z. (2006). From data mining to behavior mining. *International Journal of Information Technology & Decision Making, 5*(4), 703-711.

Dozier, C., & Jackson, P. (2005). Mining text for expert witnesses. *IEEE Software, 22*(3), 94-100.

Feldman, R., & Sanger, J. (2006). *The text mining handbook: Advanced approaches in analyzing unstructured data.* Cambridge: Cambridge University Press.

Grimes, S. (2006). Search for meaning. *Intelligent Enterprise, 9*(1), 10.

Halliman, C. (2006). *Business intelligence using smart techniques: Environmental scanning using text mining and competitor analysis using scenarios and manual simulation.* Houston, TX: Information Uncover.

Juhl, L., Saric, J., et al. (2006). Literature mining for the biologist: From information retrieval to biological discovery. *Nature Reviews Genetics, 7*, 119-129.

Karamanis, N. (2007). Text mining for biology and biomedicine. *Computational Linguistics, 33*(1), 135-140.

Köhler, J., Philippi, S., et al. (2006). Ontology based text indexing and querying for the semantic web. *Knowledge-Based Systems, 1.*

Lam, W., Chan, S., et al. (2007). Named entity translation matching and learning: With application for mining unseen translations. *ACM Transactions on Information Systems, 25*(1), 1-32.

Masao, F., Yuki, K., et al. (2005). A method of extracting and evaluating good and bad reputations for natural language expressions. *International Journal of Information Technology & Decision Making, 4*(2), 177-196.

Mittermayer, M. (2004). *Forecasting intraday stock price trends with text mining techniques.* The 37th Hawaiian International Conference on System Sciences, HI.

Monash, C. (2005). *Text mining market scoping.*

Pons-Porrata, A., Berlanga-Llavori, R., et al. (2007). Topic discovery based on text mining techniques. *Information Processing & Management, 43*(3), 752.

Porter, A. (2007). How "tech mining" can enhance R&D management. *Research Technology Management, 50*(2), 15.

Roberts, P. (2006). Mining literature for systems biology. *Briefings in Bioinformatics, 7*(4), 399-406.

San Juan, E., & Ibekwe-San Juan, F. (2006). Text mining without document context. *Information Processing & Management, 42*(6), 1532.

Trumbach, C. (2006). Addressing the information needs of technology managers: Making derived information usable. *Technology Analysis & Strategic Management, 18*(2), 221.

van Driel, M., Bruggeman, J., et al. (2006). A text-mining analysis of the human phenome. *European Journal of Human Genetics, 14*(5), 535-542.

Weber, M., Kors, J. A., & Mons, B. (2005). Online tools to support literature-based discovery in the life sciences. *Briefings in Bioinformatics, 6*(3), 277-286.

Wei, C., & Chang, Y. (2007). Discovering event evolution patterns from document sequences. *IEEE Transactions on Systems, Man & Cybernetics: Part A, 37*(2), 273-283.

Wu, B., Li, Q., et al. (2006). Finding nuggets in documents: A machine learning approach. *Journal of the American Society for Information Science and Technology, 57*(6), 740.

TERMS AND DEFINITIONS

Collocation: Collocation is defined as a sequence of words or terms that co-occur more often than would be expected by chance. Collocation is the way in which words are used together regularly.

Data Mining (DM): DM is the essential and arduous step in the process of knowledge discovery in databases with the goal of extracting high-level knowledge from low-level data.

Feature Extraction: Feature extraction refers to the extraction of linguistic items from the documents to provide a representative sample of their content. Distinctive vocabulary items found in a document are assigned to the different categories by measuring the importance of those items to the document content.

Knowledge Discovery in Databases (KDD): KDD is the nontrivial process of identifying valid, novel, potentially useful, and ultimately understandable patterns in data (Fayyad, 1996).

Natural-Language Processing: Natural-language processing is a subfield of artificial intelligence and linguistics that addresses the problems of automated generation and understanding of human languages.

Semantic Web: The semantic Web is a web of data, like a global database. The Web was designed as an information space, with the goal that it should be useful not only for human-human communication, but also that machines would be able to participate and help. The semantic Web approach aims at developing languages for expressing information in a machine-processable form.

Text Categorization: Text categorization assigns documents to preexisting categories, called topics or themes. Automatic document categorization for knowledge-sharing purposes, document indexing in libraries, Web page classification into Internet directories, and some other tasks can be accomplished by implementing categorization algorithms.

Text Clustering: Text clustering is a process of partitioning a given collection into a number of previously unknown groups of documents with similar content. Clustering allows for the discovery of unknown or previously unnoticed links in the subset of documents or terms in any particular document collection.

Text Mining (TM): Also known as intelligent *text* analysis, *text* data *mining*, and knowledge discovery in *text,* TM is an essential part of discovering previously unknown patterns useful for particular purposes from textual databases.

Thematic Indexing or Topic Tracking: Thematic indexing refers to the identification of the significant terms for a particular document collection. Indexing identifies a given document or a query text by a set of weighted or unweighted terms obtained from a document or a query text.

Chapter LV
Statistical Data and Metadata Quality Assessment

Maria Vardaki
University of Athens, Greece

Haralambos Papageorgiou
University of Athens, Greece

INTRODUCTION

Quality was defined in the ISO (International Organization for Standardization) 8402-1986 standard as "the totality of features and characteristics of a product or service that bear on its ability to satisfy stated or implied needs," which slightly changed in ISO updates. However, regarding quality in statistics, "stated or implied needs" are mainly identified by considering several quality dimensions, criteria, or components for the collection, processing, and dissemination of statistical information for the public (see, for example, Eurostat, 2002a, 2002b; Office of Management and Budget [OMB], 2002; Organization for Economic Cooperation and Development [OECD], 2003; Statistics Canada, 2003; Statistics Finland, 2002).

Statistics disseminated by national public administrations (PAs) aim at monitoring the economic and social development of their country and analyzing the current state of the economy and trends with as much accuracy, timeliness, and comparability as possible. This attempt is affected by certain constraints, some of which are as follows.

- The effort to satisfy different user categories having diverse needs and requests
- The regulations and requirements of international organizations as well as the quality standards that should be followed each time
- The strict budget and burden of human resources of each institute and the legal constraints of the countries

- The adaptation to the new technologies introduced

Therefore, currently, PAs and especially national statistical institutes (NSIs) are facing a dual task: (a) to embody harmonization and transformation procedures in their workflow processing since methodological peculiarities in the way of collecting, storing, and disseminating information may lead to inconsistencies of their statistical results, and (b) to upgrade their infrastructure with new meta information systems aiming at increasing the quality of the provided services. Since NSIs are usually the primary collectors of statistical data while other PAs are operating as secondary data sources, emphasis is given to NSIs while considering the quality of collected statistics.

On the other hand, international organizations make considerable efforts to implement a common framework for monitoring statistics between countries with as much comparability and coherence as possible. Examples are initiatives like the proposal of standard quality indicators for monitoring quality by the European Statistical Service (Eurostat, 2002b), quality guidelines for statistics dissemination by the Organization of Economic Cooperation and Development (2003) and the International Monetary Fund (IMF, 2002), the cooperation of Eurostat and IMF in presenting quality information through the Special Dissemination Standard (Eurostat, 2006), and so forth. These initiatives target in a unified approach terminology used by various countries and organizations, the integration of common indicators in their dissemination requirements, and their implementation as a benchmark for assessing the quality and sufficiency of published information.

This chapter aims at summarizing some of the latest efforts in assessing the quality of statistical results in national public administrations and international organizations in order to meet the demands for comparable, high-quality, and reliable statistics used for economy- and policy-monitoring purposes. Topics that are covered include quality criteria proposed by national and international organizations, metadata requirements for quality reporting, and transformations that should be integrated in the workflow process of public administrations' information systems for automatic manipulation of both data and metadata, thus minimizing errors and assuring the quality of results.

BACKGROUND

The quality of statistics is commonly assessed by public administrations with the use of quality dimensions and criteria, like, for example, relevance (the degree to which statistics meet current and potential users' needs), accuracy (refers to the closeness between the values provided and the unknown true values), timeliness, the accessibility of information, the comparability of the statistics (over time, across domains, and between countries), and so forth. It is worth noticing that there is a trade-off between the different components of quality, especially between timeliness and accuracy (Bier & Henning, 2001), accuracy and geographic comparability, relevance and comparability over time, relevance and accuracy, coherence for large domains and relevance for subdomains, and so forth, therefore the best balance needs to be sought.

In addition, metadata—preferably the metadata items indicated as reference metadata—play a crucial role in describing the contents and the quality of the statistical data. These are metadata relevant to all instances of data described, for example, entire collections of data, data sets from a given country, or a data item concerning a specific country and year. However, since reference metadata are sometimes produced, collected, or disseminated separately from the statistical data to which they refer, a unified approach of their dissemination highly improves the relevance and comparability of different countries' statistics.

The breakdown of quality into components is not unique or invariant over time. Organizations use slightly different sets of quality dimensions and there is a need for agencies' cooperation to develop a common quality framework in order to contribute to a harmonized approach at least by doing the following.

- Facilitating the comparison of evaluations across countries
- Enabling countries to make better use of each other's evaluation findings and reports
- Providing guidance to evaluators on the key elements required for a quality evaluation process
- Facilitating partnerships and collaboration on joint evaluations

The necessity of a common quality framework is evident when we consider that the amount of information processed by PAs is constantly growing as demands for comparable, well-timed data of high quality are increasing. At the same time, organizations operate under strict budgets and cannot indefinitely increase the workload of their personnel; therefore the statistical producer usually aims at a quality level that simply justifies the cost. However, if a set of data reported to an international organization by a national data source is assessed as not comparable in terms of international standards, it is not easy in most cases for the international organization to increase the cross-country comparability of the data since the data were produced in accordance with national standards that deviated from international ones. Therefore, international organizations' efforts in this area are often limited to only the assessment and documentation of the existing deviations from international standards (Yamada, 2004).

To overcome this problem, international organizations try to develop updated and well-established quality standards for the disseminated statistics, which, in the form of recommendations, council regulations (in European Union cases), declarations, or guidelines, are imposed or proposed to be used by national PAs or even by the international organizations under consideration in an attempt to achieve comparability and data harmonization. Examples of such efforts are made by the OECD and its *Quality Framework and Guidelines* (OECD, 2003), Eurostat with the *Standard Quality Report* (Eurostat, 2002b) and the *Standard Quality Indicators* (Linden & Papageorgiou, 2004), and the IMF with the *Data Quality Assessment Framework* (IMF, 2002). Documents and papers presenting related national quality assessment methods and practices include, among others, Statistics Finland (2002), Statistics Canada (2003), and Viggo, Byfuglien, and Johannessen (2003).

Finally, while national PAs allocate considerable resources to automate their internal procedures, international organizations try to provide them with a solid quality-assessment standard practice to integrate in their metadata-guided statistical processing. This attempt is influenced by the use of the Internet, as well as by the construction of new metadata-enabled statistical information systems (SIS). As an example of such effort in the public sector, we refer to the *European Statistics Code of Practice* (legal document Reference No. COM/2005/0217), which is addressed to governance and statistical authorities for implementation regarding professional independence, data collection, the adequacy of resources, quality commitment, statistical confidentiality, cost effectiveness, objectivity, and so forth.

QUALITY ASSURANCE FRAMEWORK AND QUALITY REPORTING

The quality assurance framework in any public administration and especially a statistical institute can be examined in two dimensions: (a) the quality of services, where total quality management (TQM), Deming's cycle, and quality function deployment (QFD) are implemented in the series of processes targeting at increasing the efficiency of the operations and customer-user satisfaction, and (b) the quality of the collection and processing of data they compile as well as the dissemination of high-quality economic indicators and, in particular, comparable and harmonized policy-making statistics, which is especially considered by NSIs.

In the latter case, the harmonization and coherence of existing statistics requires a process of reconciliation of different statistical metadata standards used in a common framework, maximizing the correspondence between statistical results and policy-making indicators. Ad hoc national and international standards, depending on the authority that develops or describes them, have been given in (Vardaki, 2004). Breaks frequently occur in time series and involve changes in standards and methods that affect the comparability of statistics over time; data made before and after the change are not fully comparable, thus endangering the coherence of statistics. Information about breaks in time series is quite an important piece of statistical metadata because of the adverse effects they can have on statistical inference based on fragmented data. Breaks can appear in space as well as in time, rendering data from different countries not fully comparable. In such cases, international practices and guidelines minimize the appearance of relevant inconsistencies.

At the same time, a set of instructions should be followed to gain better control over the organization's software development process, integrating best practices, like, for example, the hierarchy presented by the capability maturity model (CMM; *CMMI Reports and Technical Notes*, 2006).

Quality Criteria and Agencies' Cooperation

Quality in statistics is defined by national and international organizations as being comprised of a number of usually overlapping dimensions (criteria) and quality indicators.

Regarding the international organizations, some examples are as follows. The OECD (2003) proposes the following quality criteria: relevance, accuracy, credibility, timeliness, punctuality, accessibility, interpretability, and coherence. The IMF (2002) has developed its own data quality assessment framework incorporating the assurance of integrity, methodological soundness, accuracy and reliability, serviceability, and accessibility. On the other hand, Eurostat (2002b) follows six components to assess quality in statistics, namely, relevance, accuracy, timeliness and punctuality, accessibility and clarity, coherence, and finally comparability. It has also been defined as a list of *Standard Quality Indicators* (Linden & Papageorgiou, 2004), which are constantly adapted to the increasing requirements with the help of national representatives participating in regular workgroups for quality assessment.

However, national statistical institutes and other PAs have also developed their own quality frameworks, mainly taking into account the criteria proposed by the international organizations they are obliged or willing to report their results to. Some cases that are worth mentioning are the following.

In Statistics Canada (2003), the following dimensions are proposed: relevance, accuracy, timeliness, accessibility, interpretability, and coherence. Alternatively, three quality dimensions are included in the framework of FedStats (American Federal Statistical Organizations including over 100 U.S. federal organizations) in response to the OMB directive (OMB, 2002), namely, utility, objectivity, and integrity. However, while describing specific procedures of PAs like the ones of the Social Security Administration, then utility, objectivity, integrity, transparency, and reproducibility are employed to ensure the quality of the information. More quality dimensions are frequently supported by large national PAs like, for example, at the Brazilian Institute of Geography and Statistics (IGBE) where nine components are required for the assessment of quality in services and products, including exhaustiveness as a dimension. It is also interesting to examine the Korean National Statistical Office (KNSO) where efficiency is indicated as part of the quality framework, and the Swiss Federal Statistical Office (SFSO) where security and neutrality are considered among their seven quality criteria.

Finally, international organizations have proceeded in collaborations for metadata standards development for quality assurance. The Statistical Data and Metadata Exchange (SDMX) initiative is a collaborative venture sponsored by the Bank for International Settlements, the European Central Bank (ECB), Eurostat, the IMF, the OECD, the United Nations Statistics Division, and the World Bank (see SDMX, 2004). There are also initiatives toward the unification of components. For example, Eurostat recently reduced the quality framework dimensions from seven to six, removing completeness (Eurostat, 2002b).

It should also be noted that, although not usually identified as a measure of quality, the cost involved in the production and dissemination of statistics as well as the burden of respondents acts as a constraint of quality.

Table 1 illustrates a comparative analysis of several already mentioned international and national data analysis public organizations regarding the quality components they have adopted. It is worth noticing that accuracy and accessibility are considered essential by nearly all organizations, with relevance and comparability being also of high importance.

In addition, there is partial overlapping between the above criteria. For example, the methodological soundness of IMF is used as Eurostat's comparability across countries; serviceability includes parts of timeliness, punctuality, and

Table 1. Comparison of quality components used by national and international public organizations

	IMF	FedStats	OECD	Eurostat	ECB	StatCanada	SFSO	IGBE	KNSO
Integrity	√	√			√				
Methodological soundness	√								
Accuracy	√		√	√	√	√		√	√
Reliability							√		
Serviceability	√				√				
Accessibility	√		√	√	√	√		√	√
Clarity									
Relevance			√	√		√	√	√	√
Comparability				√			√	√	√
Coherence			√	√		√		√	
Timeliness			√	√		√		√	√
Punctuality			√					√	
Transparency							√	√	
Neutrality							√		
Utility		√							
Objectivity		√							
Security							√		
Availability							√		
Credibility			√						
Interpretability			√			√			
Exhaustiveness								√	
Efficiency									√

coherence; reliability enhances accuracy; integrity presupposes transparency; and finally efficiency takes into consideration the burden of personnel. Finally, it should be mentioned that although different terminologies are used, the components supported by international organizations like OECD, IMF, Eurostat, and so forth as examined above are the ones internationally approved.

Metadata and Quality Reporting

Quality reporting is the preparation and dissemination, on a regular or irregular basis, of reports conveying information about the quality of a statistical product or survey. Such reports are produced and generally published by international organizations monitoring the quality of the information collected and compiled by the national institutes. Of course, the related national PAs can also prepare more extended quality reports for their own assessment purposes, which can be internal documents or published reports.

The preparation of quality reports by a public administration presupposes that a set of metadata items has been identified as necessary to be reported for the assessment of the quality of national statistics disseminated. These metadata should reflect the entire statistical data collection process and thus, include metadata items regarding the following (Vardaki & Papageorgiou, 2004).

- Data collection directly from databases or using questionnaires and various collection methods and standards
- Data processing and analysis, including statistical editing, imputation, errors detection and correction, integration and harmonization, and the analysis of results
- Output dissemination process that consists of tabulation, publication, and reporting

Therefore, at least the following metadata items should be considered in the quality assessment reporting in order to assure comparability over time, across counties, and across domains.

- Survey or collection of information metadata (including metadata of surveys and administrative registers)
- Data storage metadata (i.e., format, location)
- Data process metadata (editing, coding, imputation, standards, etc.)
- Metadata for quality enhancement
- Metadata resulting from the integration of multiple data sources

Furthermore, it should be noted that the reported metadata should be consistent for both primary and secondary data sources and thus consider the quality assessment requirements of all public administrations.

QUALITY ASSURANCE IN PUBLIC STATISTICAL INFORMATION SYSTEMS

The quality reporting and assurance requirements discussed in the previous section as well as the metadata items that should be integrated in this framework will certainly be more effective and less costly if the procedure is automated, thus reducing the possibility of data and metadata mismatches. To automate the processing of statistical data, a set of operators or transformations must be defined and utilized for building SISs that support metadata-guided statistical processing. Examples of recent attempts for defining sets of operators are given in Papageorgiou, Pentaris, Theodorou, Vardaki, and Petrakos (2001), Denk, Froeschl, and Grossmann (2002), Scotney, Dunne, and McClean (2002), Vardaki and Papageorgiou (2004), and the references therein. Such operators are extensively used in online analytical processing (OLAP) technologies and are part of data mining techniques for extracting relevant information from large data sets or databases.

The transformations under consideration represent elementary processing steps that can be applied on statistical data tables. Their importance in an SIS is that they allow for simultaneous manipulation of both data and metadata, which results in the output of a new, automatically documented table. All such operators have the closure property, meaning that the application of a transformation on a table always produces a new table. Consequently, transformations severely reduce the possibility of data and metadata mismatches and also automatically hold the history of processes.

Several different transformations can be defined. We elected to refer to five important ones frequently used by databases' processes, namely, the following.

- **Selection:** The result of applying this transformation in a new table holding only a subset of the initial data satisfying the selection criterion
- **Projection:** The result is a new table holding only a subset of variables and indicators of the initial data
- **Group by:** Used for creating new indicators from existing data, after grouping (partitioning) the values of a table according to the distinct values of one or more existing variables denoted as grouping variables
- **Join:** applied on two tables having one or more common variables. The result is a new table having all the variables and indicators of both tables. Since the result of the operator is a new table, the indicators of this table must all have the same grouping variables.
- **Algebraic transformations:** This is a general transformation used to denote the mathematical operations involving constants (e.g., additions, multiplications, etc.) that are frequently applied into a table.

FUTURE TRENDS

There is still no unified mechanism in place for monitoring the data quality across domains and over time, at least for the data produced in the European Statistical System (ESS). In addition, the production of standard quality-reporting documents and the revision of related metadata files are essential in order to ensure the use of well-established terminology and coherent structures, and to put more emphasis on process data quality and related indicators (Eurostat, 2006).

However, the ultimate purpose would be to implement a common framework for monitoring statistics, which will be a baseline for quality assessment comparisons between different countries, as well as, for example, between USA and the European Union. Probably, a framework like the Standard Quality Indicators (Linden & Papageorgiou, 2004) should be defined from a producer's and a user's perspective, aiming at a complementary use. Such a framework will be the baseline for countries' comparability and its implementation will ensure coherence.

Finally, further considerations include the development of a composite indicator (quality barometer) measuring overall quality, defined by giving weights to representative quality indicators. Future plans should embrace transformation integration in relevant public information technologies.

CONCLUSION

The implementation of quality monitoring strategies in the collection, compilation, and dissemination of data in national statistical institutes and public administrative registers can meet the increasing demands for comparable, high–quality, and reliable statistics used for economy- and policy-monitoring purposes. We have discussed various components for the quality assessment of information produced in international statistical organizations and national agencies, and highlighted the need for cooperation and initiatives toward the unification of quality assessment criteria. A template has been examined comparing various organizations' quality frameworks.

Topics that are covered include quality criteria proposed by national and international organizations, metadata requirements for quality reporting, and transformations that should be integrated in the workflow process of public administrations' information systems for automatic manipulation of both data and metadata, thus minimizing errors and assuring the quality of results. Finally, it is depicted that trends in the future include a common, unified framework, and international organizations keep cooperating for implementing a common framework and possibly a composite indicator monitoring the overall quality.

FUTURE RESEARCH DIRECTIONS

In the cases of large data warehousing environments, the need for an integrated data-metadata model for large data-sets management has become evident, and a number of such UML (unified modeling language) or XML (extensible markup language) models have been developed and/or used by public- and private-sector organizations. However, the quality assurance of the automatic processing and interchange of various sources of information is still lagging behind since quality metrics and indicators should be developed and incorporated in the systems.

Future research directions in quality integration modeling are not only limited to statistics and statistical institutes, but are generally two-fold: (a) service- and product-development quality assessment in areas and sectors including health (bioinformatics, biobanks, etc.), business (banks, private companies, etc.), and even in the challenge Europe is facing nowadays for the New Economy, and (b) software-development life-cycle modeling to ensure software quality.

Regarding the first direction, a number of organizations performing research in areas like health, for example, insist on quality assurance for their results. In cases of multicenter, large-scale clinical trials and studies with different eligibility criteria, with a combination of trials with retrospective surveys, and so forth, a metadata model automating the stages of a trial is essential but not sufficient, unless quality metrics at least for accuracy, integrity, comparability, and punctuality are incorporated. Biobanks are compared and large data sets are processed considering thousands of variables and other metadata items while organizations try to ensure confidentiality and objectivity without sacrificing accuracy and transparency.

Furthermore, the business sector, banks, and private companies urge service and/or product quality. The cost of quality and cost of poor quality are essential components in their project control objectives. Each organization attempts to strengthen every year its quality assurance framework, aiming to obtain new or improved ISO or other quality standards. A number of banks tend to develop their own metadata models incorporating quality indicators to gain control over loan candidates and deposits, as well as performing cost-benefit analysis for new products and services. On the other hand, companies improve their logistics systems by using quality parameters for improving timeliness, serviceability, and efficiency.

In addition, Europe is currently facing a challenge: to produce indicators for the New Economy incorporating candidate and newly entered countries that have not yet been accustomed to new technologies and quality-assurance techniques. Related research cooperation programs, with a deadline of 2013, focus on the quality assessment of member state systems and methods targeting economic reform.

Finally, the second direction to quality integration refers to software-development life-cycle modeling to ensure software quality. The quality of the processes and management control methods has an important impact on software performance. Several software implementations of nuclear safety systems have failed in the past due to costly delays caused by difficulties in coordination of the development and qualification process (Kececi & Modarres, n.d.). The prediction and estimation of quality factors like safety, reliability, and security are strongly affected by software-development life-cycle models. Therefore, based on meeting the criteria for high-integrity safety-systems software-development process evaluation, a unified quality model should be defined after an evaluation of the feasibility of the quality requirements, targeting reliability (the capability of the software product to maintain its level of performance under defined conditions for a given period of time), usability, and capability to be improved or modified.

REFERENCES

Bier, W., & Henning, A. (2001). Trade-off between timeliness and accuracy: ECB requirements for general economic statistics. *Economisch Statistische Berichten (ESB), 4299*, 86.

CMMI reports and technical notes. (2006). Retrieved from http://www.sei.cmu.edu/cmmi/adoption/reports.html

Denk, M., Froeschl, K. A., & Grossmann, W. (2002). Statistical composites: A transformation-bound representation of statistical datasets. *Fourteenth International Conference on Scientific and Statistical Database Management (SSDBM)* (pp. 217-226).

Eurostat. (2002a). *Definition of quality in statistics.* Retrieved from http://forum.europa.eu.int/Public/irc/dsis/Home/main

Eurostat. (2002b). *Standard quality report.* Retrieved from http://forum.europa.eu.int/Public/irc/dsis/Home/main

Eurostat. (2006). *Quality in statistics.* Retrieved from http://www.em.gov.lv/em/images/modules/items/item_file_12629_27.-28.02.2006.quality_in_ statistics.doc

International Monetary Fund (IMF). (2002). *Data quality assessment framework and data quality program.* Retrieved from http://www.imf.org/external/np/sta/dsbb/2003/eng/dqaf.htm

Johanis, P. (2002). *Assessing the quality of metadata: The next challenge.* UNECE-CES. Retrieved from http://www.unece.org/stats/documents/2002/03/metis/19.e.pdf

Kasprzyk, D., & Lee, G. (2004). Reporting sources of error in U.S. federal government surveys. *Journal of Official Statistics (JOS), 19*(4), 343-363.

Kececi, N., & Modarres, M. (n.d.). *Software development life cycle model to ensure software quality.* Retrieved from http://www.enre.umd.edu/ctrs-lab/psam-paper2.PDF

Linden, H., & Papageorgiou, H. (2004). *Standard quality indicators.* European Conference on Quality and Methodology in Official Statistics (Q2004), Mainz, Germany.

Office of Management and Budget (OMB). (2002). *Information quality guidelines.* Retrieved from http://www.whitehouse.gov/omb/inforeg/iqg_oct2002.pdf

Organization for Economic Cooperation and Development (OECD). (2003). *Quality framework and guidelines for OECD statistical activities.* Retrieved from http://www.oecd.org/dataoecd/26/42/21688835.pdf

Papageorgiou, H., Pentaris, F., Theodorou, E., Vardaki, M., & Petrakos, M. (2001). A statistical metadata model for simultaneous manipulation of data and metadata. *Journal of Intelligent Information Systems (JIIS), 17*(2/3), 169-192.

Scotney, B., Dunne, J., & McClean, S. (2002). Statistical database modeling and compatibility for processing and publication in a distributed environment. *Research in Official Statistics (ROS), 5*(1), 5-18.

Statistical Data and Metadata Exchange (SDMX). (2004). *Standards*. Retrieved from http://www.sdmx.org/standards/index.aspx

Statistics Canada. (2003). *Quality guidelines* (4th ed.). Retrieved from http://www.statcan.ca/english/freepub/12-539-XIE/12-539XIE03001.pdf

Statistics Finland. (2002). *Quality guidelines for official statistics*. Helsinki, Finland: Author.

Vardaki, M. (2004). Statistical metadata in data processing and interchange. In J. Wang (Ed.), *Encyclopedia of data warehousing and mining* (Vol. 2, pp. 1048-1053). Idea Group Publishing.

Vardaki, M., & Papageorgiou, H. (2004). An integrated metadata model for statistical data collection and processing. *Proceedings of the Sixteenth International Conference on Scientific and Statistical Database Management (SSDBM)* (pp. 363-372).

Viggo, S. H., Byfuglien, J., & Johannessen, R. (2003). Quality issues at Statistics Norway. *Journal of Official Statistics (JOS), 19*(3), 287-303.

Yamada, T. (2004). Role of metadata in quality assurance of multi-country statistical data: In the case of UNIDO Industrial Statistics. *Conference on Data Quality for International Organizations*. Retrieved from http://unstats.un.org/unsd/accsub/2004docs-CDQIO/3i-UNIDO.pdf

FURTHER READING

Cluster of Systems of Metadata for Official Statistics (COSMOS). (n.d.). Retrieved from http://www.epros.ed.ac.uk/ cosmos/index.html

Dromey, G. (1998). *Software product quality: Theory, model, and practice*. Retrieved from http://www.sqi.gu.edu.au/docs/sqi/misc/SPQ-Theory.pdf

Environmental Data Standards Council (EDSC). (2006). *Quality assurance and quality control data standard*. Retrieved from http://www.epa.gov/edr/QAQC_01062006.pdf

European Central Bank (ECB). (2005). *Quality of public finances and growth*. Retrieved from http://www.ecb.int/pub/pdf/scpwps/ecbwp438.pdf

European Conference on Quality and Methodology in Official Statistics. (2004). Retrieved from http://q2004.destatis.de/download/Abstracts.pdf

European Conference on Quality in Survey Statistics. (2006). Retrieved from http://www.statistics.gov.uk/events/q2006/agenda.asp

Eurostat handbook on improving quality by analysis of process variables. (n.d.). Retrieved from http://epp.eurostat.ec.europa.eu/pls/portal/docs/PAGE/PGP_DS_QUALITY/TAB47143233/HANDBOOK%20ON%20IMPROVING%20QUALITY.pdf

Eurostat's quality Web site. (n.d.). Retrieved from http://epp.eurostat.ec.europa.eu/portal/page?_pageid=2273,1,2273_47140765&_dad=portal&_schema=PORTAL

Food and Agriculture Organization (FAO). (2006). Data quality measures and related stress factors: A conceptual framework to account for differences in statistical environments at country and international levels. *Conference on Data Quality for International Organizations*. Retrieved from http://faostat.fao.org/Portals/_Faostat/documents/data_quality/ FAO_CCSA_newport.pdf

Hyman, L., Lamb, J., & Bulmer, M. (2006). The use of pre-existing survey questions: Implications for data quality. *European Conference on Quality in Survey Statistics*. Retrieved from http://www.statistics.gov.uk/events/q2006/downloads/T21_Hyman.doc

MetaNet network of excellence. (n.d.). Retrieved from http://www.epros.ed.ac.uk/metanet/index.html

New Zealand Official Statistics System. (2006). *Quality protocols*. Retrieved from http://www.

statisphere.govt.nz/NR/rdonlyres/C619DEA6-BE63-413D-9CA3-C4DEC038367F/0/Quality-Protocols.pdf

Papageorgiou, H., Pentaris, F., Theodorou, E., Vardaki, M., & Petrakos, M. (2001). Modeling statistical metadata. *Thirteenth International Conference on Scientific and Statistical Database Management (SSDBM)* (pp. 25-35).

Thiyagalingam, J., & Getov, V. (2006). A metadata extracting tool for software components in grid applications. *Modern Computing 2006, JVA '06* (pp. 189-196).

Winkel, P., & Zhang, N.-F. (2007). *Statistical development of quality in clinical medicine.* Wiley.

TERMS AND DEFINITIONS

Accuracy in Statistics: This denotes the closeness of computations or estimates to the exact or true values.

Break in Time Series: When data collected in a specific year are not fully comparable with the data of the previous and/or following years, we say that we have a break in the time series.

Clinical Trial or Study: A clinical trial is a research study to answer specific questions about vaccines, new therapies, or new ways of using known treatments. Clinical trials (also called medical research and research studies) are used to determine whether new drugs or treatments are both safe and effective.

Coherence of Statistics: This describes the adequacy of statistics to be reliably combined in different ways and for various uses.

Comparability: It is the extent to which differences between statistics are attributed to differences between the true values of the statistical characteristic.

Quality Function Deployment (QFD): It is a decision-making technique used in product or service development, brand marketing, and product management transforming customer needs into engineering characteristics of a product or service (also called house of quality).

Quality Indicators: These are indicators measuring the quality of statistics produced and can be classified into being producer oriented or user oriented.

Statistical Information System (SIS): It is the information system oriented toward the collection, storage, transformation, and distribution of statistical information.

Statistical Metadata: They are data about statistical data. They describe statistical data and, to some extent, processes and tools involved in the production and usage of statistical data.

Timeliness: It reflects the length of time between the data's availability and the occurrence of the event or phenomenon they describe.

Total Quality Management (TQM): TQM is a management approach of an organization centered on quality, based on the participation of all its members, and aimed at long-term success through customer satisfaction and benefits to all members of the organization and to society.

Chapter LVI
Probability Association Approach in Automatic Image Annotation

Feng Xu
Tsinghua University, Beijing, China

Yu-Jin Zhang
Tsinghua University, Beijing, China

INTRODUCTION

Content-based image retrieval (CBIR) has wide applications in public life. Either from a static image database or from the Web, one can search for a specific image, generally browse to make an interactive choice, and search for a picture to go with a broad story or to illustrate a document. Although CBIR has been well studied, it is still a challenging problem to search for images from a large image database because of the well-acknowledged semantic gap between low-level features and high-level semantic concepts. An alternative solution is to use keyword-based approaches, which usually associate images with keywords by either manually labeling or automatically extracting surrounding text from Web pages. Although such a solution is widely adopted by most existing commercial image search engines, it is not perfect. First, manual annotation, though precise, is expensive and difficult to extend to large-scale databases. Second, automatically extracted surrounding text might by incomplete and ambiguous in describing images, and even more, surrounding text may not be available in some applications. To overcome these problems, automated image annotation is considered as a promising approach in understanding and describing the content of images.

Automatic image annotation is derived from the manual annotation for CBIR. Since the semantic gap degrades the results of image search, the text descriptions are considered. It is desired that the text and the visual features cooperate to drive more effective search. The text labels, as the high-level features, and the visual features, as the low-level features, are complementary for image content description. Therefore, automatic image annotation becomes an important research issue in image retrieval. In this chapter, some approaches for automatic image annotation will be reviewed and one of the typical approaches is described in detail. Then keyword-based image retrieval is introduced. The general applications of automatic image annotation are summarized and explained by figure examples.

BACKGROUND

As an effective way to support keyword-based image retrieval, automatic image annotation has been an active research topic in recent years. Since the purpose of image annotation is to bridge the semantic gap between low-level features and high-level concepts, the process of image annotation can be regarded as semantic concept discovery in image collections. Many sophisticated theories have attempted to drive image annotation automatically, such as statistical theory, machine learning (supervised and unsupervised methods), information theory, graph theory, and so forth.

A large number of good results have been reported. Jeon and Manmatha (2004) proposed the use of the maximum-entropy approach for automatic image annotation. Given labeled training data, maximum entropy allows one to predict the probability of a label given test data. Pan, Yang, Faloutsos, and Duygulu (2004) proposed a graph-based approach (GCap) for automatic image captioning. Carneiro and Vasconcelos (2005) introduced a supervised method to automatically annotate and retrieve images using a vocabulary of image semantics. The novel contributions include a discriminate formulation of the problem, a multiple instance learning solution that enables the estimation of concept probability distributions without prior image segmentation, and a hierarchical description of the density of each image class that enables very efficient training.

One of the most important processes is the propagation of the keywords. Jing, Li, Zhang, and Zhang (2004) proposed a keyword propagation framework to seamlessly combine the keyword and visual representations in image retrieval. Shevade and Sundaram (2004) presented a novel annotation paradigm with an emphasis on two facets: (a) semantic propagation and (b) an end-user experience that provides insight. Feng and Chua (2003) analyzed the main limitation of the supervised learning approaches and explored the use of the bootstrapping approach to tackle this problem.

Active learning is also effective in image annotation. Jin, Chai, and Si (2004) proposed a coherent language model for automatic image annotation that takes into account the word-toward correlation by estimating a coherent language model for an image. This new approach has two important advantages: (a) It is able to automatically determine the annotation length to improve the accuracy of retrieval results, and (b) it can be used with active learning to significantly reduce the required number of annotated image examples.

From the semantic discovery, Li, Goh, and Chang (2003) proposed a confidence-based dynamic ensemble (CDE) that can make dynamic adjustments to accommodate new semantics, to assist in the discovery of useful low-level features, and to improve class-prediction accuracy.

Metadata are useful in image annotation. Tsai, McGarry, and Trait (2004) presented a two-level supervised learning framework for effective image annotation. In the first-level induction stage, color and texture feature vectors are classified individually into their corresponding outputs. Then, the color and texture terms as middle-level features are classified into the target high-level conceptual classes during the second-level induction stage.

A suite of the most effective approaches for automatic image annotation is based on statistical learning, in which one of the typical approaches is the probability association method. An annotation method is implemented by classification (Fan, Gao, & Luo, 2004), in which multilevel annotation is used. Images are segmented and salient objects are detected by region classification. In this method, semantic concepts perfectly correspond to salient objects. However, the salient-object detection depends on a syntax classification tree and is difficult to be scaled up. Generative models are successful in automatic image annotation. Mori, Takahashi, and Oka (1999) proposed a co-occurrence model in which they examined the co-occurrence of words with image regions created using a regular grid. Duygulu, Barnard, Freitas, and Forsyth (2002) proposed to describe images using a vocabulary of "blobs." First, regions are created using a segmentation algorithm like normalized cuts. For each region, features are computed and then blobs are generated by clustering the image features for these regions across images. Each image is generated by using a certain number of these blobs. Their translation model applies one of the classical statistical machine translation models to translate from the set of keywords of an image to the set of blobs forming the image. Jeon, Lavrenko, and Manmatha (2003) instead assumed that this could be viewed as analogous to the crosslinguistic retrieval problem and used a cross-media relevance model (CMRM) to perform both image annotation and ranked retrieval. Lavrenko, Manmatha, and Jeon (2003) proposed the continuous-space relevance model (CRM), which assumes that every image is divided into regions and each region is described by a continuous-valued feature vector. Given a training set of images with annotations, a joint probabilistic model of image features and words is computed. Then the probability of generating a word given the image regions can be predicted. Compared with CMRM, CRM directly models continuous features, does not rely on clustering, and consequently does not suffer from granularity issues. Feng, Manmatha, and Lavrenko (2004) also proposed a probabilistic generative model that uses a Bernoulli process to generate words and a kernel density estimate to generate image features. The results showed that it outperforms CRM and other models. Blei and Jordan (2003) extended the latent Dirichlet allocation (LDA) model and proposed a correspondence LDA model that relates words and images. This model assumes that a Dirichlet distribution can be used to generate a mixture of latent factors. This mixture of latent factors is then used to generate words and regions. EM (expectation maximization) algorithm is used to estimate this model.

TYPICAL APPROACH FOR AUTOMATIC IMAGE ANNOTATION

Since the images are generally represented as the visual features, the key of automatic image annotation is associating the image features with the text labels by reasoning and learning. Nowadays, one of the typical and successful methods is based on probability association.

The goal of semantic image labeling is to, given an image I, extract, from a vocabulary W of semantic descriptors, the set of keywords or captions, w, that best describes I. Learning is based on a training set $D=\{(I_1,w_1),\ldots,(I_N,w_N)\}$ of image-caption pairs. Bayes' theorem can be used to invert the conditional dependence as:

$$p(w|I)=\frac{p(I,w)}{p(I)}=\frac{p(I|w)p(w)}{p(I)} \quad (1)$$

where $p(I)$ is interpreted as the probability density of image I and $p(I|w)$ as the probability density of I conditional upon the assignment of annotation w.

Traditionally, the joint probability density $p(I, w)$ is estimated by the parametric method while the probability densities $p(I|w)$ and $p(w)$ are estimated by the nonparametric method.

The basic idea of the parametric density estimation is to introduce a variable L that encodes hidden states of the world. Each of these states then defines a joint distribution for keywords and image features. The various methods differ in the definition of the states of the hidden variable: Some associate a state to each image in the database, while others associate it with image clusters. The overall model is of the form:

$$p_{X,W}(x,w)=\sum_{l=1}^{S} p_{X,W|L}(x,w|l)\,p_L(l) \quad (2)$$

where S is the number of possible states of L, X is the set of feature vectors extracted from I, and W is the vector of keywords associated with this image. Since this is a mixture model, learning is usually based on the EM (Dempster, Laird, & Rubin, 1977) algorithm, but the details depend on the particular definition of the hidden variable and probabilistic model adopted for $p_{X,W}(x,w)$.

The simplest model in this manner makes each image in the training database a state of the latent variable and assumes conditional independence between image features and keywords; that is:

$$p_{X,W}(x,w)=\sum_{l=1}^{N} p_{X|L}(x|l)\,p_{W|L}(w|l)\,p_L(l) \quad (3)$$

where N is the training set size. This enables individual estimation of $p_{X|L}(x|l)$ and $p_{W|L}(w|l)$, as is common in the probabilistic retrieval literature, therefore eliminating the need to iterate the EM algorithm over the entire database (a procedure of large computational complexity).

Generally, the words are associated with the image according to the posterior probability. The words describe the content of the entire image without specifying the regions, which is similar to the surrounding text of the Web images. In this type of annotation problem, the state of the hidden variable is associated with each image.

Another problem is the correspondence between the words and the specific regions in images. First, images are segmented into regions. Second, each region is described by some set of features. Usually, the image region representations are quantized so that a blob collection is obtained. Then the label associated with a region is referred to as a blob. Finally, words are predicted using regions. In this type of annotation problem, the state of the hidden variable is associated with each image region.

The typical approach of parametric density estimation adopts the generative model. The posterior probability in Equation 1 gives the annotation words. Although the annotation decisions are not always optimal in a minimum probability of error sense in some specific models, this approach has achieved impressive performance.

Since the distributions of image features will have shapes that are irregular, not resembling any simple parametric form, the nonparametric estimation approach is useful for Equation 1. In this approach, the conditional probability density $p(I|w)$ and the prior probability $p(w)$ are estimated directly from the training set.

The simplest nonparametric estimator of a distribution function is the empirical distribution function, but it is known that smoothing can improve efficiency for finite samples. Kernel smoothing, first used by Parzen (1962), is a general formulation of this. As Yavlinsky, Schofield, and Ruger (2005) proposed, the conditional probability density and the prior probability can be estimated as the sum of some certain kernel function that is placed over each point in the training set.

The nonparametric estimator of the true density that makes no prior assumptions about the true density is adopted; the irregularity will be helpful in characterizing and distinguishing the distributions under different word classes.

KEYWORD-BASED IMAGE RETRIEVAL

In multimedia information retrieval, representations of different data types (such as text and images) are used to retrieve documents that contain both. Much attention has been focused on keyword-based image retrieval, though it is an arguably more difficult task where a user submits a text query to find matching images for which there is no related text.

It is assumed that a text query $Q = \{w_i | i = 1, \ldots, k\}$ and a collection C of images are given. The goal is to retrieve the images that contain objects described by the keywords $w_1, \ldots, w_k$, then rank the images by the likelihood that they are relevant to the query. Text-retrieval systems cannot be simply used because the images $I \in C$ are assumed to have no captions.

Two types of image retrieval are implemented based on keywords. First, a simple approach to retrieving images is to annotate each image in C using the techniques described in the above section with a small number of keywords. Then the annotations are indexed and text retrieval is performed in the usual manner. This approach is very straightforward, and is quite effective for single-word queries. However, there are several disadvantages as Jeon et al. (2003) described. First, the approach does not allow users to perform ranked retrieval due to the binary nature of word occurrence in automatic annotations. The second problem with indexing annotations is that an appropriate annotation length must be decided. The number of words in the annotation has a direct influence on the recall and precision. In general, shorter annotations will lead to higher precision and lower recall since fewer images will be annotated with any given word. However, a professional user may be interested in higher recall and thus may need longer annotations. Consequently, the second method is to use probabilistic annotation. In the above section, every word w in the vocabulary is assigned a probability $p(w|I)$. Rather than matching the query against the few top words, users could use the entire probability distribution $P(\cdot|I)$ to score images using a language-modeling approach. In a language-modeling approach, users score the documents (images) by the probability that a query would be observed during a random sampling from a document (image) language model. Given the query $Q = \{w_i | i = 1, \ldots, k\}$, and the image $I = \{b_1, \ldots, b_m\}$, the probability of drawing Q from the model of I is:

$$P(Q|I) = \sum_{j=1}^{k} p(w_j|I) \quad (4)$$

where $p(w_j|I)$ is computed according to Equation 1. This model of retrieval does not suffer from the drawbacks of fixed-length annotation and allows users to produce ranked lists of images that are more likely to satisfy diverse users.

The framework of keyword-based image retrieval is illustrated in Figure 1.

APPLICATIONS

A good automatic image annotation method can enable many applications for the general public. First, images can be retrieved by the annotated keywords. For example, one can query images by the statement, "Find me all the photos with a red car in the image collection," as illustrated in Figure 2. Red color can be easily matched by the color features, but the car is difficult to be represented by the low-level features. Therefore, the annotation words are useful. Second, photos can be classified and browsed in the private album. For example, all the photos are classified according to semantic topic, from indoor to outdoor, from city to landscape. Then one can browse the photos in the same topic as illustrated in Figure 3. Third, Web image search can filter out most of the irrelevant images. Since the current Web image search is based on the surrounding text,

Figure 1. Framework of keyword-based image retrieval

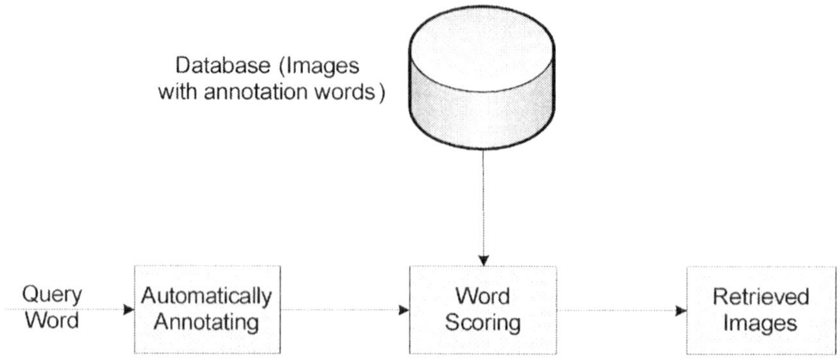

Figure 2. Example of keyword-based image retrieval

Figure 3. Example of image browse by classification

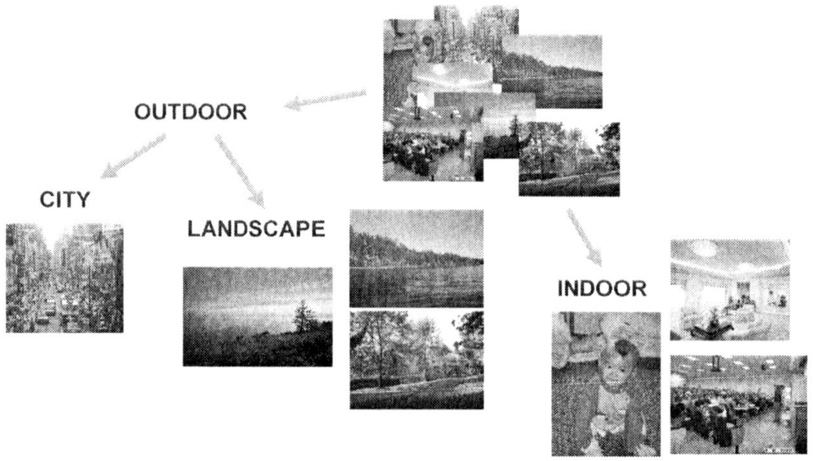

Table 1. Applications of automatic image annotation

Domain	Application	Example
General Public Domain	Keyword-based image retrieval for general image collection	Query as "find me all the red car pictures"
	Photo classification and browsing	Private photo album
	Web image search	Web image search based on content instead of surrounding text
Specialized Domain	Medical image retrieval	Medical image annotation with diagnoses results
	Satellite image retrieval	Satellite image annotation based on the analysis of the earth's surface

Figure 4. Example of annotation and retrieval of satellite images

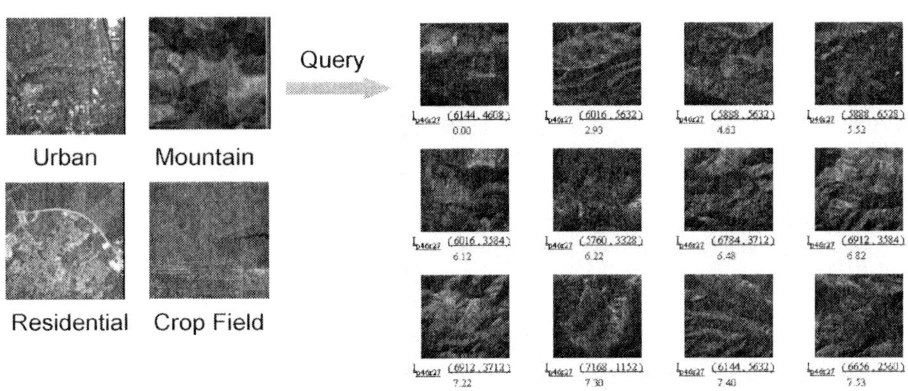

some image content is irrelevant to the query keyword. However, the automatic annotation techniques are based on the image content. If the automatic image annotation can be extended to Web image search, the search results will be more satisfactory. On the other hand, automatic image annotation results can promote some professional applications, such as medical image retrieval and satellite image retrieval. In Figure 4, each satellite image is annotated and the search result is returned according to the annotated keywords (Parulekar, Datta, Li, & Wang, 2005). Some applications of automatic image annotation are summarized in Table 1.

FUTURE TRENDS

Information retrieval based on multimodal data has been explored extensively due to the significant growth of the World Wide Web. People can access a huge amount of information from any type of modality, in which image search by keywords is an important application. In the future, automatic image annotation will also be an active research topic. Two possible trends should be focused.

1. New approaches with more effective and efficient annotation are desired, and the approaches will be extended to larger data sets.

2. In the practical scenario, the annotation approaches will drive more applications both in the general domain and specialized domain. In the Web image search, using the annotated words instead of the surrounding text is a crucial problem and needs further investigation.

CONCLUSION

Some approaches for automatic image annotation have been reviewed, and one of the typical approaches, the probability association approach, is described in detail. This approach associates the images with text keywords by posterior probability, in which parametric density estimation and nonparametric density estimation are included. For the former, images and words are related by a hidden variable and the joint distribution is estimated; for the latter, the conditional distribution and prior distribution are estimated directly from the training data. Then the posterior distribution is obtained by Bayes' theorem. Keyword-based image retrieval adopts the annotated words to search for similar images to the query. Then some current applications of automatic image annotation are summarized. In the future, the approaches will be further investigated to drive more applications.

FUTURE RESEARCH DIRECTIONS

In the future, semantics-based multimedia retrieval will still attract much attention and make more progress both in research and applications. Several specific research topics should be paid more attention.

First, image and video understanding is necessary. Both categorization and annotation are for content understanding with semantics. Many techniques in computer vision will be useful for image and video recognition. Machine learning is an alternative method, including supervised, semisupervised, and unsupervised methods. In addition to content, contextual information is also important. In multimedia information, multimodal data are often available. Mining the relationship between multimodal data will provide some contextual information. On the other hand, some traditional techniques cannot be applied on search problems directly because of the scalability. In multimedia retrieval, all the problems should be considered in a large-scale data set, even in an open environment. Large scalability may lead to low accuracy and be less efficient, so that some special techniques should be applied.

Second, a more comprehensive and practical image database is necessary for experiments in image retrieval. Most of previously-reported results have been obtained from Corel image database. Although Corel database contains plenty of images with class labels, it is specific and simple. Some successful approaches on this database may be invalid on the real data set. Currently some research experiments are conducted on real data sets. However, there is no standard database for research. A standard dataset should be comprehensive with variable concepts and practical with complex concepts. With this standard data set, all the approaches can be evaluated. Hence, a standard image database should be investigated.

Finally, multimedia information should be accessed according to affective attributes. Almost all of the current research focuses on cognitive attributes. According to semantic hierarchy, affective attributes are at the highest level for content understanding. Affective attributes convey some meaning behind the appearance of multimedia content. Although difficult, it is worthy to be investigated. At the affective level, some psychological and affective computing results will provide much help in addition to traditional techniques in computer vision and machine learning. For example, we can analyze the personal characteristics in films according to illumination distributions and photographic rules. This is an attractive and challenging topic.

REFERENCES

Blei, D. M., & Jordan, M. I. (2003). Modeling annotated data. *Proceedings of the 26th International ACM SIGIR Conference* (pp. 127-134).

Carneiro, G., & Vasconcelos, N. (2005). Formulating semantic image annotation as a supervised learning problem. *Proceedings of IEEE Computer Society Conference on Computer Vision and Pattern Recognition (Vol. 2, pp. 163-168).*

Dempster, A., Laird, N., & Rubin, D. (1977). Maximum-likelihood from incomplete data via the EM algorithm. *Journal of the Royal Statistical Society*, p. B-39.

Duygulu, P., Barnard, K., Freitas, N. de, & Forsyth, R. (2002). Object recognition as machine translation: Learning a lexicon for a fixed image vocabulary. *Proceedings of the 7th European Conference on Computer Vision* (pp. 97-112).

Fan, J., Gao, Y., & Luo, H. (2004). Multi-level annotation of natural scene using dominant image components and semantic concepts. *Proceedings of the 12th Annual ACM International Conference on Multimedia* (pp. 540-547).

Feng, H. M., & Chua, T.-S. (2003). A bootstrapping approach to annotating large image collection. *Proceedings of 5th ACM SIGMM International Workshop on Multimedia Information Retrieval* (pp. 55-62).

Feng, S., Manmatha, R., & Lavrenko, V. (2004). Multiple Bernoulli relevance models for image and video annotation. *Proceedings of IEEE Conference on Computer Vision and Pattern Recognition* (pp. 1002-1009).

Jeon, J., Lavrenko, V., & Manmatha, R. (2003). Automatic image annotation and retrieval using cross-media relevance models. *Proceedings of the 26th International ACM SIGIR Conference* (pp. 119-126).

Jeon, J., & Manmatha, R. (2004). Using maximum entropy for automatic image annotation. *Proceedings of the 3rd International Conference on Image and Video Retrieval* (pp. 24-32).

Jin, R., Chai, J. Y., & Si, L. (2004). Effective automatic image annotation via a coherent language model and active learning. *Proceedings of the 12th Annual ACM International Conference on Multimedia* (pp. 892-899).

Jing, F., Li, M., Zhang, H.-J., & Zhang, B. (2004). Keyword propagation for image retrieval. *Proceedings of the 2004 International Symposium on Circuits and Systems* (Vol. 2, pp. 53-56).

Lavrenko, V., Manmatha, R., & Jeon, J. (2003, December). *A model for learning the semantics of pictures.* Proceedings of Advances in Neutral Information Processing Systems, Whistler, British Columbia, Canada.

Li, B., Goh, K., & Chang, E. Y. (2003). Confidence-based dynamic ensemble for image annotation and semantics discovery. *Proceedings of the 11th Annual ACM International Conference on Multimedia* (pp. 195-206).

Mori, Y., Takahashi, H., & Oka, R. (1999, October). *Image-to-word transformation based on dividing and vector quantizing images with words.* Proceedings of the First International Workshop on Multimedia Intelligent Storage and Retrieval Management, Orlando, FL.

Pan, J.-Y., Yang, H.-J., Faloutsos, C., & Duygulu, P. (2004). GCap: Graph-based automatic image captioning. *Proceedings of 2004 Conference on Computer Vision and Pattern Recognition Workshop (pp. 146-155).*

Parulekar, A., Datta, R., Li, J., & Wang, J. Z. (2005). Large-scale satellite image browsing using automatic semantic categorization and content-based retrieval. *Proceedings of the IEEE International Workshop on Semantic Knowledge in Computer Vision in conjunction with IEEE International Conference on Computer Vision* (pp.1873-1880).

Parzen, E. (1962). On estimation of a probability density and mode. *Annals of Mathematical Statistics, 35*, 1065-1076.

Shevade, B., & Sundaram, H. (2004). *Incentive based image annotation* (AME-TR-2004-02). AZ: Arts Media and Engineering Program, Arizona State University.

Tsai, C.-F., McGarry, K., & Tait, J. (2004). Automatic metadata annotation of images via a two-level learning framework. *Proceedings of the 2nd International Workshop on Semantic Web in conjunction with ACM SIGIR'04* (pp. 32-42).

Yavlinsky, A., Schofield, E., & Ruger, S. (2005). Automated image annotation using global features and robust nonparametric density estimation. *Proceedings of the 4th International Conference on Image and Video Retrieval* (pp. 507-516).

FURTHER READING

Allen, N. (2001). Telling our stories in new ways. *Computers and Composition, 18*, 187-194.

Aner-Wolf, A. (2004). Extracting semantic information through illumination classification. *Proceedings of the 2004 IEEE Computer Society Conference on Computer Vision and Pattern Recognition* (pp. 1269-1274).

Batlle, J., Casalsb, A., Freixeneta, J., & Marti, J. (2000). A review on strategies for recognizing natural objects in colour images of outdoor scenes. *Image and Vision Computing, 18*, 515-530.

Boutell, M., & Luo, J. (2004). Bayesian fusion of camera metadata cues in semantic scene classification. *Proceedings of IEEE Computer Society Conference on Computer Vision and Pattern Recognition* (Vol. 2, pp. 623-630).

Chen, Y., & Wang, J. Z. (2004). Images categorization by learning and reasoning with regions. *Journal of Machine Learning Research, 5*, 913-939.

Csurka, G., Dance, C. R., Fan, L., Willamowski, J., & Bray, C. (2004). Visual categorization with bags of keypoints. *Proceedings of the 8th European Conference on Computer Vision* (pp. 11-14).

Eakins, J. P. (2002). Towards intelligent image retrieval. *Pattern Recognition, 35*, 3-14.

Feng, D., Siu, W. C., & Zhang, H. J. (2003). *Multimedia information retrieval and management.* Berlin, Germany: Springer Verlag.

Fergus, R., Perona, P., & Zisserman, A. (2003). Object class recognition by unsupervised scale-invariant learning. *Proceedings of the IEEE Computer Society Conference on Computer Vision and Pattern Recognition* (pp. II/264-II/271).

Fergus, R., Perona, P., & Zisserman, A. (2004). A visual category filter for Google Images. *Proceedings of the 8th European Conference on Computer Vision* (pp. 242-256).

Forman, G. (2003). An extensive empirical study of feature selection metrics for text classification. *Journal of Machine Learning Research, 3*, 1289-1305.

Friedman, N., Geiger, D., & Goldszmidt, M. (1997). Bayesian network classifiers. *Machine Learning, 29*, 131-163.

Hanjalic, A. (2001). Video and image retrieval beyond the cognitive level: The needs and possibilities. *Proceedings of SPIE on Storage and Retrieval for Media Databases* (Vol. 4315, pp. 30-140).

Li, F.-F., Fergus, R., & Perona, P. (2003). A Bayesian approach to unsupervised one-shot learning of object categories. *Proceedings of the IEEE International Conference on Computer Vision* (pp. 1134-1141).

Liu, X., Zhang, L., Li, M., Zhang, H. J., & Wang, D. (2005). Boosting image classification with LDA-based feature combination for digital photograph management. *Pattern Recognition, 38*, 887-901.

Lowe, D. G. (2004). Distinctive image features from scale-invariant keypoints. *International Journal of Computer Vision, 60*(2), 91-110.

Picard, R. (1998). *Affective computing*. MIT Press.

Rifkin, R., & Klautau, A. (2004). In defense of one-vs-all classification. *Journal of Machine Learning Research, 5*, 101-141.

Rubner, Y., Tomasi, C., & Guibas, L. J. (2000). The earth mover's distance as a metric for image retrieval. *International Journal of Computer Vision, 40*, 99-121.

Scholkopf, B., & Smola, A. (2002). *Learning with kernels: Support vector machines, regularization, optimization, and beyond.* Cambridge, MA: MIT Press.

Vapnik, V. (1995). *The nature of statistical learning theory.* Springer Verlag.

Vapnik, V. (1998). *Statistical learning theory.* Wiley.

Vasconcelos, N., & Vasconcelos, M. (2004). Scalable discriminant feature selection for image retrieval and recognition. *Proceedings of the IEEE Computer Society Conference on Computer Vision and Pattern Recognition* (Vol. 2, pp. 770-775).

Wang, J. Z., Li, J., & Wiederhold, G. (2001). Simplicity: Semantics-sensitive integrated matching for picture libraries. *IEEE Transactions on Pattern Analysis and Machine Intelligence, 23*(9), 947-963.

Wu, Y., Chang, E. Y., & Tsent, B. L. (2005). Multimodal metadata fusion using causal strength. *Proceedings of ACM Multimedia* (pp. 872-881).

Zhang, Y.-J. (2007). *Semantic-based visual information retrieval.* IRM Press.

TERMS AND DEFINITIONS

Automatic Image Annotation: This is the process in which images are associated with symbols (keywords or tags) automatically instead of manually being labeled as in some approaches. Most of the approaches are implemented by machine learning, pattern recognition, and computer vision. The annotated symbols describe the image content in the semantic concept level.

Content-Based Image Retrieval (CBIR): CBIR is the process by which one searches for similar images according to the content of the query image, such as color, texture, shape, and so forth.

Correspondence between Words and the Specific Regions in Images: This is the result of annotating the specific image region instead of the entire image.

Nonparametric Density Estimation: If there is no assumption about the distribution, the density is directly estimated from the training data.

Parametric Density Estimation: Assume that the images and text words are in a certain distribution. Their joint distribution is in virtue of a hidden variable. The parameters of the distribution are estimated by the EM algorithm.

Photo Classification and Browsing: This is designed for private albums. All the photos are classified into several categories corresponding to some topics. When users want to search for a photo or just randomly browse,they can first select an interesting topic.

Probability Association Approach: According to Bayes' theorem, the annotated text words for an image are selected by the posterior probability (the conditional probability of the word, given the image).

Web Image Search: This is one of the aspects of Web search. The current image search is based on surrounding text. In the future, it is desired to apply content-based search to Web images by automatic image annotation.

Chapter LVII
Online Analytical Processing and Data-Cube Technologies

Lixin Fu
University of North Carolina, Greensboro, USA

Wenchen Hu
University of North Dakota, USA

INTRODUCTION

Since the late '80s and early '90s, database technologies have evolved to a new level of applications: online analytical processing (OLAP), where executive management can make quick and effective strategic decisions based on knowledge in terms of queries against large amounts of stored data. Some OLAP systems are also regarded as decision support systems (DSSs) or executive information systems (EIS). The traditional, well-established online transactional processing (OLTP) systems such as relational database management systems (RDBMS) mainly deal with mission-critical daily transactions. Typically, there are a large number of short, simple queries such as lookups, insertions, and deletions. The main focus is transaction throughput, consistency, concurrency, and failure recovery issues. OLAP systems, on the other hand, are mainly analytical and informational. OLAP systems are usually closely coupled with data warehouses, which can contain very large data sets that may include historical data as well as data integrated from different departments and geographical locations. So the sizes of data warehouses are usually significantly larger than common OLTP systems. In addition, the workloads of OLAP are quite different from those of traditional transaction systems: The queries are unpredictable and much more complicated. For example, an OLAP query could be, "For each type of car and each manufacturer, list market share change in terms of car sales between the first quarter of 2005 and the first quarter of 2006." The purpose of these queries is not for the daily operational maintenance of data; instead, it is for deeper knowledge from data used for decision support.

Closely related to OLAP technologies are data-cube technologies. A data cube is a data model that allows data to be viewed in multiple dimensions. For example, in a large retail database (e.g., of Wal-Mart), there may be several dimensions such as time, location, store, and product that track particular sales of certain dollar amounts. We may need to know the sales by time; by location; by store; by categories; by time and location; by store, time, and category; and so forth. Actually, we may navigate by any combination of the dimensions. Furthermore, these dimensions may be hierarchical (e.g., time with day-month-year hierarchy, location with city-state-region hierarchy, product with categories, and so on). Data cubes will allow users to navigate different parts of the data at different granularity levels. For instance, users can report sales grouped by month and state, or query the total sales of product category *electronics* in the southeastern region.

OLAP and data-cube technologies have broad applications. With such decision support systems in place, enterprises can gain competitive advantages by making timely and informative business decisions based on the embedded patterns computed from large data sets. Without data warehouse and OLAP systems, the data would be separated and may have different formats. It is also very hard to maintain the currency of the databases. To answer an analytical query, we may have to coordinate with different databases stored and run on different systems. In coupling with formatting problems, data analysts may have to do it manually, which greatly reduces the overall system performance. Even if we can somehow evaluate the complex queries, the evaluation and coordination process may interfere with the existing operational OLTP systems. In view of these difficulties, the data warehousing and data-cube technologies are needed for satisfying modern data analysis requirements.

Both the total revenues in this industry and the number of vendors have experienced explosive growth in the recent past years. In academia, OLAP and data cube pose new challenges and many interesting research problems. One of the challenges is that the queries can be very complex in contrast to normal short queries in relational database systems. For example, in car sales data warehouses, one might want to know which venders or types of cars are sold fast in terms of their market share change in the past 5 years. To answer such queries, we often need to scan a large part of the overwhelming data sets. It is very challenging to evaluate complex queries against large data sets with hundreds of gigabytes (1 gigabyte = 10^9 bytes) or terabytes (1 terabyte = 1,000 gigabytes) of data. Another challenge is the notorious problem of "the curse of dimensionality." That is, when the number of dimensions of data increases, the queries may be more complex and harder to evaluate. No existing method or system so far performs efficiently on large data sets of high dimensionality.

BACKGROUND

An OLAP system is usually deployed as a part of a greater warehousing system. Data from different sources are extracted, cleaned, transformed, integrated, and loaded into a central place called a data warehouse (Chaudhuri & Dayal, 1997). The centralized data can further be partitioned into subsets of data corresponding to different departments. These smaller data sets are called data marts that are suitable for particular queries. The back-end processing steps are important because the source data more than likely contain noisy and even incorrect data, and the formats and schemas of different sources are often different. The data quality and structure of the integrated data from different sources are critical in whether we can perform meaningful data analysis. The OLAP server is a front-side data analysis tool. OLAP works on top of the warehouse database to provide sophisticated querying capabilities.

There are some other front tools such as reporting, visualizing, and data mining tools. Here, we mainly focus on OLAP. To better understand how the OLAP and cube technologies fit into the big picture of a warehousing system, a typical data warehouse and OLAP system architecture is depicted in Figure 1.

As for how to build OLAP systems, OLAP servers fall into three categories: relational OLAP (ROLAP), multidimensional OLAP (MOLAP), and hybrid OLAP (HOLAP; Han & Kamber, 2001). ROLAP servers use RDBMS or extended RDBMS systems to store and manage warehouse data, but use additional OLAP middleware to implement navigation and optimization. Metacube of Informix is based on the ROLAP approach. ROLAP servers can take advantage of the existing proven technologies of relational databases that have been used for decades. Data are stored in files and tables that are in traditional row-based records format. The query engine and related query optimization methods can be reused. The middleware provides an interface to users and parses the user queries into regular SQL (structured query language) queries, which are then evaluated by the RDBMS query execution engine. It also creates and manages derived data structures such as specialized indexes, for example, the star index and materialized views. MOLAP servers use array-based multidimensional engines to store and process data. For instance, Essbase of Arbor belongs to the MOLAP camp. MOLAP servers usually use proprietary data structures to achieve better performance. However, the OLAP query language of a product is difficult to port into other systems since there is not a standardized OLAP language for the OLAP industry. ROLAP is usually more scalable than MOLAP, but the latter holds a performance advantage. HOLAP tries to combine the benefits of both. The Microsoft SQL server OLAP Services is a HOLAP server.

The data-cube concept was first introduced by Gray et al. (1997). In the data-cube model, dimensions are the attributes to track certain numerical attributes called measures. In the following car sales example, the dollar amount is the measure while the maker, time, and location are dimensions. There are one or more fact tables and several dimension tables. Star schema and snowflake schema are data warehouse design models. In a star schema, a fact table is associated with several dimension tables, forming a star. The snowflake schema further allows the dimension tables to have hierarchies. Roll-up, drill-down,

Figure 1. Data warehouse architecture

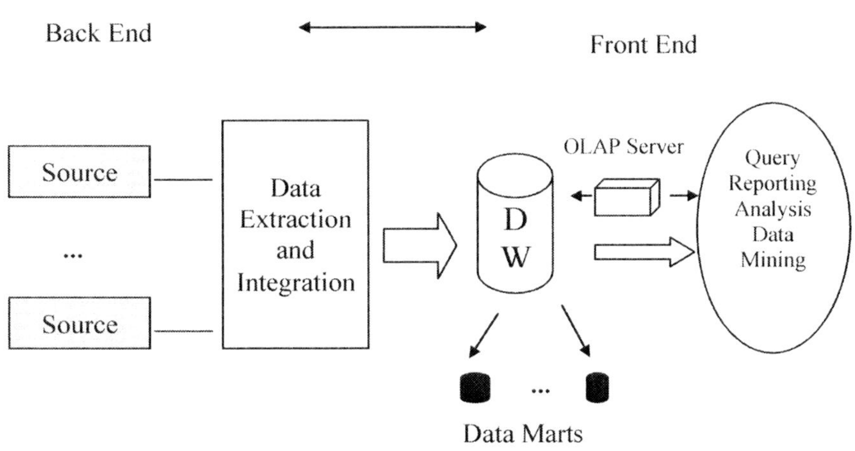

slice, and dice are common OLAP operations. Roll-up performs an aggregation up upon a dimension hierarchy or by reduction of dimensions. For example, aggregating sales from month to year is a roll-up operation. The drill-down operation is just the opposite of roll-up. For example, from yearly sales, a user drills down for more details of the sales for each location and may further drill down to sales for each vendor. The slicing operation performs a selection on one dimension of a cube. For example, accessing the total January sales is a slice operation. Figure 2 shows a data-cube example for car sales in a three-dimension diagram. We may have more dimensions but cannot visualize them directly.

OLAP and data-cube technologies have important applications in the public sector. There are many successful stories. Here we will point to two cases briefly. One case is related to data analysis for student retention. One of the major goals of many universities is to improve their retention rates and graduation rates, which are typically indicated by the first-year retention rate and 4-year and 6-year graduation rates (for part-time students). One may be interested in the rates among different categories of students, for example, in state vs. out of state, male vs. female, different ethnic groups, on campus vs. off campus, and so forth. This can be easily implemented through OLAP and cube technologies. Another case is related to NSF (National Science Foundation) grant awards analysis. One may want to know the number of awards grouped by schools, by disciplines, by regions, by amounts, by dates, and so forth, and grouped by any arbitrary combination of these dimensions. Again, OLAP and cube technologies are also suitable for solving the problem effectively.

OLAP AND DATA-CUBE COMPUTATION TECHNOLOGIES

There is abundant literature on the evaluation of OLAP queries and data cubes. We will briefly summarize some of the top algorithms and systems with good performance as well as our research findings on this subject. Since introductions and descriptions of existing OLAP systems and products are generally readily available, we will focus more on the technical, algorithmic side of the OLAP and cube systems rather than the usage and applications of the systems. In BUC (bottom-up cubing; Beyer & Ramakrishnan, 1999), a new

Figure 2. A 3-D presentation of a data cube

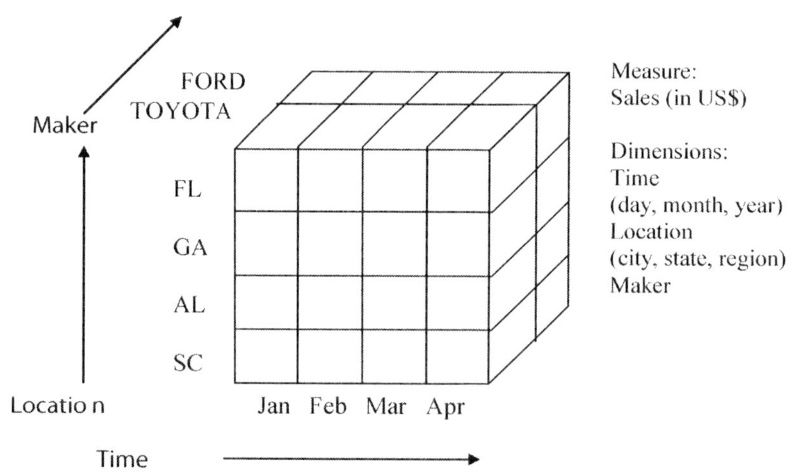

iceberg-cube problem is introduced: computing the cubes with aggregates above a threshold. The rationale is that computing only the cells that aggregate more saves time and space significantly for sparse data. The BUC algorithm computes large 1 group-bys, 2 group-bys, and so on using Apriori pruning (nicely written). The idea is inspired from PartitionedCube and Apriori. For large data sets, BUC-external switches to BUC-internal. BUC outperforms the earlier algorithms for computing sparse cubes such as ArrayCube (Zhao, Deshpande, & Naughton, 1997) and PartitionedCube (Ross & Srivastava, 1997). Unfortunately, BUC is not suitable for dense data or for highly skewed data. ArrayCube is an MOLAP algorithm that pipelines the computation of dependent cubes to save I/O (input/output) by overlapping as much as possible, fitting many partitions in memory to avoid writing intermediate results. It also uses in-memory array-based MD chunks to avoid sorting. The PartitionedCube algorithm first partitions the input data into sub data cubes according to an attribute, and then recursively partitions each subcubes according to the next attribute until the data fit in the memory when memory cube is used.

Dwarf (Sismanis, Deligiannakis, Roussopoulos, & Kotidis, 2002) gives a compressed structure with ALL pointers to compute, store, and query cubes. It removes prefix redundancy for dense cubes and suffix redundancy for sparse cubes. However, updating the data structure is complex and inconvenient. QC-tree (Lakshmanan, Pei, & Zhao, 2003) builds a structure for storing and searching for a quotient cube (Lakshmanan, Pei, & Han, 2002) in the input data. A quotient cube is an intermediate data structure computed from the input data set so that a user can navigate data at different level of granularities.

The algorithm partitions the cube cells with identical aggregate values into equivalent classes while preserving the semantics of drill-down links in the lattice structure. A quotient cube is the reduced (or summary of) lattice in terms of classes of cells. One serious and common problem with the above-mentioned algorithms and systems is that they are based on sorting the input data sets in certain ways as a preprocessing step. In real applications, the input data sets are usually much larger than the available computer memory and thus incur external sorting, which requires a large number of I/O operations (i.e., accesses to computer disks). An I/O operation is 1 million times slower than an operation in memory. Even worse, most existing algorithms need multiple scans of massive input data sets. This takes a prohibitively long time and is often infeasible.

We have given a data structure called statistics trees (STs) and an algorithm called CUBIST (cubing with ST; Fu & Hammer, 2000), introducing the star pointers for the first time. A statistics tree is a multiway, multilevel, and balanced tree where each level represents a dimension. The cardinality of a dimension is indicated by the degree of the nodes at that level. The extra star pointer is used for data cubes that do not have a constraint for that level. The leaves of the tree store the aggregated values of the data cubes indicated by the corresponding root-to-leaf paths. This chapter also gives a loading program that inserts all the input records. Once the statistics tree is initialized, a query evaluation algorithm will compute the input query and return an answer to the user. Continuous and ordinal dimensions must first be converted to integers from zero to the cardinality or size of the dimension. The advantage of the CUBIST algorithm is that the query evaluation time does not depend upon the number of records and thus the size of the input database. The disadvantage is that when the dimensions are large, the size of the statistics tree is also large.

To improve the performance of CUBIST for queries with constraints on dimension hierarchies, we have developed the algorithm CUBIST^{++} (Hammer & Fu, 2001), which uses a family of materialized ST trees. In addition to the base tree, we select a set of candidate trees that have the same dimensions as the base tree but at different granularity levels. In our greedy strategy, we roll up the dimension with the largest cardinality one after another until all dimensions are at their highest levels. A derived tree is computed from the previous one by merging the subtrees. Given a query, a matching algorithm finds the smallest tree that can provide the answer. If necessary, a query is rewritten according to the inclusion relationship. Experiments show that CUBIST^{++} is four times faster in setup and two orders of magnitude faster (seconds vs. hundreds of seconds) in the computation of queries than the current leading commercial database Oracle. Our other related work includes the optimization of large-range queries (Fu, 2002b) and the evaluation of holistic operators efficiently (Fu, 2002a; Fu & Rajasekaran, 2001).

Both CUBIST and CUBIST^{++} require that the ST trees fit into memory. However, in real-world applications, data are usually sparse and this requirement may not be met. To address this issue, our recent work on sparse statistics trees (SSTs) removes the drawback while preserving the advantages of ST trees (Fu, 2004). In SST, the data structure itself is dynamic, meaning that the branching values do not have to be contiguous. We recently proposed a new dynamic data structure called RSST (restricted sparse statistics trees) and a novel cube evaluation algorithm, which efficiently computes dense subcubes imbedded in high-dimensional sparse data sets. RSST restricts the number of nonstar values along any root-to-leaf path. In this way, the size of the RSST tree increases more slowly than those of straightforward SST or CUBIST algorithms. In this chapter we have also compared the performance of RSST with Dwarf, QC-tree, and BUC (Fu, 2006) and showed its superior performance.

FUTURE TRENDS

Despite the intensive research and great achievements, there are still some issues to resolve on OLAP and data cubes. First, we need a standard language to write OLAP queries. Currently, different vendors use different languages, which causes the difficulty of portability. Second, more effective and efficient algorithms on large warehouses with high-dimensional data are still to be explored to evaluate complex queries. Particularly, the I/O efficiency issue must be addressed. Third, data integration between OLAP, databases, and data mining to form a comprehensive information-oriented decision system will be a major trend of research.

CONCLUSION

OLAP and data cubes have been a hot research area for the past years and will continue to be. We have briefly introduced the basic concepts and principles of OLAP and data-cube systems. Specifically, we surveyed the state-of-the-art technologies on how to compute OLAP queries and data cubes efficiently. Once a few issues such as portability, efficiency, and integration are resolved, this field will promise an even brighter future. We live in an information age; how to dig out precious gold automatically from large mountains of heterogeneous, possibly noisy data will be a must to gain an advantageous edge.

FUTURE RESEARCH DIRECTIONS

One interesting research area of OLAP and data cubes is how to apply the cube computation to real-time databases. That is, how to combine the technologies of data-cube and online streaming processing—both hot topics together. Many applications need real-time processing of incoming streams of data generated from various sources. For example, many Internet sites may pump out data on a continuous basis. In weather forecasting, data from different locations and different instruments are created and transported across a network for monitoring and analysis. Traffic monitoring and temperature control of rooms in buildings are other interesting examples. In these streaming applications, data are continuously generated and processed, and rarely if at all, data are stored. Instead, only a time window of data is stored, processed, and updated. How can then data warehousing and data cubes fit in these applications since data warehouses try to store all data? First, for a trend analysis of a longer time period to find the rules of parameter changing, we have to store historical data somewhere. A data warehouse will collect the historical data from various sources. Second, a data warehouse will be suitable to analyze data in a global perspective. This is essential in the example of weather monitoring. Third, the data-cube technology can be applied to obtain data summaries of streams for streaming processing.

Another direction of data warehouse research is distributed data warehouses. Presumably, data warehouses are big, centralized, reconciled, and cleaned data copies of the data from various sources. However, when the warehouses grow too large they can become the bottleneck of data access and queries. One idea is to repartition the global data into a few warehouse sites. For example, a data warehouse for Wal-Mart could be partitioned into several submarts in large regions. In this way, data, queries, and resources may be better utilized.

REFERENCES

Beyer, K., & Ramakrishnan, R. (1999). Bottom-up computation of sparse and iceberg CUBEs. *Proceedings of the 1999 ACM SIGMOD International Conference on Management of Data (SIGMOD '99)* (pp. 359-370).

Chaudhuri, S., & Dayal, U. (1997). An overview of data warehousing and OLAP technology. *SIGMOD Record, 26*(1), 65-74.

Fu, L. (2002a). Querying and clustering very large data sets using dynamic bucketing approach. *The Third International Conference on Web-Age Information Management (WAIM'02)* (pp. 279-290).

Fu, L. (2002b, June). *Range query optimization for multidimensional Web data.* Proceedings of the 2002 International Conference on Information and Knowledge Engineering (IKE '02), Las Vegas, NV.

Fu, L. (2004). *Processing ad-hoc cube queries over sparse data efficiently and interactively.* Proceedings of ICDE '04, Boston.

Fu, L. (2006). Computing dense cubes embedded in sparse data. In D. Taniar (Ed.), *Research and trends in data mining technologies and applications: Advances in data warehousing and mining* (Vol. 1).

Fu, L., & Hammer, J. (2000). CUBIST: A new algorithm for improving the performance of ad-hoc OLAP queries. *ACM Third International Workshop on Data Warehousing and OLAP* (pp. 72-79).

Fu, L., & Rajasekaran, S. (2001). Novel algorithms for computing medians and other quantiles of disk-resident data. *IEEE International Data Engineering and Application Symposium* (pp. 145-154).

Gibbons, P. B., & Matias, Y. (1998). New sampling-based summary statistics for improving approximate query answers. *Proceedings of the 1998 ACM SIGMOD International Conference on Management of Data (SIGMOD '98)* (pp. 331-342).

Gray, J., Chaudhuri, S., Bosworth, A., Layman, A., Reichart, D., Venkatrao, M., et al. (1997). Data cube: A relational aggregation operator generalizing group-by, cross-tab, and sub-totals. *Data Mining and Knowledge Discovery, 1*(1), 29-53.

Hammer, J., & Fu, L. (2001). Improving the performance of OLAP queries using families of statistics trees. *3rd International Conference on Data Warehousing and Knowledge Discovery DaWaK 01* (pp. 274-283).

Han, J., & Kamber, M. (2001). *Data mining: Concepts and techniques*. Morgan Kaufmann Publishers.

Lakshmanan, L. V. S., Pei, J., & Han, J. (2002). Quotient cube: How to summarize the semantics of a data cube. *Proceedings of 28th International Conference on Very Large Databases (VLDB '02)* (pp. 778-789).

Lakshmanan, L. V. S., Pei, J., & Zhao, Y. (2003). QC-trees: An efficient summary structure for semantic OLAP. *Proceedings of the 2003 ACM SIGMOD International Conference on Management of Data* (pp. 64-75).

Ross, K. A., & Srivastava, D. (1997). Fast computation of sparse datacubes. *Proceedings of the 23rd VLDB Conference (VLDB '97)* (pp. 116-125).

Sismanis, Y., Deligiannakis, A., Roussopoulos, N., & Kotidis, Y. (2002). Dwarf: Shrinking the PetaCube. *Proceedings of the 2002 ACM SIGMOD International Conference on Management of Data (SIGMOD '02)* (pp. 464-475).

Zhao, Y., Deshpande, P. M., & Naughton, J. F. (1997). An array-based algorithm for simultaneous multidimensional aggregates. *SIGMOD Record, 26*(2), 159-170.

FURTHER READING

Aboulnaga, A., & Chaudhuri, S. (1999). Self-tuning histograms: Building histograms without looking at data. *Proceedings of the 1999 ACM SIGMOD International Conference on Management of Data (SIGMOD '99)* (pp. 181-192).

Acharya, S., Gibbons, P. B., & Poosala, V. (2000). Congressional samples for approximate answering of group-by queries. *Proceedings of the 2000 ACM SIGMOD International Conference on Management of Data (SIGMOD '00)* (pp. 487-498).

Agarwal, S., Agrawal, R., Deshpande, P., Naughton, J., Sarawagi, S., & Ramakrishnan, R. (1996). On the computation of multidimensional aggregates. *Proceedings of the International Conference on Very Large Databases* (pp. 506-521).

Agrawal, D., & Aggarwal, C. C. (2001, May). *On the design and quantification of privacy preserving data mining algorithms*. Paper presented at the Proceedings of the 20th ACM SIGMOD-SIGACT-SIGART Symposium on Principles of Database Systems, Santa Barbara, CA.

Chan, C. Y., & Ioannidis, Y. E. (1998). Bitmap index design and evaluation. *Proceedings of the 1998 ACM SIGMOD International Conference on Management of Data (SIGMOD '98)* (pp. 355-366).

Denning, D. (1980). Secure statistical databases with random sample queries. *ACM Transactions on Database Systems (TODS), 5*(3), 291-315.

Denning, D., & Lunt, T. (1987). A multilevel relational data model. *Proceedings of the IEEE Symposium on Research in Security and Privacy* (pp. 220-234).

Fu, L. (2005). Novel efficient classifiers based on data cube. *International Journal of Data Warehousing and Mining, 1*(3), 15-27.

Gibbons, P. B., & Matias, Y. (1998). New sampling-based summary statistics for improving approximate query answers. *Proceedings of the 1998 ACM SIGMOD International Conference on Management of Data (SIGMOD '98)* (pp. 331-342).

Gupta, H., & Mumick, I. (1999). Selection of views to materialize under a maintenance cost constraint. *Proceedings of the International Conference on Management of Data* (pp. 453-470).

Harinarayan, V., Rajaraman, A., & Ullman, J. D. (1996). Implementing data cubes efficiently. *SIGMOD Record, 25*, 205-216.

Ho, C.-T., Agrawal, R., Megiddo, N., & Srikant, R. (1997). Range queries in OLAP data cubes. *Proceedings of the 1997 ACM SIGMOD International Conference on Management of Data* (pp. 73-88).

Johnson, T., & Shasha, D. (1997). Some approaches to index design for cube forests. *Bulletin of the Technical Committee on Data Engineering, 20*(1), 27-35.

Labio, W., Quass, D., & Adelberg, B. (1997). Physical database design for data warehouses. *Proceedings of the International Conference on Database Engineering* (pp. 277-288).

Lehner, W., Sidle, R., Pirahesh, H., & Cochrane, R. W. (2000). Maintenance of cube automatic summary tables. *Proceedings of the 2000 ACM SIGMOD International Conference on Management of Data (SIGMOD '00)* (pp. 512-513).

Mumick, I. S., Quass, D., & Mumick, B. S. (1997). Maintenance of data cubes and summary tables in a warehouse. *Proceedings of the 1997 ACM SIGMOD International Conference on Management of Data (SIGMOD '97)* (pp. 100-111).

Xin, D., Han, J., Li, X., & Wah, B. W. (2003). Star-cubing: Computing iceberg cubes by top-down and bottom-up integration. *VLDB 2003: Proceedings of 29th International Conference on Very Large Data Bases* (pp. 476-487).

Yan, W. P., & Larson, P. (1995). Eager aggregation and lazy aggregation. *Proceedings of the Eighth International Conference on Very Large Databases* (pp. 345-357).

TERMS AND DEFINITIONS

Data Cube: A data cube is a multidimensional data model to view the data stored in a data warehouse.

Data Warehousing: Data warehousing is a technology to extract, clean, integrate, and load data into a central warehouse database; it uses front tools such as OLAP and data mining to query the system for decision support.

Dimension Hierarchy: This is the granularity level structure of an attribute (called a dimension) that tracks a measure. For example, in time, the dimension we may have is a year-month-day hierarchy.

Online Analytical Processing (OLAP): OLAP is mainly for analytical and informational purposes rather than operational purposes. Through a friendly interface and efficient query evaluation, OLAP can help enterprise managers make informative, strategic decisions.

Relational OLAP (ROLAP): ROLAP is a type of OLAP server that mainly uses relational technologies. Other types of OLAP servers include MOLAP (multidimensional OLAP) and HOLAP (hybrid OLAP).

Roll-Up and Drill-Down: These are common OLAP operations. Roll-up allows us to look at coarser, "big picture" data by dropping one or more dimensions or climbing up along the dimension hierarchies. A drill-down operation is the opposite of roll-up for more detailed data.

Statistics Trees: A tree data structure used to evaluate OLAP queries efficiently. The levels represent dimensions and the branching links represent attribute values of that dimensions. A star pointer represents ALL values. Dwarf trees and QC-trees are other examples of tree structures for evaluating OLAP queries.

Section V
Project Management and IT Evaluation

Information technology frequently succeeds or fails on the strength or weakness of project management. In the United States, the Bush administration's fiscal year (FY) 2007 budget increased emphasis on project management and hiring qualified project managers, backing with dollars the earlier recommendations of the Office of Management and Budget (OMB) and the Government Accountability Office for much more attention on project management. The push for project management professionalization was, in part, a reaction and solution to past information technology failures in enterprise resource planning systems and other IT arenas. In fact, in 2006, the OMB even authorized and encouraged agencies to shift personnel doing hitherto top-priority enterprise architecture systems work to work on project management instead.

Project management is often tied to enforcing the IT enterprise architecture, which reflects the IT policies at the national level and chief information officers at the state level. Illustrative was a 2005 study by the National Association of State and County Information Officers (NASCIO), which surveyed 34 state project management offices. The report endorsed a stricter approach to management of IT investments to assure investments conformed to state enterprise architectures. Implementation of such an approach, the report argued, rested on improving project management capacities through better training, certification programs, and support for career advancement by project managers. While federal and state levels have seen standardization and centralization under the banner of "enterprise architecture," there has always been an implementation gap in terms of specific IT projects at lower organizational levels. The belief reflected in the NASCIO report and in OMB emphasis on project management is that properly trained project managers can assure awareness of and compliance with mandates from central IT authorities.

Evaluation is coequal in importance with project management. Project management may be more critical for short-term IT success, but in the long run, the success of IT initiatives requires that they be proven to work in a cost-effective manner, hence the critical importance of evaluation. While evaluation is a broad topic, it is illustrated by the reliance on the Program Assessment and Rating Tool (PART) in the United States. PART was introduced in 2003 and incorporated in the federal enterprise architecture (FEA) framework for strategic planning mandated for all federal agencies. The government made submission to PART mandatory from 2005.

Congress, however, has found PART to be less than satisfactory as a tool of evaluation. For instance, in its FY 2007 consideration of e-government funding, the report of the House Appropriations Committee said that the Program Assessment Rating Tool was devoid of useful information. The committee expressed forcefully its displeasure with administrators who went through the motions of PART evaluation but who could not explain the rationale behind a program's funding level other by citing its PART score. The Bush administration was strongly encouraged by the committee to use a more meaningful system of evaluation to justify proposed program funding levels. The moral of this story is that on a worldwide basis, IT administrators can expect legislative decision makers to insist on meaningful evaluation and not to settle for symbolic evaluation mechanisms.

G. David Garson, September 2007

Chapter LVIII
Managing People and Information in Complex Organizations

Kalu N. Kalu
Auburn University Montgomery, USA

ABSTRACT

Information technology affects organizations and society itself as it redefines work content, reorganizes leadership styles and cultures, reshuffles power hierarchies, and spawns a series of both man-designed and spontaneous adaptations. Information technology oftentimes necessitates a new division of labor that creates policy problems and loss of accountability. Organizational leadership, especially in the public sector, urgently requires a theoretical as well as a practical revaluation to cope with the structural and functional changes within work and administrative organizations. This project seeks to elucidate three leadership models in the context of IT-induced changes in organizational forms and processes, namely, networked leadership, organic leadership, and gatekeeper leadership models.

INTRODUCTION

As we enter a period of dramatic change—a shift from the command-and-control organization to the information-based organization, the organization of knowledge specialists—Peter Drucker (1988, p. 53) cautions that "we can perceive only dimly, what this organization will look like; the job of actually building the information-based organization is still ahead of us—it is the managerial (administrative) challenge of the future." In the public sector, a crucial concern should be what kind of decision-making processes, administrative structure, and political responsiveness will be engendered by this transformation? To the extent that information technology decentralizes administrative power, it will have a transformational effect on the leadership role (Avison, Kendall, & Degross, 1993). The leadership function is a process that involves both managerial as well as decision-making roles, but also sets organizational goals as well as facilitates and clarifies the means for achieving them. While we have generally articulated these attributes within the classical or Weberian bureaucratic organization, how these will be manifested in the dynamic environment of IT-intensive administration is the purpose of this chapter.

In assessing the impact of the emerging technological orientation on contemporary administrative practice, we are thus confronted with a serious challenge regarding the epistemology and nature of understanding in orthodox leadership theory. However, what leaders of today and of the future would face is quite different from what used to be. They would be faced with the dual obligation of managing people and information, and at the same time securing the primary mission that informs the organization's existence. The irony is that while it is easier to manage people (by issuing orders and directives), technology, once set on its own routine, quickly takes on a life of its own and becomes more readily taken for granted. Once people are set into using it, its impersonal nature offers a means of escape from the traditional notion of an overbearing boss, but at the same time takes away from the boss a most crucial incentive of leadership (command and control). The argument is not that leaders have become moribund, but the basic fact is that much of the leadership function has become depersonalized to the extent that the traditional notions of leadership theorizing do not offer a complete portrait of what changes organizations and agencies would face in the future and how they can adapt to them.

BACKGROUND: RESTRUCTURING WORK ORGANIZATIONS

According to Laudon and Laudon (2003, p. 386, see Table 1), "New information systems can be powerful instruments for organizational change, enabling organizations to redesign their structure, scope, power relationships, work flows, products, and services." To the extent that information technology decentralizes administrative power, it will have a transformational effect on the leadership role. Organizational leaders occupy roles that are both personalized and institutionalized (Avison et al., 1993). Hence, "managers (leaders) will need to change the organization to fit the technology or to adjust both the organization and the technology to achieve an optimal fit" (Laudon & Laudon, p. 72). As technology transforms the administrative context of public administration, the principles, culture, and values that undergird its public purpose will face dramatic but uncertain changes: "While technology itself is neither enslaving nor liberating; it is the management of technology (and the information it carries) that is important" (Gabriel, Fineman, & Sims, 2000, p. 125). This is quite relevant in situations where the power of a leader to make daily decisions is isolated by a data processing system tucked away miles from the leader's desk, and also in situations where such mundane considerations and affection that require a personal presence and close proximity is removed. Suffice it then to say that the changing nature of the work environment (technology-driven division of labor) will determine how information is exchanged, how decisions are made, how new organizational forms emerge, and what type of leadership would fit into a particular organizational form.

Structure and Boundary Redefinition

One of the things that leaders do is to initiate structure, that is, exhibit a series of behaviors through which they define their roles and their subordinates' roles in achieving the organization's formal goals. While this process involves the person-in-situation, the new scenario that is advanced in this chapter supports a move toward a depersonalization of leadership roles due to the changing nature of work, and the tools needed to achieve key organizational objectives. Because of the peculiar characteristics of information technology, organizational structures and boundaries have become more fluid and dynamic. The unsettled nature of these boundaries and the frequency in which they can change has brought a greater level of uncertainty in the way tradi-

Table 1. How information technology can transform organizations (Adapted from Laudon & Laudon, 2004, p. 386)

Information Technology	Organizational Change	Leadership Model*
Global Networks Enterprise Networks	International division of labor: The operations of a firm and its business processes are no longer determined by location; the global reach of firms is extended. The cost of global coordination declines and transaction costs decline.	Networked Leadership
Distributed Computing Portable Computing	Collaborative work and teamwork: The organization of work can now be coordinated across divisional boundaries. The cost of management declines. Multiple tasks can be worked on simultaneously from different locations.	Networked Leadership
Multimedia and Graphic Interfaces	Empowerment: Individuals and work groups now have the information and knowledge to act. Business processes can be streamlined. Management costs decline. Hierarchy and centralization decline.	Organic Leadership
	Virtual organizations: Work is no longer tied to physical location. Knowledge and information can be delivered anywhere they are needed, anytime. Work becomes portable.	Networked Leadership
	Accessibility: Everyone in the organization—even senior executives—can access information and knowledge. Organizational costs decline as workflows move from paper to digital images, documents, and voice. Complex knowledge objects can be stored and represented as objects containing graphics, audio, video, or text.	Gatekeeper Leadership (Management and Monitoring of Information and Access)

**Last column added by author*

tional organizational roles relate to each other. Furthermore, the speed with which generic ideas are replaced by new information means that as functional relationships change within organizations, so will the tools needed to perform new and more sophisticated roles.

To the extent that organizational leaders and their subordinates are affected, they would need to learn new ways of thinking, coordinating, and most importantly, organizing. They will need to embrace learning organizations, but to do that they must first unlearn the old habit of doing things: "Organizing and learning will absorb increasing amounts of resources, time and effort, as information proliferates and as times and distances shrink" (Gabriel et al., 2000, pp. 264-265). Unlearning is a condition for learning: unlearning theories, unlearning habits, and unlearning lazy shortcuts that stand in the way of new understanding. It takes courage and requires the ability to drag ourselves out of our comfort zone, the zone we create with the help of our existing stock of concepts, ideas, and theories" (Gabriel et. al, 2000, p. 265). This is the paradox that is often concealed by political cliché: Old learning and old ideas can act as a hindrance to new learning and new ideas (Gabriel et al.), but in the unfolding IT-driven work environment, the choices are limited.

Hierarchy and Systems of Accountability

For the fact that "structure and hierarchy have no fixed form, they cannot function as predetermined modes of control" (Morgan, 1997, p. 266). Leaders of today have to rely less on hierarchical (vertical) power as opposed to distributed or horizontal power within or across organizational units or subunits. Nonetheless, the interactive nature of functional roles means that "leaders need to know what is important and meaningful to the people they work with, and somehow shape their beliefs or meanings in a direction that makes organizational sense" (Gabriel et al., 2000, p. 139). However, when such functional roles are distances apart but have become integral elements of an IT-driven operational routine, systems of accountability become decentralized as executive authority yields to what Terry (2003, p. 94) calls "competence authority." Thus, the leader's role in interpretation and making sense of critical organizational matters is neutralized: "As the image of the omnipotent 'boss' fades, we sometimes have to search harder in the organization for the leader" (Gabriel et al., p. 134). The distributed nature of the leadership function thus cuts across organizational units whose collective cooperation would be needed to achieve the organization's mission in a purposeful and goal-oriented direction.

BEYOND ORTHODOXY: REDEFINING THE LEADERSHIP ROLE

The fast pace in which technology has invaded the organizational work place has rendered administrative practice as a system in flux. The conventional notion of leadership regarding who decides, directs, or authorizes has become ambiguous but tentative at best. Traditional axioms, embedded cultures, and taken-for-granted everyday routines must confront the emerging realities of a new leadership ethos: "Generic management problems such as overcoming resistance to change, motivating cooperative behavior, or coordinating and integrating distinct horizontal activities" (Lynn, 1998, p. 235) will invoke new administrative learning and structural adaptation. Hence, in such organizational contexts where information technology necessitates a decentralization of administrative authority, and to the extent that they are provided with more comprehensive, immediate, and relevant data relating to their tasks, we can witness "an increase in the power of those at the periphery or local level, thereby facilitating self, rather than central control" (Kovac-Boisvert & Kouzmin, 1994). As Morgan (1997, pp. 266-267) points out, "transformational change ultimately involves the creation of new 'contexts,' in which new patterns have to emerge, but cannot be imposed." Unfortunately, "complex IT-driven tasks, with a high degree of uncertainty and variability, often confront an administrative experience which has not yet developed a formal model of the problem of departmentalism which takes into account the contingent nature of new activities" (Davis & Lawrence, 1977; Kingdon, 1973; Kouzmin, 1979; March & Simon, 1958; Thompson, 1967). Hence as "technology evolves through periods of incremental improvement or routinization, initial contingencies decrease and the order-of-magnitude of maximum achievable performance continues to rise until the next discontinuity" (Kouzmin & Korac-Boisvert, 1995, p. 107). How emerging discontinuities are managed and who does the managing have become critical questions in the unfolding administrative environment. Three leadership models are possible in the emerging organizational scenario: networked leadership, organic leadership, and gatekeeper leadership.

Networked Leadership

The networked leadership scenario would reflect organizational systems that are linked only by technology and exchange of information with very minimal individual contact; it is similar to the hub-and-spoke network used by the airline industry except that in this case, we are dealing with information, not physical or moveable objects. Information and data are pulled into a central hub for programmed decision-making, dissemination, coordination, and feedback. It draws upon integrated global networks, enterprise and mobile portal IT systems that can be linked to a central hub through the Internet or Ethernet protocols, and videoconferencing and other modes of secured work interface.

Organic Leadership

According to Morgan (1997, p. 66), "By exploring the parallels between organisms and organizations in terms of organic functioning, relations with the environment, relations between species and the wider ecology, it has been possible to produce different theories and explanations that have very practical implications for organization and management." Organic leadership reflects leaderless organizations in which decision making will be based on situational or contingency factors and a critical level of synchronization between and across various array of multiple data collection points (organizational units and subunits). In place of a "hierarchical leader specifying standards and ways of achieving goals (task-oriented behaviors), the team might set its own standards and substitute those for the leaders" (Schermerhorn, Hunt, & Osborn, 2000, p. 297), just as you would have in traditional matrix and other team-based forms of organizations. The nature of work would be one of coordination for mutual deliberation, or trial and error to deal with uncertainty, rather than one of discretionary or independent decision making. In fact, the demand of the work itself neutralizes and limits any attempt at unilateral or arbitrary action to a minimum. As the characteristics of individual workers, their jobs, and their organizations change and adapt over time, a new leadership model would be needed to accommodate both an increasing level of uncertainty and technological and information diversity in the work environment. "The management of organizations can, nonetheless, be improved through systematic attention to the needs that must be satisfied if the organization is to survive," says Morgan (p. 67), and as the needs change, so does the leadership framework that drives it.

The Gatekeeper Leadership

The gatekeeper (monitoring) leadership is situated at the boundary between the organization and its environment. It is a bridge between the internal processes within the organization and the environmental turbulence and uncertainty if faces from the outside. The critical role of the leader is to "continually gather information, reduce equivocality, provide structure, and overcome barriers" (Northouse, 2004, p. 208). The primary obligation, thus, is to network with outside organizations or agencies, secure information from internal and external sources, and structure it into a useable form so that plans can be developed and acted upon. The gatekeeper also plays a mediating role between internal organizational processes and the regulatory requirements of the external environment, and develops contingencies to deal with environmental complexity and uncertainty. Organizational leaders are equally affected by change. To the extent that many of the internal processes have essentially become rationalized and self-regulatory, the gatekeeper's role is more focused on external factors. During critical incidents such as (technology-driven) cutbacks and retrenchment, the emotional self-being and integrity of leader-follower relationships are decisive factors in organizational adaptation; hence, leaders must be capable of balancing organizational demands for stability and adaptation to external influences" (Diamond, 1992, pp. 271-272).

Table 2. Modifying the substitute for leadership framework: Emerging constructs in contemporary IT-driven contexts

Characteristics of Individuals	**Impact on Leadership**	**Leadership Models**
Experience, ability, training	Task-oriented leadership (S)	Networked
Professional orientation	Task-oriented/supportive leadership (S)	Gatekeeper
Indifference toward rewards	Motivation-oriented/supportive leadership (S)	Organic
Characteristics of Job		
Highly structured/routine	Task-oriented leadership (S)	Networked
Intrinsically satisfying	Supportive leadership (S)	Organic
Technology-driven work	Task-oriented/supportive leadership (N)	Gatekeeper
Knowledge-intensive work	Supportive leadership (S)	Gatekeeper/Networked
Characteristics of Organization		
Cohesive work group	Task-oriented/supportive leadership (S)	Organic
Low leader position	Task-oriented/supportive leadership (N)	Networked
Leader physically separated	Task-oriented/supportive leadership (N)	Networked/Organic

S = Substitute for Leadership *N = Neutralizer of Leadership*

**Last Column added by author*

ORGANIZATIONAL IMPLICATIONS OF NEW LEADERSHIP MODELS

To capture, or at best, predict, the three leadership constructs, I modify the Substitute for Leadership framework (Schermerhorn et al., 2000, p. 297; see also Keer & Jermier, 1998; Van Wart, 2005) as a way of elaborating the multiple ways that information technology can affect both structure and function in the changing work environment (Table 2). What is indicated here is that the conventional emphasis on traditional models of leadership may not be adequate to capture the various dyadic or horizontal relationships that occur in contemporary organizational work environments.

Information technology and organizations exert a reciprocal influence on one another. "While the interaction between them is, oftentimes, very complex; it is influenced by a great many mediating factors, including the organization's structure, standard operating procedures, politics, culture, surrounding environment, and management decisions" (Laudon & Laudon, 2003, p. 73). The functional changes in work processes will necessitate equivalent changes in the structure of organizations. As traditional organizational roles change, the kinds of leadership models needed to coordinate these roles will also, out of necessity, need to change (Table 3).

FUTURE TRENDS

For the simple fact that the increasing application of information technology in the private and public sectors continues to challenge traditional methods of organization and service delivery, governmental response would be reflected in an increasing use of regulations, laws, and institutions as a way of consolidating governance

Table 3. Organizational characteristics of emerging leadership constructs

	Emerging Leadership Models		
Organizational Characteristics	**Networked**	**Organic**	**Gatekeeper**
Hierarchy	Horizontal	Amorphous	Conical
Formalization	Integrative	Spontaneous	Flexible/Routine
Decentralization	High	Contingent	Discretionary
Span of Control	Wide	Transitory	Narrow
Organization Culture	Dynamic	Unstable	Durable
Communication	Reciprocal	Flexible Channels	Scripted
Decision Making	Atomized	Mutual Adjustment	Scripted
Accountability	Wide	Wide	Narrow
Environmental Scanning	Insular	Adaptive	Boundary Spanner
Strategic Planning	Scripted	Contingent	Scripted
Crisis Management	Programmed	Nonprogrammed	Programmed
OSHA	Low Uncertainty	High Uncertainty	Routine
Government Regulation	Standard	Adaptive	Standard
EEOC/Equal Opportunity	Work Factors	Environmental Factors	Organizational Factors
Workforce Diversity	Skills Driven	Politics Driven	Strategic Factors
Planning	Technology Driven	Human/Technology	Organizational Factors
Organizing	Functional Linkages	Indeterminate	SOP
Directing	Self-Directing	Adaptive	Scripted
Staffing	Skills Driven	Skills/Environmental Factors	Organizational Factors
Coordinating	Unit Autonomy	Coordination	SOP
Reporting	Centralized SOP	Contingent	SOP
Budgeting	Collective Action	Routine/Innovative	SOP

efforts within the scope of state authority. In the private sector, "organizational strategies may involve influencing the policy and regulations that shape how emergent global networks operate, the hardware that comprises the network, the content that flows through the network, or the software that mediates between the hardware and content" (Baylis & Smith, 2005,p. 626). Experts and technicians in information technology will continue to play central roles in setting the parameters for organizational action as well as regulatory policy; hence they will become enormously powerful in public- and private-sector decision making.

At the same time, the preponderance of virtual organizations and the mediating distance between leaders and subordinates would mean that authority and control would become increasingly dispersed as most organizational subunits seek to become quasi-autonomous decision-making operational turfs, none the less by default. Leadership activities would become more skills and task- oriented with a primary focus on technologically- linked teams that work independently but at the same time pool their resources together toward achieving the organizational mission: "The benefits of teams include the ability to independently select appropriate skills for a particular project, the creativity and synergy they engender, their flexibility of structure, and the fact that most of them can be easily disbanded" (Van Wart, 2005, p. 216) or reconfigured according to the demands and contingencies of the moment. Hence, the trend would reflect a gradual disappearance of vertical management and a movement toward a more decentralized horizontal managerial style. The ability of the emergent leadership model to motivate employees would be based more on instrumental rewards as opposed to the psychologically-based approaches to employee motivation.

CONCLUSION

In essence, the evolving nature of organizations will determine how information is exchanged, how decisions are made, and how new organizational forms emerge. The basis of administrative practice, especially in the public sector, would become increasingly value-neutral and impersonal; which invariably, would pose a serious challenge to the effort of the human-relations school to integrate both the formal and informal aspects of organizational work. Barrett and Greene (2001, p. 65) state, "In the complex world of IT, good planning is a necessity at all levels—to provide an entity-wide vision, to coordinate disparate efforts among agencies, to minimize technological redundancy, and to prioritize decision-making in a world in which spending possibilities are endless and resources are limited."

In the new IT-driven work environment, the key to successful strategic planning would include updating plans regularly, widening the sources of policy input, linking strategic plans to the exigencies of the budgetary process, and integrating IT planning into the wider sociopolitical framework of citizenship and value-added governance. As tempting as it may be, and as versatile as it seems to be, particularly for the administrative process in the public sector, technology remains a two-edged sword. Not only does it have major consequences regarding how leaders should lead, but it portends to transform the very essence of leadership both in theory and in practice. As the structure and boundaries of organizational work become more fluid and unsettled, the leadership model needed to properly articulate agency mission and the public interest would, invariably, become more innovative and adaptive. Leadership activities would revolve more around organizing as opposed to directing. This work, therefore, offers a pointer in a direction that seeks adaptation but at the same time opens up great possibilities for new learning and research that focuses on novel approaches to leadership theorizing, emergent organizational forms, and the central role of information technology in changing the traditional structure and norms of organizational action.

FUTURE RESEARCH DIRECTIONS

For the simple fact that organizations and societies at large involve people engaged in various activities either as individuals or as groups, the cumulative effect of these activities would have enormous consequences for the evolving social organization. As information technology permeates all aspects of social endeavor beyond the typical organization, it will seek to transform society itself and how people respond to the demands it imposes on members. There is a need to study how electronic voting affects voter participation across demographic, racial, and socioeconomic groups, and how e-filing of tax returns increases the number of those who file their tax returns on time as well as lead to a decline in unclaimed tax refunds. The Department of Treasury currently has about \$2 to \$3 billion worth of unclaimed tax revenues. In a recent research by Christopher J. Collins and Ken G. Smith (2006) titled *Knowledge Exchange and Combination: The Role of Human Resource Practices in the Performance of High-Technology Firms*, a field-study of 136 technology companies showed that commitment-based human resource practices were positively related to the organizational social climates of trust, cooperation, and shared codes and languages (organizational culture). The future will see more research focused specifically on the implication of information technology on the durability and effectiveness of the informal organization as a constructive element in organizational learning, productivity, and overall effectiveness.

In another study, Srivastava, Bartol, and Locke (2006) surveyed management teams in 102 hotel properties in the United Sates to examine the intervening roles of knowledge sharing and team efficacy in the relationship between empowering leadership and team performance. They found that empowering leadership was positively related to both knowledge sharing and team efficacy, which, in turn, were both positively related to performance. To the extent that information technology helps to advance knowledge sharing between leaders and subordinates in organizations, future research should focus on how this nuanced power play transcends eventual performance. Of equal relevance is a study that focuses on how increased application of information technology could induce work-related stress or what is called "technostress," which results from an inability to adapt to the introduction and operation of new technology (see Nykodym, Miners, Simonetti, & Christen, 1989). The frequency with which new technology is utilized in the work environment means that both leaders and subordinates will need to develop new skills needed to deal with the technical requirements of traditional job roles. Furthermore, the short time span needed to complete what may be a very intensive training and development program might create more stress for employees already reluctant to learn new ways of performing their jobs. Future research should focus on how these interconnections could affect employee motivation, performance, and potential turnover.

REFERENCES

Avison, D., Kendall, J. E., & Degross, J. I. (Eds.). (1993). *Human, organizational and social dimensions of information systems development.* Proceedings of the IFIP WG 8:2, Working Group on Information Systems Development, Amsterdam, the Netherlands.

Barrett, K., & Greene, R. (2001). *Powering up: How public managers can take control of information technology.* Washington, DC: CQ Press.

Baylis, J., & Smith, S. (2005). *The globalization of world politics: An introduction to international relations* (3rd ed.). New York: Oxford University Press.

Collins, C. J., & Smith, K. G. (2006). Knowledge exchange and combination: The role of human resource practices in the performance of high-technology firms. *Academy of Management Journal, 49*(3), 544-560.

Davis, S. M., & Lawrence, P. R. (1977). *Matrix.* London: Addison-Wesley.

Diamond, M. (1992). Hobbessian and Rousseauian identities: The psychodynamics of organizational leadership and change. *Administration & Society, 24*(3), 267-289.

Drucker, P. F. (1988). The coming of the new organization. *Harvard Business Review, 66*(1), 45-53.

Gabriel, Y., Fineman, S., & Sims, D. (2000). *Organizing and organizations* (2nd ed.). Thousand Oaks, CA: Sage.

Keer, S., & Jermier, J. (1998). Substitutes for leadership: Their meaning and measurement. *Organizational Behavior and Human Performance, 22*, 375-403.

Kingdon, D. R. (1973). *Matrix organization: Managing information technologies.* London: Tavistock.

Kouzmin, A., & Korac-Boisvert, N. (1995). Soft-core disasters: A multiple realities crisis perspective on IT development failures. In H. Hill & H. Klages (Eds.), *Trends in public sector renewal: Recent developments and concepts of awarding excellence* (pp. 89-132). Berlin, Germany: Peter Lang.

Kovac-Boisvert, N., & Kouzmin, A. (1994). The darkside of info-age social networks in public organizations and creeping crisis. *Administrative Theory and Praxis, 16*(1), 57-82.

Laudon, K. C., & Laudon, J. P. (2003). *Essentials of management information systems: Managing the digital firm* (5th ed.). Upper Saddle River, NJ: Prentice Hall.

Lynn, L. E. (1998). The new public management: How to transform a theme into a legacy. *Public Administration Review, 58*(3), 231-237.

March, J. C., & Simon, H. A. (1958). *Organizations.* New York: John Wiley.

Morgan, G. (1997). *Images of organization.* Thousand Oaks, CA: Sage.

Northouse, P. G. (2004). *Leadership: Theory and practice* (3rd ed.). Thousand Oaks, CA: Sage.

Nykodym, N., Miners, I., Simonetti, J. L., & Christen, J. C. (1989). Computerphobia. *Personnel Journal, 68*, 54-56.

Schermerhorn, J. R., Jr., Hunt, J. G., & Osborn, R. N. (2000). *Organizational behavior* (7th ed.). New York: John Wiley & Sons.

Srivastava, A., Bartol, K. M., & Locke, E. A. (2006). Empowering leadership in management teams: Effects on knowledge sharing, efficacy, and performance. *Academy of Management Journal, 49*(6), 1239-1251.

Terry, L. D. (2003). *Leadership of public bureaucracies: The administrator as conservator* (2nd ed.). Armonk, NY: M. E. Sharpe.

Thompson, J. D. (1967). *Organizations in action: Social science vase of administrative theory.* New York: McGraw-Hill.

Van Wart, M. (2005). *Dynamics of leadership in public service: Theory and practice.* Armonk, NY: M. E. Sharpe.

FURTHER READING

Agervold, M. (1987). New technology in the office: Attitudes and consequences. *Work and Stress, 1*(2), 143-153.

Bakos, J., Yannis, & Treacy, M. E. (1986). Information technology and corporate strategy: A research perspective. *MIS Quarterly.*

Bartol, K. M., & Srivastava, A. (2002). Encouraging knowledge sharing: The role of organizational reward systems. *Journal of Leadership and Organizational Studies, 9*(1), 64-77.

Castells, M. (2002). *The Internet galaxy: Reflections on the Internet, business and society.* London: Oxford University Press.

Chesbrough, H. (2001). Assembling the elephant: A review of empirical studies on the impact of technological change upon incumbent firms. *Comparative Studies of Technological Evolution, 7*, 1-36.

Danzinger, J. N., & Kraemer, K. L. (1986). *People and computers.* New York: Columbia University Press.

DiMaggio, P., Hargitai, E., Neuman, W. R., & Robinson, J. P. (2001). The Internet's effect on society. *Annual Review of Sociology, 27*, 306-327.

Foxall, G. R. (1988). Marketing new technology: Markets, hierarchies, and user-initiated innovation. *Managerial and decision economics, 9*(3), 237-250.

Fountain, J. (2001). *Building the virtual state: Information technology and institutional change.* Washington, DC: Brookings Institution.

Gold, A., Malhotra, A., & Segars, A. H. (2001). Knowledge management: An organizational capabilities perspective. *Journal of Management Information Systems, 18*(1), 185-214.

Graen, G. B., Hui, C., & Taylor, E. A. (2004). A new approach to team leadership: Upward, downward and horizontal differentiation. In G. B. Graen (Ed.), *New frontiers of leadership, LMX leadership: The Series* (Vol. 2, pp. 33-66). Greenwich, CT: Information Age Publishing.

Gronlund, A. (2000). *Managing electronic services: A public sector perspective.* Berlin, Germany: Springer-Verlag.

Haddad, C. J. (2001). *Managing technological change: A strategic partnership approach.* Thousand Oaks, CA: Sage.

Huber, G. P. (1990). A theory of the effects of advanced information technologies on organizational design, intelligence, and decision making. *Academy of Management Review, 15*(1), 47-71.

Kalu, K. N. (2001). Leadership and discretionary decision-making in a technocratic administration: Confronting a new praxis. *Administrative Theory & Praxis, 23*(4), 311-336.

Keen, P. G. W. (1991). *Shaping the future: Business design through information technology.* Cambridge, MA: Harvard Business School Press.

Kendall, K. E. (Ed.). (1999). *Emerging information technologies: Improving decisions, cooperation, and infrastructure.* Thousand oaks, CA: Sage.

Kouzmin, A., & Korac-Kakabadse, N. (2000). Mapping institutional impacts of lean communication in lean agencies. *Administration & Society, 32*, 29-69.

Landsbergen, D., & Wolken, G. (2001). Realizing the promise: Government information systems and the fourth generation of information technology. *Public Administration Review, 61*(2), 206-220.

Markus, M. L. (1983). Power, politics, and MIS implementation. *Communications of the ACM, 26*(6), 430-444.

Markus. M. L., & Robey, D. (1988). Information technology and organizational change: Causal structure in theory and research. *Management Science, 34*(5), 583-598.

Orlikowski, W. J., & Bailey, S. R. (2001). Technology and institutions: What can research on information technology and research on organizations learn from each other? *MIS Quarterly, 25*(2).

Orlikowski, W. J., & Baroudi, J. J. (1991). Studying information technology in organizations: Research approaches and assumptions. *Information Systems Research, 2*(1), 1-28.

Perry, J. L., & Kraemer, K. L. (1999). The implications of changing technology. In F. S. Lane (Ed.), *Current issues in public administration* (6th ed., pp. 182-200). New York: Bedford/St. Martin.

Pinsonneault, A., & Kraemer, K. L. (1989). The impact of technological support on groups: An assessment of the empirical research. *Decision Support Systems, 5*(2), 197-216.

Powell, W. W., & Snellman, K. (2004). The knowledge economy. *Annual Review of Sociology, 30*, 199-220.

Pradhan, J. (2002). Information technology in Nepal: What role for the government? *The Electronic Journal of Information Systems in Developing Countries, 8*(3), 1-11.

Seo, D., & La Paz, A. I. (in press). Exploring the dark side of information systems in achieving organizational agility. *Communications of the ACM.*

Taylor, J. R., Groleau, C., Heaton, L., & Van Every, E. (2000). *The computerization of work: A communication perspective.* Thousand Oaks, CA: Sage.

Tripathi, M. (2006). Transforming India into a knowledge economy through information communications technologies: Current developments.

The International Information and Library Review, 38, 139-146.

Wilheim, A. (2000). *Democracy in the digital age: Challenges to political life in cyberspace.* New York: Routledge.

Zuboff, S. (1988). *In the age of the smart machine: The future of work and power.* New York: Basic Books.

TERMS AND DEFINITIONS

Epistemology: Epistemology is the nature and scope of knowledge and understanding relative to a specific idea, field, or concept.

Gatekeeper Leadership: The gatekeeper plays a mediating or moderating role between internal organizational processes and their adaptation to external turbulence and complexity that could affect organizational effectiveness and success.

Information-Based Organization: This is an organization that relies on a progressively intensive application of information technology in the functional relationships between and within organizational units.

Leadership: Leadership is a formal organizational activity involving individual managerial and decision-making functions, employee motivation, and incentives directed at achieving organizational goals and missions.

Learning Organization: Learning is a process by which an organization adapts to new challenges in its operational environments. Members do this first by unlearning or "unfreezing" old habits, and second by accepting new methods and innovations, and incorporating these into a new process of learning (refreezing) so as to survive in an increasingly uncertain and complex environment.

Networked Leadership: This is based on organizational systems in which the operational units and control mechanisms are extensively linked and facilitated by the exchange of information through both centralized and dispersed technology-based hubs.

Neutralizer of Leadership: Neutralizers constrain a formal leader's ability to behave in certain ways, and in most cases can nullify the immediate effect of his or her actions or directives. Examples could be situations where workers have alternate resources, a leader lacks the power to impose sanctions and/or rewards, subordinates have operational autonomy, or where subordinates are distant from the leader.

Organic Leadership: This model is drawn from a biological analogy depicting contingent leadership scenarios that would be needed to accommodate an increasing level of uncertainty, nonroutine functional roles, and technological and information diversity in the new work environment.

Substitute for Leadership: The substitute-for-leadership theory posits that sometimes hierarchical authority makes no difference in organizational relationships because leaders have come to rely extensively on the expert knowledge of subordinates below them.

Chapter LIX
Human-Factors Design for Public Information Technology

Vincent E. Lasnik
Independent Knowledge Architect, USA

INTRODUCTION

This chapter examines the realm of human-factors design for public information technology in the rapidly evolving postmodern knowledge age of the 21st century, with special focus on how new research and development into human cognition, perception, and performance capabilities is changing the design function for IT systems and products. Many "one size fits all" IT designs are neither adaptive nor adaptable—promulgating a top-down technological imperialism penetrating every aspect of their use. The communication, collaboration, and interaction infrastructure of IT organizations thus remains acutely challenged with enduring problems of usability, learnability, accessibility, and adaptability. As the function and form of products undergo increasingly rigorous scrutiny, one important design goal is emerging as a paramount priority: improving the usability of products, tools, and systems for all stakeholders across the enterprise. It is therefore important to briefly describe emerging human-factor design knowledge and practices applicable to organizations that invent, incubate, innovate, prototype, and drive the creation and application of public IT. The findings here suggest the most effective strategies to manage and augment user-centered design (UCD) endeavors across a wide array of public IT products and organizations.

BACKGROUND

In the context of 21st century industrial and information product design theory and practice, user-centered design is an iterative, systematic process that focuses on constructing a user experience and responsive environment with physical and virtual affordances that are identifiable, manipulable, controllable, customizable, and adaptable from the intrinsic, subjective perspective of the conceptual model of the user (Mayhew, 1999; Moggridge, 2006; Preece, Rogers, & Sharp, 2002). This means carefully and systematically taking into account both (a) the user's subjective metamodel of his or her own experiences, actions, and information-seeking cognitive and perceptual processes, and (b) the designer's ostensibly more objective model of the user and alignment mapping to the physical affordances of the product or tool environment. Thus, in UCD, the conceptual model of the user becomes the superordinate principle guiding the IT design process for software user interfaces (UIs; Saffer, 2006; Stone, Jarrett, Woodroffe, & Minocha, 2005).

Usage-centered design is different: It focuses primarily on (a) the empirical (i.e., observable and measurable) goal-based behavior and task-driven performance requirements of users' activities, procedures, and processes, and (b) the corresponding information architecture required to optimize the effectiveness of the user-system dynamics to efficiently accomplish those functional goals (Constantine & Lockwood, 1999, 2003; Morrogh, 2003). By integrating human-factors engineering systems approaches, it may be possible to optimize the beneficent design quality of products and services from the perspective of the user's operational and instrumental task-oriented needs (Constantine, 2001; Constantine & Lockwood, 2002; Kuniavsky, 2003; Wickens, Lee, Liu, & Becker, 2004).

From the technology management perspective of the new science of user-experience design (UXD), intensive, hands-on project management is vital to the training of knowledge-age designers (Pinto, 2006). The development team needs an original design philosophy that is pliant, change embracing, and facilitates collaborative techniques, models, and skills that respect the proclivities of individual and group human behaviors (Henderson, 2000; Henderson & Harris, 2000; Kumar, 2006). To achieve this new paradigm of organizational dynamics, designers must become leaders in promoting and advocating approaches such as moving away from common functional units and rigid roles (i.e., using the agrarian-age container metaphor of silos) to cross-disciplinary, synergistic, intra-organizational open channels. According to Hughes (2003), running an organization as a collection of separate silos "can cause duplicate efforts, discourage cooperation, and stifle cross-pollination of ideas" (p. 9). For a channel model to work, however, the IT design team must first embrace user-centered human-factor methods and the collateral reorganization of the IT design process and product.

USER-CENTERED IT DESIGN PROCESSES IN HUMAN-FACTORS ENGINEERING

The cross-disciplinary field of human factors recognizes that every new IT media product is ostensibly a dynamic form of person-person and person-technology interaction that expands our communication capabilities by reframing what we know and how we act (i.e., human knowledge and behavior). The underlying three core subdomains—information design, interactivity design, and media design—each need to become integrated within a unifying architecture derived from an object-oriented, modular infrastructure organized within an evolving taxonomy of digital affordances.

Human-factors engineering recognizes (a) the holistic, ecological, and cross-disciplinary nature of human-technology system design, (b) the sociocultural, economic, and geopolitical importance of information utilization and knowledge generation, and (c) the dynamically hybrid, human-centered, user-centered, and usage-centered nature of the product form factor and interface design (Burns & Hajdukiewicz, 2004; Hofstede, 1991). Human-factor approaches strive to deeply integrate existing multidisciplinary domains including (a) systems theory, change management, and computer and information science, (b) cognitive informatics, learning, and performance, (c) philosophy, law, and ethics, (d) human physiological psychology, cognition, and perception, and (e) usability testing, industrial design, and ergonomics (Lehto & Buck, 2007; Rubin, 1994; Salvendy, 2006; Stanton, & Young, 1999; Ware, 2004; Wickens et al., 2004).

In addition, the optimal human-factors design process entails an adaptive, applied, creative, and highly sophisticated cross-disciplinary problem-solving repertoire requiring (a) a basic literacy with effective, parsimonious information design, interactivity design, and media design principles, (b) competent technology and human communication skills, (c) core knowledge of the case-based research literature regarding human information processing, behavior psychology, user-object interaction and manipulation, and usability and accessibility, and (d) a basic appreciation of aesthetics and ergonomics (Guastello, 2006; Stanton, Hedge, Brookhuis, Salas, & Hendrick, 2004; UsabilityNet, 2006).

In 1997, a working group of architects, product designers, engineers, and environmental designers (Connell et al., 1997) identified seven high-level percepts to evaluate existing product designs, refocus the future design process of new products, and educate both designers and consumers about the characteristics of more usable products and environments. They are particularly appropriate for application to all public information technology. These "Principles of Universal Design" are equitable use, flexible use, simple and intuitive use, perceptible information, tolerance for error, low physical error, and size and space for approach and use. Mapping these guidelines to our three-way human-factor design triarchy, Principles 1 and 2 are related to interaction design, 3 and 4 are associated with optimal information design, and 5, 6, and 7 are related to ergonomics, physical product form factors, and effective media design. However, a reasonable caveat is that not every principle may be relevant to every set of IT requirements, content domains, and enterprises. Each component (adapted and modified from Connell et al.) is briefly described below.

1. **Principle 1: Equitable use:** The design is useful and marketable to people with diverse abilities and capabilities.
2. **Principle 2: Flexible use:** The design accommodates a wide range of individual preferences and abilities.
3. **Principle 3: Simple and intuitive use:** The design is easy to understand and learn regardless of the user's experience, knowledge, language literacy, technical skills, or current concentration level
4. **Principle 4: Perceptible information:** The design effectively communicates necessary and sufficient information, regardless of ambient conditions or the user's cognitive and perceptual abilities.
5. **Principle 5: Tolerance for error:** The design is functionally robust and minimizes the occurrence of problems, errors, or the adverse consequences of any accidental or unintended actions.
6. **Principle 6: Low physical effort:** The design can be used efficiently and comfortably and with a minimum of physical, sensory, or cognitive fatigue.
7. **Principle 7: Size and space for approach and use:** The design affords appropriate size and space for approach, manipulation, and reach regardless of the user's physical (body/hand) size, posture, or mobility.

The International Standards Organization (ISO 13407, 1999) has outlined an iterative high-level process (*Human-Centered Design Processes for Interactive System Teams*) for effective human-factor design protocols. According to this widely adopted global ISO model, the four user-centered design activities are to (a) understand and specify the context of use, (b) specify the user and organizational requirements, (c) produce design solutions, and (d) evaluate designs against the requirements specified in Activity b.

However, it is a formidable challenge to fully integrate human factors within the IT organization. This can only be achieved when (a) every phase of the product life cycle follows the principles of professional user-centered design theory and praxis, (b) when the public IT development team is cross-trained with the proper usability skills, tools, and knowledge, (c) when the IT design team is thoroughly supported by the commitment from upper management and a dedicated human-centered infrastructure, and (d) when awareness of this culture and ethos are properly disseminated within and throughout the organization (Dumas & Redish, 1999; Jokela, 2002; Keates, 2007; Knutson, 2001; Project Management Institute, 2004; Rubin, 1994; Skelton & Thamhain, 2005; Thamhain, 2005; UsabilityNet, 2006; Venturi & Troost, 2004).

While examining ways to improve the signage, sense-of-space, self-directed way-finding, and user-centered design of interactive public information environments like museums, science centers, and shopping malls, C. G. Screven (1999) synthesized the insightful core metric of design efficiency: "the average time it takes viewers to find and process message-related information" (p. 147). Efficient IT designs facilitate users' abilities to process and absorb new information. High design efficiency is thus characterized by a high ratio of needed and salient information to unneeded and superfluous information to ease working memory load and reduce affective stressors (i.e., engineers commonly use the adage "less noise, more signal"). Intelligently designing human-centered, goal-directed IT products reduces the aversive stimuli associated with the disconnects of failure, confusion, avoidance, task time and effort, media overload, product complexity, and the frustrating emotions engendered by inefficient product design solutions (Burns, & Hajdukiewicz, 2004; Moggridge, 2006).

Specifically, efficient designs (a) conserve both mental and physical effort (i.e., working memory and time on task) needed by users to find, access, retrieve, quickly understand, and respond to messages and content, (b) reduce fatigue and maturation effects by providing intuitive, accessible affordances with low cognitive loads to quickly engage and involve the user in self-directed behavior that enhances their interactivity with the tool or system information, and (c) generally improve all aspects of the information designs themselves by systematically employing larger, easy-to-read fonts; less dense and less difficult textual content (e.g., using familiar, jargon-free vocabulary); good contrast and consistent layouts (i.e., with good chunking, white space, use of colors, clear mnemonic cues, and reduced visual clutter); and precise, unambiguous headings and labels (Mijksenaar, 1997; Tidwell, 2005).

In their insightful book *Designing from Both Sides of the Screen: Don't Impose—Respect Mental Effort*, Isaacs and Walendowski (2001) analyzed screen-based user interfaces. Designers should leave their product users as much mental energy as possible so each user can focus on his or her task goal and forget about the transparent technology entirely. Isaacs and Walendowski noted that every user choice, in fact, every click, increases working memory load, and that each additional screen object (i.e., button, field, hyperlink, media element) increments functional over-choice and visual complexity. There is also an emotional, affective technostress factor that burdens users caught in overly complex interfaces. This dilemma is particularly apparent in public information technology applications that depend upon sophisticated, interactive synchronous and asynchronous networked systems and multi-user tools. User-experience designers need to be sharply focused on developing devices and systems that reduce (not increase) working memory loads, eliminate unnecessary features, and buttress the confidence and competence of basic user task behavior (Cooper & Reimann, 2003; Hackos & Redish, 1998).

Collectively, human-factor design guidelines recommend that IT user interfaces (a) reduce way-finding memory by using visual elements like buttons, menus, icons, and legends sparingly, (b) make common tasks clearly visible and easy to find while hiding infrequent tasks (i.e., offer experienced users quick access to the common, high-priority tasks and offer less experienced users easy system start-ups and quick learnability), (c) give users feedback by combining audible and visual cues, simultaneously displaying signs of task progress and user location within the system, and finally, (d) build in good error recovery mechanisms so users can easily undo an operation, and if a system command cannot be carried out quickly, allow users to interrupt the process and return to a previously stable state. These IT system design approaches are well corroborated by other experts in the field (Cooper & Reimann, 2003; Guastello, 2006; Kalbach, 2004; Kuniavsky, 2003; Pugh, 2006; Rasmussen, Pejtersen, & Goodstein, 1994; Shneiderman, 2004; Tidwell, 2005; Vicente, 2006). While the serious, effective practice of an iterative design process involves much more than mere consideration for usability requirements per se (Nelson & Stolterman, 2003), a judicious application of the guidelines described in this chapter will support the pragmatic functional requirements of any product's user-experience portfolio and effectively accommodate the needs of as many users as possible.

FUTURE TRENDS

Today's human-factors, user-centered IT design and development teams are concerned with the mismatch between the rigidity of current conventional project management formalisms and the actual cognitive, perceptual, and intrinsically motivational richness of human lives and practices. The intention is to create pliant systems that are flexible and responsive, and that foster more effective, intuitive, and comfortable use because they better align with the tactical requirements of our work and the psychological, physiological, sensorial, and behavioral nature of human beings (ACM, 2005; Henderson, 2000; Henderson & Harris, 2000). Managers and producers of public information technology understand the need to innovate but often struggle to pragmatically support creative processes within demanding, requirements-driven business environments. Information architects, knowledge developers, product designers, and usability specialists often face similarly demanding contexts, but must resourcefully find ways to support creative projects and innovative processes reliably and successfully. In a nutshell, the optimal vision statement for public information technology should codify that people shall come first—both from the perspective within the organization functionally and operationally as well as on the bottom-line business end of the equation as clients and end users of the products and services.

These forward-thinking approaches to IT product usability are also linking the nature of our working and nonworking lives. The interesting implication is that human-factors engineering represents an ostensibly profound political and societal paradigm shift in the locus of control toward the proclivities of the person and away from the mechanics of the machine: the essence of the user-centered philosophy. In other words, human-factor models and praxis not only support, foster, and augment user-centered public IT design, but in fact embody and entail optimal IT form and function (Vicente, 2006). The emerging applied profession of human-factors engineering may make a positive, significant, and possibly decisive change in the way we will design and deliver our public information technology environments in the 21st century (Lehto & Buck, 2007). The human factors and allied usability professions are in the process of improving user-experience designs for more accessible, more truly universal design solutions (Guastello, 2006; Hassenzahl, Beu, & Burmester, 2001; Jokela, 2002; Keates, 2007; Lidwell, Holden, & Butler, 2003; Preece, Rogers, & Sharp, 2002).

CONCLUSION

Our daily lives have become increasingly belabored by a vast array of complex, intricate, and immensely powerful public information technology systems. Learning to use many of these computer-based tools, far from being transparently easy, requires a steep learning curve punctuated by psycho-emotional intimidation, trial and error, frustration, and a personal sense of belittlement in the face of the impersonal, ubiquitous and seemingly insurmountable dominance of inscrutable man-machine systems. Lowering the cognitive workload by simplifying the computer-human interface will contribute to a less stressful, more confident task performance and a more effective and efficient user experience. This is particularly salient for members of public information technology organizations who rely so critically upon their tools, software, and user interfaces to support their work environments and enterprise missions and to foster competitive, creative, and innovative knowledge workers.

By (a) simplifying and standardizing interface design affordances, metaphors, and mnemonics, (b) reducing seldom-needed collateral features, and incorporating more intuitive, familiar, parsimonious, and easily grasped mental models to reduce working memory loads while improving simple functionality, and (c) facilitating a responsive, participatory inclusion of the person or user in all IT design solutions, we can potentially empower all users to take control over their information technologies and public IT organizations (Burns & Hajdukiewicz, 2004; Henderson, & Harris, 2000; Isaacs, & Walendowski, 2001; Keates, 2007; Rowland, 2004).

In conclusion, superior human-factor engineering requires a deep understanding of the theory and practice of collaborative team leadership and participative stakeholder buy-in, as well as systems theory and the complete, concurrent, iterative public IT development life-cycle approaches from needs assessment, task analysis, and conceptual design to production, quality assurance, usability design and testing, and courseware product deliverables and evaluation (Vicente, 1999). Postmodern public information technology enterprises become successful as their communication systems give their high-tech workers confidence, trust, a true sense of stakeholdership, commitment, and collaboration, and as they value each high-performing team member. Superb management of people and technology within these enterprises needs to support the special cohesive chemistry together with good communication that promotes openness within the organizational idea-generating infrastructure to everyone at every level. Then human-factors engineering, usability testing, and user-, usage-, and person-oriented design praxis may become an active paradigm shift for administrators, clients, public officials, workers, and designers, providing a rich array of adaptable strategies for change, growth, innovation, problem solving, and competitive product invention for the public IT transformations of the new millennium (Henderson, 2000; Henderson & Harris 2000; Hughes, 2003; Rowland, 2004; Skelton & Thamhain, 2005; Thamhain, 2005).

FUTURE RESEARCH DIRECTIONS

The following two high-priority areas of formal scientific research should be pursued in the interests of expanding the current pragmatic knowledge base pertaining to improving the human-factors design of public information technology systems.

Future Research Focus One. There is an imperative need to develop an adaptive, research-based prescriptive design and development taxonomy for human-factors and ergonomics practitioners in the field. Much has already been done on the descriptive analysis in these areas—little work has been accomplished on determining which design strategies, techniques, approaches, and methods need to be applied for which particular public IT product (usage) requirements, environments, user populations, and networked distributed-media systems. To accomplish this agenda, new studies should be designed to integrate the three primary subdesign layers scaffolded by the research-based foundation of human-factors engineering (i.e., a three plus one design methodology) as follows.

1. Create prototype IT products for testing.
2. The affordances of each design layer comprise the independent variable(s); the user experience as measured by usability heuristics, performance rubrics, and other empirical metrics comprise the dependent variable(s).
3. These products must map, define, and specify each of the three subdesign components (information design, interactivity design, and media design; see basic definitions of these in the "Key Terms" section of this chapter).
4. Methodologically, each of these three design domains will overlap in production sequence as layers in a manner similar to Venn diagrams; the foundation layer is information, the middle layer is interactivity, and the top layer is media. At the center core of the combined and synthesized three-way design layer overlay is the user interface.
5. In-depth, comprehensive research analysis should entail user reaction and usability performance impacted by each design layer individually (the direct, one-way interaction); by each design layer dyad (information-interactivity, information-media, and interactivity-media), and by the confluence of all three design layers—information-interactivity-media in a single, three-way interaction.

Future Research Focus Two. A second vital set of issues to research should integrate human-factors, ergonomics, and universal-accessibility core principles and standards of practice for audio-visual-tactile user interfaces to augment the cognitive and perceptual user experience. Research into applying these standards should address how to integrate the emerging specifications of the World Wide Web Consortium (W3C) and ISO, and should also be applicable to globalization and localization of the user interface and user experience. Prototype IT products designed in conformance and compliance with these technical standards (e.g., enabling the Scalable Content Object Reference Model, SCORM, system interoperability) should be engineered to human-factors and ergonomics guidelines as well. Subsequent, advanced large-sample empirical usability testing and robust heuristic evaluations should be conducted to add more data and explanatory and inferential statistical knowledge to our growing understanding of how to promulgate and deploy optimally efficient and effective public IT systems.

REFERENCES

ACM. (2005). Ambient intelligence: Exploring our living environment. *Interactions, 12*(4), 20-58.

Burns, C. M., & Hajdukiewicz, J. R. (2004). *Ecological interface design.* Boca Raton, FL: CRC Press.

Connell, B. R., Jones, M., Mace, R., Mueller, J., Mullick, A., Ostroff, E., et al. (1997). *The principles of universal design* (Version 2.0). North Carolina State University, the Center for Universal Design. Retrieved November 3, 2006, from http://www.design.ncsu.edu:8120/cud/newweb/about_ud/udprinciples.htm

Constantine, L. L. (2001). *forUse: The Electronic Newsletter of Usage-Centered Design* (Vol. 12). Retrieved January 5, 2007, from http://www.foruse.com/newsletter/foruse12.htm#2

Constantine, L. L., & Lockwood, L. A. D. (1999). *Software for use: A practical guide to the models and methods of usage-centered design.* Boston: Addison-Wesley Professional (ACM Press).

Constantine, L. L., & Lockwood, L. A. D. (2002). Usage-centered engineering for Web applications. *IEEE Software, 19*(2), 42-50.

Constantine, L. L., & Lockwood, L. A. D. (2003). Usage-centered software engineering: An agile approach to integrating users, user interfaces, and usability into software engineering practice. *Proceedings of the 25th International Conference on Software Engineering* (pp. 746-747).

Cooper, A., & Reimann, R. M. (2003). *About Face 2.0: The essentials of interaction design.* Indianapolis, IN: Wiley Publishing.

Dumas, J., & Redish, G. (1999). *A practical guide to usability testing* (Rev. Ed.). London: Intellect Books.

Guastello, S. J. (2006). *Human factors engineering and ergonomics: A systems approach.* Mahwah, NJ: Lawrence Erlbaum Associates.

Hackos, J. T., & Redish, J. C. (1998). *User and task analysis for interface design.* New York: John Wiley & Sons.

Hassenzahl, M., Beu, A., & Burmester, M. (2001). Engineering joy. *IEEE Software*, pp. 70-76.

Henderson, A. (2000). *Pliant research.* Retrieved June 1, 2006, from http://www.pliant.org/

Henderson, A., & Harris, J. (2000). Beyond formalisms: The art and science of designing pliant systems. A talk with Austin Henderson and Jed Harris. In K. Kaasgaard (Ed.), *Software design and usability* (pp. 107-133). Copenhagen, Denmark: Copenhagen Business School Press.

Hofstede, G. (1991). *Cultures and organizations: Software of the mind.* Berkshire, England: McGraw-Hill International.

Hughes, M. A. (2003). Managers: Move from silos to channels. *Intercom*, pp. 9-11.

International Standards Organization (ISO) 13407. (1999). *Human-centered design processes for interactive system teams.* Retrieved from http://www.iso.org/

Isaacs, E., & Walendowski, A. (2001). *Designing from both sides of the screen: Don't impose—Respect mental effort.* Indianapolis, IN: Pearson Education (SAMS Publishing).

Jokela, T. (2002). Making user-centered design common sense: Striving for an unambiguous and communicative UCD process model. *ACM International Conference Proceeding Series: Vol. 31. Proceedings of the Second Nordic Conference on Human-Computer Interaction, Aarhus, Denmark* (pp. 19-26).

Keates, S. (2007). *Designing for accessibility: A business guide to countering design exclusion.* Mahwah, NJ: Lawrence Erlbaum Associates.

Knutson, J. (2001). *Project management for business professionals: A comprehensive guide.* New York: John Wiley & Sons.

Kumar, J. M. (2006). Working as a designer in a global team. *Interactions, 13*(2), 25-27.

Kuniavsky, M. (2003). *Observing the user experience: A practitioner's guide to user research.* San Francisco: Morgan Kaufman.

Lehto, M. R., & Buck, J. R. (2007). *Introduction to human factors and ergonomics for engineers.* Mahwah, NJ: Lawrence Erlbaum Associates.

Lidwell, W., Holden, K., & Butler, J. (2003). *Universal principles of design: A cross-disciplinary reference.* Gloucester, MA: Rockport Publishers.

Mayhew, D. J. (1999). *The usability engineering lifecycle: A practitioner's handbook for user interface design.* San Diego, CA: Academic Press.

Mijksenaar, P. (1997). *Visual function: An introduction to information design.* New York: Princeton Architectural Press.

Moggridge, B. (2006). *Designing interactions.* Cambridge, MA: MIT Press.

Morrogh, E. (2003). *Information architecture: An emerging 21st century profession.* Upper Saddle River, NJ: Prentice Hall (Pearson).

Nelson, H. G., & Stolterman, E. (2003). *The design way: Intentional change in an unpredictable world. Foundations and fundamentals of design competence.* Englewood Cliffs, NJ: Educational Technology Publications.

Pinto, J. K. (2007). *Project management: Achieving competitive advantage.* Upper Saddle River, NJ: Pearson/Prentice Hall.

Preece, J., Rogers, Y., & Sharp, H. (2002). *Interaction design: Beyond human-computer interaction.* New York: John Wiley & Sons.

Project Management Institute. (2004). *A guide to the project management body of knowledge* (3rd ed.). Newtown Square, PA: Project Management Institute.

Pugh, K. (2006). *Interface oriented design: With patterns.* Cambridge, MA: O'Reilly Media.

Rasmussen, J., Pejtersen, A. M., & Goodstein, L. P. (1994). *Cognitive systems engineering.* New York: John Wiley & Sons.

Rowland, G. (2004). Shall we dance: A design epistemology for organizational learning and performance. *Educational Technology Research and Development, 52*(1), 33-48.

Rubin, J. (1994). *Handbook of usability testing: How to plan, design, and conduct effective tests.* New York: John Wiley & Sons.

Saffer, D. (2006). *Designing for interaction: Creating smart applications and clever devices.* Berkeley, CA: Peachpit Press (Pearson Education).

Salvendy, G. (2006). *Handbook of human factors and ergonomics.* Hoboken, NJ: John Wiley & Sons.

Screven, C. G. (1999). Information design in informal settings: Museums and other public spaces. In R. Jacobson (Ed.), *Information design* (pp. 131-192). Cambridge, MA: MIT Press.

Skelton, T. M., & Thamhain, H. J. (2005). *Managing risk in new product development projects: Beyond analytical methods.* Proceedings of the 19th World Congress on Project Management, New Delhi, India.

Stanton, N., Hedge, A., Brookhuis, K., Salas, E., & Hendrick, H. W. (2004). *Handbook of human factors and ergonomics methods.* Boca Raton, FL: CRC Press.

Stanton, N. A., & Young, M. S. (1999). *Guide to methodology in ergonomics: Designing for human use.* New York: Routledge.

Stone, D., Jarrett, C., Woodroffe, M., & Minocha, S. (2005). *User interface design and evaluation.* San Francisco: Morgan Kaufman.

Thamhain, H. (2005). *Management of technology: Managing effectively in technology-intensive organizations.* Hoboken, NJ: John Wiley & Sons.

Tidwell, J. (2005). *Designing interfaces.* Cambridge, MA: O'Reilly Media.

UsabilityNet. (2006). *International standards for HCI and usability.* Retrieved March 2, 2007, from http://www.usabilitynet.org/tools/r_international.htm

Venturi, G., & Troost, J. (2004). Survey on the UCD integration in the industry. *Proceedings of the Third Nordic Conference on Human-Computer Interaction* (pp. 449-452).

Vicente, K. J. (1999). *Cognitive work analysis: Toward safe, productive, and healthy computer-based work.* Mahwah, NJ: Lawrence Erlbaum Associates.

Vicente, K. J. (2006). *The human factor: Revolutionizing the way people live with technology.* New York: Routledge.

Ware, C. (2004). *Information visualization: Perception for design.* San Francisco: Morgan Kaufman (Elsevier).

Wickens, C. D., Lee, J. D., Liu, Y., & Becker, S. G. (2004). *An introduction to human factors engineering* (2nd ed.). Upper Saddle River, NJ: Pearson Education.

FURTHER READING

Anders, P. (1999). *Envisioning cyberspace: Designing 3D electronic spaces.* New York: McGraw-Hill.

Baudisch, P., & Rosenholtz, R. (2003). Halo: A technique for visualizing off-screen objects. *Proceedings of SIGCHI Conference on Human Factors in Computing Systems, CHI, 5*(1), 481-488.

Bennet, A., & Bennet, D. (2004). *Organizational survival in the new world: The Intelligent Complex Adaptive System. A new theory of the firm.* Boston: Knowledge Management Consortium International Press, Butterworth-Heinemann (Elsevier).

Bias, R. G., & Mayhew, D. J. (Eds.). (2005). *Cost-justifying usability: An update for the Internet age* (2nd ed.). San Francisco: Morgan Kaufmann (Elsevier).

Carté, P., & Fox, C. (2004). *Bridging the culture gap: A practical guide to international business communication.* London: Canning (Kogan Page Ltd.).

Catani, M. B., & Biers, D. W. (1998). Usability evaluation and prototype fidelity: Users and usability professionals. *Proceedings of the Human Factors and Ergonomics Society Annual Meeting* (pp. 1331-1335).

Chauhan, V. (2006). Usability professionals: You've come a long way, baby! *Interactions, 13*(2), 14-17.

Desurvire, H. (1994). Faster, cheaper! Are usability inspection methods as effective as empirical testing? In J. Nielsen & R. L. Mack (Eds.), *Usability inspection methods* (pp. 173-202). New York: John Wiley & Sons.

Esselink, B. (2000). *A practical guide to localization.* Philadelphia: John Benjamins.

Gray, W. D., & Salzman, M. C. (1998). Damaged merchandise? A review of experiments that compare usability evaluation methods. *Human Computer Interaction, 13*(3), 203-261.

Hertzum, M., & Jacobsen, N. E. (2001). The evaluator effect: A chilling fact about usability evaluation. *International Journal of Human-Computer Interaction, 13*(4), 421-444.

Hertzum, M., Jacobsen, N. E., & Molich, R. (2002). Usability inspections by groups of specialists: Perceived agreement in spite of disparate observations. *Proceedings of the Association for Computing Machinery Special Interest Group for Computer-Human Interaction 2002* (pp. 662-663).

Jacobsen, N. E., Hertzum, M., & John, B. E. (1998). The evaluator effect in usability studies: Problem detection and severity judgments. *Proceedings of the Human Factors and Ergonomics Society* (pp. 1336-1340).

Kessner, M., Wood, J., Dillon, R. F., & West, R. L. (2001). On the reliability of usability testing. *Proceedings of the Association for Computing Machinery Special Interest Group for Computer-Human Interaction 2001* (pp. 97-98).

Kristof, R., & Satran, A. (1995). *Interactivity by design: Creating and communicating with new media.* Mountain View, CA: Adobe Press.

Krug, G. (2005). *Communication, technology and cultural change.* London: Sage Publications Ltd.

Landay, J. A., & Myers, B. A. (2001). Sketching interfaces: Toward more human interface design. *Computer, 34*(3), 56-64.

Law, E. L.-C., & Hvannberg, E. T. (2004). Analysis of combinatorial user effect in international usability tests. *Proceedings of the Association for Computing Machinery Special Interest Group for Computer-Human Interaction 2004* (pp. 9-16).

Massey, A. P., Yu-Ting, C. H., Montoya-Weiss, M., & Ramesh, V. (2001). When culture and style aren't about clothes: Perceptions of task-technology "fit" in global virtual teams. *Proceedings of the ACM Conference on Group Computing* (pp. 207-213).

Molich, R., Bevan, N., Curson, I., Butler, S., Kindlund, E., Miller, D., et al. (1998). Comparative evaluation of usability tests. *Proceedings of the Usability Professionals' Association.*

Molich, R., Meghan, R. E., Kaasgaard, K., & Karyukin, B. (2004). Comparative usability evaluation (CUE-2). *Behaviour & Information Technology, 23*(1), 65-74.

Moore, S., & Seymour, M. (2005). *Global technology and corporate crisis: Strategies, planning and communication in the information age.* New York: Routledge (Taylor & Francis Group).

Myers, B. A., Nichols, J., Wobbrock, J. O., & Miller, R. C. (2004). Taking handheld devices to the next level. *Computer, 37*(12), 36-43.

Nielsen, J. (1994). Heuristic evaluation. In J. Nielsen & R. L. Mack (Eds.), *Usability inspection methods.* New York: John Wiley & Sons.

Nielsen, J. (2000). The unbearable lightness of Web design: A talk with Jakob Nielsen. In K. Kaasgaard (Ed.), *Software design and usability* (pp. 45-76). Copenhagen, Denmark: Copenhagen Business School Press.

Norman, D. A. (2002). *The design of everyday things.* New York: Basic Books.

Singh, N., & Pereira, A. (2005). *The culturally customized Web site.* Burlington, MA: Elsevier.

Snyder, C. (2003). *Paper prototyping: The fast and easy way to design and refine user interfaces.* San Francisco: Morgan Kaufmann.

Thamhain, H. J. (1996). Best practices for controlling technology-based products. *Project Management Journal, 27*(4), 37-48.

Vogel, D., & Balakrishnan, R. (2004, October). *Interactive public ambient displays: Transitioning from implicit to explicit, public to personal.* Proceedings of Interaction with Multiple Users, UIST '04, Santa Fe, NM.

Weiss, S. (2002). *Handheld usability.* West Sussex, England: John Wiley & Sons, Ltd.

Whitehouse, R. (1999). The uniqueness of individual perception. In R. Jacobson (Ed.), *Information design.* Cambridge, MA: MIT Press.

Wilson, C. (1999). Severity scale for classifying usability problems. *Usability Interface, 5*(4).

TERMS AND DEFINITIONS

Computer-Human Interface Design (CHI): Computer-human interface design consists of the effective functional synthesis and operational integration of three overlapping subdesign domains: information design, interaction design, and media design (see collateral definitions in this "Key Terms" section). Each of these three layers must be clearly defined, represented, and manifested in the user interface design solution. These three subdesign realms and components are synthesized holistically by the conceptual usability glue of the principles of universal design. User interface affordances can be evaluated through usability heuristics and the degree to which these principles have been effectively applied and realized in the user experience—providing a coherent, logically consistent, and robust (i.e., intuitive, accessible, easy to learn and use) systems design.

Human-Factors Engineering: Human factors is an emerging applied design field that entails a synthesis of cross-disciplines from classical ergonomics (i.e., the science of work, system-person interaction, and functional and operational performance needs) and newer research gleaned from the allied fields of cognitive science, human physiological psychology, perception, learning, memory and brain-behavior science, interaction and interactivity design, product design, media design, communication design, and information design.

Information Design: Information design means understanding and clearly mapping the full scope, sequence, concepts, principles, examples, and underlying inheritance structure of the declarative and procedural facets of the content domain (i.e., the infosphere). Information design is essentially concerned with understanding the purpose, organization, context, and interrelationships within a knowledge domain—the envisioning of information to be communicated.

Interactivity Design: Interactivity design means understanding the affordances of the computer-human interrelationship from the user's perceptual and cognitive experience; and identifying and specifying the dynamic time-space transactions between the user, information, and media elements, creating a graphical user-environment interface to navigate within that is intuitive, comprehensible, robust, and engaging. The core artifact of interactivity design is the user interface. Principal ingredients of the interface design are signage, cueing, mnemonics, style and layout conventions, and the ambient conceptual metaphor.

Media Design: Media design involves the physical, functional, and operational manifestation of human-factors design. Media design is the tangible, concrete, tactile-audio-visual-sensory-motor experiential front end of the human-technology system. It requires an understanding of the multisensory nature of the user's experience and applying human learning, memory, messaging, perception, and cognition to produce effective, aesthetic multiple media that provide cognitive, perceptual, and physical affordances to improve human-machine system communications for specific audiences and organizational requirements.

Usability: The degree to which human-technological systems, artifacts, and products are appropriately and efficiently designed for the user (i.e., ease of use) is the indication of that product's usability. Various heuristics and criteria can provide an objective, empirical basis against which to measure and evaluate the level and degree of design efficiency corresponding to the key construct of usability.

Usage-Centered Design: Usage-centered design focuses primarily on the functional goal-based behavior of users and case-based structuring activities, procedures, processes, operational needs, tools, and corresponding affordances to optimize the effectiveness of the user to efficiently accomplish those work goals and requirements.

User-Centered or User-Experience Design (UCD or UXD): User-centered design focuses on constructing a user experience and environment with physical and virtual affordances that are manipulable, controllable, customizable, and adaptable from the essential perspective of the conceptual model of the user. This means both (a) the user's own internal metamodel of their own goal-directed processes, activities, and contextual (i.e., sociopsychological and physical) environment, and (b) the designer's representational model of the user-activity-environmental experience, with the former driving and superceding the latter in the design solution. Thus, the conceptual model of the user becomes the superordinate principle guiding the design process.

Chapter LX
An Overview of IT Outsourcing in Public-Sector Agencies

Anne C. Rouse
Deakin Business School, Deakin University, Australia

INTRODUCTION

For the past 15 years, governments in the developed, Western world have been contracting out, or outsourcing, services as a key part of public-sector reforms. Outsourcing has been argued to lead to cost savings, improved discipline, better services, access to scarce skills, and the capacity for managers to focus more time on the core business of their organizations (Domberger, 1998). Government outsourcing initiatives have encompassed a range of services, but given the large sums of money invested in IT assets, the outsourcing of IT services (IT outsourcing, or ITO) has been a major initiative for many agencies. Lacity and Willcocks (1998, p. 3) defined ITO as "handing over to a third party [the] management of IS/IT assets, resources and/or activities for required results." For public-sector outsourcing, this handover is usually made by way of a competitive tender. Case studies have reported ITO successes and failures (e.g., Currie & Willcocks, 1998; Rouse & Corbitt, 2003; Willcocks & Currie, 1997; Lacity and Willcocks, 2001; Willcocks & Kern, 1998), but much of the evidence presented to public-sector decision makers to justify this reform is anecdotal and unsystematic, and when investigated in depth, does not necessarily support widespread conclusions.

BACKGROUND

The policy promises associated with contracting out government services are part of a broader movement toward the privatization of public-sector services. Osborne and Gaebler (1993) in their influential book *Reinventing Government* argued that governments should "steer, not row the boat" (p. 25); in other words, they should ensure that services are provided to the public, not necessarily provide the services themselves. This suggestion resonated with governments around the globe that were anxious to reduce public expenditure and risks. The move to outsource was also a response to arguments that through economies of scale, scope, and specialization, private-sector vendors could deliver outsourced services at a lower cost than governments themselves (Domberger, 1998). Initial forays into public-sector outsourcing involved relatively simple and straightforward services (like garbage collection or hospital cleaning), which were easy to specify and to measure. However, a growing vendor market, improvements in communications technologies, and emerging skills shortages that raised the cost of IT labor (and threatened salary relativities within public-sector agencies) were drivers for the move to outsource IT (Hodge & Rouse, 2006). Both project-based services (like the development of a new system) and routine support services (such as desktop and mainframe support, and the maintenance of legacy systems) became candidates for outsourcing.

It is important to distinguish outsourcing from another key public-sector reform: privatization. While both may involve handing over public assets to the private sector, privatization is a once-off, irreversible sale of a state-owned asset. Governments generally retain some regulatory control over the provision of the privatized service, but retain no governance control and no operating risk (Jensen & Stonecash, 2005). In contrast, outsourcing is contracted for a specific period, after which governments might select an alternative vendor, or even return to providing the service in-house. The latter is theoretically possible, though in practice it is rarely contemplated because of the financial costs and organizational disruption associated with re-insourcing. With outsourcing, governments retain responsibility for governance of the outsourced function and for specifying what is required while allowing the vendor to decide how to provide this. This means that, in practice, governments largely retain most of the risk associated with the outsourced function.

EMPIRICAL EVIDENCE ABOUT GOVERNMENT OUTSOURCING OUTCOMES

It is not yet clear whether the outsourcing of government services (including ITO) has delivered on the theoretical promise. Anecdotal case studies of success are reported (e.g., Savas, 2000), but many of these considered only preliminary experiences. They may also be atypical.

Before the success of outsourcing can be established, the nature of success needs to be defined. This depends on what was expected from the strategy in the first place (Parasuraman & Grewal, 2000). Expectations for complex services with substantial impact on organizational performance are multifaceted and go beyond simple cost comparisons.

Because of the multifaceted nature of expectations, outsourcing usually results in mixed outcomes as is illustrated by the cases cited in the first paragraph. Rouse's (2006) survey of 240 public- and private-sector purchasers found that while IT outsourcing provided access to scarce skills and high levels of technical service quality, it failed to provide substantial cost savings, leading to generally low levels of overall satisfaction, the result of failure to meet stated or unstated expectations, according to marketing theory (e.g., Parasuraman & Grewal, 2000).

Another problem with determining success is that while outsourcing is known to be risky (Aubert, Patry, & Rivard, 2002; Gewald, Wüllenweber, & Weitzel, 2006), until potential downsides are encountered, decision makers may fail to recognize the level of risk. They may then perceive the arrangement to be more successful than it really is. According to Lacity and Willcocks (1998), perceptions of outsourcing success diminish the longer the arrangement lasts as many costs do not become apparent for some time. Purchasers risk vendor lock in (Wikipedia, 2006), where they find that they have no choice but to continue with an existing vendor because of high switching costs, or because few (or no) alternative bidders can be found. Another important risk, heightened for public-sector outsourcing because of public expectations, involves threats to the privacy and confidentiality of citizens' records that are handed over to vendors. Increasingly in

Europe, Australasia, and some U.S. states, privacy legislation is raising the stakes in relation to such records, and recent data protection failures by outsourced vendors (such as CardSystems in the United States) have increased community concerns about this issue.

Outsourcing success is often defined in terms of whether or not costs have been saved compared to those of in-house delivery. Lacity and Willcocks (1998) reported that this reason for outsourcing IT appeared in 80% of the cases they studied. However, establishing whether costs are reduced when complex services (like IT) are outsourced is a technically complex and expensive exercise (Rouse & Corbitt, 2003). Transaction cost theory (Williamson, 1979) notes that two forms of costs are involved: production and transaction costs. Production costs (sometimes labeled transformation costs) are the direct costs of production, that is, of transforming inputs into outputs. Transaction costs are the costs of dealing with the marketplace, and include the costs of finding, contracting with, monitoring, and controlling the activities of the supplier. In general, with outsourcing, production costs are reduced because of competition, while transaction costs are often increased (Ang & Straub, 1998) as are the notional costs associated with the risks associated with the strategy: risk exposure costs. Very few of the studies on outsourcing have considered transaction costs as well as production costs when exploring savings (Hodge, 2000). Added to these costs must be the costs of absorbing risks (risk exposure), which are normally calculated as the probability of the downsides occurring, multiplied by the costs of these downsides (Aubert, Dussault, Patry, & Rivard, 1999). According to Rouse and Corbitt (2003), the risk exposures for complex outsourcing (like ITO) are much higher than generally recognized.

EMPIRICAL EVIDENCE FOR OUTSOURCING SUCCESS

Public-Sector Outsourcing

Even when only production costs savings are considered, there are mixed findings about government outsourcing (of IT and other services). The Australian Industry Commission (1996) reviewed 203 international studies of government outsourcing and concluded that the extent of savings varied widely, and that there was evidence of cost increases following outsourcing in some cases. When reviewing quantitative studies of government outsourcing using the technique of meta-analysis, Hodge (2000) established that some types of services achieved much better cost savings than others. He calculated that average savings of between 6 and 12% were obtained (this contrasts strongly with the 20% to 30% anecdotally quoted by outsourcing proponents). Hodge found evidence for substantial production cost savings (of between 19% and 30%) in the areas of garbage collection, and cleaning and maintenance services. Such simple services are easy to define and measure, and involve relatively unskilled staff with little bargaining power. However, Hodge found limited research into the cost outcomes for complex services (like IT), and in the few he found, average cost savings estimates ranged from an 8% saving to a 24% increase.

IT Outsourcing

Despite the rapid growth of ITO in the public and private sectors, there is still no consensus in the academic literature on the extent of cost savings from contracting out IT services. There is also limited literature on whether government IT outsourcing achieves better or worse outcomes than those achieved by the private sector. In contrast to the relatively easy-to-measure services reported above, for IT services, the technical complexity of the tasks carried out by staff is high, the professional language of solutions is obscure, and the rate of change in development is substantial. Establishing cost savings in these circumstances is difficult.

Possibly because of these difficulties, most research into ITO has involved singular cases studied at one point of time, which may not be representative of wider experiences. There are few survey-based studies of ITO outcomes, and of these, even fewer have targeted public-sector agencies. Little research has differentiated between the once-off, bespoke development of a new system on the one hand, and the ongoing delivery of IT services, on the other. The notion of savings in the former case is fuzzy because, since the move to post-Internet systems architectures, few public-sector agencies have the in-house skills to develop applications at the level of complexity required for government administration. Thus, comparisons of in-house vs. outsourced delivery become impossible. Furthermore, the bespoke nature of systems development means that each system's costs are unique. When the costs of ongoing IT services are compared, the rate of technological changes in IT means it is rare to be able to compare in-house and external delivery costs with any precision, even when only production costs are considered. Rouse and Corbitt's (2003) longitudinal study of the Australian government's IT outsourcing established that it is relatively easy to get the business-case cost projections wrong; they reported that inaccurate cost projections (particularly the costs of risks) were a key reason the Australian government was forced to abandon its IT outsourcing initiative.

As with other forms of outsourcing, case study research into ITO has revealed widely varying outcomes. Willcocks, Lacity, and Fitzgerald (1997) reported that for 41 cases of outsourcing, there were 23 instances where some cost savings were achieved (i.e., 56%), with savings being mixed in five instances (12%) and savings not being achieved in 13 cases (31%). Savings could not be determined in eight further cases. In a study of 7,500 government outsourcing contracts published by CTC Consultants (1999), Simon Domberger, a strong proponent of government outsourcing, reported an average increase in costs of 8.6% when IT services were outsourced. Aubert, Patry, and Rivard (1999) in their longitudinal study of Canadian IT outsourcing found that in 49% of firms costs rose. Willcocks and Currie (1997) also noted that in some cases, government outsourcing costs rose, in part because the private sector often paid higher salaries than the public sector. This was an explanation given by Domberger (as cited in CTC Consultants), too, for the generally poor outcomes for ITO outsourcing that he observed.

The study by Rouse and Hodge (in press) statistically contrasted public-sector and private-sector agencies' ITO experiences. These authors analyzed a survey of 240 IT directors and CIOs (chief information officer) for Australia's largest public- and private-sector firms. Just over a third of respondents reported unequivocal satisfaction, however, only a minority reported cost savings, and only a small minority (7%) reported substantial cost savings. A sizeable minority (22%) reported cost increases from ITO. Rouse and Hodge investigated 27 individual outcome measures in that survey (including cost savings) and found that for the large majority of outsourcing outcomes, no statistical difference existed in perceived levels of performance between public- and private-sector firms. There were no statistically significant differences for the key success measures: technical benefits, strategic benefits, technical service quality, cost savings, business flexibility, economies of scale, and access to skilled personnel. Nor were there statistical differences in outsourcing satisfaction or perceptions of overall value: Government respondents reported the same relatively poor outcomes as did those in nongovernment organizations.

FUTURE TRENDS

In view of the relatively dismal outcomes of large-scale outsourcing of IT by governments, many large, single-vendor contracts have not been renewed. Typically, governments now break apart the contract and deal with different suppliers for different IT services, and so the prevailing outsourcing arrangement involves a series of selective or best-of-breed contracts. This strategy appears to be a reaction to academic advice that selective outsourcing is less risky (e.g., Lacity & Willcocks, 2001), though empirical studies have failed to confirm this proposition. A larger number of selective contracts are argued to increase transaction costs (Currie & Willcocks, 1998), and in future research such costs should be included in cost analyses. Future research should also explore the comparisons that can be used to evaluate cost savings because once an agency has outsourced, it soon becomes impossible to compare in-house and outsourced costs. Research should also continue to explore reasons for the failures of many agencies to reap the theoretical benefits of outsourcing.

There is an increasing trend in the literature to consider the risks of IT outsourcing (e.g., Aubert et al, 2002; Gewald et al., 2006; Rouse & Corbitt, 2003) and to look at the way perceptions of risk are related to whether decision makers are proponents of outsourcing or not. At this stage, discussions are largely theoretical, but in the future, more quantitative evaluation of risks should be carried out. Evidence from Ang and Straub (1998) suggests that when organizations choose to outsource, they tend to de-emphasize transaction costs, while those that consider but reject outsourcing tend to focus on transaction costs. A similar effect may occur with the perceptions of risk, and this too provides a fruitful avenue for future research.

FUTURE RESEARCH DIRECTIONS

In the 15 years or so since IT outsourcing emerged as an academic topic, new variations have been taken up by the private sector. Two important variations are business process outsourcing (BPO) and offshore outsourcing (offshoring). In practice, because of problems achieving substantial cost savings with onshore outsourcing, there is pressure on firms to consider offshore delivery of both IT and business processes. While growth in the IT outsourcing market had, by 2004, slowed (Gartner, 2005), the growth in new outsourcing forms (offshoring and BPO) is reportedly strong. Consequently, public-sector agencies, too, will be encouraged to explore these options in the continued search for reduced business costs.

Offshore outsourcing, in particular, while benefiting developing countries and offering the promise of substantial savings, involves significant additional risks for purchasers, so it is likely to be of particular interest to researchers in the future. For public-sector purchasers, the issue of managing the privacy of citizens records sent to other legal and cultural jurisdictions will be particularly critical. Future studies of outsourcing risk will need to establish typical risk exposures for on- and offshore outsourcing, and the effectiveness of risk minimizing strategies. It is also important that research into offshore outsourcing be undertaken by independent academic researchers as well as vendors.

A detailed review by Dibbern, Goles, Hirschheim, and Jayatilaka (2004) of the academic outsourcing literature to 2001 illustrated how little systematic quantitative research into outsourcing had been undertaken, and how much of this had concentrated on the reasons behind sourcing decisions rather than the outcomes. The predominant research methodology continues to be case studies, and there have been few theory-testing studies in the literature and hardly any studies that have statistically tested propositions related to outsourcing practices. At the same time, a large number of trade-based books have now been published on how to successfully outsource. These are based on the personal experience of the author rather than on any empirical research.

Given the emphasis on individual and largely exploratory case studies and on practitioner opinion, there are substantial opportunities for future outsourcing research that shifts the emphasis to theory testing. There is a need for research that uses outsourcing outcomes as the dependent variables, and uses alternative research methods (including quantitative methods). Such research will allow for disconfirming propositions. In particular, future research should begin to explore which of the many prescriptions offered by researchers and consultants for ensuring successful outsourcing do generalize widely to public- and private-sector firms in the community. Researchers are also encouraged to investigate the measurable effects managerial decisions and behaviors have on outsourcing outcomes.

There is opportunity for research that systematically examines differences in outcomes and management practices across different types of outsourcing (e.g., BPO and ITO; offshore and onshore outsourcing). There is also opportunity for research that explores experiences in both the private and public sectors, as the latter sector has not received the same level of attention, despite its widespread use of outsourcing.

CONCLUSION

IT costs form a large component of government expenditure, and governments around the world have sought to rein in these costs by outsourcing. From the evidence to date, though, achieving costs savings by outsourcing IT is relatively unlikely. Some of the other strategic benefits of outsourcing (such as being able to redirect attention to core business) also appear difficult to achieve in real life (Rouse & Corbitt, 2003). Earlier researchers (e.g., Lacity & Hirschheim, 1995) argued that it is substantially more challenging to manage outsourcing arrangements than is generally recognized, and this observation is supported by the research cited above. It seems that rapidly changing business requirements resulting from dynamic community demands, together with unexpectedly high transaction costs and risks, substantially reduce the theoretical likelihood of success. Given the evidence to date, public-sector agencies need to proceed more cautiously down the road of IT outsourcing, ensuring that their cost projections include both transaction and production costs, and making financial provisions for the high levels of risks that appear to be involved in contracting out complex services.

REFERENCES

Ang, S., & Straub, D. W. (1998). Production and transaction economies and IS outsourcing: A study of the US banking industry. *MIS Quarterly, 22*(4), 535-552.

Aubert, B., Dussault, S., Patry, M., & Rivard, M. (1999). *Managing the risks of IT outsourcing.* Proceedings of the 32nd Hawaii International Conference on System Sciences, HI.

Aubert, B., Patry, M., & Rivard, S. (1999). L'impartation des services informatique au Canada: Une comparaison 1993-1997. In M. Poitevin (Ed.), *Impartition: Fondements et analyses* (pp. 202-220). Montreal, Canada: University of Laval Press.

Aubert, B., Patry, M., & Rivard, S. (2002). Managing IT outsourcing risk: Lessons learned. In R. Hirschheim, A. Heinzl, & J. Dibbern (Eds.), *Information systems outsourcing: Enduring themes, emergent patterns and future directions* (pp. 155-176). Berlin, Germany: Springer.

Australian Industry Commission. (1996). *Competitive tendering and contracting by public sector agencies: Report No. 48.* Melbourne, Australia: AGPS.

CTC Consultants. (1999). *Government outsourcing: What has been learnt?* Sydney, Australia: CTC Consultants.

Currie, W., & Willcocks, L. (1998). Analysing four types of IT sourcing decisions in the context of scale, client/supplier interdependency and risk mitigation. *Information Systems Journal, 8*(2), 119-144.

Dibbern, J., Goles, T., Hirschheim, R., & Jayatilaka, B. (2004). Information systems outsourcing: A survey and analysis of the literature. *ACM SIGMIS Database, 35*(4), 6-102.

Domberger, S. (1998). *The contracting organization: A strategic guide to outsourcing*. Oxford: Oxford University Press.

Gartner. (2005). *Outsourcing drives IT services growth.* Retrieved from http://www.gartner.com/5_about/press_releases/pr2004.jsp

Gewald, H., Wüllenweber, K., & Weitzel, T. (2006). The influence of perceived risks on banking managers' intention to outsource business processes: A study of the German banking and finance industry. *Journal of Electronic Commerce Research, 7*(2), 78-96.

Hodge, G. A. (2000). *Privatization: An international review of performance.* Boulder, CO: Westview Press.

Hodge, G. A., & Rouse, A. C. (2006). Outsourcing government information technology services: An Australian case study. In G. Boyne, K. Meier, L. O'Toole, Jr., & R. Walker (Eds.), *Public service performance: Perspectives on measurement and management.* London: Palgrave McMillan.

Jensen, P. H., & Stonecash, R. E. (2005). Incentives and the efficiency of public sector outsourcing contracts. *Journal of Economic Surveys, 19*(5), 767-787.

Lacity, M. C., & Hirschheim, R. (1995). *Beyond the information systems outsourcing bandwagon: The insourcing response.* New York: Wiley.

Lacity, M. C., & Willcocks, L. (1998). An empirical investigation of information technology sourcing practices: Lessons from experience. *MIS Quarterly, 22*(3), 363-408.

Lacity, M., & Willcocks, L. (2001). Inside mega contracts: South Australian and Dupont. In M. Lacity & L. Willcocks (Eds.), *Global IT outsourcing: In search of business advantage* (pp. 40-88). New York: Wiley.

Osborne, D., & Gaebler, T. (1993). *Reinventing government: How the entrepreneurial spirit is transforming the public sector.* Reading, MA: Addison-Wesley Publishing.

Parasuraman, A., & Grewal, D. (2000). Serving customers and consumers effectively in the 21st century: A conceptual framework and overview. *Journal of the Academy of Marketing Science, 28*(1), 9-16.

Rouse, A. C. (2006). *Explaining I.T. outsourcing purchasers' dissatisfaction.* Proceedings of 10th Pacific Asia Conference on Information Systems (PACIS), Kuala Lumpur, Malaysia.

Rouse, A. C., & Corbitt, B. (2003). The Australian government's abandoned infrastructure outsourcing program: What can be learned? *Australian Journal of Information Systems, 10*(2), 81-90.

Savas, E. S. (2000). *Privatization and public-private partnerships.* NJ: Chatham House Press.

Wikipedia. (2006). *Vendor lock in.* Retrieved from http://en.wikipedia.org/wiki/Lock_in

Willcocks, L., & Currie, W. L. (1997). Information technology in the public services: Towards the contractual organization? *British Journal of Management*, 107-120.

Willcocks, L., & Lacity, M. C. (1998). *Strategic sourcing of information systems: Perspectives and practices.* Chichester, United Kingdom: Wiley.

Willcocks, L., Lacity, M. C., & Fitzgerald, G. (1995). Information technology outsourcing in

Europe and the USA: Assessment issues. *International Journal of Information Management, 15*(5), 333-351.

Willcocks, L., Lacity, M., & Fitzgerald, D. (1997). IT outsourcing in Europe and the USA: Assessment issues. In L. Willcocks, D. Feeny, & G. Islei (Eds.), *Managaing IT as a strategic resource* (pp. 306-358). New York: McGraw Hill.

Willcocks, L. P. & Kern, T. (1998). IT outsourcing as strategic partnering: The case of the UK Inland Revenue. *European Journal of Information Systems, 7*(1), 29-45.

Williamson, O. E. (1979). Transaction cost economics: The governance of contractual relationships. *Journal of Law and Economics, 22*, 233-261.

FURTHER READING

Bahli, B., & Rivard, S. (2005). Validating measures of information technology outsourcing risk factors. *Omega, 33*(2), 175-187.

Carmel, E., & Tjia, P. (2005). *Offshoring information technology: Sourcing and outsourcing to a global workforce*. New York: Cambridge University Press.

Earl, M. J. (1996). The risks of outsourcing. *Sloan Management Review, 37*(3), 26-32.

Grover, V., Cheon, M. J., & Teng, J. T. C. (1996). The effect of service quality and partnership on the outsourcing of information systems functions. *Journal of Management Information Systems, 12*(4), 89-116.

Halvey, J. K., & Melby, B. M. (2000). *Business process outsourcing: Processes, strategies and risks.* Hoboken, NJ: Wiley.

Halvey, J. K., & Melby, B. M. (2005). *Information technology outsourcing transactions: Process, strategies, and contracts.* Hoboken, NJ: Wiley.

Hirschheim, R., Heinzl, A., & Dibbern, J. (2002). *Information systems outsourcing in the new economy: Enduring themes, emergent patterns and global challenges.* Berlin, Germany: Springer-Verlag.

Hirschheim, R., Heinzl, A., & Dibbern, J. (2006). *Information systems outsourcing: Enduring themes, new perspectives and global challenges* (2nd ed.). Berlin, Germany: Springer-Verlag.

Kern, T., & Willcocks, L. P. (2000). Contract, control and presentiation in IT outsourcing: Research in thirteen UK organizations. *Journal of Global Information Management, 8*(4), 15-29.

Kern, T., & Willcocks, L. P. (2002). *The relationship advantage: Information technologies, sourcing, and management.* Oxford: Oxford University Press.

Lacity, M. C., & Hirschheim, R. (1993). *Information systems outsourcing: Myths, metaphors and realities.* Chichester, England: Wiley.

Lacity, M. C., Willcocks, L., & Feeny, D. F. (1995). Information technology outsourcing: Maximising flexibility and control. *Harvard Business Review,* 84-93.

Lacity, M., Feeny, D., & Willcocks, L. (2004). Commercializing the back office at Lloyd's of London: Outsourcing and strategic partnerships revisited. *European Management Journal, 22*(2), 127-140.

Lee, J. N., Huynh, M. A., Kwok, R. C., &, Pi, S. M. (2003). IT outsourcing evolution: Past, present, and future. *Communications of the ACM, 46*(5), 84-89.

Lee, J.-N., & Kim, Y.-G. (1999). Effect of partnership quality on IS outsourcing: Conceptual framework and empirical validation. *Journal of Management Information Systems, 15*(4), 29-61.

Lee, J.-N., Miranda, S. M., & Kim, Y.-M. (2004). IT outsourcing strategies: Universalistic, contingency and configurational explanations of success. *Information Systems Research, 15*(2), 110-131.

Looney, J. A. (1998). *Outsourcing state and local government services: Decision-making strategies and management methods.* Westport, CT: Quorum Books.

Rouse, A. C., & Corbitt, B. J. (2003). *Minimising risks in IT outsourcing: Choosing target services.* Proceedings of the Seventh Pacific Asia Conference on Information Systems, Adelaide, South Australia.

Rouse, A. C., & Corbitt, B. J. (2006a). Analysis of a large-scale IT outsourcing failure: What lessons can we learn? In M. Khosrow-Pour (Ed.), *Outsourcing and offshoring in the 21st century: A socio-economic perspective.* Idea Group Publishing.

Rouse, A. C., & Corbitt, B. J. (2006b). Business process outsourcing. In R. Hirschheim, A. Heinzl, & J. Dibbern (Eds.), *Information systems outsourcing: Enduring themes, emergent patterns and global challenges* (2nd ed.). Berlin, Germany: Springer-Verlag.

Rouse, A. C., & Hodge, G. A. (2006). *Rethinking risk: A strategy for improving public sector sourcing performance.* Paper presented at the Determinants of Performance in Public Organization International Conference, Hong Kong, China.

Saunders, C., Gebelt, M., & Hu, Q. A. (1997). Achieving success in information systems outsourcing. *California Management Review, 39*(2), 63-79.

Timbrell, G., Hirschheim, R., Gable, G. G., & Underwood, A. (1998). Government IT and T insourcing/outsourcing: A model and guidelines. *Proceedings of the 9th Australasian Conference on Information Systems.* Retrieved from http://eprints.qut.edu.au/archive/00004491/01/4491.pdf

Walker, B., & Walker, B. C. (2000). *Privatisation: Sell off or sell out?* Sydney, Australia: ABC Books.

Williamson, O. E., & Masten, S. E. (1999). *The economics of transaction costs: Elgar critical writings reader.* London: Edward Elgar Publishing.

TERMS AND DEFINITIONS

Business Process: A business process is a set of interrelated organizational activities performed by a number of individuals with the goal of generating customer value.

Business Process Outsourcing (BPO): BPO is the outsourcing of relatively complex business processes or activities that are supported by information technologies.

IT Outsourcing (ITO): ITO is the outsourcing of IT services. The term is usually used in contrast to business process outsourcing, where the business function or process (including the IT that supports it) is outsourced. ITO includes the outsourcing of unique, once-off systems development projects, as well as the outsourcing of ongoing IT services, such as mainframe hosting, desktop support, telecommunications installation and maintenance, or maintenance and support of legacy systems.

Offshoring: This is offshore outsourcing or cross-national outsourcing, where the vendor and client operate in different countries.

Outsourcing: Outsourcing is the provision, at an agreed price, of specified services by an external vendor that is contracted to manage the day-to-day activities (and related assets and resources) so as to meet agreed performance and quality standards. Outsourcing involves specifying what will be done rather than how it will be done.

Privatization: Privatization is the conversion of a government-owned enterprise to private ownership and operation. The theory behind privatization is that private enterprises run more effectively and offer better service.

Production Costs: The costs of the processes involved in creating and distributing goods or services

Risk: Risk is the potential harmful or undesirable consequences (downsides) that might arise in the future from a decision or course of action. Examples in the context of ITO include the release of confidential data, loss of organizational knowledge, and reduced business flexibility.

Risk Exposure: Risk exposure is the likelihood or probability of an undesirable future event, multiplied by the magnitude (e.g., costs) of the consequences of the event.

RE = Probability(event) x Consequences(event)

Transaction Costs: Transaction costs are the costs of contracting with a vendor through the marketplace in contrast to coordinating and managing service provision in-house (i.e., through the hierarchy). Key costs include finding, choosing, contracting with, monitoring, and controlling the work of the vendor, as well as coordinating the vendor's activities with others being carried out by the purchaser.

Chapter LXI
E-Health, Local Governance, and Public-Private Partnering in Ontario

Jeffrey Roy
Dalhousie University, Canada

ABSTRACT

The purpose of this chapter is to undertake a critical examination of the emergence of e-health in the Canadian Province of Ontario. More than solely a technological challenge, the emergence and pursuit of e-health denote a complex governance transformation both within the province's public sector and in terms of public-private partnering. The Ontario challenge here is complicated by the absence of formal regional mechanisms devoted to health care, a deficiency that has precipitated the creation of Local Health Integration Networks (LHINs) to foster e-health strategies on a subprovincial basis, as well as ongoing difficulties in managing public information technologies. With respect to public-private partnering, a greater regionalization of decision-making and spending authorities, within transparent and locally accountable governance forums, could provide incentives for the private sector to work more directly subprovincially, enjoying greater degrees of freedom for collaboration via more manageable contracting arrangements.

INTRODUCTION

The purpose of this chapter is to undertake a critical examination of the emergence of electronic health (e-health) in the Province of Ontario from two interrelated dimensions: first, the emergence of Local Health Integration Networks as the regionalization vehicle for governance reform within a province-wide health care system, and secondly, the usage of public-private partnering to pursue the realization of e-health mechanisms. There is no more profoundly consequential and complex example of public information technologies being deployed than in the realm of health care organization and delivery.

In many respects, the two concepts of e-health and e-government are interrelated and coevolving layers of both organizational and institutional governance processes. As the single largest funding envelope of public-sector activity, particularly at the provincial level, the digital transformation of health care is also highly consequential for the digital transformation of the public sector as a whole (Roy, 2005, 2006).

The chapter is organized as follows. Following this introduction, the second section reviews the main contours of e-health. Then we examine the conceptual challenges of public-private-sector partnerships. The fourth section provides an assessment of the e-health experience to date in Ontario from the two aforementioned dimensions of governance change. The fifth section then provides some conclusions as to the lessons learned from this case study.

The Emergence of E-Health[1]

More than a mere technical apparatus for providing information, the Internet has also become an associational infrastructure, enabling knowledge and power to be more widely distributed and contested (Courchene, 2005; Paquet, 1997). One specific result is a lessening of tolerance for secrecy as individuals and new forms of associational movements mobilize around specific issues and interests (Dwyer 2004; Evans 2002). Governments themselves have not been immune or ignorant to these pressures for reform, responding increasingly with calls for more public participation and citizen engagement (Coleman & Norris, 2005; Oates, 2003; Oliver & Sanders, 2004).

The application of a digital and interoperable information infrastructure carries the potential to enable faster and more integrated forms of care for the patient on a scale that could profoundly transform structures and performance (Hurley, Baum, & van Eyk, 2004; Prisma, 2004). Indeed, a centerpiece of e-health is the electronic health record—a basis for revolutionary improvements in information management, patient responsiveness, and service delivery capacities:

> An electronic health record (EHR) provides each individual in Canada with a secure and private lifetime record of their key health history and care within the health system. The record is available electronically to authorized health care providers and the individual anywhere, anytime in support of high quality care.
>
> The Electronic Health Record Solution is a combination of people, organizational entities, business processes, systems, technology and standards that interact and exchange clinical data to provide high quality and effective healthcare.[2]

This passage usefully underscores the manner by which, as a basis for such change, the introduction of online mechanisms externally and new forms of digital interoperability internally require more than technological design as benefit realization is dependent on complex and multidimensional reforms (Fountain, 2001; Scholl, 2005). In terms of e-health and the EHR specifically (like many other areas of e-government but more acutely than most given the sensitivity of information and privacy), offsetting concerns about technical flaws and security glitches, leading to inappropriate access to personal information, are prevalent and of great sensitivity politically (Gath, 2004; Mundy, 2004).

With regards to health care organization and service delivery, it is the combination of the EHR, greater interoperability across all segments of the health care system, and telemedicine that comprise the parameters of system-wide transformation. Such transformation includes not only how services are delivered through new organizational channels, but also how power is organized and deployed across the major stakeholder groups of health care, notably governments providing oversight and regulatory direction, delivery bodies such as hospitals and clinics, professional groups such as physicians and nurses, and communities at large (Eng & Beauchamp 2004).

The EHR enables more efficient and citizen-centric decision-making mechanisms through a much greater ability to share and access information about a patient that is the basis of any diagnosis and treatment. In turn, telemedicine offers the potential to deliver service outcomes in locations, particularly in remote jurisdictions, where actual medical facilities and staff may not be readily available (Demiris, 2004). Permeating both of these components is the need for a digital and organizational infrastructure capable of quickly and securely managing information flows across a complex system to facilitate client-centric outcomes (Patton, 2005).

This need for a system-wide coordination to introduce such standards underlines a major governance challenge common to e-health and e-government more generally, namely, the need for central coordination in a manner that respects the autonomy and need for flexibility across different components of the health care system. The degree to which those responsible for health care planning and technological design (typically a CIO- [chief information officer] type role) can thus realize interoperability through collaborative means (i.e., orchestrating change as opposed to imposing it in a more hierarchical fashion) is a major determinant of system-wide transformation, and it underscores one reason why the existence and degree of high-level political leadership is so central in this regard (Culbertson, 2005; Dutil, Langford, & Roy, 2005; Langford & Roy, 2006).

The expansion of information availability and oversight capacities facilitated by an online world are momentous forces in altering traditional roles and responsibilities in health care. Patients now often engage in self-diagnosis prior to visiting a physician, and while there is undoubtedly a potential benefit stream in more informed and aware clients and users of the health care system, offsetting concerns lie in the accuracy and reliability of the information circulating, particularly in cyberspace (Randeree & Rao, 2004). There is widening evidence, however, that medical experts face a less deferential and more inquisitive public than in the past (Allsop, 2003).

The same is true for governments holistically in terms of the public's role as both a voter (in the representational mindset of democracy) and a stakeholder to be engaged in democratic governance more actively. As health care costs continually rise in tandem with growing demands for more sophisticated care, public-sector investments are under more scrutiny as performance reporting becomes more prevalent (Rosenbord, 2003). Similarly, difficult political and policy questions about the rules and reasonable expectations sought in health care are increasingly viewed as areas requiring a more direct form of engagement on the part of the public than merely deferring to the decisions of government managers and political leaders (reflecting the pressures for citizen engagement from a more informed public in a manner not unlike the changing power relations and balance between physicians and patients).

More transparency also means that stakeholders working with governments in the organizing of e-health systems will face more scrutiny and pressures for openness. Given e-health's reliance on a digital infrastructure, and by extension a significant role for the private sector in creating and maintaining this infrastructure, the widening scope and heightened complexity of public-private partnerships are a case in point. The decline in deferential trust accorded to both government and industry is thus a major challenge, one requiring a more direct effort to both inform and engage the citizenry in deliberations about choices, means, and outcomes (Eggers, 2005).

A corresponding rise in those determinants of trust that are based more on direct experience and encounters than expertise and deferential authority, coupled with the rise of online connectivity, are also facilitating the creation of new relationships between citizens, activists, and health care users. The formation of such communities can be driven by a desire to influence government decision making or it can be more peer focused, such as support communities for individuals encountering similar health conditions (Josefsoon,

2005). Moreover, the level of engagement between citizens as users of health care and the governance processes underpinning planning and decision making is very much intertwined with political legitimacy. A forceful case has been made that the public has not been well utilized as a stakeholder, more often than not the recipient of communication strategies by health care bodies and political leaders as opposed to genuine engagement and contribution (Ableson & Eyles, 2002).

Here there is some convergence between schools of thought from management and governance generally and e-health specifically with respect to the need to widen involvement and participation of key stakeholder groups in order to effectively align human, organizational, institutional, and technological variables in a coherent manner (Borins, 2004; Fountain, 2004; Woodward, 2003).

Public-Private Partnering

There are two major sets of reasons underpinning the growing prominence of public-private partnerships for the creation and maintenance of various forms of infrastructure, both new and old. They may be summarized as financing and investment on the one hand, and innovation and performance on the other hand. Both dimensions of seeking to combine and align public and private interests may also be interlinked within the confines of a particular governance undertaking.

Regarding the financing of new infrastructure, the attractiveness of leveraging private pools of capital investment is rooted in a similar context of new public management that arose during the 1980s, encouraging governments to look to industry for managerial techniques and governance practices. A key factor in this trend had been the view that excessive government bureaucracy leads to an inefficient allocation of resources for the jurisdiction and its governance system as a whole: Two alternative paths of recourse thus include either reforming government internally or privatizing specific government functions (thereby shifting them from the public to the private realm). What both paths shared was an emphasis on efficiency and greater sensitivity to bottom-line measures of government spending, including accumulated debt and annual deficits.

Throughout the 1980s (and in many OECD [Organization for Economic Cooperation and Development] countries continuing into the 1990s), this growing fiscal sensitivity resulted in constraints on public investment perhaps more severe than at any time since well prior to the post-WWII reconstruction period largely financed by direct government taxation and investment.

The example of the United Kingdom is illustrative, where by 1997 the British government reported the lowest levels of public infrastructure spending since the 1970s, the result being deterioration of facilities, equipment, and service standards across schools, hospitals, and other facets of traditionally public-sector assets such as roadways and public transportation. In Canada, estimates of the current infrastructure gap range anywhere from \$50 billion to \$125 billion, with at the very least a consensus that current levels of public-sector spending cannot keep pace with the refurbishment needs of the country's aging infrastructure (TD Economics, 2006).[3]

The inability of the marketplace to respond to such decline is indicative of what economists term a market failure. Many such aspects of local and national infrastructure are collective in nature—of use by everyone (and all or many companies) for functions of critical importance that nonetheless lack competitive structures and pricing mechanisms to warrant private investment (as there would be little hope of generating an economic return). Yet, at the same time, markets and communities suffer collectively if reparation is not forthcoming, a function invariably demanding public-sector action. The question that emerges in such a context is whether or not a jurisdiction can find ways to leverage the potential benefits of private investment and competition for the pursuit of aims that are essentially collective by nature, and thus more characteristic of traditional forms of public goods warranting government investment and control.

Inspired by the warnings of Jane Jacob's on the potentially corrupting and ill-performing hybrids of mixing the two sectors (as many, but not all traditional forms of public infrastructure are of a more guardian orientation than that of the commercial syndrome), traditionalists defending separation and clarity would respond to such a question in the negative: Unless a particular aspect of infrastructure can be shown to be well suited to market pricing and investment (in which case the government should relinquish its involvement), the resulting public good demands clear government action and financing that is direct and unambiguous.

Conversely, defenders of integrative models of public-private activity point to the possibility of generating value from aligning complementary perspectives in a transparent manner. The potential benefits are well summarized in a recent report by TD Canada Trust and they include greater flexibility for governments in planning infrastructure development, freeing up governments to focus on what they do best, improving the care of public assets, maintaining service quality through innovation, shifting risk from taxpayers to the private sector, and the potential for synergies by combining project components through a single contracting party (then empowered to coordinate the project more freely than would otherwise be the case if government managed each separate project variable).

While the concept of a P3 typically denotes private-sector involvement in the construction and/or maintenance of a new capital asset to be used for public-interest purposes, such arrangements can take many forms. P3s fall short of privatization, which implies a relinquishing of government involvement in favor of market-based ownership and private-sector actors (thereby removing the conditions for partnership. Most P3s typically fall in the middle ground of the diagram, with various financing schemes involving long-term leasing arrangements and in some cases, provisions as to whether the asset will revert to private or public ownership at the end of the project term.

In the United Kingdom, the government introduced a scheme known as the Private Finance Initiative (PFI). Started by conservatives but maintained and expanded under the purview of Tony Blair and his Labour Government, the purpose of this program has been to create infrastructure of a public purpose through mechanisms leveraging private-sector involvement in financing, construction, and maintenance. Seeking a middle ground between direct government control and outright privatization, PFI seeks opportunities to share responsibilities and risks, creating new assets via payment schemes and commitments underwritten by the stable involvement of government authorities.

PFI has not replaced direct public-sector provision, accounting for only a modest portion of overall infrastructure spending, but it has become an increasingly prominent—and controversial—aspect of new infrastructure development across the United Kingdom. Defenders of the initiative point to the flourishing of new infrastructure projects (meeting public-interest needs) that has been enabled by leveraging private-sector capital investment and project management competencies while shifting much of the financial risk associated with these new ventures to industry.

Can Risk be Shared?

Under PFI, if a company in the United Kingdom faces cost overruns in completing the construction of a new facility within the agreed-to timeframe, it must absorb those costs, reducing its rate of return (and thereby providing a strong performance incentive to remain on time and on budget). In comparison to those projects administered directly by government authorities (i.e., situating the public-private governance to the lower left quadrant of the diagram, perhaps contracting out limited aspects of construction to private companies but nonetheless retaining full ownership and control), studies demonstrate that PFI initiatives enjoy stronger performance and fewer failures, and the program itself has been exported to many other countries in Europe and elsewhere (including Canada, a point returned to below).

Yet, PFI is not without critics and controversy. The first PFI initiative led to the construction of the Skye Bridge in Scotland, connecting mainland Scotland to the island of Skye (and shutting local ferry services as a result). The arrangement proved controversial since its inception, with significant cost overruns incurred by governments as private-sector operators proved incapable of sustaining profits with toll charges that proved politically unpalatable. While the initiative began under the British national government (then under conservative rule), the since-created Scottish government eventually terminated the partnership and removed the tolls, reverting the bridge to a more traditional model of government control at a much greater expense than initially envisioned.

While such spectacular failures have been rare, the financial implications of PFI remain complex and contested. From the government's perspective, in particular, an advantage of PFI or a similar public-private variant is the avoidance of upfront costs, a politically attractive prospect to any government facing short-term scrutiny over spending (usually gauged by immediate budget projections and results for which annual metrics of deficits and/or surpluses represent the most closely scrutinized performance indicator, not unlike the private sector's reliance on quarterly profits). The offsetting costs for such upfront off-loading is a long-term commitment to fixed payments of one sort or another (usually specified by leasing arrangements). Many observers contend that the cost-benefit analysis with respect to financing and return over the lifetime of the asset in question is proving to be more art than science and it may well be that a final analysis of such quantitative results may not be forthcoming for some time to come.

There are also ongoing questions about total costs of borrowing when investments are required for new asset construction. A key PFI rationale, as noted, has been the heightened constraints on public-sector borrowing following dramatic increases in public debt that occurred in many countries throughout the 1970s and 1980s (continuing in some jurisdictions to this day). However, when left to private companies to raise capital, it may be that borrowing costs rise since individual companies are generally unable to secure the most advantageous interest rates enjoyed by government borrowers. In essence, then, according to some observers, government may merely be avoiding upfront costs on its balance sheet but contributing to higher overall financing costs for the infrastructure initiative over its total lifetime.

Skeptics of these new governance models, both within and outside of the public sector, will continue to scrutinize such arrangements and such scrutiny is important and should be viewed as not entirely unwelcome. More than ultimately leading to a stark endorsement of public or private means in terms new of infrastructure development, the analyses and counterarguments put forth by various parties (with nonetheless varying motivations and degrees of objectivity) are indicative of the sorts of governance pressures for transparency and accountability that are becoming more commonplace across all sectors (a theme discussed in previously). Along with uncertainties pertaining to cost and financing, however, are equally important questions of a more strategic nature pertaining to innovation and performance.

Innovation and Performance

As infrastructure becomes more strategic, complex, and technologically sophisticated, questions pertaining to specialized skills and capacities and the sorts of performance outcomes being sought rise in importance. It is for such a reason that a program such as PFI specifically targets those areas where risk is high. If an asset is straightforward and relatively inexpensive to build, a traditional contracting approach between public owners and private companies may well suffice; if uncertainty is high, so too is the need for leading-edge expertise and innovative solutions.

The example of highways and road tolls personify the complexities of governance and the range of both financing and performance variables at play. In Ontario, for instance, the construction of a new toll highway in the Greater Toronto Area that began in 1993 involved an innovative partnership scheme largely because of the desire to create a more technologically sophisticated solution to driver tolls than the traditional ticketing-booth method.

At the same time, the Government of Ontario sought to fix its costs when tendering the project, thereby shifting risk to the private-sector developers, although initial financing for the project would be arranged by a provincial crown corporation on the grounds of securing lower costs of borrowing (Borins, 2004). Later in 1999, the Government of Ontario would sell its stake in the 407 system, moving closer to full privatization. Such a move would prove politically contentious, and while few doubt the technical success of the 407 experience, debates continue as to the financing and the politics of the scheme.

Indeed, the specter of privatization would shadow the conservative government's efforts in Ontario to embrace public-private partnering for infrastructure development, extending such efforts into the realms of education and health care. Such debate and tension would come to a head in the 2003 election campaign when a proposed PFI-type initiative for a new hospital in Ottawa drew much criticism: The long-term lease agreement stipulated that despite guaranteed public-sector usage of the facility, ownership would ultimately revert to private owners at the end of the 30-year deal.

The liberals criticized such an arrangement as unacceptable privatization (in the particularly sensitive health care realm), promising change. Once in power, their solution was a highly nuanced modification in the leasing agreement that would see public ownership ultimately retained in an otherwise unchanged partnership arrangement of private financing and upfront risk for a guaranteed, long-term annual payment stream. Since then, the liberals have, not unlike the Labour Party in the United Kingdom, sought to entrench PFI-type arrangements in a more mainstream, politically palatable template: the Infrastructure Planning, Financing and Procurement Framework (IPFP).

While Ontario has proven to be one of North America's most politically volatile jurisdictions over the past two decades (in terms of political leaders shifting dramatically across the ideological spectrum), it has also become indicative of the mainstream expansion of private-sector activity across the realm of public infrastructure. New hospitals in Ontario are now being constructed under collaborative, P3-type arrangements with the private sector, and the end determination of whether such deals ultimately generate net benefits for both companies and taxpayers must await a final account some 25 to 30 years hence.

The main point, however, is less the ideology surrounding such partnerships (that are clearly becoming mainstream vehicles in jurisdictions with governments of every political stripe) and more the governance complexities of making such projects work, particularly with respect to complex IT-based e-health systems integrating public- and private-sector processes. An early e-government report by the OECD (2001) underlined the hidden threat to e-government as poor management of IT projects generally in large organizational settings, and follow-up work explored the compounding difficulties, many of them discussed in this section, of collaborative endeavors involving multiple sectors (Allen, Paquet, Juillet, & Roy, 2005). Ontario's performance in this regard is examined further below.

Assessing E-Health in Ontario

The Government of Ontario (2005) defines e-health as "achieving better health outcomes by transforming health systems and business practises through the investment in and more comprehensive use of information and information technology." In terms of the realms of service and security, Ontario's e-health efforts may be summarized (and somewhat simplified) in thee major directions: (a) efforts to create new e-health competencies and capacities within the core bodies of the provincial government with health care responsibilities, (b) efforts to realize interoperability and an EHR-type infrastructure to better serve the public users at the community level and in doing so, balance province-wide systemic reform with the localized dimension to health care organization, accountability, and delivery, and (c) efforts to address the particular circumstances of remote parts of the province, notably northern regions and communities (despite the importance of this third direction, it is the first two that are the focus of this chapter).

Regarding the first direction, the provincial Office of E-Health was formally established in 2004. This new office is akin to a central policy unit guiding the overall evolution of e-health within the core provincial public service and across the extended health care system. In this latter realm, the office works closely with its predecessor organization that has since become an autonomous public agency, Smart Systems for Health (SSH), a provincial body focused on developing and introducing IT-based technological solutions in health care (and in doing so, working more directly with health care practitioners and their communities[4]).

The purpose of the e-health office today, then, is essentially to provide a CIO capacity for the health care system as a whole in order to guide system-wide reforms pertaining to new technologies. The head of this office reports directly to the deputy minister responsible for the provincial Ministry of Health and Long-Term Care (the appointed department head who, in turn, reports directly to the political minister).

The e-health office also serves as the secretariat and coordinating body for the Ontario E-Health Council, a forum that is actually a collection of four separate councils with specific areas of focus (continuing care, laboratories, physicians, and hospitals). Four additional councils have also been proposed and their status is under consideration by the government (pharmacies, public health, regional integration, and program integration). It is these councils that comprise the extended and comprehensive network of sectors, professions, and organizational bodies that make up Ontario's health care system. The council mechanisms are meant to reflect the separate needs of the groups such as physicians and hospitals, notwithstanding the danger of fragmentation:

> *While the e-Health Council format provides valuable support for projects within each sector, it may also cause the creation of virtual silos that may impede or restrict the sharing of important information. To prevent this, the region must be aware of what is going on within each sector and work cooperatively to share projects.* (Health Care Network of Southeastern Ontario, 2005, p. 4)

The latter segment of this quote—the invocation of a regional concerted approach—underscores one of the most central quandaries facing e-health in Ontario, namely, the geographic alignment of health care operations and delivery across central (provincial), regional, and local dimensions. Identified as the second major direction of provincial efforts at the outset of this section, the problem is a familiar one to CIOs and students of e-government alike: striking the balance between system-wide coordination that is demanded if interoperability is to be realized and a requisite level of flexibility and autonomy that permits individual organizations and subnetworks of health care providers to innovative and act in a client-centric manner.

In the case of Ontario, this challenge is somewhat unique in comparison to other provinces since there are no regional health care authorities with formal decision-making autonomy between the province as a whole and community-level care providers and facilities such as physicians, clinics, hospitals, and the like.[5] The provincial e-health office and the provincial CIO structures represent the province-wide perspective on health care matters, whereas locally and regionally a variety of largely informal, advisory bodies (District Health Councils) promote coordination and dialogue for specific subprovincial zones while also providing input to the provincial government.

Whereas the formation of such movements represents a bottom-up emergence of governance mechanisms to address shared externalities, both positive and negative, the province has also responded with a formalized strategy to instill more local coordination through the creation of a province-wide set of LHINs. The purpose of these bodies is to facilitate interoperability and integrated health care delivery in a collaborative manner without imposing a new layer of centralized, regional authority on the system. Even those engaged in e-health acknowledge that "the impact of the LHINS on Ontario's e-Health agenda has not yet been defined" (Health Care Network of Southeastern Ontario, 2005, p. 7). Indeed, an important governance design question is the shape of relations between the new LHIN network and the proposed e-Health Council on Regional Integration.

There is an expectation at this point in time that the LHIN will become a vehicle to promote a shared-services approach to a more common IT infrastructure that, in turn, can facilitate system-wide perspectives on resource planning and delivery within a given jurisdiction (Government of Ontario, 2005). In doing so, however, it is clear that the provincial government is walking on eggshells in attempting to facilitate provincial guidance and stronger local coordination in a manner that is not interpreted as a threat to key stakeholders with their own territorial and operational autonomy. Hospitals are one key stakeholder group. Their views pertaining to the LHIN model would see strong support at first glance, but this is also conditional on the LHIN not undermining their own governance structures and authority:

The hospitals of Ontario and the OHA (Ontario Hospital Association) are strong supporters of increased integration of the health care system and believe that efforts to improve integration should build on current system strengths and successes. Hospitals also support the establishment of LHINs that will focus on engaging communities in health system transformation by enhancing and supporting local capacity to plan, coordinate and integrate the delivery of health services at the community level. In addition, the OHA fully endorses the government's commitment to maintaining local independent governance including the voluntary role of hospital trustees. (Ontario Hospital Association, 2005, p. i)

The backdrop shaping this position is the contentious relationship between hospitals, health care groups generally, and the previous conservative-led governments in power from 1995 to 2003 that preferred a heavy-handed approach to government restructuring (driven less by an interest in e-health and more by an overarching agenda of tax cuts and spending reductions). In health care specifically, a number of hospital consolidations were imposed across the province, leading some hospitals to fight such moves (i.e., smaller hospitals fused into larger ones) while others positioned themselves as larger health care centers with more responsibility and autonomy. Importantly, the absence of regional authorities in Ontario meant that power throughout this process and since has been shared between the province centrally and individual hospitals locally.

With respect to e-health, the hospitals have not only positioned themselves as supporters of the LHIN model as a complement to their own authority, but also as a critic of the province's lack of more forceful and political interest in IT-led transformations of the health care system as a whole (Ontario Hospital Association, 2005). Part of this interest may no doubt be ascribed to a genuine attachment to the potential of e-health to improve medical systems, but it should also be viewed as a position that complements the hospital's own agenda in seeking more direct funding from the province to invest in their own operations through their own autonomous governance structures.

There is evidence to suggest that the foundational e-health work being undertaken by the province is not translating into wider public learning and support. Public opinion research in Canada suggests that it is in Ontario over the past 3 years where the decline in confidence accorded to the provincial government has been the steepest.[6] Elected on a campaign of democratic renewal, promising more openness and direct public engagement in governing, the provincial liberals have acted on a number of their pledges. In the realm of health care, however, the government has sought a more directly interventionist approach in crafting a message of reassurance and refurbishment through more taxation and improved public-sector delivery (dismissing, for example, more flexibility through private-sector care). While such an approach has prioritized health care spending, it raises the issue of whether the Government of Ontario is adequately preparing the populous for the significance of e-health in terms of health care organization and delivery associated with online connectivity and digital technologies.

This question, in turn, needs to be examined from two complementing planes. At the macro level of the system as a whole, some groups such as the Ontario Hospital Association and the private sector have conveyed the view that the province has not accorded sufficient attention politically to e-health. Notwithstanding the self-interest motive at play, there is some merit to this view when one considers the evolution of the current government's approach to health care management during their first mandate.

First, the centerpiece of their strategy has been a new health care levy (or tax) designed to expand funding for the existing system, albeit in ways that achieve specific improvement targets laid out by the province. These targets, however, are focused on user outcomes and the communication of service improvements, with the overall tone of the political message being one of reassurance as opposed to systemic change. While the LHIN represents a notable governance innovation, the e-health agenda generally has not been accorded a high degree of political visibility or new public funding (Ontario Hospital Association, 2005). This tone mirrors, by and large, the government approach toward e-government and service transformation, which has been to become more cautious on large-scale, IT-led transformations due to a view that such ventures in the past have yielded more problems and failures than clear improvements.[7]

Here the question of whether the Government of Ontario is acting transparently with respect to health care reform is an important one. At one level, for those stakeholders and informed observers engaged in e-health areas, there is ample information about the strategies and mechanisms deployed (and the rationale for doing so). Yet, at the same time, the absence of more political attention devoted to e-health and both the opportunities and risks associated with new digital technologies suggests less a desire to withhold information or mislead the public than a preference for a form of positive-laden clarity (i.e., the message of government succeeding) over a willingness to embrace uncertainty and complexity. The risk of such a direction, however, is a further erosion of public legitimacy and trust as such efforts are viewed as manipulative and politically deceitful at worst, partial and incomplete at best (Paquet, 2004; Reed, 2004; Reid, 2004).

At the community level, then, the creation of the LHIN raises the issue of whether or not such a mechanism will be sufficiently empowered to orchestrate a level of systemic change on a subprovincial level (i.e., the 14 regions each denoted with an LHIN). While the OHA and the province view the LHIN as an important vehicle for community mobilization and engagement in health care transformation (a view supported by the increasingly participative determinants of governance legitimacy and positive change), it is also the case that the public must be convinced of the usefulness of doing so. A weak regional mechanism with little authority to instill change may well undermine the credibility of the system, viewed once again as a vehicle for provincial intervention and communication as opposed to genuine consultation and engagement (Woodward, 2003).

The government provides a counterargument rooted in incrementalism: the LHIN as a starting point for dialogue and consultation across a diverse province where the needs of different regions are varied. Accordingly, the difficult context faced by the LHIN, if it is to serve as a vehicle for community involvement and dialogue, has been well summarized by Ableson and Eyles (2002) in their assessment of public participation in the governance of health care in Canada (put forth in their original form as four concluding statements).

- Citizen domination by powerful groups interested in involving the public when it suits their purpose;
- Policy-makers touting citizen governance as a critical element to achieve more responsive decision making while using these structures as instruments of cost-cutting and restructuring;
- The ability for only the most educated and sophisticated and arguably the most unrepresentative and biased "publics" to participate as citizen governors; and
- An increasingly cynical public, weary of the pre-determined illegitimate public consultation processes...seeking more accountable consultation. (p. vi)

It is precisely this mood that was captured in the present Ontario government's electoral platform of 2003 that emphasized the need for more meaningful citizen engagement. Since taking power, however, the creation of the 14 LHIN bodies and the appointment of initial chairs and board members (nine in each region), a process that was complete by June 2006, has proven to be carefully orchestrated by the provincial government. For instance, all board chairpersons were selected and appointed directly by the province, as were an initial set of members. The province then used a process of local selection to form a pool of candidates for the final section while retaining its authority to render the final decision in each case. Such an approach raises questions about the degree of local engagement enjoyed by the networks at the outset of their mandates.

Private-Sector Partnering

From the private-sector vantage point, the creation of the regional LHINs has done little to alter their involvement in e-health architecture and prospective technology solutions. There are two reasons. First, the largely centralized nature of the design process used to date has not dramatically altered the decision-making structures of health care spending in Ontario and, and result (the second reason), major procurement and policy decisions pertaining to IT usage and e-health remain at the provincial level.

It bears noting once again that many of the most sophisticated heath care systems are highly regionalized, including countries such as those across Scandinavia who in many ways can be compared to a province such as Ontario (as they are smaller in both population and territory). Accordingly, the usage of a private-sector-run health authority in Stockholm was not a national decision but rather a regional one. In the United Kingdom, a much larger country, there has been a federated effort to empower separate regional health authorities with their own distinct partnering arrangements (coordinated by an overarching national policy framework).

In Ontario, by contrast, the government has itself recognized its own weaknesses in managing large IT projects both in-house and via private partners, albeit doing so early in its mandate by way of an external review commission (that not only sought improvements but could be cast as a retroactive look at the previous government's failures). Nonetheless, the review commission, headed up by a former national auditor general, had very little by way of specific improvements to offer with respect to public-private partnering beyond the need to consult industry and improve the relationship in going forward (Dutil et al., 2005).

Some reluctance on the part of the province to turn to a greater role for the private sector is not without some understanding in light of trends elsewhere, including Canada. In British Columbia, for instance, where the provincial government has been perhaps the most aggressive in embracing public-private partnering across both traditional infrastructure and IT and organizational systems, a recent outsourcing initiative aimed at improving the service delivery apparatus of the health insurance systems has created some controversy as to whether performance is being improved or not (Williams, 2006). Even the industry-friendly, generally protechnology publication offered indirect warnings by virtue of its April 2006 cover story on the State of Maine's failed IT partnership in the realm of health care.

Yet, despite such risks, it remains apparent that most governments are ill-equipped to proceed entirely through in-house solutions in the realms of e-government, e-health, and IT architecture generally. A key issue in the Ontario experience is whether the risks of greater partnering, if and when they are pursued, are likely to be compounded in light of the centralized nature of IT management and health care organization within the ministry and its affiliate bodies.

CONCLUSION AND FUTURE RESEARCH DIRECTIONS

The Province of Ontario is hardly alone in facing a variety of technological, organizational, and political challenges as it seeks to orchestrate health care reform. E-health in particular creates tensions in the immediate term between the need for stability and incremental progress on the one hand (as governments in power look to reassure the public and ensure voter support at the next electoral encounter), and the potential for system-wide transformation on the other.

There is a body of evidence in e-government and IT management demonstrating that in the absence of significant pressure to modify the existing structures of power and authority, the application of new technologies will result by and large in a strengthening of existing arrangements (Kraemer & King, 2003). With respect to the adaptation of large-scale public-sector health care systems, this view of technological incrementalism seems consistent with the manner by which the provincial government appears reluctant to share power locally and regionally on the one hand, and through more innovative governance models involving the private sector on the other hand.

Clearly consequential for Ontario's fledging LHINs, such incrementalism can only weaken bottom-up innovation and experimentation. As digital technologies permeate wider segments of public-sector operations, and as further democratic innovation is pursued (in light of the signs of eroding trust at these levels), the deployment of new technology and its alignment with organizational and political structures will grow in scope and complexity. The risk of federal and provincial technocracies is real since administratively larger governments have typically adapted more slowly than subnational ones (Goldsmith & Eggers, 2004). The enterprise architecture of a public sector in a federal environment is complicated by the need to sort out roles and assign resources and authority in a manner that either respects or explicitly seeks agreement to overcome the limits of sovereign autonomy at each political and organizational level enjoined within the system as a whole.

While the province is beginning to create many aspects of a solid technical and organizational infrastructure for e-health, what remains problematic is the political landscape. What is therefore required is a much stronger exploration of the means by which public and community engagement can be both expanded and leveraged as a means toward creating the conditions for (a) a higher level of trust among the province's citizenry as a whole (that at present is highly skeptical of the government's message of reassurance and incremental improvement) and (b) stronger forms of public engagement at the local and regional level to orchestrate the sorts of shared processes required to underpin complex change with mechanisms for socializing learning, shared risk, and collective change.

In terms of public-private partnering, a greater regionalization of decision-making and spending authorities, within transparent and locally accountable governance forums, could provide incentives for the private sector to work more directly subprovincially, enjoying greater degrees of freedom for collaboration via more manageable contracting arrangements. Such an approach does not need to be fragmented or displace a provincial role; rather, it calls for provincial coordination to provide an overall policy and interoperability framework within which these new partnership models can flourish.

Finally, with respect to future research directions, what would emerge as an imperative is the undertaking of interdisciplinary efforts to enjoin what have until now typically been separate realms of the technology of electronic health on the hand, and the governance of health care delivery on the other. The success of e-health is very much intertwined with public-sector governance and, as this chapter has demonstrated, the capacities of local and regional communities to engage the public that is at once a recipient of health care services, a partner in the formation of health care strategies, and a voter overseeing the usage of public resources and the stewardship of managers and elected officials. Researchers must therefore delve into the nexus between technological adaptation and civic engagement in order to better understand the new governance landscape of health care systems in an increasingly digital and networked world.

REFERENCES

Ableson, J., & Eyles, J. (2002). *Public participation and citizen governance in the Canadian health system* (Discussion Paper No. 7). Commission on the Future of Health Care in Canada. Retrieved from http://www.hc-sc.gc.ca/english/pdf/romanow/pdfs/Abelson_E.pdf

Allen, B. A., Paquet, G., Juillet, L., & Roy, J. (2005). E-government as collaborative governance: Structural, accountability and cultural reform. In M. Khosrow-Pour (Ed.), *Practising e-government: A global perspective* (pp. 1-15). Idea Group Publishing.

Allsop, J. (2003). Evaluating user involvement in primary healthcare. *International Journal of Healthcare Technology and Management, 5*(1/2), 34-44.

Bajkowski, J. (2005). Ill wind blows through Australia's e-health adoption. *IT World Canada.* Retrieved from http://www.itworldcanada.com

Batini, C., Cappadozzi, E., Mecella, M., & Talamo, M. (2002). Cooperative architectures. In W. J. McIver & A. K. Elmagarmid (Eds.), *Advances in digital government: Technology, human factors and policy.* Boston: Kluwer Academic Publishers.

Bliemel, M., & Hassanein, K. (2004). E-health: Applying business processes reengineering principles to healthcare in Canada. *International Journal of Electronic Business, 2*(6), 625-643.

Borins, S. (2004). A holistic view of public sector information technology. *Journal of E-Government, 1*(2), 3-29.

Cairncross, F. (2002). *The company of the future.* Cambridge: Harvard Business School Press.

Charih, M., & Robert, J. (2004). Government online in the Federal Government of Canada: The organizational issues. *International Review of Administrative Sciences, 70*(2), 373-384.

Coe, A. (2004). *Government online in Canada: Innovation and accountability in 21st century government.* Unpublished master's thesis, Kennedy School of Government, Cambridge, MA.

Coleman, S. (2003). The future of the Internet and democracy beyond metaphors, towards policy. In *Promise and problems of e-democracy: Challenges on online citizen engagement.* Paris: E-Government Project.

Coleman, S., & Norris, D. (2005). A new agenda for e-democracy. *International Journal of Electronic Government Research, 1*(3) 69-82.

Courchene, T. J. (2005). "E-the-people": Reflections on citizen power in the information age. *Policy Options, 26*(3), 43-50.

Culbertson, S. (2005). E-government and organizational change. In M. Khosrow-Pour (Ed.), *Practising e-government: A global perspective.* Idea Group Publishing.

Demiris, G. (2004). Electronic home healthcare: Concepts and challenges. *International Journal of Healthcare, 1*(1) 4-16.

Dutil, P., Langford, J., & Roy, J. (2005). *E-government and service transformation relationships between government and industry: Developing best practises.* Toronto, Canada: Institute of Public Administration.

Dwyer, P. (2004). The rise of transparency networks: A new dynamic for inclusive government. In J. Halligan & T. Moore (Eds.), *Future challenges for e-government.* Canberra, Australia: Government of Australia.

Eggers, W. (2005). *Government 2.0: Using technology to improve education, cut red tape, reduce gridlock and enhance democracy.* New York: Rowman and Littlefield Publishers.

Eng, T., & Beauchamp, N. (2004). *Striving for critical mass.* Proceedings of the Fourth Annual eHealth Developer's Summit, Seattle, WA.

Evans, K. G. (2002). Virtual dialogue and democratic community. *The Transformative Power of Dialogue, 12*, 157-177.

Fountain, J. E. (2001). *Building the virtual state: Information technology and institutional change.* Washington, DC: Brookings Institution Press.

Fountain, J. E. (2004). Digital government and public health. *Public Health Research, Practise, and Policy, 1*(4), 1-5.

Gath, S. (2004). Electronics health records for Australia: Some legal and policy issues. In J. Halligan & T. Moore (Eds.), *Future challenges for e-government.* Canberra, Australia: Government of Australia.

Gibbons, R. (2004). Federalism and the challenge of electronic portals. In L. Oliver & L. Sanders (Eds.), *E-government reconsidered: Renewal of governance for the knowledge age.* Regina, Canada: Canadian Plains Research Center.

Goldsmith, S., & Eggers, W. D. (2004). *Governing by networks: The new shape of the public sector.* WA: Brookings Institution Press.

Government of Ontario. (2005). *Local health integration networks* (Bulletin No. 13). Ministry of Health. http://www.health.gov.on.ca

Health Care Network of Southeastern Ontario. (2005). *Southeastern Ontario information technology & communications strategy, 2005-09.* Retrieved from http://www.seohealthnet.com

Hurley, C., Baum, F., & van Eyk, H. (2004). Designing better health care in the South: A case study of unsuccessful transformational change in public sector health reform. *Australian Journal of Public Administration, 63*(2), 31-41.

Josefsoon, U. (2005). Coping with illness online: The case of patients' online communities. *The Information Society, 21,* 143-153.

Koch, C. (2005, March 1). A new blueprint for the enterprise. *CIO Magazine.*

Kraemer, K., & King, J. L. (2003). *Information technology and administrative reform: Will the time after e-government be different?* Irvine, CA: Center for Research on Information Technology and Organizations.

Langford, J., & Roy, J. (2006). E-government and public-private partnerships in Canada: When failure is no longer an option. *International Journal of Electronic Business, 4*(2), 118-135.

McMillan, M. L. (2004). *Financial relationships between regional and municipal authorities: Insights from the examination of five OECD countries* (IIGR Working Paper No. 3). Kingston: Queen's University.

Mieczkowska, S., & Hinton, M. (2004). Barriers to e-health business processes. *International Journal of Healthcare, 1*(1) 47-59.

Mundy, D. (2004). Electronic transmission of prescriptions: Towards realizing the dream. *International Journal of Healthcare, 1*(1) 112-125.

Oates, B. J. (2003). The potential contribution of ICT's to the political process. *Electronic Journal of E-Government, 1*(1).

Oliver, L., & Sanders, L. (Eds.). (2004). *E-government reconsidered: Renewal of governance for the knowledge age.* Regina, Canada: Canadian Plains Research Center.

Ontario Hospital Association. (2005). *Transformation agenda risks and opportunities report: E-health as the strategic enabler.* Retrieved from http://www.oha.com

Ontario Hospital eHealth Council. (2002). *An update on data and technology standards in Ontario.* Ontario Hospital Association. Retrieved from http://www.oha.com

Ontario Hospital eHealth Council. (2004). *Home telehealth in Ontario.* Ontario Hospital Association. Retrieved from http://www.oha.com

Organization for Economic Cooperation and Development (OECD). (2001). *The hidden threat to e-government, avoiding large government IT failures* (PUMA Policy Brief 8).

Paquet, G. (1997). States, communities and markets: The distributed governance scenario. In T. J. Courchene (Ed.), *The nation-state in a global information era: Policy challenges.* Kingston: John Deutsch Institute for the Study of Economic Policy.

Paquet, G. (2004). There is more to governance than public candelabras: E-governance and Canada's public service. In L. Oliver & L. Sanders (Eds.), *E-government reconsidered: Renewal of governance for the knowledge age.* Regina, Canada: Canadian Plains Research Center.

Patton, S. (2005, March 1). Sharing data, saving lives. *CIO Magazine.*

Pavlichev, A., & Garson, G. D. (Eds.). (2004). *Digital government: Principles and best practises.* Hershey, PA: Idea Group Publishing.

Prisma. (2004). *Implications of Pan-European best practise in eHealth service delivery.* European Union. Retrieved from http://wwwiprisma-eu.net

Randeree, E., & Rao, H. R. (2004). E-health and assurance: Curing hospital Websites. *International Journal of Healthcare, 1*(1), 33-46.

Reed, B. (2004). Accountability in a shared services world. In J. Halligan & T. Moore (Eds.), *Future challenges for e-government.* Canberra, Australia: Government of Australia.

Reid, J. (2004). Holding governments accountable by strengthening access to information laws and information management practices. In L. Oliver & L. Sanders (Eds.), *E-government reconsidered: Renewal of governance for the knowledge age.* Regina, Canada: Canadian Plains Research Center.

Rosenbord, L. D. (2003). A facilitated approach to developing collaborative action in primary healthcare. *International Journal of Healthcare Technology and Management, 5*(1/2), 63-80.

Roy, J. (2005). Services, security, transparency and trust: Government online or governance renewal in Canada? *International Journal of E-Government Research, 1*(1), 48-58.

Roy, J. (2006). *E-government in Canada: Transformation for a digital age.* Ottawa, Canada: University of Ottawa Press.

Roy, J. (2007). E-health in Ontario: A multi-dimensional governance transformation. *International Journal of Health Care Technology and Management, 8*(1/2), 66-84.

Scholl, H. (2005). Motives, strategic approach, objectives and focal points in e-government-induced change. *International Journal of E-Government Research, 1*(1), 59-78.

TD Economics. (2006). *Creating the winning conditions for public-private partnerships in Canada.* Retrieved from http://www.td.com/economics/special/db0606_p3s.pdf

Wickramasinghe, N., & Misra, S. K. (2004). A wireless trust model for health care. *International Journal of Healthcare, 1*(1), 60-77.

Williams, L. (2006). Tech to the rescue? *CIO Government Review.*

Woodward, V. (2003). Participation the community work way. *International Journal of Healthcare Technology and Management, 5*(1/2), 3-19.

TERMS AND DEFINITIONS

E-Government: E-government is the usage of news policy tools and organizational processes involving digital technologies in order to improve public-sector capacities.

E-Health: E-health is the usage of new technologies to improve health care organization and service delivery.

Electronic Health Record (EHR): EHR provides each individual with a secure and private lifetime record of their key health history and care within the health system.

Governance: It is the mechanism of coordinating resources, making decisions, and structuring accountability.

Identity Management: This involves policies and technologies that enable authenticated identities to be verified in order to confirm and enable access or transactions between individuals and organizations.

Interoperability: It is the ability of different information and computer systems to exchange data and enable communication and coordination across different organizations or subsystems within an organization in order to be participative in shared governance systems.

Local Health Integration Networks (LHIN): LHINs are flexible bodies created to facilitate interoperability and integrated health care delivery in a collaborative manner without imposing a new layer of centralized, regional authority on the system.

Chapter LXII
Implementing a Sound Public Information Security Program

Stephen K. Aikins
University of South Florida, USA

INTRODUCTION

The evolving nature of information security threats such as cybercrime, as well as the need to ensure the confidentiality and privacy of citizen information and to protect critical infrastructure call for effective information security management in the public sector. According to Evers (2006), the FBI (Federal Bureau of Investigation) estimates that cybercrime will cost businesses an estimated $67.2 billion per year. Citizens' privacy and the security of their personal information have become issues of increasing concern as headlines of data security breaches and identity thefts abound in the mainstream media. For example, in 2005, 9.3 million U.S. citizens, about 4.25% of the population, were victims of identity theft and fraud, costing approximately $54.4 billion (Council of Better Business & Javelin Strategy & Research, 2006).

E-government applications have made it easier for citizens to conduct business online with government agencies, although their trust in the ability of governments to keep that information private is low. Considering the amount of citizen information held by governments at all levels and the steps needed to address potential homeland-security and IT-related threats to critical infrastructure, the need for effective means of safeguarding public agency data has become an issue of paramount importance. In addition, the need to ensure integrity and availability of public information resources is crucial to many government operations. As a result, several states are recognizing the importance of information security and privacy in their state IT strategic plans (National Association of State Chief Information Security Officers [NASCIO], 2006).

BACKGROUND

Almost two decades after the Computer Security Act was signed into law, federal IT security reviews indicated continuing risks to federal operations (U.S. General Accounting Office [GAO], 2000, 2001, 2002). This appears to be happening despite the escalating cost of federal IT security spending, which is expected to increase from $4.2 billion in 2003 to $6 billion in 2008 (Walker,

2003). A key requirement for effective planning and management of public organizations' information security is the implementation of a public information security program.

Several public agencies such as the National Institute of Standards and Technology (NIST), the Office of Management and Budget (OMB), the National Security Agency (NSA), the GAO, and NASCIO have published numerous security documentations that serve as sources of reference for public organizations in managing the security of their information resources. However, a recent survey by NASCIO (2006) revealed that about 30% of the state chief information security officers (CISOs) were unfamiliar with major cybersecurity-related documents. This chapter discusses the elements of an effective information security program and how it could be implemented by state and local governments to mitigate their security vulnerabilities, threats, and exploits.

ELEMENTS OF AN INFORMATION SECURITY PROGRAM

The implementation of an effective information security program begins with a risk assessment and the development of an enterprise-wide information security plan. State and local governments should understand their environment and conduct IT risk assessment. This is done to determine their security needs and formulate plans that include strategic goals to protect critical infrastructure and citizen privacy. Once the plan is in place, an information security program that embodies security management structure and comprehensive policy, related standards, and procedural guidelines should be developed. GAO (2001) outlines the following elements of an information security program as critical.

1. Periodic risk assessment
2. Documented entity-wide security program plan
3. Security management structure with clearly assigned security responsibilities
4. Effective security-related personnel policies
5. Security program evaluation

Perform Periodic Risk Assessment

Understanding the risks of the public organization is crucial in determining the proper security policies, procedures, guidelines, and standards to put in place to ensure adequate information security controls. The IBM Foundation for the Business of Government (2002) argues a risk assessment should include a complete inventory of critical systems and assets as well as a gap analysis between the actual and ideal levels of IT security. Therefore, the risk assessment should include a review of such broad areas as employee management and training; information systems, including network and software design and information processing, storage, transmission, and disposal; and detection, prevention, and response in the case of attacks, intrusions, and failures (NSA, 2002).

Effective risk assessment should have three major components: threat assessment, vulnerability assessment, and asset identification. In a survey of State CISOs, NASCIO (2006) found that although 73% of the respondents reported they have conducted risk assessments on systems that are homeland-security-critical assets, 76 to 84% reported they have inadequate or no information regarding threats from "internal ineptitude" and "internal maliciousness," which are potentially the most dangerous aspects of security breaches. Assessing the threats posed by a malicious insider (e.g., disgruntled employee), accidental insider (e.g., poorly trained or curious employee), malicious outsider (e.g., hacker, industrial espionage), and nature (e.g., fire, flood) will be useful in identifying and assessing the government agency's vulnerabilities (Hurd 2001; NIST, 2002).

Vulnerability assessment should focus on key areas of information security, including identification and authentication, account management, auditing, virus protection, configuration management, physical environments, personnel security, incident handling, and security awareness training (NIST, 2002). Once the public entity has assessed its vulnerability, the importance of each asset to that organization should be defined, and a rating system for confidentiality, integrity, and availability should be developed. After completing these three steps, the threats to the public entity's systems can then be compared to the vulnerabilities identified and balanced against the need and cost to protect the confidentiality, integrity, and availability (NIST, 1998). A good risk assessment clarifies the posture of agency security need and can serve as a source of justification for increased funding (Gartner, 2004).

Document Entity-Wide Security Program

NASCIO (2006) found that only 47% of responding State CISOs in its recent survey had good documented information security guidelines in place. With pressures from legislatures for government agencies to be strictly accountable for IT expenditures, as well as private and public data security breaches remaining in the headlines, clearly defined programs can clarify the agencies' security posture and help make the case for funding.

A good entity-wide security program requires documentation of the security policy and related procedures, guidelines, and standards that will equip the program managers and their information security officers with the tools needed to implement the policy (U.S. GAO, 2001). A good program includes guidelines and standards for authorization and authentication, logging, auditing and monitoring, vulnerability and patch management, and virus management. Aligning security policy with management controls, operational controls, and technical controls is useful in ensuring effective vulnerability assessment mapping (NIST, 1998; NIST, 2000).The State of Minnesota, for example, has initiated an aggressive enterprise-wide information security program enabling it to launch IT standards and a resource management program, and set hardware and software standards.

Providing visible and regular security awareness training, including e-mail updates and newsletters, is critical to effective enforcement of the program. To ensure adequate understanding of the entity's security posture, the security program should provide for a central management of incident handling. The program should also provide for compliance reviews and enforcement of the policies, procedures, and standards (OMB, 2000). This could be accomplished through self-assessment and reporting, vulnerability and penetration testing, site security reviews, and a tool that queries agents on every desktop to give the security configuration status (NIST, 2000, 2001; NSA, 2002; Wood, 2001).

Establish Security Management Structure with Clearly Defined Responsibilities

Clearly defined management structure and security roles and responsibilities as part of the security program could enhance enforcement (NIST, 1995; U.S. GAO, 2001). The management structure could vary depending on the nature of the government and its agencies, as well as its IT governance model. For example, in the State of Ohio, information technology is managed from two perspectives: from the perspective of the state as an enterprise covering all agencies, and from the perspective of the Office of Information Technology (OIT) as the primary IT service and infrastructure provider to the state agencies. This management structure enabled the OIT to issue a state IT security policy that requires agencies to perform security vulnerability assessment of the major agencies' computing and network systems (NASCIO, 2006). In Michigan, the Office of Enterprise Security is accountable to the director of the Michigan Department of Information Technology for identifying, managing, and mitigating the state's IT security risks and vulnerabilities.

Depending on the size of the public entity, there could be as many as six key players in the management of information security. These include the CISO who is responsible for the overall management, implementation, and enforcement of the IT security program, and the system program manager, who is responsible for life cycle planning of the system. There is also the information system security officer who is responsible for administrative and operational aspects of the system, and the system administrator who is responsible for day-to-day care and feeding of the system. There could also be the agency security personnel responsible for the management of physical access to all organizational facilities, including the IT data center and all other buildings hosting the IT department. Another key player could be a designated approval authority who is a senior executive with the ultimate responsibility for funding, configuration, and operation of the system (OMB, 2000). Finally, there are the business owners and functional managers who help to set the requirements for the level of protection needed for their processes or data. Effective information security management depends on clear coordination and understanding between these stakeholders (Wood, 2001).

Develop and Implement Effective Security-Related Policies

In general, department managers and supervisors are charged with keeping employees informed about policies and programs that pertain to their work, including those that govern information security and privacy. Policies, related standards, and procedures should spell out clearly the required actions to secure the agencies' information assets, and enforcement procedures and the consequences of noncompliance. In addition, employees must be trained to be reasonably well aware of the precautions they should take and ethics they should uphold in using information systems, e-mail, and the Internet in terms of cybersecurity.

A well-developed and effective implementation of information technology polices and standards could lead to savings. As part of its enterprise-wide information security program, Minnesota successfully implemented the state's first ever desktop standards through a public-private partnership with an expected savings of $24 million per year. The CISO should work with various departments within the entity such as human resources, legal, and contractors to help put in place controls such as background checks, nondisclosure agreements, termination and transfer procedures (e.g., return of equipment and ID, termination of user ID), regular vacations and shift rotations, and so forth. Background checks and termination and transfer procedures, if properly implemented, are critical in minimizing insider risks (NIST, 1996).

Monitor the Effectiveness of the Security Program and Make Necessary Changes

Once the public entity has the information security program in place, there is the need to monitor the effectiveness of the program to determine whether it is operating as intended. This can be done through reliance on a combination of self-reporting and hands-on review such as a tailored version of NIST 800-26 reviews with supporting documentation, vulnerability and system scanning of technical controls, random on-site checks of operational and technical controls, specific security policy compliance reviews, and audit finding reviews. In Nebraska, the CIO's office has partnered with the state auditor's office to provide IT risk assessment and application testing. As a result of tying the results of IT assessments to the financial audits, a higher level of attention is paid to the outcome of the IT assessment within each state agency.

Once the program monitoring is completed, it is important to coordinate with system administrators, security officers, business and system program managers, and upper level executives to determine a viable solution to the compliance problems identified (Wood, 2001). This calls for prioritization and initial tackling of the critical issues that require immediate management attention.

FUTURE TRENDS

The information technology threat environment is constantly changing, but the efforts of many governments at all levels to adapt to these changes and implement adequate countermeasures have been constrained by inadequate budgetary resources. As the need for change management to deal with these threats has become increasingly glaring, a number of states like Kansas, Minnesota, and Michigan have initiated enterprise-wide information security programs that include risk assessment, policy guidelines and standards, as well as countermeasures that address known threats. However, as stated earlier, the National Association of State Chief Information Officers found in its 2006 strategic cybersecurity survey that roughly 30% of state CIOs were unfamiliar with existing cybersecurity-related documents and strategies. Promotion of these documents, especially at the local government level, will be important in helping to develop effective information security programs in future.

Considering the even more limited resources of many local governments, an effective way of addressing the information security threats in the future will be resource alignments in which local governments take advantage of existing national and state government resources in order to enhance economies of scale. Recognizing the importance of information security initiatives in today's highly threatening environment, the National Association of State Chief Information Officers has conducted studies and developed guidelines and recommendations to assist members to take actionable steps and to make the business case for increased information security funding. It is expected that more and more states and local governments will take advantage of these resources as information security breaches continue to make the headlines and pushes security concerns to the forefront.

In order to compete with other service areas for funding, state information security officers will have to align information security with government business needs. For example, they will have to demonstrate how improved security can enhance protection for and reliability of information in critical government functions like tax assessments, revenue collection, budgeting, public safety, health, and education. In addition to understanding the security needs, they will also have to demonstrate expertise in taking possible proactive steps in preventing breaches.

CONCLUSION

The growing threat of information security breaches is an issue of grave concern to both governments and citizens. With finite government resources and the drain of entitlements and other significant discretionary spending, information security will continue to compete with other services and programs for much needed taxpayer dollars. This calls for innovativeness and efficiency on the part of CISOs in managing risks. The key to successful outcomes are well documented, and so are effectively implemented enterprise-wide information security programs that align information security with the business needs of governments. State and local governments and related agencies should avail themselves with the plethora of existing information security documents and strategies to help understand their environments, perform risk assessments, and put in place information security programs to manage risks effectively. This will happen if the implemented programs are enforced and their effectiveness evaluated on a periodic basis.

FUTURE RESEARCH DIRECTIONS

With the number of resources being made available by NIST, NASCIO, and other agencies, future research will be needed to determine the extent of utilization of these resources at the state and local government levels, as well as the impact of such utilization on the adoption of information security programs; the prevention, detection, and reduction of security breaches; as well as changes in information security funding.

For those state governments that are pioneers in adopting information security programs and action steps to reduce threats, case studies will be beneficial to ascertain whether the intended savings and benefits from information security investments have been realized and whether their practices could serve as models and benchmarks for future information security investment projects. Such studies could include analysis of what went well and lessons learned for the purposes of developing a reservoir of documented information security best practices and experiences to help guide future investment decisions and adoption practices.

Considering the enormity and the constant nature of information security vulnerabilities, threats, and exploits, an information security management consortium consisting of federal, state, and local government agencies, private-sector experts, and university professors is needed to effectively address the risks facing the United States and the rest of the world. The consortium could have a research wing, the purpose of which should include empirical investigations into potential and emerging threats and how best to leverage its resources to improve problem solving. Another area of research could be operational alignment of the existing agencies to enhance efficiency. Properly constituted, such a consortium will bring to bear the expertise of all members on pertinent issues and provide an avenue for cross fertilization of ideas, effective problem solving, and management. The consortium can also partner with international organizations in the field of information security to research into potential global antidotes to the cybersecurity threats and exploits.

REFERENCES

Council of Better Business & Javelin Strategy & Research. (2006). *New research shows identity fraud growth is contained and consumers have more control than they think.* Retrieved February 16, 2007, from http://www.bbbonline.org/IDTheft/safetyQuiz.asp

Evers, J. (2006). *FBI wants businesses' help in fighting cyber crime.* Retrieved February 16, 2007, from http://news.com.com/FBI+wants+businesses+help+to+fight+cybercrime/2100-7348_3-6040521.html

Gartner, Inc. (2004). *Summary report: Assessing of agency compliance with enterprise security standards* (Prepared for the North Carolina State CIO). Retrieved, January 31, 2007, from http://www.iso.scio.nc.gov.pdf/Summary RportFV02.pdf

Hurd, B. E. (2001). *The digital economy and the evolution of information assurance.* Retrieved October 16, 2005, from http://www.itoc.usma.edu/Workship/2001/Authors/Submitted_Abstracts/paperWIC3(20).pdf

National Association of State Chief Information Security Officers. (2006). *The IT security business case: Sustainable funding to manage the risks.* Retrieved from http://www.nascio.org/nascioCommittees/securityprivacy/members#publications

National Institute of Standards and Technology. (1995). *An introduction to computer security: The NIST handbook* (NIST SP 800-12). Retrieved January 21, 2006, from http://csrc.nist.gov/publications/nistpubs/800-12/handbook.pdf

National Institute of Standards and Technology. (1996). *Generally accepted principles and practices for securing information technology systems.* Retrieved October 14, 2005, from http://csrc.nist.gov/publications/nistpubs/800-14.pdf

National Institute of Standards and Technology. (1998). *Guide for developing information security plans for information technology systems.* Retrieved November 26, 2006, from http://csrc.nist.gov/publications/nistpubs/800-18/Planguide/PDF

National Institute of Standards and Technology. (2000). *Federal information technology security assessment framework.* Retrieved November 26, 2005, from

http://www.cio.gov/Documents/federal%5Fit%F security%5Fassessment%5Fframework%5Fframework %5F112800%Ehtml

National Institute of Standards and Technology. (2001). *Security self-assessment guide for information technology systems* (NIST SP 800-26). Retrieved January 2006 from http://csrc.nist.gov/publications/nistpubs/800-26/sp800-26.pdf

National Institute of Standards and Technology. (2002). Risk management guide for information technology systems. Retrieved November 26, 2005, from http://csrc.nist.gov/publications/nistpubs/800-30/sp800-30.pdf

National Security Agency. (2002). *Infosec assessment methodology.* Retrieved January 26, 2007, from http://www.iatrp.com/

Office of Management and Budget. (2000). *Management of federal information resources* (OM Circular A-130, November 28, 2000). Retrieved December 15, 2005, from http://www.whitehouse.gov/omb/circulars/a130/a130trans4.html

Sans Institute. (2002). *The twenty most critical Internet security vulnerabilities* (Version 2.504.2). Retrieved March 7, 2006, from http://www.sans.org/top20.html

United States General Accounting Office. (2000). *Computer security: Critical federal operations and assets remain at risk* (T-AIMD-00-314).

United States General Accounting Office. (2001a). *Computer Security: Improvements needed to reduce risk to critical federal operations and assets* (GAO-02-231T).

United States General Accounting Office. (2001b). *Federal information system control audit manual* (GAO/AIMD-12.19.6). Retrieved March 7, 2006, from http://www.gao.gov/special.pubs/ail2.19.6.pdf

United States General Accounting Office. (2002). *Computer security: Progress made but critical federal operations and assets remain at risk* (GAO-03-303T).

Walker, R. (2003). As threats rise, feds shelter their IT. *Government Computer News.*

Wood, C. C. (2001). *Information security policies made easy.* Houston, TX: Pentasafe Security Technologies, Inc.

FURTHER READING

Allen, J. (2003). *Making compelling business case for investing in information security.* U.S. Computer Emergency Readiness Team (US-CERT). Retrieved from http://www.cert.org/features/green/business_case.html

Anderson, A. (2006). Effective management of information security and privacy. *Educause Quarterly.* Retrieved from http://www.educause.edu/ir/library/pdf/EQM0614.pdf

Appendix F: Cyber-security. (2006). *2006 Michigan IT Strategic Plan.* Retrieved from

http://www.michigan.gov/documents/AppendixF_149547_7.pdf

Federal Agency Security practices. (n.d.). *Federal Agency Security Program Manager's Forum.* Retrieved from http://www.csrc.nist/gov/fasp/index.html

Gordon, L., Loeb, M. P., Lucyshyn, W., & Richardson, R. (2005). *CSI/FBI computer crime and security survey.* Retrieved from http://www.gocsi.com/press/20050714.jhtml

Heiman, D. (2002). *Public sector information security: A call to action for public sector CIOs.* NASCIO. Retrieved from http://www.businessofgovernment.org/main/publications/grant_reports/details/index.asp?GID=51

Jarrett, T. (2005). *Securing cyberspace: Efforts to protect national information infrastructures continue to face challenges.* Testimony before the Subcommittee on Financial Management, Government Information and International Security of the Senate Committee on Homeland Security and Government Affairs. Retrieved from http://hsgac.senate.gov/_files/071905Jarrett.pdf

National Association of State Chief Information Security Officers (NASCIO). (2003). *Business case and beyond: A primer on state government IT business cases.* Retrieved from http://www.amrinc.net/nascio/publications/shoppingCart/index.cfm#business

National Association of State Chief Information Security Officers (NASCIO). (2004). *Enterprise Architecture Development Tool-Kit, v.3.0.* Retrieved from http://www.nascio.org/nascioCommittees/EA

National Association of State Chief Information Security Officers (NASCIO). (2005). *The year of working dangerously: The privacy implications of wireless in the state workplace: Parts I and II.* Retrieved from http://www.nascio.org/nascioCommittees/privacy

National Association of State Chief Information Security Officers (NASCIO). (2006a). *Born of necessity: The CISO evolution. Bringing the technical and the policy together.* Retrieved from http://www.nascio.org/nascioCommittees/securityprivacy/members#publications

National Association of State Chief Information Security Officers (NASCIO). (2006b). *Findings from NASCIO's strategic cyber security survey.* Retrieved from http://www.nascio.org/publications/documents/NASCIO-CyberSec_Survey_Findings.pdf

National strategy to secure cyberspace: A White House report. (2003). Retrieved from http://www.whitehouse.gov/pcipb

Ponemon Institute and the CIO Institute of Carnegie Mellon University. (2004). *Privacy trust survey of the United States Government.* Retrieved from http://cioi.web.cmu.edu/research/

2004PrivacyTrustSurveyoftheUnitedStatesGovernmentExecutiveSujjayV.6.pdf

Ross, R., Jackson, A., Katzke, S., Toth, P., & Rogers, G. (2006). *Guide for assessing security controls in federal information systems* (NIST Special Publication No. 800-53A, 2nd public draft). Retrieved from http://csrc.ncsl.nist.gov/publications/drafts/SP800-53A-spd.pdf

State of Kansas, IT security self-assessment, systems questionnaire. (n.d.). Retrieved from http://www.da.ks.gov/itec/itsec/Security_SelfAssessment.doc

State of Maryland, standards self-assessment checklist. (2004). *State information technology policy and standards, Version 1.2* (p. 27). Retrieved from http://www.dbm.maryland.gov/dbm_publishing/public_content/dbm_taxonomy/

security/prevention/itsecuritypoliciesjuly2003.pdf

State of Montana Information Technology Strategic Plan 2006 update. (2006). Retrieved from http://itsd.mt.gov/stratplan/MT_IT_Strategic_Plan__Update_2006_Govenor's_draft.doc

State of North Carolina, Office of the State CIO, Strategic Initiatives Office, Risk Management Program. (n.d.). Retrieved from http://www.iso.scio.nc.gov/SecurityAssessment.htm

State of Texas, Department of Information Resources. (n.d.). *Texas Project Delivery Framework.* Retrieved from http://www.dir.state.tx.us/pubs/framework/index.htm

Stoneburner, G., Goguen, A., & Feringa, A. (2002). *Risk management guide for information technology systems: Recommendations of the National Institute of Standards and Technology.* Retrieved from http://csrc.nist.gov/publications/nistpubs/800-30/sp800-30.pdf

Swanson, M. (2001). *Security self-assessment guide for information technology systems* (NIST Special Publication No. 800-26). Retrieved http://csrc.nist.gov/publications/nistpubs/800-26/sp800-26.pdf

Swanson, M., Hash, J., Wilson, M., & Kissel, R. (2005). *Guide for information security program assessments and reporting form* (NIST Special Publication No. 800-26, Rev. 1, initial public draft). Retrieved from http://csrc.nist.gov/publications/drafts/Draft-sp800-6Rev1.pdf

U.S. Office of Management and Budget. (2000). *Incorporating and funding security information system investments.* Retrieved from http://www.whitehouse.gov.omb/memoranda/m00-07.html

U.S. Office of Management and Budget. (2005). *Mapping your investments to the federal enterprise architecture.* Retrieved from http://www.whitehouse.gov/omb/egov/documents/Mapping_Investments.pdf

TERMS AND DEFINITIONS

Authentication: Authentication is the process of identifying an individual, usually based on a user name and password. In security systems, authentication is distinct from authorization, which is the process of giving individuals access to system objects based on their identity. Authentication merely ensures that the individual is who he or she claims to be, but says nothing about the access rights of the individual.

Authorization: Authorization is the privilege granted to an individual by management to access information based upon the individual's clearance and need-to-know principle. It is the granting to a user, program, or process the right of access.

Configuration: Configuration is the relative or functional arrangement of components in a system. It is the way a system is set up, or the assortment of components that make up the system. Configuration can refer to hardware or software, or the combination of both.

Configuration Management: This is the management of security features and assurances through the control of changes made to a system. It is a procedure for applying technical and administrative directions and surveillance to identify and document the functional and physical characteristics of an item or system, control any changes to such characteristics, and record and report the change, process, and implementation status.

Identification: Identification is the process that enables the recognition of an entity (subject or object) by a computer system, generally by the use of unique machine-readable user names.

Information Security Plan: It is a document that provides a road map for the goals to be accomplished in securing the information assets of an organization. The information security plan provides the basic blueprints for documenting an information security program.

Information Security Policy: This is a document that outlines the rules, laws, and practices that regulate how an organization will manage, protect, and distribute its sensitive information (both corporate and client information). It lays the framework for the computer-network-oriented security of an organization.

Information Security Program: It is a documented set of information security policies, procedures, guidelines, and standards implemented to provide the road map for effective information security management practices and controls.

Information Security Standards: This is a set of documents that outline the criteria and specific level of performance regarding the actions needed to be taken to secure the information assets of an organization.

Management Controls: Management controls are actions taken to manage the development, maintenance, and use of the system, including system-specific policies, procedures, and rules of behavior, individual roles and responsibilities, individual accountability, and personnel security decisions.

Operational Controls: These are day-to-day procedures and mechanisms used to protect operational systems and applications. They address security methods that focus on mechanisms that primarily are implemented and executed by people (as opposed to systems). Operational controls affect the system and operational environment.

Patch: A patch is a section of software code that is inserted into a program to correct mistakes or to alter the program.

Security Management: This is the process of monitoring and controlling access to network resources. This includes monitoring usage network resources, recording information about the usage of resources, detecting attempted or successful violations, and reporting such violations.

Technical Controls: These are hardware and software controls used to provide automated protection to the information technology system or applications. Technical controls operate within the technical system and applications.

Threat: A threat is any circumstance or event with potential cause for harm to a system in the form of destruction, disclosure, modification of data, and/or denial of service. It is the potential for the exploitation of a vulnerability. Threats arise from internal failures, human errors, attacks, and natural catastrophes. The examination of all actions and events that might adversely affect a system or operation is known as threat analysis.

Vulnerability: A vulnerability is a weakness in a network computer system's security procedures, administrative controls, system design, implementation, internal controls, or so forth that could be exploited by a threat for one to gain unauthorized access to information, to disrupt critical processing, or to violate a system security policy. It is a flaw that may allow harm to occur to an information technology activity.

A measurement of vulnerability, which includes the susceptibility of a particular system to a specific attack and the opportunities available to a threat agent to mount that attack, is known as vulnerability assessment.

Chapter LXIII
Evaluation of E-Government Web Sites

Michael Middleton
Queensland University of Technology, Faculty of Information Technology, Australia

INTRODUCTION

In recent times, the popularity of the Internet has led to e-government practices being widely recognized as an important option for service to the general public. In response, various tiers of government from national to local level have sought opportunities to engage the public through Web sites.

Many governments now provide some level of access to government through Web interfaces, for example, through access to resources such as publications and government data. In some cases there are services provided that may be executed online. For example, users may provide personal information for licensing or to undertake payments. There continues to be a diversity of implementation quality and levels for such services.

The facilitation of e-government has been characterized in various ways. For example, the European Union has seen it in terms of four main tasks: the development of Internet-based services to improve access to public information and services, the improvement of the transparency of public administration by using the Internet, the full exploitation of information technology within public administration, and the establishment of e-procurement (Strejcek & Theilb, 2003). More recently, the United Nations (UN), noting that ICTs may be used to transform its internal and external relationships, has also identified four similar but distinct areas: internal processes such as record keeping, electronic service delivery, virtual communities for digital democracy, and e-business opportunities such as procurement (United Nations Department of Economic and Social Affairs, 2005).

Legislation that supports e-government may address many aspects of its implementation. For example, a regulatory environment for electronic contracts, regulation of telecommunications, digital signatures, and consumer protection is being developed by different states. In terms of access to public information and services, the USA has tackled the issue with an E-Government Act that provided for an office of electronic government within its Office of Management and Budget along with minimum standards of information for the public on federal agency sites (Jaeger, 2004; Matthews, 2002).

The UN has also produced participation and readiness indexes in order to indicate the extent of participation in, and development toward, e-government (United Nations Department of Economic and Social Affairs, 2004). These indexes are among a number approaches to measuring e-government performance. A comparison of methods for assessing implementation has been made by Janssen, Rotthier and Snijkers (2004). They have used the term "supply oriented eGovernment measurements" for evaluations that focus on delivery, typically through the Internet.

This is closest to the second of the four UN areas, that of service delivery, and is the focus of what is described in the following. The intent here is to provide an overview of different approaches to Web site evaluation in order to suggest further application and development of evaluation instruments.

BACKGROUND

Evaluation instruments are useful to governments at all levels in order to provide for benchmarking, and detailed assessment and comparison between Web sites. Such instruments may also help governments in developing nations to direct their online strategies by reference to analytical tools for evaluating Web sites.

It has been noted by Sharma (2004) that a number of e-government benchmarking studies have been limited by a focus solely upon the supply side. Likewise, Holland, Bongers, Vandeberg, Keller, and te Velde (2005) have pointed out that the measurement of e-government must take account of more than the supply side. Beyond the provision of services, there should also be consideration of policy including the regulatory environment, prerequisites such as Internet penetration, and internal government functioning such as intranet development. However, as the focus here is on services as presented via the Web, two main types of evaluation are relevant for consideration. These are, first, approaches to Web site design and evaluation in general, and second, approaches to examining the performance of e-government as delivered via the Internet.

In the case of Web site design and evaluation, there are many examples of guidance. These may take the form of online checklists (Ciolek & Goltz, 1996-2006; World Wide Web Consortium [W3C], 1999). There are also many general texts on the subject that provide direction in matters of information architecture and design, style, and information quality in Web site development (Benyon, Turner, & Turner, 2005; Lazar, 2006; Rosenfeld & Morville, 2002).

A great deal has been written on e-government online delivery practices, however, in this work the focus is on the evaluation of delivery that makes some reference to methods for testing the delivery. For example, a need for the effective benchmarking of e-government implementations was suggested by Kaylor, Deshazo, and van Eck (2001). They conducted studies on local governments in the USA, and focused on the functions and services that cities typically provide. The model they used contains detailed questions on services delivered online. It also used a four-point scale system to measure the presence and the degree of implementation of online services.

Korsten and Bothma (2005a, 2005b) have evaluated South African government Web sites for content and usability. They also studied the portal *South African Government Online*, which provides a gateway to government information. Usability was differentiated for first-time users and frequent users, where the focus was on efficiency and satisfaction. Web sites were assessed with regard to site-level criteria that included the home page and site-wide design, information architecture, navigation, search capability, linking strategy, overall writing style, page templates, and layout. Specific issues relating to individual pages including downloading time, coding problems, and error messages were considered to be outside the scope, as were accessibility and downtime.

The criteria used have been detailed by Korsten (2003). She considers content that is well written, comprehensive, current, of high quality and authoritative, to be a fundamental element of an effective Web presence. Additionally, Web sites must cater for a wide range of audiences and discharge the host institution's objectives relating to communication and information dissemination through publishing.

Another Web site evaluation instrument whose use has been reported in the literature is one used to support the e-Qual (formerly known as WebQual) method. This has been utilized to evaluate a number of UK government sites (Barnes & Vidgen, 2002, 2004). The associated questionnaire seeks Likert-scale responses to 23 questions on usability, information quality, and service interaction. The e-Qual approach has been refined by the use of comment analysis in association with the traditional survey data. This has been found to provide a useful approach to triangulation, thereby strengthening Web quality assessment (Barnes & Vidgen, 2005). Choudrie and Ghinea (2005) have also adopted a dual evaluative approach using what they termed an integrated sociotechnical perspective by utilizing participant evaluation along with use of Web diagnostic tools for the sites of four countries.

The Center for Public Policy at Brown University has conducted ongoing research that provides annual reports on comparative performance of e-government sites. These have been national (West, 2006b) and international (West, 2006a), using a set of criteria relating to the presence of various features dealing with information availability, service delivery, and public access. Among the criteria questions are those that seek the presence of online publications, databases, audio or video clips, alternative languages or translation capability, commercial advertising, premium fees, user payments, disability access, privacy policy, security features, digital signatures, credit card payments facility, feedback options, automatic e-mail updates, Web site personalization, and personal digital assistant (PDA) access.

Similarly, the Accenture (2004) company has assessed advances that different countries have made in their e-government capacity, and compares the different approaches countries have taken. Accenture also publishes reports on innovations in e-governance that the surveyed countries have undertaken for better service for their citizens.

One of the more detailed instruments reported is that of Melitski, Holzer, Kim, Kim, and Rho (2005). They have used five main categories for evaluation of e-government sites: security and privacy, usability, content, service, and citizen participation. Within these five categories, there are a total of 92 questions, 47 of which use a four-point scale. This approach has been extended by Henriksson, Yi, Frost, and Middleton (2006). It is instruments such as these whose elements have been consolidated to form the basis for evaluation criteria that are included in the following section.

WEB SITE EVALUATION

The generic approach and specific e-government approach to evaluation naturally have a certain amount of overlap, but they are considered separately here, so the generic evaluation is given a brief summary overview in order to introduce the specific.

Generic Web Site Evaluation

Methods for Web site evaluation based upon the design and architecture principles referenced above use a variety of characterizations. For example, Edwards (1998) sees evaluation in terms of access, quality, and ease of use. Alexander and Tate (2003-2006) use the categories authority accuracy, objectivity, currency, and coverage, for

Table 1. A summary of generic Web site evaluation categories

Criterion	Example of factor	Examples of check
Functionality	Site maps	-Is there a summary of site organization by showing broad categories of pages?
Authority	Affiliation	-Do the authors indicate who their employer is? -Is an organization responsible for governance of the site?
Validity	Referring links	-How many other sites provide links to this one?
Obtainability	Format support	-Does the site display all its aspects on the browser that is in use? -Does the site require plug-ins for full functionality?
Relevance	Currency	-Is there an indication of when it was last updated? -Is there an indication of how frequently it is updated?
Substance	Evidence	-Are statements supported by illustrations, quoted sources, linked Web sites?

which they elaborate different subcriteria for different Web site types such as informational sites. Many of the evaluation categories are consolidated by Middleton (2002), and an extract drawn from these is shown in Table 1.

The categories are briefly outlined as follows.

- Functionality refers to how effectively a site is designed in order to help you navigate around it. It is concerned with such matters as layout, link activity, error-free markup, and user assistance facilities such as a help function, site map, and search facility. It is also concerned with support such as the provision of text for images for users who are restricted in their capabilities.
- Authority refers to the trustworthiness of the information carried at the site, and how reliable it is thought to be based upon what is known of the individual or organization responsible for its production. Evaluation considers such factors as the creators, their credentials and affiliations, whether there is editorial oversight, whether the site makes intellectual property claims, and what its funding and viability are.
- Validity is an indication of the extent to which a site is considered useful by other parties. It takes into account such factors as ratings, the extent of links referring to the site (for example, listing in sites that provide gateways to the site in question), reviews of the site, and the amount of usage.
- Obtainability refers to the ease with which a site may be recalled and displayed. It takes into account factors such as format support, load aspects, metadata, naming, and speed. It also takes into consideration security matters and costs that may be involved.
- Relevance accounts for the information requirements of a user and how pertinent to them a site is. It involves the audience to which a site is directed, as well as such matters as balance, currency, and depth of content.
- Substance assesses the significance of the site for producing unbiased and reliable content. It is therefore concerned with accuracy, extent and detail of coverage, readability, supporting evidence such as references, and the extent of explanation of content.

A complete explanation of these criteria accompanied by examples of checks to be performed for factors is provided on a website called FAVORS (Queensland University of Technology, 1999-2006).

E-Government Service Evaluation

The factors that influence the quality of government Web sites can be placed into six categories: (a) security and privacy, (b) usability, (c) content, (d) services, (e) citizen participation, and (f) features. The first five of these categories and a number of the security and privacy questions are based upon factors outlined by Melitski et al. (2005). These have been extended by applying generic material as outlined in the section above to the government site context by including an increased number of factors in the categories, and by adding an additional features category. Table 2 gives an example of an element in each category and the type of question that may assist in checking for the element's application.

- **Security and privacy** are concerned with the existence and quality of any privacy policy presented on a government Web site. It takes into account the security of data transmission to the site and the site's servers. Furthermore, this category is concerned with the use of cookies in identifying and monitoring users and whether the Web site is still usable when cookies are disabled. The internal security measures taken within the government department itself are also of interest.
- **Usability** is the broadest of the six categories and derives mainly from the generic functionality category. The areas examined range from the readability of a Web site's text fields to whether the site employs a consistent style through the usage of cascading style sheets. The ease of using the Web site's navigation system is estimated, and the robustness of forms encountered is assessed. As government sites are intended for general public use, overall accessibility is embraced within this category and takes into account disability access and backward compatibility with older systems. The user friendliness of the Web site is observed by looking at factors such as the presence of help pages, and whether the site is available in more than one language.
- **Content** is judged on the amount of public information available on the Web site. The amount of horizontal integration between various government agencies is also assessed, along with an estimate of the amount of information available about the dealings of these agencies. The logical grouping of information for easy access to diverse groups within society is also observed.
- **Services** comprise two subcategories: services for citizens and services for businesses. In each of these subcategories, the availability of payment, registration, and

Table 2. Summary of e-government evaluation categories

Category	Example of element	Examples of check
Security/privacy	Privacy policy	-Does the Web site policy explicitly state the use of personal data in relation to third parties?
Usability	Disability access	-Is the Web site W3C Standard Priority 1 compliant for vision-impaired users?
Content	Public information	-Does the Web site offer access to databases containing regularly updated public information?
Services	Business	-Does the Web site offer online registration?
Citizen participation	Business	-Does the Web site offer online surveys or opinion polls?
Features	Personal pages	-Can these be customized based upon characteristics and preferences of individual users?

application services is observed. For businesses, the presence of online tendering is examined, and for citizens, the availability of online recruitment is considered.

- **Citizen participation** examines the extent to which citizens are able to communicate both with the government agency and with each other through the Web site. The availability of opinion polls, bulletin boards, and satisfaction surveys is observed. The existence of a government strategy to educate citizens about the online channel and the presence of any government incentives to drive the usage of the e-government Web sites are also included.
- **Features** include assessment for the availability of personal pages and the degree to which the government agency allows each citizen to create his or her own space on the Web site, the time taken for the agency to answer questions made online and the nature of such answers, and the presence of commercial advertising, external links, and advanced search capabilities.

FUTURE TRENDS

Although generic Web site evaluation instruments are now mature, their adaptation to e-government and in particular, government Web sites, requires development in line with the increasing capabilities of those sites and innovation in public-sector facilities. Instruments such as that which have been developed by Henriksson et al. (2006) take account of best practices in Web site design and have been especially tuned to assess the areas of importance to public administration. However, they must be continually refined in order to provide better tools for evaluation. For example, they need to take account of the following:

- Specific criteria for Web site development standards developed by groups such as W3C, which should be embodied in evaluation checklists as the standards are promulgated.
- Refining approaches to the scalability of questions, for example, by making use of readability measures that have been developed for other contexts, and by developing gradations of executability for site functionality.
- Improving approaches to developing checklists so that an appropriate balance is maintained between those factors that can be determined online by visiting a Web site, and those factors such as security ones, which require internal access for insight into the workings of a government agency.
- Adapting evaluation instruments so that they take account of the legal environment to which a particular government Web site is subjected.
- Adapting evaluation to deal with services at some tiers of government that implement a decentralized approach across multiple agencies and sites.
- Incorporating the use of automatic analysis tools to deal with appropriate factors in order to reduce the manual time spent on analysis.

CONCLUSION

As the number of government Web sites proliferates, so must the ability to evaluate those sites be refined. Typically, the criteria that are developed should test if quality content is being made more amenable by developing a Web site that provides straightforward navigability and an information architecture that facilitates browsing or searching. Future development of the Web sites must take into account regulatory constraints, and make certain of transaction security. Yet, this development must also ensure that a digital divide is not perpetuated by providing information visibility to users who have a wide range of computer and information literacy.

General tools for Web site evaluation need to be associated with specific approaches to measuring electronic delivery of government services. These measurements have initially focused on the functionality of sites allied with the quantity and quality of information provided. However, increasing attention is being paid to services, either for citizens through participation and personalization or for enterprises (government or business) by support of business processes.

In addition to evaluating design, typography, and consistent approaches to page layout that contribute to the look and feel of Web sites, criteria must be developed to consider the following:

- The extent of citizen access, sometimes termed universal access, including availability to those without personal equipment
- The extent of coordinated dissemination of information through a whole-of-government approach
- The extent of metadata support underlying the organization of pages so that they may be identified in focused search engines
- The extent to which the security of the environment reassures citizens of privacy and data protection
- The extent to which interfaces may be personalized

The examples provided in this chapter offer an introduction to a structured approach to Web site evaluation that derives from generic site evaluation, and then establishes a framework for government site evaluation. The examples, together with the references that are provided, give an insight into the development of instruments that may be used to measure government Web sites, and lead to their optimization for the user environment that they are meant to service.

FUTURE RESEARCH DIRECTIONS

Further research in the area can be considered from two viewpoints. First, the area of services delivery requires more analysis of delivery modes accompanied by a study of factors influencing effective service provision. This should lead to refinements in instruments used for evaluation, and improved approaches to the ways in which they can be implemented. Associated with this, there should be more concentration on user analysis so that perceptions of effectiveness of e-government facilities are sought from those who make use of them as well as those who provide them.

Second, there should be more connection between the analysis of the service aspects and the other sustaining areas of digital e-government, namely, those supporting internal processes such as digital record keeping, the development of virtual communities for exercising citizens' input, and the advancement of government-to-government and government-to-business opportunities including administration and procurement. It is to be anticipated that such investigation will take the form of case studies, social and technical analysis, and the development of guiding models for different levels of jurisdiction.

REFERENCES

Accenture. (2004). *eGovernment leadership: High performance, maximum value*. Retrieved August 23, 2005, from http://www.accenture.com/xdoc/en/industries/government/gove_egov_value.pdf

Alexander, J., & Tate, M. A. (2003-2006). *Evaluate Web pages*. Retrieved June 26, 2006, from http://www.widener.edu/Tools_Resources/Libraries/Wolfgram_Memorial_Library/Evaluate_Web_Pages/659/

Barnes, S., & Vidgen, R. (2002). An integrative approach to the assessment of e-commerce quality. *Journal of Electronic Commerce Research, 3*(3), 114-127.

Barnes, S., & Vidgen, R. (2004). Interactive e-government: Evaluating the Web site of the UK Inland Revenue. *Journal of Electronic Commerce in Organizations, 2*(1), 42-46.

Barnes, S., & Vidgen, R. (2005). Data triangulation in action: Using comment analysis to refine Web quality metrics. *Proceedings of the 13th European Conference on Information Systems, Regensburg, Germany.* Retrieved September 26, 2006, from http://www.webqual.co.uk/papers/comment.pdf

Benyon, D., Turner, P., & Turner, S. (2005). *Designing interactive systems: People, activities, contexts, technologies.* Harlow, United Kingdom: Addison-Wesley.

Choudrie, J., & Ghinea, G. (2005). Integrated views of e-government Website usability: Perspectives from users and Web diagnostic tools. *Electronic Government, An International Journal, 2*(3), 318-333.

Ciolek, T. M., & Goltz, I. M. (1996-2006). *Information quality WWW virtual library.* Retrieved January 24, 2006, from http://www.ciolek.com/WWWVL-InfoQuality.html

Edwards, J. (1998). *The good, the bad and the useless: Evaluating Internet resources.* Retrieved June 28, 2006, from http://www.ariadne.ac.uk/issue16/digital/

Henriksson, A., Yi, Y., Frost, B., & Middleton, M. (2006). *Evaluation instrument for e-government Websites.* Paper presented at Internet Research 7.0: Internet Convergences, Brisbane, Australia. Retrieved June 26, 2006, from http://eprints.qut.edu.au/archive/00003113

Holland, C., Bongers, F., Vandeberg, R., Keller, W., & te Velde, R. (2005). Measuring and evaluating e-government: Building blocks and recommendations for a standardized measuring tool. In M. Khosrow-Pour (Ed.), *Practicing e-government: A global perspective* (pp. 179-198). Hershey, PA: Idea Group/OECD.

Jaeger, P. T. (2004). Beyond section 508: The spectrum of legal requirements for accessible e-government Web sites in the United States. *Journal of Government Information, 30*(4), 518-533.

Janssen, D., Rotthier, S., & Snijkers, K. (2004). If you measure it they will score: An assessment of international eGovernment benchmarking. *Information Polity, 9*(3/4), 121.

Kaylor, C. R., Deshazo, R., & van Eck, D. (2001). Gauging e-government: A report on implementing services among American cities. *Government Information Quarterly, 18*(4), 293-307.

Korsten, H. (2003). *An evaluation of and a model for South African government Websites.* Unpublished doctoral dissertation, University of Pretoria, Pretoria, South Africa.

Korsten, H., & Bothma, T. J. D. (2005a). Evaluating South African government Web sites: Methods, findings and recommendations (Part 1). *South African Journal of Information Management, 7*(2).

Korsten, H., & Bothma, T. J. D. (2005b). Evaluating South African government Web sites: Methods, findings and recommendations (Part 2). *South African Journal of Information Management, 7*(3).

Lazar, J. (2006). *Web usability: A user-centered design approach.* Boston: Pearson Addison Wesley.

Matthews, W. (2002). House passes compromise e-government bill. *Federal Computer Week, 16*(41), 13.

Melitski, J., Holzer, H., Kim, S.-T., Kim, C.-G., & Rho, S.-Y. (2005). Digital government worldwide: An e-government assessment of municipal Web sites. *International Journal of Electronic Government Research, 1*(1), 1-19.

Middleton, M. (2002). *Information management: A consolidation of operations, analysis and strategy.* Wagga Wagga, Australia: CSU Centre for Information Studies.

Queensland University of Technology. (1999-2006). *FAVORS.* Retrieved June 28, 2006, from http://www.favors.fit.qut.edu.au/

Rosenfeld, L., & Morville, P. (2002). *Information architecture for the Word Wide Web* (2nd ed.). Cambridge, MA: O'Reilly.

Sharma, S. K. (2004). Assessing e-government implementations. *Electronic Government, An International Journal, 1*(2), 198-212.

Strejcek, G., & Theilb, M. (2003). Technology push, legislation pull? E-government in the European Union. *Decision Support Systems, 34*(3), 305-313.

United Nations Department of Economic and Social Affairs. (2004). *Global e-government readiness report 2004: Towards access for opportunity.* Retrieved January 24, 2006, from http://unpan1.un.org/intradoc/groups/public/documents/un/unpan019207.pdf

United Nations Department of Economic and Social Affairs. (2005). *World public sector report 2005: Unlocking the human potential for public sector performance.* Retrieved January 24, 2006, from http://unpan1.un.org/intradoc/groups/public/documents/un/unpan021616.pdf

West, D. (2006a). *Global e-government 2006.* Retrieved August 20, 2006, from http://www.insidepolitics.org/egovt06int.pdf

West, D. (2006b). *State and federal e-government in the United States, 2006.* Retrieved August 20, 2006, from http://www.insidepolitics.org/egovt06us.pdf

World Wide Web Consortium (W3C). (1999). *Checklist of checkpoints for Web content accessibility guidelines.* Retrieved January 24, 2006, from http://www.w3.org/TR/WCAG10/full-checklist.html

FURTHER READING

Al-Hakim, L. (Ed.). (2007). *Global e-government: Theory, applications and benchmarking.* Hershey, PA: Idea Group Publishing.

Asgarkhani, M. (2005). Digital government and its effectiveness in public management reform: A local government perspective. *Public Management Review, 7*(3), 465-487.

Australian Government Information Management Office. (2006). *Responsive government: A new service agenda.* Retrieved April 11, 2006, from http://www.agimo.gov.au/publications/2006/march/introduction_to_responsive_government

Bekkers, V., & Homburg, V. (Eds.). (2005). *The information ecology of e-government: E-government as institutional and technological innovation in public administration.* Amsterdam: IOS.

Bertelsmann Foundation. (2002). *Balanced e-government.* Retrieved September 30, 2005, from http://www.begix.de/en/studie/studie.pdf

Böhlen, M., Gamper, J., Polasek, W., & Wimmer, M. A. (Eds.). (2005). *E-government: Towards electronic democracy: International Conference, TCGOV 2005, Bolzano, Italy, March 2-4, 2005. Proceedings.*

Chadwick, A. (2006). *Internet politics: States, citizens, and new communication technologies.* New York: Oxford University Press.

Curtin, G. G., Sommer, M. H., & Vis-Sommer, V. (Eds.). (2003). *The world of e-government.* New York: Haworth.

De, R. (2005). E-government systems in developing countries: Stakeholders and conflict. *Electronic Government, Proceedings* (Vol. 3591, pp. 26-37).

Deakins, E., & Dillon, S. M. (2002). E-government in New Zealand: The local authority perspective. *The International Journal of Public Sector Management, 15*(4/5), 375.

Drèuke, H. (Ed.). (2005). *Local electronic government: A comparative study.* London: Routledge.

Edmiston, K. D. (2003). State and local e-government: Prospects and challenges. *American Review of Public Administration, 33*(1), 20-45.

Garcia, A. C. B. M. C., & Pinto, F. B. (2005). A quality inspection method to evaluate e-government sites. In M. A. T. R. Wimmer, A. Gronlund, & K. V. Andersen (Eds.), *Lecture notes in computer science: Vol. 3591. Electronic government: 4th International Conference, EGOV 2005* (pp. 198-209). Berlin, Germany: Springer-Verlag.

Gil-Garcia, J. R., & Pardo, T. A. (2005). E-government success factors: Mapping practical tools to theoretical foundations. *Government Information Quarterly, 22*(2), 187-216.

Guangwei, H., & Weijun, Z. (2004). Research on the survey and evaluation method of e-government Websites. *Journal of the China Society for Scientific and Technical Information, 23*(4), 495-501.

Guijarro, L. (2005). Policy and practice in standards selection for e-government interoperability frameworks. In *Electronic Government, Proceedings* (Vol. 3591, pp. 163-173).

Gupta, M. P., & Jana, D. (2003). E-government evaluation: A framework and case study. *Government Information Quarterly, 20*(4), 365-387.

Hadzilias, E. A. (2005). A methodology framework for calculating the cost of e-government services. In *E-Government: Towards Electronic Democracy, Proceedings* (Vol. 3416, pp. 247-256).

Henriksson, A., Yi, Y., Frost, B., & Middleton, M. (in press). Evaluation instrument for e-government Websites. *Electronic Government: An International Journal.*

Ho, A. (2002). Reinventing local government and the e-government initiative. *Public Administration Review, 62*(4), 434-444.

Huang, W., Siau, K., & Wei, K. K. (Eds.). (2005). *Electronic government strategies and implementation.* Hershey PA: Idea Group.

Irani, Z., Love, P. E. D., Elliman, T., Jones, S., & Themistocleous, M. (2005). Evaluating e-government: Learning from the experiences of two UK local authorities. *Information Systems Journal, 15*(1), 61-82.

Iyer, L. S., Singh, R., Salam, A. F., & D'Aubeterre, F. (2006). Knowledge management for government-to-government (G2G) process coordination. *Electronic Government, An International Journal, 3*(1), 18-35.

Jaeger, P. T. (2006). Assessing Section 508 compliance on federal e-government Web sites: A multi-method, user-centered evaluation of accessibility for persons with disabilities. *Government Information Quarterly, 23*(2), 169-190.

Kampen, J. K., Snijkers, K., & Bouckaert, G. (2005). Public priorities concerning the development of e-government in Flanders. *Social Science Computer Review, 23*(1), 136-139.

Khosrow-Pour, M. (Ed.). (2005). *Practicing e-government: A global perspective.* Hershey, PA: Idea Group.

Kim, T. H., Im, K. H., & Park, S. C. (2005). Intelligent measuring and improving model for customer satisfaction level in e-government. In *Electronic Government, Proceedings* (Vol. 3591, pp. 38-48).

Koh, C. E., & Prybutok, V. R. (2003). The three ring model development of an instrument for measuring dimensions of e-government functions. *The Journal of Computer Information Systems, 43*(3), 34.

Kunstelj, M., & Vintar, M. (2004). Evaluating the progress of e-government development: A critical analysis. *Information Polity, 9*(3, 4), 131.

La Porte, T. M., Demchak, C. C., & de Jong, M. (2002). Democracy and bureaucracy in the age of the Web: Empirical findings and theoretical speculations. *Administration & Society, 34*(4), 411-446.

Larsen, B., & Milakovich, M. (2005). Citizen relationship management and e-government. *Electronic Government, Proceedings* (Vol. 3591, pp. 57-68).

McGovern, G., Norton, R., & O'Dowd, C. (2002). *The Web content style guide: An essential reference for online writers, editors, and managers.* Harlow: Financial Times Prentice Hall.

McMahon, R. (2005). E-government: Effects on the netologically disadvantaged. *Electronic Government, An International Journal, 2*(4), 460-471.

McMahon, R., & Bressler, R. (2005). E-government: Do audits aid the netologically disadvantaged. *Electronic Government, An International Journal, 2*(4), 413-425.

Shackleton, P., Fisher, J., & Dawson, L. (2006). E-government services in the local government context: An Australian case study. *Business Process Management Journal, 12*(1), 88-100.

Sun, S.-Y., Ju, T. L., & Chen, P.-Y. (2006). E-government impacts on effectiveness: A survey study of an e-official-document system. *Electronic Government, An International Journal, 3*(2), 174-189.

Wood, F. B., Siegel, E. R., LaCroix, E.-M., Lyon, B. J., Benson, D. A., Cid, V., et al. (2003). A practical approach to e-government Web evaluation. *IT Professional, 5*(3), 22-28.

Zhu, X., & Gauch, S. (2000). Incorporating quality metrics in centralized/distributed information retrieval on the World Wide Web. *Proceedings of the 23rd Annual International ACM SIGIR Conference on Research and Development in Information Retrieval* (pp. 288-295).

TERMS AND DEFINITIONS

Cookie: A cookie is a facility that enables a Web server to send a Web browser a packet of data that will be returned by the browser each time it accesses the same server. It may include any data the server is set to determine, and is often used to authenticate a registered user of a Web site without requiring them to sign in again every time they access it.

Encryption: Encryption involves any procedure used for converting plaintext into cipher text (encrypted message) in order to prevent any but the intended recipient from reading the data. It may then be carried, for example, by secure sockets layer (SSL), a protocol that uses a secure hypertext transmission method designed to provide encrypted communications on the Internet.

Executability: This is the extent to which a user may interact with a service function via a Web site. This may range from nonexistent through information display, information download, partial executability (in which a user may submit digital material but not receive responses), and fully executable in which mutual citizen-agency interaction takes place with a validation of the transaction provided.

Information Architecture: It is the arrangement of information in a structured way for Web site interface presentation based upon the technical architecture in databases and static files.

Navigation: Navigation is the process of following a path in a database to find desired information. It is usually applied to the exploration of a hypertext system, or a database that has graphic representation via a Web site.

Privacy Policy: A Web site's official statement on the type of information collected on the site, how the information will be used, how the person can access this data, and the steps for having the data removed. A privacy statement will also usually include information regarding systems that are in place to protect the information of visitors.

Readability Measures: These are analytical measures based upon algorithms such as the Fog Scale and the Flesch-Kincaid grade level that estimate the extent to which text is comprehensible.

Chapter LXIV
IT Evaluation Issues in Australian Public-Sector Organizations

Chad Lin
Curtin University of Technology, Australia

INTRODUCTION

Public-sector organizations are one of the top spenders in information technology (IBM, 2006). According to an IDC report, global public-sector IT spending will exceed $138 billion in 2006, representing 12.2% of overall IT spending (IBM). In the United States, public-sector IT spending is likely to grow to $92 billion in 2010 from $71 billion in 2005 (Pulliam, 2005). Despite the huge and growing IT spending by public-sector organizations, the resulting benefits from these IT spending are still not clearly understood (Gunasekaran, 2005). This is often due to the poor IT investment evaluation process implemented by these public-sector organizations (Hall, 1998). In other words, there is a lack of understanding of the impact of the proper IT investment evaluation processes of IT projects in the public-sector organizations. The IT investment evaluation is an ongoing process that seeks to identify best practice and use it as a basis for evaluating public-sector IT project performance in order to set up clear goals and identify areas for improvement (Gunasekaran, 2005). For example, without undertaking proper IT investment evaluation processes, organizations are at the risk of failing to establish clear IT project goals and design. Therefore, research in the public-sector organizations is becoming critical, especially in how these organizations evaluate their IT projects and ensure that benefits expected from these projects are eventually delivered.

The main objective of this chapter is to identify evaluation issues that are critical in the implementation of IT projects by public-sector organizations. A key contribution of the chapter is to identify and examine evaluation issues and other key factors faced by public-sector organizations undertaking IT projects. The key issues presented are of interest to senior public-sector executives concerned with making decisions about IT investments and realizing IT benefits.

BACKGROUND

IT Investment Evaluation

While organizations continue to invest heavily in IT, research studies and practitioner surveys report contradictory findings on the effect of the expenditures on organizational productivity (Osei-Bryson & Ko, 2004; Thatcher & Pingry, 2004). Therefore, it is not difficult to see that the measurement of the business value of IT investment has been the subject of considerable debate by many academics and practitioners (Sugumaran & Arogyaswamy, 2004). Although some IT productivity studies have produced inconclusive and negative results, and the interpretation of the results may have depended on many factors (e.g., Zhu, 2004), many research studies have indicated that IT spending is directly related to organizational performance (e.g., Hu & Quan, 2005).

In addition, the complex role and scope of IT investment decision-making processes are often the major constraints and difficulties in IT investment evaluation and benefits realization processes (Lin, Lin, Huang, & Kuo, 2006; Sugumaran & Arogyaswamy, 2004; Tsao, Lin, & Lin, 2004). Many private-sector IT projects fail to deliver what is expected of them because most organizations focus on implementing the technology rather than the adoption of the tools necessary to help to track and measure the IT projects (Hillam & Edwards, 2001). For example, a study by Sohal and Ng (1998) has found that in large Australian organizations, the potential of IT has not been utilized to meet the competitive challenges due to inadequate and inappropriate evaluation of the proposed IT projects. Moreover, they have reported that 59% of the responding organizations did not determine whether expected benefits were being realized.

There have also been a lot of reports on public-sector IT project failures. One of the major reasons for IT project failure is that most organizations fail to properly monitor and evaluate IT projects (Ballantine & Stray, 1998; Domberger, Fernandez, & Fiebig, 2000; Perrin & Pervan, 2004). It should be understood that IT investment evaluation in the public sector is highly complex, due in part to legal requirements that govern organizational processes (Khalfan, 2003), but also because it is a very politically sensitive process with many stakeholders holding very different and often conflicting perspectives (Allen, Kern, & Mattison, 2002; Heeks, 1999). While IT investment evaluation processes in the private sector is generally seen as something normal, there are special characteristics of the public sector that makes it inappropriate or extremely difficult (Bannister, 2001; Kouzmin, Loffler, Klages, & Korac-Kakabadse, 1999). Sullivan and Ngwenyama (2005) have found that some public-sector guidelines do not effectively address IT investment performance monitoring and evaluation. According to Jones and Hughes (2001), IT investment evaluation techniques are not widely used in public-sector organizations. However, according to Forrester Research, only 55% of public-sector organizations have intended to increase their efforts in evaluating their IT investments (IBM, 2006). Hence, the inability of many organizations to measure and apply IT both inter- and intra-organizationally is resulting in missed opportunities and a lack of business value (van Grembergen & van Bruggen, 1998).

IT Benefits Realization

While IT investment evaluation processes are important, they are insufficient in terms of ensuring that the benefits identified and expected by organizations are eventually realized and delivered (Lin, Pervan, & McDermid, 2005). The essence of benefits realization is to organize and manage so that the potential benefits arising from the use of IT can actually be realized (Ward, Taylor, & Bond, 1996).

Seddon, Graeser, and Willcocks (2002) have indicated that the identification and measurement of benefits is the most difficult issue in evaluating IT. According to Ward et al. (1996), very few organizations have a benefits realization approach. Much attention is paid to ways of justifying investments, with little effort being expended to ensuring that the benefits expected are realized (Ballantine & Stray, 1998). For example, a survey by Forrester Research indicated that only 51% of public-sector organizations had considered making some serious efforts in realizing the expected benefits of their IT investments (IBM, 2006). As the result, there is a massive imbalance between IT investment and benefits derived from that investment (Love, Irani, Standing, Lin, & Burn, 2005).

While the search for benefit identification can contribute to the success of an IT investment, organizations have often found it difficult to evaluate them and as a result tend to use notional arbitrary values for assessing benefits (Lin & Pervan, 2003; Standing & Lin, 2007). The use of a formal benefits realization methodology (e.g., Cranfield Process Model of Benefits Management; Ward et al., 1996) is important in assisting organizations to ensure that their expected benefits are delivered (Changchit, Joshi, & Lederer, 1998; Lin et al., 2005).

RESEARCH METHODOLOGY AND FINDINGS

Research Objectives and Methodology

Before the case study was conducted, a pilot survey was carried out to first obtain an overview of current Australian service industry practices and norms in managing IT benefits and evaluation. Questionnaires were sent to IT managers in Australian public-sector organizations. The pilot survey results show some similarity to much of the non-Australian studies (e.g., Ward et al., 1996; Willcocks & Lester, 1997). In summary, a variety of informal IT investment evaluation methodologies were used and most users were not involved in IT investment evaluation and implementation. Respondents had different reasons and success measurements or benchmarks for IT investments. Moreover, while about two thirds of the survey respondents indicated that they had ever used an evaluation methodology, only about one third had ever utilized a benefits realization methodology to ensure their expectations were realized eventually. While the survey was useful in obtaining an overview of the IS and IT evaluation practices of the large public-sector organizations, case studies were needed to investigate detailed issues such as the use of the IT investment evaluation and benefits realization methodologies and their effects on IT project implementation.

An in-depth case study was conducted on two public-sector organizations in Australia. The case-study method was chosen because it enables the researcher to examine the context of the evaluation processes and better understand the responses given in the interviews through observation (Silverman, 2001). The first organization (Case A) had more than 10 major IT projects running concurrently and many of them were contracted out to external IT vendors. On the other hand, the second organization (Case B) had only three major IT projects and only one was contracted out. Case A had adopted an informal IT investment evaluation methodology but without any IT benefits realization methodology. Case B also used an informal IT investment evaluation methodology but with a formal IT benefits realization methodology. In total, 20 key participants (CEOs [chief executive officers], CIOs [chief information officers], IT managers, and project managers) were interviewed, including some from their major external IT contractors. The interviews focused on both organizations' major IT projects, the IT investment evaluation methodology deployed, and benefits realization process used. All interviews were taped and the transcripts were sent to the interviewees for validation. Other data collected included some of the actual contract documents, planning documents, and some minutes of relevant meetings. More than 200 pages of transcripts were analyzed. Qualitative content analysis was used to analyze the data from the case studies. The analysis of the case-study results was conducted in a cyclical manner and the results were checked by other experts in the field.

Case-Study Findings

A number of issues emerged from the analysis of the text data, and some of the key issues surrounding the use of evaluation methodologies are presented below in some detail.

Lack of Use of Formal IT Investment Evaluation Methodology

Most of the case-study participants claimed that a methodology or process was in place for investment evaluation. However, closer examination of the participants' responses reveals that there was a lack of formal IT investment evaluation methodology or process used.

Most of the participants from the case-study organizations claimed formal IT investment evaluation methodologies or processes were used for evaluating the IT projects. However, closer examination of the participants' responses and project documents revealed otherwise. Documents such as service-level agreements (SLAs), monthly reports, standard contract management, and public-sector guidelines provided by organizations were stated by most participants as the IT investment evaluation methodology or process used for evaluating IT projects. Most of these measurements were related to the contract conditions specified in the SLAs within each project and no formal IT investment evaluation methodology, process, or technique (e.g., information economics) was mentioned. In reality, only informal IT investment evaluation processes (e.g., cost-benefit analysis) were used. However, several participants mistakenly thought project control and evaluation mechanisms specified within the SLAs constituted their IT investment evaluation methodology or technique. Furthermore, this may be also due to the fact that both case-study organizations were unable to introduce a formal IT investment evaluation methodology because they were required to follow the public-sector IT project contract guidelines.

Conflict between Motivations and Success Criteria for IT Projects

There appeared to be a conflict between both organizations' motivations for investing in IT projects and the criteria for determining the success of these projects. Access to the required technical expertise was cited by most participants as one of the motivations for investing in these projects. Therefore, one can expect that getting the required expertise and cost saving should be mentioned by at least half of the participants as their criteria for determining the success of these IT projects. However, this was not the case. None of the participants mentioned getting the required technical expertise as one of the criteria for determining the success of the IT projects. Cost saving was not explicitly mentioned by any participant.

It seemed that the participants had different expectations regarding the IT projects. Alternatively, the participants may have felt that the IT projects had already brought in the required technical expertise and, therefore, should not be used as one of the criteria for determining the success of the projects.

Lack of User Involvement in IT Project Implementation and Evaluation

User involvement has a positive influence on the successful outcome of system implementation. This implies that getting users involved in the project implementation and evaluation processes may improve their attitudes toward the system, and enhance the importance and relevance users perceive about the system. However, none of the participants was involved with any of the original IT project justification and negotiation processes. It appeared that the IT project justification process was handled by other units within both organizations.

There appeared to be an "organizational memory gap" where units within both organizations possessed knowledge of different sorts (i.e., investment evaluation and benefits realization) of the entire IT system's development cycle. However, the knowledge did not seem to be shared by all units because different units participated in different stages of the IT project development cycle. It is arguable that both organizations' project implementation and evaluation processes would be even more successful if the participants were involved in the original IT project justification and negotiation processes as well as the benefits realization process.

General Lack of Commitment by Contractors

There was a general lack of commitment by external IT project vendors. Most external vendors' criterion for determining the success of the external contracts seemed to be maximization of profit and revenue. The contractors' lack of commitment can also be demonstrated by the fact that they either did not know (or care?) why the organizations selected external IT vendors. This was despite the fact that all of the external contracts were in partnership type of arrangements.

This result appears to confirm the studies conducted by several researchers, which indicate that not only are many organizations from the private or public sector skeptical about partnerships (Hancox & Hackney, 2000), but also the partnership type of contract is not the most successful because the profit motive is not shared (Lacity & Willcocks, 1998).

FUTURE TRENDS

IT evaluation must be considered as a continuous activity as the IT itself evolves and adapts over time. More successful organizations in the future are likely to be the ones that persistently evaluate their new IT initiatives in order to gain the expected benefits. These include the use of formal IT investment evaluation and benefits realization methodologies and the formulation of effective strategies to assess their IT initiatives from the technical, social, and economic perspectives. These organizations will invest only in those IT projects that are likely to deliver productivity gains.

DISCUSSIONS

As mentioned earlier, the effective deployment of appropriate IT investment evaluation and benefits realization methodologies are critical to the successful outcomes for IT projects. The results from this study indicate that most organizations have suffered from poor IT investment evaluation practices. A number of issues have emerged from the data and some key issues have been presented in this chapter. These include the lack of use of formal IT project evaluation processes, conflicting motivations and different perceptions of success of the IT projects by stakeholders, lack of user involvement in IT project evaluation, and general lack of commitment by external IT vendors.

FUTURE RESEARCH DIRECTIONS

According to Carr (2003), IT has become a commodity because it has become widespread, as has happened to other innovations such as engines and telephones. IT has become the infrastructural technology and, therefore, is often subject to overinvestment and causes economic troubles such as the "Internet Bubble" (Carr). Carr's views on IT are not shared by many IT practitioners and academics who argue that IT still has a lot to offer in the future and can deliver competitive advantages to organizations (Evans, 2003). More recent evidence suggests that many organizations simply got carried away with IS and IT and spent money unwisely in the late 1990s. According to a study by the McKinsey Global Institute, more successful organizations analyzed their economics carefully and spent on only those IS and IT applications that would deliver productivity gains, sequencing their investments carefully through a disciplined approach with innovative management practices (Farrell, 2003).

The need for better methods of IS and IT investment evaluation has arisen from problems such as the productivity paradox where existing measures fail to reveal the gains made from these investments. IS and IT investment evaluation may also be needed for project justification, project comparisons, control, learning, and competitive advantage. Similarly, different approaches to benefits realization are also needed. The benefits of IS and IT can only be fully realized when systems and available technology are applied to specific and relevant tasks, which in turn are aligned with the business strategy (Andresen et al., 2000). Moreover, recent research indicates that formal approaches are not often used (Lin & Pervan, 2003; Lin, Huang, & Tseng, 2007) and that the application of structure and discipline to the process will improve the measurement of IS and IT benefits in organizations and lead to more effective investment of organizations' scarce resources in key elements of information systems and technology.

Finally, the study took place at a particular point in time. Further research could be conducted to capture the opinions of respondents at various stages of the IS and IT project development process. Alternatively, our study could be replicated in a few years time to examine how IS and IT benefits realization and investment evaluation have changed and are being managed in light of emerging technologies such as e-commerce. Nevertheless, some key issues have been presented by the research and these may be helpful to practitioners and researchers in this field.

REFERENCES

Allen, D., Kern, T., & Mattison, D. (2002). Culture, power and politics in ICT outsourcing in higher education institutions. *European Journal of Information Systems, 11*, 159-173.

Andresen, J., Baldwin, A., Betts, M., Carter, C., Hamilton, A., Stokes, E., et al. (2000). A framework for measuring IT innovation benefits. *Electronic Journal of Information Technology in Construction, 5*, 57-72.

Ballantine, J., & Stray, S. (1998). Financial appraisal and the IS/IT investment decision making process. *Journal of Information Technology, 13*, 3-14.

Bannister, F. (2001). Dismantling the silos: Extracting new value from IT investments in public administration. *Information Systems Journal, 11*, 65-84.

Carr, N. G. (2003). IT doesn't matter. *Harvard Business Review, 8*(1), 4-50.

Changchit, C., Joshi, K. D., & Lederer, A. L. (1998). Process and reality in information systems benefit analysis. *Information Systems Journal, 8*, 145-162.

Domberger, S., Fernandez, P., & Fiebig, D. G. (2000). Modelling the price, performance and contract characteristics of IT outsourcing. *Journal of Information Technology, 15*, 107-118.

Evans, B. (2003). Business technology: IT doesn't matter? *InformationWeek.* Retrieved from http://www.informationweek.com/story/showArticle.jhtml?articleID=9800088

Farrell, D. (2003). The real new economy. *Harvard Business Review, 81*(10), 104.

Gunasekaran, A. (2005). Benchmarking in public sector organizations. *Benchmarking: An International Journal, 12*(4).

Hall, R. (1998). New electronic communication from local government: Marginal or revolutionary? *Local Government Studies, 24*, 19-33.

Heeks, R. (1999). *Reinventing government in the information age.* London: Routledge.

Hillam, C. E., & Edwards, H. M. (2001). A case study approach to evaluation of information technology/information systems (IT/IS) investment evaluation processes within SMEs. *The Electronic Journal of Information Systems Evaluation, 4*(2).

Hu, Q., & Quan, J. J. (2005). Evaluating the impact of IT investments on productivity: A causal analysis at industry level. *International Journal of Information Management, 5*(1), 39-53.

IBM. (2006). Government in an era of transformational opportunity. *IBM Investor Relationships.* Retrieved from http://www.ibm.com/investor/viewpoint/features/2006/09-05-06-1.phtml

Jones, S., & Hughes, J. (2001). Understanding IS evaluation as a complex social process: A case study of a UK local authority. *European Journal of Information Systems, 10*, 189-203.

Khalfan, A. (2003). A case analysis of business process outsourcing project failure profile and implementation problems in a large organisation of a developing nation. *Business Process Management Journal, 9*(6), 745-759.

Kouzmin, A., Loffler, E., Klages, H., & Korac-Kakabadse, N. (1999). Benchmarking and performance measurement in public sectors towards learning for agency effectiveness. *The International Journal of Public Sector Management, 12*(2), 121-144.

Lacity, M. C., & Willcocks, L. P. (1998). An empirical investigation of information technology sourcing practices: Lessons from experience. *MIS Quarterly*, pp. 363-408.

Lin, C., Huang, Y., & Tseng, S. (2007). A study of planning and implementation stages in electronic commerce adoption and evaluation: The case of Australian SMEs. *Contemporary Management Research, 3*(1), 83-100.

Lin, C., Lin, K., Huang, Y., & Kuo, W. (2006). Evaluation of electronic customer relationship management: The critical success factors. *The Business Review, 6*(2), 206-212.

Lin, C., & Pervan, G. (2003). The practice of IS/IT benefits management in large Australian organizations. *Information and Management, 41*(1), 13-24.

Lin, C., Pervan, G., & McDermid, D. (2005). IS/IT investment evaluation and benefits realization issues in Australia. *Journal of Research and Practices in Information Technology, 37*(3), 235-251.

Love, P. E. D., Irani, Z., Standing, C., Lin, C., & Burn, J. (2005). The enigma of evaluation: Benefits, costs and risks of IT in small-medium sized enterprises. *Information and Management, 42*(7), 947-964.

Osei-Bryson, K., & Ko, M. (2004). Exploring the relationship between information technology investments and firm performance using regression splines analysis. *Information and Management, 42*(1), 1-13.

Perrin, B., & Pervan, G. (2004, May). *Performance monitoring systems for public sector IT outsourcing contracts.* Proceedings of the 15th International Conference of the Information Resources Management Association (IRMA 2004), New Orleans, LA.

Pulliam, D. (2005). *Pace of information technology spending to slow, report predicts.* National Journal Group Inc. Retrieved from http://www.govexec.om/dailyfed/0505/050405p1.htm

Seddon, P., Graeser, V., & Willcocks, L. (2002). Measuring organizational IS effectiveness: An overview and update of senior management perspectives. *The Database for Advances in Information Systems, 33*(2), 11-28.

Silverman, D. (2001). *Interpreting qualitative data* (2nd ed.). London: Sage.

Sohal, A. S., & Ng, L. (1998). The role and impact of information technology in Australian business. *Journal of Information Technology, 13*, 201-217.

Standing, C., & Lin, C. (2007). Organizational evaluation of the benefits, constraints and satisfaction with business-to-business electronic commerce. *International Journal of Electronic Commerce, 11*(3), 107-153.

Sugumaran, V., & Arogyaswamy, B. (2004). Measuring IT performance: "Contingency" variables and value modes. *The Journal of Computer Information Systems, 44*(2), 79-86.

Sullivan, E. W., & Ngwenyama, O. K. (2005). How are public sector organizations managing IS outsourcing risks? An analysis of outsourcing guidelines from three jurisdictions. *Journal of Computer Information Systems, 45*(3), 73-87.

Thatcher, M. D., & Pingry, D. E. (2004). Understanding the business value of information technology investments: Theoretical evidence from alternative market and cost structure. *Journal of Management Information Systems, 21*(2), 61-85.

Tsao, H., Lin, K. H., & Lin, C. (2004). An investigation of critical success factors in the adoption of B2BEC by Taiwanese companies. *The Journal of American Academy of Business, 5*(1/2), 198-202.

van Grembergen, W., & van Bruggen, R. (1998). Measuring and improving corporate information technology through the balanced scorecard. *Electronic Journal of Information Systems Evaluation, 1*(1). Retrieved from http://is.twi.tudelft.nl/ejise/indpap.html

Ward, J., Taylor, P., & Bond, P. (1996). Evaluation and realization of IT benefits: An empirical study of current practice. *European Journal of Information Systems, 4*, 214-225.

Willcocks, L., & Lester, S. (1997). Assessing IT productivity: Any way out of the labyrinth? In L. Willcocks, D. F. Feeny, & G. Islei (Eds.), *Managing IT as a strategic resource* (chap. 4, pp. 64-93). London: The McGraw-Hill Company.

Zhu, K. (2004). The complementarity of information technology infrastructure and e-commerce capability: A resource-based assessment of their business value. *Journal of Management Information Systems, 21*(1), 167-202.

FURTHER READING

Anderson, J., & Van Crowder, L. (2000). The present and future of public sector extension in Africa: Contracting out or contracting in? *Public Administration and Development, 20*, 373-384.

Apte, U. M., Sobol, M. G., Hanaoka, S., Shimada, T., Saarinen, T., Salmela, T., et al. (1997). IS outsourcing practices in the USA, Japan and Finland: A comparative study. *Journal of Information Technology, 12*, 289-304.

Barthelemy, J. (2003). The hard and soft sides of IT outsourcing management. *European Management Journal, 21*(5), 539-548.

Barthelemy, J., & Geyer, D. (2004). The determinants of total IT outsourcing: An empirical investigation of French and German firms. *The Journal of Computer Information Systems, 44*(3), 91-97.

Burnes, B., & Anastasiadis, A. (2003). Outsourcing: A public-private sector comparison. *Supply Chain Management: An International Journal, 8*(4), 355-366.

Cilek, P., Fanko, W., Koch, S., Mild, A., & Taudes, A. (2004). A hedonic wage model-based methodology for evaluating the benefits of IT investments in public-sector organisations. *The Journal of Enterprise Information Management, 17*(4), 269-275.

Currie, W. (1996). Outsourcing in the private and public sectors: An unpredictable IT strategy. *European Journal of Information Systems, 4*, 226-236.

Dean, A. M., & Kiu, C. (2002). Performance monitoring and quality outcomes in contracted services. *International Journal of Quality & Reliability Management, 19*(4), 396-413.

Dos Santos, B. L. (1994). Assessing the value of strategic information technology investments. In L. Willcocks (Ed.), *Information management: The evaluation of information systems investments.* London: Chapman & Hall.

Douglas, V. (1999, May 10). Fahey under fire over fat fees and dubious savings. *Informationweek*, pp. 20-25.

Fink, D., & Shoeib, A. (2003). Action: The most critical phase in outsourcing information technology. *Logistics Information Management, 16*(5), 302-311.

Gordon, M. L., & Walsh, T. P. (1997). Outsourcing technology in government: Owned, controlled, or regulated institutions. *Journal of Government Information, 24*(4), 267-283.

Hirschheim, R., & Lacity, M. (2000). The myths and realities of information technology insourcing. *Communications of the ACM, 43*(2), 99-107.

Huang, Y., Lin, C., & Lin, H. (2005). Techno-economic effect of R&D outsourcing strategy for small and medium-sized enterprises: A resource-based viewpoint. *International Journal of Innovation and Incubation, 2*(1), 1-22.

Kakabadse, A., & Kakabadse, N. (2001). Outsourcing in the public services: A comparative analysis of practice. *Capability and Impact, Public Administration and Development, 21*, 401-413.

Kuo, W., Lin, C., Hsu, G., & Huang, Y. (2006). An empirical study of resource contribution in SMEs alliance. *Journal of Global Business Management, 2*(2), 103-111.

Lacity, M. C., & Willcocks, L. (1997). Information systems sourcing: Examining the privatization option in USA public administration. *Information Systems Journal, 7*, 85-108.

Laitinen, E. M. (2002). A dynamic performance system: Evidence from small Finnish technology companies. *Scandinavian Journal of Management, 18*, 65-99.

Lee, B., & Barua, A. (1999). An integrated assessment of productivity and efficiency impacts of information technology investments: Old data, new analysis and evidence. *Journal of Productivity Analysis, 121*, 21-43.

Lewis, B. R., & Byrd, T. A. (2003). Development of a measure for the information technology infrastructure construct. *European Journal of Information Systems, 12*, 93-109.

Lin, C., & Huang, Y. (2007). An integrated framework for managing eCRM evaluation process. *International Journal of Electronic Business, 5*(3).

Lin, C., Huang, Y., Cheng, M., & Lin, W. (2007). Effects of information technology maturity on the adoption of investment evaluation methodologies: A survey of large Australian organizations. *International Journal of Management, 24*(4).

Lin, K., & Lin, C. (2007). Evaluating the decision to adopt RFID systems using analytic hierarchy process. *The Journal of American Academy of Business, 11*(1), 72-78.

Lin, K., Lin, C., & Tsao, H. (2005). IS/IT investment evaluation and benefit realization practices in Taiwanese SMEs. *Journal of Information Science and Technology, 2*(4), 44-71.

McIvor, R. (2000). A practical framework for understanding the outsourcing process. *Supply Chain Management, 5*(1), 22.

Misra, R. B. (2004). Global IT outsourcing: Metrics for success of all parties. *Journal of Information Technology Cases and Applications, 6*(3), 21-34.

O'Looney, J. (1998). *Outsourcing the city: State and local government outsourcing.* New York: Quorum Books.

Parker, M. M., Benson, R. J., & Trainor, H. E. (1988). *Information economics.* London: Prentice Hall.

Remenyi, D., Sherwood-Smith, M., & White, T. (1997). *Achieving maximum value from information systems: A process approach.* Chichester, England: John Wiley & Sons.

Standing, C., Burn, J., & Lin, C. (2006). Case study: Information systems in Western Australian universities. *Australasian Journal of Information Systems, 14*(1), 251-260.

Standing, C., Guilfoyle, A., Lin, C., & Love, P. E. D. (2006). The attribution of success and failure in IT projects. *Industrial Management and Data Systems, 106*(8), 1148-1165.

Strassman, P. A. (1990). *The business value of computers.* New Canaan: The Information Economics Press.

Tallon, P. P., Kraemer, K. L., & Gurbaxani, V. (2000). Executives' perceptions of the business value of information technology: A process-oriented approach. *Journal of Management Information Systems, 16*(4), 145-173.

Willcocks, L., & Currie, W. (1997). Contracting-out information technology in the public sector context: Research and critique. *Journal of the Australian and New Zealand Academy of Management, 2*(2), 34-49.

Willcocks, L., Fitzgerald, G., & Lacity, M. (1996). To outsource it or not? Recent research on economics and evaluation practice. *European Journal of Information Systems, 5*, 143-160.

Willcocks, L. P., Lacity, M. C., & Kern, T. (1999). Risk mitigation in IT outsourcing strategy revisited: Longitudinal case research at LISA. *Journal of Strategic Information Systems, 8*, 285-314.

Young, S. (2005). Outsourcing in the Australian health sector: The interplay of economics and politics. *International Journal of Public Sector Management, 18*(1), 25-36.

TERMS AND DEFINITIONS

Benchmarking: This refers to the identification of historical data against which a data set can be compared now and in the future.

Cost-Benefit Analysis: This is a technique or approach used to compare the various costs associated with the expected benefits.

IT Benefits Realization: It is a managed and controlled process of benchmarking, involving implementing and adjusting the expected results and continuously adjusting the path leading from IT investments to expected business benefits.

IT Project: This is an organizational initiative that employs or produces IT or IT-related assets.

Organizational Memory: It is also called corporate knowledge. It refers to the repository where hard data and soft information are stored for future use. The soft information can be in the form of tacit know-how, expertise, biases, experiences, and anecdotes.

Performance Measurement: Performance measurement involves the data that will be gathered, analyzed, reported, and utilized to make business decisions. It is also used to justify business spending, report progress toward established business objectives, and identify areas for improvement.

Preinvestment Justification: These are approaches or techniques that are used to assess organizations' potential IT investments before decisions are made to invest.

Chapter LXV
Performance and Accountability in E-Budgeting Projects

Gabriel Puron-Cid
Rockefeller College of Public Affairs and Policy, University at Albany, SUNY, USA

J. Ramon Gil-Garcia
Centro de Investigación y Docencia Económicas, Mexico

INTRODUCTION

An influential theoretical tradition in information systems research suggests that information and communication technology has the power to transform organizational structures and individual behaviors. This approach has been called "technological determinism." In contrast, recent studies have found evidence of more complex relationships between information technologies and the organizational and institutional contexts in which those technologies are embedded (Fountain, 2001; Kling & Lamb, 2000; Orlikowski & Baroudi, 1991). The theories that Orlikowski and Iacono (2001) have categorized as the "ensemble view" explain that information technologies should not be conceptualized as physical artifacts only, but that the social relations around those artifacts should also be considered. In addition, the relationship between information technologies and social structures is at least bidirectional, and therefore organizational characteristics and institutional arrangements also have an impact on government ICT projects (Fountain; García, 2005; Kraemer, King, Dunkle, & Lane, 1989). As a result of this embedment of ICT in government settings, certain characteristics of the information technologies are expected to reflect important aspects of the institutional and organizational environment and, therefore, help preserve the status quo instead of promoting change (Fountain; Kraemer et al.).

In the last decade, the Mexican federal government has attempted to significantly transform its administrative processes and improve the quality of the services it provides through the use of ICT (Organisation for Economic Co-operation and Development [OECD], 2003; Puron-Cid & Gil-García, 2004). This trend toward service quality and results (performance) has been reflected in numerous organizational transformations and the implementation of performance-oriented budgeting (Arellano-Gault & Gil-García, 2004; Arellano-Gault & Puron-Cid, 2004; Petrei, 1997; World Bank, 1997). Accountability and control are indeed always concerns for government agencies, particularly for the Ministry of Finance, and therefore some tensions between performance and accountability within budgetary reform will exist. Based on the analysis of three federal initiatives, this chapter argues that due to the embedment of ICT in government institutional and organizational environments, the tensions between performance and accountability become also reflected in the goals, features, and functionality of e-budgeting projects (see "Key Terms"). Furthermore, the prevalence of accountability for finance and fairness (accountability bias) already identified in the literature (Behn, 2001) is also reflected in the formal goals, general characteristics, and technical capabilities of the e-budgeting systems. The cases thus support the general hypothesis that information technologies do not necessarily have the power to transform government radically, at least not in the case of e-budgeting initiatives.

This chapter is organized into six sections, including this introduction. The second section provides an overview of the importance of accountability and its tension relation with performance. It also explains the accountability-bias argument. The third section describes the research method and design. Next the chapter presents the analysis of three e-budgeting projects in Mexico, highlighting specific aspects of these projects related to performance and accountability. The fifth section identifies certain future trends in relation to this topic, and finally, the sixth section provides final comments and suggests areas for additional research.

BACKGROUND: ACCOUNTABILITY AND PERFORMANCE

Scholars and practitioners in government have emphasized the tensions between accountability and performance, where accountability usually prevails over performance, producing what is called accountability bias (Behn, 2001). The current characteristics of ICT applications in government reflect multiple power struggles and negotiations among the actors involved in making decisions and creating rules regarding the design, implementation, and use of these systems (Bovens & Zouridis, 2002; Fountain, 2001; Heeks, 1998; Kraemer & King, 2003; Newcomer & Caudle, 1991; Puron-Cid & Gil-García, 2004). It is expected that the prevalence of accountability is also reflected in some characteristics of government IT projects. In the following sections, we define accountability and its bias. As performance is a multidimensional concept, we consider accountability bias to be any kind of impact on performance as a consequence of privileging accountability in the design, development, and use of ICT applications in government.

Defining Accountability

Accountability has been considered to be one of the most important features of democratic governments (Behn, 2001). In recent reviews of the history of different governments, Light (1993) and Rosenbloom (2001) considered accountability as one of the main democratic values. In fact, the key actors in this democratic scene, such as Congress, the Executive, and the Bureaucracy, must interpret and practice accountability and usually do so in different ways (Aberbach & Rockman, 2000; Wood & Waterman, 1991). Scholars have offered several distinct definitions and classifications of accountability (Behn; Fesler & Kettl, 1991; Shafritz, 1988). Based on three e-budgeting initiatives, this chapter demonstrates how government information systems reflect the tensions between what Behn calls different forms of accountability: finance, fairness, use of power, and performance (see "Key Terms").

Tensions between Accountability and Performance

Traditionally, political and organizational systems have established rules, procedures, and standards to accomplish different types of accountability (Aberbach & Rockman, 2000; Anechiarico & Jacobs, 1996; Behn, 2001; Derthick, 1990; Kearns, 1996, 1998; Light, 1993). In the case of the budgetary process and the management of public resources, holding people accountable for performance while also holding them accountable for finance and fairness creates a dilemma, namely, that accountability rules for finance and fairness can hinder performance (Behn).

This tension is considered one of the classic dilemmas in public administration and is described in different ways by different researchers (Self, 1972). Mosher (1980) depicted the problem as a conflict between accountability and the values of experimentation, inventiveness, and risk taking. Moe (1984) explained that bureaucrats are constrained by multiple rules and control mechanisms that then have a negative impact on their work, activities, responsibilities, and overall performance. Romzek and Dubnick (1987) noted that "the essence of this dilemma was the inability of entities to be accountable [to] many masters and manage the government's business under conditions of multiple accountability relationships and systems."

March and Olsen (1995) observed this tension as risk aversion in terms of paying more attention to finance and fairness in the short term than to performance in the long term. Anechiarico and Jacobs (1996) suggested a trade-off between maintaining the integrity of political decisions (accountability) and attaining public administration efficiency (performance). Finally, this tension is also present in the tide of reforms sponsored by international organizations, reforms that can bring potential conflicts between traditional notions of public administration and accountability and the emerging forms of public management that stress performance strongly (Arellano-Gault, 1999; Behn, 2001; Light, 1997; Lynn, 1998; OECD, 1995; Ricucci, 2001; World Bank, 1997).

Accountability Bias

The accountability environment of government can be described as a constellation or group of forces—legal, political, sociocultural, and economic—that place pressure on organizations and the people working in them to engage in certain activities and refrain from others (Kearns, 1996). Behn (2001) describes these tensions as accountability bias: It is easier and clearer to codify accountability for finance or fairness in explicit rules than accountability for performance, which usually presents a challenge of defining multidimensional aspects of public organizations and a need for performance measurements to be created or defined before their incorporation into the systems. Then, it can be expected that accountability holders concentrate their efforts and resources to develop and use ICT infrastructure and tools to monitor finance and fairness and give much less attention to performance.

PERFORMANCE AND ACCOUNTABILITY IN E-BUDGETING INITIATIVES

Three e-budgeting projects are included in our analysis: (a) the Digital Signature for Budgetary Transactions and Procedures Project, (b) the Integral Process for Programming and Budgeting Project, and (c) the Government Strategic Planning Project. The following sections describe each of these initiatives, emphasizing aspects related to performance and accountability as reflected in the formal documents, general characteristics, and technical features of these systems. Some background information about the budgetary reform in Mexico is also provided.

Budgetary Reform and E-Budgeting Projects

During the last decade, many governments have attempted to transform their organizational structures and improve the quality of their services by using ICT as an instrument for administrative reform (Kraemer & King, 2003; OECD, 2002, 2003). The budget process has been part of this wave of changes occurring since 1998, through an initiative called Budgetary Reform (Giugale, Lafourcade, & Nguyen, 2001; e-Strategia Consulting Group, 2002a; World Bank, 1997). In Mexico, these changes included new budgetary rules (performance-oriented budgeting) and ICT tools for budgetary control and decision making (Arellano-Gault & Gil-Garcia, 2004; Arellano-Gault & Puron-Cid, 2004; Petrei, 1997; Puron-Cid & Gil-Garcia, 2004; World Bank).

The new e-budgeting systems in Mexico were designed to endow public managers with more rational tools to calculate their annual budgets that were based on functional categories, metrics of performance, and expected results. ICT applications were expected to play an important role in the implementation of this new model for the budget cycle (OECD, 1995; e-Strategia Consulting Group, 2002a).

Digital Signature for Budgetary Transactions and Procedures Project

During 2002, the Ministry of Finance (SHCP) created a project team to modernize budgetary transactions and procedures. This team discovered several problems: (a) slow response to budgetary procedures, (b) impractical budgeting procedures for users, (c) discretional application of budgetary rules, and (d) lack of analysis, budgetary impact on government goals, and objectives. In sum, there were too many official document-oriented procedures that were causing inefficiencies and low performance (SHCP, 2003f).

The team proposed to use ICT applications to improve government performance while still maintaining budgetary control according to the existing regulations and responsibilities of the Ministry of Finance. The Digital Signature for Budgetary Transactions and Procedures Project (DSBT) was designed and implemented in fiscal year 2003, and it is still operating with few adjustments. Today, most of the budgetary transactions are operated using this system.

By analyzing the system manual and some budgetary regulations (SHCP, 2002a; SHCP, 2003e), it was possible to identify the following specific features. The goal of the DSBT is to facilitate budgeting management of the budgetary appropriations (SHCP, 2003f). Specifically, this e-budgeting project attempts to improve communication and the workflow between the Ministry of Finance and all other involved public organizations. This ICT tool also seeks a delegation and flexibility of budgetary operations (called BO) but without losing data control, transaction security, and process transparency. Digital signatures are used to ensure security standards during transaction transmissions, auditing requirements, and supervising protocols.

We argue that accountability was the most important criterion in defining the system requirements and priorities for the DSBT in terms of high response, utility for multi-users, deregulation, security, and paperless orientation. Based on an analysis of the SHCP official information, namely, manuals, regulations, procedures, memorandums, and presentations, we were able to identify the following system features that matched the accountability-bias description.

According to the diagnostic report (SHCP, 2003f) and the budgetary regulations (SHCP, 2002a), the system was designed to improve administrative efficiency for budgetary procedures and analysis of the impact of budgetary adjustments in government goals. However, the manual suggests that the system certainly improves administrative efficiency by translating and programming the budgetary regulations into the system's rules (SHCP, 2002b). However, the system does not provide any application to evaluate the impact of these transactions in government performance. The system is mostly finance oriented and not very useful for agencies to use to evaluate their performance. It is almost exclusively useful for SHCP and its focus on budgetary control and regulations.

The diagnostic report (SHCP, 2003f) and the rules for the Ministry of Finance (SHCP, 2003e) advocate the need to provide tools for external users, such as Congress, citizens, and other agencies. For technical reasons offered in the manual (SHCP, 2002b), the final features of the system mainly reinforces a dominant legal authority and the roles of the executives in the Ministry of Finance over the public agencies for many budgetary procedures. Therefore, the system is limited to the Ministry's procedures and administrative needs (mostly related to accountability and control) and does not include appropriate features to evaluate the performance of the agencies.

In all of the manuals and regulations, there is no evidence of any application available for long-term analysis of budget, neither for the budgetary effects on performance of programs or projects. The budgetary information is limited only to the current fiscal year. It is not possible with the present tools in the system to evaluate information of previous budgets or budgeting trends, or perform comparative analysis for detecting problems, identifying alternatives, or proposing solutions. The system focuses mainly on the short-term activities of the Ministry of Finance and does not contain, as initially planned, tools for other agencies to use to evaluate their activities in relation to their budgets.

Integral Process for Programming and Budgeting Project

The Ministry of Finance analyzes programming and budgeting project procedures annually (SHCP, 2003d). The main problems identified during the 2004 budget project process were (a) the lack of internal coordination and collaboration among SHCP subunits and (b) the large number and diversity of public organizations that had to bring their budget projects into line (public resources) within proper programming structures (goals for performance). Some of the results of the presence of these problems were (a) useless planning exercises by the agencies that were incompatible with their programming structures, (b) conflicting and disarticulated budget project integration, and (c) unrealistic budgets for real public financial needs (SHCP, 2003b).

The Integral Process for Programming and Budgeting Project (IPPB) attempts to improve the budgetary management process in a sequential and integral process among the different levels of authority in the Ministry of Finance and public agencies. The IPPB includes three modules: (a) programming, (b) integration and authorization, and (c) authorized appropriation and accountability reports (SHCP, 2003b).

For the complex analysis that involves the IPPB (Puron-Cid & Gil-García, 2004), the present section only focuses on the first module called programming, where the budgetary project is integrated for the Congress through the use of the Integration Budget Project (IBP) procedure. The IBP consists of budgetary allocation according to a strategic plan, programming structure, and financial needs. The system consists of an interactive Web application that is available to public administrators and Ministry executives who have specific profiles and levels of access. Every IBP document must be registered in the system to comply with the procedure described in the manual (SHCP, 2003d).

After examining the manual and the regulations (SHCP, 2003a, 2003b, 2003c, 2003d), we found evidence of the accountability-bias effect in the IPPB system.

Previous analysis established the need for coordination to integrate any budget project to the Congress in terms of congruency between strategic planning, programming structure, and performance goals in order to allocate resources. However, the final design and use of the system highlights the operational needs of the Ministry of Finance more than the needs of the Congress and the agencies so as to bridge their budgets with their plans, programming structures, and financial needs. The Ministry of Finance reinterpreted the requirements of information from the Congress in terms of more budgetary controls that favor the Ministry over the agencies. This interpretation of the role of the Ministry of Finance in the budgetary operations made the IPPB a much more finance-oriented tool for the Ministry to use rather than a performance and planning tool for other agencies.

In addition, the original design proposes an integral and interactive application to support federal agencies in the integration process. However, the position and responsibilities of the Ministry of Finance over public funds prevailed in the final features of the IPPB. By analyzing manuals and guides (SHCP, 2003a, 2003c, 2003d), it is common to find applications to monitor the integration process across the agencies and the annual controls for budgetary balance instead of reporting tools that can offer information or assistance for programming or performance evaluation. The IPPB was significantly influenced by the predominant administrative role of the Ministry of Finance, which is shaped by accountability regulations over the course of the whole budgetary cycle.

Government Strategic Planning Project

After the first budget experience in the present administration in 2000, the President's Office (Oficina de la Presidencia de la República, OPR) and the Ministry of Finance perceived that the executive policies were dispersed and disarticulated throughout the federal governmental structure (e-Strategia Consulting Group, 2002b). Therefore, the budgetary process became a strategic factor for success of the President's strategies and plans (e-Strategia Consulting Group, 2002a).

The objective of the Government Strategic Planning Project (GSP) is to facilitate the strategic planning process among the executive and operative levels of government through the budgetary process (e-Strategia Consulting Group, 2002a). The GSP is empowered by an external provider who collaborates directly with the OPR and the Ministry of Finance.

The GSP provides ICT tools for planning across agencies to define standard strategic information. The role of the executive through the OPR in this process is to establish a group of projects for each agency to be included in the next programmatic structure and budget project (e-Strategia Consulting Group, 2002b). The OPR is responsible for defining methodology, formats, and norms. The Ministry of Finance is responsible for integrating these elements into the programming process that eventually appears in the budget project chapter. The GSP was designed to assist public executives with project-management tools and the monitoring of strategic planning and budget projects, including a panel of indicators for strategic and administrative performance. After examining the manuals and guides (e-Strategia Consulting Group, 2002a, 2002b), we found proofs of an accountability-bias impact on the GSP.

The GPS design prioritizes an articulation of efforts among the OPR, the Ministry of Finance, and agencies to bridge the planning process to the budgetary cycle. However, the dominant role of the Ministry of Finance in terms of the reinterpretation of information requirements and regulations and its constant emphasis on budgetary control importantly influenced final OPR decisions for more finance-related tools in the system.

Similarly, the budgetary operations of the agencies through Ministry of Finance procedures were critical to confirm the Ministry's domination of the final features in the GSP. The prevalence of control over the agencies' activities, the need of administrative effectiveness in these processes, and the annual integration of the budget in the short-term finally emphasized the existing role of the Ministry of Finance, allowing less room for new initiatives from the OPR. The GSP was finally shaped by the dominant purposes of the Ministry of Finance agenda and its operational needs. The finance-oriented accountability in the regulations and the role of the Ministry of Finance were more clearly incorporated into the system than were the President's need to oversee the performance of the agencies.

FUTURE TRENDS

There is an increasing investment in technology for government operations and services in developed and developing countries. Many of these projects attempt to improve government performance and efficiency. The budget cycle has often been part of these new waves of reform, which do include the more extensive use of ICT. This trend is expected to continue in the near future, leading to more investments and more complex e-budgeting initiatives. However, some of the institutional and organizational features of government have imposed important restrictions on e-budgeting projects, causing them not to be useful for evaluating the performance of agencies or to encourage Congressional or Presidential political control. In our cases, the systems were only useful for the Ministry of Finance and mainly designed for accountability and financial control, even when performance assessment was part of the initial goals and objectives. It is a key issue, therefore, to identify precisely what factors cause the prevalence of accountability over performance in order to better understand this phenomenon and increase the value of ICT investments. Despite great expectations about the transformational power of ICTs, it seems that organizational and institutional constraints will continue having an important influence on the design, implementation, and use of e-government initiatives in general and e-budgeting projects in particular.

CONCLUSION

Across the case studies examined here, the role of the Ministry of Finance in the budgetary cycle was predominant for e-budgeting projects, even when the original objectives of the systems included important performance aspects. The prevalence of accountability for finance, alternatively giving much less attention to performance, influenced the characteristic of the systems that consistently serve as administrative and control tools for the executives of the Ministry of Finance rather than providing useful applications for agency managers to use to support their daily budgetary tasks and evaluate their organizations' performance. In addition, the use of these systems favored the Ministry of Finance's operations and helped to accomplish the existing budgetary regulations instead of improving political control by the Congress or the Presidency. Therefore, the systems were only useful in terms of accountability and control for the relationship between the Ministry of Finance (as principal) and other agencies (as agents), but not for the relationship between the Ministry of Finance (as an agent) and its principals.

The focus on accountability for finance is also a common characteristic of e-budgeting systems and emphasizes the continuity of existing models of administration and the centralization of rules, procedures, and processes. The existing technical and organizational features suggest that the designers of the systems were not able to change most of the existing rules or to incorporate creativity, experimentation, inventiveness, and risk taking into the characteristics of the e-budgeting systems. Instead, the systems concentrated mostly on administrative control and accountability for finance, which were precisely the most important values for the Ministry of Finance. There was no evidence of appropriate tools to evaluate the consistency of public expending relative to the political decisions of Congress or the Executive. In all the cases, the systems were designed to manage short-term projects and low-risk activities that were involved in the budgetary cycle rather than long-term and high-risk performance evaluation, which is normally more difficult to measure.

FUTURE RESEARCH DIRECTIONS

A common practice in the literature has been to consider information technology as a homogeneous theoretical construct with uniform and unidirectional effects on organizational and social settings. One of the challenges in this area is to find adequate ways to classify projects, operationalize measures, collect data, and test results in order to make comparable generalizations of diverse types of ICT projects across different governmental and managerial needs, including budgeting and financial management. Future studies should develop classifications and test how the effects of institutional and organizational factors are similar or different in various organizational contexts and among organizations dealing with different problems. Similarly, the accountability bias was a useful framework for the analysis of e-budgeting projects. Future research should explore the usefulness of this theoretical framework when studying other types of e-government projects, including interorganizational initiatives at different levels of government.

This chapter uses analysis of documents as the primary research method. Documents such as systems manuals and budgetary regulations were examined. Using this research method, we were able to identify the specific features, system requirements, and priorities of each project to evaluate the prevalence of accountability over efficiency (response time, functionality, deregulation, security, and paperless orientation). However, there are limitations in using analysis of documents in particular and as a single research method in general. There is a great opportunity for multimethod approaches combining qualitative and quantitative methods. Future research should analyze some of the factors that do result in accountability bias for e-budgeting projects through the use of multimethod approaches (Gil-García & Pardo, 2006).

Finally, there are conceptual frameworks in different disciplines such as sociology, psychology, communications, and economics that may help to understand how public managers and executives define formal goals, make decisions about general characteristics, and define technical capabilities of the e-budgeting systems in government. A multidisciplinary discussion would enrich the field with complementary and contrasting concepts and approaches to the studies of information and communication technologies in organizational settings. Future studies should explore these opportunities.

ACKNOWLEDGMENT

This work was partially supported by the National Science Foundation under Grant No. 0131923. Any opinions, findings, and conclusions or recommendations expressed in this material are those of the authors and do not necessarily reflect the views of the National Science Foundation.

REFERENCES

Aberbach, J. D., & Rockman, B. A. (2000). *In the Web of politics: Three decades of the U.S. Federal executive.* Washington, DC: Brookings Institution Press.

Anechiarico, F., & Jacobs, J. B. (1996). *The pursuit of absolute integrity: How corruption control makes government ineffective.* Chicago: University of Chicago Press.

Arellano-Gault, D. (1999). De la administracion publica a la nueva gestion publica: Cinco dilemas. *Revista Conmemorativa del Colegio Nacional de Ciencias Politicas y Administracion Publica, 1*, 35-47.

Arellano-Gault, D., & Gil-García, J. R. (2004). Public management policy and accountability in Latin America: Performance-oriented budgeting in Colombia, Mexico, and Venezuela (1994-2000). *International Public Management Journal, 7*(1), 49-71.

Arellano-Gault, D., & Puron-Cid, G. (2004). Mexico. Reforma al sistema presupuestal: Una reforma atrapada por las inercias. In *Mas alla de la reinvencion del gobierno: Fundamentos de la nueva gestion publica y presupuestos por resultados en America Latina.* Mexico: Editorial Porrua and CIDE.

Behn, R. (2001). *Rethinking democratic accountability.* Brookings Institution Press.

Bovens, M., & Zouridis, S. (2002). From street-level to system level bureaucracies: How ICT is transforming administrative discretion and constitutional control. *Public Administration Review, 62*(2), 174-183.

Derthick, M. (1990). *Agency under stress: The Social Security Administration in American government.* Washington, DC: Brookings Institution Press.

e-Strategia Consulting Group. (2002a). *Guía de referencia para la administración de proyectos presidenciales en el spe.* Author.

e-Strategia Consulting Group. (2002b). *Manual de orientación del sistema de planeación estratégica y das-g.* Author.

Fesler, J. W., & Kettl, D. F. (1991). *The politics of the administrative process.*

Fountain, J. E. (2001). *Building the virtual state: Information technology and institutional change.* Washington, DC: Brookings Institution Press.

Gil-García, J. R. (2005). *Enacting state Websites: A mixed method study exploring e-government success in multi-organizational settings.* Unpublished doctoral dissertation, University at Albany, State University of New York, New York.

Gil-García, J. R., & Pardo, T. A. (2006, January). *Multi-method approaches to digital government research: Value lessons and implementation challenges.* Paper presented at the 39th Hawaii International Conference on System Sciences (HICSS), HI.

Giugale, M. M., Lafourcade, O., & Nguyen, V. H. (2001). *Mexico: A comprehensive development agenda for the new era.* Washington, DC: The World Bank.

Heeks, R. (1998). *Information systems and public sector accountability.* Manchester, United Kingdom: Institute for Development Policy and Management, University of Manchester.

Kearns, K. P. (1996). *Managing for accountability.* Jossey-Bass.

Kearns, K. P. (1998). Institutional accountability in higher education: A strategic approach. *Public Productivity and Management Review, 22*(2), 141.

Kling, R., & Lamb, R. (2000). IT and organizational change in digital economies: A sociotechnical approach. In I. E. B. B. K. (Ed.), *Understanding the digital economy: Data, tools, and research.* Cambridge, MA: The MIT Press.

Kraemer, K. L., & King, J. L. (2003, September). *Information technology and administrative reform: Will the time after e-government be different?* Paper presented at the Heinrich Reinermann Schriftfest, Post Graduate School of Administration, Speyer, Germany.

Kraemer, K. L., King, J. L., Dunkle, D. E., & Lane, J. P. (1989). *Managing information systems: Change and control in organizational computing.* San Francisco: Jossey-Bass.

Light, P. (1993). *Monitoring government: Inspectors general and the search for accountability.* Washington, DC: Brookings Institution Press.

Light, P. (1997). *The tides of reform: Making government work, 1945-1995.* Yale University Press.

Lynn, L. E. (1998). A critical analysis of the new public management. *International Public Management Journal, 1*(1), 107-123.

March, J. G., & Olsen, J. P. (1995). *Democratic governance.* Free Press.

Moe, T. M. (1984). The new economics of organization. *American Journal of Political Science, 28*, 739-777.

Mosher, F. C. (1980). The changing responsibilities and tactics of the federal government. *Public Administration Review, 40*(6).

Newcomer, K. E., & Caudle, S. L. (1991). Evaluating public sector information systems: More than meets the eye. *Public Administration Review, 51*, 377-384.

Organisation for Economic Co-Operation and Development (OECD). (1995). *Budgeting for results: Perspectives on public expenditure management.* Paris: Author.

Organisation for Economic Co-Operation and Development (OECD). (2002). *OECD e-government project.* Paris: Author.

Organisation for Economic Co-Operation and Development (OECD). (2003). *The e-government imperative.* Paris: Author.

Orlikowski, W. J., & Baroudi, J. J. (1991). Studying information technology in organizations: Research approaches and assumptions. *The Information Systems Research*, 1-29.

Orlikowski, W. J., & Iacono, C. S. (2001). Research commentary: Desperately seeking the "it" in IT research: A call to theorizing the IT artifact. *Information Systems Research, 12*, 121-134.

Petrei, H. (1997). *Presupuesto y control: Pautas de reforma en América Latina.* Washington, DC: Banco Interamericano de Desarrollo.

Puron-Cid, G., & Gil-García, J. R. (2004). Enacting e-budgeting in Mexico. *Public Finance and Management, 4*(2), 182-217.

Ricucci, N. (2001). The old public management versus the new public management: Where does public administration fit in? *Public Administration Review, 61*, 172-175.

Romzek, B. S., & Dubnick, M. J. (1987). Accountability in the public sector: Lessons from Challenger tragedy. *Public Administration Review, 47*(3), 228.

Rosenbloom, D. H. (2001). History lessons for reinventors. *Public Administration Review, 61*, 161-165.

Self, P. (1972). *Administrative theories and politics.*

Shafritz, J. M. (1988). *The Dorsey dictionary of American government and politics.* Dorsey Press.

SHCP. (2002a). *Lineamientos normativos y de operación para la transferencia en línea de las adecuaciones presupuestarias internas vía Internet* (Internal Document No. VIII-2002). Author.

SHCP. (2002b). *Manual de normas presupuestarias para la administración pública federal* (D.O.F. Publication No. 3-IX-2002). Author.

SHCP. (2003a). Guia de acceso al proceso integral de programacíon y presupuesto (Internal Document No. 31-VII-2003). Author.

SHCP. (2003b). *Guía funcional del proceso integral de programación y presupuesto* (Internal Document No. VII-2003). Author.

SHCP. (2003c). *Lineamientos operativos de concertación de estructuras programáticas 2004* (Internal Document No. 04-VII-2003). Author.

SHCP. (2003d). *Manual de programación y presupuesto* (Internal Document No. X-2003). Author.

SHCP. (2003e). *Oficio circular por el que se establecen los lineamientos para la operación de los sistemas electrónicos de la subsecretaría de egresos, mediante la utilización de firma electrónica* (D.O.F. Publication No. 05-III-2003). Author.

SHCP. (2003f). *Presentación para capacitación del sistema sicp-sicgp con firma electrónica* (Internal Document No. 31-III- 2003). Author.

Wood, B. D., & Waterman, R. W. (1991). The dynamics of political control of the bureaucracy. *American Political Science Review, 85*(3), 801-828.

World Bank. (1997). *World report.* Washington, DC: Author.

FURTHER READING

Atkinson, R. D., & Leigh, A. (2003). Customer-oriented e-government: Can we ever get there? In G. G. Curtin, M. H. Sommer, & V. Vis-Sommer (Eds.), *The world of e-government* (pp. 159-81). New York: Haworth Press.

Attewell, P. (2001). The first and second digital divides. *Sociology of Education, 74*(3), 252-259.

Brown, M. M., & Jeffrey, L. B. (1998). Public sector information technology initiatives: Implications for programs of public administration. *Administration & Society, 30*(4), 421-442.

Carvin, A. (2004). *E-government for all: Ensuring equitable access to online government services.* Newton, MA: EDC Center for Media & Community & NYS Forum, Rockefeller Institute of Government.

Chengalur-Smith, I., & Duchessi, P. (1999). The initiation and adoption of client-server technology in organizations. *Information & Management, 35*, 77-88.

Clark, D. D., Guillet, S. E., Lehr, W., Sirbu, M., & Fountain, J. (2003). *Local government stimulation of broadband: Effectiveness, e-government, and economic development.* KSG.

Cresswell, A. M. (2004). *Return on investment in information technology: A guide for managers.* Albany, NY: Center for Technology in Government, University at Albany, SUNY.

Cresswell, A. M., & Pardo, T. A. (2001). Implications of legal and organizational issues for urban digital government development. *Government Information Quarterly, 18*, 269-278.

Dawes, S. S., Gregg, V., & Agouris, P. (2004). Digital government research: Investigations at the crossroads of social and information science. *Social Science Computer Review, 22*(1), 5-10.

Dawes, S. S., Pardo, T., & DiCaterino, A. (1999). Crossing the threshold: Practical foundations for government services on the World Wide Web. *Journal of the American Society for Information Science, 50*(4), 346-353.

Dawes, S. S., Pardo, T. A., Simon, S., Cresswell, A. M., LaVigne, M., Andersen, D., et al. (2004). *Making smart IT choices: Understanding value and risk in government it investments.* Albany, NY: Center for Technology in Government.

Fletcher, P. D., Holden, S. H., & Norris, D. F. (2001). E-government: Planning, funding, and outsourcing. Washington, DC: International City/County Management Association.

Garson, G. D. (Ed.). (2003). *Public information technology: Policy and management issues.* Hershey, PA: Idea Group Publishing.

Gil-Garcia, J. R., & Helbig, N. (2006). Exploring e-government benefits and success factors. In A.-V. Anttiroiko & M. Malkia (Eds.), *Encyclopedia of digital government.* Hershey, PA: Idea Group Inc.

Gil-Garcia, J. R., & Luna-Reyes, L. F. (2006). Integrating conceptual approaches to e-government. In M. Khosrow-Pour (Ed.), *Encyclopedia of e-commerce, e-government and mobile commerce.* Hershey, PA: Idea Group Inc.

Gil-Garcia, J. R., & Pardo, T. A. (2005). E-government success factors: Mapping practical tools to theoretical foundations. *Government Information Quarterly, 22*(2), 187-216.

Gubbins, M. (2004, April 8). Global IT spending by sector. *Computing*, p. 28.

Heeks, R. B. (2006). *Implementing and managing eGovernment: An international text.* London: Sage Publications.

Heeks, R. B., & Bhatnagar, S. C. (2001). Understanding success and failure in information age reform. In R. B. Heeks (Ed.), *Reinventing government in the information age* (pp. 49-74). London: Routledge.

Holden, S. H. (2003). The evolution of information technology management at the federal level: Implications for public administration. In G. D. Garson (Ed.), *Public information technology: Policy and management issues* (pp. 53-73). Hershey, PA: Idea Group Publishing.

Jennings, E. T. (2002). E-government and public affairs education. *Chinese Public Administration Review, 1*(3/4).

Lazer, D., & Binz-Scharf, M. C. (2004). *Information sharing in e-government projects.* Boston: National Center for Digital Government, Harvard University.

Lee, G., & Perry, K. L. (2002). Are computers boosting productivity? A test of the paradox in state governments. *Journal of Public Administration Research and Theory, 12*(1), 77-102.

Luna-Reyes, L. F., Zhang, J., Gil-Garcia, J. R., & Cresswell, A. M. (2005). Information systems development as emergent socio-technical change: A practice approach. *European Journal of Information Systems, 14*(1), 93-105.

McDaniel, E. A. (2003). Facilitating cross-boundary leadership in emerging e-government leaders. *InSITE: "Where Parallels Intersect."*

Pardo, T. A., Cresswell, A. M., Thompson, F., & Zhang, J. (2006). Knowledge sharing in cross-boundary information system development in the public sector. *Information Technology and Management, 7*(4), 293-313.

Pinsonneault, A., & Kraemer, K. L. (2002). Information technology and middle management downsizing: A tale of two cities. *Organization Science, 13*(2), 191-208.

Rocheleau, B. (2000). Prescriptions for public-sector information management: A review, analysis, and critique. *American Review of Public Administration, 30*(4), 414-435.

West, D. M. (2005). *Digital government: Technology and public sector performance.* Princeton, NJ: Princeton University Press.

Zhang, J., Cresswell, A. M., & Thompson, F. (2002). *Participant's expectations and the success of knowledge networking in the public sector.* Paper presented at the AMCIS Conference, TX.

TERMS AND DEFINITIONS

Accountability: According to Robert Behn (2001), individuals exercise accountability in four ways: For finance, when we establish detailed expectations about how public officials will handle public resources; for fairness or equity, when we create values, principles, and ethical standards to ensure that government and its employees treat its citizens fairly; for use (or abuse) of power, when we create rules to limit the discretion of public officials and to prevent those officials from abusing their power and discretion in finances or fairness; and finally, for performance, when we define the expectations for the actual outcomes that public officials will achieve using public resources and their invested power.

Accountability Bias: This is the expected partiality from accountability holders used to concentrating their efforts and resources on building ICT infrastructure for monitoring finance and fairness, thus giving much less attention to performance. Codifying accountability for finance or fairness in explicit rules is normally easier than codifying accountability for performance in government.

Administrative Reform: It is any initiative to improve the management performance of any public organization or institution in government by using managerial techniques, best practices, and recommendations.

Budgetary Cycle: It is a process of the management of funds and resources during a period of time that involves planning, programming, integrating, presenting a project, authorizing appropriations, calendaring funds, and controlling, evaluating, and auditing according to a group of rules, systems, procedures, transactions, standards, manuals, policies, and regulations.

Digital Signature: A digital signature is any procedure of encryption for the purpose of information or transactional safety, which is intended to be equivalent to a hand-written signature.

E-Budgeting: E-budgeting is any ICT application or tool for budgetary functions, procedures, or services across the budgetary cycle (planning, programming, budgeting, appropriations, control, and evaluation of financial resources).

E-Project: An e-project is any initiative that involves the design, implementation, and use of ICT applications for institutional or organizational purposes.

ICT Embedment: The term is used to describe how information technologies do not operate in a vacuum or in isolation of their context. Instead, information technologies affect and are affected by organizational structures and processes, as well as institutional arrangements.

Performance: Performance involves a set of measurements that indicate the level of how an individual, group, organization, or institution is achieving a goal or a set of goals.

Chapter LXVI
A Model for Reengineering IT Job Classes in State Government

Craig P. Orgeron
Mississippi Department of Information Technology Services, USA

INTRODUCTION

For public-sector administrators burdened with the task of recruiting and retaining information technology (IT) professionals, these are difficult times. A shortage of IT personnel combined with intense demand for new technology skills has made recruiting and retaining staff harried pursuits; additionally, the demand for technical workers in corporate America keeps rising (Pawlowski, Datta, & Houston, 2005). This demand for workers with leading-edge IT skills is exacerbated by the looming retirement of seasoned government workers, estimated at a 30% reduction in public-sector workforce across state governments by 2006 (Council of State Government [CSG], 2002). Despite the mounting demands on IT to be leveraged in state governments as a cost-reducing and efficiency-increasing tool (Levinson, 2003), even with economic recovery (Information Technology Association of America [ITAA], 2004) many scholars and industry analysts fear a widening shortage in available IT professionals (Pawlowski et al.). Pawlowski et al. suggest that for state governments, more so than private-sector firms, the problem has become acute, heightened by not only recruitment and retention barriers (CSG, 2000), but also by an ideological backlash against contracting for IT services with offshore firms (Hira, 2004). In recent research, barriers to recruitment (low base salaries, lack of qualified candidates, a poor image of civil service, and limited advancement opportunities) and retention (inability to compete with the private sector, low base salaries, insufficient reward systems, and lack of advancement opportunities) were documented through a survey of 400 IT professionals working in state agencies and universities (Pawlowski et al.). The ubiquitous nature of information technology at all levels of government and the core requirement to recruit and retain qualified technology professionals calls for an expansion in the body of research; this research can provide invaluable insight into the success and failure in public-sector information technology human resource practices. The intent of this research is the utilization of the DeMers' (2002) seven-pronged approach to critically examine Mississippi state government agencies with the expected result of assessing the effectiveness and efficiency of the IT personnel classification system. This leading-edge and highly effective IT personnel classification system, designed specifically to improve IT recruitment and retention, was implemented by the State of Mississippi in partnership with the Hay Group, an internationally known human resource consultancy.

BACKGROUND

Information technology has become crucial in the innovation of government service delivery in the day-to-day operations of many public-sector agencies at the federal, state, and local level (Heiman, 2002; Modesitt, 2002). Indeed, public-sector agencies at all levels depend on information technology in order to accomplish their varied missions (Babcock, Bush, & Lan, 1995; Fletcher, 2000). Specifically, state governments have invested heavily in information technology. To that end, at least 420,000 IT personnel, representing more than 20% of executive-branch state workers, are employed throughout the 50 states (Brown & Brudney, 1998). Varying authors have noted the tension between private- and public-sector organizations in recruiting and retaining experienced IT professionals (Agarwal & Ferratt, 1999). Careful and systematic analysis of research conducted finds that many scholars have discussed and agreed that examination of existing public and private IT recruitment and retention strategies can aid in the formulation of a more effective, forward-thinking human resource policy (DeMers, 2002; Lan, Riley, & Cayer, 2005; Pawlowski et al., 2005). Indeed, DeMers sets forth a seven-pronged approach toward IT recruitment and retention, created from an assimilation of "realistic government strategies" (DeMers, p. 28). The objective of DeMers' best-practice approach allows public-sector agencies the ability to build human resource policies to compete with the private sector for the recruitment and retaining of the best and brightest IT professionals.

According to a United States Department of Commerce report (1998) entitled *America's New Deficit: The Shortage of Information Technology Workers*, 1,134,000 new IT positions will be created between 1996 and 2006, and an additional 240,000 already existing positions will have to be filled due to retirements. According to the *America's New Deficit* study, the reasons for the shortage are varied, including a general lack of interest in the field and a belief that there is an excess of IT workers already. According to a related United States Department of Commerce report entitled *The Digital Work Force: Building Information Technology Skills at the Speed of Innovation* (1999), information technologies represent more than 25% of the growth in the current U.S. economy, and the entire information industry employs almost 7.4 million people with an average salary of $64,000. The *Digital Work Force* study also reports that job growth in the IT field will increase at a rate of 137,800 jobs per year; an industry that grows so fast needs workers, but fewer people are entering the IT field. Inherent differences between managing public and private IT organizations have long been recognized (Cats-Baril & Thompson, 1995). Businesses, individual citizens, and nongovernmental organizations empowered by the Internet are creating new challenges that public agencies will not be able to meet unless they become much more technologically savvy (Naim, 2000). State governments are faced not only with a shortage of information technology workers, but also with the prospect of losing out to corporations in the competition to hire these workers. Government agencies simply do not have the budget, flexibility, or compensation infrastructure to offer company cars and huge bonuses, and stock options are nonexistent (Goodridge, 2000; Pawlowski et al., 2005).

In recent years, a wealth of research has emerged that has identified the primary causes of why information technology employees leave their employers. These factors fall into five broad categories: (a) poor quality of work life, (b) compensation below market level, (c) lack of training and development opportunities, (d) bad management, and (e) an inability to advance one's career without going into management (Longenecker & Scazzero, 2003). Additionally, researchers have found that the "civil service system emphasizing rules and regulations, control systems, political context, and limited autonomy and flexibility can serve as a barrier to creating outcome-oriented human resource management in the public sector" (Kim, 2005, p. 138). To that end, as described by Kim, many public-sector agencies are leveraging their first-rate perks, including "job stability and security, flexibility, and their social- and civic-service orientation" (p. 138) to retain experienced IT professionals. Yet, according to Kim, even with these retention-based efforts many public-sector organizations are not maintaining adequate levels of senior-level IT professionals, and have thus, in many cases, turned to alternative strategies for diminishing IT employee turnover. Hence, for state governments to stem the tide of IT employee turnover, many states have placed significant effort in understanding specific job characteristics affecting retention (Bruce & Blackburn, 1992; Pawlowski et al., 2005; Rainey, 1997).

The recruitment of IT staff by states is often made difficult for a variety of reasons (CSG, 2000). Success in the hiring of IT personnel must be based upon a clear understanding of the marketplace and the needs and desires of the IT candidates (Murray, 1999). Restrictive merit systems, noncompetitive salaries, and a negative perception of public service impede recruiting efforts. Centralized civil service systems have been criticized for obstructing and impeding the ability of agencies or departments with special skill requirements from responding quickly to labor market opportunities (Dawes, 1994). Civil service systems often become more focused on procedural correctness than on the end results. To be successful, public agencies must have selection systems in place that are designed to enable swift selection from among the best-qualified candidates and allow agencies to shape their workforces to meet their changing missions (Pynes & Bartels, 1996). Dawes puts forth specific recommendations, which include developing new approaches to testing, exploring alternatives to written tests for some occupations, and recognizing professional or technical credentials and educational degrees as qualifiers for selected positions.

Information Technology Personnel in Mississippi

The research surveyed indicates that government agencies have struggled with the recruitment and retention of IT professionals and have thus been unable to benefit from the efficiencies of a highly effective IT staff. As documented by DeMers (2002), utilizing pragmatic public-sector strategies affords state governments the capacity to compete with the private sector. Clearly, the body of knowledge regarding the application of creative hiring and retention practices for IT personnel in the public sector argues that flexible hiring practices, advanced hiring techniques, increased employee recognition, and the availability of professional development training provide a means of attracting and retaining top-notch IT professionals (CSG, 2000; Pawlowski et al., 2005). Table 1 shows the seven-step approach developed by DeMers from experience with a myriad of public- and private-sector strategies for IT personnel recruitment and retention.

Table 1. Seven-step approach for IT recruitment and retention (DeMers, 2002)

Approach 1	Allow flexibility of hiring practices.
Approach 2	Employ technologically advanced hiring techniques such as Web-based applications and database skill tracking.
Approach 3	Enable an organization-wide commitment to hiring qualified IT staff.
Approach 4	Advocate an increase in employee recognition through the use of bonuses and innovative awards.
Approach 5	Fund professional development training.
Approach 6	Examine the significance of environment and innovation.
Approach 7	Stress the importance of publicity for both an area and its government.

In 1997, the Mississippi Department of Information Technology Services (ITS) contracted the Hay Group, an internationally known human resource consultancy, to conduct a detailed review of the classification structure, role definition, compensation levels, and IT organizational structure for the Mississippi state government. ITS, along with many other state government agencies, recognized that the current job classifications were out of date and did not reflect the true nature of the work being done, and that the existing compensation structure and processes did not enable the state to attract, retain, and reward the quality and caliber of IT employees needed to meet the business needs of the Mississippi state government. For the State of Mississippi, the creation of a leading-edge job classification structure, compensation plan, and organizational framework that would allow the state to attract, retain, and reward high-performing IT professionals was the primary strategic objectives. These IT professionals are necessary to sustain the information technology business requirements of the state and to provide first-class, customer-oriented service. It is critical to appreciate that the DeMers' model focuses sharply on an assimilation of "realistic government strategies" (DeMers, 2002, p. 28). Thus, no single, magic bullet will repair a recruitment and retention system that is culturally entrenched in a government agency, or the government as a whole. Rather, the impetus of the DeMers' best-practice approach allows government agencies the ability to combine multiple, realistic human resource policies to compete with the private sector and leverage its existing strengths for the recruitment and retaining of the best and brightest IT professionals.

As noted by DeMers (2002), flexibility is a term used to describe an organization's ability to provide flexible recruiting, as well as to retain qualified, existing employees. Specifically, however, DeMers notes that flexibility is focused on the availability of variable pay in response to real-time market conditions. Resulting from the IT review undertaken, the Mississippi State Personnel Board established a Special Compensation Plan for the purpose of attracting, retaining, and developing competent information technology professionals. This Special Compensation Plan, designed by ITS and the State Personnel Board, has become the focal point in producing change in the recruitment and retention of the best and brightest IT professionals for Mississippi state government. The Special Compensation Plan provides methods for employment, promotion, and reassignment that are responsive to organizational needs and offers flexibility in the negotiation and adjustment of salaries. In this regard, the State of Mississippi has implemented a model to reward individual achievement. Salary increases for in-class movement under the Special Compensation Plan are awarded for achievement of educational objectives, the development of additional technical skill sets, or documented evidence of increasing complexity of work goals (Mississippi State Personnel Board [MSPB], 2006).

DeMers' (2002) description of new technology includes the design, development, and implementation of Web-based employment applications: "utilization of web-based job boards, and database skill tracking" (p. 30). The automation of the recruitment process allows human resource departments in state government to gain access to a wider array of applicants, track their skills, and hire them faster. The Special Compensation Plan provides methods for recruitment and appointment. The Plan states that the hiring of new employees into information technology positions are exempted from the formal Certificate of Eligibles process established by the State Personnel Board, provided that the applicant meets the minimum qualifications of the classification of the position (MSPB, 2006). As described in DeMers' second approach, the State of Mississippi employs Web-based hiring techniques. The State of Mississippi, via the State Personnel Board, implemented an e-application that enables the collection of a full-range of relevant information on a prospective applicant, such as educational attainment, professional experience, and familiarity with leading-edge information technologies. Similarly, Web-based job board advertisements have provided increased visibility for information technology jobs open in Mississippi state government. As noted by DeMers, the implementation of Web-based employment applications, utilization of Web-based job boards, and database skill tracking can make the process "easy and productive for both the recruiter and the recruit" (p. 32).

The fourth and fifth steps in the DeMers (2002) approach are employee recognition and skill acquisition and education, respectively. According to DeMers, employee recognition and skill training is a crucial factor for decreasing the turnover rate among existing IT employees. However, DeMers notes that potential recruits often show apprehension that their expertise with leading-edge technology will fade if they accept state government employment. As noted by DeMers, a report published by the ITAA suggested that "training after the employee is hired is rated significantly more effective than pre-hire methods of training" (p. 34). Indeed, "84% of managers rated on the job training as effective or very effective compared to 41% rating pre-hire training as high" (p. 34). DeMers cites a program in the State of Kansas whereby established bonuses reward not only specific skills but also the completion of successful projects; furthermore, the program "encourages motivated IT professionals to acquire new mission critical skills" (p. 33). In the State of Mississippi, under the direction of the State Personnel Board, an Information Technology Professional Development Committee (ITPDC) has been instituted. The ITPDC provides recommendations to the State Personnel Board on specific personnel actions within the field of information technology. The ITPDC, composed of 10 members, has specific responsibility to review and recommend the level of information technology positions required within a state agency, as well as to review and recommend the appropriateness of educational requirements associated with information technology job classifications. The ITPDC has enjoyed much success with its interagency approach to addressing employee recognition and skill acquisition and education, respectively, in the Mississippi state government. Specifically, the ITPDC has been deemed successful in the reward of employees who have attained additional education and skill sets that directly add value to their ability to perform the duties and tasks of their positions (MSPB, 2006).

According to DeMers (2002), the work environment component of employment by IT professionals has largely been ignored by public administration researchers. In fact, relatively little research simultaneously examines both indicators of the work environment such as job satisfaction or perceived job characteristics and market conditions such as perceived job alternatives or pay competitiveness on IT worker turnover (Thatcher, Stepina, & Boyle, 2003). Of course, many public-sector employees desire a dynamic work environment, though that is often a shifting concept to clearly describe. For the purpose of this research, work environment is defined as "a catchall for innovative programs that make employment more enjoyable" (DeMers, p. 35). As DeMers describes, telecommuting remains one of the most sought after work environment perks sought by public-sector information technology personnel. Though DeMers cited numerous examples from the private sector, the research did not reveal vast adoption of telecommuting or other work environment perks offered by state governments; this is true for the Mississippi state government as well: Very few work environment perks are offered to information technology personnel.

Lastly, DeMers (2002) notes that it is necessary for public agencies to make information available to recruits both actively and passively, beyond simply posting job information on Web pages and third-party job boards. Interestingly, DeMers advocates that public agencies recruit individuals not actively seeking employment in the government arena. DeMers cites an example from the City of San Jose; the city used banners pulled from planes at local sporting events as a means of advertising the benefits of city employment. In addition, the city also "purchased advertising space at local movie theaters in an attempt to create interest among passive citizens" (DeMers, p. 37). The State of Mississippi has not attempted these kinds of techniques, nor was any evidence uncovered to suggest that the state would use them in the future. DeMers notes that "government's lower pay, slower response time, inflexibility, lack of performance rewards, and sometimes stifling environment hurt its ability to recruit qualified employees of any kind" (p. 38). However, when marketing, DeMers states that the public sector should accentuate its work environment assets: stability, comparatively low time demands, good retirement benefits, and low-stress environment.

FUTURE TRENDS

Numerous recent studies have recounted approaches for public-sector agencies to consider in the methods used to recruit, retain, appraise, and compensate government workers, including IT professionals (Lan et al., 2005; Lipiec, 2001; Pawlowski et al., 2005; Perry, Wise, & Martin, 1994; Roberts, 2002). Still, in addition to exposure to Internet-based technology currently leveraged in the development of electronic government applications, results of a recent survey "show that work exhaustion, an emphasis on participatory management, and opportunities for advancement were statistically significant variables affecting state government IT employee turnover intentions, and that salary satisfaction was not a statistically significant factor" (Kim, 2005, p. 137). Given that, while efforts to boost public-sector salaries for IT professionals are warranted, "as states continue to improve their compensation programs, it is equally important to look beyond financial incentives as the primary long-term strategy for recruitment and retention" (Pawlowski et al., p. 90). The focal point of designing a thriving IT workforce in the public sector is enabled by harnessing employee motivation received from managers and the subsequent feeling that the employee is "an important part of the organization" (Pawlowski et al., p. 90). Thus, a work environment that fosters both creativity and autonomy, while harnessing a sense of accomplishment is a target for attracting top IT talent (Pawlowski et al.; Smits, McLean, & Tanner, 1993). The capacity of a state government to "become an employer of choice will be dependent upon dual strategies of improved compensation practices and excellence in other human resource management practices" (Pawlowski et al., p. 91).

CONCLUSION

The uniquely crafted information technology personnel classification system in Mississippi state government was implemented to aid in the recruitment and retention of information technology professionals. For this research, the IT personnel classification system was appraised via the DeMers' seven-step approach toward IT recruitment and retention, created and defined from an assimilation of "realistic government strategies" (DeMers, 2002, p. 28). The State of Mississippi is one of several states that have recognized and responded to the IT labor crisis in a variety of ways. The work completed by the Mississippi Department of ITS and the Hay Group, as assessed by the DeMers' seven-step approach toward IT recruitment and retention, embodies a progressive relationship between public and private sectors to bring contemporary human resource concepts and practices to the recruitment and retention of information technology personnel. The approaches of organization-wide commitment to recruiting, environment, innovation, and publicity, as outlined by DeMers, uncovered little, if any, innovation on the part of the Mississippi state government. In addition to the lack of innovation within several categories in the DeMers seven-step approach, the overhauled information technology personnel classification system, as does traditional job descriptions, depicts an "artificially static view of work and organization" (Klingner & Nalbandian, 1998, p. 106). Given the effort in the State of Mississippi, limited innovation has been initiated since the originating endeavor, thus allowing the work originally accomplished to become out of date, as is the case in many public-sector reengineering projects. Additionally, as is the case with traditional job descriptions, the updated classification system "promotes a hierarchical and control-oriented relationship between the organization and its employees which works against employee involvement and 'ownership' of the organization or its mission" (Klingner & Nalbandian, p. 106). This fact, while arguably unavoidable in the public sector, has dampened the enthusiasm for the overhauled information technology personnel classification system, considered, at least initially, to be a dramatic transformation in the management of IT job classes. Thus, the effort to review the classification structure, role definition, compensation levels, and IT organizational structure for the Mississippi state government ultimately resulted in a more effective "position management, rather than management of work or employees" (Klingner & Nalbandian, p. 106). Yet, given these constraints, largely common across public-sector job classification systems, the effort to review the classification structure, role definition, compensation levels, and IT organizational structure for Mississippi, and the subsequent implementation of proposed recommendations has been largely successful. Specifically, the newly overhauled program for the recruitment and retention of information technology personnel in the State of Mississippi faired well in the approach toward flexibility, new technology, employee recognition, and skill acquisition and education. There are, of course, no easy answers or simple solutions. Each approach examined by DeMers requires some resource allocation; taken in aggregate, the seven steps form a strategy for dealing with the difficult issue of information technology recruitment and retention. This research shows that much progress has been made in enabling the state to attract, retain, and reward the quality and caliber of IT employees needed to meet and accomplish the business of Mississippi.

FUTURE RESEARCH DIRECTIONS

As agency missions in the public sector become more dependent on job functions such as IT, government executives, as well as human resource managers, will be challenged to recruit and retain qualified and motivated civil servants. To that end, many personnel systems will require a functional overhaul. The single greatest impetus to collectively reform public personnel systems is rooted in concepts and best practices captured in the National Performance Review (Executive Office of the President, 1993). There is evidence that points to state governments leveraging the reform recommendations contained in the National Performance Review, which include decentralized hiring practices, a reduction of procedural restrictions in the management of human resources, a renewed emphasis on merit-based performance, and increased management flexibility (Hays, 2004). Specifically, with regard to a future-oriented research agenda, considering the reinvention concepts as a foundation, scholars will need to devote attention to recruitment, infamously restrictive for public-sector managers vying for exceptional talent in the job market. Related to recruitment, the retention of high-quality employees is crucial; research topics inclusive of pay schedules, performance reviews, and work environments should be entertained with respect to employee retention. Regarding of the position classification of public employees, scholars should focus on job descriptions that "promote cross-training, reassignments, and the ability of managers to use workers where they can be most effective" (Hays, p. 260). Scholars may also find emerging research opportunities in the arena of employee training and development, "perhaps the most neglected function in public agencies" (Hays, p. 261). Lastly, another research area that has not received adequate attention is succession planning for skilled, tenured public-sector managers. Hays notes that the "current generation of public managers is nearing retirement, and many are leaving as soon as they are eligible due to buy-outs, fiscal pressures, and generous pension plans that may soon fade into history" (p. 264). Public management scholars would be encouraged to focus on the development of innovative leadership development programs; these programs "need to address special leadership concerns of public agency managers, including creative thinking, collaboration, cross-organizational team building, and leading for results" (Ingraham & Getha-Taylor, 2004).

REFERENCES

Agarwal, R., & Ferratt, T. W. (1999). *Coping with labor scarcity in information technology: Strategies and practices for recruitment and retention* (Practice-driven research in IT management series). Cincinnati, OH: Pinnaflex Educational Resources.

Babcock, T., Bush, M., & Lan, Z. (1995). Executive use of information technology in the public sector: An empirical examination. *Journal of Government Information, 22*, 119-130.

Brown, M., & Brudney, J. (1998). Public sector information technology initiatives. *Administration & Society, 30*, 421-443.

Bruce, W. M., & Blackburn, J. W. (1992). *Balancing job satisfaction and performance.* Westport, CT: Quorum Books.

Cats-Baril, W., & Thompson, R. (1995). Managing information technology projects in the public sector. *Public Administration Review, 55*, 559-566.

Council of State Governments (CSG). (2000). *Technical difficulties: Hiring and keeping IT employees in state government.* Retrieved August 30, 2006, from http://www.csg.org

Council of State Governments (CSG). (2002). *State employee worker shortage: The impend-*

ing crisis. Retrieved September 2, 2006, from http://www.csg.org

Dawes, S. (1994). Human resource implications of information technology in state government. *Public Personnel Management, 23*, 31-47.

DeMers, A. (2002). Solutions and strategies for IT recruitment and retention: A manager's guide. *Public Personnel Management, 31*, 27-40.

Executive Office of the President. (1993). *From red tape to results: Creating a government that works better and costs less.* Washington, DC: U.S. Government Printing Office.

Fletcher, P. (2000). Governmental information systems and emerging computer technologies. In G. D. Garson (Ed.), *Handbook of public information systems* (pp. 577-596). New York: Marcel Decker.

Goodridge, E. (2000). Uncle Sam wants you for IT. *Information Week, 7*, 160-164.

Hays, S. (2004). Trends and best practices in state and local human resource management. *Review of Public Personnel Administration, 24*, 256-275.

Heiman, D. (2002). *Public-sector information security: A call to action for public-sector CIOs.* Washington, DC: PricewaterhouseCoopers.

Hira, R. (2004). White collar jobs move overseas: Implications for states. *Spectrum: The Journal of State Government, 77*, 12-18.

Information Technology Association of America (ITAA). (2004). *Adding value growing careers: The employment outlook in today's increasingly competitive IT job market.* Retrieved September 2, 2006, from http://www.itaa.org/

Information Technology Association of America (ITAA) & Virginia Polytechnic Institute. (1998). *Help wanted: A call for collaborative action for the new millennium.* Retrieved August 30, 2006, from http://www.itaa.org/

Ingraham, P., & Getha-Taylor, H. (2004). Leadership in the public service: Models and assumptions for leadership development in the federal government. *Review of Public Personnel Administration, 24*, 95-112.

Kim, S. (2005). Factors affecting state government information technology employee turnover intentions. *American Review of Public Administration, 35*, 137-156.

Klingner, D. E., & Nalbandian, J. (1998). *Public personnel management: Contexts and strategies* (4th ed.). Upper Saddle River, NJ: Prentice Hall.

Lan, G., Riley, L., & Cayer, N. (2005). How can local government become an employer of choice for technical professionals? *Review of Public Personnel Administration, 25*, 225-242.

Lipiec, J. (2001). Human resources management perspective at the turn of the century. *Public Personnel Management, 30*, 137-146.

Longenecker, C., & Scazzero, J. (2003). The turnover and retention of IT managers in rapidly changing organizations. *Information Systems Management, 20*, 59-66.

Mississippi State Personnel Board (MSPB). (2006). *Administrative polices and procedures for the special compensation plan for information technology classification.* Retrieved August 30, 2006, from http://www.spb.state.ms.us/SPB Documents/SPB/SPB pubs.asp

Modesitt, C. (2002). *Bridging the gap between citizens and local government with information technology: Concepts and case studies.* Washington, DC: National Civic League.

Murray, J. (1999). Successfully hiring and retaining IT personnel. *Information Systems Management, 16*, 18-25.

Naim, M. (2000). The digital drain. *Foreign Policy, 120*, 120-122.

Pawlowski, S., Datta, P., & Houston, A. (2005). The (gradually) changing face of state IT jobs. *Communications of the ACM, 48*, 87-91.

Perry, J., Wise, L. R., & Martin, M. (1994). Breaking the civil service mold: The case of

Indianapolis. *Review of Public Personnel Administration, 14*, 40-54.

Pynes, J., & Bartels, L. (1996). The times they are a changing. *Public Productivity and Management Review, 20*, 121-136.

Rainey, H. G. (1997). *Understanding and managing public organizations.* San Francisco: Jossey-Bass.

Roberts, G. (2002). Employee performance appraisal system participation: A technique that works. *Public Personnel Management, 31*, 317-332.

Smits, S., McLean, E., & Tanner, J. (1993). Managing high-achieving information system professionals. *Journal of Management Information Systems, 9*, 103-120.

Thatcher, J., Stepina, L., & Boyle, R. (2003). Turnover of information technology workers: Examining empirically the influence of attitudes, job characteristics, and external markets. *Journal of Management Information Systems, 19*, 231-261.

United States Department of Commerce, Office of Technology Policy. (1998). *America's new deficit: The shortage of information technology workers.* Retrieved August 30, 2006, from http://www.ta.doc.gov/Reports/itsw/itsw.pdf

United States Department of Commerce, Office of Technology Policy. (1999). *The digital work force: Building information technology skills at the speed of innovation.* Retrieved August 30, 2006, from http://www.ta.doc.gov/Reports/itsw/digital.pdf

FURTHER READING

Ashbaugh, S., & Miranda, R. (2002). Technology for human resources management: Seven questions and answers. *Public Personnel Management, 31*, 7-21.

Ban, C., Drahnak-Faller, A., & Towers, M. (2003). Human resource challenges in human service and community development organizations. *Review of Public Personnel Administration, 23*, 133-153.

Bennan, E., Bowman, J., West, J., & Van Wart, M. (2001). *Human resource management in public service: Paradoxes, processes, and problems.* Thousand Oaks, CA: Sage Publications, Inc.

Coursey, D. (2005). Human resource management challenges in government information technology. *Review of Public Personnel Administration, 25*, 203-206.

Coursey, D., & McCreary, S. (2005). Using technology in the workplace. In S. Condrey (Ed.), *Handbook of human resource management in government* (2nd ed., pp. 189-214). San Francisco: Jossey-Bass.

Fountain, J. (2001). *Building the virtual state: Information technology and institutional change.* Washington, DC: Brookings Institution.

Garson, G. (2003). *Public information technology: Policy and management issues.* Hershey, PA: Idea Group Publishing.

Hays, S., & Kearney, R. (2001). Anticipated changes in human resource management: Views from the field. *Public Administration Review, 61*, 585-597.

Heeks, R. (Ed.). (1999). *Reinventing government in the information age: International practice in IT-enabled public sector reform.* New York: Routledge.

Helton, K., & Soubik, J. (2004). Pennsylvania's changing workforce: Planning today with tomorrow's vision. *Public Personnel Management, 33*, 459-473.

Ito, J. (2003). Career mobility and branding in the civil service: An empirical study. *Public Personnel Management, 32*, 1-22.

Johnson, G., & Brown, J. (2004). Workforce planning not a common practice, IPMA-HR study finds. *Public Personnel Management, 33*, 379-388.

Kellough, J., & Selden, S. (2003). The reinvention of public personnel administration: An analysis of the diffusion of personnel management reform in the states. *Public Administration Review, 63*, 165-176.

Lewis, G., & Zhenhua, H. (2005). Information technology workers in the federal service: More than a quiet crisis? *Review of Public Personnel Administration, 25*, 207-224.

Light, P. (1999). *The new public service.* Washington, DC: Brookings Institution.

McEntee, G. (2006). The new crisis of public service employment. *Public Personnel Management, 35*, 343-346.

Ott, J., & Dicke, L. (2001). Challenges facing public sector management in an era of downsizing, devolution, dispersion and empowerment: And accountability? *Public Organization Review, 1*, 321-339.

Peled, A. (2001). Outsourcing and political power: Bureaucrats, consultants, vendors and public information technology. *Public Personnel Management, 30*, 495-515.

Ressler, S. (2006). Recruiting and retaining young IT leaders. *Public Manager, 35*, 49-52.

Riccucci, N. (2005). *Public personnel management: Current concerns, future challenges* (4th ed.). New York: Longman.

Schuh, A. (2006). Institutional values: The foundation for civil service change. *Public Personnel Management, 35*, 49-69.

Thompson, F., & Miller, H. (2003). New public management and bureaucracy versus business values and bureaucracy. *Review of Public Personnel Administration, 23*, 328-343.

Turban, E., Leidner, D., McLean, E., & Wetherbe, J. (2005). *Information technology for management: Transforming organizations in the digital economy.*

West, J., & Berman, E. (2001). From traditional to virtual HR. *Review of Public Personnel Administration, 21*, 38-65.

Wright, B., & Davis, B. (2003). Job satisfaction in the public sector: The role of the work environment. *American Review of Public Administration, 33*, 70-90.

TERMS AND DEFINITIONS

Civil Service System: This is a model for managing a bureaucracy in which individuals are selected for employment in the government on the basis of either competitive examinations or special qualifications, such as professional training.

Electronic Government: This is the transformation of internal and external business processes toward customer-centricity based upon service delivery opportunities offered by new communication technologies (such as Web-based technologies) to better fulfill the purposes of government to provide efficiency and effectiveness as well as fairness and equitability.

Flex Time: Flex time is a variable work timetable, in contrast to a traditional work arrangement, which allows employees to set their own schedules.

Human Resource Management: This describes the functions within an organization that include the employment of suitable staff and the administration of the employment relationships, as well as both the strategic and operational view of personnel requirements.

Perk: A perk is an incidental benefit awarded for certain types of employment.

Special Compensation Plan for Information Technology: It was used in the State of Mississippi to provide methods for employment, promotion, and reassignment that are responsive to organizational needs and offers flexibility in the negotiation and adjustment of salaries (MSPB, 2006).

Telecommute: The human resource practice of working off site, often at home, and communicating with the primary office in a different location via a personal computer equipped with communications software.

Section VI
Selected Readings

Concluding the *Handbook of Research on Public Information Technology* is a "selected reading" collection of 10 refereed journal articles for additional insight into the realm of information technology in the public sector. These articles come highly recommended and introduce innovative applications, trends and technologies within this fast growing area of information science and technology.

Chapter LXVII
Developing a Generic Framework for E-Government

Gerald Grant
Carleton University, Canada

Derek Chau
Carleton University, Canada

ABSTRACT

Electronic government (e-government) initiatives are pervasive and form a significant part of government investment portfolio in almost all countries around the world. However, understanding of what is meant by e-government is still nascent and becomes complicated because the construct means different things to different people. Consequently, the conceptualization and implementation of e-government programs are diverse and are often difficult to assess and compare across different contexts of application. This paper addresses the following key question: Given the wide variety of visions, strategic agendas, and contexts of application, how may we assess, categorize, classify, compare, and discuss the e-government efforts of various government administrations? In answering this question, we propose a generic e-government framework that will allow for the identification of e-government strategic agendas and key application initiatives that transcend country-specific requirements. In developing the framework, a number of requirements are first outlined. The framework is proposed and described; it is then illustrated using brief case studies from three countries. Finally, findings and limitations are discussed.

INTRODUCTION

E-government (electronic government) is increasingly a global phenomenon that is consuming the attention of politicians, policy makers, and even ordinary citizens. Governments around the world have made and continue to make massive financial and political commitments to establishing e-government (Accenture, 2004). A report by the United Nations (UN World Public Sector Report, 2003) indicates that by 2003, over 173 countries had developed government Web sites. Additionally, many countries (including Canada, Germany, Malaysia, Norway, the UK, and the U.S.) have embarked on ambitious multi-year programs to create more citizen-centered, effective, and efficient governments (Accenture, 2004).

E-government is predicated on leveraging the capabilities and power of IT to deliver services provided by governments at local, municipal, state, and national levels. While early conceptions of e-government have largely focused on electronic service delivery as the key feature of the phenomenon, a closer examination suggests a more complex set of circumstances. Beyond service delivery, e-government offers additional channels of interaction among governments, businesses, and citizens, separately or collectively. For example, individual citizens may interact with government electronically by filing their income tax documents online. Governments in delivering services may do so directly or indirectly through intermediaries such as banks, postal outlets in private businesses, and by other means. Consequently, any e-government effort must meet the needs of a diverse set of stakeholders that operate in the political, business, or civic spheres of influence. E-government, however, is more than a technological phenomenon. Whether through deliberate choice or passive acceptance, it is transformative in nature, affecting the management of human, technological, and organizational resources and processes. Consequently, the implementation of e-government is a monumental change effort.

The drive to implement e-government has resulted in the adoption of many e-government visions and strategic agendas (Accenture, 2004). However, each vision is driven by its own unique set of social, political, and economic factors and requirements. Consequently, the mission and objectives that emanate from these e-government visions variously manifest strong focus on one or two elements. For example, the United States has placed a major focus on service delivery and on increasing cross-functional efficiencies (OMB, 2003). The South African government's e-government program is heavily weighted towards service delivery, while e-government efforts in the United Kingdom have tended to balance several strategic objectives.

A key factor driving the achievement of any e-government program is the vision of e-government, articulated and adopted by a government administration. Coupled with actual developments undertaken by the administration, the articulated vision (expressed in documents, objectives, frameworks) greatly helps to describe the e-government space. However, these efforts are not necessarily well articulated nor well coordinated. In large part, this is due to how electronic government is conceptualized. With each administration articulating its own view, it becomes difficult to identify, assess, and understand what is being accomplished under the e-government aegis. While some e-government strategic agendas focus primarily on service delivery issues, others may focus more on creating internally efficient systems and processes. Still others may adopt a more comprehensive view, incorporating issues such as constituent relationship management and e-democracy. Understanding what is meant by e-government becomes complicated because the construct means different things to different people. Although each of these views of e-government may be legitimate, there is a need for some common understanding to allow for assessment, comparison, and explanation of current efforts vis-à-vis past and future investment in the e-government enterprise.

This article addresses the following key question: Given the wide variety of visions, strategic agendas, and contexts of application, how may we categorize, classify, assess, compare, and discuss the e-government efforts of various government administrations? In answering this question, we see the need for a mechanism that will facilitate the articulation and discussion of current issues and concepts related to e-government. We believe this instrument would ideally transcend country-specific requirements and identify experiences and elements that could be transferred across contexts of application. For example, we should be able to describe and discuss the e-government efforts in a country such as Malaysia and make some broad comparisons with similar efforts in the United Kingdom. Therefore, we propose the development of a generic framework that can be used to categorize, classify, and compare electronic government visions, strategic agendas, and application initiatives. Such a framework, rather than seeking to rigidly constrain or categorize e-government activities, should act as a lens to focus attention and awareness on underlying issues and elements that could be debated, discussed, and further developed. Clearly, our main objective is to find a way to make sense of the plethora of perspectives and developmental agendas populating the e-government space. Our proposed framework should be viewed as a first step in this process. It represents another way to consider e-government efforts and provide a starting point for integrating current experiences and knowledge.

This article is organized as follows. Following this introduction, section one (Literature Review) focuses on developing a working operational definition for e-government that will underpin the development of a generic e-government framework. Key requirements for the development of such a framework are identified and discussed. A framework is proposed. Section two (Methodology) provides insight into the development of the framework. We illustrate, in section three, the application of the framework. Here, we use it to categorize, classify, and discuss the e-government visions and implementation efforts of three nations: the United States, the United Kingdom, and Malaysia. Section four presents the findings from the case studies. In section five we discuss the practical and theoretical implications of applying the framework. Possible future roles and directions will also be considered.

LITERATURE REVIEW

Defining E-Government

Definitions of e-government abound in the literature. Some definitions narrowly focus on using ICTs, particularly the Internet, to deliver more efficient and effective government services, while others view e-government as a broad-based effort to transform government and governance. In the examples below, e-government is characterized as:

- the use of technology to enhance the access to and delivery of government services to benefit citizens, business partners, and employees (Deloitte Research, 2000, p. 4);
- electronic information-based services for citizens (e-administration) with reinforcement of participatory elements (e-democracy) to achieve objectives of balanced e-government (Bertelsmann Foundation, 2001, p. 4);
- the use of information and communication technologies, particularly the Internet, as a tool to achieve better government (OECD, 2003, p. 63); and
- the use of information and communication technologies in all facets of the operations of a government organization (Koh & Prybutok, 2003, p. 34).

These definitions, while useful in describing e-government in a broad-based manner, offer little insight into deeper issues and considerations relating to the construct. On the one hand, those definitions that focus exclusively on the service delivery component of e-government efforts, fail to capture the more complex aspects of transforming government or acknowledge the role of the information and information technology elements. Such a one-sided focus tends to skew the e-government development and deployment agenda. Consequently, most implementation activities center around service delivery concerns with little emphasis on real transformation of the services themselves or the processes associated with their delivery (Poostchi, 2002). On the other hand, definitions that are too broad make it difficult to determine what really constitutes e-government and, as a consequence, may confuse the treatment of the issue.

For e-government to be properly understood and applied, we believe that it needs to be more comprehensively conceptualized (Caldow, 2001). However, the nascence of the e-government phenomenon, coupled with the complexities associated with the public sector context, contribute to the multiple interpretations and confusion surrounding the concept. Our review of academic, practitioner, and a variety of government publications suggests that any conceptualization of e-government needs to address a variety of concerns beyond the service delivery elements (Chadwick & May, 2003; Marche & McNiven, 2003; OECD,

Table 1. E-government operational definition

Characteristic	Description	References
Strong service delivery and information provision component	Electronic Services and Information provision provide the chief mode of interaction	Deloitte Research, 2000; Bertelsmann Foundation, 2001; World Markets Research Centre, 2001; Accenture, 2002, 2004; Koh & Prybutok, 2003; Layne & Lee, 2001 Reddick, 2004; OECD, 2003
	Transaction and feedback effected via services and information provision components	
E-government is a transformation effort	Represent multiple levels of engagement	Osborne and Gaebler, 1992; Rais Abdul Karim, 1999; OECD, 2003; Accenture, 2004;
	Cuts across functional and organizational boundaries	
	Digital age public sector reform	
	Demands new forms of interaction between citizens and government	
Diverse number of solutions and patterns of development	Country specific	UK Cabinet Office, 2000a; Corrocher & Ordanini, 2002; OMB, 2001; OMB, 2003; Accenture, 2002, 2004; OECD, 2003.
	Implementation differs across contexts of application (political, social, economic)	
	Multiple patterns of development prevail	
IS/IT Based development but not limited to IS/IT	IS/IT infrastructure essential in deploying an e-government program	Box, 1999; Guy, 2001; Heeks, 1999; UK Cabinet Office, 2000a; Chadwick & May, 2003.
	Leverages IS/IT capabilities to deliver systems and services	
	Overlapping functionality and knowledge	
	Added complexities from public sector context	
	IS/IT knowledge insufficient to explain and predict future trends	
Convergence of integration, sophistication, and maturity	Extends beyond service automation, and efficiencies to integrated service offering	Deloitte Research, 2000; Bertelsmann Foundation, 2001; Accenture, 2002, 2004; Koh & Prybutok, 2003; Layne & Lee, 2001; Working Group on E-Government, 2002;
	Integrative efforts and requirements increasing with added functionality and citizen centric design	
	Increasing complexity and functionality requires commensurate development of understanding and knowledge of relationships between e-government and other functional areas and organizational concepts including IS/IT contributions	
	Asymptoting towards higher levels of service interaction and maturity	
International Phenomenon	Diversity of e-government realizations	Accenture 2002, 2004; Deloitte Research, 2000; Basu, 2004; Ke & Wei, 2004;
	Crosses geographical boundaries	
	Adaptable to country specific requirements	
	Growing number of implementations and developments worldwide	

2003). E-government is a detailed and complex development that is difficult to conceptualize. What is known and understood is mostly of a descriptive and anecdotal nature. The end result is that e-government implementations have yet to realize the upper stages of maturity and that the understanding and knowledge of the area is still in the process of formation.

Developing an Operational Definition for E-Government

Our review of the e-government literature (frameworks, models, white papers, government documents, etc.) suggests several characteristics that should be taken into consideration when defining e-government. These are identified and listed in Table 1.

Strong Service Delivery and Information Component

Most e-government programs emphasize a strong service delivery and information provision component, particularly in the initial stages (Accenture, 2004; Bertelsmann Foundation, 2001; Deloitte Research, 2000; World Markets Research Centre, 2001). Citizen experiences with customer-centric information and service offerings via the Internet have resulted in an increased demand on government administrations to organize information, services, and government functions around the citizen (Deloitte & Touche, 2000). The breadth and maturity of information and service offerings are also increasing where a significant number of nations with high levels of maturity have been measured (Accenture, 2002, 2004). For example, transaction level services have been observed, categorized, and represented in several measurement frameworks (Accenture, 2002; Koh & Prybutok, 2003) and models (Layne & Lee, 2001). These include services such as tax filing and payment, postal agency bill payments, and license renewal and registration. Portals such as the U.S. www.consumer.gov and the Canadian www.canada.gc.ca, provide access to a broad range of information and services, reflecting a "cradle to grave" philosophy that supports citizens' information and service needs throughout their lives.

E-Government as a Transformational Endeavor

Most operational definitions of e-government betray an underlying transformational or reformation theme that ranges from more effective services delivery to greater participation through relationship building with stakeholders. They embrace many aspects of the transformational agenda promoted under the rubric of the "new public management," which calls for the reinvention of government (Osborne & Gaebler, 1992). The transformation agenda focuses on the need for governments to more effectively manage inputs, processes, and outputs of the public administration organization, and envisions broad classes of institutional reform (Osborne & Gaebler, 1992; Rais Abdul Karim, 1999). These include:

- Increased efficiencies in government operations;
- Decentralization of services and administration;
- Increased accountability;
- Improved resource management; and
- Marketization and leveraging of market forces to enhance public sector and private sector relationships

Research by the OECD (2003b) suggests that e-government can be an important catalyst to public sector reform agendas, whether as a tool of reform, a catalyst for change initiatives, or an instrument for improving processes and governance. The recent report by Accenture (2004) implies that to get more value from e-government investments, governments will need to embrace a more ambitious transformation agenda.

Diverse Number of Solutions and Contexts of Application

Changes and transformational efforts can be undertaken across many dimensions and are often a reflection of the unique political, social, and economic needs and capacities of the hosting nation or government administration. We refer to this as the context of application. Corrocher and Ordanini (2002) suggest that different patterns (asymmetric and symmetric) of development exist, depending on the particular economic and administrative situation of the nations in question.

We anticipate that e-government as a public sector and technology-enabled initiative will be subject to contextual factors similar to those experienced by other public sector initiatives, and also will exhibit multiple patterns of development. We see examples of this in the differing foci and patterns of development in nations such as the U.S., the UK, Malaysia, and South Africa. In some nations, e-government developments have a market and efficiencies emphasis (OMB, 2001, 2003). In others, increasing citizen awareness and access to services are given priority. Still others take a balanced approach to e-government development (UK Cabinet Office, 2000).

Electronic Government, Information, and IT

There is a special relationship among e-government, information, and IT. Information permeates all organizational activities and is used by all members of the organization, from the front line to back room, impacting every organizational function (Lacity & Willcocks, 1998; Ward & Peppard, 2002). This is particularly true for government organizations that are charged with managing (in the public interest) multiple stakeholders across the social, political, and economic domains. Information is a key resource for the operation of government and generates key inputs for producing the outputs of policy and public action (Box, 1999; Guy, 2001). Accurate and timely information about the external environment and stakeholder requirements are at the heart of effective decision-making, policy development, and administration.

A strong relationship also exists between e-government and the use of information technology and systems. E-government, like e-business, would be impossible without the technological platform provided by modern information and communication technologies. Perhaps the most significant capability that is enabled by IT is the creation of a new interaction and communication channel. The connectivity element of IT provides another conduit for information and feedback between government agencies, departments, and stakeholders through the application of standardized Web browsers, workflow, project management, and customer relationship management technologies, among others (Koh & Prybutok, 2003). The use of real time communication and data processing technology also allows for almost instantaneous exchange and feedback that cuts across geography, time, and organizational boundaries. The IT infrastructure effectively enables the rapid propagation of information and data throughout the e-government network to all connected parties, increasing both the quality and quantity of information received.

This unique combination of increased efficiency, information quality and quantity, and organizationwide distribution and connectivity creates an effect that goes beyond the support of government operations. The use of IT creates the potential for change and reinforces the transformation elements of e-government, providing a medium for the realization of electronic ideas, goals, and objectives (Heeks, 1999). However, e-government is not principally driven by technology concerns, but rather must reflect the operational context and obligations of the public sector (Chadwick and May, 2003; UK Cabinet Office, 2000). IT systems are enablers of e-government. The inclusion of these systems and technologies within e-government is not the final objective.

Integration, Service Sophistication, and Maturity

Electronic service delivery is undoubtedly a key component of any electronic government effort. However, governments have begun to recognize the need to move beyond front end efficiencies to a more sophisticated model where saving "money should not be the broad vision that motivates e-government" and where the implementation is more than just automated service delivery and a series of Web presences (Pacific Council on International Policy, 2002). The ultimate goal of many government efforts is to present one view of government, regardless of the point of access, through an integrated and secure service and interaction environment. This represents an evolution of the service contract between citizens and government and is also driven by constituent relationship management (CRM) efforts aimed at serving citizens and other stakeholders better (Accenture, 2002). Consequently, e-government is expected to impact every area of the organization (Bertelsmann Foundation, 2001; Deloitte Research, 2000) and crosses political and functional boundaries. The effort is beyond the scope of any one agency, and ultimately, the degree of integration an administration achieves will strongly determine how much value is brought to itself and its citizens (Bertelsmann Foundation, 2001).

Integration of applications and services across governments are relatively more complex and problematic than similar integration in private businesses. Integration efforts in government require cross agency cooperation, which is not necessarily forthcoming or legally permitted (Marche & McNiven, 2003). In many governments, individual ministers and agencies are charged with executing the responsibilities assigned to them through legislation and are, therefore, not eager or able to expend resources on cross-agency arrangements that were not anticipated or provided for in budgetary allocations and mandates (OECD, 2003). The difficulty encountered in deploying an integrated services platform is partly responsible for the slowdown in e-government advances in many countries (Accenture, 2004). Any definition of e-government, therefore, needs to encompass a whole-of-government view that envisions an integrated network of applications and services that will provide a seamless service delivery and transaction environment to which there is 'no wrong door.'

The maturity and breadth of e-government services are on the rise (Accenture, 2002; 2004). The reach and range of e-government applications and other developments are increasing in terms of both scope and functionality. Implementations have begun to move towards full transaction level experiences between citizens and government where communication can occur in duplex mode (i.e., feedback is given bi-directionally by both government and citizens). Transaction level services, such as tax filing and payment and postal-agency-based bill payments, have been observed, categorized, and represented in measurement frameworks (Accenture, 2002, Koh & Prybutok, 2003) and models (Layne & Lee, 2001). Service sophistication and maturity in the e-government area parallel developments in the IS/IT sphere (Nolan & Gibson, 1974; Somogyi & Galliers, 1987). There has also been a shift from an internal to an external focus. This includes the creation of citizen-centric services in response to citizen demands that stem from Internet-based encounters (Deloitte Research, 2000). This shift is evidenced in the growing focus on CRM efforts, which seek to organize services and government functions around the citizen. Emerging initiatives in service personalization extends this trend (Accenture, 2004).

E-government service maturity will continue to change and evolve in keeping with changing stakeholder requirements. This maturation process suggests that conceptualizations of e-government should not be limited to the services and applications that currently exist. Any definition or framework that seeks to describe or explain e-government phenomena must be sufficiently robust to accommodate the evolution of activities and applications without requiring a total reconstitution of the frameworks or models previously developed.

International Phenomenon

E-government is an international phenomenon that is undertaken by a diverse array of government administrations (Basu, 2004; Chadwick & May, 2003; Ke & Wei, 2004; OECD, 2003). Studies from independent consultants detail the efforts of both developed and developing nations to deploy e-government services and applications (Accenture, 2002, 2004; Deloitte Research, 2000). These initiatives have inherent benefits that apply to all administrations, regardless of economic and social background, although there is great variability in how the implementation is undertaken. Governments around the world are convinced that e-government efforts can provide that engine for deep and valuable economic, social, political, technological, and strategic transformation due to its broad scope (OECD, 2003). Consequently, we are now witnesses to the proliferation of e-government implementation around the world, superseding geographical as well as cultural boundaries. This means, therefore, that as we conceptualize e-government, we need to be cognizant of its international dimension and that it has implications for more substantive economic, social, political, and cultural impacts.

Based on the preceding discussion and our understanding of published material on the subject, we propose a working operational definition of e-government that expands the limited view present in most practitioner definitions. We define electronic government as follows.

A broad-based transformation initiative, enabled by leveraging the capabilities information and communication technology; (1) to develop and deliver high quality, seamless, and integrated public services; (2) to enable effective constituent relationship management; and (3) to support the economic and social development goals of citizens, businesses, and civil society at local, state, national, and international levels.

Developing a Generic Framework for E-Government

The operational definition of electronic government implies a number of complex issues. From our research, we have observed that every government has its own vision of what constitutes the construct and its own approach to implementing that vision. However, we feel that there is a common need to characterize and identify the direction and dimensions of each of these approaches. Certain commonalities and challenges exist in every e-government undertaking. Our goal is to develop a generic e-government framework (GEF) that will help to overcome and to restate these challenges. To do this, we first identify key requirements for developing the framework. We then propose a framework, identifying and discussing its various features and functionality.

Requirements for a Generic E-Government Framework

E-government deployment is influenced by diverse factors. Consequently, in developing a generic framework, we need to establish a set of criteria that should inform and shape what factors constitute the framework, its requirements, and features, and how they are arranged and relate to each other. We believe a generic e-government framework should meet the following requirements.

a. *Provide a "noise free" representation of e-government*

To respond to and represent the desires of a variety of stakeholder groups, an e-government program must embrace and satisfy the desires of citizens, businesses, civil society, and policymakers, while taking into consideration the requirements of existing political structures and operating processes. As a result, a significant amount of "noise" and interference generated by political, social, and technological factors and agendas, are injected into the process of identifying, analyzing, and deciding what projects and processes to adopt in executing the e-government program.

E-government efforts inherit problems similar to those found in the IS/IT field, where technical jargon and definitions are confusing and a large number of terms are used inconsistently for the same concepts (Ward & Peppard, 2002). Technology issues, including technology jargon, can also obscure the true situation (Luftman, 1996; Keen, 1991). As a result, there are often disconnects between the points of view of key participants (i.e., policymakers and technology experts). The resulting interference makes it difficult to determine the true situation surrounding the overall strategy and transformation effort (Osborne & Gaebler, 1992). A nonpartisan view would aid greatly in optimizing planning and implementation activities. Therefore, it is vital to have a high-level framework that has the ability to capture a more objective representation of e-government. Such a framework can then be shared and easily referenced across political, ideological, and technological boundaries, providing a common basis for informed discourse about issues relating to the e-government agenda.

b. *Enable identification and articulation of e-government goals and objectives*

Effective coordination and organization of an e-government program requires clear understanding of goals and objectives. The power of setting clear goals and a shared mission statement is potentially one of the most significant acts that an administration can undertake in the reform process (Osborne & Gaebler, 1993). These are not always easy to ascertain, given the many vagaries involved in the vision development and realization process. In order to maximize support and success, the vision must be shared and communicated effectively (Cufaude, 2003). The articulation of goals and objectives also helps to meet the requirement of creating a shared vision and has the powerful effects of (1) communicating the fundamental purpose and mission of the effort; (2) creating a common understanding and commitment to the overall effort; and (3) integrating and aligning different functional areas. Therefore, a framework that will aid in the articulation and identification of common goals and objectives will have significant benefits.

c. *Identify the gap between the present and the future states of e-government deployment*

Understanding and identifying the gap between current and future states are key elements in the strategic management process and provide an effective way of monitoring the progress of e-government initiatives. The distance between reform initiatives and the current realities of the public sector is often of vital importance in determining the success and failure of reform initiatives (Heeks, 1999). Mapping the progress from "the way things are now" to "the way things ought to be" also allows decision makers to weigh the potential progress of each area against the level of future development required by the e-government vision. It can also assist policymakers and administrators in analyzing the potential benefits and impacts of committing resources and implementation effort as they engage in the planning process.

Beyond the determination of success and failure, the mapping of current reality against the mission statement of the future also generates the energy for change that is a requirement for any transformation process. In effect, the transformation process needs both a vision and a picture of the present to move forward. Therefore, we have another compelling argument for the creation of a new representation of e-government efforts that allows planners and implementers to measure and map the current state of the implementation against its intended result.

d. *Support prediction of future trends affecting e-government initiatives*

Electronic government is a reform effort that is breaking new ground in many areas. For example, beyond the ability to access information and perform basic electronic transactions, citizens in some jurisdictions are demanding more customized products and services rather than acceding to the traditional public institution 'one size fits all' approaches (Osborne & Gaebler, 1992). The emphasis of technology-enabled service delivery has shifted towards providing the right systems and services that users need and want rather than purely emphasizing operational efficiencies (Friedman, 1994). Trends are towards increasing functionality, specialization, and integration (Bertelsmann, 2001; Nolan & Gibson, 1974). New funding arrangements and horizontal and vertical integration are some of the many new elements that are being implemented (Accenture, 2001; Layne & Lee, 2001). As a result, there are no pre-established roadmaps; an international standard or format does not exist (Bertelsmann, 2001).

Beyond citizen-focused initiatives, electronic government also requires the balancing of diverse elements across strategic and operational domains. Changes in the technology field can significantly affect the direction and progress of applications development by either enhancing or limiting choices or functionality. Planners and decision makers must maintain a high level of awareness of required technology and applications change (Nolan & Gibson, 1974). Strategic foresight, coupled with an understanding of the technology and application changes required, is essential to managing internal and external operational and strategic constraints. Consequently, a framework for e-government, acting as a diagnostic tool, should be helpful in predicting the impact of future trends and requirements. In this way, the potential effect of future events can be anticipated and taken into account throughout the entire development life cycle.

e. *Be transferable across different contexts of application*

Every nation has its own functional, social, and administrative objectives to fulfill. As a result, each nation's vision will differ with respect to the strategic priorities of the policymakers and the jurisdiction they represent, giving a unique flavor and direction for each e-government endeavor. Therefore, every e-government program should be viewed and assessed with respect to its context of application (Corrocher & Ordanini, 2002). A greater understanding of motivations and resulting patterns of development in different settings can facilitate the process of comparing approaches and provide a rational means of setting the reform of public administration on course for efficiency and transparency, with clear orientation towards its citizens (Bertelsmann, 2001). It is vitally important to distinguish patterns of development and motivations for e-government and identify transferable elements. Common experiences and practices from one nation's realization could be incorporated into another's, resulting in the creation of a synergistic learning capability. This would be invaluable, given that electronic government is an evolving and pioneering effort where all countries can be considered as being in the early stages of development (Pacific Council on International Policy, 2002). The ability to leverage the experiences and lessons learned by other administrations and selectively identify the applicable elements of other nations would create a synergistic learning and knowledge network that would reduce planning and strategizing efforts. A generic framework that encapsulates these principles would go a long way to improve the discourse about how e-government is being developed across different jurisdictions and contexts.

f. *Support a system representation of strategic agendas and implementation efforts*

A system representation of e-government is required to capture the system's nature of the concept. Systems are one of the common units of analyses within the e-government endeavor. Systems must be balanced across the implementation and are also an area where mapping efforts can be applied and gaps can be identified. The impact and effects of future needs and requirements also have a direct effect on the e-government systems. Given that the operation of e-government depends significantly on the effective management of a variety of systems, a generic framework should capture details of electronic government at this level.

g. *Provide a functional representation of e-government objectives*

Another common unit of analysis is at the functional level. Goals, objectives, and future needs and requirements are typically articulated in the form of functional capacities. In addition, gaps in functionality provide the first indicators that the realization of the e-government vision is not on course. Functional capacities are also used in the comparison of international efforts. To account for these realities the framework must maintain a capability to identify functional capabilities at a high level in a way that reflects the primary motivations and objectives of the overall e-government program. Therefore, a functional representation of e-government is a necessary requirement, supporting several types of analytical efforts.

h. *Support reusability and expandability of framework constructs*

The analysis and consideration of electronic government also has an implicit requirement for reusability and expandability. E-government is an evolving phenomenon that reflects the changing needs and requirements of a society. The mapping of current development against the future is an ongoing effort and must be periodically reviewed and revised. As a result, the generic framework also must be able to capture new data and information about new developments on an ongoing basis. In brief, the framework must classify and describe the ongoing activities at a high level and provide a functional representation that can aid in the planning and implementation process. With regards to the changing nature of e-government, the framework should act as a "sliding window" that reveals the relationship between current initiatives and the overall vision. By meeting these requirements, we are seeking to create a new model for viewing e-government programs as a contiguous whole, while providing a starting point for discussing current knowledge and practices and extending the boundaries of these two areas.

A Generic E-Government Framework (GEF): A Proposal

In Figure 1, we present a proposal for a generic framework for e-government. The framework comprises a number of features that attempt to provide a comprehensive representation of e-government endeavors that meet the requirements identified and discussed earlier. Following a discussion of some of the key features of the framework presented in Figure 1, we discuss how the framework was developed.

GEF Framework Features

The GEF model presented in Figure 1 displays a number of features that, we believe, enhance its usefulness.

Graphical Representation

A graphical representation was chosen, since it provided the best balance between detail and abstraction of e-government visions and implementation activities. From our analysis of other models and frameworks in the IS/IT and e-government areas, a graphical representation or hybrid representation (text plus graphics) was often utilized to better illustrate key details and concepts, including:

- levels of abstraction;
- complex relationships and interactions;
- multiple dimension spanning developments; and

Figure 1. A generic framework for electronic governmen

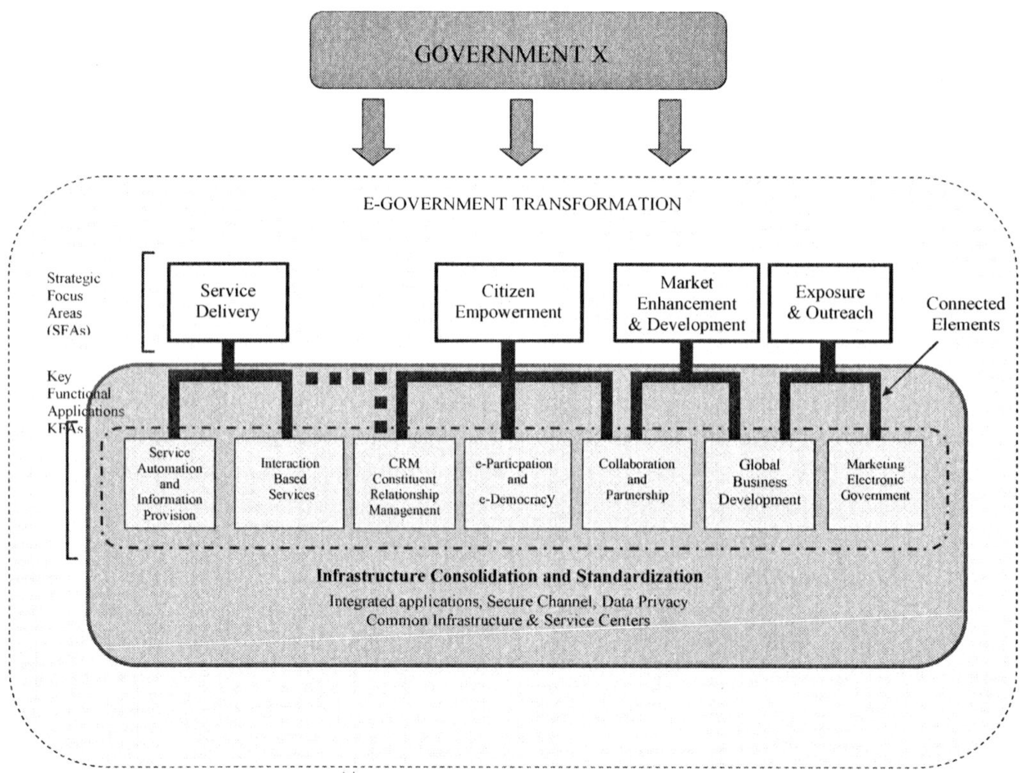

- systems and functional perspective.

For example, the four-stage EDP model (Nolan & Gibson, 1974) uses a combination of text and graphical elements to provide varying levels of abstraction with respect to growth elements and management techniques over the model's four development stages. Graphical illustrations were also used to describe the dynamics of the IS function within user organizations (Friedman, 1994), as well as the interconnection between technology, human, and business elements (Alter, 2002). With respect to e-government developments, the graphical representation is more direct. Koh and Prybutok (2003) directly depict the three-ring model for measuring the dimensions of e-government functions in graphical form. Similarly, Layne and Lee (2001) provide a graphical representation of functional development mapped against overall integration and development complexity in their four-stage model of fully functional e-government. A pictorial view was also deemed to be the most effective way of communicating in a common language that provides a functional perspective free of technical language jargon and document-based artifacts. Such a framework would be easier to share and disseminate across administrations and development contexts, and it reduces the number of implicit assumptions and uncertainties. Our hope is that such a representation would be subject to less interpretation errors and could be debated and discussed with greater facility than a traditional text-based document.

Modularity, Flexibility, and Scalability

The model illustrated in Figure 1 provides a system level representation of a generic Government X's implementation or vision. Strategic focus areas (SFAs) and key functional applications (KFAs) are represented as stand-alone blocks and sub-blocks that represent vertical and horizontal elements of electronic government vision and implementation. The basic security and computing infrastructure platform was also designed to meet the same requirements. These are stand-alone elements that can be reused and interconnected in a variety of ways. This modularity enables reuse and ease of modification and also significantly supports scalability and flexibility capabilities.

By virtue of its flexibility and modularity, the framework can be expanded and modified to represent a diverse array of e-government visions of developments through the selection of SFA clusters and by interconnecting these with relevant developmental areas. In this way, customized views can be built to provide a contingency capability that allows for differentiation and representation of different development perspectives and development patterns. This allows for multiple applications of the framework to different implementations and vision plans and also meets the requirement for transferability across contexts. Note also that the model classifies efforts by function or end objective and not by departmental or agency boundaries, and thus provides additional flexibility in considering electronic government developments.

Application of the framework is not limited to the pre-defined SFAs and key application areas. New SFA and KFA blocks can be created or interchanged, and interconnections between elements also can be readily changed to reflect new relationships and developments as they arise over time. The framework is not a static construct with rigid classifications; the key application areas and SFAs given are only meant as starting points for future investigations. The framework is customizable, not only across contexts of application, but also across different development periods where it can be reapplied to the same implementation periodically. This scalability and ease of reapplication underline the need for longitudinal analysis and continual monitoring and environmental scanning.

METHODOLOGY

Formulating Key Application Areas and Identifying Strategic Agenda Clusters

The conceptualization of the generic framework was a multi-phased process and began with the study of information age agendas proposed by

Heeks (1999). These were identified as increased efficiency, decentralization, increased accountability, improved resource management, and marketization. These agenda items are, in effect, the horizontal motivating elements that are shared across functional and departmental lines. We inferred from this that every electronic government initiative could be considered in some way to fulfill one or more of these agendas.

To build upon these findings, we then identified prominent areas of electronic government development by analyzing e-government vision and white paper documents of various nations, along with independent consulting reports and academic research. Initially, we focused on developed nations (US, Canada, France, Denmark), but further expanded the analysis to include developing and developed nations (Malaysia, Singapore, Malta, Mauritius, South Africa, United Kingdom). This level of analysis highlighted a number of key functional applications and represents a progression in the framework development process from high-level motivations to more concrete implementation aspects. Table 2 outlines the e-government applications initially identified from the literature investigated.

The next step was the refinement of the application areas to include operational and infrastructure components, and human and collaborative elements that were not explicitly identified in the reviewed material. These components act as bridging and enabling elements to many of the other areas and must necessarily be acknowledged as essential areas of e-government development. See Appendix 1 for a detailed description of the application areas.

In Table 3 some key refinements introduced into the conceptualization of the framework at this stage were:

- Separation of services into interactive and automation and information based efforts. This demarcation parallels the evolutionary progression of services towards greater maturity and sophistication and allows for the measurement of efforts with differing levels of each.

Table 2. Identification of e-government functional applications

E-Government Functional Applications (Initial)	Sources
Interaction based services	Bertilsmann, 2001, Layne, & Lee, 2001; OECD, 2003
Seamless service delivery and automation	Accenture 2001, 2002; Working Group E-gov., 2002; Word Markets Research, 2001
Integration of information, services and agencies	Accenture 2002, Government of Canada, 2002, Koh & Prybutok, 2003
Information organization and content aggregation	Layne, & Lee, 2001, Koh & Prybutok, 2003, Working Group E-gov., 2002
CRM: Constituent Relationship Management	Accenture, 2001, Deloitte Research, 2000, Government of Canada, 2002
Democracy and Participation	UK Online Action Plan, 2001, Government of Canada, 2002,
Transparency and Constituent Connectivity	
Exposure and outreach	Accenture, 2001, Heeks, 1999; Chadwick and May, 2003; OECD, 2003
Global Business Development	MAMPU Flagship Applications, 2002, CIMU White Paper, 2002, Accenture, 2002, Working Group E-gov., 2002
Data and security protection	Accenture, 2002, Working Group E-gov., 2002, Government of Canada, 2002, UK Online Action Plan, 2001

Table 3. E-government functional applications (refined)

E-Government Functional Applications (Initial)	E-Government Key Functional Applications (Refined)
Interactive services	Interactive Services
Seamless service delivery & automation	Service Automation & Information Provision
Integration of information, services and agencies	Infrastructure consolidation & Standardization
Information organization & content aggregation	CRM Development
CRM: Constituent Relationship Management	e-democracy & e-participation
Democracy & Participation	Collaboration & Partnership Programs
Transparency & Constituent Connectivity	Marketing e-government
Exposure & outreach	Global Business Development
Global Business Development	
Data & Security protection	

- Recognition of a common infrastructure and security platform that provides a baseline for developing internal efficiency, reliability, and acceptance for IT and human systems. This platform addresses the need for a high degree of integration between technology, organizational and human systems.
- Recognition of ICT as a determining factor in the participation and democracy developmental areas by the inclusion of the "e" prefix
- Recognition of collaborative elements involved in the planning, rollout and adoption of E-Government initiatives and services. This can also be seen as the acknowledgment of soft integration elements not defined in the basic infrastructure platform.
- Addition of Marketing of E-Government as another key area that supports the adoption and diffusion of initiatives but is not intended to replace the marketization agenda presented earlier.

At this stage, we have identified the generic areas of development that an administration can potentially undertake. However, the framework, as it stood, did not meet the requirements for transferability across different contexts of application. To meet this exigency, we created a classification scheme entitled Strategic Focus Areas (SFAs) that could be used to identify high-level e-government vision objectives that would be applicable across different government administrations. Each group incorporates a number of relevant functional applications. The SFAs are identified in Figure 1 as:

- Service Delivery
- Citizen Empowerment
- Market Enhancement and Development
- Exposure and Outreach

Each SFA provides a suggestive mapping between KFA and higher-level agendas. SFA clustering represents an initial interpretation of the strategies and directions employed in current e-government programs and, at best, is an informed estimate of current efforts. In addition to these four groupings, we introduce the horizontal dimension of the infrastructure consolidation and standardization. Given the level of coupling between groupings and an integrated and secure infrastructure, each SFA's associated developmental area is interconnected with the integrated platform. We note one caveat, however. The growing importance and impact of security and privacy concerns within e-government may soon merit their own Strategic Focus Area.

SFA Analytical Capabilities

The model is designed to provide the flexibility to consider developments at different levels of abstraction. Figure 1 represents a high-level cat-

Table 4. Generic framework breakout capability

Service Delivery **Service Auto & Info Interactive Services CRM**	**Citizen Empowerment** **E-Particpation/Democracy Collaboration/Partnership CRM**	**Market Enhancement & Development Collaboration/Partnership Globalization**	**Exposure and Outreach Globalization Marketing E-Gov.**	**Infrastructure Consolidation and Standardization**
Service Automation & Info SA-PIT: Public information SA-Transport: www.transport.gov.za (train schedules, road construction updates) UK-WAP wireless services (Land Registry) **Interactive Services** SA-Education: www.education.pwv.gov.za Www.unisa.ac.za (online ente + fees) SA-Taxes: www.mytax.co.za (filing public/private, view correspondence, forms) US-Postal: www.moversguide.com (follow-up procedure) CAN: Revenue Netfile: private/citizen filing, paperless: www.netfile.gc.ca **CRM** SA-Multilanguage and Literacy Level delivery mechanisms US-CRM ** Labor: www.ajb.org MAL-Citizen Central, user group focused info (community, young adult, parent) http://www.myeg.com.my	**eParticpation/Democracy** US-Central Gov't Portal: www.FirstGOv.gov (figures, account driven/ legislative docs search) US-Census/Library Congress: www.census.gov, www.thomas.loc.gov UK-Democracy: Citizen space UK-Democracy: live debate coverage of parliament + feedback encouraged, 12 month trial: www.parliamentative.tv: SA: Voting and registration services and information and results updates: www.elections.org.za **Collaboration/Partnership** Fin: interactive public discussion forum hosted by ministry: www.otakantaa.fi/kaynnissa.cfm UK: Online Media Campaign coincides w/ 2005 service launch	**Collaboration/Partnership** US-Bus/Agency Proc. Portal: procurement portal for business and agencies: www.FedBizOpps.gov MAL: Government Supplier and Vendor Commerce site http://home.eperolehan.com.my/ **Global Business Development** MALTA: Partnering w/ Global firm to develop common ICT infrastructure UK-digital key infrastructure to enable eCommerce, one certification authority SA-PIT: public information terminal → example of Reach focus + provide access to masses	**Global Business Development** MAL: Cyber Jaya, technology showcase, integrated infrastructure, open invitation to international firms to share knowledge openly… **Marketing E-Gov.** SA: Alternative Technologies ITV, WAP, KIOSK SA-Multilanguage and Literacy Level delivery mechanisms SA-Smartcard & Population Registry → example of Reach focus + brings EGOV to masses	**Internal efficiencies and procurement** SA: Consolidate buying power of state, common procurement platform US: 24 month high pay off initiatives, internal efficiencies and federal infrastructure US; Internal Efficiency and Effectiveness Portfolio MAL: Generic Office Environment (Paperless) MAL: Electronic Procurement (Internal Supply Chain initiative)

egorization of general trends and directions that could be used to generate awareness and discussion. Lower-level differentiation would consist of analyzing actual implementation initiatives and nesting them within the appropriate key functional application areas. This ability to decompose the elements of the functional application areas is useful for operational and strategic analyses. This decomposition technique can be applied for the following:

a. Verification of direction and strategy against actual implementation activities on an ongoing basis

This constitutes a top down application of the GEF. An objective view of e-government is created when implementation activities are nested within SFAs. This view provides a measure of the progress of the implementation relative to strategic objectives and can be used in conjunction with predefined qualitative or quantitative criteria (e.g., usage rates or degree of operational readiness). If applied on a continuing basis, this application can be utilized as a dynamic check that reveals how far strategic objectives have been realized, based on the degree of completion within key application areas.

b. Vision identification for emerging e-government efforts

This represents a bottom-up application. Key initiatives can be identified and used to form functional application areas. These can then be used to create appropriate SFA clusters that can be used to define vision objectives and directions. The application of GEF in such a manner would be ideal for situations where e-government initiatives are ad hoc and an overall vision or strategy has not yet been articulated.

In Table 4, we provide some examples of the decomposition of the GEF using e-government initiatives and activities from five nations. Various activities are identified and placed under the appropriate SFA and KFA headings. This mapping then gives the relative degree of activity in each SFA and KFA. As presented, the depiction gives an overall view of e-government initiatives internationally. However, each nation's relative activity level could also be determined only by considering its specific activities. For example, South African efforts focus mainly on Service Delivery and Exposure and Outreach SFAs, with minor activity elsewhere.

Table 5. GEF features and requirements

Framework Features	Key Benefits	Requirements Supported
Graphical representation	Differing levels of abstraction	System perspective
	Illustration of complex relationships and interactions	Noise free representation
	Multi-dimensional view	Transferability and across contexts of application
	Common alignment medium	Functional representation of E-government
Modularity, Flexibility, Scalability	Stand alone vertical and horizontal elements	System perspective
	Flexible interconnection	Functional Representation of E-government
	Customizable	Reusability and Expandability
	Capture capability (strategic developments, developments)	Mapability of present against overall objectives
	Longitudinal analysis and ease of reapplication	Transferability across contexts of application
Breakout Capability	Differing levels of abstraction	Reusability and expandability
	Strategic & operational Applications	Mapability of present against overall objectives
	Diagnostic capabilities	

Consolidated GEF Features and Requirements

A mapping between the requirements and GEF features is given in Table 5 to conclude our discussion.

E-government is an ongoing endeavor that is constantly evolving. We expect that the rate of change will continue to accelerate, given the potential for new technological advances and the complexity of government processes and citizen needs and requirements. To accommodate the fluid nature of the effort, future oriented tools and methodologies must be scalable and have the capability to measure progress on a continuing basis. The framework must act as a sliding window that can be used to update key stakeholders of the current state of the vision. Therefore, a framework or conceptual model also must have the freedom to classify and reclassify ongoing developments as the implementation and vision mature.

CASE STUDIES

To further illustrate the application of the framework, we used it to study the e-government programs of three countries: the United States; the United Kingdom; and Malaysia. The case studies are presented in brief and should not be considered as the complete representation of all the e-government efforts in the countries selected. Our aim is simply to illustrate the main features of the framework. In Table 6, we outline the key features of each of the cases. Information used in the table was gleaned from published government documents (white papers, reports, etc.) typically found on government Web sites and from other publicly available sources. Data presented here were gathered in 2002 and 2003. Note that some of the information since might have been updated since then.

We begin the table by first identifying the published title for e-government vision and the principal agency responsible for executing the vision. We then briefly outline key e-government initiatives undertaken by each government administration under the rubric of the SFAs. We should note that the visions and initiatives here represent activities at the national/federal level only. Once the initiatives have been listed, we provide a qualitative assessment of how much emphasis is placed on them by the government administration in question. We classify the emphases as major, balanced, or minor. As noted earlier, each government administration may place a different emphasis on an application area. The emphasis placed depends on the strategic objectives being pursued, the history and context influencing the choices being made, as well as the level of e-government implementation experience and maturity. Most government administrations give priority to service delivery efforts because they are able to deliver "quick wins" in this area (Accenture, 2002, 2004). However, as they grow in e-government deployment maturity and the service delivery application areas become more fully functional, they tend to move on to other areas of focus.

FINDINGS

We now present some general observations and comments with respect to overall e-government development. From the above, the generic framework was applied to the three nations and provided a good initial mapping of their e-government development efforts. The modularity feature provided a high degree of freedom in classifying the different initiatives and strategic objectives of each vision, which mapped well to the predetermined and SFA and KFA clusters. The case outlines also uncovered a number of potentially key developmental themes including:

- varying degree of centralization
- lack of balanced development
- service delivery SFA as the most prevalent development cluster

Similar to the measurement of digital divide dimensions by Corrocher and Ordanini (2002), there were significant differences in how ad-

Table 6. Case study summaries

	United States	United Kingdom	Malaysia
Vision Title:	Information Super Highway Updated with Expanded Electronic Government 2001 (1993-present)	Information age Government (1998-present)	Electronic Government (1997-present)
Principal Driver:	Office of Management and Budget	Office of the e-Envoy	Malaysian Administrative Modernization and Management Planning Unit (MAMPU)
Strategic Focus Area			
Service Delivery	**Major**	**Balanced**	**Major**
	Government to Citizen Portfolio: Consumer portal with diverse free and pay based benefits & services (Education, tax, forms, postal)	UK Online Centers: 6000 online center gateway to introduce e-Government services by 2002	PMO Office—Paperless environment: Internally focused program to create electronic seat of Government.
	Government to Business Portfolio: Expanded tax products for business, international trade licensing and regulation	Transaction based services: Postal & Education	Centralized public service offerings: Human Resources, Electronic Procurement
		Alternate technology services: WAP wireless services	Automated service pilot programs: including interaction public service/citizen based services (knowledge sharing, labour, licensing)
Citizen Empowerment	**Minor**	**Balanced**	**Minor**
	eVoting	PIU web based policymaking and parliament web TV –governance and public participation integration efforts	KIOSK development principally to meet service delivery objectives
	Service oriented based segmentation	Web access to Government legislation and initiative status	Articulated CRM efforts: Rough segmentation of targeted groups
	Business centric collaboration & partnership	UK Online Centers basic skills training and framework for bringing e-Government to a national audience.	
Market Enhancement & Development	**Major**	**Balanced**	**Minor**
	Government to Business Portfolio: Streamlined support process, E-Business communication enhancement, one-stop business compliance provision.	Citizen focused development: Extensive government wide CRM efforts to identify and segment user groups	Marketing of Malaysia as a technological R&D enter for international development.
	Core Process Identification and High Payoff Initiatives: 24 high payoff initiatives across 28 lines of business	Collaboration and Partnership: Dedicated E-Commerce group to develop E-Commerce environment with public, private stakeholders	Technology component of E-Government is significantly articulated.
		Action plans to overcome regulatory/legal barriers and enhance connectivity to the global community	

continued on following page

Table 6. continued

Exposure & Outreach	Minor	Balanced	Major
	Consumer portal: A single point of access to federal information sources online.	Strategic marketing plan: Online media campaign for 2005 service launch, E-Government branding & high profile marketing of services to users at local and international arenas	Cyberjaya: Smart CityMultimedia fully wired oasis designed to attract innovative companies from around the world
			PMO Office—Generic Office Environment: Showcase a fully integrated, distributed and scalable deployment of multimedia information technology
			Multimedia Super Corridor (MSC): 20 year transformation effort to build and create a knowledge based society and technology utopia
Infrastructure consolidation and standardization	**Major**	**Minor**	
	Government to government portfolio: Integrated federal architecture for IT efficiency (information, processes, resources)	E-government interoperability framework	
	Internal efficiency and effectiveness portfolio: Commercial best practices application		
Overall Assessment	A market driven vision with high pay off applications developed on a case by case basis to maximize internal efficiencies across 28 lines of business. Strong focus on support services and streamlining processes to develop the business environment. A diverse and large array of services offered with citizen engagement predominantly focused on linking users with product offerings.	A balanced and integrated approach supported by a wide variety of services for private citizens, business and the public service coupled to extensive segmentation and customization CRM efforts. A clearly articulated and integrated marketing strategy to maximize exposure and outreach at local and international levels along with ongoing collaboration to create a conducive E-Commerce framework	An outreach and exposure based vision that is also service oriented. Integrated with the Multimedia Super Corridor (MSC) transformation effort to build and create a knowledge-based society and technology utopia. Significant showcasing and marketing of technological areas of excellence and innovation including paperless environments, cyber smart cities at the international level. Centralized services and pilot applications serve both public service and private citizens.

Table 7. Framework requirement evaluation

Framework Requirement	Successfully Demonstrated
Noise free representation	Partial
Transferability and across context of application	Yes
Functional representation of E-government objectives	Yes
System representation	Partial
Reusability and Expandability	Partial
Mapability of present against overall objectives	No, untested

ministrations choose to develop their visions of electronic government. Development efforts were undertaken in both symmetric and asymmetric fashions. Certain nations, such as the United Kingdom, focused on more integrated and distributed efforts (symmetric) across all SFAs, while others focused only on a few of the SFA efforts to meet specific contexts of application (asymmetric).

Patterns of development also reflected the degree of centralized direction that each nation followed. Most nations followed a long-term approach, with the exception of the United States, which drives its implementation based on a 24-month-long initiative with clear and measurable returns.

There is also a distinct lack of balanced development. SFA development was more prevalent in areas with more well defined and measurable impacts and benefits. Most nations did not pursue a balanced development across all dimensions, but chose one or more key areas on which to concentrate their efforts. The overall US and UK visions for e-government represented the two endpoints of the centralization spectrum. Service Delivery SFA initiatives were present for all nations, however. exposure and outreach and market enhancement SFA clusters were the next most prevalent. The weakest SFA was citizen empowerment. This supports the observation made by Chadwick and May (2003) that the consultative and participatory focus of e-government efforts were the least developed and often overlooked. We believe that the development and performance of the former are more measurable (usage rates, penetration levels, revenue generated) than the latter, and that a relationship exists between measurability and the frequency of implementation. Additionally, there may be a relationship between the maturity of the vision (infrastructure, service sophistication and diversity, degree of articulated centralized direction) and the level of symmetric development. From our findings, therefore, we can confirm the following:

- There is a strong services component in e-government visions and realizations.
- There is a prevalence of a practitioner perspective that focuses on "quick wins."
- There are many different ways to conceptualize and implement e-government.

DISCUSSION AND CONCLUSION

Framework Capabilities and Requirements

We now discuss the implications of findings on framework capabilities and requirements. Six initial requirements were suggested and incorporated into the framework design. Of these, five were fully or partially demonstrated by the first application of the generic framework, and one was not.

From this application, we observed that the framework provided:

- a mapping of diverse electronic government elements to a common perspective;
- the ability to compare and differentiate underlying goals and themes between different implementations; and
- the ability to draw general conclusions and compare differences and similarities across implementations.

In our application of the framework, we were able to represent higher-level objectives as Strategic Focus Areas and Key Functional Applications. These provide the common elements that are flexible enough to classify the specific elements of each initiative, yet not introduce too great a level of detail. As a result, interpretation and jargon "noise" effects were minimized. The profiles are highly customizable and allow for the creation of a common view of electronic government that could be easily shared and compared.

For example, in the U.S. and Malaysian profiles, we were able to identify key areas of strategic focus. Both nations had a similarly strong focus on the service delivery component, but differed on the other dimensions. The U.S. e-government program has a strong market enhancement and infrastructure consolidation and standardization focus, whereas the Malaysian development's other area of concentration lay in the exposure and outreach area. Therefore, different areas of strategic focus and activities were captured, and different patterns of development were observed by comparing levels of strategic concentration (minor, major) and related key functional application activities. U.S. development tended to be more internalized and focused on providing maximum efficiencies and economic benefits over a shorter period (24-month high payoff initiatives), while Malaysian efforts reflected a more externalized approach to raise global awareness of Malaysian society and technology offerings over an extended period (20 years). Some potential contextual factors were also highlighted during this process. Perhaps U.S. efforts reflect a more established base of applications and development, while Malaysian efforts are more focused on growth and enhancement of emerging technical and social conditions.

In a similar fashion, country profiles were created for all three nations and used to identify patterns of development that highlighted both similarities and differences in implementation activities and strategic areas of focus. We observed a number of general trends and developments.

- Differing patterns of development
- Varying degrees of centralization
- Lack of Balanced Development
- Service Delivery SFA as the most prevalent development cluster

We were able to identify these because the framework was expandable and reusable across the e-government programs studied. We successfully used the breakout capabilities to analyze and classify the activities and articulated objectives. In this manner, we were able to perform a mixed analysis with some qualitative (articulated objectives) and quantitative (achievements, implementations) elements. The built-in modularity, scalability, and flexibility features then provided the means to identify patterns of development in a simplified yet inclusive manner. As a result, we were able to consider these patterns at a manageable level of abstraction and draw general conclusions that transcend the specific activities of each e-government endeavor and that could be shared across contexts of application.

Limitations

However, we also observed the following shortcomings of the framework:

- Lack of support for a full systems representation
- Potential noise effects could be present
- Case study represents a static application

The generic framework only provides partial systems representation of e-government. The interconnection of key application areas and SFAs provides a high-level system representation of overall objectives and some of the relationships between different areas of development. By its very nature, it is more functionally orientated and not optimized towards representing system connections and interrelationships. Profiles are designed to provide a common perspective based on analyzing findings from material that tends to describe developments from a functional or capabilities viewpoint. Consequently, these common elements are abstracted from the actual systems and relationships employed by the administrations under study. For example, the relationships and connectivity of the IS/IT function with the executive and public service branch of government are not detailed. Only high-level objectives and relationships are depicted as interconnected SFAs and KFAs. This level of abstraction is required in order to maintain the common perspective and ability to transcend application contexts. Therefore, for an analysis of the actual systems, additional models and tools will be required to complement the application of the GEF.

Another post application discovery was the lack of filtering for potential bias and inconsistencies in vision claims and achievements included in the country-specific profiles. The profiles did present a common view that filtered out technical jargon and multiple interpretation artefacts, but did not provide any checks on the validity of the data that was used in profile construction. Initially, our intention was that a "noise-free" representation would be achieved by virtue of reviewing several sources from both involved and independent parties; additionally, profiles were envisioned to be generated based on a substantial body of achieved, as well as articulated, objectives. However, most developments were in the initial stages, and, therefore, profiles were based almost exclusively on the latter. Consequently, this application may contain political noise artefacts and inconsistencies and only offers a best attempt at "noise-free" depiction based on the data available.

The case studies only represent a static application at one point in time. The expandability and reusability requirement has only been confirmed with respect to the application to different e-government efforts, but not over the dimension of time. As a result, the measurability of e-government maturity requirement is untested, given that vision objectives and achievements were combined instead of measuring the current state against the intended vision. In conclusion, the framework was successful in providing a common perspective that transcends any one e-government offering, but must be supported by additional analytical tools to provide a full systems perspective. It must also be reapplied to fully test its applicability over time.

In addition to these shortcomings, there are a number of questions still to be addressed. For example, if service delivery and a practitioner perspective are the basis for e-government developments, what direction will future developments take? Is balanced development across all areas necessary for superior performance? Additionally, what are the ultimate potential and benefits of application areas such as Citizen Empowerment? Currently, initiatives in this area are the weakest (Chadwick & May, 2003). We argue that, in the end, some form of balanced development will be necessary. There are only a limited number of "quick-win" initiatives available, and most of these have already been exploited in advanced countries (Accenture, 2004).

Ultimately, electronic government development and maturity must reflect the changes in the political, social, and economic orientation of the hosting nation. Therefore, it must evolve beyond its current state. However, this will require additional knowledge, experience, and deliberation. New technology and organizational infrastructure will also need to be developed. We hope that the generic framework can be refined and reapplied to identify some of these upcoming trends and developments, and we look forward to the emergence of additional tools and models that will move the e-government consciousness closer to this point of maturity.

REFERENCES

Accenture (2001). eGovernment leadership: Innovation delivered.

Accenture (2002). eGovernment leadership: Realizing the vision.

Accenture (2004, May). *eGovernment leadership: High performance, maximum value.* E-Government Executive Series.

Alter, S. (2002). *Information systems: Foundations of e-business* (4th edition). Upper Saddle, NJ: Prentice Hall.

Basu, S. (2004). E-government and developing countries: An overview. *International Review of Law, Computers & Technology*, 18(1), 109-132.

Bertelsmann Foundation (2001). Balanced e-government: E-government—Connecting efficient administration and responsive democracy.

Box, R. (1999). Running government like a business: Implications for public administration theory and practice. *American Review of Public Administration*, 29(1), 19-43.

Brodie, J. (1999). *Critical concepts: An introduction to politics*. Scarborough, Canada: Prentice Hall; Allyn and Bacon.

Caldow, J. (2001). *Seven e-Government leadership milestones*. Working paper - Institute of Electronic Government, IBM Corporation.

Chadwick, A., & May, C. (2003, April 27). Interaction between states and citizens in the age of the Internet: "E-government" in the United States, Britain, and the European Union. *Governance*, 16(2), 271-300.

Corrocher, N., & Ordanini, A. (2002). Measuring the digital divide: A framework for the analysis of cross-country differences. *Journal of Information Technology*, 17(1), 9-19.

Cufaude, J. (2003). Creating the future while managing the present. *Association Management*, 55(8), 28-34.

Davies, A., & Heeks, R. (1999). Different approaches to information age reform. In R. Heeks (Ed.), *Reinventing government in the information age* (pp. 9-12). London and New York: Routledge.

Deloitte Research – Public Sector Institute. (2000). *At the dawn of e-government: The citizen as customer.*

Friedman, A. (1994). The stages model and the phases of the IS field. *Journal of Information Technology, 9*, 76-88.

Guy, J.J. (2001). *People, politics and government: A Canadian perspective*. Scarborough, Ontario: Prentice Hall.

Heeks, R. (1999). Reinventing government in the information age. In R. Heeks, (Ed.), *Reinventing government in the information age* (pp. 9-12). London and New York: Routledge.

Ke, W., & Wei, K.K. (2004, June). Successful e-government in Singapore. *Communications of the ACM*, 47(6), 95-99.

Keen, P.G.W. (1991). *Shaping the future: Business design through information technology.* Boston: Harvard Business School Press.

Koh, C.E., & Prybutok, V.R. (2003). The three ring model and development of an instrument for measuring dimensions of e-government functions. *Journal of Computer Information Systems*, 43(3), 34-39.

Lacity, M.C., & Willcocks, L.P. (1998). *Strategic sourcing of information systems: Perspectives and practices*. Chicester, UK; New York: Wiley.

Layne, K., & Lee, J. (2001). Developing fully functional e-government: A four stage model. *Government Information Quarterly*, 18, 122-36.

Luftman, J.N. (1996). *Competing in the information age: Strategic alignment in practice.* New York: Oxford University Press.

Marche, S., & McNiven, J.D. (2003). E-government and e-governance: The future isn't what it used to be. *Canadian Journal of Administrative Sciences*, 20(1), 74-86.

Nolan, R., & Gibson, C. (1974). Managing the four stages of EFP growth. *Harvard Business Review, 52*(1), 76-78.

OECD (2003). The case for e-government: Excerpts from the OECD Report "The e-government imperative." *OECD Journal on Budgeting*, 3(1), 62-96.

Office of Management and Budget (OMB) (2003). Implementing the president's management agenda for e-government: E-government strategy, April. Retrieved July 30, 2004: *http://www.whitehouse.gov/omb/egov/2003egov_strat.pdf*

Osborne, D., & Gaebler, T. (1992). *Reinventing government: How the entrepreneurial spirit is transforming the public sector.* New York: Plume.

Pacific Council on International Policy (2002). Roadmap for e-government in the developing world: 10 questions e-government leaders should ask themselves. *Report of the Working Group on e-government in the developing world.*

Poostchi, M. (2002). *Implementing e-government: Potential impact on organization structure, business processes, and costs.* MBA Thesis. Carleton University.

Rais Abdul Karim, M. (Ed.) (1999). *Reengineering the public service: Leadership and change in an electronic age.* Subang Jaya, Malaysia: Pelanduk Publications.

Reddick, C.G. (2004). A two-stage model of e-government growth: Theories and empirical evidence for U.S. cities. *Government Information Quarterly*, 21, 51-64.

Somogyi, E.K., & Galliers, R.D. (1987). Applied information technology: From data processing to strategic information systems. *Journal of Information Technology*, 2, 30-41.

UK Cabinet Office (2000). E-government: A strategic framework for public services in the information age. Central IT Unit, April.

United Nations World Public Sector Report 2003: E-government at the crossroads (2003). Retrieved April 2004: *http://unpan1.un.org/intradoc/groups/public/ documents/un/unpan012733.pdf*

Ward, J., & Peppard, J. (2002). *Strategic planning for information systems. Wiley Series in information systems.* West Sussex, UK: John Wiley & Sons.

World Markets Research Centre (2001). *Global e-government survey.* Providence, Rhode Island: Brown University.

ADDITIONAL REFERENCES

E-Government Vision Documents and White Papers

Malaysia

Electronic government flagship applications (2002). Retrieved June 2002: *http://www.mampu.gov.my/mampueng/Ict/flagship.htm*

ISP framework version 1.0. Retrieved December 2002: *http://www.mampu.gov.my/mampueng/ICT/ISPlan/ISPlan.htm*

ISP template version 1.0. Retrieved December 2002: *http://www.mampu. gov.my/mampueng/ICT/ISPlan/ISPlan.htm*

PMO office: Generic office environment. Retrieved July 2002: *http://www.mampu .gov.my/mampueng/Corporat/profile/eg/goe.htm*

Human resources management information system. Retrieved July 2002: *http://www.mampu.gov.my/mampueng/Corporat/profile/eg/hrmis.htm*

Electronic procurement (internal supply chain). Retrieved July 2002: *http://www.mampu.gov.my/mampueng/Corporat/profile/eg/ep.htm*

Malta

White paper on the vision and strategy for the attainment of e-government (n.d.). Retrieved July 2002: *http://www. cimu.gov.mt/htdocs/content.asp?c=34*

Maltese exchange. Retrieved July 2002: *http://www.cimu.gov.mt/eGovWP contents.asp*

Government portal architecture. Retrieved July 2002: *http://www.cimu.gov.mt/e GovWPcontents.asp*

National email. Retrieved July 2002: *http://www.cimu.gov.mt/eGovWP _contents.asp*

South Africa

e-governemnt policy, second draft 2001 version 3.2. Department of Public and Administrations. Republic of South Africa. Retrieved July 2002: *www.dpsa. gov.za/e-gov/2001docs/e-govpolicyFramework.htm*

Smart card and population registry. Retrieved July 2002: *http://www. dpsa.gov.za/e-gov/2001docs/e-govpolicyFramework.htm and http://www.dpsa.gov.za/e-gov/e-govindex.htm*

PIT – Public information terminal. Retrieved July 2002: *http://www.dpsa.gov. za/e-gov/2001docs/e-govpolicyFramework.htm and http://www.dpsa.gov.za/e-gov/e-govindex.htm*

Transportation information services. Retrieved July 2002: *www. transport.gov.za*

United States

First gov your first click to the US Government (2002). Retrieved July 2002: *www.firstgov.gov*

E-government strategy: Simplified delivery of services to citizens (2002). Office of Management and Budget. Retrieved July 2002: *www.whitehouse.gov/OMB*

Core process identification and high payoff initiatives. Retrieved July 2002: *http://www.firstgov.gov*

Department of Labor Website. Retrieved July 2002: *www.ajb.org*

Consumer portal. Retrieved July 2002: *www.consumer.gov*

Federal business opportunities. Retrieved July 2002: *www.FedBizOpps.gov*

United Kingdom

UK online action plan (2001). Retrieved December 2002: *http://www.e-envoy.gov.uk/ukonline/progress/actplan/table.htm*

Department of Trade and Industry (1999). Building the Knowledge Driven Economy. United Kingdom. Retrieved June 2002: *http://www.dti.gov.uk/comp/competitive/wh_int1.htm*

Electronic government services for the 21st century (2000). Retrieved June 2002: *http://www.cabinet-office.gov.uk/innovation/2000/delivery/intro.htm*

UK e-commerce services for the 21st century (2001). Retrieved June 2002: *http://www.cabinet-office.gov.uk/innovation/1999/ecomm.html*

Postal services. Retrieved July 2002: *www.consignia.com*

Parliament Web TV. Retrieved July 2002: *www.parliamentlive.tv*

APPENDIX A: KEY E-GOVERNMENT APPLICATION AREAS

Service Automation and Information Provision

This refers to efforts that are primarily concerned with automating existing government services. Typically, existing services are duplicated to provide an alternate communication channel. Additionally, implementation programs are skewed towards the online aggregation and publishing of materials and information. The default standard is towards information quantity and richness versus organization for usage.

Interactive Services

These constitute development efforts that are implemented for providing a broad range of services and a high level of functionality. Initiatives focus on providing information and content that is transactional in nature and that offer a higher level of interaction. Communication capability is performed in duplex mode (i.e., both citizens and government have the capacity to provide feedback to one another).

CRM Development

Another refinement in service delivery is to add citizen centricity to the design and development effort. Constituent Relationship Management (CRM) techniques, such as focus groups, need analysis feedback and field-testing, which are integral parts of the action plan. Constituent or user targeting and segmentation efforts are also prevalent, and sites are structured around the needs and requirements of citizens and business. Not only are services offered, but applications also offer value-added services and may provide proactive advisory capabilities, as well. Service integration and user-friendly interfaces also characterize CRM service development.

Collaboration and Partnership Programs

Advances in fostering cooperation and joint initiatives between internal agencies and external organizations are the focus. Partnerships are encouraged and the risks and rewards are shared. Often, service delivery and maintenance are distributed between government and private industry. External stakeholders can also have a significant role in determining and plotting out vision strategies and objectives. Stakeholders also work cooperatively to implement and realize the vision.

Infrastructure Consolidation and Standardization

Internal transformation efforts relate to the growth and implementation of initiatives that aid in reorganizing internal processes to improve efficiency and decision-making effectiveness. Core processes are analyzed and optimized for online delivery. Organizational changes are also brought about to enable these efforts and include modifying reward programs, evaluation procedures, and procedures for resource allocation. Redundant process and information are also reduced or eliminated.

E-Democracy and E-Participation

Citizens are informed and educated about the decision-making process and programs to increase the transparency and responsiveness of government as a whole. Citizen feedback and involvement in day-to-day governance is encouraged as much as possible. Additionally, access to legislation and the decision-making process is more prevalent, and efforts seek to bring government closer to the population and to as wide an audience as possible.

Marketing E-Government

This overlaps to some degree with E-Democracy and citizen centricity objectives. Citizens and business again are informed and educated. However, developments in this area are targeted at promoting and marketing the visions and services. Comprehensive plans to introduce and advocate electronic government services and technology are put into place. Consumer confidence and trust are key objectives, and dedicated resources are allocated to the overall strategy. The measuring of service and CRM performance is another key feature.

Global Business Development

The principal thrust of globalization is to increase global connectivity. A high level of partnership and fostering of relationships internationally are central to these efforts. A main activity is the development and encouragement of e-commerce and business ventures. Programs also reflect a high degree of effort towards establishing links and contacts across physical and state boundaries.

This work was previously published in Journal of Global Information Management, Vol. 13, No. 1, edited by F. Tan, pp. 1-30, copyright 2005 by IGI Publishing, formerly known as Idea Group Publishing (an imprint of IGI Global).

Chapter LXVIII
A Web Query System for Heterogeneous Government Data

Nancy Wiegand
University of Wisconsin–Madison, USA

Isabel F. Cruz
University of Illinois at Chicago, USA

Naijun Zhou
University of Wisconsin–Madison, USA

William Sunna
University of Illinois at Chicago, USA

ABSTRACT

This paper describes a Web-based query system for semantically heterogeneous government-produced data. Geospatial Web-based information systems and portals currently are being developed by various levels of government along with the GIS community. Typically, these sites provide data discovery and download capabilities but do not include the ability to pose DBMS-type queries. One of the main problems in querying distributed government data sources is the difference in semantics used by various jurisdictions. We extend work in schema integration by focusing on resolving semantics at the value level in addition to the schema or attribute level. We illustrate our method using land use data, but the method can be used to query across other heterogeneous sets of values. Our work starts from an XML Web-based DBMS and adds functionality to accommodate heterogeneous data between jurisdictions. Our ontology and query rewrite systems use mappings to enable querying across distributed heterogeneous data.

INTRODUCTION

Governmental data are increasingly are being produced and distributed over the Web. Integrating and querying these data will greatly help improve governmental decision making. However, most current Web-based practices rely on keyword search engines and do not consider the heterogeneous problem in data sources. This paper presents a study of deploying powerful Database Management System (DBMS) technology to improve capabilities for data search and query and to use ontology approaches for data semantics. We give an overview of our system and address the problem of mediating between highly heterogeneous information developed independently by many different government units. We focus on geospatial data in general and on diverse land use coding systems in particular. To be able to map between heterogeneous values found in land use attributes, we extend work on semantic integration by resolving semantics at the *value* level of individual attributes in addition to the schema level.

Web sites are currently being developed by many levels of government to serve geospatial data. A recent example from the federal government is Geospatial One-Stop (2003), which was initiated to have all geospatial data and information from federal agencies along with many state, local, tribal, and private agencies accessible from one portal. Other examples of geospatial clearinghouses and portals at the national level include the Alexandria Digital Library and the Federal Geographic Data Committee (FGDC) Clearinghouse. In addition, there are many geospatial Web sites being produced at the state, county, and local levels. For example, state level examples for Wisconsin include the Wisconsin Land Information Clearinghouse (WiscLinc) and the prototype Wisconsin Land Information System (WLIS).

WLIS, for example, will allow central access to distributed data sets that remain under local government control and reside on local and county servers across the state (WLIS Project Team, 2000). The problem is that without state-mandated standards, data sets produced by local and county governments are highly heterogeneous. As one moves across jurisdictional boundaries, not only do database schemas vary, but also the definitions and acceptable values of attributes change significantly. In fact, most of the effort required to integrate diverse geospatial data lies with the nonspatial attributes. That is, integration problems caused by the use of different coordinate systems, for example, are more easily solved (WLIS Project Team, 2000).

We began our work in the context of WLIS but are extending it to a larger scale such as needed for Geospatial One-Stop. The typical purpose of WLIS and other geospatial Web sites is to enable search and download capabilities for geospatial data and services. However, such sites are limited or lacking in their ability to allow full DBMS-type querying over the content of distributed government data sources. Instead, querying in these sites is restricted to selecting a few metadata fields for the purpose of locating data sources. Sites that do allow DBMS querying on source data content provide an explicit connection over the Web to a backend DBMS containing the data of a single data source. Otherwise, to query data source content, a user has to download the data into a local Geographic Information System (GIS) or DBMS. To enhance these government Web sites, we are working to support full-fledged DBMS-type querying over distributed data sources.

This paper discusses our approach as embodied by a prototype Web-based query system in which we focus on resolving semantic heterogeneities between the attributes of related data sets. To design our system architecture, we first consider characteristics of government-produced geospatial data. Next, we discuss the semantic heterogeneity problem in general and then present our specific application problem concerning land use codes. We then discuss ontology integration methods including our semi-automatic solution. Our existing working system using land use data examples is described in the last section.

WEB DBMS DESIGN FOR DISTRIBUTED GEOSPATIAL GOVERNMENT DATA

Special considerations of data models and architectures are needed for designing a Web-based distributed query system for government-produced geospatial data. Although some characteristics are not unique to this application, traditional DBMS and current Web architectures do not accommodate these characteristics. We determined that to provide the necessary functionality, our Web query system needs to recognize the following characteristics: multiple inherent data set organizations, such as theme, jurisdiction, and spatial extent; existence of separate metadata files; spatial functionality requirements; and heterogeneity in schemas and data content.

Geospatial data produced by government agencies have various inherent data set organizations. For example, GIS data sets tend to be based on a theme (also called a data category or channel) such as land use, transportation, hydrography, and so forth. In addition, data sets characterize a particular jurisdiction. Jurisdictions range from cities, towns, and villages to counties, regions of various types, the state, and the federal level. These base organizations (theme and jurisdiction) often are used in geospatial portals as main search criteria. A Web-based DBMS can take advantage of such information to determine data sets involved in a query, eliminating the need for the user to identify and specify exact data sources as is required in typical DBMSs.

Geospatial data often have separate metadata files that describe the data source in many ways. Theme, jurisdiction information, type of data such as raster or vector, and temporal aspects are examples of metadata. This type of metadata provides more information than typical DBMS schemas and can be queried separately. A common format for metadata is the FGDC's Content Standard for Digital Geospatial Metadata (CSDGM), often referred to as the FGDC standard. A Web DBMS for geospatial data needs to be able to handle separate metadata files and their associations with the actual data. Challenges regarding metadata have previously been recognized (Maier & Delcambre, 1999).

Another characteristic of geospatial data is implicit or explicit spatial extent. Explicit spatial coordinates may exist to represent the data at the data set level or the record level. A full geospatial Web-based query system would include spatial query processing, spatial indexes, and functionality such as buffering and overlay. Because that is not the focus here, we design and implement a subset of spatial capabilities.

Finally, a Web-based query system needs to resolve the heterogeneity between data sources created by different government jurisdictions. This is our main focus, and we are particularly concerned with semantic heterogeneity at the value level. For example, land use descriptions, that vary by jurisdiction, need to be integrated over multiple jurisdictions need to be integrated for comprehensive planning purposes.

RELATED WORK ON HETEROGENEITY

This section discusses selected prior work on mediating between heterogeneous data sources. We also further discuss the level of semantics at which we are currently working, which is the value level.

GIS Semantic Interoperability

Types of interoperability relevant to geospatial data and GISs previously have been identified, and the difficulties at the semantic level have been noted (Bishr, 1998). In particular, Bishr's highest level of interoperability proposes seamless communication between remote GISs without prior knowledge of their semantics.

To help realize GIS interoperability, the Open Geospatial Consortium (OGC) was formed in 1994. OGC has extended the eXtensible Markup Language (XML) (Bray, Paoli, Sperberg-McQueen, Maler, & Yergeau, 2004) to develop the Geography Markup Language (Cox, Daisey, Lake, Portele, & Whiteside, 2003) to further help achieve geospatial interoperability. GML uses a standard markup for spatial representations, although variations exist. However, in GML, the representation and meaning of the *nonspatial* elements do not follow a standard and may be described in any manner. As a result, GML does not solve semantic problems for nonspatial properties (just as XML does not). In this regard, OGC recommends the formation of *information communities* that share a data dictionary and metadata schema (OGC Topic 14, 1999).

Ontologies have been proposed as a solution for semantic integration (Fensel, 2001), and this is currently a very active area of research within geospatial and other communities. An ontology is a shared and machine-executable conceptual model in a specific domain of interest (Bussler, Fensel, & Maedche, 2002). Ontology engineering, which is methodology for developing ontologies (Staab & Studer, 2004), includes automatic creation of ontologies, as explored by Malyankar (2002), for example. Ontology-driven GIS has been proposed for geographic information integration, especially between GIS and remote sensing systems (Fonseca, Egenhofer, & Agouris, 2002). Their proposal recognizes the difficulties of creating and imposing standards similar to the difficulties we found regarding a statewide land information system. Instead, they assume communities will commit to common ontologies, which will be used to characterize and locate information sources.

An example of work being done by government agencies on national standards related to land parcel data is the National Integrated Land System (NILS). NILS is an effort between the BLM and the USDA Forest Service to manage cadastral records and land parcel information specifically for use in geographic information systems. Also, a new XML standard related to land information exchange for land development and transportation professionals is LandXML. LandXML is being used for civil engineering applications, for example.

However, until additional standards are developed or information communities are formed, many GIS data sets will continue to be independently developed and heterogeneous. Furthermore, legacy data sets may never be converted to a new standard.

DBMS Semantic Integration

Heterogeneity in Database Management Systems has received extensive attention (Bouguettaya, Benatallah, & Elmagarmid, 1998). Various types of heterogeneity have been identified. *Syntactic* heterogeneity can be solved by mapping between data models, such as between a relational model and an object-oriented model. *Schematic* heterogeneity is handled by schema integration and is important when there are semantically similar objects of interest. *Semantic* heterogeneity concerns discrepancies in the meaning, interpretation, and intended use of the same or related data (Sheth & Larson, 1990).

Most work on semantic integration has focused on the schema level (Rahm & Bernstein, 2001). For example, Clio is a tool for managing schema integration (Hernandez, Miller, & Haas, 2001; Miller et al., 2001). Because of the difficulty to fully automate semantic decisions, Clio combines user intervention with automated techniques. An interesting feature of Clio is that it provides actual data values for review to help with mapping decisions.

An XML query system using ontologies has been developed (Theobald & Weikum, 2000). In this system, if the user chooses a special similarity operator, query processing will include semantically similar terms obtained from a knowledge base developed using WordNet. Use of the similarity operator produces ranked results for the similar words. In our application, however, the land use code mappings that are needed to identify similar terms cannot be found in a general collection such as WordNet. Also, there is a greater need to present the user with precise semantic nuance information instead of retrieval relevance rankings. As a result, we needed to develop a precise ontology mapping method.

DBMS Heterogeneity at the Value Level

Prior research on schema integration has recognized semantic problems at the value level. By value level, we mean the values in the domain of an attribute. Bouguettaya et al. (1998) present three representational differences for value level conflicts: differences in the expression (e.g., 4.0 vs. A); differences in units (e.g., miles vs. kilometers); and differences in precision (e.g., cardinality differences such as low, medium, high vs. a range with five choices). These types of representational differences usually can be resolved using straightforward formulas or algorithms.

Other types of heterogeneity at the value level are not easily resolved. The land use coding systems in our application include categories such as agriculture, commercial, and residential. The systems are often hierarchical with each category being subdivided into more specific land uses. As above, there are differences in the expression of land use codes (e.g., agriculture codes beginning with *A* vs. beginning with *9*). And, units and precision vary (e.g., hectares vs. acres and six subcategories for agriculture vs. 11). But, in addition, the meanings of codes between different local data sources cannot be directly compared. For example, a coding scheme for one jurisdiction in which the *commercial* category is divided into *commercial sales* and *commercial services* cannot easily be compared to another code scheme divided into *commercial intensive* and *commercial nonintensive*.

VALUE LEVEL SEMANTIC PROBLEMS FOR LAND USE DATA

One of the most immediate purposes of the Wisconsin Land Information System, for example, is to support comprehensive land use planning. Wisconsin, similar to other states, has passed *smart growth* legislation requiring local governments to develop land use plans. Of the many types of data sets needed to create a land use plan, such as transportation, environmental corridors, wetlands, and so forth, current land use information is of prime importance. However, land use data is one of the most problematic types of data because of its heterogeneity.

Land use codes are oftentimes found in GIS data sets. The data may be parcel based in which each polygon forms a parcel or may be such that each polygon covers an area having the same land use without regard for parcel boundaries. In either case, there is great variability in what other attributes exist in a data set containing a land use attribute.

The largest problem, however, is that city and county governments and regional planning commissions develop their own coding systems for land use. Historically, a standard coding system was never imposed, and individual communities preferred to develop land use codes that more closely represented the particular land uses in their jurisdictional area. A multi-dimensional coding system called the Land Based Classification System (LBCS) (Everett & Ngo, 1999) was developed by the American Planning Association to help provide a standard. However, to date, it has not been widely adopted.

Table 1 shows example land use codes in Wisconsin. The synonyms (*Lucode*, *Tag*, *Lu1*, and *Lu_4_4*) for the land use attribute are resolved more easily than determining whether the code descriptions share common definitions. Value level semantic resolution is needed because the descriptions are not exact matches; each description slightly varies from one another. For example, the 8110 code of the City of Madison makes no

Table 1. Heterogeneity in land use codes

Planning Authority	Attribute Identifier	Land Use Code	Description of Code
Dane County RPC	Lucode	91	Cropland/ Pasture
Racine County (SEWRPC)	Tag	811 815	Cropland Pasture and Other Ag
Eau Claire County	Lu1	AA	General Agriculture
City of Madison	Lu_4_4	8110	Farms

distinction between cropland and farm buildings; whereas, the Dane County Regional Planning Commission (RPC) has a separate code for farm buildings. Eau Claire County's most specific code that would include cropland is at the general agriculture level, which also includes various other subcategories.

Comprehensive planning between neighboring communities requires mapping between coding systems. An example query needed as part of a land use decision may be to *find all lands with a particular land use over a watershed spanning several counties*. The problem of resolving land use codes is a significant one. Not only are the ramifications important within a state, they also are important for planning efforts between states or even between countries, such as between the U.S. and Mexico (Ganster & Wright, 2000).

One solution to resolving differences in meanings of land use codes is only to compare codes at a general level, such as commercial, residential, or agriculture, and not to try to resolve subcategories. Even at this general level, a system to automatically make comparisons between diverse coding systems is extremely valuable for comprehensive planning, because, currently, efforts to resolve codes are done currently by hand on a case by case basis. We developed a method, however, to keep comparisons between the meanings of subcategories for codes as precise as needed.

VALUE LEVEL SEMANTIC INTEGRATION USING ONTOLOGY METHODS

Strategies for Semantic Integration: Global-As-View and Local-As-View

Data integration to solve schematic heterogeneity has taken two general approaches: Global-As-View (GAV) and Local-As-View (LAV). In GAV, each entity in a global schema is associated with a view over the data sources. Contrary to this, in LAV, a source is defined as a view over the global schema. Our work is more similar to the LAV approach

Figure 1a. Ontology DTD

```
<!ELEMENT database      (table+)>
<!ELEMENT table         (tuple+)>
<!ELEMENT tuple         (attrname+)>
<!ELEMENT attrname      (attrvalue*)>
<!ELEMENT attrvalue     (attrvalue*)>

<!ATTLIST database  id CDATA #REQUIRED>
<!ATTLIST table     id CDATA #REQUIRED>
<!ATTLIST tuple     id CDATA #REQUIRED>
<!ATTLIST attrname  id CDATA #REQUIRED>
<!ATTLIST attrvalue id CDATA #REQUIRED>
```

in that we consider a global ontology of master attributes and values, which are then mapped to local attributes and values. A global ontology, available through the user interface, is beneficial for querying heterogeneous data sets because the user can select from provided ontology terms.

To support the LAV approach, we use a table-based DTD to define the ontology (Figure 1a) (Cruz, Rajendran, Sunna, & Wiegand, 2002). A unique feature of our approach is that the ontology DTD includes an optional subelement—attrvalue—to hold ontology values for attributes with heterogeneous domains. The attrvalue element can have nested attrvalue elements to describe any level of subcategories, such as needed for land use coding systems. We present a subset of the values in the global ontology for the land use code attribute (Figure 1b). Our vocabulary con-

Figure 1b. Ontology for land use code values

```
<attrname id= "land_use_code">
  <attrvalue id= "Commercial">
    <attrvalue id= "Commercial-Scale>
      <attrvalue id= "Commercial-Scale-Intense"/>
      <attrvalue id= "Commercial-Scale-NonIntense"/>
  </attrvalue>
  <attrvalue id= "Commercial-Function>
      <attrvalue id= "Commercial-Function-Sales"/>
      < attrvalue id= "Commercial-Function-Service"/>
  </attrvalue>
    ...
  <attrvalue id= "Other"/>
</attrvalue>
<attrvalue code= "Residential">
    ...
</attrvalue>
...
</attrname>
```

sists of about 200 different terms obtained from a subset of around a dozen land use databases that we collected.

Another unique feature to our approach, in addition to providing a method to allow value level representations, is that the global ontology does not specify a *standard* set of land use code values, which can be a contentious issue. Instead, it is a potential composite of all values, including synonyms and various overlapping categorical terms that might be used in a query. Including multiple categorizations in the ontology provides a solution to the problem of a domain being categorized differently in various coding systems. For example, in Figure 1b, the commercial code includes *both* the *scale* and *function* subcategories.

Ontology Integration Methods

Given the semantic differences between the domains for land use coding systems, it is not possible to resolve completely the discrepancies in the level of precision that we need using fully automatic methods. For example, algorithms that involve string matching either will not work or will not capture the needed semantics. That is, *cropland* will not match *agriculture*, although cropland is a subset of agriculture. Other types of advanced automatic matching methods involve rankings of results using probabilities. For example, we experimented with modifications to the Naïve Bayesian classifier to automatically match categories by comparing the occurrence of terms in their subcategories (Zhou, 2003). Others have also used similarity measures to produce probabilities (Doan, Madhavan, Domingos, & Halevy, 2002). However, returning answers with attached probabilities for an application involving land use planning may not be sufficient or appropriate if, for example, a land use planner needs to know as precisely as possible where and how much cropland exists over a multi-jurisdictional area. We also experimented with Formal Concept Analysis (Ganter & Wille, 2004) to form a concept lattice as a means of relating broad categories in the various land use coding systems (Zhou & Wiegand, 2004). Although the results were interesting, they were not precise enough to use for automatic resolutions between coding systems. We concluded that a semi-automatic approach would provide the most accurate results for ontology integration.

Semi-Automatic Ontology Alignment

We developed a tool to map the global ontology to each local schema and the values of its land use coding system (Figure 2). Using this tool, a domain expert first performs initial mappings manually between concepts in the global ontology and concepts in the local schema. Based on these mappings and the user's request, the tool can perform a semi-automatic deduction process to generate more mappings (Cruz & Rajendran, 2003; Cruz, Sunna, & Chaudhry, 2004). The user can commit the new mappings generated by the tool or override them. The user can resume the process of manual mapping and can invoke the semi-automatic deduction process anytime.

Concepts are mapped using the following mapping types: exact—the connected concepts are equivalent in their meaning; approximate—the connected concepts have similar meanings but are not quite exact; no mapping—a concept in the global ontology does not have a candidate match in meaning in the local schema; superset—the concept in the global ontology is more general in meaning or contents than a concept or a group of concepts in the local schema; and subset—a concept or a group of concepts in the global ontology is less general in meaning or contents than a concept in the local ontology.

The semi-automatic deduction process establishes mappings between concepts based on mappings of their children. For example, in Figure 3, vertices *auto parts* and *construction and electrical supplies* in a part of a global ontology on the left are mapped using mapping types *exact* and *superset* to vertices *auto parts* and *electrical supplies* in a part of a local schema on the right. The mapping type between their parents *manufacturing* and *production* can be deduced to be *superset* based on the mapping between the children, because we consider that the content of the parent is the aggregation of the contents of its children. All

Figure 2. Tool to create an agreement file

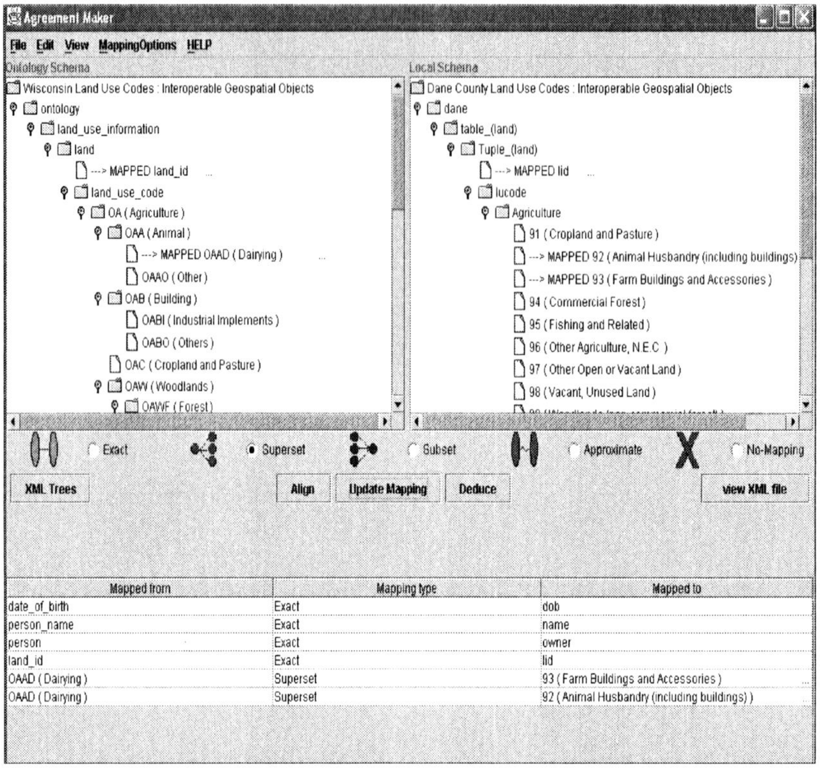

the children of *manufacturing* are mapped to all children of *production*. This is the Fully Mapped (FM) case.

The Partially Mapped (PM) case occurs if there are some children in the global ontology that cannot be mapped to any of the children in the local schema. For example, in Figure 4, vertices *auto parts* and *electrical* on the left are mapped to vertices *auto parts* and *electrical supplies* on the right using mapping type *exact* for both mappings. But the vertex *construction material* in the global ontology on the left cannot be mapped to any concept in the local schema. As a result, vertex *manufacturing* is automatically mapped using mapping type *superset* to the vertex *production*. Detailed specifications of the deduction process for all possible combinations of vertex mappings, the resulting mappings for their parents and the assumptions upon which the process works have previously been described (Cruz and Rajendran, 2004).

Preliminary experiments were performed to test the effectiveness of the semi-automatic deduction process. The automatic deduction process yielded 20% of the total mappings when two fairly large shallow ontological trees were mapped to each other. More experiments are being run to study the effect of the depth and the width of ontological trees on the performance of the deduction process.

The tool automatically generates an *agreement* file in XML for each local mapping. XML tags and attributes are used within the agreement file to record the semantics of the mappings (Figure 5). For example, the attribute value OAAD (Ontology Agriculture) maps as a superset to two local values for Dane County. And, the ontology code for Multi-Family maps as a subset to Residential. RDF and OWL have emerged as Semantic Web technologies since we implemented our system in XML, but XML was sufficient for our needs. Information from the agreement files is used to generate subqueries sent into Niagara.

Figure 3. Semi-automatic ontology integration: A fully mapped case

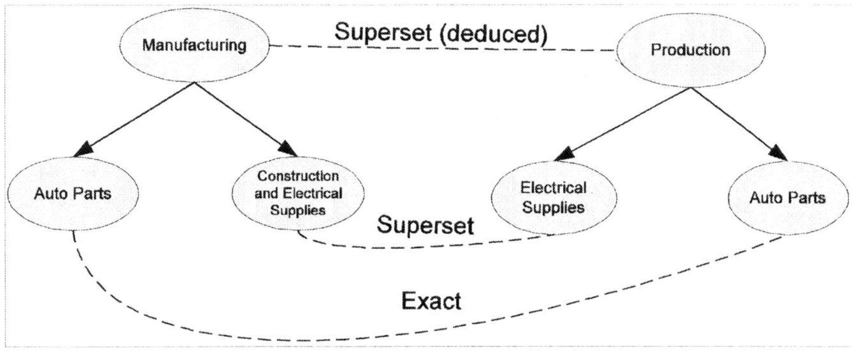

Figure 4. Semi-automatic ontology integration: A partially mapped case

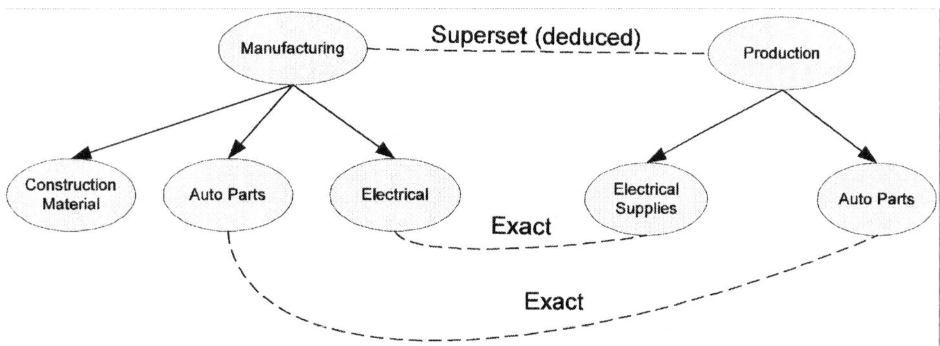

Figure 5. Fragment of an agreement file

```
<attrvalue id="OAAD" mapping="Superset">
    <localvalue>91</localvalue>
    <localvalue>92</localvalue>
</attrvalue>

<attrvalue id="ORMF" mapping="NoMapping">
    <resolve_to>Residential</resolve_to>
</attrvalue>
```

ONTOLOGY-BASED DBMS WEB QUERY SYSTEM

In this section, we present the functionality and flow of our Web query system that extends government portals and clearinghouses such as Geospatial One-Stop or WLIS by providing full DBMS querying over the internal content of the distributed geospatial data sources. We introduce details of the system from the aspects of data provider, system design, and user. Although we illustrate our method using land use codes, we are not limited to that domain. Instead, the method can be generalized to capture semantic differences for any theme, attribute, and set of attribute values.

System Overview

Our system is based on the search and query engines of Niagara, an XML *Internet* DBMS system (Naughton et al., 2001). Contrary to an HTML engine, the Niagara search engine allows *text-in-context* searching in addition to keyword searching. That is, rather than just typing in a keyword, such as *cropland*, one can add context to limit the search by typing, for example, *LandUseCode* ***contains*** *cropland*. This search will yield the URL(s) of the data set(s) that contain a value of *cropland* for an element (attribute) named *LandUseCode*.

Figure 6. System architecture

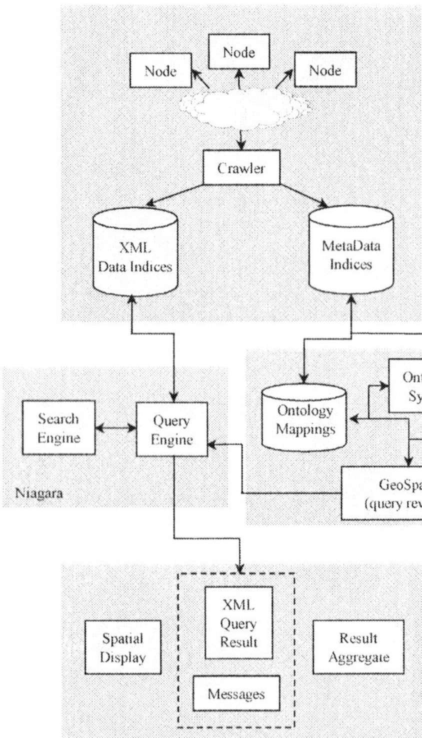

In addition to the search engine, Niagara has a query engine that allows users to pose full DBMS queries using an XML query language, such as XML-QL (Deutsch, Fernandez, Florescu, Levy, & Suciu, 1998). The query engine produces answers to queries rather than URLs. For example, it can return the name of the county that has the greatest acreage of cropland.

Although a system such as Niagara has great potential for Web-based querying, it also has limitations. A significant limitation is that it cannot handle the heterogeneity that exists among conceptually similar data sources that are represented differently. Furthermore, it is not designed to take advantage of the unique characteristics described earlier for government-produced geospatial data—that is, inherent data set organizations such as government jurisdiction and theme, the existence of separate metadata files, and spatial information. For example, although Niagara has an "IN*" statement allowing the user to pose a query over an entire Web space without specifying particular data sources, we modify this idea by extracting metadata information from the user to determine appropriate data sets.

Our system extends the Niagara architecture to support semantic integration (Figure 6). Our modifications include the metadata indexes and ontology mappings, a query rewrite system in an ontology component, and enhanced output displays (Wiegand, Zhou, Cruz, & Sunna, 2004; Wiegand, Zhou, Cruz, & Rajendran, 2002). As described further in the following sections, we provide a custom Graphical User Interface (GUI), and we modified the XML-QL query language to support querying through an ontology. Briefly, our custom GUI captures the user query along with metadata to locate appropriate data sources. Our ontology system locates data sources and their *semantic agreement files,* which contain the correspondences between the land use codes, to perform lookups for query rewriting. Our system supports list and graphical output displays and provides additional semantic information to the user.

Registering Spatial Databases to the Query System

Although Niagara will crawl any XML data found on the Web, it also can range over a subset of the Web. For our prototype, because we need additional information from the data providers, we designed our system assuming a registered set of data producers who include metadata, URLs of data sources, and other related information. An approach requiring registration and authentication also ensures only authorized data are available.

We assume the distributed data are marked up in XML. For our test data, we use land use data sets, which typically are in ArcView GIS (Environmental Systems Research Institute [ESRI]) shapefile format. We converted the spatial and nonspatial components of each data set to one XML file by embedding the spatial coordinates within each feature. We also calculated and included the bounding box extent for each feature to use for our MapObjects (ESRI) spatial display of the results. Figure 7 shows sample XML data for a land parcel in Eau Claire County having a land use code of AR, farm residence.

Figure 7. XML source data

```
<EauClaireLandUseData>
  <LandParcel>
    <area> 1704995.587470 </area>
    <perimeter> 5223.944820 </perimeter>
    <id> 258 </id>
    <lu1> AR </lu1>
    ...
    <town> Wilson </town>
    <xycoords> 477229.236863, ...</xycoords>
    <extent> 477229.236, , , 295553.507 </extent>
  </LandParcel>
  ....
</EauClaireLandUseData>
```

Indexing Data, Metadata, and Ontology Information

Base XML data files are crawled and indexed into inverted lists by Niagara (Figure 6). Our system adds metadata and ontology mapping indexes to the Niagara architecture to supplement the base data index. That is, each land use data set has an associated metadata file (also in XML) and an agreement file. Our minimal metadata currently consists of theme, jurisdiction type, and jurisdiction name, and we create metadata for data sets not already having associated FGDC metadata files. Although all data and their associated files are locally maintained by their providers, the information they contain is centrally indexed. We build an index network from which all data and index information can be retrieved given a few known metadata values. For example, given a land use type, data records together with their schema, metadata, and ontology mappings can be retrieved.

User DBMS Query

Figure 8 shows the initial user interface to our system, which is modeled after Geospatial One-Stop. However, we have an additional link that allows a user to *query* data sources (*Query Distributed Data Content*). For the query option, there are two subsequent steps: metadata selection and database query. Metadata selection is currently designed for Wisconsin jurisdications. Users can choose Wisconsin jurisdiction types (county, city,

Figure 8. User interface

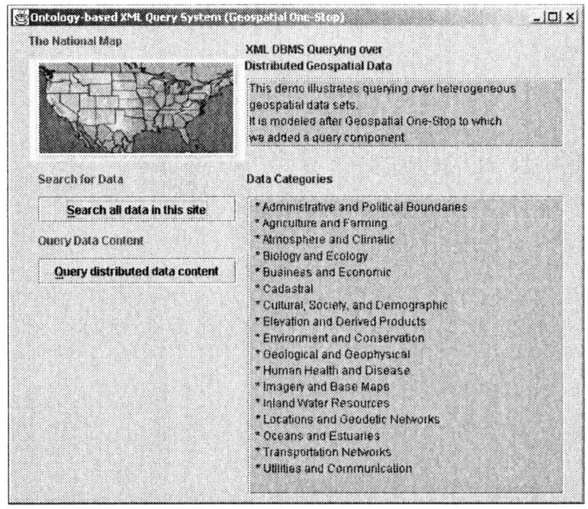

and/or town) and jurisdiction names over which a query will range. All jurisdictions of a type can be chosen (e.g., all counties in the state), or a subset can be specified using dropdown lists or by clicking on a map (limited now to Wisconsin counties). Finally, the user selects one or more themes to query, and the global ontology schemas and values for those themes are presented, allowing the user to pose a DBMS query by selecting terms. Our system currently supports full queries on a land use ontology.

Query Rewrite and Execution

We give an example of our query rewrite with a typical query in a land use application—*Find all cropland in Dane, Racine, and Eau Claire counties*. This type of query is different from a traditional DBMS query, because more than one data source is identified, but there is no join. Instead, the same predicate is applied over multiple data sources. Because the data sources represent geographic areas, we call this type of query a *GeoQuery*. After a user poses a query using an ontology, our system applies a query rewrite method to solve the semantic heterogeneity problem across multiple databases. To indicate the query should consult our ontology component, we developed a *GeoSpace* statement (Figure 9) as a formal representation of the XML-QL query.

Figure 9. BNF for a GeoSpace statement

```
Query ::= Geospace WherePart ConstructPart
        | WherePart ConstructPart ;
Geospace ::= GEOSPACE id = SourceList;
SourceList ::= SourceList, Source | Source;
Source ::= string;
GEOSPACE ::= string;
id ::= string;
```

Figure 10. GeoSpace in an XML-QL query

```
GEOSPACE  Area ="www.co.wi.us/Dane.xml,
                www.co.wi.us/Racine.xml,
                www.co.wi.us/EauClaire.xml"
WHERE <$*>
        <Area:LandUseCode> "cropland" </>
        </> ELEMENT_AS $a
CONSTRUCT $a
```

Figure 11. A generated subquery

```
WHERE <$*>
            <Lucode> "91" </Lucode>
            </> ELEMENT_AS $a
IN www.co.dane.wi.us/Dane.xml
CONSTRUCT $a
```

An example query with a GeoSpace statement is shown in Figure 10. The GeoSpace statement includes a variable—in this instance, *Area*—to hold the list of URLs for the data sources needed in the query. The variable *Area* is also used in the body of the query as a qualifier for generic ontology terms. The syntax "WHERE <$*>" indicates that the XML-QL query ranges over any nested XML element structure having (the equivalent of) a LandUseCode element.

When the query is submitted for execution, a *GeoSpace Interpreter* consults the agreement files (ontology mappings) to translate qualified ontology terms to local terms, and it rewrites the user query into subqueries in local terms specific to a data source. Subqueries are sent into Niagara for execution. An example subquery pertaining to Dane County is shown in Figure 11.

Query Result Display and Semantic Output Messages

Our ontology system reassembles Niagara's results and aggregates by data source. Various summary statistics are calculated such as total land acreage in cropland for each jurisdiction. As a spatial data query system, our system also provides graphical displays of query results using MapObjects (ESRI). Semantic relation information is additionally conveyed, so users can understand what level of semantic interoperability is achieved. For example, *cropland* does not map exactly to Dane County's *cropland/pasture* code (Figures 10 and 11). However, the user will know that a superset is being returned, because our output explicitly includes the query value and the mapped local code(s) for each data set involved in the query.

SUMMARY AND CONCLUSION

Data produced by local governments, in particular, tend to be highly heterogeneous. However, government operations such as land use planning that affect a multi-jurisdictional area require data integration for querying and analysis purposes. Many levels of government are producing geospatial Web sites, such as the Federal Geospatial One-Stop and the Wisconsin Land Information System, that are used for locating data sources. Our goal is to greatly enhance the capabilities of these sites to include query support over data content. To do this, we developed new technology for semantic integration within an Internet query system. We extended work in schema integration by focusing our efforts on resolving differences at the value level. This was needed to be able to query across the many different land use coding systems in use in Wisconsin, for example. However, our method is general enough to be applicable to heterogeneous domains of any attribute, and our framework is complete to handle any data.

We developed a tool to aid local experts in mapping a global ontology to their local schemas and values. The tool automatically generates an XML agreement file in which semantic relationships are stored using XML tags. To formally represent a typical type of query in our application in which the same predicate is applied over multiple data sets, we extended XML-QL with a GeoSpace statement. We have demonstrated our system to government partners and they are extremely interested in the potential of our work regarding automatic or semi-automatic ontology alignment and the ability to do query processing on heterogeneous data sets distributed across the state. Our system achieves the technical goal of designing and implementing a Web-based query system that, in particular, solves the problem of semantic heterogeneity among distributed and independently developed government data sources.

ACKNOWLEDGMENT

This work was partially supported by the Digital Government Program of NSF, Grant No. 091489.

REFERENCES

Alexandria Digital Library. (n.d.). Retrieved August 4, 2004: *http://webclient. alexandria. ucsb.edu*

Bishr, Y. (1998). Overcoming the semantic and other barriers to GIS interoperability. *International Journal of Geographical Information Science, 12*(4), 299-314.

Bouguettaya, A., Benatallah, B., & Elmagarmid, A. (1998). *Interconnecting heterogeneous information systems.* Boston: Kluwer Academic Publishers.

Bray, T., Paoli, J., Sperberg-McQueen, C., Maler, E., & Yergeau, F. (2004). *Extensible markup language (XML) 1.0 (third edition), W3C recommendation 04 February 2004.* Retrieved August 4, 2004: *http://www.w3.org/TR/2004/REC-xml-20040204/*

Bussler, C., Fensel, D., & Maedche, A. (2002). A conceptual architecture for semantic Web enabled Web services. *SIGMOD Record, 31*(4), 24-29.

Content Standard for Digital Geospatial Metadata (CSDGM), Federal Geographic Data Committee (FGDC). Retrieved August 4, 2004: *http://www. fgdc.gov/metadata/meta data.html*

Cox, S., Daisey, P., Lake, R., Portele, C., & Whiteside, A. (2003). *OpenGIS® geography markup language (GML) implementation specification.* Retrieved August 4, 2004: *http://www.opengis. org/docs/02-023r4.pdf*

Cruz, I.F., & Rajendran, A. (2003). Exploring a new approach to the alignment of ontologies. *Proceedings of the Semantic Web Technologies for Searching and Retrieving Scientific Data Workshop, 2nd International Semantic Web Conference*, Sanibel Island, Florida, October 20-23 (pp. 7-12).

Cruz, I.F., Rajendran, A., Sunna, W., & Wiegand, N. (2002). Handling semantic heterogeneities using declarative agreements. In A. Voisard, & S. Chen (Eds.), *Proceedings of ACM GIS* (pp. 168-174).

Cruz, I.F., Sunna, W., & Chaudhry, A. (2004). Ontology alignment for real-world applications. *Proceedings of the National Conference on Digital Government Research*, Seattle, Washington, May 24-26 (pp. 393-394).

Deutsch, A., Fernandez, M., Florescu, D., Levy, A., & Suciu, D. (1998). *XML-QL: A query language for XML.* Retrieved August 4, 2004: *http://www. w3.org/TR/NOTE-xml-ql*

Doan, A., Madhavan, J., Domingos, P., & Halevy, A. (2002). Learning to map between ontologies on the semantic Web. *Proceedings of the WWW2002*, Honolulu, Hawaii, May 7-11.

Environmental Systems Research Institute (ESRI). (n.d.). Retrieved August 4, 2004: *http://www.esri. com*

Everett, J., & Ngo, C. (1999). Land-based classification standards—Federal role. *Proceedings of the American Planning Association National Planning Conference.* Retrieved August 4, 2004:

http://www.asu.edu/caed/proceedings99/LBCS/EVERETT.HTM

Federal Geographic Data Committee (FGDC) Clearinghouse. (n.d.). Retrieved August 4, 2004: *http://www.fgdc.gov/clearinghouse/clearinghouse.html*

Fensel, D. (2001). *Ontologies: Silver bullet for knowledge management and electronic commerce*. Berlin: Springer-Verlag.

Fonseca, F., Egenhofer, M., Agouris, P., & Camara, G. (2002). Using ontologies for integrated geographic information systems. *Transactions in GIS*, *6*(3), 231-257.

Ganster, P., & Wright, R. (eds.) (2000). San Diego-Tijuana international border area planning atlas. *Institute for Regional Studies of the Californias, San Diego State University.* Retrieved August 4, 2004: *http://www-rohan.sdsu.edu/~irsc/atlas/atlashom.html*

Ganter, B. & Wille, R. (2004). *Formal concept analysis: Mathematical foundations*. Springer Verlag.

Geospatial One-Stop (2003). Retrieved August 4, 2004: *http://www.geo data.gov and http://www.geo-one-stop.gov*

Hernandez, M., Miller, R., & Haas, L. (2001). Clio: A semi-automatic tool for schema mapping, demo. *Proceedings of the 2001 ACM SIGMOD International Conference of the Management of Data*, Santa Barbara, California, May 21-24 (p. 607).

LandXML. (n.d.). Retrieved August 4, 2004: *http://www.landxml.org*

Maier D., & Delcambre, L. (1999). Superimposed information for the Internet. *Proceedings of the ACM SIGMOD Workshop on the Web and Databases (WebDB '99)*, Philadelphia, Pennsylvania (pp. 1-9).

Malyankar, R. (2002, May). Vocabulary development for markup languages—A case study with maritime information. *Proceedings of the WWW2002*, Honolulu, Hawaii.

Miller, R., et al. (2001). The Clio project: Managing heterogeneity. *SIGMOD Record*, *30*(1), 78-83.

National Integrated Land System (NILS). (n.d.). Retrieved August 4, 2004: *http://www.blm.gov/nils*

Naughton, J., et al. (2001). The Niagara Internet query system. *IEEE Data Engineering Bulletin*, *24*(2), 27-33.

Open GIS Consortium (OGC), Inc. (n.d.). Retrieved August 4, 2004: *http://www. opengeospatial.org*

OpenGIS® Abstract Specification (1999). Topic 14: Semantics and information communities, version 4. *Open GIS Consortium.* Retrieved August 9, 2004: *http://www.opengis.org/docs/99-114.pdf*

Rahm, E. & Bernstein, P. 2001. A survey of approaches to automatic schema matching. *VLDB Journal, 10*(4), 334-350.

Sheth, A.P., & Larson, J.A. (1990). Federated database systems and managing distributed, heterogeneous, and autonomous databases. *ACM Computing Surveys*, *22*(3), 83-226.

Staab, S. & Studer, R. (eds.) (2004). *Handbook on ontologies*. Springer.

Theobald, A., & Weikum, G. (2000). The index-based XXL search engine for querying XML data with relevance ranking. *Proceedings of EDBT 2000* (pp. 477-495).

Wiegand, N., Zhou, N., Cruz, I.F., & Rajendran, A. (2002). Querying heterogeneous GIS land use data over the Web. *Proceedings of GIScience 2002 Abstracts*, Boulder, Colorado (pp. 207-210).

Wiegand, N., Zhou, N., Cruz, I.F., & Sunna, W. (2004). Ontology-based geospatial XML query system. *Proceedings of the National Conference on Digital Government Research,* Demo (pp. 289-290).

Wisconsin Land Information Clearinghouse (WiscLinc). (n.d.). Retrieved August 4, 2004: *http://wisclinc.state.wi.us*

Wisconsin Land Information System (WLIS) Core Node Pilot Project. (n.d.). Retrieved August 4, 2004: *http://wlis.dnr.state.wi.us/wlis*

Wisconsin Land Information System (WLIS) Project Team (2000). Final report of the Wisconsin land information system project team. Retrieved August 9, 2004: *http://wlis.dnr.state.wi.us/wlis/downloads/background/wlis_project_team_report_sep2000.pdf*

Zhou, N. (2003). Automatic ontology mapping of categorical information. *Proceedings of the National Conference on Digital Government Research*, Boston, Massachusetts (pp. 401-404).

Zhou, N. & Wiegand, N. (2004). *Formal concept analysis for semantic integration.* Technical Report.

This work was previously published in International Journal of Electronic Government Research, Vol. 1, No. 2, edited by M. Khosrow-Pour, pp. 64-82, copyright 2005 by IGI Publishing, formerly known as Idea Group Publishing (an imprint of IGI Global).

Chapter LXIX
Digital Government Worldwide:
An E-Government Assessment of Municipal Web Sites

James Melitski
Marist College, Poughkeepsie, USA

Marc Holzer
Rutgers University – Campus at Newark, USA

Seang-Tae Kim
Sungkyunkwan University, South Korea

Chan-Gun Kim
Rutgers University – Campus at Newark, USA

Seung-Yong Rho
Rutgers University – Campus at Newark, USA

ABSTRACT

This article evaluates the current practice of digital government in large municipalities worldwide. The study assesses 84 cities from around the world that use a five-stage e-government framework. Our research and methodology goes beyond previous research by utilizing 92 measures that were translated into the native language of each city. In addition, the assessment of each municipal web site was conducted by a native speaker of the municipality's language between June and October of 2003. We reviewed relevant e-government literature for evaluating Web sites nationally and internationally, and discussed our sample selection, methodology, theoretical framework, findings, and recommendations. Our results indicate that Seoul, Hong Kong, Singapore, New York, and Shanghai are the top five large cities for providing digital government opportunities to citizens online. Our research also suggests a difference in the digital government capabilities among the 30 developed nations belonging to the Organization for Economic Cooperation and Development (OECD) and lesser developed (non-OECD) nations.

ASSESSING MUNICIPAL WEB SITES

What are the objectives and rationale for public sector services? Some scholars have suggested a list of questions that public administrations have faced, including "How can the public sector achieve efficiency and effectiveness, at the same time balancing those concerns with equity in service delivery?" (Holzer & Gabrielian, 1998, p. 49) and "How can the public sector bring about a more honest dialogue between citizens and their governments?" (Nathan quoted in Holzer & Gabrielian, 1998, p. 79). Since public organizations should be efficient and effective (i.e., productive internally), and should pursue such democratic values as equality, equity, and participation for a better society externally, both dimensions are important to service delivery.

Technological utopians (Blanchard & Horan, 1998; Dyson et al., 1994; Firssen, 1997; Klein, 1999; Winner, 1997) have suggested that information and communication technologies (ICTs) are conducive to both efficient and effective public organizations. In addition, they have argued that ICTs enable citizens to engage in policy deliberation (see Holzer et al., 2004). Following this logic, e-government researchers have examined in recent years how public organizations are using the Internet. They have often sought to answer two questions: (1) Why do public organizations adopt new initiatives such as e-government programs? (2) Why are some initiatives more successful than others?

One way that researchers determine success is to assess performance of organizations that adopt e-government criteria by developing such criteria and conducting a content analysis of government web sites. Unfortunately, most of this literature focuses on state and federal governments in the U.S. in terms of examining trends in digital government (the Center for Digital Government and Microsoft Corp. 2002, 2003). At the local level, a notable survey was conducted of local government managers in conjunction with the International City/Country Management Association and Public Technologies Inc. (Holden et al., 2003; Norris et al., 2001).

Little research has been conducted on analyzing the worldwide movement to digital government from a comparative perspective. Researchers at Brown University, led by Darrell West, have conducted a content analysis of US states and federal government web sites in the US since 2000; they also completed in 2001 a worldwide analysis of central government web sites. A summary of the results was published recently in the *Public Administration Review* (West, 2004). West's research finds an improvement of digital service delivery at federal, state, local, and international levels.

Previous research, however, lacks a comprehensive framework for evaluating digital government. Such studies have paid attention to a few aspects of digital service delivery, comparing limited aspects of public organizations. They have not provided specific exemplars of practices and conditions necessary to successfully reproduce each best practice. Furthermore, their research that evaluates web site content consists of only 27 dichotomous variables (West 2004). This research attempts to take a more comprehensive approach by utilizing 92 measures, of which 45 are dichotomous and 47 are measures that use a four-point scale.

This research also utilizes a theoretical framework that is consistent with e-government and e-government literature. In 2002, Moon developed a framework for e-government analysis that consists of five stages:

1. Information dissemination/catalogue
2. Two-way communication
3. Service and financial transactions
4. Vertical and horizontal integration
5. Political (citizen) participation

Based on Moon's research, one can imply performance improvement as a progression from "Stage 1 Information Dissemination" through "Stage 5 Citizen Participation." From a theoretical perspective, Ho (2002) describes performance improvement as a paradigm shift from a bureaucratic paradigm toward an e-government paradigm. According to Ho, "the new (e-government) paradigm transforms organizational principles in government. While the bureaucratic model emphasizes top-down management and hierarchical communication, the new model emphasizes teamwork, multidirectional networks, direct communication between parties, and a fast feedback loop" (Ho, 2002).

Ho argues that while the shift between paradigms is occurring at the city level, socioeconomic and organizational barriers are slowing the process to the point where city government web sites are not reaching their fullest potentials. In contrast, Melitski (2003) argues that e-government and the use of the Internet by public organizations is value neutral. While Melitski's information technology (IT) and public administration paradigms are similar to Ho's bureaucratic and e-government paradigms, Melitski argues that adoption of Internet technologies does not automatically progress to open, accountable government (e.g., the public administration paradigm).

Instead, Melitski argues for the existence of two competing paradigms similar to Burrell and Morgan (1979). Melitski argues that organizational and cultural factors influence whether public managers will use the Internet and e-government to exert central control over their organization (IT paradigm), or decentralize and empower their organization (public administration paradigm). In other words, while other e-government theorists argue that adoption of e-government leads to the idealistic use of technology to empower citizens, we believe that competing paradigms within public organizations may hinder such a paradigm shift. Despite our value neutral view of technology, we do believe that the greatest potential for Internet use in public organizations lies in applications designed to facilitate open communication between agencies and create dialogue between citizens and their government. This research uses a five-stage continuum based on previous research, with citizen participation as the fifth stage.

Along with these theoretical movements, our society has been engaged in an ongoing transformation process from an industrial to an information based society. Rapid change in ICTs has further expedited this trend. Moreover, technological change creates new challenges and opportunities for social and political organization (Kamarck & Nye, 2002; O'Looney, 2002). In order to facilitate efficiency and effectiveness in digital government, public organizations have begun to apply performance measurement to examine digital government initiatives.

Even though there has been a growing use of digital government, there are also certain problems that prevent efficient and effective implementation. For instance, in terms of the digital divide, there has always been a gap between those people and communities that can make effective use of ICTs and those that cannot. Now more than ever, unequal adoption of technology excludes many from reaping the fruits of the economy (Norris, 1999). In addition, there are recent calls for increased security, particularly of our public information infrastructure. Concern over the security of the information systems underlying government applications has led some researchers to the conclusion that e-government must be built on a secure infrastructure that respects the privacy of its users (Kaylor, 2001).

INTERNATIONAL DIGITAL GOVERNMENT EFFORTS

Digital government development is now constant and conspicuous. It has received considerable attention through a steady stream of events at the national and international levels (Bertelsmann Foundation, 2003; DigitalGovernance.org Initiative). The Bertelsmann Foundation conducted research on "Balanced E-Government," and their international study identifies criteria of success for outstanding e-government performance in local government administration. The Bertelsmann project differentiates between e-administration and e-democracy. E-administration is represented by "transaction of user oriented services offered by public institutions that are based on information and communication technologies." E-democracy is "digitally conveyed information and the political influence exerted by citizens and business on the opinion-forming process of public (institutions)." Furthermore, the study also measures how far the concepts of e-administration and e-democracy have been integrated by public agencies online.

Digital government has become a high priority throughout the world. No country wants to be left behind in the movement to improve government through electronic delivery of information and services (Pardo, 2000). While most of the research on digital government has focused on advanced countries, the World Bank E-Government web site focuses on digital government in developing countries (www1.worldbank.org/publicsector/egov). The World Bank provides cases studies as a source of ideas in the areas of better service delivery to citizens, improved services for business, transparency and anticorruption efforts, empowerment through information, and efficient government purchasing.

In addition to the World Bank, the Digital-Governance.org initiative focused on digital governance in developing countries in terms of building accountable and democratic governance institutions using ICTs. It presents five generic e-governance models: broadcasting model, critical flow model, comparative analysis model, e-advocacy model, and interactive service model, as well as many case studies in developing countries.

In 2001, an international report on national web sites was published by the United Nations and the American Society for Public Administration in consultation with the National Center for Public Productivity at Rutgers University — Campus at Newark. The report, "Benchmarking E-government: A Global Perspective," used a framework similar to our research. According to the report, "National government websites were analyzed for the content and services available that the average citizen would most likely use. The presence or absence of specific features contributed to determining a country's level of progress. The stages (emerging web presence, enhanced web presence, interactive presence, transactional web presence, and fully integrated web presence) present a straightforward benchmark which objectively assesses a country's online sophistication" (UN/ASPA, 2001:1).

Digital government has become a new part of the government structure. However, parochial perspectives limit opportunities to increase experimentation, innovation, and organizational learning pertinent to digital government. It is important to understand existing gaps in government theory and practice, including both traditional and digital perspectives, between Western and non-Western nations (Welch & Wong, 1998). Fortunately, the global study of digital government is advancing, and such efforts may contribute to its continued development.

In this context, our research evaluates the current practices of digital governments in municipalities worldwide. This research focuses on the evaluation of current practices on the supply side (government), not the demand side (citizen). Our emphasis is on the evaluation of each city government's web site in terms of security, usability, and content of web sites, the type of online services currently being offered, and citizen response and participation.

SAMPLE

This research examines cities throughout the world based on their population size, the total number of individuals using the Internet, and the percentage of individuals using the Internet. The cities were selected using International Telecommunication Union's (ITU) "Internet Indicators" (2002). The ITU data lists the online population for each of 196 countries[1], and our initial sample consisted of the largest municipalities within the 98 UN member countries with an online population greater than 100,000. For example, in the U.S. and South Korea, New York and Seoul were chosen, respectively. In addition, Hong Kong SAR and Macao SAR were added to the 98 cities selected, since they have been considered independent countries for many years and have high percentages of Internet users.

The rationale for selecting the largest municipalities stems from the e-government literature, which suggests a positive relationship between population and e-government capacity at the local level (Moon, 2002; Moon & deLeon, 2001; Musso et al., 2000; Weare et al., 1999). Table 1 is a list of the 100 cities selected.

*Table 1. 100 cities selected by continent (2004 Population in 1000s)***

Asia (30) Country	Pop.
Almaty (Kazakhstan)	1025.7
Amman (Jordan)	1308.3
Baku (Azerbaijan)*	1240.8
Bangkok (Thailand)	6709.2
Beirut (Lebanon)	446.3
Bishkek (Kyrgyzstan)*	841.1
Colombo (Sri Lanka)	669.7
Dhaka (Bangladesh)	9363.1
Dubai (United Arab Emirates)	940.6
Ho Chi Minh (Vietnam)	3452.1
Hong Kong SAR (Hong Kong SAR)	6855***
Istanbul (Turkey)	9631.7
Jakarta (Indonesia)	8987.8
Jerusalem (Israel)	708.5
Karachi (Pakistan)	10889
Kuala Lumpur (Malaysia)	1440.3
Kuwait City (Kuwait)*	152.1
Macao SAR (Macao SAR)	445***
Manama (Bahrain)	154.7
Mumbai (India)	12623
Muscat (Oman)*	880.2
Nicosia (Cyprus)	200.7
Quezon City (Philippines)	10330
Riyadh (Saudi Arabia)	3822.6
Seoul (Korea)	9551.8
Shanghai (China)	13279
Singapore (Singapore)	3499.5
Tashkent (Uzbekistan)	2299.4
Tehran (Iran)	7317.2
Tokyo (Japan)	8273.9

Europe (34) Country	Pop.
Amsterdam (Netherlands)	742.3
Athens (Greece)	762.1
Belgrade (Serbia and Montenegro)	1126.9
Berlin (Germany)	3396.3
Bratislava (Slovak Republic)	428.8
Brussels (Belgium)	983.9
Bucharest (Romania)	1897.1
Budapest (Hungary)	1729.8
Copenhagen (Denmark)	1100.7
Dublin (Ireland)	1027.9
Helsinki (Finland)	590.6
Kyiv (Ukraine)	2598.0
Lisboa (Portugal)	560.7
Ljubljana (Slovenia)	258.7
London (United Kingdom)	7465.1
Luxembourg City (Luxembourg)	79.8
Madrid (Spain)	3290.9
Minsk (Belarus)*	1682.9
Moscow (Russia)	11247
Oslo (Norway)	799.2
Paris (France)	2107.6
Prague (Czech Republic)	1165.2
Reykjavik (Iceland)	116.5
Riga (Latvia)	687.7
Rome (Italy)	2453.1
Sarajevo (Bosnia and Herzegovina)	602.5
Sofia (Bulgaria)	1084.7
Stockholm (Sweden)	1264.8
Tallinn (Estonia)	372.1
Vienna (Austria)	1504.1
Vilnius (Lithuania)	544.0
Warsaw (Poland)	1676.6
Zagreb (Croatia)	682.3
Zurich (Switzerland)	351.7

North America (12) Country	Pop.
Ciudad de Mexico (Mexico)	8705.1
Guatemala City (Guatemala)	999.4
Havana (Cuba)*	2359.2
Kingston (Jamaica)*	594.5
New York (United States)	8134.8
Panama City (Panama)	445.8
Port-of-Spain (Trinidad & Tobago)	50.6
San Jose (Costa Rica)	346.8
San Salvador (El Salvador)	513.4
Santo Domingo (Dominican Republic)*	2240.5
Tegucigalpa (Honduras)	470.5
Toronto (Canada)	4558.8

Africa (12) Country	Pop.
Algiers (Algeria)*	2004.0
Cairo (Egypt)	1790.7
Cape Town (South Africa)	8113.6
Casablanca (Morocco)*	2984.1
Dakar (Senegal)*	3741.2
Dar-es-Salaam (Tanzania)*	2613.7
Harare (Zimbabwe)*	1976.4
Lagos (Nigeria)*	8682.2
Lome (Togo)*	695.1
Nairobi (Kenya)	2504.4
Port Louis (Mauritius)	143.6
Tunis (Tunisia)*	704.7

South America (10) Country	Pop.
Asuncion (Paraguay)	539.2
Buenos Aires (Argentina)	11928
Caracas (Venezuela)	1719.6
Guayaquil (Ecuador)	2044.7
La Paz (Bolivia)	850.0
Lima (Peru)	8380.3
Montevideo (Uruguay)	1346.9
Santa Fe De Bogota (Colombia)	6981.5
Santiago (Chile)	4434.9
Sao Paulo (Brazil)	10333

Oceania (2) Country	Pop.
Auckland (New Zealand)	374.3
Sydney (Australia)	4305.5

* Official city web site unavailable

** Population data from the 2004 World Gazetteer (except for Hong Kong and Macao): www.world-gazetteer.com

*** Population data for Hong Kong and Macao from the 2004 World Sourcebook: http://www.odci.gov/cia/publications/factbook/

For our purposes, the main city home page was defined as the official web site where information about city administration and online services is provided by the city. City web sites typically included information about the city council, mayor, and executive branch of the city. Separate home pages for agencies, departments, or the city council were examined only if the sites were linked to the menu on the main city home page. If the web site was not linked, it was excluded from evaluation.

Sixteen of the initial 100 cities were excluded from our research for lack of an official city web site: eight in Africa (67%), four in Asia (13.33%), one in Europe (2.94%), and three in North America (25%). As a result, this research evaluated only 84 of the 100 cities initially selected.

METHODOLOGY

Our instrument for evaluating city and municipal web sites builds on previous research that identifies content, transactional services, and citizen participation as critical components of e-government (Moon, 2001). Furthermore, in recent years many U.S. citizens have become more aware of the need for increased security and privacy of government. A recent poll conducted by Hart-Teeter in conjunction with the Council for Excellence in Government (2003) found that Americans are cautiously aware of possible risks associated with digital government. The Hart-Teeter poll states:

> *Nearly 44% of Americans strongly agree that if they submit personal information about themselves to government websites, government will be able to provide them with better services.... This concern about privacy and security translates into a cautionary tone from Americans: a 54% majority think that government should proceed slowly in relying on the Internet for communication between citizens and government.* (Hart-Teeter, 2003, p. 2)

In addition, we have added an additional area of emphasis for our analysis that examines web

Table 2. E-government measures

E-government Category	Number of Key Concepts	Raw Score	Weighted Score	Keywords
Security/ Privacy	19	28	20	Privacy policies, authentication, encryption, data management, and use of cookies
Usability	20	32	20	User-friendly design, branding, length of homepage, targeted audience links or channels, and site search capabilities
Content	19	47	20	Access to current accurate information, public documents, reports, publications, and multimedia materials
Service	20	57	20	Transactional services involving purchase or register, interaction between citizens, businesses and government
Citizen Participation	14	39	20	Online civic engagement, internet based policy deliberation, and citizen based performance measurement
Total	92	203	100	

site usability. Our final instrument consists of five components: (1) security and privacy; (2) usability; (3) content; (4) services; and (5) citizen participation. Table 2 summarizes the measures used in our research to assess a web site's capabilities in each of those five categories.

Previous e-government research varies in the use of scales to evaluate government web sites. For example, while West (2000, 2001, 2004) uses an index consisting of about 27 dichotomous (yes or no) measures, other assessments use a four-point scale (Kaylor, 2001) for assessing each measure. Our research instrument goes well beyond previous research, utilizing 92 measures, of which 45 are dichotomous. For each of the five components in our theoretical framework, the study applies 14 to 20 measures, and each measure was coded on a four-point scale of increasing technological sophistication (0, 1, 2, 3) (see Table 3). Furthermore, in developing an overall score for each municipality, we have equally weighted the five categories to avoid skewing the research in favor of a particular category (regardless of the number of questions in each category). The remaining 47 measures were scored according to the scale in Table 3. The dichotomous measures in the "service" and "citizen participation" categories correspond with values on our four-point scale of "0" or "3"; dichotomous measures in "security/ privacy" or "usability" correspond to ratings of "0" or "1" on our four-point scale.

Our instrument places a higher value on some dichotomous measures due to the relative value and technical complexity of the different e-government services being evaluated. For example, evaluators using our instrument in the "service" category were given the option of scoring web sites as either "0" or "3" when assessing whether a site allowed users to access private information online (e.g., educational records, medical records, point total of driving violations, lost property). "No access" equated to a rating of "0." Allowing residents or employees to access private information online was a higher order task that required more technical competence, and was clearly an online service, or "3," as defined in Table 3.

On the other hand, when assessing a site's privacy statement or policy, evaluators were given the choices of scoring the site as "0" or "1." The presence or absence of a security policy was clearly a content issue that emphasized placing information online, and corresponded with a value of "1" on the scale outlined in Table 3. The differential values assigned to dichotomous categories were useful in comparing the different components of municipal web sites with one another.

To ensure reliability, each municipal web site was assessed by two evaluators in the site's native language, and, in cases where a significant variation (+ or – 10%) existed on the raw score between evaluators, web sites were analyzed a third time. Furthermore, an example for each measure indi-

Table 3. E-government scale

Scale	Description
0	Information about a given topic does not exist on the website
1	Information about a given topic exists on the website (including links to other information and e-mail addresses)
2	Downloadable items are available on the website (forms, audio, video, and other one-way transactions, popup boxes)
3	Services, transactions, or interactions can take place completely online (credit card transactions, applications for permits, searchable databases, use of cookies, digital signatures, restricted access)

cated how to score the variable. Evaluators were also given comprehensive written instructions for assessing web sites.

FRAMEWORK

This section details our theoretical framework and discusses specific measures used to evaluate web sites. The discussion of security and privacy examines privacy policies and issues related to authentication. Discussion of the usability category involves traditional Web pages, forms, and search tools. The content category is addressed in terms of access to contact information, public documents, multimedia, time-sensitive information, and disability access. The section on services examines interactive services, services that allow users to purchase or pay for services, and the ability of users to apply or register for municipal events or services online. Finally, the measures for citizen participation involve examining how local governments are engaging citizens and providing mechanisms for citizens to participate in government online.

The first part of our analysis examined the security and privacy of municipal web sites in two key areas: privacy policies and authentication of users. In examining municipal privacy policies, we determined whether policies were available on every page that accepted data, and whether or not the word "privacy" was used in the link to such policies. We were also interested in determining if privacy policies identified the agencies collecting the information, and whether the policy identified exactly what data were being collected on the site.

Our analysis determined if the intended use of the data was explicitly stated on the web site. The analysis examined whether the privacy policy addressed the use or sale of data collected on the web site by outside or third party organizations. Our research also determined if there was an option to decline the disclosure of personal information to third parties[2]. This included other municipal agencies, other state and local government offices, or businesses in the private sector. Furthermore, we examined privacy policies to determine if third party agencies or organizations were governed by the same privacy policies as the municipal web site. We also determined whether users had the ability to review personal data records and contest inaccurate or incomplete information.

In examining factors affecting the security and privacy of local government web sites, we addressed managerial measures that limit access of data and assure that they were not used for unauthorized purposes. The use of encryption in the transmission of data, as well as the storage of personal information on secure servers, was also examined. We also determined if web sites used digital signatures to authenticate users. In assessing how or whether municipalities used their web sites to authenticate users, we examined whether public or private information was accessible through a restricted area that required a password and/or registration.

A growing e-government trend at the local level is for municipalities to offer their web site users access to public, and in some cases private, information online. Other research has discussed the government issues associated with sites that choose to charge citizens for access to public information (West, 2001). We add our own concern about the impact of the digital divide if public records are available only through the Internet or if municipalities insist on charging a fee for access to public records. Our analysis specifically addresses online access to public databases by determining if public information such as property tax assessments or private information like court documents is available to users of municipal web sites. In addition, there are concerns that public agencies will use their web sites to monitor citizens or create profiles based on the information they access online. For example, many web sites use "cookies" or "web beacons"[3] to customize web sites for users, but the technology can also be used to monitor Internet habits and profile visitors to web sites. Our analysis examined municipal privacy policies to determine if they addressed the use of cookies or web beacons.

This research also examined the usability of municipal web sites. Simply stated, we wanted to know if sites were "user-friendly." To address usability concerns, we adapted several best practices and measures from other public and private sector research (Giga, 2000)[4]. Our analysis of usability examined three types of web sites: traditional Web pages, forms, and search tools. To evaluate traditional Web pages written using hypertext markup language (html), we examined issues such as branding and structure (e.g., consistent color, font, graphics, page length, etc.). For example, we looked to see if all pages used consistent color, formatting, "default colors" (e.g., blue links and purple visited links), and underlined text to indicate links. We also examined whether system hardware and software requirements were clearly stated on the web site.

In addition, our research examined each municipality's home page to determine if it was too long (two or more screen lengths) or if alternative versions of long documents such as .pdf or .doc files were available. The use of targeted audience links or "channels" to customize the web site for specific groups such as citizens, businesses, or other public agencies was also examined. We looked for the consistent use of navigation bars and links to the home page on every page. The availability of a "site map" or hyperlinked outline of the entire web site was examined. Our assessment also examined whether duplicated link names connected to the same content.

We examined online forms to determine their usability in submitting data or conducting searches of municipal web sites. We looked at issues such as whether field labels aligned appropriately with fields, whether fields were accessible by keystrokes (e.g., tabs), or whether the cursor was automatically placed in the first field. We also examined whether required fields were noted explicitly, and whether the tab order of fields was logical. For example, after a user filled out his or her first name and pressed the tab key, did the cursor automatically go to the surname field? Alternatively, did the page skip to another field such as zip code, only to return to the surname later?

We also checked to see if form pages provided additional information about how to fix errors if they were submitted. For example, did users have to reenter information if errors were submitted, or did the site flag incomplete or erroneous forms before accepting them? Also, did the site give a confirmation page after a form was submitted, or did it return users to the home page?

Our analysis also addressed the use of search tools on municipal web sites. We examined sites to determine if help was available for searching a municipality's web site, or if the scope of searches could be limited to specific areas of the site. Were users able to search only in "public works" or "the mayor's office," or did the search tool always search the entire site? We also looked for advanced search features such as exact phrase searching, the ability to match any or all words, and Boolean searching capabilities (e.g., the ability to use and/or/not operators). Our analysis also addressed a site's ability to sort search results by relevance or other criteria.

Content is a critical component of any web site. No matter how technologically advanced a web site's features are, if its content is not current, if the site is difficult to navigate, or if the information provided is not correct, then it is not fulfilling its purpose. When examining web site content, our research examined five key areas: contact information, public documents, disability access, multimedia materials, and time-sensitive information.

When addressing contact information, we looked for information about each agency represented on the web site. In addition, we also looked for the availability of office hours or a schedule of agency office hours. In assessing the availability of public documents, we looked for the availability of the municipal code or charter online. We also looked for content items such as agency mission statements and minutes of public meetings. Other content items included budget information and publications. Our assessment also examined whether web sites provided access to disabled users either through "bobby compliance" (disability access for the blind; see http://www.cast.org/bobby) or disability access for deaf users via a TDD phone service. We also checked to see if sites offered content in more than one language.

Time-sensitive information that was examined included the use of a municipal web site for emergency management, and the use of a web site as an alert mechanism (e.g., terrorism alert or severe weather alert). We also checked for time-sensitive information such as job vacancies or a calendar of community events. In addressing the use of multimedia, we examined each site to determine if audio or video files of public events, speeches, or meetings were available.

A critical component of e-government is the provision of municipal services online. Our analysis examined two different types of services: (1) those that allow citizens to interact with the municipality, and (2) services that allow users to register for municipal events or services online. In many cases, municipalities have developed the capacity to accept payment for municipal services and taxes. The first type of service examined, which implies interactivity, can be as basic as forms that allow users to request information or file complaints. Local governments across the world use advanced interactive services to allow users to report crimes or violations, customize municipal home pages based on their needs (e.g., portal customization), and access private information online such as court records, education records, or medical records. Our analysis examined municipal web sites to determine if such interactive services were available.

The second type of service examined in this research determined if municipalities have the capacity to allow citizens to register for municipal services online. For example, many jurisdictions now allow citizens to apply for permits and licenses online. Online permitting can be used for services that vary from building permits to dog licenses. In addition, some local governments are using the Internet for procurement, allowing potential contractors to access requests for proposals or even bid for municipal contracts online. In other cases, local governments are chronicling the procurement process by listing the total number of bidders for a contract online, and in some cases listing contact information for bidders.

This analysis also examined municipal web sites to determine if they had the capacity to allow users to purchase or pay for municipal services and fees online. Examples of transactional services across the United States include the payment of public utility bills and parking tickets online. In many jurisdictions, cities and municipalities allow online users to file or pay local taxes, or pay fines such as traffic tickets. In some cases, cities around the world are allowing their users to register or purchase tickets to events in city halls or arenas online.

While this research evaluates a city's capacity or ability to implement transactional services, it should be noted that the research does not account for the total number of transactions a city offers. Cities that offer three transactional services received the same score as cities with 20 services. In addition, we recognize that not all transactions are equal, and technological sophistication among different transactional services varies. In other words, while we evaluate a city's capacity to implement basic transactional services, we do not determine whether the transactional service implemented is one of greater or lesser technological sophistication.

Finally, perhaps the most untapped area of e-government involves using the Internet to engage citizens in democratic processes. Citizen participation in government is a ripe area for e-government, in part because the Internet is a convenient mechanism for citizen users to engage their government, and because of the potential to decentralize decision making. Despite that potential, very few public agencies offer online opportunities for civic engagement. We looked at several ways public agencies at the local level were involving citizens. For example, do municipal web sites allow users to provide online comments or feedback to individual agencies or elected officials?

Our analysis examined whether local governments offer current information about municipal government online or through an online newsletter or e-mail listserv. We also examined the use of Internet-based polls about specific local issues. In addition, our research examined whether communities allow users to participate and view the results of citizen satisfaction surveys online. For example, some municipalities used their web sites to measure performance and published the results of performance measurement activities online.

Other municipalities used online bulletin boards or other chat capabilities for gathering input on public issues. Most often, online bulletin boards offer citizens the opportunity to post ideas, comments, or opinions without specific discussion topics. In some cases, agencies attempt to structure online discussions around policy issues or specific agencies. Our research looked for municipal use of the Internet to foster civic engagement and citizen participation in government.

This study does have some limitations — unique cultural, customary, and institutional considerations — even though we have made concerted attempts to reduce them. We do offer this research as progress in solving the problems of developing reliable and valid evaluation criteria for digital government.

FINDINGS & RECOMMENDATIONS

Table 4 lists the top 20 cities in digital government. The table lists city scores in each of the five categories of our framework. The maximum score for each category was 20, and the maximum total score was 100. Of the top five cities, four ranked first in at least one category in our framework.

Table 4. Top 20 cities in digital government

Ranking	City	Country	Score	Privacy	Usability	Content	Service	Participation
1	Seoul	Republic of Korea	73.48	11.07	17.50	13.83	15.44	15.64
2	Hong Kong SAR	Hong Kong SAR	66.57	15.36	19.38	13.19	14.04	4.62
3	Singapore	Singapore	62.97	11.79	14.06	14.04	13.33	9.74
4	New York	United States	61.35	11.07	15.63	14.68	12.28	7.69
5	Shanghai	China	58.00	9.64	17.19	11.28	12.46	7.44
6	Rome	Italy	54.72	6.79	14.69	9.57	13.16	10.51
7	Auckland	New Zealand	54.61	7.86	16.88	11.06	10.35	8.46
8	Jerusalem	Israel	50.34	5.71	18.75	10.85	5.79	9.23
9	Tokyo	Japan	46.52	10.00	15.00	10.00	6.14	5.38
10	Toronto	Canada	46.35	8.57	16.56	9.79	5.79	5.64
11	Helsinki	Finland	45.09	8.57	15.94	11.70	6.32	2.56
12	Macao SAR	Macao SAR	44.18	4.29	17.19	11.91	7.72	3.08
13	Stockholm	Sweden	44.07	0.00	13.75	14.68	10.00	5.64
14	Tallinn	Estonia	43.10	3.57	13.13	12.55	6.67	7.18
15	Copenhagen	Denmark	41.349	4.643	13.438	9.787	5.789	7.692
16	Paris	France	41.338	6.429	14.375	7.660	5.439	7.436
17	Dublin	Ireland	38.85	2.50	13.44	11.28	7.02	4.62
18	Dubai	United Arab Emirates	37.48	7.86	10.94	7.87	8.25	2.56
19	Sydney	Australia	37.41	6.79	12.19	9.15	5.44	3.85
20	Jakarta	Indonesia	37.28	0.00	16.56	9.79	6.32	4.62

For example, Seoul excelled in service delivery and citizen participation, Hong Kong ranked highest in Privacy/Security and usability, and New York led all cities in providing content on its municipal web site.

Tables 5-10 list the top 10 cities in the categories of privacy/security, usability, content, service delivery, and citizen participation.

Our research also suggests a difference in the digital government capabilities between the 30 developed nations belonging to the Organization for Economic Co-operation and Development (OECD) and lesser-developed (non-OECD) nations.

For example, Table 10 shows that although the average score for digital government in municipalities throughout the world is 28.49 out of 100, the average score in OECD countries is higher (36.34) while the average score in non-OECD countries is lower (24.26). Whereas 19 of 28 cities in OECD countries are above the world average, only 16 of 52 cities in non-OECD countries are above that average. Interestingly, 32 of 52 cities in non-OECD countries are below the average score for that group of countries.

There were also regional differences. For example, 67% of cities in Africa, 13% in Asia, 3% in Europe, and 25% in North America do not have official city web sites. Interestingly, every city selected in South America had its own official web site. In addition, this research seems to suggest that city governments on every continent, except Africa, are actively developing their capabilities in digital government.

A one-way ANOVA (Table 11) suggests a difference in the level of digital government at the municipal level between OECD and non-OECD countries at a significance level of 0.05. This is consistent with our concern over the disparity in e-government between governments in developed versus lesser-developed countries.

The apparent gap between developed and underdeveloped countries suggests the need for international organizations such as the UN and cities in advanced countries to attempt to bridge the digital divide. We recommend developing a comprehensive policy for bridging that divide. A comprehensive policy should include capacity

Table 5. Top 10 cities in privacy and security

Rank	City	Country	Score
1	Hong Kong SAR	Hong Kong SAR	15.36
2	Singapore	Singapore	11.79
3	New York	United States	11.07
3	Seoul	Republic of Korea	11.07
5	Tokyo	Japan	10.00
6	Shanghai	China	9.64
7	Helsinki	Finland	8.57
7	Toronto	Canada	8.57
9	Auckland	New Zealand	7.86
9	Dubai	United Arab Emirates	7.86

Table 6. Top 10 cities in usability

Rank	City	Country	Score
1	Hong Kong SAR	Hong Kong SAR	15.36
2	Singapore	Singapore	11.79
3	New York	United States	11.07
3	Seoul	Republic of Korea	11.07
5	Tokyo	Japan	10.00
6	Shanghai	China	9.64
7	Helsinki	Finland	8.57
7	Toronto	Canada	8.57
9	Auckland	New Zealand	7.86
9	Dubai	United Arab Emirates	7.86

Table 7. Top 10 cities in content

Rank	City	Country	Score
1	Hong Kong SAR	Hong Kong SAR	19.38
2	Jerusalem	Israel	18.75
3	Seoul	Republic of Korea	17.50
4	Macao SAR	Macao SAR	17.19
4	Shanghai	China	17.19
6	Auckland	New Zealand	16.88
7	Jakarta	Indonesia	16.56
7	Toronto	Canada	16.56
9	Vienna	Austria	16.25
10	Helsinki	Finland	15.94

building for municipalities, including information infrastructure, content, applications, and access for individuals. Parallel to improving citizens' access to digital government, it is important to develop relevant content for citizens and innovative applications in digital government considered as best practices throughout the world.

The data we have developed underscore several concerns. First, given the low scores on privacy (mean 2.53; median 1.07) and participation (mean 3.26; median 2.18), cities worldwide need to work diligently to increase web site security and to encourage citizen participation. There are many established criteria for improved Web security, and an increasingly rich and accessible set of best practices studies on citizen participation.

Second, the apparent gap between developed and underdeveloped countries suggests the need for international organizations such as the U.N. and the World Bank, as well as cities in the more advanced countries, to work assiduously to bridge the digital divide within countries and between countries. The digital divide is a challenge that democratic and democratizing societies must address, and it refers to the divide between those with web access and web-related skills, and those without such capacities. Even though the online population worldwide is increasingly reflective of communities offline, the reality of a digital divide means that certain segments of the population are effectively excluded from online access and public policy deliberation.

Thus, the divide undermines the Internet as a mainstream and inclusive participatory medium as it disproportionately impacts lower socio-economic individuals who have historically played an insignificant role within the public policy process. We recommend the development of comprehensive policies to bridge that divide. A comprehensive policy should include capacity building for government web sites, including information infrastructure, content, applications, and access for individuals and their representative organizations. Parallel to improving citizens' access to digital government, it is important to develop relevant content and to emulate innovative applications and best practices of digital government throughout the world.

Table 8. Top 10 cities in service delivery

Rank	City	Country	Score
1	New York	United States	14.68
1	Stockholm	Sweden	14.68
3	Singapore	Singapore	14.04
4	Seoul	Republic of Korea	13.83
5	Hong Kong	Hong Kong	13.19
6	Tallinn	Estonia	12.55
7	Macao	Macao	11.91
8	Helsinki	Finland	11.70
9	Dublin	Ireland	11.28
9	Shanghai	China	11.28

Table 9. Top 10 cities in citizen participation

Rank	City	Country	Score
1	Seoul	Republic of Korea	15.44
2	Hong Kong SAR	Hong Kong SAR	14.04
3	Singapore	Singapore	13.33
4	Rome	Italy	13.16
5	Shanghai	China	12.46
6	New York	United States	12.28
7	Auckland	New Zealand	10.35
8	Stockholm	Sweden	10.00
9	Sao Paulo	Brazil	9.12
10	Sofia	Bulgaria	8.42

Table 10. Comparison by OECD membership

Rank	City	Country	Score
1	Seoul	Republic of Korea	15.64
2	Rome	Italy	10.51
3	Singapore	Singapore	9.74
3	Tegucigalpa	Honduras	9.74
5	Jerusalem	Israel	9.23
6	Auckland	New Zealand	8.46
7	Copenhagen	Denmark	7.69
7	New York	United States	7.69
9	Paris	France	7.44
9	Shanghai	China	7.44

Table 11. Comparison by OECD membership

	OECD countries	Non-OECD countries
Above 36.58	12	8
36.34	**Average Score in OECD countries**	
36.58–28.49	8	7
28.49	**Average Score Throughout the World**	
28.49–24.55	2	5
24.26	**Average Score in Non-OECD Countries**	
Below 24.55	6	32

Table 12. ANOVA OECD membership

	Sum of Squares	Df	Mean Square	F	Sig.
Between Groups	2654.411	1	2654.411	13.696	.000
Within Groups	15117.039	78	193.808		
Total	17771.450	79			

Table 13. Descriptive statistics for the 84 cities surveyed

	Privacy	Usability	Content	Service	Participation
Min	0	3.44	0.43	0	0
Max	15.36	19.38	14.68	15.44	15.64
Mean	2.53	11.45	6.43	4.82	3.26
Median	1.07	11.72	5.635	4.2105	2.18

Note: Maximum score for each category was 20

ACKNOWLEDGMENT

Additional research support was provided by:

- Lung-Teng Hu, Ph.D. Student, Rutgers University-Newark
- Yong-Kun Lee, Ph.D. Student, Sungkyunkwan University
- Jong-Seok Kim, Master's Candidate, New York University
- Young-jin Shin, Ph.D. Student, Sungkyunkwan University
- Eun-Jin Seo, Ph.D. Student, Sungkyunkwan University
- Min-young Ku, M.A. Student, Sungkyunkwan University
- Stephen Ablan, Master's Candidate, New York University

REFERENCES

Bertelsmann Foundation. (2001). *Balanced e-government.* Retrieved December 24, 2003: http://www.begix.de/en/index. html

Blanchard, A., & Horan, T. (1998). Virtual communities and social capital. *Social Science Computer Review, 16*, 293-307.

Burrell, M. G. (1979). *Sociological Paradigms and Organizational Analysis*. London: Heinemann.

Dyson, E., Gilder, G., Keyworth, G., & Toffler, A. (1994). Cyberspace and the American dream: A magna carta for the knowledge age. Release 1.2, Progress and Freedom Foundation, Washington DC, August 22, *www.townhall.com/pff/position.html*

Frissen, P. (1997). The virtual state: Postmodernisation, informatisation, and public administration. In B. D. Loader, *The Governance of Cyberspace* (pp. 111-125). London: Routledge.

Giga Consulting. (2000). *Giga scorecard analysis of the New Jersey Department of Treasury.* Unpublished report to the NJ Department of Treasury. Retrieved from: www.forrester.com

Hart-Teeter. (2003). *The new e-government equation: Ease, engagement, privacy and protection.* A report prepared for the Council for Excellence in Government.

Ho, A. (2002). Reinventing local governments and the e-government initiative. *Public Administration Review, 62*(4), 434-444.

Holden, S.H., Norris, D.F., & Fletcher, P.D. (2003). Electronic government at the local level: Progress to date and future issues. *Public Performance & Management Review, 26*(4), 325-344.

Holzer, M. & Vatche, G. (1998). Five great ideas in American public administration. In J. Rabin, W. B. Hildreth, & G. J. Miller (Eds.), *Handbook of Public Administration* (2nd ed.). New York: Marcel Dekker, Inc. (pp. 49-101).

Holzer, M., Melitski, J., Rho, S.-Y., & Schwester, R. (2004). *Restoring trust in government: The potential of digital citizen participation.* Washington, DC: IBM Center for The Business of Government.

Kaylor, C. et al. (2001). Gauging e-government: A report on implementing services among American cities. *Government Information Quarterly, 18,* 293-307.

Klein, H.K. (1999). Tocqueville in cyberspace: Using the Internet for citizen associations. *The Information Society, 15,* 213-220.

Melitski, J. (2003). Capacity and e-government performance: An analysis based on early adopters of Internet technologies in New Jersey. *Public Performance and Management Review, 26*(4), 376-390.

Moon, M. J. (2002). The evolution of e-government among municipalities: Rhetoric or reality? *Public Administration Review, 62*(4), 424-433.

Moon, M. J., & deLeon, P. (2001). Municipal reinvention: Municipal values and diffusion among municipalities. *Journal of Public Administration Research and Theory, 11*(3), 327-352.

Musso, J. et al. (2000). Designing Web technologies for local governance reform: Good management or good democracy. *Political Communication, 17*(1), 1-19.

Norris, D.F., Fletcher, P.D., & Holden, S. (2001). *Is Your Local Government Plugged In? Highlights of the 2000 Electronic Government Survey.* Washington, DC: International City/Country Management Association.

Norris, P. (1999). Who surfs? New technology, old voters and virtual democracy. In Kamarck & Nye (Eds.), *Democracy.com? Governance in a Networked World* (pp. 71-94). Hollis, NH: Hollis Publishing Company.

Pardo, T. (2000). *Realizing the Promise of Digital Government: It's More Than Building a Web Site.* Albany, NY: Center for Technology in Government.

United Nations; American Society of Public Administration (2001). *Bench-marking e-government: A global perspective.* Retrieved from: http://www. aspanet.org/about/pdfs/Bench markingEgov.pdf

Weare, C. et al. (1999). Electronic democracy and the diffusion of municipal Web pages in California. *Administration and Society, 31*(1), 3-27.

Welch, E. & Wong, W. (1998). Public administration in a global context: Bridging the gaps of theory and practice between Western and non-Western nations. *Public Administration Review, 58*(1), 40-50.

West, D. M. (2000). *Assessing e-government: The Internet, democracy, and service delivery by state and federal governments.* Retrieved from: http:// www.insidepolitics.org/egov treport00.html

West, D. M. (2001, October). *WMRC global e-government survey.* Retrieved from: http://www. insidepolitics.org/egovt01int.html

West, D. M. (2002). *Global e-government.* Retrieved from: http://www. insidepolitics.org/egovt02int.PDF

West, D. M. (2003). *Global e-government.* Retrieved from: http://www.insidepolitics.org/egovt03int.pdf

West, D. M. (2003). *Urban e-government.* Retrieved from: http://www.insidepolitics.org/ egovt03city.pdf

West, D. M. (2004). E-government and the transformation of service delivery and citizen attitudes. *Public Administration Review, 64*(1), 15-27.

Winner, L. (1997). Technology today: Utopia or dystopia. *Social Research, 64*(3), 989-1017.

ENDNOTES

1 International Telecommunication Union. (2002). Internet indicators: Hosts, users and number of PCs. Retrieved June 12, 2003, from http://www.itu.int/ITU-D/ict/statistics/

2 The New York City privacy policy (www.nyc.gov/privacy) defines third parties as follows: "Third parties are computers, computer networks, ISPs, or application service providers (ASPs) that are non-governmental in nature and have direct control of what information is automatically gathered, whether cookies are used, and how voluntarily provided information is used."

3 The New York City privacy policy (www.nyc.gov/privacy) gives the following definitions of cookies and Web bugs or beacons: "Persistent cookies are cookie files that remain upon a user's hard drive until affirmatively removed, or until expired as provided for by a pre-set expiration date. Temporary or "Session Cookies" are cookie files that last or are valid only during an active communications connection, measured from beginning to end, between computer or applications (or some combination thereof) over a network. A web bug (or beacon) is a clear, camouflaged or otherwise invisible graphics image format ("GIF") file placed upon a web page or in hyper text markup language ("HTML") e-mail and used to monitor who is reading a web page or the relevant email. Web bugs can also be used for other monitoring purposes such a profiling of the affected party."

4 Additional information about public sector web site usability can be found online at the U.S. Department of Human Services site at www.usability.gov. Examples of private sector usability criteria and benchmarks include Moffitt at: http://www.unt.edu/benchmarks/archives/2002/august02/access.htm and Nielsen at http://www.useit.com/alertbox/990711.html.

This work was previously published in International Journal of Electronic Government Research, Vol. 1, No. 1, edited by M. Khosrow-Pour, pp. 1-18, copyright 2005 by IGI Publishing, formerly known as Idea Group Publishing (an imprint of IGI Global).

Chapter LXX
User Help and Service Navigation Features in Government Web Sites

Genie N. L. Stowers
San Francisco State University, USA

ABSTRACT

This article examines the user help and service navigation features in government Web sites and compares them across levels of government. These features are critical to ensuring that users unfamiliar with government are able to successfully and easily access e-government services and information. The research finds clear patterns in the use of similar help and navigation features across governments, leading to a conclusion that these features are diffusing in the public sector Web development field. The article concludes by stating that Web developers should work to overcome a second digital divide, one of a lack of knowledge of Web site organization and government structure. Users need to be actively assisted to find information by Web developers.

USER HELP AND SERVICE NAVIGATION FEATURES IN GOVERNMENT WEB SITES

This article reports on efforts to make American state, local, and federal e-government portals more user-friendly by providing user help, service navigation, and organizational structures to assist potentially novice users in finding e-government information and services.

Once users have access to the Internet and learn how to use computers, they still have to understand how to navigate Web sites and find the information or services they need. Then, they have to understand how to interact with the Web site so that they can access those services. Governments need to provide more proactive user help features, service navigation features, and organizational structures to actively assist users in finding information and services they desire; otherwise, they can create a second digital divide, one between those who understand Web site structure and organization structure, and those who do not. As Hargittai (2003, p. 3) puts it, many a Web developer "wrongly assumes that gaining access to the Internet obliterates any potential inequality that may result from lack of access to the new medium. There are factors beyond mere connectivity that need to be considered when discussing the potential implications of the Internet for inequality. In addition to relying on basic measures of access to a medium, one needs to consider more nuanced measures of use such as user 'skill'. " 'Skill' is defined as the ability to locate content online effectively and efficiently".

USABILITY IN PUBLIC SECTOR WEB SITES

Today, West (2005) suggests that there is a great degree of variation among the organization and structure of current public sector Web sites, and that not all sites are organized in a user-friendly fashion. Indeed, there is little formal focus on these elements, and their importance sometimes goes unheeded. Many government portals and Web sites are designed with government workers in mind, not the ordinary users without experience in government or with the use of Internet services.

Bridging the "digital divide" does not mean just making computers themselves accessible, but also involves making the Web sites themselves more user-friendly and easy to use—removing barriers due to lack of experience with the Internet (Nielsen, 2000; Rosenfeld & Morville, 1998). Designers and developers of public sector Web sites must assume that those using their sites have limited training and experience and will need sites that are easy to use and designed with usability and effective information architecture in mind. They must also consider that the design lessons developed for private sector e-commerce sites might not necessarily work for public sector sites.

User help, service navigation, and organizational structure are critical features of any public sector main portal that is dedicated to having users find its services and information. The presence or absence of these features on public sector sites can greatly affect the ability of a user to find information and services that might be available on the site and to effectively use those services.

The usability of the e-government portal interface is an important feature of human-computer interaction; to many users, the interface of the main portal is, in fact, the only important part (Singh & Kotze, 2002). Usability is typically defined as "the measure of the quality of a user's experience when interacting with a product or system — whether a Web site, a software application, mobile technology, or any user-operated device. Usability is a combination of factors that affects the user's experience with the product or system, including: ease of learning, efficiency of use, memorability, error frequency and severity, and subjective satisfaction" (U.S. Department of Health and Human Services, 2005).

Other factors that can be incorporated into usability include effectiveness, a match between the system and the real world, user control, safety, utility, flexibility, robustness, and consistency and usefulness of navigation (Nielsen, 2000; Singh & Kotze, 2002). We can also argue that usability includes adequate help features (including embedded help, interactive help, or manuals) and an information architecture that is descriptive, broad, and shallow for users to "click through" rather than relying upon a deep structure (Kitajima, Blackmon, & Polson, 2000, 2005; Nielsen, 2000).

Since the beginning of the World Wide Web, empirical studies have reported low rates of successful information and retrieval (Nielsen, 2000) and wide variation in the lengths of time taken for success (Hargittai, 2003). When Hargittai (2003) tested user ability to find the IRS 1040 tax form (given an unlimited amount of time), 93% could find the form, but the time required varied from 30 seconds to almost nine minutes. Of those participating, 60% used a search engine and 40% tried a specific URL. Among the problems encountered, particularly by those who were significantly older and by more recent users, were confusion about URLs and about page design layout.

Jenkins, Corritore, and Wiedenbeck (2003) identified four groups of users who utilized different search strategies based upon their level of expertise in subject matter and with the World Wide Web. Those who were domain or content and Web novices searched broadly first but did little evaluations of their findings. Domain experts but Web novices searched broadly first but were able to evaluate their results more thoroughly for accuracy. Domain and Web experts first looked deeply, utilizing their expertise, and were able to follow those deep trails and evaluate their findings. Those who were experts on both domain and the Web were able to quickly find and identify the information which was needed.

As Kitajima, Blackmon, and Polson (2000) describe it, if a user has a 90% chance of finding and selecting the correct link at each level, and there are five levels to go before they can access their desired services or content, the chance of successfully finding that information falls to .53 (.9 6) or 53% rather than the 81% chance of success if there are only two levels to move through.

Users typically seek to improve these odds by being goal-driven and focused upon descriptions of content and links that match with their understanding of reality rather than necessarily utilizing search facilities or navigation aids (Kitajima, Blackmon, & Polson, 2000, 2005). They seek out "information scent", defined as "the imperfect, subjective, perception of the value, cost or access path of information sources obtained from proximal cues, such as Web links, or icons representing the content sources" (Chi, Pirolli, & Pitkow, 2000, p. 2).

Typically, users perform this through a two-stage process. The first is an "attention" process where the user seeks to separate a Web page into sections based on labels, layout, and information on the page. To be effective in laying out information scent to guide user behavior, the layout and labels have to be able to direct the user to the appropriate section with labels that make sense for them. The second step is the "action selection" stage, where the user decides upon which link to choose. Clearly, here the appropriate labels are crucial to user success. Successful navigation thus requires gaining the user's attention and leading them to the correct selection of the appropriate link at each hierarchical level of the Web site (Blackmon, Kitajima, & Polson, 2005).

For many users seeking online government information, conducting a successful search for information means solving an unfamiliar problem (Blackmon, Kitajima, & Polson, 2005). In essence, they know too little about government and how it is structured to be able to successfully navigate and make link choices on many government Web sites.

There are numerous difficulties with this task, some of them based upon the knowledge of and familiarity with the labels themselves. Takeuchi and Kitajima (2002) effectively illustrate that, at the very least, there are gender differences in the understanding of many technical words, and these differences are further accentuated when viewed across cultural divisions. Given that there are many other differences in levels of understanding of information and a wide variety of quality in labeling and the laying of information scents, it is clear that government Web designers have a daunting task.

To overcome these many differences in abilities and understanding of how to use the technology and content, Web developers must develop effective site structures that reflect the users' views of the content at that site, not just the organization's own view of itself (based upon its organizational chart) (Nielsen, 2000). Plus, many gaps in user knowledge can also be filled with effective help systems like live chat, online learning and tutorials, online manuals, and well-structured designs which seek to define choices in terms that inexperienced users might know (Shneiderman & Hochheiser, 2001).

Usability features include those which assist the user in finding information, finding services, and in finding their way around the Web site. They include the following:

- navigation (features that assist the user in moving around the site);
- labeling (how the content is labeled, again so that the user knows how to find information);
- searching systems (the usefulness of the search features) (Rosenfeld & Morville, 1998); and
- visible help features, including a help page, frequently asked questions (FAQs) about the site, site maps (pages that literally provide a map of the entire site), and tutorials on using the site.

This previous research is important to understanding the project reported upon here, but is still not sufficient to allow us to generate meaningful hypotheses of the more specific topic explored here, user help features. Therefore, the research reported here will be structured around research questions.

STRUCTURING RESEARCH QUESTIONS ABOUT USER HELP FEATURES

Before we can identify research questions about user help features, we must identify these features. Initially, standard content analysis techniques were used to identify existing user help, navigation, and information architecture features on the Web portals. Agency and government portals were visited, features were identified and categorized, and a comprehensive list was developed. Once the list was developed, each portal to be studied was visited and coded as to the presence or absence of each feature.

Table 1 presents the types of user help features identified on government portal sites as well as a brief explanation of each. These include information about the site, an explicit Help section, FAQs (Frequently Asked Questions), information in other languages, and site maps. These features are organized in two sections according to whether or not they would be relatively easy to implement or require few resources. Thus, simple e-mail linkages for contacting the agency, to additional help, to information about the site, to user tips, and to an e-mail or comment section to provide feedback about the site would be easy to implement. Indices, site maps, FAQs, and search engines also would require minimally more work but little technical expertise to implement.

The most reasonable explanation for widespread user help features is that the features which are easiest and cheapest to produce will be utilized most frequently. There is no reason to believe that

Table 1. User help features

Feature	Explanation
Easiest and Requires Fewest Resources To Implement	
About the Site	Link to information about the site
Contact Us	Information and links to allow the user to contact the agency for more information or for help with the site
FAQs	Includes answers to Frequently Asked Questions
Feedback	Invites users to give them feedback about the site
Help	Explicit agency-provided help with the site
Index	An index of information, data, and agencies available
Search	Search engine to allow users to search the site
Site Map	Visual representation of the entire Web site
User Tips	Helpful hints on how users can use the site
More Technically Difficult or Resource-Heavy To Implement	
Live Help	Links to live chat with agency representative to provide assistance
Other Languages	Site provides information in other languages
Text Version	An alternate site is provided in text

Table 2. Service navigation aid features

Feature	Explanation
Agency Information	Listings of all agencies in directory form
Answers A to Z	Alphabetized listings of answers to questions
Calendars	Calendars of government activities and events
Contact Information	Linkages to direct contact information for agencies
Do you know how I do ___ …?	List of questions organized according to major service areas from the citizen's point of view, stating "how do I do x or y?"
E-Government Services	Direct link from home page to all e-government services
Events	Link to information on major events
Facilities Locator	Direct linkage to way to locate government offices
Featured Link / Spotlight	Many sites have featured programs or linkages
Hot Topics	Link to information on what are considered currently important issues
Most Visited / Frequently Requested Site	Links to or listings of the most frequently visited sites, indicating the importance of that information
Popular Services / Major Programs	Highlighting of popular services or major programs
Quick Links	Listing of the commonly-asked questions in prominent format
Special Initiatives	Current, new, or special initiatives from the agency
What's New	Listing of new items posted on the site

this pattern would differ across levels of government. Therefore, the first research question is:

R1: The user help features which require the least technical abilities and fewest resources to implement will be found more frequently across all levels of government. The features which require the most technical abilities and greatest levels of resources to implement will be found least often.

Table 2 provides a listing of the various portal features used to provide users with assistance in finding agency online services. These features are not as common as the user help features listed above. They include agency or government calendars leading to information, as well as various ways to link to services (for example, Answers A to Z, Do You Know?, Facilities Locators, Frequently Requested Site, Featured Links, Quick Links, and What's New).

We already know that well-planned formatting leads to success in finding sought-after information or services (Blackmon, Kitajima, & Polson, 2005) since users seek "information scent", or clues to the information they want (Chi, Pirolli, & Pitkow, 2000). Further, Web site developers can structure a site's portal entryway to separate users into knowledgeable consumers or users who might not know much about government. Thus, they are able to take advantage of the fact that users with experience and expertise typically utilize different strategies to find information (Jenkins, Corritore, & Wiedenbeck, 2003). Different agencies have used these principles to structure entry into their Web sites in different ways. This information can be used to structure service navigation schemes or the overall information organization of the entire Web portal.

However, this research is clearly exploratory, and there are few theoretical or practical reasons to expect one type or distinguish one type of service navigation scheme from another. There is no clear difference in the amount or level of technical expertise or resources needed to develop each scheme; they are just different ways of concep-

Table 3. Types of information and service organization on government Web portals

Type of Information Architecture	Description.. Site is Organized Around:
Audience / Market	The needs of particular audiences or markets; for example, Firstgov.gov has information organized around Online Services for Citizens, for Businesses, and for Governments.
E-Government Services / Links to Agencies	The services, tasks, or functions offered by the agency
Topics / Issues	Various topics, often just miscellaneous listings of topics
Hybrid Site	Combinations of all of the above

tualizing services and setting up the information scent discussed above. However, the most basic of the service navigation schemes are the ones which provide only basic description and require no re-conceptualization, such as E-Government Services linkages and Links to Agencies; therefore, we would suggest that these would be most popular. There would be no expectation that the usage of these labeling systems would differ from one level to another level of government.

R2: The E-Government Services/Links to Agencies service navigation labeling systems would be found most commonly among government agency Web portals, no matter the level of government.

Table 3 identifies the information architecture, or structure, of systems of various Web site portals, in other words, how access to the information is organized. The various possible ways in which the Web portal can be organized include an audience/market orientation (the now familiar Citizen/Visitor/Business/Government), according to the types of services or tasks available, the kinds of topics or issues, or a hybrid of several types.

The audience/market orientation is one in which the Web portal's navigation scheme is segmented into a separate set of linkages for each potential audience. For example, the audience-oriented FirstGov.gov site has four tabs leading to four different sets of site features: For Citizens, For Businesses and Non-Profits, For Federal Employees, and Government-to-Government. States with audience/market orientations will often have their sites segmented according to the purpose of a visitor (Access Washington's Living in Washington, Working/Employment, Doing Business, Education/Learning, and Visiting/Recreation).

A portal guiding their visitors according to the types of services or tasks available will have navigation features listing the types of services provided by the agency and providing links to information or services on those areas. Portals guiding users according to topics or issues set up navigation according to subject matter dealt with within the agency or government.

One of the few theoretical suggestions as to how these features would be clustered is by Ho (2002), who suggests that the system of information architecture used is a function of whether an agency is traditionally organized with a bureaucratic paradigm (in which case the information architecture would be structured according to a traditional listing of agencies) or whether it has moved to the more efficient e-government paradigm emphasizing a customer service orientation (with a structure according to the Web site audience or market).

However, Ho's hypothesis also suggests that there is necessarily a direct and strong linkage between design ideas within an agency's technology branch and the organizational sophistication of the overall agency, which is unlikely. Instead, staffs from these two areas are unlikely to communicate often (this is, in fact, one of the most commonly-cited breakdowns of technological systems, that there is little communication between technology developers and end users). Therefore, no research question is posited for these site features.

As discussed in the research methodology section, the components of these features on each government's main Web portal were identified for this project, their presence or absence on the portal was coded, and basic analysis was conducted.

PROJECT METHODOLOGY

The research project discussed here utilized a cross-sectional comparison that focused upon a review of federal, state, and local e-government portals, and comparisons between them. All federal agency portals from executive agencies, cabinet agencies (including sub-agencies with their own domain name), and independent agencies were included in the study. Federal boards and commissions were not included. All 50 states plus Washington, D.C. were included in the analysis, along with all cities over 100,000 in population. This resulted in 43 federal sites, 51 state sites, and 47 urban sites. The data was collected during summer of 2005.

The first stage of this analysis was to identify the user help features, service navigation features, and types of information architecture, or organization and presentation of information, that are currently being used on public sector Web sites, focusing upon the home portal of each portal. (While accessibility is also a crucial aspect of usability, it was not part of the overall project and is not reported here.)

Portals were the initial points of entry for users, as they define the usability and information architecture features for the entire site. Therefore, they are the most crucial part of an agency or government's entire Web site. The identification of help or navigation features was accomplished by content analysis of federal, state, and local home pages and the construction of coding sheets including the identified features. The presence of various features was determined through the examination of the site's portal, as this is the main entryway and where users would need these features.

All coding was conducted by one individual, the author, which is a shortcoming of this research. To attempt to overcome this issue, the author double-checked the results; of course, a simple "yes" or "no" check-off for each feature is a much less complex coding task than having to code an arbitrary scale of the effectiveness of a feature. All features were working at the time of the coding. Sixty-four variables were coded, along with three additive indices.

The author recognizes that a simple count does not address the issue of whether or not a feature is well-designed or not; however, this research is the first step in investigating this phenomena, and the first step should be whether a feature exists or not. Later, additional research should be conducted on the effectiveness of these features across jurisdictions.

USABILITY AND HELP FEATURES

The research reported here explores the simple research questions discussed above and is descriptive and exploratory in nature.

Descriptive Results

Table 4 presents basic descriptive data on user help features. As can be seen, most governments utilize more than one help feature, up to a maximum of six different features on the same portal, with state governments utilizing the most user help features. One federal and one local agency utilized none.

Table 5 reports descriptive data on service navigation features. An average of 5.1 features per government Web portal is used, with federal agencies utilizing an average of 4.3 and state agencies utilizing the highest average number, 5.6 service navigation features per site. The minimum number on a site was one for federal and local, two for state. The maximum number utilized was quite high—seven features for federal agencies, eleven for state, and ten for local agencies.

Exploration of Research Questions

The next part of the analysis is the exploration of the research questions and then, more exploratory

Table 4. Distribution of user help features across level of government

	Total	Federal	State	Local
N	141	43	51	47
Mean Number of Features	3.7 features	3.7 features	4.3 features	3.1 features
Standard Deviation	1.36	1.35	1.30	1.17
Minimum Number of Features	0	0	2	0
Maximum Number of Features	6	6	6	6

Table 5. Distribution of service navigation features across level of government

	Total	Federal	State	Local
N	141	43	51	47
Mean Number of Features	5.1 features	4.3 features	5.6 features	5.3 features
Standard Deviation	1.78	1.59	1.62	1.85
Minimum Number of Features	1	1	2	1
Maximum Number of Features	11	7	11	10

Table 6. Distribution of help features by level of government (Ranked by most frequently used by all jurisdictions)

User Help Feature	Total	Federal (% Sites With Feature)	State (% Sites with Feature)	Local (% Sites with Feature)	Chi-Square	Probability
		Easiest and Requires Fewest Resources To Implement				
Search	97.9%	97.7%	100%	95.7%	2.139	0.343
Contact Us	70.2	65.1	72.5	72.3	0.769	0.681
Site Map	***48.2***	***69.8***	***52.9***	***23.4***	***20.043*** ***	***0.000***
Help	***33.3***	***25.6***	***58.8***	***12.8***	***25.021*** ***	***0.000***
FAQs	19.9	27.9	21.6	10.6	4.355	0.113
About the Site	***18.4***	***11.6***	***31.4***	***10.6***	***8.901*** **	***0.012***
Feedback on Site	15.6	4.7	21.6	19.1	5.744	0.057
Index	12.8	20.9	5.9	12.8	4.744	0.093
User Tips	2.8	2.3	2	4.3	0.526	0.769
		More Technically Difficult or Resource-Heavy To Implement				
Other Languages	***25.5%***	***41.9***	***11.8***	***25.5***	***11.11*** **	***0.004***
Text Version	***18.4%***	***4.7***	***31.4***	***17***	***11.17*** **	***0.004***
Live Help	***9.2%***	***0***	***19.6***	***6.4***	***11.39*** **	***0.003***

Help features which are present at significantly different levels across government levels are in bold italics.

* *Statistically different and significant at the .05 level*
** *Statistically different and significant at the .01 level*
*** *Statistically different and significant at the .000 level*

analysis. Clearly, the first research question can be supported, as the easiest and least resource-intensive types of user help features were found much more frequently (Table 6). Among all levels of government, the most commonly-seen help feature was a search engine (found in 97.9% of all sites investigated, with no significant differences among levels of government). This was followed by invitations to Contact Us, found in 70.2% of sites, also with no significant differences across types of government. Site maps and Help areas were also found very commonly but exhibited different patterns across governments. Site maps were used most frequently by federal agencies and only by less than one-quarter of local agencies. Help areas were created most frequently by state agencies (58.8%), followed by one-quarter of federal agencies and only 12.8% of local agencies. User tips were very seldom utilized as user help features by any level of government.

Also as suggested in Research Question 1, those user help features that would require more resources or more technical sophistication were found less frequently on government Web portals. However, two of them (the site presented in Other Languages and an alternate Text Version, both very resource-intensive features) were available in 25.5% and 18.4% of all sites, respectively, and there were significant differences across types of governments. Federal agencies were much more likely to have sites available in other languages, and text versions were more frequently found at state sites.

Table 7 presents the distribution of service navigation features by level of government. As suggested, the very basic E-Government Services

Table 7. Distribution of service navigation features by level of government (Ranked by most frequently used by all jurisdictions)

Service Navigation Feature	Total	Federal (% Sites With Feature)	State (% Sites with Feature)	Local (% Sites with Feature)	Chi-Square Statistic	Probability Level
E-Government Services	*60.3%*	*16.3%*	*72.5%*	*87.2%*	*52.2 ****	***0.000***
Featured Links	***60.3***	***44.2***	***66.7***	***68.1***	***6.7 ****	***0.035***
Link to Agencies	***51.8***	***25.6***	***52.9***	***74.5***	***21.5 ******	***0.000***
Popular Services	***35.5***	***32.6***	***54.9***	***17.0***	***15.6 ******	***0.000***
Do You Know / How I Do ___?	31.9	18.6	37.3	38.3	5.1	0.080
Calendars	***27.0***	*7*	***33.3***	***38.3***	***12.8 *****	***0.002***
Link to Contacts	27.0	20.9	27.5	31.9	1.4	0.500
Events	***23.4***	***18.6***	***15.7***	***36.2***	***6.5 ****	***0.038***
What's New	22.7	27.9	17.6	23.4	1.4	0.492
Quick Links	19.1	16.3	27.5	12.8	3.7	0.154
Special Initiatives	14.9	16.3	15.7	12.8	0.3	0.879
Most Visited	***12.8***	***2.3***	***15.7***	***19.1***	***6.3 ****	***0.042***
Facilities Locator	***10.6***	***30.2***	***3.9***	***0.0***	***25.4 ******	***0.000***
Hot Topics	9.2	4.7	11.8	10.6	1.6	0.454
Answers A to Z	3.5	4.7	3.9	2.1	0.5	0.798

Table 8. Distribution of information or service organization available by level of government (Ranked by most frequently used by all jurisdictions)

Type of Organization Available	Total	Federal (% Sites With Feature)	State (% Sites with Feature)	Local (% Sites with Feature)	Chi-Square Statistic	Probability Level
Audience	35.5	14.0	49.0	40.4		
Services, Processes	34.8	44.2	43.1	17.0		
Hybrid	17.7	7.0	5.9	40.4		
Topics or Issues	11.3	34.9	2.0	2.1		
					67.7	.0000

was present in 60.3% of all government sites, but more surprisingly, was seldom found on federal sites (16.3% only). It was very common on state and local sites (72.5% and 87.2%), however, and the differences between all three levels of government was statistically significant.

Featured Links, Links to Agencies, and Popular Services were the next most commonly found across all levels of government, but again there were significant differences across those levels in where it was used. Featured Links were found on two-thirds of state and local sites; Agency Links were found in three-quarters of local sites, approximately one-half of the state sites, but on only one-third of the federal sites.

Features like Calendars and Events were most commonly found on state and local sites while Facilities Locators, not surprisingly, were most often found on federal sites but very seldom on state or local sites (governments evidently presume that their residents know where these government facilities are located).

Finally, Table 8 presents the distribution of information organization types across levels of government. The most commonly-utilized organizational scheme is the Audience/Market scheme, but that is because it is used by practically one-half of all states and 40% of all large cities in their Web portals. Federal agencies utilize this type only 14% of the time. A structure breaking down information by the types of services or processes offered is utilized far more often by federal agencies (44.2%) and by most of the rest of the states not using the Audience scheme (43.1%). Only 17% of the large cities used this type. Cities most frequently used a hybrid type of portal (in 40.4% of the cases), while states and federal agencies seldom used this. Finally, another third (34.9%) of federal agencies organized their information around topics or issues, a scheme avoided by states and local governments.

Clearly, the differences here are significant statistically and substantively. The types of information organization schemes utilized are a function of the types of services provided and the site managers' perceptions of their audiences. Federal agencies seem to focus on what they can offer users rather than be organized according to any anecdotal perception of their audience's identity (FirstGov.gov is a significant exception). State agencies focus on the services they offer or provide a user perspective. Cities, on the other hand, have fewer resources with which to work, which might explain the high number of hybrid sites, which are less organized. Still, 40% of local portals have taken the audience approach.

These initial results focus upon identifying user help, service navigation, and information architecture features used by the public sector. This is the first step in identifying which of these features ultimately are effective and really are helpful in assisting the general public in understanding these public sector portals and their services, and how to navigate and use them.

CONCLUSION

From the results, it appears that similar patterns do exist across levels of government in the types of user help and information organizational structure utilized. More technically-difficult features appear to be utilized by larger levels of government, so financial and staff resources are clearly determining patterns. However, there are many user help features that require little technical expertise so it is hard to explain their usage by the simple existence of resources in larger governments or agencies. In addition, it appears that states are leading the way in offering multiple types of features (see tables 4 and 5) and in offering the arguably more user-friendly audience-based type of information and service organizational structure.

Given the patterns found for some features, it appears that diffusion of these innovations and features is occurring across jurisdictions and within levels of government. Local government IT professionals meet and know one another through conferences, professional associations, and other informal networks, as do those at the federal and state levels. Certain features are discussed and popularized among IT professionals as important and useful for assisting users. Then, other governments in a network follow up and develop that feature for their own Web site. Or, Web managers visit the Web portals of their sister governments, see a feature they like that works well for their own level of government, and move to adopt it. However, there is no sense, from these results, that there is any systematic usability testing being utilized in the Web development process.

The development of user help and service navigation features, as well as systematic usability testing on Web portals, is crucial if governments really intend to effectively utilize e-government and provide electronic services. Deservedly, much focus is put upon the differences still existing between classes of users due to their access to computers and the Internet. Obviously, the inability of some groups of users to access e-government services reduces the equity of these services.

However, it should be recognized that another digital divide exists. Even if users have access to computers and the Internet, in order to fully utilize e-government services, they need government agency Web sites that can be understood and navigated successfully by everyone, not just by those who have knowledge and understanding about how government agencies and services work and are organized.

Effective user help and service navigation features can remove this second divide by allowing novice users or users unused to contacting government to understand and fully utilize e-government services and information. We should not create the "other digital divide"; we should work to ensure that all can access government services in an online context.

REFERENCES

Blackmon, M. H., Kitajima, M., & Polson, P. G. (2005). Tool for accurately predicting Web site navigation problems, non-problems, problem severity, and effectiveness of repairs. In *Proceedings of the Conference on Human Factors in Computing Systems (pp.31-40).* Retrieved July 29, 2005, from http://staff.aist.go.jp/kitajima.muneo/English/PAPERS(E)/CHI2005.pdf

Blackmon, M. H., Polson, P. G., Kitajima, M., & Lewis, C. (2002). *Cognitive walkthrough for the Web.* Retrieved July 29, 2005, from http://staff.aist.go.jp/kitajima.muneo/English/PAPERS(E)/CHI2002.pdf

Chi, E. H., Pirolli, P., & Pitkow, J. (2000). The scent of a site: A system for analyzing and predicting information scent, usage, and usability of a Web site. In *Proceedings of CHI 2000.* ACM Press. Retrieved July 29, 2005, from http://www-users.cs.umn.edu/~echi/papers/chi2000/scent.pdf

Cohen, S. A., & Eimecke, W. B. (2001). *The use of the Internet in government service delivery.* PricewaterhouseCoopers Foundation for the Business of Government. Retrieved August 22, 2002, from http://endowment.pwcglobal.com/pdfs/CohenReport.pdf

Daabaj, Y. (2002). An evaluation of the usability of human-computer interaction methods in support of the development of interactive systems. In *Proceedings of the 35th Hawaii International Conference on System Sciences.*

Dillon, A. (2001). *Beyond usability: Process, outcome, and affect in human-computer interactions.* Canadian Journal of Information and Library Science, 26(4), 57–69.

Hargittai, E. (2003). *Serving citizens' needs: Minimizing online hurdles to accessing government information. IT and Society,* 1(3, Winter, 2003), 27 – 41. Retrieved July 29, 2005, from http://www.ITandSociety.org

Ho, A. T.-K. (2002). Reinventing local governments and the e-government initiative. *Public Administration Review, 62(4),* 434-444.

Huang, C. J. (2003). Usability of e-government Web sites for people with disabilities. In *Proceedings of the 36th Hawaii International Conference on System Sciences.*

Jansen, B.J., & Pooch, U. (2000). Web user studies: A review and framework for future work. *Journal of the American Society of Information Science and Technology, 52(3),* 235–246. Retrieved August 1, 2005, from http://jimjansen.tripod.com/academic/pubs/wus.pdf

Jenkins, C., Corritore, C. L., & Wiedenbeck, S. (2003). Patterns of information seeking on the Web: A qualitative study of domain expertise and Web expertise. *IT and Society, 1(3, Winter, 2003),* 64–89. Retrieved July 29, 2005, from http://www.ITandSociety.org

Jones, C. P. (2003). Usability and information design. In *Proceedings of the Annual Conference for the Society for Technical Community: Vol. 50 (pp. 333–338).*

Kitajima, M., Blackmon, M. H., & Polson, P. G. (2000). A comprehension-based model of Web navigation and its application to Web usability analysis. In S. McDonald, Y. Waern, & G. Cockton (Eds.), People and computers XIV - Usability or else! In *Proceedings of HCI 2000 (pp. 357-373).* Springer. Retrieved July 29, 2005, from http://staff.aist.go.jp/kitajima.muneo/English/PAPERS(E)/HCI2000.pdf

Kitajima, M., Blackmon, M. H., & Polson, P. G. (2005). Cognitive architecture for Web site design and usability evaluation: *Comprehension and information scent in performing by exploration. HCI International, 2005.* Retrieved July 30, 2005, from http://staff.aist.go.jp/kitajima.muneo/English/PAPERS(E)/HCII2005-CoLiDeS.html

Lazar, J., Bessiere, K., Ceaparu, I., Robinson, J., & Shneiderman, B. (2003). Help! I'm lost: User frustration in Web navigation. *IT & Society, 1(3, Winter, 2003),* 18–26. Retrieved July 29, 2005, from http://www.ITandSociety.org

Nielsen, J. (2000). Designing Web usability: *The practice of simplicity.* Indianapolis, IN: New Riders Publishing.

Norris, P. (2001). *Digital divide: Civic engagement, information poverty, and the Internet worldwide.* New York: Cambridge Press.

Paciello, M. G. (2000). *Web accessibility for people with disabilities.* Lawrence, KS: CMP Books.

Pearrow, M. (2000). Web site usability handbook. Rockland, MA: Charles River Media, Inc.

Pew Research Center (2002). Getting serious online. P*ew Internet and American Life Project.* Retrieved August 30, 2005, from http://www.pewinternet.org/reports/pdfs/PIP_Getting_Serious_Online3ng.pdf

Pew Research Center (2002). Daily Internet Activities. Retrieved August 30, 2005, from http://www.pewinternet.org/reports/chart.asp?img=Daily_Internet_Activities.jpg

Pew Research Center. (2002). Internet Activities. Retrieved August 30, 2005, from http://www.pewinternet.org/reports/chart.asp?img=Internet_Activities.jpg

Reiss, E. L. (2000). *Practical information architecture.* New York: Addison Wesley.

Rosenfeld, L. (2000). Special report: Design usability—Seven pitfalls to avoid in information architecture. *Internet World Magazine.* Retrieved July 29, 2005, from http://www.internetworld.com/magazine.php?inc=121500/12.15.00feature3long.html

Rosenfeld, L., & Morville, P. (1998). *Information architecture for the World Wide Web Sebastopol*, CA: O'Reilly and Associates.

Shneiderman, B., & Hochheiser. (2001). *Universal usability as a stimulus to advanced interface design. Human-Computer Interaction Lab*, University of Maryland. Retrieved August 1, 2005, from http://www.cs.umd.edu/hcil/pubs/tech-reports.shtml

Singh, S., & Kotze, P. (2002). Towards a framework for e-commerce usability. In *Proceedings of the 2002 Annual Research Conference of the South African Institute of Computer Scientists and Information Technologist on Enablement through Technology*. Retrieved July 29, 2005, from http://portal.acm.org/citation.cfm?id=581508&CFID=51211042&CFTOKEN=76008125

Takeuchi, H., & Kitajima, M. (2002). Web contents evaluation based on human knowledge of words. *International Conference on Soft Computing and Intelligent Systems*. Retrieved July 29, 2005, from http://staff.aist.go.jp/kitajima.muneo/English/PAPERS(E)/SCIS2002Takeuchi.pdf

U.S. Department of Commerce (2002). *A nation online: How Americans are expanding their use of the Internet*. Retrieved February 15, 2002, from http://www.ntia.doc.gov/ntiahome/dn/index.html

U.S. Department of Commerce (2000). *Falling through the net: Toward digital inclusion*. Retrieved February 21, 2001, from http://www.esa.doc.gov/fttn00.pdf

U.S. Department of Health and Human Services (2005). *Usability basics at usability.gov*. Retrieved August 4, 2005, from http://www.usability.gov/basics/index.html

U.S. Office of Management and Budget E-Government Task Force. (2002).

E-government strategy: *Simplified delivery of service to citizens*. Retrieved from

http://www.whitehouse.gov/omb/inforeg/egov-strategy.pdf

West, D. M. (2005). *Global e-government, 2005*. Retrieved October 28, 2005, from http://www.insidepolitics.org/egovt05int.pdf

West, D. M. (2005). *State and federal e-government*, 2005. Retrieved October 15, 2005, from http://www.insidepolitics.org/egovt05us.pdf

This work was previously published in International Journal of Electronic Government Research, Vol. 2, Issue 4, edited by M. Khosrow-Pour, pp. 24-39, copyright 2006 by IGI Publishing, formerly known as Idea Group Publishing (an imprint of IGI Global).

Chapter LXXI
An Empirical Study on the Migration to OpenOffice.org in a Public Administration

B. Rossi
Free University of Bolzano-Bozen, Italy

M. Scotto
Free University of Bolzano-Bozen, Italy

A. Sillitti
Free University of Bolzano-Bozen, Italy

G. Succi
Free University of Bolzano-Bozen, Italy

ABSTRACT

The aim of the article is to report the results of a migration to Open Source Software (OSS) in one public administration. The migration focuses on the office automation field and, in particular, on the OpenOffice.org suite. We have analysed the transition to OSS considering qualitative and quantitative data collected with the aid of different tools. All the data have been always considered from the point of view of the different stakeholders involved, IT managers, IT technicians, and users. The results of the project have been largely satisfactory. However the results cannot be generalised due to some constraints, like the environment considered and the parallel use of the old solution. Nevertheless, we think that the data collected can be of valuable aid to managers wishing to evaluate a possible transition to OSS.

INTRODUCTION

Open Source Software (OSS) and Open Data Standards (ODS) emerged in recent years as a viable alternative to proprietary solutions. There are many cases in which the adoption of OSS has proven advantageous for companies deciding to adopt it in replacement or in conjunction with closed solutions. The limitation of these migrations for our point of view is that they were very often server-side oriented and not supported by empirical evidence of the benefits of the new solution. In this sense, there are very few case studies that report successful transitions on the desktop side (ZDNet, 2005) and some are still underway (Landeshauptstadt München, 2003; Stadt Wien, 2004). It is our opinion that the reason of the apparent different results in the two fields is due to the nature of OSS development (Feller & Fitzgerald, 2001) that leads to repercussions on the resulting usability (Nichols & Twidale, 2003).

When comparing OSS and proprietary software and when comparing software solutions in general, it is impossible to get a global index referring to quality in order to compare two solutions (Fenton & Pfleeger, 1997).

If we consider the most important aspects under which it is significant to analyse software, as:

- Reliability
- Performance
- Price
- Security
- Interoperability
- Usability
- Extendibility
- Functionalities
- Privacy protection

The categories have to be balanced with the requirements of the environment and users in which the solution is deployed. Where the aspects of security, reliability, and extendibility are of key importance, OSS has proven a valid solution, if not superior to proprietary solutions. Where functionalities, usability, and in general user interaction acquires importance as on the client side, OSS has yet to prove as a valid alternative. Price is a controversial issue as there is the need not only to evaluate the license price but also the software maintenance and other costs inherited from the migration. These considerations originated the study we propose.

The purpose of the study is to evaluate in a rigorous way the introduction of OSS in a working environment, following the criteria of a controlled experiment from the selection of the sample to the evaluation of the results. We selected a sample of 22 users from different offices in the public administration target of the experiment. We divided the sample in two groups, one to be migrated, the other to be used as a control group. The results obtained seem to report that the initial reduction of productivity is not as consistent as we thought, also taking into account that half of the users considered the introduced solution as offering less functionality than the proprietary one.

STATE OF THE ART

There are many studies available evaluating the Total Cost of Ownership (TCO) of OSS. The original model derived from the work of the Gartner Group in 1987 and has since then been inserted in different models. The TCO model helps managers by considering not only the cost of purchase but also further costs as maintenance or training.

All the studies are not unanimous as the savings that can be reached with the adoption of OSS (Robert Frances Group, 2002; The Yankee Group, 2005). One of the reasons is probably the different weight given to costs and benefits that are difficult to measure. Two of such measures are, for example, the risks of lock-ins and the development of local economies. The risks of entering a mechanism of lock-in, for example, by relying only on a single software supplier or storing massive amounts of data by means of closed data standards are real and must be considered in a TCO model evaluating a transition (Shapiro & Varian, 1999). On the other side, the adoption of OSS can be of benefit to local software companies that can exploit the possibility given by the available source code and open data standards. Also in this case, the amount of this kind of externality is difficult to quantify.

Considering OSS, there are many projects worth mentioning, we will name here two of the most famous and see how they perform on the market against proprietary solutions:

- the Apache Web server[1]
- the Mozilla Firefox Web browser[2]

Table 1 shows that the Apache Web server detains almost 70% of the whole market share (Netcraft Survey, 2005). As virus attacks of the last years have proven (CERT, 2001), one of the reason of such wide adoption is the security proposed by the Apache architecture.

Table 2 shows the market share of the Mozilla Firefox browser between January and April 2005.

Table 1. Web servers in September and October 2005 (Netcraft Survey, 2005)

Developer	September 2005	Percent	October 2005	Percent	Change
Apache	49598424	69.15	52005811	69.89	0.74
Microsoft	14601553	20.36	15293030	20.55	0.19
Sun	1868891	2.61	1889989	2.54	-0.07
Zeus	584598	0.82	585972	0.79	-0.03

Table 2. Browsers market share ("Browser Market Share Study," itproductivity.org, 2005)

Browser	January 2005 (%)	April 2005 (%)
Internet Explorer	84.85	83.07
Firefox	4.23	10.28
Mozilla	4.48	3.81
Netscape	3.03	0.92
AOL	2.20	0.85
MSN	0.58	0.67
Opera	0.34	0.41
Total	99.71	100.01

Table 3. Large scale migrations to OSS of public administrations

Region	Clients to migrate	Side	Distribution
Extremadura	80,000	Desktop/Servers	gnuLinex
Munich	14,000	Desktop	Debian
Vienna	7,500	Desktop	Wienux (Debian/KDE)
Largo, FL	900	Desktop/Servers	Linux KDE 2.1.1

As it can be seen also in this case the software is gaining constant market shares in the last months. The software is still behind in market shares but it represents an important competitor for the market dominator, Microsoft Internet Explorer.

These are surely two of the most popular OSS that emerged during the last few years; there are many more that can compete with proprietary solutions. By looking at these and other examples, we can conclude that OSS already could represent an important alternative to proprietary software.

Another important consideration on OSS is represented by the cases in which a large migration has been performed or is in the process of being performed. Having a look at the different case studies available for the migration to OSS, we summarise the most famous during these years in Table 3; three are European, while one is U.S.-based.

One of the most remarkable deployments of OSS on the desktop side is surely the one of the Extremadura region in Spain, recently installing 80,000 Linux systems, 66,000 for the educational system and 14,000 for administrative workstations. The local administration created their Linux distribution called gnuLinex.[3] According to their IT department, the savings have been of the order of €18M (ZDNet, 2005). Another case of success is the one of the city of Largo, FL where the migration has involved 900 clients; the savings have been estimated at $300,000-$400,000 (Newsforge, 2002). The migration of the city of Munich and the one of the city of Vienna are currently underway (Landeshauptstadt München, 2003; Stadt Wien, 2004). As the delay of the Munich migration seems to demonstrate, a transition to OSS is not a process to underestimate. There are also cases where the proprietary solution has been considered as more convenient, like the city of Nürnberg, where according to their own migration study the transition from Windows 2000/Office 2000 to Windows XP/Office XP was considered €4.5M cheaper than the transition to Linux/OpenOffice.org (Stadt Nürnberg, 2004).

A final consideration on studies performed on OSS usability. Of certain interest for our study, albeit a little dated, is the experimentation conducted by the Berkeley University in November-December 2001 (Everitt & Lederer, 2001), comparing two different solutions in the office automation field, namely Sun StarOffice Writer 5.2 and Microsoft Word 2000. Authors report about an experiment on 12 users, regarding the user interface integration. As a result of the study, the two products were comparable, although the Microsoft solution proved to be more satisfactory and easier to use.

THE STUDY

Our study has been inserted into this framework; the intention is to contribute to the field with a solid and sound analysis of a real transition to OSS on the client side, specifically the analysis of a migration in the office automation field in one public administration.

In particular the study related the introduction of the OpenOffice.org[4] suite. The suite offers comparable functions as the one offered by Microsoft Office.[5] It is composed of several applications, a text-processor, a spreadsheet, software for presentations, for drawing operations and for the creation of formulae. The only functionality missing in the version installed was the possibility to create small local databases. In the organisation where we performed the study, this was a feature rarely employed by users and, in general, deprecated by IT managers. We focused our analysis mainly on word-processors and spreadsheets.

The experiment was performed on 22 users of a public administration (PA) during the transition to OSS. In the following sections we expose the methodology adopted, the tools employed, and the main results obtained from the qualitative and quantitative data collected. The limitations and possible future additional work is listed at the end of the article. The overall sample of 22 users has been selected from three departments of the PA under exam. Some constraints had to be followed, for example, the fact that the head of the different offices posed a limitation on the number of the available workers per office. Table 4 represents the different groups, with two office directors per each group as part of the sample. The average age of participants to both groups was uniform between groups and has not influenced the results; users were selected from such departments in a random way with the limitations described previously. Regarding the protocol, the selection of the experimental groups has been done in a way to enable that the participants were, when possible, in some way in relation with each other, physically near and if possible coming from the same organisational units, to take advantage of possible network externalities that arise in terms of document exchange and reciprocal help (Shapiro & Varian, 1999).

One group experimented with the introduction of OpenOffice.org (our treatment X, in Figure 1), while the other group was used as a control group. The experimental design followed an experimental pretest-posttest control group design (Campbell & Stanley, 1990).

A questionnaire has been submitted to both groups before (O1) and after (O2) the introduction of OpenOffice.org to evaluate the effects of the experimentation on the attitude towards OSS. The activities of both groups have been constantly monitored by an automatic system for data collection (Sillitti, Janes, Succi, & Vernazza, 2003) that permitted the gathering of a series of objective process data (the series of observations O3,i).

In some other cases where there has not been the possibility to have a control group and a proper randomisation of the sample, a "quasiexperimental" and a "one-shot" design have been employed (Campbell & Stanley, 1990). We are aware that in

Table 4. The selected sample and distribution among groups

Group	Women	Men	Total	Departments	Notes
Group 1	6	3	9	3	Only using MS Office
Group 2	9	4	13	3	Using MS Office and OpenOffice.org
Total	15	7	22	3	-

Figure 1. Experimental design adopted

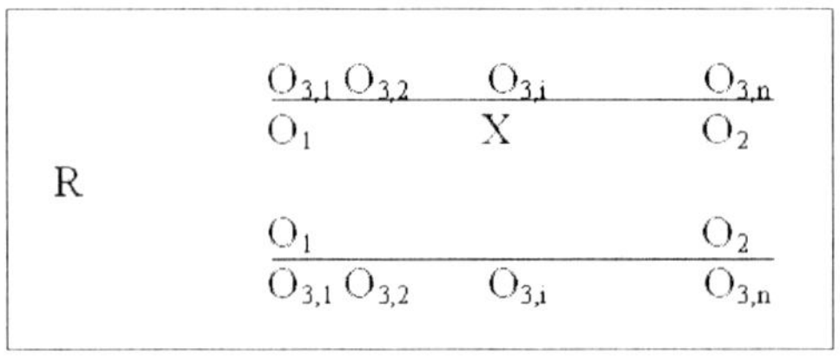

this way the results obtained are less extendible to the general case and more subject to exogenous effects.

TIME EVOLUTION OF THE EXPERIMENT

The experiment lasted for 32 weeks; during the first 10 only Microsoft Office was monitored and the different system dependencies were collected. OpenOffice.org was introduced in group 2 after week 10 and during the 23rd week of experimentation OpenOffice.org has been associated with Microsoft Office formats .doc and .xls. The results of the choice will be exposed in the subsequent sections. Figure 2 shows a graphical representation of the evolution of the experimentation.

In detail, the steps performed during the experimentation were the following:

1. Selection of the participants to the experiment;
2. Submission of the questionnaires on the attitude towards OSS;
3. Motivational seminar on the reasons of the experimentation;
4. Identification of the OpenOffice.org experimental group and control group;
5. Analysis of the most used documents and the possible software dependencies;
6. Installation of OpenOffice.org and translation in the OpenOffice.org format of the most used documents and on a per request basis;
7. Installation of the monitoring and data collection system to define the situation before the transition;
8. Training, performed on a single day, trying to focus on the different approach proposed by the new software; users were instructed on how to perform the usual office automation tasks;
9. Start of the OpenOffice.org data collection;
10. Support given to users through an online forum and a hotline;
11. Periodic verification meetings with users of OpenOffice.org to identify possible problems;
12. Automatic start of OpenOffice.org with files with Microsoft Office extension starting from week 23;
13. Submission of the final questionnaires.

Two types of questionnaires have been submitted to users. The first one identical before and after the experimentation, to understand the attitude towards OSS and the effects of the experimentation on such attitude; the second one has been submitted only at the end, where all the final results of the project have been collected and more information for the replication of the experiment have been determined. The Goal Question Metrics (GQM) paradigm (Basili, 1995) was employed in every phase of the project, from the overall design to the creation of the questionnaires. The GQM is a

Figure 2. Evolution of the experiment expressed in weeks

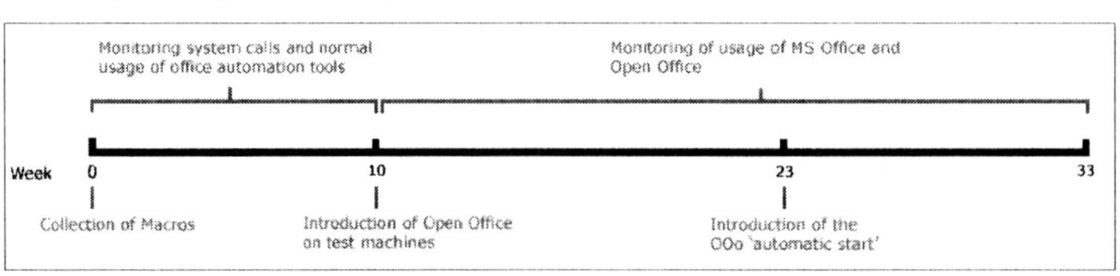

methodology that was developed at the University of Maryland in the mid-1980s that relates the goals of an organisation to a set of questions. Questions are further associated to a set of metrics. In this way it is always possible to evaluate whether a goal has been reached and what are the informational needs of a certain goal are.

SOFTWARE EMPLOYED

The tools used during the experimentation were useful to assess the evolution of the experiment and in particular to gather quantitative and objective data about the migration process. In particular, two applications were employed for the ex-ante analysis and one was continuously employed during the transition to monitor the usage of the proposed solutions.

- PROM (PRO Metrics), a noninvasive monitoring tool was used to evaluate the usage of OpenOffice.org and Microsoft Office during all the transition process (Sillitti et al., 2003). Metrics of interest were the number of documents handled and time spent per single document. The software has been running during all weeks of the experimentation, permitting us to acquire objective data on the experimentation.
- DepA (Dependency Analyser) has been employed to evaluate at the beginning of the project the existing dependencies of Microsoft Office in terms of called and calling programs (Rossi & Succi, 2004). The program is a simple agent running on workstations to determine the calls from different applications, collecting in this way information on the different interrelations between applications. The program has been running on client desktops for the first 10 weeks.
- FLEA (FiLe Extension Analyser) has been used to perform a scan of the data standards available on the users' drives and analyse the eventual presence of macros. The software permits us to collect information on the type of extension, date of creation, date of last access, size of the file, and for particular extensions also information about the macros contained. The scan was performed at the beginning of the experimentation.

All tools deployed are not noninvasive in order not to bias the results. From the final questionnaires emerged that users did not notice the presence of any external software during the experimentation.

DATA ANALYSIS

In this section we report the results of the data collection activities. In particular we can distinguish the data collection across a temporal boundary (*ex-ante, during, and ex-post*) and between *qualitative* and *quantitative* data.

The biggest effort during the project has been to monitor constantly the users during the experimentation. To gather objective data on the migration, we used the PROM software. Data collected included the time spent on documents and the number of documents opened using the selected office automation suite. A more fine-grained analysis on the function utilised has not been performed. During every phase of the project, the quantitative data collected has been backed with qualitative data coming from interviews and questionnaires. As a

Table 5. Type of data collected during the experimentation

	Ex-ante	During	Ex-post
Qualitative	Interviews/questionnaires	Periodic meetings for feedback	Interviews/Questionnaires
Quantitative	Collection of data standards (FLEA), Collection of dependencies (DepA)	Monitoring of SW usage (PROM)	Number of OOo files created during the project.

side effect, we noticed that the periodic meetings performed with users caused a small increase in the usage of the open source solution during the immediate subsequent days.

We will briefly review all the data collected, starting from the analysis of the existing situation, performed at the beginning of the experimentation.

EX-ANTE ANALYSIS

The aspects we analysed for an overview of the existing situation were concerned with the presence of interoperability issues in the users' environment and the presence of possible dependencies in the form of macros inside office automation documents. Macros are a series of commands inserted in the form of code inside documents, to perform a series of repetitive actions. They are generally very common in office automation documents, to permit the automation of repetitive tasks. As the usage in OpenOffice.org of macros written for Microsoft Office is not possible—at least at the time the experimentation was carried out—this is an interoperability issue. Macros need, in this way, to be completely rewritten.

The number of templates in the preexisting format represents another interoperability issue. Our software for data collection granted us the possibility to evaluate the number of this type of documents, but not the complexity, another factor to take into account when there is the need to migrate a document. The collection of such data has to be crossed with interviews with the IT personnel to evaluate the real relevance of the macros discovered and the real necessity of the conversion of templates.

The first step for performing the initial analysis of the experimentation environment was the one related to the presence of macros inside documents and the distribution of the documents. Another important issue was to find the number of templates available. This analysis has been performed statically at the beginning of the project. In the evaluation of macros impact, Microsoft Word and Microsoft Excel documents of the participants to the project were considered. Two different locations were considered:

- Users' drives
- Network drives

In the last location, both normal documents and templates were considered. Table 6 reports a summary of the results. We found 25.810 Word documents and 2.192 Excel documents. Among these, only 2 Word documents (0.01%) and 49 Excel documents (2.24%) contained macros. Moreover, our tool has identified a high number of Excel documents protected by password (near 16% of the total). In this case, it is not possible to determine whether they contain macros.

The second step has been the identification of the software dependencies that existed in the office automation environment. A dependency is either a call to an external application (outgoing call) or a call from an external application to the office automation suite (incoming call). As the dynamic evaluation of the calls, two different typologies have been considered:

- Applications that call Microsoft Word or Excel (Figure 3)

Table 6. Number of documents and macros during the pretransition phase; LOC = Lines of Code, CNO = Could Not Open

Location	Microsoft Word				Microsoft Excel			
	Files	Macros	LOC	CNO	Files	Macros	LOC	CNO
Users' driver	19144	2	12	-	1367	8	1070	14
Network driver	4484	-	-	-	816	43	21482	331
Network drives (templates)	2182	-	-	-	9	3	10197	-

Figure 3. Number of incoming dependencies of Microsoft Word (left) and Microsoft Excel (right)

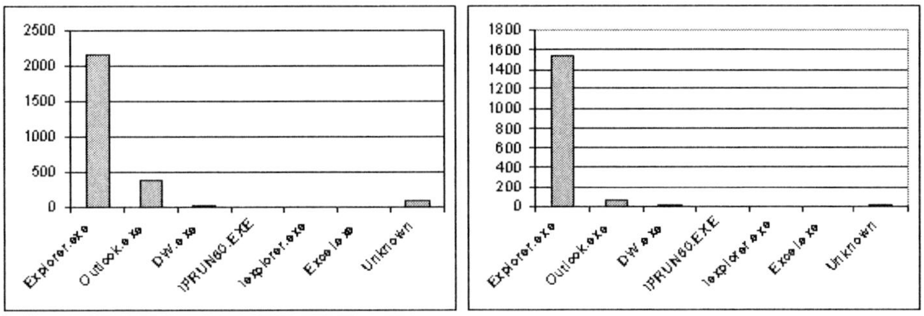

In this category we discovered that 80% of the times, Microsoft Word was called from explorer.exe which means a normal start from its icon or a file on the file manager. Furthermore, 12% of the times it was called from the e-mail client Outlook. Microsoft Excel was called 95% of the times by explorer.exe and 4% of the times from Outlook (for a total of 99% of the calls).

- Applications called from Microsoft Word or Excel (Figure 4)

74% of the global calls have been towards printer drivers. Almost 11% of the calls of Microsoft Word and Excel have been towards the program to report problems in Microsoft applications, and about 6% for the help guide.

Further interviews with IT managers confirmed the situation outlined by data collection tools. Globally, the system environment of the experimentation was less turbulent than we had thought initially. Templates, macros, and dependencies collected were not so critical to increase significantly the migration costs.

Figure 4. Number of outgoing dependencies for Microsoft Word/Excel

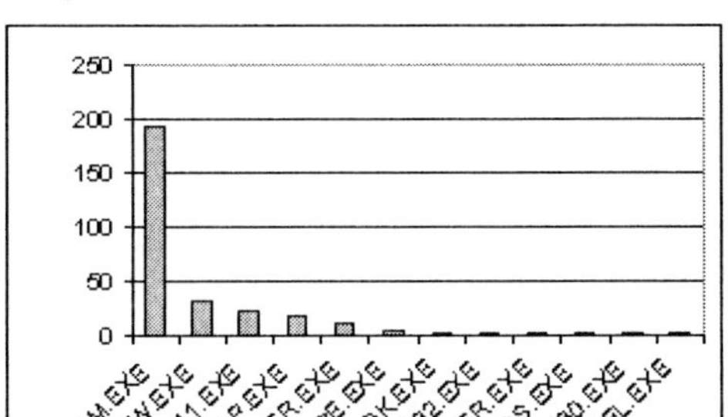

ONGOING EXPERIMENT ANALYSIS

The experimentation has been monitored constantly by PROM software. Figure 5 shows two different measures of productivity, the percentage of documents opened by using OpenOffice.org and the percentage of time spent within the OpenOffice.org suite. As an example, a percentage of 5% means that users spent in that week 95% of the time using Microsoft Office.

From the data collected, we can notice, in particular, two effects:

- As expected, the level of adoption of the new software has been increased by the decision to associate the Microsoft Office file formats with OpenOffice.org. We expected to have complaints and reports of incompatibilities deriving from this decision. What happened was instead that users learned when it was convenient for compatibility reasons to adopt one solution or the other.
- Even after 32 weeks of experimentation, the time spent with OpenOffice.org was below 25% of the total time dedicated to the two suites for office automation. Also to note is the fact that the time and documents of Figure 5 are inclusive of the Microsoft Office documents opened with OpenOffice.org.

Figure 5. Increase in OpenOffice.org usage. On the X-axis there is the week of the project; OpenOffice.org has been inserted during week 10; and the automatic association has been activated during week 23. In blue the percentage of opened files using OpenOffice.org is represented and in orange the percentage of average time devoted to OpenOffice.org among users that effectively used OpenOffice.org.

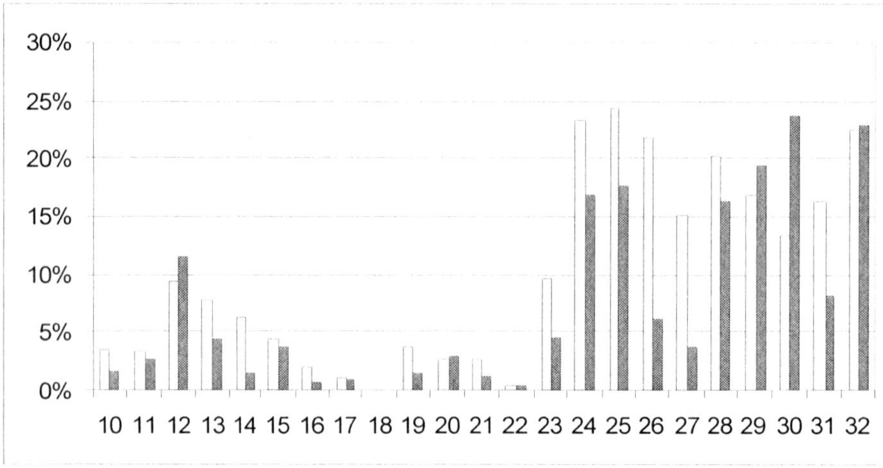

It is noteworthy that, during the experimentation, we did not benefit fully from the network effect that can be raised by the growing number of documents in one format and the subsequent exchange between users (Shapiro & Varian, 1999). In a broader migration such effects can also have an impact increasing the usage of the new platform proposed. In our experimentation users were in some way constrained in the adoption of the new format, as they could not exchange the documents with the users not participating in the experimentation.

We also posed two questions to evaluate the impact on productivity, according to the GQM methodology:

1. Did the usage of OpenOffice.org caused a reduction in the number of documents used per day? We studied the correlation between the number of documents used each day and number of documents opened with OpenOffice.org. A negative effect on the usage of OpenOffice.org had to produce a negative impact on the usage of the office automation documents and a significant negative correlation between these two variables; that is, the more documents are handled with OpenOffice.org, the less they are globally handled. The correlation in question has been of -0.08, therefore we exclude that the usage of OpenOffice.org has reduced the number of documents handled daily.
2. Did the usage of OpenOffice.org caused an increase in the time devoted to each document? We studied the correlation between the time spent managing all the documents and the OpenOffice.org ones. A negative effect on the usage of OpenOffice.org has to create a significant positive correlation; that is, it should be evident that the more time spent with OpenOffice.org, the more time is spent globally managing documents, as OpenOffice.org required more time to accomplish the same tasks. This correlation has been determined in -0.04, therefore it has to be excluded that the usage of OpenOffice.org has increased the global effort to handle documents. The comparison with the control group confirmed furthermore that the evolution of the usage of documents among the test group and the control group has been consistent, excluding the presence of exogenous factors.

EX-POST ANALYSIS

At the end of the experimentation, the evaluation of the attitude towards OSS and in general the evaluation of the project has been performed. We submitted one questionnaire to users in order to evaluate their attitudes towards OSS and the knowledge that was acquired after the transition. We submitted also the same questionnaire to the control group to ensure that no exogenous effects biased the results. The questionnaire was designated to answer to the following two questions:

- What is the user perception of OSS at the end of the experiment?
- Has the user modified his/her perception of OSS at the end of the experiment?

All figures of this section represent the ex-ante situation on the left and the ex-post situation on the right. In this way it should be easier to evaluate the change of users' attitudes.

The *first question* that has been submitted was whether the Open Source concept has become more familiar after the experimentation. The result in this case is quite obvious; at the end the users had a clearer idea of the concept of OSS. It may be surprising the initial number of users claiming to know OSS, but this is due to the preproject meetings with IT managers explaining the reasons of the experimentation.

The *second question* enters the heart of the matter, questioning about the perception of OSS. In this case an interesting phenomenon has been discovered. At the beginning one group had no opinion on OSS (almost half of the interviewed). At the end of the experiment, almost all users have an opinion: those that were positive maintained the same opinion and the uncertain were divided into three groups almost of the same size, those with a positive opinion, those with a negative one, and those that had no opinion. Nevertheless, at the end of the experiment only a small part of the participants had a negative opinion on OSS.

Figure 6. Question 1: How familiar are you with the expression Open Source Software? Possible answers: (a) very well, (b) well, (c) neither nor, (d) not well, (e) not at all.

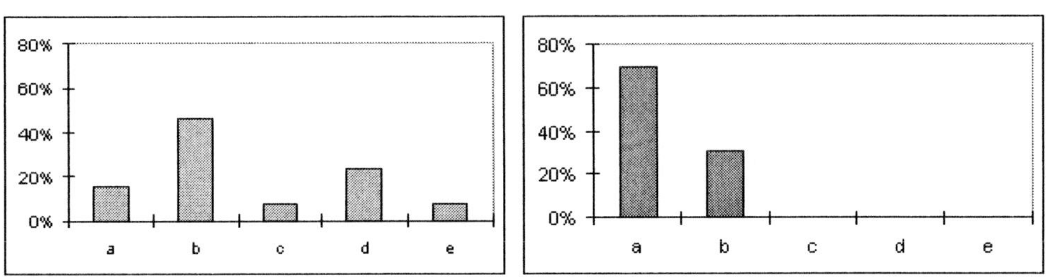

Figure 7. Question 2: How do you perceive the expression Open Source Software? Possible answers: (a) as something negative, (b) as something positive, (c) neither positive nor negative.

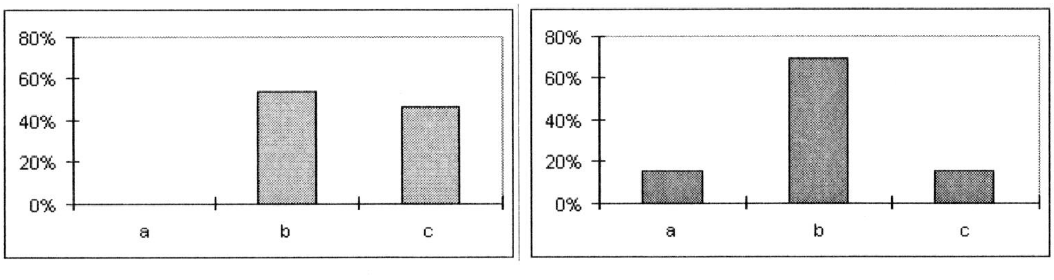

The *third question* focuses on the importance of the diffusion of the software in use. In this answer we have a strong movement towards a bigger knowledge; for example, the category "very important" has gone from 0 to almost 40%. The experimentation in the usage of OpenOffice.org has strongly increased the consciousness of the participants on the importance of the usage of well established software.

The *fourth question* poses the problem of the direct substitution and asks the user how much the user is reluctant to abandon the application in use in favour of an OS solution. In this case the user in favour maintained the same opinion, while reluctant people became more reluctant; also in this case users had a clearer idea of OSS after the experimentation. More than half of the interviewed users were still positive towards a possible transition.

The *fifth* and *sixth questions* present a slightly different nature. The aim is to find whether the experimentation changed the perception on the requirements of the software to be adopted and used. Question 5 focuses on the factors to consider when a new product is adopted and question 6 discusses the more important aspects of an efficient usage. In both cases the role of the training and support is evidenced as important, while other aspects as security, privacy, and availability of source code are considered less important. We can conclude that the effect of the OpenOffice.org introduction has increased the perception of the importance of the training. From one side, this can be obvious: the introduction of a new instrument requires always a training period, especially if it partially substitutes an old one. We must also point out that all the interviewed people had already performed their training with the office automation tools

Figure 8. Question 3: How important is it that the application you use is established and widely used? Possible answers: (a) very important, (b) important, (c) of moderate importance, (d) of little importance, (e) not important.

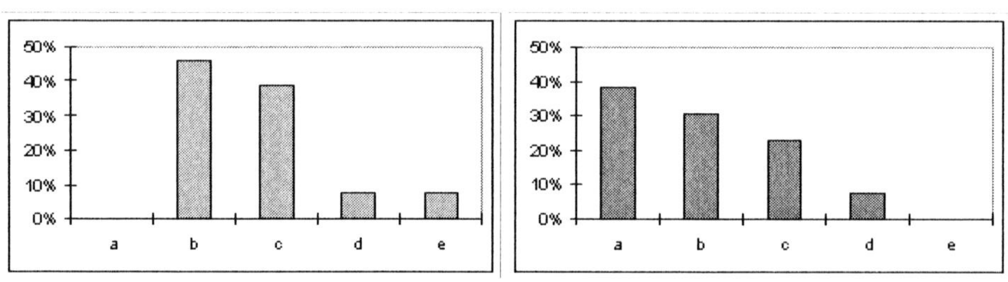

Figure 9. Question 4: You are reluctant to give up the use of application software that you are using to in favour of an OSS alternative! Possible answers: (a) totally agree, (b) agree, (c) neither, (d) disagree, (e) totally disagree.

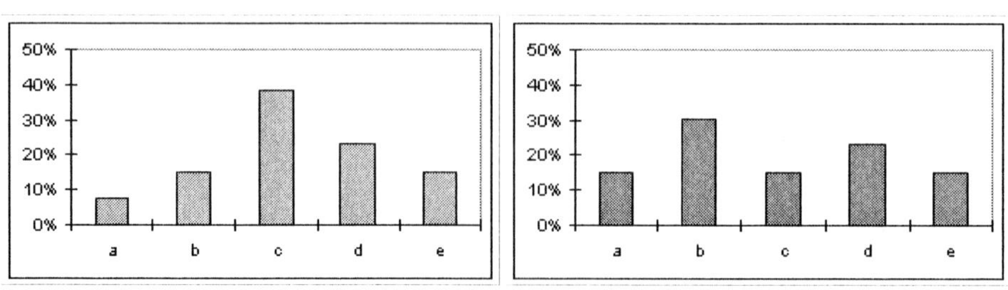

Figure 10. Question 5: How important do you find the following factors when you use a new IT-platform? Factors considered are: (a) support and training, (b) easiness of use, (c) interoperability, (d) source code available, (e) functionalities, (f) security, (g) privacy.

<table>
<tr><th>Position</th><th>Before the experiment</th><th>After the experiment</th></tr>
<tr><td>1</td><td>Easiness of use</td><td>Easiness of use</td></tr>
<tr><td>2</td><td>Functionalities</td><td>Support and training</td></tr>
<tr><td>3</td><td rowspan="3">Support and training, interoperability, security</td><td>Functionalities</td></tr>
<tr><td>4</td><td>Interoperability</td></tr>
<tr><td>5</td><td>Security</td></tr>
<tr><td>6</td><td>Privacy</td><td>Privacy</td></tr>
<tr><td>7</td><td>Source code available</td><td>Source code available</td></tr>
</table>

Figure 11. Question 6: The biggest advantages you perceive with OSS are: Factors considered: (a) better support and training, (b) it is easier to use, (c) stability, (d) better functionalities, (e) better security.

<table>
<tr><th>Position</th><th>Before the experiment</th><th>After the experiment</th></tr>
<tr><td>1</td><td>Easiness of use</td><td>Easiness of use</td></tr>
<tr><td>2</td><td rowspan="2">Better functionalities, more stable</td><td>Better support and training</td></tr>
<tr><td>3</td><td rowspan="2">Better functionalities, more stable</td></tr>
<tr><td>4</td><td>Better support and training</td></tr>
<tr><td>5</td><td>Better security</td><td>Better security</td></tr>
</table>

some time before, therefore such perception should already be present. It can be concluded that OSS has additionally stimulated the curiosity of participants, to the point to ask more questions about the tools used; such approach, if confirmed, can go in favour of people who claim that the adoption of OSS brings more "shared" knowledge.

The *last question* proposed before and after the experimentation is a sort of summary and deals with the motivations that the user would have to use OSS. It is interesting to note that near OSS supporters a new group emerged also absorbing neutral users towards a more negative opinion.

Some questions about the overall evolution of the migration have been submitted to users at the end of the project. Two questions are interesting for our evaluation of the migration, both related to the functionalities of OpenOffice.org and the possible full migration to the new solution proposed. We must point out that the experimentation has been performed with version 1.1.3 of OpenOffice.org; the latest release would, probably, obtain better results.

Question 8 faces the problem of the choice between the two proposed solutions in a general way. It asks whether the functionalities offered by the two suites are equivalent. Some users answered that Microsoft Office offers more functionalities than OpenOffice.org 1.1.3. In some way, the surprise may be that half of the users considered the set of functionalities offered equivalent.

Question 9 contextualises the problem. It tries to evaluate the impact of a possible substitution of Microsoft Office with OpenOffice.org. In this case almost all the participants in the test considered the migration as possible, even though the majority sustained later that this operation requires some effort and is not only a simple substitution.

A final evaluation of the experimentation has been performed on the number of files generated by the users adopting the new data standard supplied by OpenOffice.org. Table 7 contains a

Figure 12. Question 7: Which motivations do you have to use Open Source Software? Possible answers: (a) You believe it is right to support OSS initiatives, (b) You find that today's market dominance of a single software vendor is wrong, (c) other: specify, (d) I have no motivation to use Open Source Software.

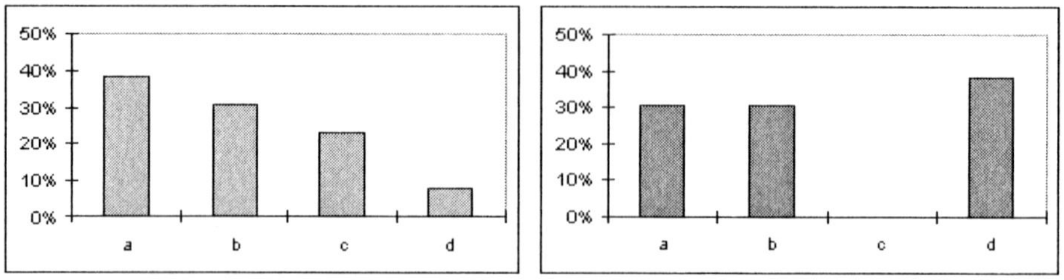

Figure 13. Question 8: How do you evaluate the functionalities of OpenOffice.org with respect to the Microsoft Office ones? Possible answers: (a) widely superior, (b) superior, (c) equal, (d) inferior, (e) widely inferior.

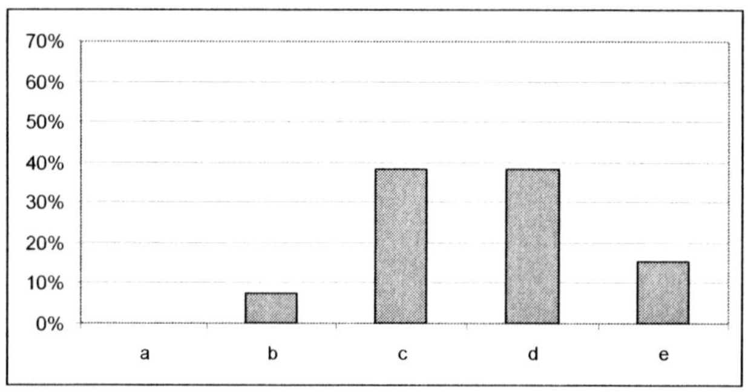

summary of all the different files created during the experimentation in the two different formats proposed by the OpenOffice.org suite for text processors and spreadsheets. Obviously this kind of static analysis represents only a small subset of the usage of the open solution, as users had also the freedom to open Microsoft Office proprietary formats using OpenOffice.org. For technical reasons FLEA could not be employed in this type of scan to give us more fine-grained data.

LIMITATIONS

This study represents the results of a single experience and such results cannot be systematically generalised, as the essential comparative aspect is missing. As already mentioned, the PA under exam has imposed some constraints on the selection of the sample. The office automation field, in particular, may not be fully comparable to other desktop environments where open source solutions are not as strong as OpenOffice.org. Furthermore, this study does not focus on a complete substitution of the old solution, rather on the evaluation of the coexistence of both solutions. A further step might be the evaluation of the effects deriving from a complete migration.

CONCLUSION

The migration to OSS described in this article has to be taken with care before generalising the results to other similar cases. In particular the migration has been restricted to the OpenOffice.org platform and to the PA field. The migration approach has been the more gradual as possible, maintaining the proprietary solution in parallel with the new one.

The results obtained from the experimentation have been encouraging for the introduction of OSS

Figure 14. Question 9 – In this moment, if Microsoft Office is removed, are you still able to perform the same tasks? Possible answers: (a) yes, (b) yes but with some problems, (c) no.

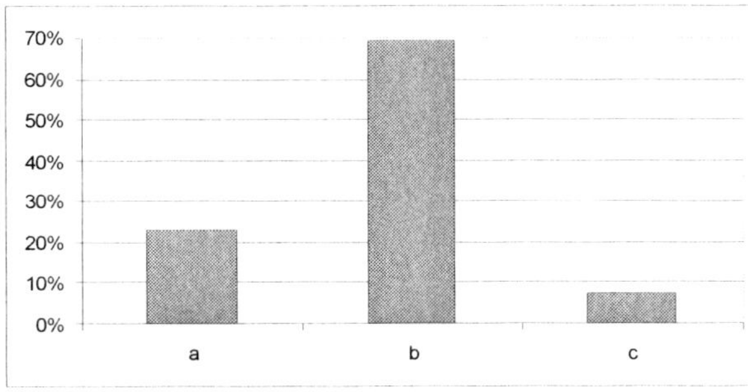

Table 7. Number of documents created during the experimentation

	Writer documents	Calc documents
Department 1	27	2
Department 2	223	34
Department 3	164	12
Total	414	48

on the desktop-side. Data collected during the experimentation shows that the usage of the new platform increased during the whole period, reaching at the end 25% of the total office automation tasks. Proprietary software remained the preferred solution for users. The impact on productivity has been minimal also due to the similarities of the software considered. Users acquired a better understanding of OSS after the experimentation and tended to have, in general, a positive vision of the whole movement. Software used has been considered adequate for the transition, although a sort of lack of functionalities emerged from the opinions of the users. More recent releases of OpenOffice.org should solve these problems.

ACKNOWLEDGMENT

We acknowledge Dr. Hellmuth Ladurner for his precious help and support. Acknowledgments also go to all the users involved, participants in the experiment, technical personnel, and supervisors; without their constant effort and their availability, this study would not have been possible.

REFERENCES

Basili, V. (1995). Applying the goal/question/metric paradigm. Experience factory. In *Software quality assurance and measurement: A worldwide perspective* (pp. 21-44). International Thomson Publishing Company.

Campbell, D.T., & Stanley, T.D. (1990). *Experimental and quasi-experimental design.* Houghton Mifflin Company.

CERT. (2001). Advisory CA-2001-19: Code Red Worm. Retrieved June 15, 2006, from http://www.cert.org/advisories/CA-2001-19.html

Everitt, K., & Lederer, S. (2001). *A usability comparison of Sun StarOffice Writer 5.2 vs. Microsoft Word 2000.* Retrieved June 15, 2006, from http://www.sims.berkeley.edu/courses/is271/f01/projects/WordStar/

Feller, J., & Fitzgerald, B. (2001). *Understanding Open Source Software development.* Addison-Wesley.

Fenton, N.E., & Pfleeger, S.L. (1997). *Software metrics: A rigorous and practical approach* (2nd ed.). PWS Publishing Company.

Gartner Inc. (2003). *Distributed computing chart of accounts*. Retrieved June 15, 2006, from http://www.gartner.com/4_decision_tools/modeling_tools/costcat.pdf

Landeshauptstadt München. (2003). *Clientstudie der Landeshauptstadt München*. Retrieved June 15, 2006, from http://www.muenchen.de/aktuell/clientstudie_kurz.pdf

Netcraft Survey. (2005). Retrieved June 15, 2006, from http://news.netcraft.com/archives/web_server_survey.html

Newsforge. (2002). *Largo loves Linux more than ever*. Retrieved June 15, 2006, from http://www.newsforge.com/print.pl?sid=02/12/04/2346215

Nichols, D.M., & Twidale, M.B. (2003, January). The usability of Open Source software. *First Monday, 8*(1). Retrieved June 15, 2006 from http://www.firstmonday.org/issues/issue8_1/nichols/

Robert Frances Group. (2002). *Total cost of ownership for Linux Web servers in the enterprise*. Retrieved June 15, 2006, from http://www.rfgonline.com/subsforum/LinuxTCO.pdf

Rossi, B., & Succi, G. (2004). *Analysis of dependencies among personal productivity tools: A case study*. Undergraduate Thesis, Free University of Bolzano-Bozen.

Shapiro, C., & Varian, H.R. (1999). *Information rules: A strategic guide to the network economy*. Harvard Business School Press.

Sillitti, A., Janes, A., Succi, G., & Vernazza, T. (2003, September 1-6). Collecting, integrating and analyzing software metrics and personal software process data. In *Proceedings of EUROMICRO 2003*, Belek-Antalya.

Stadt Nürnberg. (2004). *Strategische Ausrichtung im Hinblick auf Systemunabhängigkeit und Open Source software*. Retrieved June 15, 2006, from http://online-service.nuernberg.de/eris/agendaItem.do?id=49681

Stadt Wien. (2004). *Open Source software am Arbeitsplatz im Magistrat Wien*. Retrieved June 15, 2006, from http://www.wien.gv.at/ma14/pdf/oss-studie-deutsch-langfassung.pdf

The Yankee Group. (2005). 2005 *North American Linux TCO survey*. Retrieved June 15, 2006, from http://www.yankeegroup.com

ZDNet. (2005). *Extremadura Linux Migration case study*. Retrieved June 15, 2006, from http://insight.zdnet.co.uk/software/linuxunix/0,39020472,39197928,00.htm

ENDNOTES

1. Apache Software Foundation, http://www.apache.org
2. The Mozilla Firefox project, http://www.mozilla.com/
3. gnuLinex, http://www.linex.org/
4. OpenOffice.org, http://www.openoffice.org
5. Microsoft Office, http://www.microsoft.com/office/editions/prodinfo/default.mspx

This work was previously published in International Journal of Information Technology and Web Engineering, Vol. 1, Issue 3, edited by G. I. Alkhatib and D. C. Rine, pp. 64-80, copyright 2006 by IGI Publishing, formerly known as Idea Group Publishing (an imprint of IGI Global).

Chapter LXXII
Organisational Challenges of Implementing E-Business in the Public Services:
The Case of Britain's National Mapping Agency

Francesca Andreescu
University of Greenwich, UK

ABSTRACT

Underpinning £136 billion of economic activity in the United Kingdom, Britain's National Mapping Agency is a commercialising public sector organisation having trading fund status and existing in the intersection of two different spheres—the public and the private. Recognised as a leading participant in the geographic information industry, within which it is forging partnerships with key private sector companies, the organisation has enthusiastically grasped e-business as an all-embracing phenomenon and implemented a new strategy that transformed the way it did business. Drawing on longitudinal data gathered over a period of four years, this article explores the processes of strategic and organisational transformation engendered by e-business implementation in this organisation and discusses the successful elements, as well as some of the challenges to its change efforts.

INTRODUCTION

A common theme within the management literature in recent years has been the take up of private sector management strategies and practices by public sector organisations, designed to increase efficiency, performance, and cost economy in the activities they performed. In the United Kingdom, more specifically, in the context of significant changes in their operating environments and pressures to increase efficiency and accountability, public sector organisations have been urged to experiment with new organising ideas, structures, and processes and transform the way they do business, by taking the opportunities and meeting the challenges that e-technologies and e-ways of working presented. As a result, public sector organisations have embraced e-business and have made innovative uses of Internet technologies to invent new business models or to enhance existing practices. E-business has been seen as a way of transforming these bureaucratic, centralised, and reactive organisations and their capabilities. Whilst the Internet created new commercial opportunities for public sector organisations, e-business was thus about exploiting those opportunities.

This article draws on findings from a study conducted over a period of four years in a commercialised public sector organisation to reveal the processes of strategic and organisational transformation engendered by e-business during the implementation of a complex structural and cultural change programme aimed at reshaping this organisation and rethinking how it provided value to its customers. The discussion will examine the dilemmas and constraints identified by managers in the interpretation of the e-business strategy concept and why its implementation in practice can be challenging. Whilst the Internet offers a technological solution, the findings of this case study suggest that the successful implementation of a wider e-business strategy depends on managing simultaneously a number of projects which cross organisational boundaries and link organisational and technological factors.

The article is divided into five main sections. The first section reviews recent e-business research and highlights that studies treating the concept of e-business as an all-embracing phenomenon and analysing in depth its implications are relatively rare. The second section of the article describes the methodology used in the study. Information on the contextual developments within the case study organisation is followed by a discussion of the research findings. The case study is used as a background for discussing some of the challenges and constraints that this commercialising organisation faces in implementing a wider e-business strategy. Finally, the concluding discussion highlights key lessons learnt and implications for practitioners.

E-BUSINESS AND ORGANISATIONAL CHANGE: REVOLUTION OR E-VOLUTION?

Increasing environmental pressures, global economic uncertainties, changes in public and community expectations, and pressures to increase public accountability have provided the momentum for British public sector organisations to examine the effectiveness of their management structures, systems, and processes. The emphasis is on achieving efficiency, effectiveness, and economy in the activities performed by public organisations and on developing their ability to compete with private sector organisations. As a result, many public sector organisations are now existing in the intersection of two different spheres—the public and the private (Kickert, 2001). They fit neither in the strictly public realm of state action nor in the strictly private realm of commercial relationships. They are expected to function like businesses—to be efficient, customer-driven, and client-oriented—yet they perform tasks that are inherently public. How to strengthen organisational capabilities in order to confront successfully the competitive pressures becomes, consequently, one of the biggest challenges for these organisations.

Research into appropriate e-business models has grown significantly over the past few years, with authors taking both theoretically and empirically based approaches to the development of taxonomies of business models suitable for the new economy. A number of business models focused upon individual business transactions that use the Internet as a medium of exchange, including both business-to-business and business-to-consumer (e.g., Becker & Berkemeyer, 2005; Carlton, 2001; Clay, 2001; Clegg, Chu, Smithson, Henney, et al., 2005; Gao, 2005; Garicano, 2001; Scott Morton, 2001; Smith, 2001). Interest has also tended to focus on new startups (Chaston, 2001; Clarke & Flaherty, 2004; Colombo, 2001) and on traditional organisations moving towards integrating electronic marketing and sales, purchasing, or customer service with their current businesses (e.g., Barnes, Hinton, & Mieczkowska, 2005; Bhaskar, 2005; Chen & Leteney, 2000; Hansen, 2000; Kotha, Rajgopal, & Rindova, 2001; Lee & Wang, 2001), or on the technology itself (Day & Schoemaker, 2000; Smith, 2001). Much research into the use of e-commerce, furthermore, has tended to focus on larger firms (Dutta & Segev,

1999), new business models for digital content (Barnes & Hunt, 2001; Boddy & Macbeth, 2000; Daniel, Wilson, & Myers, 2002; Mahadevan, 2000; Van der Wiele, Williams, Van Iwaarder, Wilson, & Dale, 2002), and the growth and development of dot-coms (Benoy, Cook, & Javalgi, 2001; Clay, 2001). Further studies revealed how the Internet has made possible types of business models previously very hard, or impossible, to implement (Mahadevan, 2000; Rayport, 1999; Timmers, 2000).

A key concern is how strategy can be developed in hypercompetitive markets where the speed of change makes traditional forms of analysis impractical (Hoffman & Novak, 2000; Ordanini & Pol, 2001; Venkatraman, 2000). Eisenhardt (1998, 1999) and Yoffie and Cusumano (1999a, 1999b) address this issue with concepts derived from complex systems theory and emergent strategy making. E-business has also confirmed the significance of the resource-based view of the firm. Competencies, such as knowledge management and the ability to integrate complex sets of technological and business skills, are identified as success factors in a number of case studies (e.g., Feeny, 2001; Harris, Coles, Dickson, & McLoughlin, 1999; Kotha, 1998; Sauer, 1993). Various studies also addressed the risks of Internet ventures, barriers to implementation, success factors, and steps needed to manage technology-driven change (e.g., Barua, Konona, Whinston, & Yin, 2001; Eisenhardt, 1999; Kotha et al., 2001; Porter, 2001).

In general, existing research has focused on issues related to the digital content provision (particularly online provision) and technologies or technology-based change generically, rather than focusing specifically on the organisational transformation required for successfully making the change to e-business. This topic is critically important because the majority of organisations are not startups, and many are not solely concerned with e-commerce and electronic markets. Rather, most organisations are traditional businesses which must grapple with finding a new architecture to meet the imperative of remaining competitive in an increasingly Internet-enhanced economy. Their concern is the adoption of e-business as an all embracing phenomenon, in other words, transforming key business processes with Internet related technologies (Deise, Nowikow, King, & Wright, 2000; Symonds, 1999). In particular, within the literature drawn on public sector organisations, the issue of how public sector organisations undergoing commercialisation can successfully make the transition from traditional approaches to e-business by taking advantage of e-technologies has received little attention.

Building upon these arguments, this article explores the processes of strategic and organisational transformation engendered by e-business implementation through an in-depth case study of a commercialising British public sector organisation within the geographic information industry. On doing so, the study aims to provide fresh insights into the internal transformation processes which occurred in an organisation evolving from the classical, bureaucratic, and centralised "public sector model" towards a new organisational form through embracing e-business as a corporate philosophy. We also aim to see whether practice had overtaken theory and, if so, what enhancements to existing theory could be learned from the practitioners in the field.

The definition of *e-business* adopted in this research takes the view that e-business represents:

> *the way in which organisations can gain value from the Internet technologies and encompasses not only e-commerce—selling and buying over a network, but also the way people within an organisation work together, the sharing of information and effective communication, the transactions and connections across a supply chain, between suppliers and distributors and consumers, as well as the relationships between individuals and institutions.* (Symon, 2000, p. 6)

Thus, unlike other authors (e.g., Clegg et al, 2002; Poon & Swatman, 1999) who use the terms more or less interchangeably, this study seeks to distinguish between e-commerce and e-business. E-business is not just the sharing of business information, maintaining business relationships, and conducting business transactions by means of Internet-based technology; it is also about the organisation's social environment and the relationships between people and technologies. Such a perspective highlights the complex nature of the notion and shows that e-business goes beyond e-commerce, in that when implemented successfully, it transforms an organisation and its capabilities entirely.

RESEARCH APPROACH

The research reported here is drawn from findings from a four-year study of organisational change in Britain's National Mapping Agency, carried out between 2001 and 2004. The study adopted a longitudinal perspective on change concerned with the holistic and processual character of organisational transformations over time (Pettigrew, 1985, 1990).

An inductive research strategy was employed, which was both iterative and developmental. The research aim was not to confirm hypotheses, but to understand the *process* of e-strategy implementation and the perceptions of those involved and affected. What was important was the process by which the changes were introduced, the reaction by organisational members to those changes, and their perception of them.

Data Collection and Data Types

The time period for data collection was between 2001 and 2004. This research involved three main types of data: in-depth interviews, documentary data, and nonparticipant observation.

Data were collected from the organisation at two time points during the research period to track the internal changes over time:

- Time 1 (2001/2002), corresponded to the official adoption of the new "business model")
- Time 2 (2003/2004) corresponded to the incorporation and consolidation of strategic changes, allowing for change to become partially "anchored" in new social structures and practices

A total of 89 interviews were conducted with the main actors involved in the strategic initiative programmes and in the implementation of change, such as deputy chief executive, corporate strategists, members of the top and middle management, other individual organisational members, and management consultants (Table 1). Most respondents had been with the organisation for a considerable period of time. This was supplemented with analysis of documentary evidence, including board minutes, strategy documents, reports of the steering committee, project teams, minutes of follow-up meetings, business plans, as well as nonparticipant observation.

During the field study, the researcher had access to the main participants, formal and informal meetings, existing minutes, and documentation highlighting some of the historical, processual, and contextual issues relevant to the e-business

Table 1. Number of respondents participating in interviews in Phase 1 and Phase 2

Position of Interviewee	Number in Time 1	Number in Time 2
CEO	1	1
Strategy Directors and Strategy Managers	6	5
Senior Managers		8
Senior Consultants	14	2
Project Managers	3	10
Line Managers	21	6
Individual Organisational Members	8	2
(Sales and Finance)	2	
Total Interviews = 89	55	34

strategy implementation. In addition, the interviews emphasised both individual and shared interpretations of key participants concerning actions, events, views, beliefs, aspirations, and motives. All interviews were tape-recorded.

The following section will introduce the case study organisation and present the results.

Research Site

Britain's National Mapping Agency (NMA) is a quasiautonomous agency within the geographic information industry with trading fund status. It employs approximately 1,850 staff, 1,350 of whom are based at the head office, whilst the rest—cartographic surveyors and territorial sales representatives—are dispersed among a network of 80 local offices around the country.

NMA is recognised as a leading participant in the geographic information industry, within which it is forging partnerships with key private sector companies. Its principal activities are twofold: the maintenance of the National Topographic Database by recording and storing measurements of new roads, houses, and so forth, and the creation of products from it, such as paper map series and digital datasets used in geographic information systems (GIS).

The organisation offered an excellent opportunity to study the organisational change required in transforming a former government agency into an e-business, culturally, commercially, and technically. Confronted by powerful pressures to improve organisational performance under the government modernisation agenda, NMA implemented a complex e-business strategy, combined with a huge investment in technology new product development, which were designed to radically change the organisation's structure, management, and knowledge processes. To take advantage of the opportunities that e-technologies and e-ways of working presented, NMA charted an ambitious organisational transformation in which e-business was seen as a catalyst for change and e-strategy as a route map.

This knowledge-intensive organisation is a particularly interesting example of how a public organisation managed to overcome the constraints of its business context to fashion its own destiny. Unlike other public sector organisations with stable, incremental environments, NMA is operating in conditions of low environmental stability, with frequent, rapid changes in geographic information systems technology. Due to the emergence of new digital technology, the geographic information industry is on the verge of rapid growth, particularly in the market for location-based services. The overlay of layers of data to create new views creates good commercial opportunities for NMA, such as in the correlation of geographic, commercial catchment area and sociodemographic data for use in supermarket home delivery services.

All of these trends make the geographic information industry very different from the more traditional consumer and industrial markets in which many other public organisations operate. With an increasingly challenging environment, pressures to develop e-business under the government e-strategy in the public sector and emergence of new technologies, NMA is closer to the "relentlessly changing organisations" model of Brown and Eisenhardt (1998) in the high-velocity computer industry. There are these particular "high-tech" and "e-business" features of NMA that make this public sector organisation such an interesting case for management research in general, and for e-business change implementation in particular.

Key Facts About NMA

- Modern data collection using the geographic positioning system (GPS) and location information.
- Turnover from operating activities: £110 millions in 2004; most of the income comes from computerised geographic data, which is used extensively in both the private and public sector, with around £136 billion of Britain's GDP underpinned by it.
- Core markets by 2004: Public sector and utilities (32%); land and property (5%); consumer (12%); commercial markets (mobile

communications and wireless; large retailers; banking, finance and insurance; transport and distribution) (51%).

- Has operated as a trading fund since April 1999, providing a greater degree of commercial flexibility and increased responsibility for its business planning and finances. As a trading fund the business has to make a profit but does not receive a subsidy from the taxpayer.
- A potential change in status towards a government-owned plc. was proposed in 2002 and rejected because it did not deliver the necessary benefits to the organisation. It was decided that it was in the public interest for NMA to remain a trading fund. However, enhanced financial freedoms and flexibilities have been granted by the government through a revised framework document in 2003.

Results

External Context

The *E-government Strategic Framework* (April 2001) set out a series of guiding principles for public sector organisations centred upon building services around citizens choices, making government and its services more accessible electronically and managing information and knowledge in more efficient ways to ensure easier online access and more effective use of all services. It set a series of e-government policies and targets for quasiautonomous agencies, stating as main objectives that 90% of low-value procurement transactions and 100% of document management should take place electronically by 2004 and that 100% of services should be available electronically by 2005. In order to meet these aims, public sector organisations must innovate within a common framework and manage their services as a business, focusing on cost effectiveness and funding mechanisms.

In line with these targets, Britain's national mapping agency was granted trading fund powers by Parliament in 1999 to give it direct responsibility for its own finances and freedom to develop new initiatives. In effect, this meant that NMA would remain obliged to serve the government by providing information across Britain whilst earning revenues in a commercial and increasingly competitive marketplace, reducing dependence on the taxpayer. Such a status provided the organisation with the opportunity to operate and compete commercially by earning commercial revenues for its geographical information in order to be self-funding, as well as be more accountable for the efficiency and effectiveness of its operations.

Internal Context

The organisation had a long history of unsuccessful reorganisations and frequent changes of Chief Executives. Since 1993, NMA has launched three different reorganisation initiatives under different governments, all of them recognised by managers and staff as "spectacularly unsuccessful."

Similar to other public sector entities undergoing public sector reform in the form of commercialisation, the efficiency and effectiveness of management processes were major challenges. NMA was a vertically integrated organisation, with an excessive degree of specialisation, rigid hierarchical divisions, and divided areas of activity with niches and boundaries that served no useful purpose. Underlying many of the problems of inefficiency and high costs was the monopoly situation that all costs could eventually be passed on to the market. The organisation was also a classic example of public service culture and organisational systems and processes. NMA's administrative structure based on departments and well-defined job categories had effectively prevented the organisation from operating in accordance with its own objectives and values. It was realised that, especially in the relationship between NMA's employees and its customers, too much importance was being given to resolving bureaucratic issues, to the detriment of customer service. In short, the internal structure worked against the integration of main business processes.

Drivers for Change

NMA has expanded considerably in recent years into commercial and leisure markets, both in the

U.K. and internationally. The environment in which the organisation operated was characterised by emerging opportunities for the rapid expansion of the digital market and, in particular, location-based services offered via the Internet. That sat alongside its activities in the mature market for traditional paper-based mapping.

The severe market competition and threat of product substitution through the mass expansion of digital information and the new status of trading fund acted as drivers for revenue maximisation and for placing greater emphasis on increasing the utilisation of geographical data. A key aspect of becoming a trading fund was to move towards performance targets and a culture of measuring, and rewarding achievement linked to the business vision. This new "business model" meant that NMA had to strike the right balance between maintaining consistent and accurate geographical information for the whole of Great Britain whilst ensuring its operations are funded by earning income and generating profits from the licensing of data to both the public and private sectors. The organisation was also required to make an average return on the capital it employs—on average around £40 million—of at least 5.5% a year and to pay an annual dividend to the government based on each year's trading results. In response to this challenge, a series of organisation change initiatives began.

The Change Agenda: From Bureaucracy to E-Business

With the advent of a new Chief Executive Officer recruited from the commercial sector in September 2000, considerable impetus for change was being evidenced. A reevaluation of the business from the customers' perspective was completed and the need for the organisation to develop innovative products and services that could be delivered electronically was identified. The review undertaken by the executive team identified that the greatest hindrance to achieving NMA's corporate goals were its structures and work practices. Another major change that had to occur was a shift from the old culture of public monopoly to the culture of a market-oriented, customer-focused, and self-financing organisation. The nature and direction of the required cultural shift was a radical change for many employees, who had spent virtually all their careers in the relative security, comfort, and complacency of the old "public sector ethos" culture. The "cultural inertia" among the majority of employees, at all levels, was one of the major challenges to management in trying to achieve the transformation to the new system of efficient business operations.

Following the review, a new vision formed the foundation on which the organisation could be transformed into an e-business: *NMA and its partners will be the content provider of choice for location based information in the new information economy.* In October 2000, a cross-functional team from across NMA was established to develop the vision into a new strategy for the organisation. The team used the mission statement as a starting point for designing the structure and process of the change programme and translating it into a new e-strategy.

Fundamentally, the e-strategy was about transforming the business commercially, technologically, and culturally, by implementing a new business model, combined with a multimillion pound investment in technology and new product development. The main strategic priorities were:

- Commercial revenue—increase commercial revenue from existing assets
- Reduce costs and waste
- Invest in new brands, infrastructure, and capability
- Grow data products and help partners to develop their products
- Aggressive marketing for products
- Grow partners and enable them to add value to products
- Build the best data to enable "joined-up geography"

The key emphasis was on better knowledge management, focusing on the needs of businesses and individuals, and helping partners to create radically new products underpinned by data maintained by NMA. At the heart of the new strategy was the idea of NMA working together with partners to become the content provider of choice for location-based information. This meant establishing commercial agreements with various partners in which NMA was providing the geographical data and the partners were developing the software required for customising this data in different ways and translating it into innovative products and services under NMA's brand.

A series of *objectives* were established:

- Delivering excellence in all aspects of the business, employing e-business principles to exceed customer expectations
- Identifying, developing, and maintaining effective strategic partnerships
- Ensuring that the business strategy is clearly understood by staff, customers, partners, and the wider community
- Establishing NMA as the centre of excellence for innovation in location-based information
- Developing a business of progressive people with skills appropriate to an e-business
- Changing the internal culture

A range of projects were identified that would exploit e-business technology and approaches to improve performance. An initial assessment of costs, benefits, and timescales were prepared. At the end of the four-week period, NMA Executive and Nonexecutive Directors approved the strategy. More detailed planning and evaluation of implementation costs and benefits followed as development work began.

A major feature of the e-strategy implementation was the intention to place the organisation at the forefront of the new information economy by embracing cutting-edge technology for supplying geographical data and enhancing the versatility of NMA data. This involved the implementation of a groundbreaking new concept of mapping and the development of new products, by transforming the map-making process so that electronic data could be available to customers within 24 hours of being surveyed. The key aim was to replace the traditional paper map products with large-scale electronic mapping, so that most of the products and services offered by the organisation could be delivered electronically; digital mapping now accounts for some 80% of the organisation's turnover.

Amongst the most pioneering products were a digital database and online service named Master Map, featuring definitive digital data for the whole of Great Britain and an online integrated product called Pre-Build TM. The Master Map database provides intelligent and accessible data with the flexibility to link information across and between organisations, whilst Pre-Build TM offered highly-detailed digital mapping pinpointing buildings and roads tailored to the needs of utilities and telecommunication companies.

The successful implementation of the new strategy pivoted on the adoption of *e-business as a corporate philosophy.* As the Chief Executive remarked:

e-business is key to our future success, opening huge new opportunities for us and our partners. It requires new ways of working and both individual and team efforts right across the business. We have the best data to underpin the Master Map of Britain. Our e-initiatives will ensure we can create and supply that data when, where and how our customers want it—and at the same times e-enable ourselves. (Chief Executive, 2001)

Collecting, maintaining, and delivering geographical data was at the forefront of NMA's activity and the implementation of the new e-business strategy acted as a driver for the transformation of its core business processes—data collection and management. The e-strategy was thus seen as the necessary framework for driving forward business change. As some senior managers argued:

The "E" strategy allows us to reassess how we manage the collection and delivery of our data to remain at the forefront of the industry, offering agility and flexibility to our customers. (Director—Data Collection and Management, 2001)

Table 2. Projects under the e-strategy

Strategic Initiative	Corresponding Projects
Putting the customer first	*Customer Web sites* *New Web site for the organisation* *Customer Relationship Management* *On-line Service* *Digital Mapping*
Strategic alliances	*Establishment* *Joined-up government* *Alliance Extranet*
The new mapping agency	*New ways of working and Project Platinum* *Knowledge management* *"Help yourself" (personalised online support for all employees)* *Raising the return (a new financial model)*
Developing the market	*Developing the Digital National Geographic Database* *E-Brands* *Location-based standards* *E-Business channels* *Market Development team* *Pricing and licensing*
Enabling infrastructure	*Enhancing the IT infrastructure* *Off-site 24/7 availability* *Enterprise Wide Software Suite (ESS)*

The Digital Maps business cannot grow enough without the e-strategy. This work is critical because it will allow us to create and deliver more innovative products much faster to our customers. It will allow us to become far more efficient and cost effective across a wide range of activities. (Director—Digital Brands, 2001)

As the main supplier of geographical information in Britain, NMA needed not only to implement tangible customer benefits and to advance online services, but also to change the organisation's internal culture to a customer-led one. The prevailing view amongst over 90% of senior executives interviewed was that e-business was not only about electronic service delivery, but also that "e" should become embedded in the employees' ways of working, in terms of approach and attitude:

For the future NMA, there is no business but e-business! We must become a more agile organisation able to respond to our customers and partners needs at "internet-speed." ... The IT technology is the engine room of this change providing the infrastructure, information systems and user support in transforming the organisation. However, if we are to succeed in achieving our strategic aims and becoming an e-business, it is essential that we develop new ways of working. We must improve our day-to-day business practices and ensure that we get the best out of people, knowledge, systems and facilities. (Chief Technology Officer, 2001)

The process of strategy formulation resulted in a series of 21 investment projects that were grouped into 5 strategic initiatives reflecting their interconnected nature (Table 2).

Putting the customer first initiative involved the adoption of e-business principles and technology to ensure that each customer and partner is managed at segment and individual levels. In the words of the Initiative Manager:

This initiative is critical because it will allow us to create and deliver more innovative products much faster to our customers. It will allow us to become far more efficient and cost effective across a wide range of activities. (Initiative Manager, 2001)

Customers were offered online access to a wide range of mapping data, product demonstrations to show the versatility of NMA data and tailor-made Web gateways into the mapping agency, each fostering improved, more focused customer service. These gateways included facilities for the online ordering and delivery of existing data products at any time of the day or night or requests for special mapping surveys. Each customer Web site held information specific to that customer or partner as well as access to generic information and functionality available to wider groups.

By December 2002, the implementation of a portal Web infrastructure environment increased the efficiency of personalisation and customisation provided to customers. In parallel, the NMA Web site was redeveloped to become a gateway for location-based services and information and an enterprisewide software was implemented to allow better customer relationship management. Users of the new Web site were able to access location-based information and services either directly provided by NMA or indirectly by partners and account holders (customers and partners) could order digital and graphic mapping online.

The *strategic alliance initiative* involved the establishment of a strategic alliance to help drive the location-based information industry forward in a cohesive manner and develop collaborative working between NMA and other parts of the government with the help of e-business technology. It involved joined-up geography by using NMA data and referencing framework to combine other location-based information from other government bodies, for example, land ownership, local authorities, addresses, field parcels, and land use. It also marked a change in the way NMA was making available its datasets to users, by enabling partners to commercialise this data, on behalf of NMA, in a more flexible way. The initiative manager talks of the overall project as follows:

This initiative ensures that our NMA has the right strategic relationships to help grow the geographic information industry. Our organisation holds an important position in the location based information industry but must work with key players in government and the private sector to realise the vision. (Initiative Manager, 2001)

The new mapping agency initiative focused on the people implications of the transformation of NMA into an e-business. The Project Manager states:

Whilst each of the other four strategic initiatives delivers in its own way significant change to the business, this initiative is the one that touches every single person in NMA. These projects are all closely related to our people and the way we do things. The focus is on simple and more effective ways of working whilst focusing on the needs of the customer. (Initiative Manager, 2001)

A programme called "New Ways of Working" addressed issues associated with the current organisational structure, people, culture, communication, and the way employees worked. The clear target was to make these elements more streamlined, adaptive, responsive, and customer-driven. This included changing the existing working practices, the implementation of new performance management, and reward systems focused on rewarding performance, changing the way information and knowledge are captured, coordinated, and made readily available within the organisation (knowledge management), and the implementation of a new software which allowed employees to manage their personnel records online whilst also eliminating unnecessary paperwork, procedures, administration, and costly support functions.

The organisation needed new competencies and skills among existing managers, so that they could drive forward the change programme. Current management capabilities were characterised by excellent technical abilities but poor people management skills, especially in terms of managing change and risk. It was considered that, in order to change the culture of the organisation, leaders and management teams had to develop themselves in readiness to embrace the new challenges and opportunities facing NMA. Therefore, a new programme entitled "Project Platinum" was designed to help leaders understand how they could influence the culture of the organisation, identify the competencies and skills required in leaders, and set in place a programme which could develop the behaviours supporting those competencies. As part of this initiative, a set-piece event—*NMA Experience*—was organised in December 2001. The event was attended by all the employees and was designed to explain to everyone the new vision and values of the organisation as an attempt to change the strong supportive civil service culture, rich in custom and practice, develop a new culture in line with the new direction of the organisation, and encourage creative and innovative behaviours. The core new values were identified as customer focused, quick, working together, able to take some risks, interested and excited by challenge, personally accountable, commercially oriented, and rewarded for results.

Developing the market initiative involved developing new partnerships and using new channels to reach new customers. In the past, NMA focused on an established core of customers in a relatively mature market with sectors such as central government, local government, and utilities. These customers increasingly expected better quality products and services in a market that was becoming more competitive. The organisation needed thus not only to develop the existing markets but also to find new markets and work with partners to develop new applications that will provide benefits to end customers. This involved adopting a proactive brand strategy, with a focus on digital location-based information and the launch of a new idea of geographic database—Master Map. Innovative in concept, Master Map was not a map in the traditional sense but a digital map framework through which customers could access the precise mapping data they needed. It offered a high level of flexibility and a complete reference system for Britain's geographical data. As the programme manager comments: "The initiative supports customers evolving needs, develops existing markets and opens new opportunities to ensure that NMA is the content provider of choice" (Initiative Manager, 2001).

Enabling infrastructure initiative involved building a robust new infrastructure of systems to underpin the e-business. A considerable amount of infrastructure has been put in place to support the whole of the e-strategy but particularly the Master Map idea. The Internet, extranet, and intranet applications were all upgraded and, in order to enhance customer benefit and operational efficiencies, the old systems were replaced with a single, integrated, enterprisewide software application platform. This integrated software package, called *Enterprise-Wide Software Suite* (ESS), offered a single repository for all NMA's data and was implemented in association with technology partners. One of the programme managers expressed a commonly held view:

The Enabling Infrastructure provides the foundation for the success of the e—Strategy. The application and technical environment that we build must provide the efficiencies that allow us to operate in an increasingly dynamic and delivery focused organisation. Information Technology (IT) provides the infrastructure, information systems and user support in transforming the organisation. Without a robust IT infrastructure none of the e-business activities will be sustainable. To a lesser or greater extent, we have all been frustrated when a system let us down, whether it be our own personal Internet Service Provider or a corporate system. As our business becomes increasingly dependent on IT systems, we have to avoid those frustrating (and potentially damaging) failures, as it is through the Enabling infrastructure initiative that we aim to do this. (Programme Manager, Enabling Infrastructure, 2002)

IMPLEMENTATION ISSUES

Organisational Restructuring

In order to successfully implement the e-business strategy, the structure of the organisation was reviewed and reorganised in November 2001. As the CEO summed up the rationale for this strategic initiative:

The need for accurate, reliable locational information underpins so many of the new services coming on stream and in Britain, no one has better locational information than us. ... But to stay at the forefront of the geographical industry we must keep pace with the market. That's why we're not only investing in e-business initiatives but have already put in place a whole new organisational structure to make it a reality. (Chief Executive, 2001)

The realignment of internal group structures and board responsibilities resulted in:

- The establishment of two brands businesses, based around distinct customer groups—Digital and Graphic Brands. The two brands' businesses were focused on introducing new and innovative ways of working with commercial and government partners to meet different customer group needs. Amongst such innovative approaches were the establishment of a joint-venture company with a commercial partner, with the aim of providing consistent and maintained points of interest data for the industry and an estimated £35 million content deal with a mobile phone operator that would allow mobile users to access coloured maps featuring real-time displays of various locations.
- The creation of a Business Change group that was charged with championing the transformation of the way the organisation did business and in particular managing the implementation of the e-business strategy.

Ownership of the Strategy

Ownership, accountability, and leadership were essential elements of the successful implementation of the NMA e-business strategy. As change was intended to be transformational and to affect all the aspects of the organisation and the levels within it, the entire programme has been top-down driven, with the provision of a clear, sustained direction that was well resourced and coordinated. The instigators of the transformation were the leaders of the organisation and the Strategy and Operating Board—including Executive and Nonexecutive Directors—had been heavily involved in the e-business strategy and monitor its implementation. In addition, each strategic initiative had a director-level owner who was accountable to the board for delivering the benefits of that initiative. Full-time initiative managers who focused on coordinating activity within their initiative have been appointed.

At project level, business owners have been identified, who were champions for their projects within the implementation. Project owners were responsible for ensuring that their projects delivered the benefits anticipated in the strategy. Where IT projects were involved in the delivery, the business owners worked in close conjunction with IT Programme and Project Managers.

Risk Management, Change Control, and Financial Monitoring at Appropriate Levels

Mechanisms have been implemented to ensure the adequate management of risks, costs, and change control during the implementation. The Operating Board received updates on implementation progress, including costs, on a fortnightly basis with a more detailed review undertaken six-weekly through a business health check exercise. In addition, a weekly implementation steering group (chaired by the Director of Business Change and including the Initiative Owner Directors) monitored strategic level risks, costs, and implementation progress. Significant changes to project contracts and business cases were approved by initiative owners and reported to the steering group. Furthermore, programme and project boards have been established within each initiative and these dealt with the day-to-day detail of implementation monitoring, cost control, and minor change control.

Internal Communication

In order to engage all employees in the business transformation associated with the implementation of the e-business strategy, considerable effort has been put into a coordinated programme of internal communication, which included:

- Face-to-face briefings with all staff in December 2000 and June 2001, including interactive and multimedia demonstrations of live and prototype systems
- Face-to-face briefings on quarterly basis with all field staff from December 2000 onwards
- Fortnightly update briefings at Operating Board—cascade briefed by managers to all staff and reported on Intranet
- A dynamic intranet site—regularly updated with project aims and progress
- Internal branding of the implementation activity to help focus all staff on the business transformation

Further Restructuring

In May 2002, a new Human Resources Director, recruited from the commercial sector, was appointed to drive forward the people side of the change programme. At her initiative, in August 2002, a team of senior managers undertook an eight-week review exercise (entitled "Emerald City") which involved looking forward to the future and identifying the challenges and opportunities that the organisation was likely to face in three to five years' time and how the business could be driven forward.

Following this review, in September 2002, the board announced a further restructuring of the organisation to help develop stronger teams and networks around the core processes (Figure 1) and to create a more flexible structure, with more flexible processes and communication patterns. This was accompanied by a review of staffing levels in different functional and subfunctional areas and 300 people were, consequently, released. A consequence of this restructuring was that a number of old divisions and functions were either eliminated or merged, in order to obtain a leaner, flatter structure and increase overall efficiency of the business.

The proposed new structure involved merging the Digital and Graphic Brands businesses into a single Sales and Market Development Group and creating a separate Programmes and Products Group, each headed by a Director. The Business Change Group activities were absorbed within other parts of the organisation. To give greater integration to corporate communications, the Corporate Communications Department has been integrated into the Human Resources and Corporate Services Group led by the HR Director. Minimal changes were introduced in the other groups.

As a result of these changes, the new structure due to be implemented starting with November 2002 incorporates seven major groups (Figure 2): strategy; human resources and corporate services; finance; information systems, Web, research and innovation; data collection and management; programmes and products; and sales and market development.

The previous structure created in November 2001 in relation to the e-strategy implementation served its purpose of focusing the organisation of work on developing new products and markets and gave an impetus to particular projects. It allowed NMA to strengthen its digital offering and also gave the graphic side of the business the confidence and space to develop, and between them both business groups could identify notable successes.

The new structure implemented in September 2002 offered a much higher level of functional flexibility. It gave clarity to the end-to-end processes of the business—from collecting data, through the production processes, and on the supply of data to partners and customers, whilst allowing the development of stronger cross-functional teams and networks around core processes. The number of hierarchical levels between top management and business groups teams has been substantially reduced and the seven groups have been organised along business processes, giving a lot of operational freedom to Group Managers. This freedom was balanced by a stronger planning process in the organisation, with group teams working with the strategy people on the overall planning.

The different cross-functional teams created meant increased horizontal communication between groups as well as vertical between the top management team and group teams, facilitated by

Figure 1. Core business processes in NMA

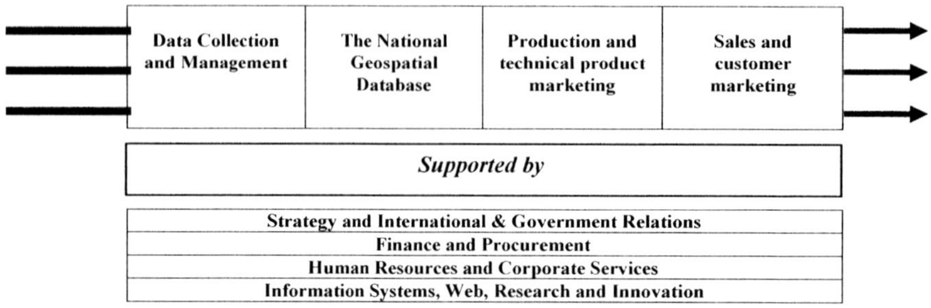

Figure 2. The new organisational structure

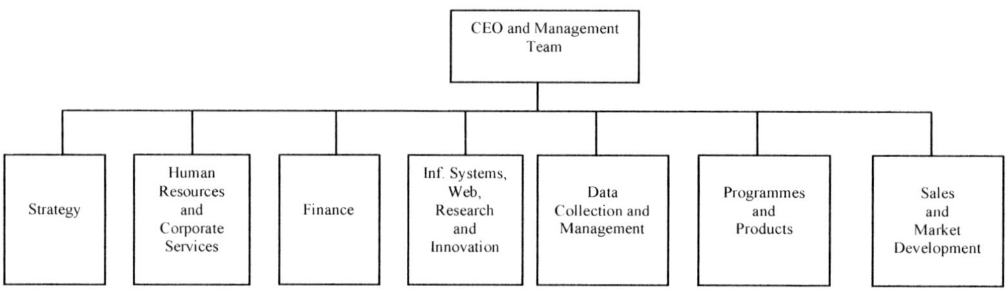

the use of modern information technology. The new organisation of work was trying to combine the strengths of a functionally arranged organisational structure, offering a better coordination of the core business process with the flexibilities in terms of vertical communication offered by a process-based structure.

The transition from the old structure to the new one was a lengthy process. The old structure was effectively being moved to the new structure on a level by level basis. As employees in the positions made redundant under the voluntary redundancy scheme were leaving the organisation, the remaining positions were being rearranged in the new structure and staff were notified about the new positions. Transition structures were being used to prop up the old structure and keep the day-to-day operations going. The implementation of the new structure was finalised in August 2003.

In parallel with these structural changes, in order to track and predict customer, market, and brand profitability, a Corporate Balanced Scorecard with six performance dimensions (financial performance; quality of service; flexibility; competitiveness; resource utilisation; and innovation) has been introduced as a way of consolidating corporate performance measures and focus them upon core strategy components. The aim of introducing the balanced scorecard, in addition to other measurement tools such as customer satisfaction surveys, employee opinions, and monthly business health checks, was to provide the management board with the means to monitor the progress of the business on an on-going basis. In addition, the strategy team could liaise better with individual business planners (Business Groups' Directors) for coordinating business processes across teams and establish integrated performance measures.

By December 2004, all the 21 projects comprising the e-strategy were fully completed and their success benchmarked against their key deliverables. A new business strategy 2005-2008, focused on how NMA will be meeting customer needs in the next four years, was created, building on some of the success aspects of the previous e-strategy: the creation of better data collection, maintenance and management systems as well as the development of new products and geographic solutions through partnerships with other public and private organisations. An event chart of the NMA "journey" is presented in Figure 3.

An overall assessment of the change efforts driven by the e-business implementation between 2000 and 2004 suggests the e-strategy implementation was a success. The progress made towards transforming the way the organisation worked was acknowledged by customers, partners, suppliers, and e-business experts, and employees noticed a marked improvement in their working environment. In addition to this feedback, the e-strategy was awarded five stars by the Government Office of the E-Envoy in 2004 and this rating indicated that the NMA's strategy was seen as a successful plan of action that has largely been met with key deliverables offering customers and staff new benefits. An operating profit of £9.4 million was forecasted by April 2005 thanks to careful management of costs, growth in revenue, and rigorous prioritisation of investments.

LESSONS LEARNED

The digital revolution offered huge opportunities for the organisation to improve the services that it provided to its customers, enhance its interaction with partners, and revolutionised the way people worked: first, by redrawing the way in which those services are provided to capture the full benefits of technology and, second, by tailoring the services to the needs of individual citizens, customers, and businesses. Electronic service delivery enabled NMA to become far more responsive and flexible, as well as creating the opportunity to harvest significant efficiency benefits.

The steps taken to meet the organisational challenges of implementing the e-business strategy across the organisation therefore provide a list of best practices for this particular situation (see Table 3). Several success factors relevant to e-business implementation emerged from this account:

First, one major lesson from this experience was that a successful organisational transformation involving e-business implementation requires clear leadership from the top management team. The NMA e-strategy has been created as the strategic blueprint to develop the business and firmly

Figure 3. Event chart, e-strategy implementation and follow-up (2000-2004)

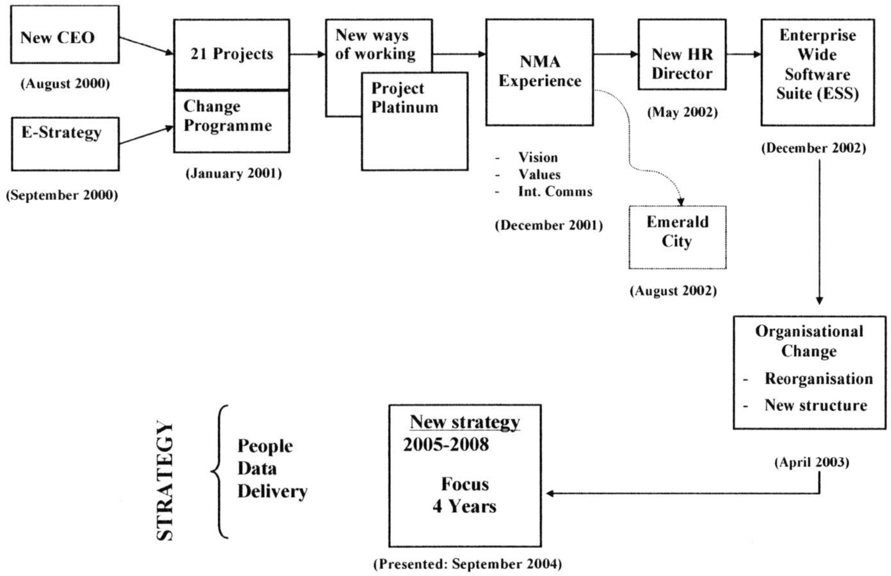

Table 3. Best practices for the implementation of the e-business strategy

No.	*Organisational Challenges*	*Steps Taken to Meet Organisational Challenges*	*Data from NMA*
1	Being "halfway" towards the private sector as a public sector executive agency moving towards a competitive commercial model	- Design a strategy that would capitalise on the unique position of the NMA on the market, as the biggest geographical information provider in U.K. with market-ready cutting-edge technology and high levels of internal capability - Establish strategic alliances to help drive the location-based information industry forward in a cohesive manner - Develop collaborative working between NMA and other parts of the government	"What we needed was a strategy that recognised our unique position. Something that enabled the organisation to have learning and, at the end of the experience, the learning would be resident in the organisation" (Corporate Strategist, 2001) "Who are our competitors? There is no single competitor for us. Because we are responsible for the national infrastructure of geographical information, there is no single other organisation who could and would want to replicate that, because it is hugely expensive to replicate that" (Senior manager, 2002)
2	Need to develop and communicate a clear e-business vision and the concept behind the change to the organisation as a whole and to all stakeholders, especially end users (customers and partners)	Communicate the why, where, and how of the change to the people involved in the 21 projects and to all employees by using mobilising events such as "NMA Experience." This builds confidence in the projects, lets the team know where they stand and where they are headed, and encourages commitment to the cause through the use of various internal communication mechanisms	"The top team and the board decided 'Right, this is our new strategy, this is were we are going, and this is our vision. We need to communicate that to everybody'" (Project Platinum Manager, 2002) "The essentials are around being absolutely clear about what it is you are trying to achieve and why — and I don't just mean the reorganisation. I mean: where do you want to be as a business?" (Senior manager, 2003) "What this event [NMA Experience] really did was to move the senior management up in the eyes of the workforce. It helped them understand that there was skill and ability in our senior team, and they were all committing to doing things in a different way and start leading the business more effectively" (Project Manager, 2002)
3	Create a feeling of ownership for the e-strategy at project level and a commitment at all levels of the organisation	- Get the project leaders and initiative owners involved early in the e-strategy projects - Communication events important in creating belief and feeling of ownership	"We put this plan together, represented by a railway journey. It's a single-track railway, a one-way journey, because we wouldn't be going back. It didn't have a starting-point because change has been going on forever, and we couldn't say if or when we would finish" (Chief Executive, 2001)
4	Need new effective communication channels between the project teams and between the Sales and Marketing teams and customers	- The project management teams were put in place to develop channels for and manage the communication between the different parties. Weekly, fortnightly, and quarterly status meetings help to keep all parties updated on each other's progress and on the progress of the e-strategy implementation as a whole	"After about three months we had improved the relationship between the project teams and the steering group. The steering group felt more comfortable and more confident in the ability of the teams to deliver" (Director of Business Change, 2002) "Communication forms the grounding for all the organisational work I have done. The communication, consultation and involvement strategy is what will make it happen" (Programme Manager, 2003)

continued on following page

Table 3. continued

No.	*Organisational Challenges*	*Steps Taken to Meet Organisational Challenges*	*Data from NMA*
5	Manage different customer segments: retain traditional loyal customers (public sector and utilities) whilst developing emerging markets (telecomm, retail, and insurance) and commercial partnerships	- From products to relationships: shift from a customer relationship management (CRM) focused on products or processes to a CRM philosophy focused on customer segments and the solutions they require - Identify the most profitable customer groups - Focus NMA's activity entirely on improving core business processes (data collection and management) and involve commercial partners in translating this digital data into business solutions that meet end users' needs through partnership agreements	"We need partners who would come and help us find/exploit certain niches in the market place. They are very well financed — e.g. Microsoft, big mobile operators and by enlarge our strategy is and will be in the future to partner with some of these companies rather than compete with them. So partnership development is an important part of our strategy, previously we worked with small partners, now we are trying to work with bigger ones, to get them develop solutions for us" (Senior Manager, 2002) "We place the customer rather than the product or process at the centre of the organisation to develop a stronger link between our different groups of customers and our data collection and management side of the business" (Business Improvement Manager, 2002)
6	Establish the right model of organisational design for the organisation	- Design and implement the right structure for an e-business starting from NMA's core business processes - Focus on core organisational competences: data collection, data management, exploitation of new technologies, and partner/customer management	"The normal practice would be: you take the external consultancy methodology cookbook and you apply things from it and other projects that you worked for, and you get a sense of the right way to do things … but this organisation is different and we wanted the structure to reflect what we do, not what consultants want us to do" (Board Member responsible for the structural change, 2003) "We did not want an off-the-shelf structure. Consultants came with a whole series of structural models, they came with the toolkit but didn't know how to fit it" (Strategist, 2003) "Don't expect everything to work without some adjustment and don't be afraid to review changes at an early stage to keep the reorganisation on track" (Business Group Director, 2003)
7	Top management commitment and the business case	- CEO with experience and personally identified with the e-strategy project - Have a multifunctional leadership team that is from sales, marketing, and IT -Involve senior management from sales and marketing in the strategy implementation	"The fundamentals are you need to have a really clear leader of the structure, somebody who has a very clear vision about what the endgame looks like" (Senior Manager, 2002) "Sales and Marketing senior management buy-in was absolutely fundamental for the process to work. … There must be a vision, there must be a strategy and there must be support behind it" (Senior Change Manager, 2003)
8	Political resistance to change of various stakeholders and managing simultaneously their diverse expectations	- Consistent communication allied to the use of facilitated workshops	"Consistency of message and purpose is one of the most important success factors in making change happen. Crystal-clear purpose, understood by all, including 'what it means for me,' should be made explicit" (NMA Employee, 2002)

continued on following page

Table 3. continued

No.	Organisational Challenges	Steps Taken to Meet Organisational Challenges	Data from NMA
9	External "customer acceptance" barriers and problems	- Communicate consistently with end users, at the beginning to build confidence, and throughout to communicate progress and to get feedback - Use customer relationship management to rebuild the confidence of customers who are confused about who they are actually buying products and services from	"The changes in our business processes — for example, procurement, reporting and customer relationship management, were so massive that the smallest error could have potentially serious consequences during business processes switching, damaging customer relationships and delivery channels for a lengthy period of time. Communicating proposed changes to our customers, users and clients was essential. They demanded honest, consistent and up-to-date information whether the news were good or bad. (Business Improvement Manager, 2002) "It was important to ensure all the time our customers, users and clients that we had a back-up or disaster recovery plan should something go wrong during the transition" (Sales and Marketing Manager, 2002)
10	Aligning the objectives of the 21 projects with the overall objectives of the e-business strategy and establishing timelines	- People involved in the projects have clear understanding of their roles and responsibilities - Good project management to avoid duplications and conflicting business objectives	"this great big machine called project planning comes in and it takes up vast amounts of time and systems space, because of all these critical paths which chunter away. Actually this is too big right now, and frightening people. (Senior Manager, 2002)
11	Blending major change with major continuity	- Integrate the e-commerce strategy with the business strategy and with the core operations from the start	"We needed to be able to adapt to shifting circumstances in market conditions and identify potential changes in course sooner rather than later" (Senior Marketing Manager, 2003)

position it in the new information economy. The strategy was transforming the business at all levels, culturally, technically, and commercially. Fundamental to all of this activity was the requirement to create the environment in which NMA could successfully deliver its strategy for the business. This has required the Senior Management Team to clearly articulate the vision, purpose, goals, and values for the organisation and to communicate them clearly businesswide. It also required pulling together the leadership, communication, and engagement activity, whilst ensuring that all existing projects, initiatives, and everyday activities were aligned and integrated with this. This high level strategic activity was also about leveraging what was already in place and, most importantly, maintain consistency across cultural, behavioural, and leadership approaches.

Second, the case of Britain's National Mapping Agency shows that, in practice, the transition from government monopoly to commercial organisation whilst embracing e-business as a corporate philosophy can be extremely challenging to achieve. Although e-business has enabled NMA to tap new customers and new revenues and opened up a space for importation of private sector practices into NMA, the strong public interest for its activities was still present. Yet the organisation was expected to operate commercially, cover its costs, and build up reserves through its own commercial style operations. That situated the organisation in the intersection of two different spheres—the public and the private. Becoming an e-business, in this context, required collaborative working not only with commercial partners but also with different parts of the government. The "in-between" situation thus tested to the full extent the capability of the organisation to lead and manage change, especially in terms of finding the perfect balance between fulfilling its still strategic role as national agency and providing high-quality services to its customers in a dynamic marketplace.

One of the senior managers interviewed described this situation with the following words:

"We [as an organisation] want to behave as if we were situated in the commercial business sector, but we cannot escape our origins" (Senior Manager, 2004).

Third, the case findings demonstrate that successful organisational transformation involving e-business implementation relies on changing some fundamental business processes and attitudes. Close cooperation between many different sets of people—from middle managers to programmers, and from technical architects to system users within the organisation—is needed. This convergence of business process, creative, and technical skills created in NMA a new dimension for teamwork, which in turn shifted the culture of the organisation from "knowledge is power" to "sharing knowledge is power." Technology can be an important enabler but not a driver of knowledge sharing.

Finally, one key challenge in NMA was how to blend major change with major continuity. In this respect, a major lesson learnt from this organisation's experience was that it is essential to integrate the e-commerce strategy with the business strategy and with the core operations from the start. This echoes the findings of Dutta and Segev (1999) that successes result from close partnerships between commercial and IT managers, and that companies making e-commerce central to their organisation do better than those that make it an afterthought.

CONCLUSION

This article aimed to reveal the processes of strategic and organisational transformation engendered by e-business during the implementation of a complex structural and cultural change programme aimed at reshaping a commercialised public sector organisation and rethinking how it provided value to its customers. The discussion examined the dilemmas and constraints identified by managers in the interpretation of the e-business strategy concept and why its implementation in practice could be challenging. Whilst the Internet offers a technological solution, the findings of this case study suggest that the successful implementation of a wider e-business strategy depends on managing simultaneously a number of projects which cross organisational boundaries and linking together organisational and technological factors.

Whilst this reflective account may be unique, it does, however, provide pointers to other large organisations undertaking a similar e-transformation and reflects on the degree of organisational transformation required by traditional organisations in meeting this imperative and successfully making the change to e-business. In particular, the findings illustrate that an e-business strategy is not just about technology. It also embraces the business challenges that result from managing change in a fast moving environment, as well as the important issues of people, organisation, culture, communication, and how an organisation must create a process for delivering innovation.

Further empirical field studies in other settings would enrich the concepts developed in this study and would produce a definitive list of best practices. The case highlights, however, the complex nature of the notion of e-business in a public sector context and shows that when implemented successfully, it can transform entirely these organisations and their capabilities.

REFERENCES

Barnes, D., Hinton, M., & Mieczkowska, S. (2005). Enhancing customer service operations in e-business: The emotional dimension. *Journal of Electronic Commerce in Organizations, 3*(2), 17-33.

Barnes, S., & Hunt, B. (2001). *E-commerce and e-business: Business models for global success.* Oxford: Butterworth-Heinemann.

Barua, A., Konona, P., Whinston, A., & Yin, F. (2001). Driving e-business excellence. *Sloan Management Review, 43*(1), 36-45.

Becker, S. A., & Berkemeyer, A. (2004). A case study on a security maturity assessment of a business-to-business electronic commerce organization. *Journal of Electronic Commerce in Organizations, 2*(4), 1-19.

Benoy, J., Cook, R., & Javalgi, R. (2001). Marketing on the Web: How executives feel, what businesses do. *Business Horizons, 44*(4), 32-40.

Bhaskar, R. (2004). A customer relationship management system to target customers at Cisco. *Journal of Electronic Commerce in Organizations, 2*(4), 1-19.

Boddy, D., & Macbeth, D. (2000). Prescriptions for managing change: A survey of their effects in projects to implement collaborative working between organisations. *International Journal of Project Management, 18*, 297-306.

Brown, S. L., & Eisenhardt, K. M. (1998). The art of continuous change: Linking complexity theory and time-paced evolution in relentlessly shifting organisation. *Administrative Science Quarterly, 42*, 1-34.

Carlton, D. W. (2001). Free riding and sales strategies for the Internet. *The Journal of Industrial Economics, 49*(4), 521-540.

Chen, S., & Leteney, F. (2000). Get real! Managing the next stage of Internet retail. *European Management Journal, 18*(5), 519-528.

Chaston, I. (2001). The Internet and e-commerce: An opportunity to examine organisational learning in progress in small manufacturing firms? *International Small Business Journal, 19*(2), 13-30.

Clarke, I., & Flaherty, T. B. (2004). Challenges of transforming a traditional brick-and-mortar store into a bricks-and-clicks model: A small business case study. *Journal of Electronic Commerce in Organizations, 2*(4), 74-87.

Clay, K. (2001). Prices and price dispersion on the Web: Evidence from the online book industry. *The Journal of Industrial Economics, 49*(4), 441-462.

Clegg, C. W., Chu, C., Smithson, S., Henney, A., et al. (2002). *E-business prospects: Findings from an expert panel*. London: Department of Trade and Industry.

Colombo, M. G. (2001). Technology-based entrepreneurs: Does Internet make a difference? *Small Business Economics, 16*(3), 177-190.

Daniel, E., Wilson, H., & Myers, A. (2002). Adoption of e-commerce by SMEs in the UK: Towards a stage model. *International Small Business Journal, 20*(3), 253-270.

Day, G., & Schoemaker, P. (2000). Avoiding the pitfalls of emerging technologies. *California Management Review, 42*(2), 8-33.

Deise, M. V., Nowikow, C., King P., & Wright, A. (2000). *Executive's guide to e-business, from tactics to strategy.* New York: John Wiley & Sons.

Dutta, S., & Segev, A. (1999). Business transformation on the Internet. *European Management Journal, 17*(5), 466-476.

Eisenhardt, K. M. (1998). Time pacing: Competing in markets that won't stand still. *Harvard Business Review, 76*(2), 59-70.

Eisenhardt, K. M. (1999). Patching: Restitching business portfolios in dynamic markets. *Harvard Business Review, 77*(3), 72-83.

Feeny, D. (2001). Making business sense of the e-opportunity. *Sloan Management Review, 42*(2), 41-52.

Gao, J. (2005). E-commerce issues in Australian manufacturing: A newspaper medium perspective. *Journal of Electronic Commerce in Organizations, 3*(4), 20-41.

Garicano, L. (2001). The effects of business-to-business e-commerce on transaction costs. *The Journal of Industrial Economics, 49*(4), 463-486.

Hansen, M. (2000). Networked incubators: Hothouses of the new economy. *Harvard Business Review, 78*(5), 74-84.

Harris, L., Coles, A. M., Dickson, K., & McLoughlin, I. (1999). Building collaborative networks. In P. Jackson (Ed.), *Virtual working: Social and organisational dynamics* (pp. 33-46). London: Routledge.

Hoffman, D., & Novak, T. (2000). How to acquire customers on the Web. *Harvard Business Review, 78*(3), 179-183.

Kickert, W. (2001). Public management of hybrid organisations: Governance of

quasi-autonomous executive agencies. *International Public Management Journal, 4*, 135-150.

Kotha, S. (1998). Cometing on the Internet: The case of Amazon.com. *European Management Journal, 16*(2), 212-222.

Kotha, S., Rajgopal, S., & Rindova, V. (2001). Reputation building and performance: An empirical analysis of the top-50 pure Internet firms. *European Management Journal, 19*(6), 571-586.

Lee, H. L., & Wang, S. (2001). Winning the last mile of e-commerce. *Sloan Management Review, 42*(4), 54-62.

Mahadevan, B. (2000). Business models for Internet-based e-commerce: An anatomy. *California Management Review, 42*(4), 55-69.

Ordanini, A., & Pol, A. (2001). Infomediation and competitive advantage in B2B digital marketplaces. *European Management Journal, 19*(3), 276-285.

Pettigrew, A. M. (1985). *The awakening giant: Continuity and change in ICI.* Oxford: Basil Blackwell.

Pettigrew, A. M. (1990). Longitudinal field research on change. Theory and practice.

Organization Science, 1, 267-292.

Poon, S., & Swatman, P. (1999). An exploratory study of small business Internet commerce issues. *Information and Management, 35*, 9-18.

Porter, M. (2001). Strategy and the Internet. *Harvard Business Review, 79*(2), 63-78.

Rayport, J. (1999). The truth about Internet business models. *Strategy and Business, Third Quarter*(16), 1-3.

Sauer, C. (1993). *Why information systems fail: A case study approach.* Henley-on-Thames: Alfred Waller.

Scott Morton, F. (2001). Internet car retailing. *The Journal of Industrial Economics, 49*(4), 501-520.

Smith, M. D. (2001). Consumer decision-making at an Internet shopbot: Brand still matters. *The Journal of Industrial Economics, 49*(4), 541-559.

Symon, C. (2000). The future at your fingertips. In S. Rock & J. Reeves (Eds.), *Building a successful e-business* (pp. 6-11). London: IBM Business Guide, Caspian Publishing.

Symonds, M. (1999, June 26). Business and the Internet: Survey. *The Economist*, pp. 1-44.

Timmers, P. (2000). *Electronic commerce.* Chichester, UK: John Wiley & Sons.

Van der Wiele, T., Williams, R., Van Iwaarder, J., Wilson, M., & Dale, B. (2002, September). *The e-business research network: Summary of the results of the Dutch pilot survey.* Paper presented at the British Academy of Management Conference.

Venkatraman, N. (2000). Five steps to a Dot.com strategy: How to find your footing on the Web. *Sloan Management Review, 15*(3), 15-29.

Yoffie, D., & Cusumano, M. (1999a). Judo strategy: The competitive dynamics of Internet time. *Harvard Business Review, 77*(1), 70-81.

Yoffie, D., & Cusumano, M. (1999b). Building a company on Internet time: Lessons from Netscape. *California Management Review, 41*(3), 8-28.

This work was previously published in International Journal of E-Business Research, Vol. 2, Issue 4, edited by I. Lee, pp. 39-60, copyright 2006 by IGI Publishing, formerly known as Idea Group Publishing (an imprint of IGI Global).

Chapter LXXIII
Public Administrators' Acceptance of the Practice of Digital Democracy:
A Model Explaining the Utilization of Online Policy Forums in South Korea

Chan-Gon Kim
Rutgers University–Newark, USA

Marc Holzer
Rutgers University–Newark, USA

ABSTRACT

The Internet provides a new digital opportunity for realizing democracy in public administration, and this study raises a central question: What factors determine public officials' acceptance of the practice of digital democracy on government Web sites? We focused on online policy forums among many practices of digital democracy. To gauge public officials' behavioral intentions to use online policy forums on government Web sites, we examined individual and organizational factors, as well as system characteristics. We administered a survey questionnaire to Korean public officials and analyzed a total of 895 responses. Path analysis indicates that three causal variables are important in predicting public officials' intentions to use online policy forums: perceived usefulness, attitudes toward citizen participation, and information quality. We discuss implications of this study for practices and theories of digital democracy.

INTRODUCTION

Today the Internet is changing the operation of governments. A large number of citizens can access a large volume of information simultaneously and conduct online transactions with government agencies 24 hours a day and 7 days a week. In addition, citizens can register their opinions on government Web sites through online discussions and online polls anywhere and anytime. Thus the concept of digital democracy is emerging. New electronic means have the potential to increase citizen participation in government and to ensure that citizens' preferences are reflected in the policy-making process.

Despite the fact that digital democracy is possible in public agencies, there are wide variations in adopting and implementing practices of digital democracy among government agencies at the federal, state, and local levels. Decisions at the organizational level do not necessarily bring changes in the attitudes and behaviors of individual public administrators. In other words, policy adoption is different from program implementation, and factors affecting these two are also different (de Lancer & Holzer, 2001). Successful innovation implementation is determined by human factors, or end users' acceptance of the innovation (Nedovic-Budic & Godschalk, 1996). Organizational members can reject or not fully utilize an innovation (Leonard-Barton & Deschamps, 1988). The literature on implementation has indicated that street-level bureaucrats have considerable resources with which to influence policy outcomes (Hill, 2003; Lipsky, 1980). While some research has examined the adoption of e-government at the organizational level (Ho & Ni, 2003; Ho, 2002; Moon, 2002; Weare, Musso, & Hale, 1999), little research has been done at the micro level with regard to attitudes and behaviors of public administrators toward digital democracy.

This study examines why and how public administrators accept the practice of digital democracy on government Web sites when they make and implement public policies. Since public administrators offer and maintain government Web sites, supplying the space for digital democracy on a government Web site and utilizing it is a prerequisite for such democracy in public administration. The major research question of this study is: What factors determine public administrators' acceptance of the practice of digital democracy on government Web sites? More specifically, this study focuses on a single practice of digital democracy and aims to examine the impact of individual, organizational, and system characteristics on administrators' intentions to use online policy forums on government Web sites.

DIGITAL DEMOCRACY IN PUBLIC ADMINISTRATION

Citizens' involvement in public affairs through the Internet has brought about the use of several essentially similar terms, such as "digital democracy," "electronic democracy," "e-democracy," "virtual democracy," "teledemocracy," and "cyberdemocracy." This study uses the term "digital democracy" to describe the use of government Web sites for citizens' participation in public affairs. The main characteristic of the new information and communication technology (ICT) is digital data transfer (Hague & Loader, 1999), and "digital democracy" is defined as "a collection of attempts to practice democracy without the limits of time, space, and other physical conditions, using ICT or computer-mediated communication instead, as an addition, not a replacement for, traditional analogue political practices" (Hacker & van Dijk, 2000, p. 1).

Online citizen participation can enrich democratic processes and build public trust by enabling public agencies to receive broader and more diverse opinions from citizens than those available through traditional means of off-line participation (Holzer, Melitski, Rho, & Schwester, 2004). Through online discussions, members of the public can learn from each other, and public administrators can become better informed, sometimes through the experience and hidden expertise of the public (Coleman & Gotze, 2001). Several scholars have suggested typologies of digital democracy (Kakabadse, Kakabadse, & Kouzmin, 2003; Norris, 2005; Tsagarousianou, 1999). With regard to the current state of digital democracy, information disclosure on government Web sites is full-fledged, and many agencies are receiving feedback on policy issues from citizens through the Internet. However, online discussion is just emerging, and decision making through government Web sites such as electronic referenda is still relatively infrequent in government (Norris & Moon, 2005; Kim, 2004).

Online Policy Forums

An "online policy forum," or an online discussion forum, is a place on the government Web site where public officials or citizens can post discussion topics on policy issues and exchange their views on those topics over a period of time. Online policy forums can take several formats. Public officials can participate in forums as discussants or citizens can discuss issues among themselves without officials' participation. Discussion topics can be offered by the government or registered online by citizens. There are also two types: issue-based forums and policy-based forums. At an early stage of policy making, issue-based forums are organized to collect ideas and opinions. At a later stage of policy-making, policy-based forums are offered to solicit responses about a draft policy (OECD, 2003).

Although online policy forums are still emerging and not universally utilized yet in public agencies, there are several exemplary cases of online discussion forums around the world (Holzer et al., 2004; OECD, 2003; Coleman & Gotze, 2001). At the central government level, the National Dialogue of Public Involvement was implemented by the Environmental Protection Agency (EPA) in 2001 to offer online discussions between public administrators and citizens (www.network-democracy.org/epa-pip) with 1,261 message postings in 10 days (Beierle, 2002; Holzer et al., 2004). The Hansard Society e-democracy program has been piloting a series of online discussion forums (www.tellparliament.net) for the UK Parliament since 1998 (Coleman, 2004). At the state level, Minnesota offered an online policy forum, Issue Talk (http://issuetalk.state.mn.us), from January 7 to 18 in 2002, inviting more than 600 comments and ideas about the state budget shortfall (Minnesota Planning, 2002). Cases at the local government level include online forums for the city of Kalix, Sweden (www.kalix.se), for the North Jutland County in Denmark (www.nordpol.dk), and for Bologna, Italy (www.comune.bologna.it) (OECD, 2003; Coleman & Gotze, 2001).

CONCEPTUAL FRAMEWORK

Since a government Web site can be viewed as an information system (IS) for public administrators, the theories of information system use can be applied to explain and predict public administrators' use of such sites. Kling and Jewett (1994) classify theories of information systems use into two broad types: rational systems models and natural systems models. The rational systems model views organizations as instruments designed to pursue specific goals and considers the efficiency of achieving those goals the most important value. By contrast, the natural systems model assumes that organizational members share a common interest in the survival of the organization, and that organizational behavior is oriented toward the pursuit of this end. In this model, organizations resemble natural systems that are like living organisms (Kling & Jewett, 1994; Scott, 1992). We conducted a comprehensive literature review, and an updated classification is presented in Table 1. The prevailing theory of information systems use is based on the rational systems model, and the Technology Acceptance Model (Davis, 1989) has been the dominant model for an individual's technology acceptance (Adams, Nelson, & Todd, 1992; Mathieson, Peacock, & Chin, 2001).

Based on previous research on an individual's technology acceptance and utilization of information systems, this study proposes a model to explain public administrators' acceptance of online policy forums on government Web sites when public agencies introduce such forums in their organizations. Since the characteristics of the Internet are different from other information technologies, these factors have been considered in formulating the conceptual framework of this study. Previous information technology innovations were mainly used by organizational members without interaction with citizens; but using a government Web site for purposes of digital democracy requires interaction between public administrators and citizens. Thus, when studying online dialogue, factors affecting users' attitudes and behaviors should be considered in contexts different from those utilized in studying other information technologies.

The basic constructs of this study are "perceived usefulness" and "behavioral intention," which are derived from the Technology Acceptance Model (Davis, 1989) and the Theory of Planned Behavior (Ajzen, 1985, 1991). The dependent variable in this study is a public administrator's behavioral

Table 1. Theories of information systems use

Theories	Research	Variables affecting IS Use
1. Rational Systems Explanations		
A. IS Implementation Research	Kwon & Zmud (1987)	individual, structural, technological, task-related, environmental factors
	Lucas, Ginzberg, & Schultz (1990)	user acceptance, system characteristics, management support, user knowledge of system purpose and use, organizational support, etc.
B. IS Success Model	DeLone & McLean (1992, 2003)	information quality, system quality, service quality
C. Application of the Theory of Planned Behavior	Ajzen (1985, 1991)	attitude, subjective norms, perceived behavioral control
D. Technology Acceptance Model	Davis (1989)	attitude, perceived usefulness, perceived ease of use
E. Application of Innovation Diffusion Theory	Rogers (1995)	relative advantage, compatibility, complexity, trialability, observability
2. Natural Systems Explanations		
A. Cultural/political perspectives	Kling (1980), Kling and Jewett (1994)	power politics, coalition building, forwarding agendas
	Walsham (1993)	interpretive approach, organizations as cultures and political systems
B. Sociotechnical Systems Theory	Kraemer, Dutton, & Northrop (1981), Danziger, Dutton, Kling, & Kraemer (1982)	political, socio-economic technological environment, political/administrative system attributes, computer package (hardware, software, procedures, management policies), orientation of computing
	Danziger & Kraemer (1986)	organizational environment, computer package, user characteristics
C. Theory of Technology Enactment	Fountain (2001)	objective information technology, organizational forms, institutional arrangements, enacted technology

intention to use online policy forums on a government Web site. A public administrator's behavioral intention to use such forums is considered a predictor for actual use of online policy forums. The public administrator's perceived usefulness of online policy forums is an intervening variable that mediates the relationship between independent variables and the behavioral intention. We assume that independent variables have impacts on the dependent variable directly or indirectly through perceived usefulness. A survey of the literature on variables that affect individuals' attitudes toward, and use of, information technology generated a substantial number of factors (Anandarajan, Simmers, & Igbaria, 2000; Davis, 1989; DeLone & McLean, 1992, 2003; Finlay & Finlay, 1996; Igbaria, Guimaraes, & Davis, 1995; Lucas, 1978; Ranerup, 1999; Thong & Yap, 1995). Among them, nine factors are considered important in predicting a public official's perceived usefulness and behavioral intention to use online policy forums. These independent variables can be divided into three broad categories: (1) individual factors, (2) organizational factors, and (3) system characteristics. Individual factors include Internet attitudes, attitudes toward citizen participation, and knowledge about digital democracy. Organizational factors refer to supervisor support, IS department support, and innovation-supportive organizational culture. System characteristics include the ease of use of online policy forums, information quality, and perceived risk in online discussion. Taking account of all relationships between these factors, the conceptual framework

Figure 1. A model of public administrators' acceptance of online policy forums on government Web sites

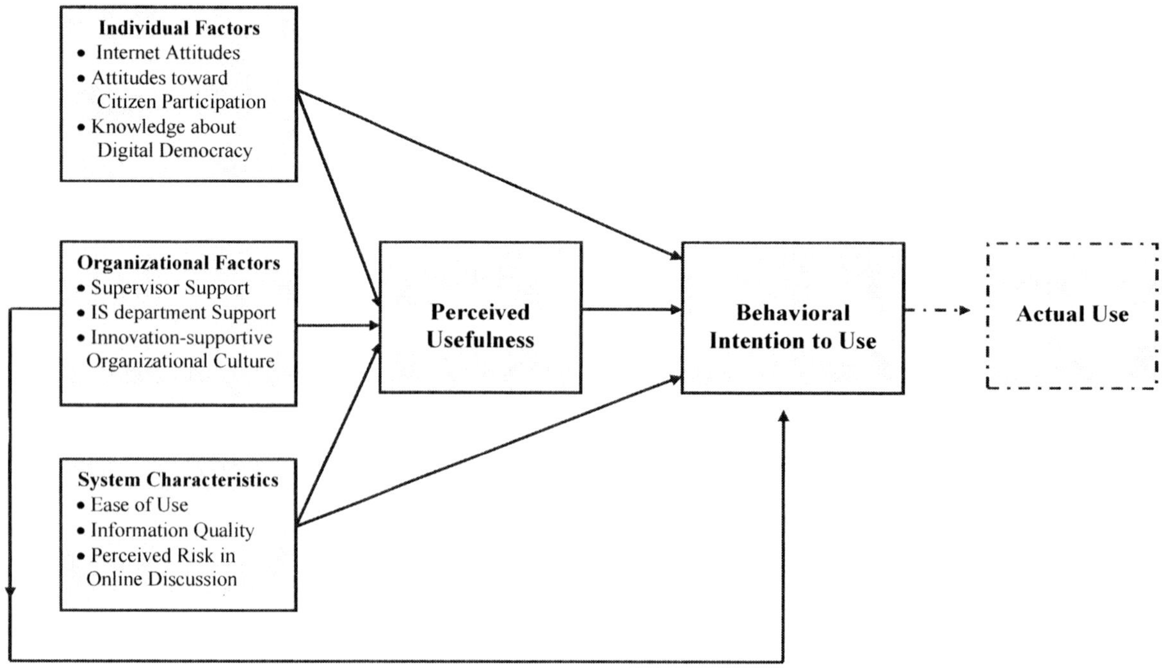

of this study is presented in Figure 1. According to empirical research, there is a close relationship between intention and behavior (Davis, 1989; Davis, Bagozzi, & Warsaw, 1989; Sheppard, Hartwick, & Warsaw, 1988). This study focuses on intentions and relevant factors but does not measure actual use of online policy forums. However, behavioral intention can be used as a surrogate for predicting actual use of online policy forums.

Individual Factors

Previous research found that favorable Internet attitudes are associated with the frequent use of the Internet (Anandarajan et al., 2000; Spacey, Goulding, & Murray, 2004). Thus we expect that administrators' Internet attitudes will influence the perceived usefulness of online policy forums and behavioral intentions to use online policy forums.

- **Hypothesis 1-1.** A public administrator's favorable Internet attitudes will positively affect his/her perceived usefulness of policy forums.
- **Hypothesis 1-2.** A public administrator's favorable Internet attitudes will positively affect his/her behavioral intention to use online policy forums.

To implement digital democracy, public administrators must interact with citizens and allow citizen participation in policy making and implementation through the government Web site. Wang (2001) found that both managers' and public administrators' willingness to be accountable was related to increased citizen participation. Thus, public administrators' favorable attitudes toward citizen participation are prerequisite to the use of practices of digital democracy.

- **Hypothesis 2-1.** A public administrator's favorable attitudes toward citizen participation will positively affect his/her perceived usefulness of online policy forums.
- **Hypothesis 2-2.** A public administrator's favorable attitudes toward citizen participa-

tion will positively affect his/her behavioral intention to use online policy forums.

Research on the use of MIS has shown that education, training, experience, and skills of individuals using the technology are associated with perceived usefulness and actual use of information systems (Agarwal & Prasad, 1999; Igbaria, 1990, 1993; Igbaria et al., 1995; Igbaria, Parasuraman, & Baroudi, 1996; Nelson & Cheney, 1987). Thong and Yap (1995) found that businesses with CEOs who are more knowledgeable about information technology (IT) are more likely to adopt IT. Research found that knowledge about the Internet affects their use of the Internet (Finlay & Finlay, 1996). If public administrators are knowledgeable about digital democracy, they will understand the importance of digital democracy and perceive the usefulness of practices of digital democracy as high and use online policy forums frequently.

- **Hypothesis 3-1.** A public administrator's high level of knowledge about digital democracy will positively affect his/her perceived usefulness of online policy forums.
- **Hypothesis 3-2.** A public administrator's high level of knowledge about digital democracy will positively affect his/her behavioral intention to use online policy forums.

Organizational Factors

In MIS research, organizational support—such as manager support and information center (IS department) support—was found to affect system usage (Anandarajan et al., 2000; DeLone & McLean, 2003; Igbaria et al., 1995; Igbaria et al., 1996; Igbaria, 1990, 1993; Lucas, 1978; Thompson, Higgins, & Howell, 1991). Supervisors may encourage or discourage subordinates to use online policy forums in their work. In addition, an IS department that is in charge of managing the government Web site may facilitate implementing practices of digital democracy in agencies.

- **Hypothesis 4-1.** Supervisor support for using online policy forums will positively affect a public administrator's perceived usefulness of online policy forums.
- **Hypothesis 4-2.** Supervisor support for using online policy forums will positively affect a public administrator's behavioral intention to use online policy forums.
- **Hypothesis 5-1.** IS department support for using online policy forums will positively affect a public administrator's perceived usefulness of online policy forums.
- **Hypothesis 5-2.** IS department support for using online policy forums will positively affect a public administrator's behavioral intention to use online policy forums.

As long as a certain culture exists within an organizational unit, the activities of organizational members can be influenced by the culture. According to Subramaniam and Ashkanasy (2001), innovation takes place when organizational members are opportunistic, not constrained by many rules, and willing to take risks and experiment with new ideas. According to previous research, businesses with more innovative CEOs are more likely to adopt IT (Thong & Yap, 1995), and top managers' risk-taking propensity is positively associated with IT innovativeness (Moon & Bretschneider, 2002). Since online policy forums are new innovations, public administrators who work in an innovative organizational culture may try new inventions.

- **Hypothesis 6-1.** Innovation-supportive organizational culture will positively affect a public administrator's perceived usefulness of online policy forums.
- **Hypothesis 6-2.** Innovation-supportive organizational culture will positively affect a public administrator's behavioral intention to use online policy forums.

System Characteristics

The influence of perceived ease of use on perceived usefulness and behavioral intention is derived from the Technology Acceptance Model (Davis, 1989). Public administrators have several means of gathering information from citizens in the decision-making process, such as face-to-face meetings, telephone conversations, or government Web sites. Thus perceived ease of use of online policy forums is directly related to the use of online policy forums.

- **Hypothesis 7-1.** A public administrator's positive perception of the ease of use of online policy forums will positively affect his/her perceived usefulness of online policy forums.
- **Hypothesis 7-2.** A public administrator's positive perception of the ease of use of online policy forums will positively affect his/her behavioral intention to use online policy forums.

Previous research found that the quality of information had significant influence on the perceived usefulness of an information system (Klobas, 1995; Kraemer, Danziger, Dunkle, & King, 1993; Lin & Lu; 2000). We can view the government Web site as an information system that produces information for public administrators when citizens register their opinions on online policy forums. Public administrators judge whether the information provided by online citizens is reliable and valid, or whether the online information is of uncertain quality. If the quality of online information is high, then public administrators may perceive the usefulness of online policy forums positively and continuously use those forums. Therefore, the following hypotheses are formulated:

- **Hypothesis 8-1.** A public administrator's perception of high information quality of online policy forums will positively affect his/her perceived usefulness of online policy forums.
- **Hypothesis 8-2.** A public administrator's perception of high information quality of online policy forums will positively affect his/her behavioral intention to use online policy forums.

Online relationships are established between users of the Internet when they are engaged in electronic conversation through a chat room or a discussion forum. The lack of face-to-face contact leads to greater anonymity in online interactions and online citizens might behave with less good will (Friedman, Kahn, & Howe, 2000). If public administrators perceive a high risk in using online discussion forums, they might not write on online forums.

- **Hypothesis 9-1.** A public administrator's perception of high risk in online discussions will negatively affect his/her perceived usefulness of online policy forums.
- **Hypothesis 9-2.** A public administrator's perception of high risk in online discussions will negatively affect his/her behavioral intention to use online policy forums.

The Impact of Perceived Usefulness on Behavioral Intention

The importance of perceived usefulness as one of the determinants of the intention to use an information system has been stressed by the Technology Acceptance Model (Davis, 1989). Perceived usefulness influences user acceptance of the information system because of the value of outcomes from using the system. Public administrators can utilize online information submitted by citizens through online discussion on the government Web site. If public administrators perceive the usefulness of online policy forums as positive, they will use online policy forums more frequently.

- **Hypothesis 10.** A public administrator's positive perception of the usefulness of online policy forums will positively affect his/her behavioral intention to use online policy forums.

RESEARCH METHODOLOGY

Sample and Data Collection

The unit of analysis in this study is individual public administrators, and the population of this study is defined as public administrators who work in public agencies that have adopted online policy forums, and make and implement public policies in their agencies in South Korea. Our focus is on individual public administrators' use of online policy forums in South Korea, which is the leader in broadband penetration in the world (Organization for Economic Cooperation and Development, 2001) and places second in terms of Internet usage rate among its population (International Telecommunication Union, 2004). South Korea obtained a fifth-place ranking in terms of an e-government readiness index and was sixth in terms of the e-participation index constructed by the United Nations[1] (2004). South Korea has been vigorously promoting e-government and digital democracy, with many public agencies adopting online policy forums. All Ministries except one among 18 Ministries offer online policy forums, and 12 upper-level local governments among 16 offered online policy forums as of January 2005. Thus South Korea is a particularly good case for the study of digital democracy

This study mixed purposive sampling and cluster sampling. To select appropriate public agencies, we used several criteria: the frequency of online policy forums, the number of message postings per forum, and the highest and average number of message postings per forum. Then, a total of 13 public agencies were selected, including four central government ministries, two upper-level local governments, and seven lower-level local governments. Among 18 ministries at the central government of South Korea, four ministries were relatively active as shown in Table 2 in terms of the frequency of online forums and the number of message postings, and these ministries were selected for the survey: the Ministry of Information and Communication, the Ministry of Government Administration and Home Affairs, the Ministry of Unification, and the Ministry of Health and Welfare. Among them, the Ministry of Unification's "Online Public Hearing" (www.unikorea.go.kr) is the most active, offering six online forums in 2004, with 731 participants on average per forum. Discussion topics were offered by the government or registered by citizens on government Web sites. Most online forums lasted for 15 to 30 days, and any citizens or officials can post messages. We applied the same methodology to selecting several local governments. Among 16 upper-level local governments, the Seoul Metropolitan Government and Gyeonggi Province were actively promoting online policy forums and were selected for the survey. Seoul Metropolitan Government's "Cyber Policy Forum" (http://forum.seoul.go.kr) provided discussion topics every month in 2004, with an average number of 120 participants per forum. Gyeonggi Province offered five online policy forums in 2004, with 82 participants on average per forum (http://www.gg.go.kr/0502new/news/join/dojung/dojung01/index.html). Among 232 lower-level local governments, seven district offices were deemed appropriate for this study: Gangnam, Gangdong, Guro, Jungnang, Seongbuk, Yangchon, and Gangseo.

Then we selected several divisions at each public agency. Selected divisions were those that posted discussion topics on their agency's Web site or those related to discussion topics registered by citizens. A total of 34 divisions were selected in the central government, 29 divisions in upper-level local governments, and 31 divisions in lower-level local governments. We mailed questionnaires to a manager at each agency in central and local governments between February 11th and 15th, 2005. Then these managers distributed the questionnaires to all public administrators who make and implement public policies in their divisions, which had posted discussion topics or had topics registered by citizens on government Web sites for the past two years. Questionnaires were distributed to 300 officials at the central government, 320 at upper level local governments, and 390 at lower-level local governments. Thus the total sample selected for this study was 1,010 as presented in Table 3.

Table 2. Statistics of Online Policy Forums for 18 Ministries in South Korea, 2004

Ministry	Selection of discussion topics	Online forums with message postings 21 ~ 50	Online forums with message postings above 50	The highest number of message postings per forum
Unification	Offered by government	0	6	1,257
(average 731)				
Information and Communication	Offered by government	0	2	99
(average 96)				
Government Administration and Home Affairs	Offered by government	0	2	1,281 threads (average more than 817)
Health and Welfare				
	Offered by government	0	2	167
(average 120)				
Gender Equality and Family	Offered by government	3	2	110
(average 60)				
Education and Human Resources Development	Offered by government	2	1	106
Construction and Transportation	Offered by government	0	1	258
Agriculture and Forestry	Offered by government	0	1	252
Finance and Economy	Offered by government	0	1	85
Science and Technology	Offered by citizens	1	0	11
Labor	Offered by government	1	0	29
Culture and Tourism	Offered by government	1	0	18
Commerce, Industry and Energy	Offered by both government and citizens	1	0	39
Foreign Affairs and Trade	Offered by government	1	0	36
Maritime Affairs and Fisheries	Offered by government	1	0	27
Environment	Offered by government	0	0	10
Justice		0	0	0
National Defense		0	0	0

Questionnaires were accompanied by a cover letter that stated that participation was voluntary and that responses were anonymous, encouraging honest responses for this study. We did not ask a respondent's name, phone number, resident registration number, address, or date of birth. After respondents completed the questionnaires, they voluntarily returned them by mail. After excluding incomplete questionnaires, we collected 895 questionnaires, and the response rate was 88.6% across governments.

Measurement and theSurvey Instrument

This study used a five-point Likert-type questionnaire to measure the attitudes and beliefs of public administrators. We combined several questions to measure a variable and created a composite measurement by summing individual items for each variable. Questionnaire items are summarized in the Appendix. Factor analysis and Cronbach alpha coefficients showed the unidimensionality

Table 3. Distribution and collection of the questionnaire

Level of government	Agency	Number of divisions for survey	Distribution	Collection	Response rate
Central Government Ministries	Ministry of Information & Communication	8 divisions	70	62	88.6%
	Ministry of Government Administration & Home Affairs	8 divisions	90	86	95.6%
	Ministry of Unification	9 divisions	70	64	91.4%
	Ministry of Health & Welfare	9 divisions	70	65	92.9%
	Sub-total	34	300	277	92.3%
Upper-level Local Governments	Seoul Metropolitan Government	22 divisions	240	230	95.8%
	Gyeonggi Province	7 divisions	80	69	86.3%
	Sub-total	29	320	299	93.4%
Lower-level Local Governments	Gangnam District Office	12 divisions	120	80	66.7%
	Gangdong District Office	3 divisions	40	23	57.5%
	Jungnang District Office	3 divisions	55	50	90.9%
	Guro District Office	3 divisions	40	39	97.5%
	Seongbuk District Office	5 divisions	60	59	98.3%
	Yangchon District Office	4 divisions	60	54	90.0%
	Gangseo District Office	1 division	15	14	93.5%
	Sub-total	31	390	319	81.8%
	Total	**94**	**1,010**	**895**	**88.6%**

and reliability of the instrument. Variables of this study are as follows.

- **Negative Internet attitudes:** A public administrator's negative attitudes toward the Internet.
- **Attitudes toward citizen participation:** A public administrator's willingness to allow citizen participation in the policy-making process.
- **Knowledge about digital democracy:** A public administrator's knowledge about digital democracy.
- **Supervisor support:** The degree to which a public administrator's supervisor emphasizes citizen input through online policy forums in policy processes and encourages employees to use online policy forums in their work.
- **IS department support:** The degree to which IS department supports a public administrator's using online policy forums in public agencies.
- **Innovation-supportive organizational culture:** The degree to which a public administrator works in an innovative organizational culture in public agencies.
- **Perceived ease of use:** The degree to which a public administrator expects the use of online policy forums to be free of effort.
- **Information quality:** The degree to which online information submitted by citizens is valuable and of high quality.
- **Perceived risk in online discussion:** The degree to which a public administrator perceives risks when communicating with citizens online.

- **Perceived usefulness:** A public administrator's subjective perception that using online policy forums will increase his/her job performance.
- **Behavioral intention:** The degree to which a public administrator has the intention to use online policy forums in his/her work.

RESULTS

Descriptive Statistics

Following factor analysis and reliability tests, appropriate constructs were established and the descriptive statistics for 11 research variables are presented in Table 4. On average, public officials in South Korea seemed to believe that organizational culture is moderately innovative ($M = 3.68$), and they tended to have moderately high behavioral intentions to use online policy forums in the near future ($M = 3.55$). However, they think that they have only a little knowledge about digital democracy ($M = 2.58$), perceived low risk in online discussion ($M = 2.83$), and low supervisor support for using online policy forums ($M = 2.89$). When we examined a correlation matrix, perceived usefulness and behavioral intention have positive relationships with several variables. None of the independent variables show correlations above 0.8 among themselves, which implies that multicollinearity would not be a problem in regression analysis.

Path Analysis

To test hypotheses, we analyzed data using SPSS and employed path analysis. Path analysis was developed by Sewall Wright as a method for examining relationships among all variables and testing causal models when multiple variables are involved in a theoretical model (de Vaus, 1986; Loehlin, 1998; Pedhazur, 1997). In path analysis, a path diagram graphically displays the pattern of causal relationships among a set of variables. An arrow from one variable to another indicates a direct effect, and a two-headed curved arrow indicates the correlation between two variables. We assume that the relations among the variables in the path model are linear and additive; the residual of each endogenous variable is not correlated with one another or with other endogenous variables; there is a one-way causal flow in the model; and the variables are measured on an interval scale without error. Then path analysis can be reduced to the solution of several multiple linear regression analyses (Pedhazur, 1997, p.771). When we examined the assumptions of multiple regres-

Table 4. Descriptive statistics for research variables

Variable	N	Mean	Std. Deviation
Negative Internet Attitudes	891	3.52	.95
Information quality	515	3.07	.63
Perceived usefulness	512	3.24	.64
Perceived risk in online discussion	883	2.83	.80
Supervisor support	861	2.89	.75
IS department Support	867	2.99	.81
Attitudes toward citizen participation	891	3.36	.73
Organizational culture	892	3.68	.68
Knowledge about digital democracy	892	2.58	.83
Ease of use	508	3.42	.64
Behavioral intention	889	3.55	.67

sion, they were also met, including normality of residuals, linear relationships between variables, homoscedasticity, and no perfect collinearity.

In path analysis, each path is given a path coefficient, a beta weight (standardized regression coefficient) in regression analysis that shows how much impact the variable has on another variable. Since these path coefficients are standardized numbers, they can be compared with each other in terms of the degree of importance of each variable.

To control for the effects of other known influences on regression models, we examined two variables: age and gender. When we removed these two control variables in regression analysis, R^2 for the model without control variables was similar to R^2 the original regression model with control variables, and the magnitude of the regression coefficients changed little. Among research variables, Internet attitudes, innovation-supportive organizational culture, and perceived risk in online discussion had no significant impacts on either perceived usefulness or behavioral intention. Thus these independent variables were removed in path analysis.

The initial path analysis produced all path coefficients regardless of statistical significance or meaningfulness of coefficients. To trim the path model and make it more parsimonious, insignificant or unimportant path coefficients can be removed from the model. Accordingly two criteria were used in deleting a few path coefficients: the significance and importance of the coefficient. Path coefficients not significant at the 0.1 level were deleted, and path coefficients less than 0.05 were deleted from the model. Thus three paths were removed from the original path model: the path from knowledge about digital democracy to perceived usefulness, the path from supervisor support to behavioral intention, and the path from information quality to behavioral intention. All path coefficients in the final model are statistically significant at the 0.05 level, R^2 for the model predicting perceived usefulness is 0.572, and R^2 for the model predicting behavioral intention is 0.417. This means that 57% of the variation of perceived usefulness is explained by five independent variables, and 42% of the variation of behavioral intention is explained by four variables. The final path model is presented in Figure 2.

The total causal effect of each predictor on behavioral intention was calculated by adding the direct and indirect effects in the final path model. To obtain indirect effects, we multiply the path coefficients of all of the indirect routs. The results of effect analysis are presented in Table 5. Total causal effects for all predictor variables are

Figure 2. Final path model

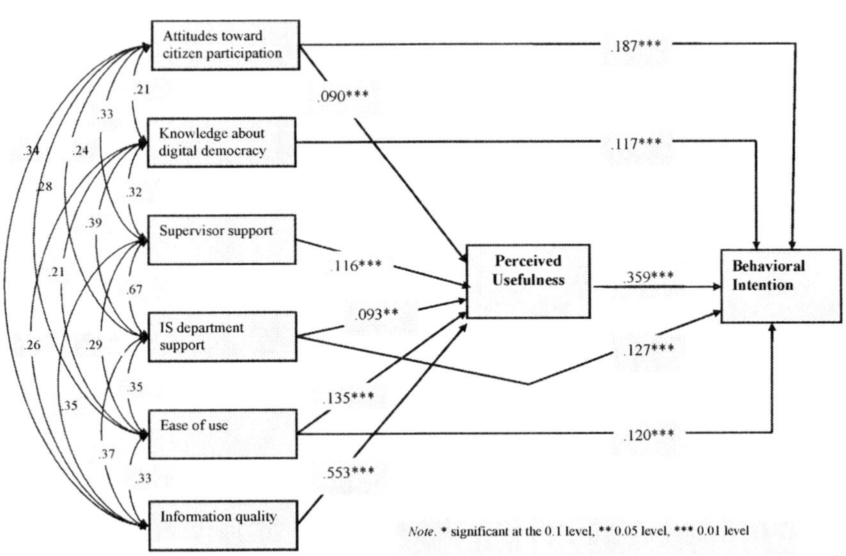

Table 5. Decomposition of effects for the final path model

Causal variable	Endogenous Variable	
	Perceived Usefulness	Behavioral Intention
Attitudes toward citizen participation		
Direct effect	.090*	.187*
Indirect effect		.032*
Total causal effect	.090*	.220*
Knowledge about digital democracy		
Direct effect		.117*
Indirect effect		
Total causal effect		.117*
Supervisor support		
Direct effect	.116*	
Indirect effect		.042*
Total causal effect	.116*	.042*
IS department support		
Direct effect	.093*	.127*
Indirect effect		.034*
Total causal effect	.093*	.160*
Ease of use		
Direct effect	.135*	.120*
Indirect effect		.048*
Total causal effect	.135*	.168*
Information quality		
Direct effect	.553*	
Indirect effect		.199*
Total causal effect	.553*	.199*
Perceived usefulness		
Direct effect		.359*
Indirect effect		
Total causal effect		.359*
R2	.572	.417

significant at or below the 0.05 level. With regard to the magnitude of the total causal effect of each predictor on behavioral intention, the order of importance is as follows: (1) perceived usefulness (0.359), (2) attitudes toward citizen participation (0.220), (3) information quality (0.199), (4) ease of use (0.17), (5) IS department support (0.16), (6) knowledge about digital democracy (0.168), and (7) supervisor support (0. 042).

In path analysis, model-implied or model-predicted correlations between two variables using path coefficients should reproduce the original correlations or observed correlations (Heise, 1969; Klem, 1995; Kline, 1998; Pedhazur, 1982; Schumacker & Lomax, 1996), and it is desirable to have correlation residuals with absolute values less than 0.1 (Kline, 1998). We calculated a predicted correlation in a path model by adding causal effects—direct and indirect effects—and non-causal effects—spurious and unanalyzed effects. Spurious effects occur when a third variable has causal paths to both an independent variable and a dependent variable, while unanalyzed effects occur due to effects from correlations between pairs of source variables (Davis, 1985; Klem, 1995; Kline, 1998; Pedhazur, 1982). In our model, correlations range from 0.21 to 0.39 between pairs of source variables, and these effects were considered in analyzing the impact of independent variables on dependent variables.

The final path model appears to fit the data fairly well. Applying the criterion that the difference between the original and reproduced correlations should not exceed 0.1, we find that correlation residuals in the absolute values for all correlations are well below the 0.1 criterion (Table 6). Thus, the final path model reproduced all of the observed correlations, and the model is relevant in predicting public administrators' behavioral intention to use online policy forums in South Korea. The final path model confirms that "perceived usefulness" mediates between some predictors and "behavioral intention." Information quality does not directly affect behavioral intention but affects it indirectly through perceived usefulness. Perceived usefulness provides only a partial mediation for attitudes toward citizen participation, supervisor support, IS department support, and ease of use.

CONCLUSION

This study examined what factors determine public administrators' acceptance of online policy forums on government Web sites for digital democracy and how individual, organizational, and system characteristics affect public officials' intentions to use online policy forums in South Korea. Hypotheses 2-1, 2-2, 3-2, 4-1, 5-1, 5-2, 7-1, 7-2, 8-1, and 10 were supported, but hypotheses 1-1, 1-2, 3-1, 4-2, 6-1, 6-2, 8-2, 9-1, and 9-2 were not supported at the 0.05 significance level.

First, perceived usefulness of online policy forums is the strongest factor affecting public administrators' behavioral intentions to use online policy forums. Path analysis reveals causal relationships between behavioral intention, perceived usefulness, and other predictors. Perceived usefulness has been found to play a mediating role between some predictors and behavioral intentions.

Second, public administrators' favorable attitudes toward citizen participation are positively associated with the perceived usefulness of online policy forums and their intentions to use online policy forums. If public administrators have negative attitudes toward citizen participation, online policy forums cannot be utilized in the policy-making process.

Third, the information quality of online policy forums is the major factor affecting public administrators' perceived usefulness of online policy forums. It has the largest impact on perceived usefulness among the nine factors.

Fourth, perceived ease of use of online policy forums is a predictor for perceived usefulness of online policy forums and behavioral intentions to use online policy forums. If public administrators feel that online policy forums are easy to access and use compared to other methods of gathering citizens' opinions, they will utilize online policy forums more frequently.

Fifth, IS department support for using online policy forums is related to the perceived usefulness of online policy forums and behavioral intentions to use online policy forums. Public officials may perceive online policy forums as useful when IS departments encourage officials to consider citizens' opinions in the policy-making process.

Sixth, public administrators' knowledge about digital democracy is positively associated with their behavioral intention to use online policy forums. In other words, the more knowledgeable public officials are about digital democracy, the more likely they are to use online policy forums for digital democracy in public administration.

Seventh, Internet attitudes, innovation-supportive organizational culture, and perceived risk in online discussion are not predictors for either perceived usefulness of online policy forums or behavioral intention to use online policy forums. Considering the fact that South Korean public administrators are heavy users of the Internet, Internet attitudes may have no impact on our model. Unlike other discussion forums operated in the private sector, the government's online policy forums may strongly regulate messages posted on their Web sites, so public administrators may not perceive much risk when they write in online policy forums. As South Korea has been promoting administrative reforms at all public agencies, innovation-supportive organizational culture may not be an important factor.

Since digital democracy is still emerging for many public agencies, the results of this research can be helpful for successful implementation of the concept. Path analysis reveals that perceived usefulness, attitudes toward citizen participation, and information quality are the major determinants of behavioral intention among individual, organizational, and information system factors. Policy makers, elected officials, and managers should focus on increasing the level of those three factors in order to facilitate digital democracy. Leaders within public administration organizations should pay attention to online policy forums and utilize information provided by citizens in the policy-making process so that public administrators may perceive the usefulness of those policy forums. Since public administrators' use of online policy forums involves citizen participation in the policy-making process through government Web sites, officials' favorable attitudes toward citizen participation are indispensable to digital democracy. On the part of citizens, they should understand policy issues and provide good discussions on policy issues through government Web sites so that public administrators can perceive the usefulness of online policy forums and utilize them. This was consistent with the analysis of comments from respondents who emphasized that the quality of information, mature citizenship, and citizens' competence in policy issues are prerequisite to the success of digital democracy. Many officials commented that opinions on online policy forums were often posted by narrow, self-interested parties, and some officials complained that abusive or malicious opinions were posted on government Web sites.

Theories of digital democracy have hypothesized that the Internet has a potential to broaden and deepen citizens' participation in decision making in government and improve the quality of decisions by ensuring deliberative public debate. Although several studies have been conducted at the organizational level to find characteristics of agencies that have adopted practices of e-government, research on individual public administrators is rare. This research underscores several implications for developing theories of digital democracy. First, this study suggests that the acceptance of practices of digital democracy at the individual level should be distinguished from the adoption of such practices at the organizational level. This study also finds that the level of individual public administrators' acceptance of practices of digital democracy varies within an agency that has adopted those practices. Second, this study indicates that the causal path model is valid in explaining public administrators' behavioral intentions to use online policy forums. This model can be extended to public administrators' acceptance of other practices of e-government or digital democracy, such as online opinion polls/surveys, online public hearings, and electronic town meetings. As these practices take place online, there are no essential differences between online forums and other practices.

The generalizability of this study across countries is limited because the samples were selected from public officials in South Korea. We expect that individual, organizational, and IS system characteristics will differ between public officials in South Korea and other countries, and one previous study did show that the pattern of relationships between variables in IS research was different between countries (Igbaria & Zviran, 1991). Thus comparative, cross-national research is necessary to more fully understand the implementation process for digital democracy. In addition, future research might compare public administrators' willingness to use the practice of digital democracy between public administrators who work at agencies that adopted such practices and those who work at agencies that did not introduce such practices in their organizations.

REFERENCES

Adams, D. A., Nelson, R. R., & Todd, P. A. (1992). Perceived usefulness, ease of use, and usage of information technology: A replication. *MIS Quarterly, 16*-(2), 227-247.

Agarwal, R., & Prasad, J. (1999). Are individual differences germane to the acceptance of new information technology? *Decision Sciences, 30*(2), 361-391.

Ajzen, I. (1985). From intention to actions: a theory of planned behavior. In J. Kuhl, & J. Beckmann (Eds.), *Action control: From cognition to behavior* (pp. 11-39). NY: Springer-Verlag.

Ajzen, I. (1991). The theory of planned behavior. *Organizational Behavior and Human Decision Processes, 50*, 179-211.

Anandarajan, M., Simmers, C., & Igbaria, M. (2000). An exploratory investigation of the antecedents and impact of interne usage: An individual perspective. *Behaviour & Information Technology, 19*(1), 69-85.

Baron, R. M., & Kenny, D. A. (1986). The moderator-mediator variable distinction in social psychological research: conceptual, strategic, and statistical considerations. *Journal of Personality and Social Psychology, 51*(6), 1173-1182.

Beierle, T. C. (2002). *Democracy on-line: An evaluation of the national dialogue on public involvement in EPA decisions*. Retrieved February 17, 2005, from http://www.rff.org/Documents/RFF-RPT-demonline.pdf

Coleman, S. (2004). Connecting parliament to the public via the Internet. *Information, Communication & Society, 7*(1), 1-22.

Coleman, S., & Gotze, J. (2001). *Bowling together: Online public engagement in policy deliberation.* Hansard Society. Retrieved October 14, 2004, from http://bowlingtogether.net/bowlingtogether.pdf

Danziger, J. N., Dutton, W. H., Kling, R., & Kraemer, K. L. (1982). *Computers and politics: High technology in American local governments.* New York: Columbia University Press.

Danziger, J. N., & Kraemer, K. L. (1986). *People and computers: The impacts of computing on end users in organizations.* New York: Columbia University Press.

Davis, J. A. (1985). *The logic of causal order.* Beverly Hills, CA: Sage.

Davis, F. D. (1989). Perceived usefulness, perceived ease of use, and user acceptance of Information Technology. *MIS Quarterly, 13*(3), 319-340.

Davis, F. D., Bagozzi, R. P., & Warsaw, P. R. (1989). User acceptance of computer technology: a comparison of two theoretical models. *Management Science, 35*(8), 982-1003.

de Lancer Julnes, P., & Holzer, M. (2001). Promoting the utilization of performance measures in public organizations: An empirical study of factors affecting adoption and implementation. *Public Administration Review, 61*(6), 693-708.

DeLone, W. H., & McLean, E. R. (1992). Information systems success: The quest for the dependent variable. *Information Systems Research, 3*(1), 60-95.

DeLone, W. H., & McLean, E. R. (2003). The DeLone and McLean model of information systems success: A ten-year update. *Journal of Management Information Systems, 19*(4), 9-30.

De Vaus, D. A. (1986). *Surveys in social research.* London: George Allen & Unwin.

Finlay, K., & Finlay, T. (1996). The relative roles of knowledge and innovativeness in determining librarians' attitudes toward and use of the Internet: A structural equation modeling approach. *Library Quarterly, 66*(1), 59-83.

Fountain, J. E. (2001). *Building the virtual state: Information technology and institutional change.* Washington, DC: Brookings Institution Press.

Friedman, B., Kahn, P. H., & Howe, D. C. (2000). Trust online. *Communications of the ACM, 43*(12), 34-40.

Gutmann, A., & Thompson, D. (1996). *Democracy and disagreement.* Cambridge, MA: The Belknap Press of Harvard University Press.

Hacker, K. L., & van Dijk, J. (2000). What is digital democracy? In K. L. Hacker, & J. van Dijk (Eds.), *Digital democracy: Issues of theory and practice* (pp. 1-9). Thousand Oaks, CA: Sage Publications.

Hague, B. N., & Loader, B. D. (Eds.). (1999). *Digital democracy: Discourse and decision making in the information age.* London: Routledge.

Heise, D. R. (1969). Problems in path analysis and causal inference. *Sociological Methodology, 1*, 38-73.

Hill, H. C. (2003). Understanding implementation: street-level bureaucrats' resources for reform. *Journal of Public Administration Research and Theory, 13*(3), 265-282.

Ho, A. T. (2002). Reinventing local governments and the e-government initiative. *Public Administration Review, 62*(4), 434-444.

Ho, A. T., & Ni, A. Y. (2003). Explaining the adoption of e-government features: A case study of Iowa County Treasures' Office. *American Review of Public Administration, 34*(2), 164-180.

Holzer, M., Melitski, J., Rho, S., & Schwester, R. (2004). *Restoring trust in government: The potential of digital citizen participation.* Report of IBM Center for the Business of Government. Retrieved October 25, 2004, from http://www.businessofgovernment.org/pdfs/HolzerReport.pdf

Igbaria, M. (1990). End-user computing effectiveness: A structural equation model. *Omega, 18*(6), 637-652.

Igbaria, M. (1993). User acceptance of microcomputer technology: An empirical test. *Omega, 21*(1), 73-90.

Igbaria, M., Guimaraes, T., & Davis, G. B. (1995). Testing the determinants of microcomputer usage via a structural equation model. *Journal of Management Information Systems, 11*(4), 87-114.

Igbaria, M., Parasuraman, S., & Baroudi, J. J. (1996). A motivational model of microcomputer usage. *Journal of Management Information systems, 13*(1), 127-143.

Igbaria, M., & Zviran, M. (1991). End-user effectiveness: A cross-cultural examination. *Omega, 19*(5), 369-379.

International Telecommunication Union. (2004). *Internet indicators: hosts, users, and number of PCs.* Retrieved February 11, 2005, from http://www.itu.int/ITU-D/ict/statistics/at_glance/Internet03.pdf

Kakabadse, A., Kakabadse, N. K., & Kouzmin, A. (2003). Reinventing the democratic governance project through information technology? A growing agenda for debate. *Public Administration Review, 63*(1), 44-60.

Kim, S.-T. (2004). *E-government: Theories and strategies.* Seoul, Korea: Bummunsa. (In Korean)

Klem, L. (1995). Path analysis. In L. G. Grimm, & P. R. Yarnold (Eds.), *Reading and understanding multivariate statistics* (pp. 65-97). Washington, DC: American Psychological Association.

Kline, R. B. (1998). *Principles and practices of structural equation modeling.* NY: Guilford Press.

Kling, R. (1980). Social analyses of computing: Theoretical perspectives in recent empirical research. *Computing surveys, 12*(1), 61-108.

Kling, R., & Jewett, T. (1994). The social design of work life with computers and networks: A natural systems perspective. In M. C. Yovits (Ed.), *Advances in computers* (Vol. 39; pp. 239-293). San Diego, CA: Academic Press.

Klobas, J. E. (1995). Beyond information quality: Fitness for purpose and electronic information resource use. *Journal of Information Science, 21*(2), 95-14.

Kraemer, K. L., Danziger, J. N., Dunkle, D. E., & King, J. L. (1993). The usefulness of computer-based information to public managers. *MIS Quarterly, 17*(2), 129-148.

Kraemer, K. L., Dutton, W. H., & Northrop, A. (1981). *The management of information systems.* New York: Columbia University Press.

Kwon, T. H., & Zmud, R. W. (1987). Unifying the fragmented models of information systems implementation. In R. J. Boland, & R. A. Hirschheim (Eds.), *Critical issues in information systems research* (pp. 227-251). New York: John Wiley & Sons.

Leonard-Barton, D., & Deschamps, I. (1988). Managerial influence in the implementation of new technology. *Management Science, 34*(10). 1252-1265.

Lin, J. C., & Lu, H. (2000). Towards an understanding of the behavioural intention to use a Web site. *International Journal of Information Management, 20*, 197-208.

Lipsky, M. (1980). *Street-level bureaucracy: Dilemmas of the individual in public services.* New York: Russell Sage Foundation.

Loehlin, J. C. (1998). *Latent variable models: An introduction to factor, path, and structural analysis* (3rd ed.). Mahwah, NJ: Lawrence Erlbaum Associates.

Lucas, H. C. (1978). Empirical evidence for a descriptive model of implementation. *MIS Quarterly, 2*(2), 27-41.

Lucas, H. C., Ginzberg, M. J., & Schultz, R. L. (1990). *Information systems implementation: testing a structural model.* Norwood, NJ: Ablex Publishing.

Mathieson, K., Peacock, E., & Chin, W. W. (2001). Extending the technology acceptance model: the influence of perceived user resources. *The Data Base for Advance in Information systems, 32*(3), 86-112.

Minnesota Planning. (2002). *Issue talk: State budget shortfall.* Retrieved January 12, 2005, from http://www.mnplan.state.mn.us/pdf/2002/IssueTalkSummary.pdf

Moon, M. J. (2002). The evolution of e-government among municipalities: Rhetoric or reality? *Public Administration Review, 62*(4): 424-433.

Moon, M. J., & Brestchneider, S. (2002). Does the perception of red tape constrain IT innovativeness in organizations?: Unexpected results from simultaneous equation model and implications. *Journal of Public Administration Research and Theory, 12*(2), 273-291.

Nedovic-Budic, Z., & Godschalk, D. R. (1996). Human factors in adoption of geographic information systems: A local government case study. *Public Administration Review, 56*(6), 554-567.

Nelson, R. R., & Cheney, P. H. (1987). Training end users: an exploratory study. *MIS Quarterly, 11*(4), 547-559.

Norris, D. F. (2005). Electronic democracy at the American grassroots. *International Journal of Electronic Government Research, 1*(3), 1-14.

Norris, D. F., & Moon, M. J. (2005). Advancing e-government at the grassroots: Tortoise or hare? *Public Administration Review, 65*(1), 64-75.

Organization for Economic Cooperation and Development. (2001). *The development of broadband access in OECD countries.* Retrieved February 14, 2005, from http://www.oecdwash.org/DATA/DOCS/broadband_access.pdf

Organization for Economic Cooperation and Development. (2003). *Promise and problem of e-democracy: Challenges of online citizen engagement.* Retrieved October 18, 2004, from http://www1.oecd.org/publications/e-book/4204011E.PDF

Pedhazur, E. J. (1982). *Multiple regression in behavioral research* (2nd ed.). New York: Holt, Rinehart and Winston.

Pedhazur, E. J. (1997). *Multiple regression in behavioral research* (3rd ed.). Forth Worth, TX: Harcourt Brace College Publishers.

Ranerup, A. (1999). Internet-enabled applications for local government democratisation. In R. Heeks (Ed.), *Reinventing government in the information age* (pp. 177-193). London: Routledge.

Rogers, E. M. (1995). *Diffusion of innovations* (4th ed.). New York: The Free Press.

Schumacker, R. E., & Lomax, R. G. (1996). *A beginner's guide to structural equation modeling.* Mahwah, NJ: Lawrence Erlbaum Associates.

Scott, W. R. (1992). *Organizations: Rational, natural, and open systems* (3rd ed.). Englewood Cliffs, NJ: Prentice Hall.

Sheppard, B. H., Hartwick, J., & Warsaw, P. R. (1988). The theory of reasoned action: A meta-analysis of past research with recommendations for modification and future research. *Journal of Consumer Research, 15*(3), 325-343.

Singleton, R. A., & Straits, B. C. (2005). *Approaches to social research* (4th ed.). New York: Oxford University Press.

Spacey, R., Goulding, A., & Murray, I. (2004). Exploring the attitudes of public library staff to the Internet using the TAM. *Journal of Documentation, 60*(5), 550-564.

Subramaniam, N., & Ashkanasy, N. (2001). The effects of organizational culture perceptions on the relationship between budgetary participation and managerial job-related outcomes. *Australian Journal of Management, 26*(1), 35-54.

Thompson, R. L., Higgins, C. A., & Howell, J. M. (1991). Personal computing: Toward a conceptual model of utilization. *MIS Quarterly, 15*(1), 125-143.

Thong, J., & Yap, C. (1995). CEO characteristics, organizational characteristics and information technology adoption in small businesses. *Omega, 23*(4), 429-442.

Tsagarousianou, R. (1999). Electronic democracy: rhetoric and reality. *Communications, The European Journal of Communication Research, 24*(2), 189-208.

United Nations. (2004). *UN global e-government readiness report 2004*. Retrieved December 10, 2004, from http://www.unpan.org/egovernment4.asp

Walsham, G. (1993). *Interpreting information systems in organizations*. Chichester, UK: John Wiley & Sons.

Wang, X. (2001). Assessing public participation in U.S. cities. *Public Performance & Management Review, 24*(4), 322-336.

Weare, C., Musso, J. A., & Hale, M. L. (1999). Electronic democracy and the diffusion of municipal Web pages in California. *Administration & Society, 31*(1), 3-27.

ENDNOTE

[1] E-government readiness index is calculated by averaging the Web measure index, the telecommunication infrastructure index and the human capital index. The e-participation index evaluates the extent of information provision on government Web sites and citizens' online participation in policy making.

This work was previously published in International Journal of Electronic Government Research, Vol. 2, Issue 2, edited by D. F. Norris, pp. 22-48, copyright 2006 by IGI Publishing, formerly known as Idea Group Publishing (an imprint of IGI Global).

Chapter LXXIV
E-Mexico:
Collaborative Structures in Mexican Public Administration

Luis F. Luna-Reyes
Universidad de las Américas-Puebla, México

J. Ramon Gil-Garcia
University at Albany, USA

Cinthia Betiny Cruz
Universidad de las Américas-Puebla, México

ABSTRACT

After six years of challenges and learning pushing forward the e-Government agenda in Mexico, the Presidential succession brought an opportunity for assessing the current progress, recognizing the main unsolved problems, and planning the vision for the future of e-Government in Mexico. This case provides a rich description of the e-Mexico system, including its main objectives and goals, governance structures, IT infrastructure, collaboration processes, main results, and current challenges. Some background information about Mexico is also provided at the beginning of the case. Playing the role of a consultant working for the new Mexican CIO, the reader is asked to evaluate the current situation and help in the design of a work plan, including a proposal for organizing the ICT function, the main strategic objectives, and some specific lines of action for the next six years.

INTRODUCTION

Three years of presidential election campaign finally came to an end on July 2, 2006. Aspirants from the three main political parties worked hard to attract voters' preferences since 2003, but everything got resolved in a single election day. Results were so close that the Federal Elections Institute decided not to pronounce any winner on the basis of their "fast count" program, but to wait for the complete counting of votes. For the first time since 1929, the Institutional Revolutionary Party (PRI) was not the first force in both the House of Representatives and the Senate. Actually, PRI became the third political force with about 21% of the legislators in the House of Representatives. The National Action Party (PAN) became the first political force with about 42%, and the Party of the Democratic Revolution (PRD) became the second force with about 25%.

Just a couple of weeks after the election, Pedro Torres,[1] who was going to be appointed by the elected President to organize the Information and Communication Technologies (ICT) function in the Federal Government for the next six years, was gathering information about the current state of digital government in Mexico. He needed to prepare an assessment of the current progress and needs, and to present a work plan, including a proposal for organizing the Information and Communication Technologies (ICT) function, the main strategic objectives and some specific lines of action. He asked for your advice as a consultant in this process. The following sections in the document constitute a summary of the information Pedro had gathered and shared with you to work in this assessing and planning process.

BACKGROUND

The official name of Mexico is the United Mexican States and is a federal republic formed by 31 states and a Federal District, which is Mexico City. There are three levels of government: federal, state, and municipal. Each level has certain degree of political and administrative autonomy. Municipalities have an elected council chaired by the municipal president. This council—called "cabildo"—has both executive and legislative functions. At the state level, there is a Governor, representing the executive branch, a state legislature, and a state judicial branch headed by the state supreme court of justice. Finally, at the federal level the president is the head of the Executive branch; she is elected by democratic direct voting for a six-year period without possibility of reelection. The legislative branch is conformed by the Senate and the House of Representatives, 128 senators and 500 representatives. The judicial branch is represented by the Supreme Court with 11 Justices. Supreme Court Justices are elected by the House of Representatives every 15 years. The legal system is a combination of the Roman and French systems (Lowe, Armstrong, & Mathias, 2002). Politically, Mexico was governed by the same political party (PRI) from 1929 to 2000 in a quasi-single-party system.

Table 1. Mexico's Politico-Administrative Regime

Key Feature	Mexico
State Structure	Federal Fairly Centralized Co-ordinated
Executive Government	Intermediate (formerly Majoritarian)
Minister/Mandarin Relations	Separate Fairly Politicized
Administrative Culture	Predominantly *Rechtsstaat*
Diversity of Policy Advice	Mainly Political Appointees and civil servants Increasingly consultants, academics and corporations

The country's borders are with the United States of America to the north and with Guatemala and Belize to the south. The Mexican territory spans 1,964,375 square kilometers.

Mexico's politico-administrative regime includes characteristics similar to the United States, Canada, and France, among others. Table 1 summarizes the main characteristics using the framework developed by Pollitt and Bouckaert (2000). Regarding the basic structure of the state, as mentioned before, Mexico is a federal system by constitution and the autonomy of state and local governments is clearly established. However, for more than 60 years a single political party dominated the three levels of government and there was a *de facto* centralization of power around the federal government. A decentralization process started in 2000, but there are still examples of this quasi-federal regime. Regarding the horizontal co-ordination at the federal level, two ministries have historically "called the shots" as far as administrative reform is concerned: the Ministry of Finance and the Ministry of Public Administration (former Office of the Federal Comptroller).

Regarding the nature of executive government, Mexico is in a transition period from a mostly majoritarian regime to a more consensual one (probably intermediate). For many years, Mexican presidents had a significant majority of the legislature from the same political party. They rarely included people from other parties as heads of a ministry or agency. Starting in the late 90's, this situation is changing and the different between the party winning the election and the second force has become very small. In fact, in 2000 President Fox included in his cabinet individuals identified with another political party (PRI).

The relationship between executive politicians (ministers) and senior civil servants is very interesting in Mexico. The Mexican Civil Service is very new and before it was established only very low hierarchical levels were not political appointees (they were union members). With the creation of the civil service, some political appointees decided to change their career paths to senior civil servants. Therefore, public servants are separate from political appointees but their careers are already fairly politicized.

Similarly to France and Germany, the philosophy and culture of governance in Mexico follow what has been called a Rechtsstaat perspective. That is, the state is conceptualized as a central legal and administrative force that integrates society around it. In these cases, civil servants are trained in specific laws that have been developed specifically to guide the functioning of government. This conception is slowly changing following New Public Management trends, at least at the level of political discourse, but it is still predominant.

Finally, regarding the diversity of sources of policy advice, specifically administrative reform issues, political appointees, and recently civil servants, have been the main sources of reform initial ideas for a long time. However, other groups such as management consultants, academics, and corporations are increasingly taking the role of sources of policy advice. This trend has become more evident since 2000, when President Fox (with a long private corporation background) was elected.

Mexico's total population was 103.1 million inhabitants in 2005 (INEGI, 2006b). About 53 million are female and 50.1 million are male. About 25% of the population lives in rural areas, 14 % in semi-urban localities, and 61% in urban cities. One quarter of the population resides in cities of 500,000 inhabitants or larger, with the biggest human concentration in the Federal District (Palacios, Lara, & Kraemer, 2003). The Metropolitan area of Mexico City, including population officially living in the Federal District and the State of Mexico, is home of nearly 21 million people.

Gross National Product (GNP) for 2005 was 8,374,348.5 million pesos (about $800 billion US dollars), which represented a 3% increase from 2004 (INEGI, 2006a). The Mexican Economy shifted from an imports' substitution model between the 30s and the 70s to trade liberalization in the 80s and 90s. In the last few years, there has been an important focus on the Small and Medium Enterprises (SMEs), which account for most of the business establishments in the country (Palacios Lara & Kraemer, 2003). Main economic activities in the country are commerce, personal services, and manufacturing. These three activities account for about 75% of the GNP.

Although the World Bank classifies Mexico as a Middle income country (World Bank, 2005), the country faces several problems. According to the World Policy Institute (2000), Mexico had an underfunded educational system, and an even poorer healthcare system, resulting in low educational levels and a high infant mortality index. Also in 2000, the country had one of the lowest levels of rural development in Latin America, and it was below average in attracting foreign investment, and also in its tourism industry. When compared with other Latin American countries in its same income level, Mexico is the lowest in number of telephones per capita, yet has some of the most expensive rates for domestic calls. In addition, there existed a restrictive environment for new business creation. Finally, Mexico was considered one of the nations in the world with high levels of corruption (World Policy Institute, 2000).

In 2000, the first president from an opposition political party —Vicente Fox from PAN—was elected. Given the country problems, some of the main challenges faced by the Fox administration were to boost economic growth, reduce poverty, and improve Mexico's international competitiveness. To respond to these and other challenges, President Fox main strategy has focused on a plan to upgrade infrastructure, modernize the tax and labor systems, and reform the energy sector. Proposals on these topics have been discussed in the House of Representatives in previous years without reaching consensus in any of them. Therefore, the new elected president, who will take office at the end of 2006, will face very similar challenges.

SETTING THE STAGE

The National Institute of Informatics, Geography and Statistics (INEGI) played a leadership role in Information Policy from the 80s to 2002. One of the main objectives of the Institute was to promote and regulate ICT development in the Federal Government. According to one of the current program managers, INEGI attempted to centralize control over ICT-related purchases and contracts. Other Federal agencies opposed this attempt, and as a result, INEGI decided to follow a "no-policy" strategy. President Fox started in 2000 a very ambitious program to promote the Mexican Digital Society and the use of ICT to improve government services. One important component of the program oriented mainly to promote a digital society was called the e-Mexico system, and was housed at the Ministry of Communications and Transportation. The program component related to the use of ICT in government was lead initially by the President's Office for Innovation. As a result of some policy and process changes described in the following sections, the Office of the Federal Comptroller (SECODAM) became the Ministry of Public Administration in 2002. The new ministry took responsibility of important aspects of Information Policy in Mexico. Actually, program managers working in this direction

Table 2. Main project objectives of e-Mexico

e-Mexico: Main Project Objectives
• To generate value alternatives through a technological system with social content, offering opportunities made feasible by ICT to improve the quality of life of all Mexicans.
• To be a communication channel to integrate and harmonize in a one-stop window services in four initial areas (e-Learning, e-Health, e-Economy, and e-Government).
• To create synergies among public and private agents, allowing content and services integration to create public value.
• To provide to citizens knowledge, opportunities and services in Education, Health, Economy and Government, resulting in personal development inside their own communities, and promoting a closer relationship with government.
• To offer alternative and more flexible communication channels with the citizen using modern ICT.
• To reduce intermediaries, opening direct communication channels with the entity responsible of service offering.
• To develop a technical system with social content, promoting an integral social development.
• To incorporate isolated communities to social development using modern ICT to deliver basic education, health, economic and government services.
• To develop a showcase of Mexican culture and values for interested persons abroad.
• To become the place to connect citizens with public administration, public and private organisms as well as non-profits.
• To promote an IT-enabled government, allowing the creation of opportunities, breaking down barriers, and promoting efficiency.
• To provide experience in Internet-projects implementation, developing a unique "portal for internet portals" containing links to information and services.
• To provide advice based upon world best practices on Internet government services to promote the offering of basic government services through the Internet.
• To provide the technological infrastructure to develop Internet services in a fast, easy and safe way, allowing the evolution of government presence from informational to transactional and combining open standards for interoperability among government entities.

in the President's Office for Innovation moved to the Ministry of Public Administration to give continuity to the programs. INEGI kept policy responsibility only for geographical and statistical systems (i.e., national census), but ICT applications to government became a responsibility of the newly created Ministry of Public Administration (see the Appendix for a brief description of these and other agencies involved in e-Mexico).

The e-Mexico system is an "umbrella" initiative at the center of the Mexican strategy to develop government services and applications for all society. The mission of e-Mexico is to "be an agent of change in the country, integrating efforts from diverse public and private actors in the elimination of the digital divide and other socio-economic differences among Mexicans, through a system with technical and social components to offer basic services on education, health, commercial interchange, and government services, being at the same time leaders in Mexican technological development" (e-México, 2003b).

President Fox administration assumed as one of its main objectives the promotion of ICT use among Mexicans. The e-Mexico system was conceived as a way to provide universal access to information, knowledge and government services as a strategy to create a more democratic and participative society where economic and social benefits were better distributed (e-México, 2003b).

The project started as a direct initiative of President Fox, who in his initial address to the Nation on December 1st, 2000 instructed the Minister of Communications and Transportation to start the initiative:

I instruct the Minister of Communications and Transportation, Pedro Cerisola, to start as soon as possible the e-Mexico project, so the information and communications revolution acquires a truly national character, reducing the digital divide among governments, private organizations, households and individuals, reaching up to the last corner of our country.

The main rationale of e-Mexico was the widely accepted belief that ICT offer national economies with opportunities to grow, to develop, and to create sustainable competitive advantages. Moreover, ICT use in government is associated with benefits such as cost savings, better programs, more transparency and accountability, and improved democracy (6, 2001; Dawes, 1996; OECD, 2003). In this way, the e-Mexico initiative was driven by several problems and challenges faced by President's Fox administration, and it was looking to coordinate government actions to promote economic development, improve transparency and democracy through the use of ICT. Other important driver of the project was also the global trend of ICT applications in government as a tool to promote the "new public management" (Arellano-Gault, 2000).

E-Mexico objectives were developed on the basis of information collected from three main sources. First, a diagnosis of the ICT situation in Federal Government agencies was conducted, finding what a project participant described as a "fifteen year lag in infrastructure compared to Mexican private organizations." Second, current practices research looking for e-gov experiences in Latin America and the rest of the world were conducted. For instance, the initial team took into consideration experiences from Singapore, Korea, Canada, Brazil, Cuba, and England. Finally, they conducted during 2001 a public forum involving more than 900 participants from academia, public administration, private sector, and non-profit organizations. The forum produced more than 140 different documents and proposals, which were considered together with the current practices and the given status of ICT in the Mexican government to develop the e-Mexico strategy. Table 2 lists the main e-Mexico project objectives (e-México, 2003a).

The e-Mexico project is closely related with other presidential initiatives associated with the President's Office for Innovation and the Ministry of Public Administration, who are in charge more specifically of ICT use in government. One such initiative is the Good Government Agenda —created in 2002—which has created synergy with e-Mexico in facilitating government reform. Synergies were generated particularly because one of the main objectives of the Good Government Agenda was to create a digital government to facilitate access to government information and services anytime and anywhere (INNOVA, 2002).

DESCRIPTION OF THE CASE

The proposed goals were ambitious. Actually, project leaders in e-Mexico and other federal government agencies believe that ICT use in government is an instrument to create a more democratic society by giving access to information and services to the entire population, including those small and remote sites regularly difficult to access. The goal was not only to reduce the digital divide, but to create social and economic impacts through the access to information and public services. Moreover, the project was intended to contribute to knowledge creation through the creation of a main portal and several sub-portals based upon particular interests of diverse Mexican communities, reaching 80% of the Mexican population through the 20% higher-impact services (e-México, 2003a).

However, to reach the vision, project participants faced important challenges. One of the main challenges resulted from the initial explorations was related to starting a project with a clear vision for the long run, but allowing concrete results also in the short run. As one of the interviewees commented,

...to truly take the country to the information society is a change that took Korea 40 years, so Mexico made the bet to make this change in at least 25 years, currently [after the first five years] we have the technology that will allow us to make a faster progress. We know that what we are doing in this period is only setting the foundations to build faster upon the things that we have created and did not exist when we started.

Other important challenges were related to the digital divide. In Mexico, as in many other countries, there is a high correlation between the digital divide, and other social "divides" that exist in the whole country (e-México, 2003b). Developing countries lack the appropriate technological and human infrastructures, as well as relevant content in the local language to create a significant social impact. As mentioned above, one of the interviewees commented that through the initial assessment, they found a 15-year lag in Federal Ministries and government agencies' computer infrastructures. Just to mention a couple of examples, more than 50% of PC computers in Mexican government had a Pentium II processor or older in 2001 (INEGI, 2001), and there are only 3.6 million Internet connections for 93.9 million people older than six years (AMIPCI, 2005). Moreover, the problem of government innovation not only resides in building technical capabilities, but also in public services redesign and modernization (e-México, 2003b).

The General Strategy

E-Mexico strategy was organized around three main "axes" or lines of action, and with a value-oriented and collaboration focus. The three main axes were (1) to create infrastructure that allows citizens to connecting to the Internet, (2) to produce relevant content, and (3) to develop a technical architecture for government. The focus on value creation and collaboration is reflected in the coordination nature of e-Mexico. The following sections include a description of each of the three action streams, and the collaborations in the process.

Connectivity

The first line of work of e-Mexico was related to the creation of a connectivity infrastructure to cover most of the country. E-Mexico representatives have been working together with telecommunication companies to promote investment in the communications infrastructure in the country, increasing in this way the number of phone lines in Mexico.

Additionally, the e-Mexico system has worked in the deployment of 7,200 Digital Community Centers (DCC), following models that they found operational from experiences in Brazil and Peru, but also following previous successful experiences in the country with educational programs using satellite communications. Although the country geography posed interesting technical challenges, the group has been also highly interested in the social and community component, as one of the participants commented,

...the most impressive were the results from efforts in Cuba. I went there for a meeting about the Information Society, and they presented all their work models. Their digital community centers had an impact even with all their financial restrictions, there were only three computers, one for the center manager and two for other users, but they were taking advantage of that. We considered that the important part was their social network model. We liked the idea to have it installed in some sort of library. France was declaring little success in their model of community centers, Peru had a similar model but in very early stages, but Cuba had a big success. We thought that part of the success was that they were placing the center in an established organization with somebody taking care of it.

In this way, and taking advantage of the opportunity of using the PANAMSAT satellite system, the group worked together with several government agencies to deploy the DCC based on a satellite network, and locating them in already-established community centers such as public libraries, centers for adult education, but mainly in elementary and medium-high schools (about 6,000 out of the 7,200 DCC are located in schools). According to one of the project participants, about 8,000 well-collocated DCC would be enough to serve most communities with more than 1,000 habitants. However, the same participant commented "we have to think very well about the location of the centers, although our goal is 10,000 community centers, there are more than 200,000 towns along the country, about 150,000 of them with less than 1,000 habitants."

Given the important proportion of DCC established in schools, e-Mexico program collaborated closely with the Ministry of Education during the process. Main challenges during the early stages were technical and logistic, how to place a satellite plate in a donkey or how to install it in a cardboard roof, or how to make the satellite network work in not-state-of-the-art computers. Currently, the challenges are more associated with the sustainability of the DCC, getting people to use them, and to find ways to help communities to generate applications that create wealth and community development. These activities require collaboration with the Ministry of Education, individual schools, citizens, private companies, and non-profit organizations.

Contents

One known problem about information on the Internet is the fact that an important proportion of it is in English. In this way, the second main line of work in e-Mexico involved the creation of relevant contents for people to access. Initially, they worked in the development of the main e-Mexico Portal, and four sub-portals, e-learning, e-health, e-economy, and e-government. The portal project involved a collaboration process with the State Ministries associated to each of the four main "pillars," as people in e-Mexico calls each content area. In fact, there is a contact person in each one of the related Ministries that works together with e-Mexico in the Ministry of Communications and Transportation to coordinate content creation or the integration of currently existing content into the portals.

The four portals were designed to support the main objectives of the e-Mexico System (see Table 2). The e-learning portal has the objective to offer new options to access education and training, promoting education for everyone as a way to personal development. E-health portal intends to increase public health by eliminating barriers to access to wellbeing information and services such as social security. The e-economy portal has the goal to promote the development of the digital economy in Mexico, particularly oriented to the micro, small, and medium enterprises (mSMEs), as well as to promote a digital culture among consumers. Finally, the e-government portal is a medium to offer government information and services (e-México, 2003b).

Following the same spirit of the DCC, e-Mexico staff collaborated with government agencies in content creation and integration, leaving the final responsibility of content management to the Ministry of Education, Health, Economy, or Public Administration, who are actually the content owners. However, although there is one main content owner, many organizations are involved in each sub-portal. As one of the participants commented,

...of course learning is coordinated by the Ministry of Education, but e-Learning goes beyond schools... education, training and culture. You have to include the Ministry of Education, you have to include the state education authorities, the National Council for Science and Technology (CONACYT), the National Council for Culture and Arts (CONACULTA), public and private universities, the poet associations, the National Council for Educational Promotion (CONAFE)... This is important, it is very important to understand that the Ministry of Education only provides services to towns with a population greater than 500. Unfortunately, most of the 200,000+ towns in the country have less than 500 habitants. In those places operates a strategy from the National Council for Educational Promotion (CONAFE). They do not have any school, they are not organized in grades... They use a model for literacy based on a multi-grade approach.

Although the initial plan involved the creation of these four portals, the e-Mexico system has created 12 different content portals, all involving participation of many organizations. For example, the e-Migrant portal was created with the collaboration of 27 different agencies inside and outside government. The experience in content integration has lead to a standard process that has been called "the portal factory." A key player in the creation of portals has been INFOTEC, an applied research center, which has developed as part of its activities tools to design content portals based upon group processes and semantic networks.

Systems

The last main strategy from e-Mexico was the creation of valuable systems. The first and more visible system was the e-Mexico portal itself. One of the interesting design features of the portal was

Figure 1. Network of relationships around e-Mexico system and digital government in Mexico (Luna-Reyes, Gil-García, & Cruz, 2006, p. 2380)

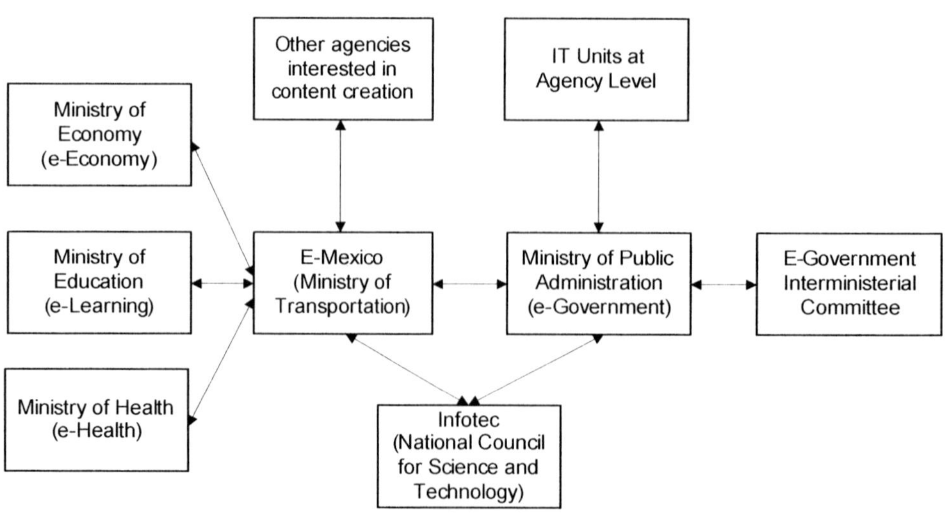

its orientation to the Mexican citizen, and how it was organized around people's life, home, family, taxes, education, health, etc.

The less visible, but not less important, system is conformed by an architecture to facilitate government interoperability and services development. Initially, the group got involved in the definition of requirements and the development of a neural access point, and a data center (e-México, 2003b). During the last year, the group has been involved in requirements definition and the acquisition of a Virtual Private Network for all federal agencies, and an e-services infrastructure based upon the two main technologies in the market, .NET and J2EE. As expressed by another project participant, "the number of convergent (interoperable) systems is still low, and all this architectures are oriented to support true convergence among government agencies."

An important element related to the technical infrastructure is that most of it is outsourced. The DCC monitoring system, the data center, the VPN, and other hardware and communications systems are all outsourced. This situation required collaboration and coordination between the e-Mexico group and a great number of public and private organizations. It is important to mention that e-Mexico systems and infrastructure are not mandatory to other ministries and agencies at the Federal level. They are currently used only by those agencies, which choose to do so.

Collaboration and Value Creation[2]

E-Mexico has been since the beginning a collaborative process, and it is reflected in the network of agencies involved in the digital government project in Mexico (see Figure 1). E-Mexico Coordination, which resides in the Ministry of Communications and Transportation, works closely with the Ministries of Economy, Education, Health, and Public Administration. In the last couple of years, many other agencies and organizations had shown interest in developing specialized content portals for communities such as the native Mexicans, the community of emigrants to the US, women or people with disabilities.

The Digital Government and IT Unit (Ministry of Public Administration) worked in close coordination with the agency-wide IT units at the federal level. Much of the coordination work has been done with the participation of Ministries and CIOs in an e-government network, which last December was formalized into an e-government Inter-ministerial Committee. The main objectives of the committee, as well as all subcommittees around it, are to share experiences, and to develop policy to be applied to all the Public Administration. As mentioned in previous sections, INFOTEC has given technical support in content creation. INFOTEC has also collaborated through research on current practices and technological trends, functioning as a consultant of both e-Mexico and the Ministry of Public Administration, and as a partner in the development of Internet applications.

An interesting result that this horizontal coordination effort has brought is the change in focus from a vertical, hierarchical approach to a value model. One of the participants mentioned that one of their main lessons from the initial public forum was about working together horizontally,

"The first thing we found out was the need to work together. It could not be done piece by piece, but we had to do something strange. That is, instead of creating a new Ministry or a new National Institute, we had to align the process horizontally with the people in charge of doing it... and we thought that to do it, we had to focus in three great areas [..] So, e-Mexico could have been born as a new entity, but the idea was to do it with the existing structures, asking people to do the things they had to do, and coordinating and aligning efforts from organizations and agencies working the same topic."

Another important characteristic of the value model was that any interested agency could approach with project ideas, increasing the probability of project success. Other participant commented

The advantage of a value-based model is that people looks for us when they are interested in doing something, and then things get done. I am not in the hierarchy above them, and that's perfect, because we are understanding for the first time in Mexico, the meaning of collaboration among powers.

As one other participant commented

the beauty of this is that we can do a lot with 13 people in the structure of middle- and high-level managers, and about 25 unionized personnel. So, the ratio of the administrative cost compared to the total budget was just 3.6% last year.

The coordination, planning, and implementation of any project follow a four-step process: Digital Participation, Strategic Planning, Project Management, and Operation. Digital Participation involves the inter-institutional relationships with ministries, agencies and other organizations. It is in this first stage where new project ideas are generated. During the Strategic Planning stage, ideas start to be developed, assessing social impacts, costs, benefits, and alignment with the general e-Mexico Strategy, building a plan. When an idea passes these initial filters, the technical committee of the e-Mexico endowment reviews the project and makes a funding decision. Once funds are available, the idea becomes a project, and moves to the Project Management stage, where following Project Management Institute standards, the group of agencies deploys and implements the project. The last stage involves the operation of the new system or content portal. Most of this operation is external, that is, they are managed by other ministries or agencies. The four stages are organized in a loop of continuous improvement. One of the participants commented, "we deliver, and then we go back to the inter-institutional relationships… to close the loop and start a continuous process of improvement" (see Figure 2).

Governance

According to one of the program managers, e-Mexico and the Good Government Agenda promoted the creation of the Digital Government Network, an informal group with the participation of the CIOs from federal ministries, other agencies, and the e-Mexico coordinator. This group interpreted Digital Government as an axis to support other guiding principles for good government such as transparency, accountability, professionalization, service quality or cost efficiency, starting a series of projects under the leadership of the President's Office for Innovation. When the Ministry of Public Administration was created in 2002, this Ministry's Digital Government and IT Unit kept leadership of this group (actually, the responsible of the strategy at the Office for Innovation took charge of the Digital Government and IT unit).

The main projects of the Network were initially oriented to promote savings, to facilitate interoperability, and to re-define the IT function at the government level. For example, they promoted a unique licensing agreement between Microsoft and all Federal agencies creating important savings for all of them. On the other hand, conversations inside the network made participants realize that about 90% of the IT budget was devoted to control applications, maybe because agency CIOs reported directly to the internal agency comptroller. Moreover, they found out that the decentralization of the IT function in several agencies had promoted the lack of a clear overall IT strategy inside each of them.

Positive experiences and savings with the Digital Government Network, together with research on best practices, lead the group to the creation of an E-government Interministerial Committee,

Figure 2. Coordination process at e-Mexico

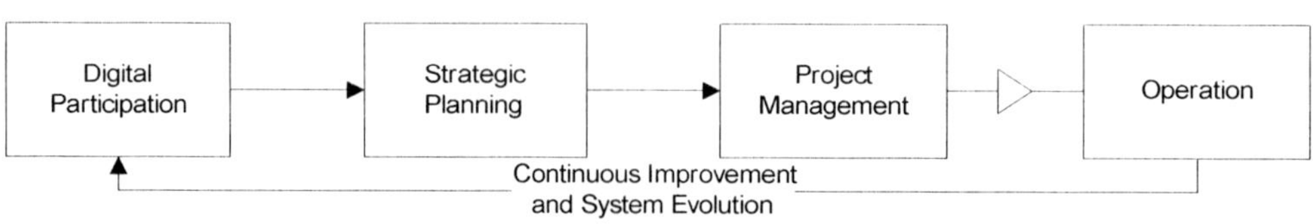

Figure 3. Structure of the e-government interministerial committee

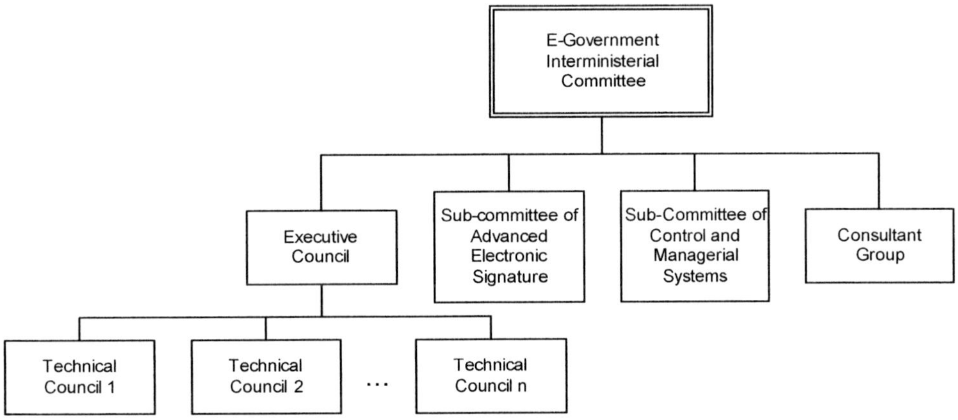

which became a formal body last December (see Figure 3). Committee members are all federal ministers plus the directors of other important institutions such as the Mexican Oil Company (PEMEX), the Mexican Institute for Social Security (IMSS), the Internal Revenue Service (SAT), the National Council for Science and Technology (CONACYT), the President's Office for Innovation, and the Federal Commission for Electricity (CFE). The committee president is the Minister of Public Administration, and the executive secretary of the Committee is the Director of the Digital Government and IT Unit from the same ministry. The Committee develops general policy and strategy (Becerra, 2006).

The Digital Government Network, became the Executive Council of the Committee. Besides the Plenary Sessions, the Executive Council is organized in several technical councils in charge of creating recommendations on important themes such as IT function organization, Security, IT Procurement, Privacy or Interoperability. The Interministerial Committee also supports its functions in two sub-committees in charge of two key IT topics, electronic signatures and Control and Managerial Systems. The first sub-committee members are the representatives from the Ministry of Public Administration, the Ministry of Economy, and the Internal Revenue Service. The Control and Managerial Systems Sub-committee members are representatives from the Ministry of Finance and the Ministry of Public Administration. Finally, the Consultant group will be conformed by members from academia, the private sector, and other members of the civil society.

Although the Interministerial Committee may have an important impact on the Federal Government IT strategy and policy, each Ministry or Agency currently develops its own strategic plan and negotiates its IT budget directly with the President's Office. Some political actors are concerned about the survival of the Committee after the presidential succession, arguing that it had not enough time to consolidate as an institution, and that most members from both the Committee and the Executive Council will change when the elected president brings his own Cabinet.

Main Results, Lessons Learned and Challenges

The e-Mexico project and other associated initiatives have been successful in several ways and to a different extent in several areas of work. According to participants in the project, they have accomplished about 95% of the objectives at the beginning of President Fox Administration (see Table 2). Several of these objectives are closely related with the creation of a "portal of portals" with information and services in four related areas: e-government, e-economy, e-health, and e-learning. The current e-Mexico portal (www.emexico.gob.mx) was not only successful creat-

Figure 4. English version of the e-Mexico portal

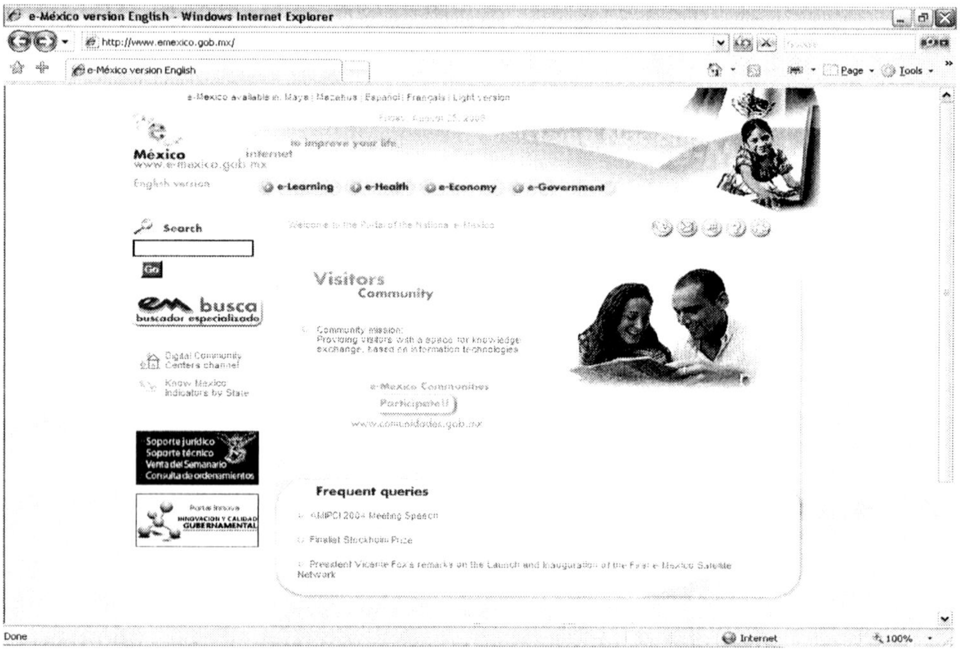

ing these four content areas, but in the creation of many others related to specific interest groups (see Figure 4). The portal contains more than 7,000 Web pages organized in about 15 content portals, with a monthly traffic of about 1.5 million hits. About 1,000 government services can be done in some extent through the Internet. These services constitute alternative communication channels with citizens. The portal has been the main place where synergies among public and private partners have been created through the "portal factory," where public and private organizations, as well as non-profits, have joined efforts to provide valuable content and services to Mexicans. The portal has been also the main tool to develop a showcase of Mexican culture offering contents in English and French, as well as in some Mexican Indian languages such as Mayan and Mazahua.

In order to incorporate isolated communities to social development using ICT, e-Mexico has started the deployment of a network of 7,200 DCC with an estimated number of 5.5 million visitors per month. According to surveys about Internet use, and the expert opinion of some of the marketing companies developing the surveys, e-Mexico has had an important impact on Internet penetration in Mexico. Four out of the 17 million people connected to the Internet does so through a DCC.

The level of success has been different in each of the four main e-Mexico areas. The area of e-health, for example, has had a limited impact because of the lack of resources. However, they have managed to create some important relationships with universities and research centers piloting technologies for telemedicine. Through these initial tests, they have figured out that the same technologies can be used for training and administration of medical centers in rural areas.

The area of e-learning has been closely related to the DCC deployment. Current challenges in the area are less related to the technical aspects of the installation of DCC, and more associated with the sustainability of each Center, and the challenge of creating programs to promote the DCC as a wealth and development factor in each community.

The area of e-economy has been working in the promotion of the supply and demand in the software and IT industry to promote economic development. The work stimulating the supply side has promoted the creation of 19 IT clusters in 19 Mexican States. On the demand side, the group has coordinated projects to show the benefits of using IT in traditional business models. Most of these projects are still in a prototype stage, and it is difficult to assess their impact.

The area of e-government has made important progress in terms of creating and formalizing an initial governance structure based on the Interministerial Committee for Digital Government, and in terms of the development of an initial e-services architecture to support interoperability. The basic architecture includes a government services framework with guidelines for service development, interoperability and security standards, the organization of content using semantic Web technology, the use of Identity Federation and Liberty Project standards for authentication, and a dual technology platform supporting J2EE and .NET standards. However, as of October 2006, all existing services are offered by single agencies and there is almost no sharing of ICT resources among agencies.

The evaluation of the ICT strategy is an area that can be improved. Given that the emphasis during the last six years has been on developing the basic infrastructure for e-government, most indicators of progress are focusing on project deliverables and complying with project timelines. Assessment of accomplishing 95% of initial objectives is based upon this kind of indicators. However, e-government impact measures are missing in this evaluation scheme, and should be included to support sustainable development of the Mexican ICT strategy.

Finally, there are also other important challenges for the future. Many public managers recognize the need of a much better regulatory environment. Although some important regulations have been created, such as the Law regulating the Access to Government Information, some of the participants commented that "legislators are not in complete 'synchrony' with digital government," making the process slow, or even creating new legislation that makes digital government implementation more complicated. Another challenge recognized by some participants is posed by different institutional arrangements inside Ministries, or assumptions that made collaboration complicated. For example, the centralized structure of the Ministry of Communications and Transportation has to coordinate with the decentralized education system, which some times make the coordination difficult.

ACKNOWLEDGMENT

The research reported here is supported by the Consejo Nacional de Ciencia y Tecnología (CONACYT-Mexico) grant SEP-2004-C01-46507. The views and conclusions expressed in this paper are those of the authors alone and do not necessarily reflect the views or policies of CONACYT.

REFERENCES

6, P. (2001). E-governance. Do digital aids make a difference in policy making? In J. E. J. Prins (Ed.), *Designing e-government. on the crossroads of technological innovation and institutional change* (pp. 7-27). The Hague, Netherlands: Kluwer Law International.

AMIPCI. (2005). *Estudio AMIPCI de Internet en México 2005.* Retrieved October, 2005, 2005, from http://www.amipci.org.mx/docs/Presentacion_Estudio_AMIPCI_2005_Presentada.pdf

Arellano-Gault, D. (2000). Challenges for the new public management. Organizational culture and the administrative modernization program in Mexico City (1995-1997). *American Review of Public Administration, 30*(4), 400-413.

Becerra, J. L. (2006). Comisión Intersecretarial para el Desarrollo del Gobierno Electrónico ¿Cómo Funcionará este Modelo Normativo? *Política Digital, 5,* 12-14.

Bogdanor, V. (Ed.). (2005). *Joined-up government.* New York: Oxford University Press.

Dawes, S. S. (1996). Interagency information sharing: Expected benefits, manageable risks. *Journal of Policy Analysis and Management, 15*(3), 377-394.

e-México. (2003a). *El Sistema Nacional e-México: Sistema de Participación Digital*. Retrieved January, 2006, from http://www.emexico.gob.mx/wb2/eMex/eMex_El_Sistema_Nacional_eMexico_un_Sistema_de_Par

e-México. (2003b). *Resumen ejecutivo del sistema nacional e-México*. Retrieved January, 2006, from http://www.emexico.gob.mx/wb2/eMex/eMex_Resumen_ejecutivo_del_Sistema_Nacional_eMexic

INEGI. (2001). *Estructura Porcentual de las Computadoras Personales de la Administración Pública por tipo de Procesador por cada nivel de la Administración Pública*. Retrieved October 2005, from http://www.inegi.gob.mx/est/contenidos/espanol/rutinas/ept.asp?t=tinf003&c=3425

INEGI. (2006a). *Información económica agregada*. Retrieved 2006, from http://www.inegi.gob.mx/inegi/contenidos/espanol/acerca/inegi324.asp?c=324

INEGI. (2006b). *Mujeres y Hombres en Mexico 2006*, Retrieved 2006, from http://www.inegi.gob.mx/prod_serv/contenidos/espanol/bvinegi/productos/integracion/sociodemografico/mujeresyhombres/2006/MyH_x_1.pdf

INNOVA. (2002). *Agenda Presidencial de Buen Gobierno en México*. Retrieved March, 2006, from http://www.innova.gob.mx/ciudadanos/innovacion/index.php?contenido=515&lang=es

Janssen, M., & Cresswell, A. M. (2005, January 3-6). *The development of a reference architecture for local government*. Paper presented at the 38th Hawaii International Conference on System Sciences, Hawaii.

Janssen, M., & Joha, A. (2006, August 4-6). *Governance of Shared Services in Public Administration*. Paper presented at the Americas Conference on Information Systems, Acapulco, Mexico.

Klijn, E. H., & Koppenjan, J. F. M. (2000). Public management and policy networks: Foundations of a network approach to governance. *Public Management, 2*(2), 135-158.

Klijn, E. H., Koppenjan, J. F. M., & Termeer, K. (1995). Managing networks in the public sector: A theoretical study of management strategies in policy networks. *Public Administration, 73*(3), 437-454.

Luna-Reyes, L. F., Gil-García, J. R., & Cruz, C. B. (2006, August, 4-6). *Collaborative Digital Government in Mexico: Some Lessons from Federal Web-Based Inter-Organizational Information Integration Initiatives*. Paper presented at the AMCIS 2006, Acapulco, Mexico.

Lowe, Armstrong S., & Mathias, A. (2002). *Informe de Pais Mexico*, 2006, from http://www.missingkids.com/en_US/publications/Mexico_S.pdf

OECD. (2003). *The e-government imperative*. Paris, France: Organisation for Economic Co-operation and Development.

Palacios Lara, J. J., & Kraemer, K. L. (2003). Globalization and e-commerce IV: Environment and policy in Mexico. *Communications of the AIS, 11*, 129-185.

Pollitt, C., & Bouckaert, G. (2000). *Public management reform: A comparative analysis*. Oxford, UK: Oxford University Press.

World Bank. (2005). *Mexico Country Brief*. Retrieved 2006, from http://iris37.worldbank.org/domdoc/PRD/Other/PRDDContainer.nsf/WB_ViewAttachments?ReadForm&ID=85256D2400766CC78525715600596034&

World Policy Institute. (2000). *Mexico: A statistical evaluation of government performance*. Retrieved 2006, from http://www.worldpolicy.org/globalrights/mexindex.html

ENDNOTES

1 This case is based on the findings from 15 semi-structured interviews to e-Mexico program managers. Interviewees include project managers and CIOs from the ministries of Communications and Transportation (3), Public Administration (3), Economy (1), Health (1), Education (1), Finance (2), the President's Internet System (1), the Institute for Access to Information (2), and staff from INFOTEC (1), a public center for innovation involved in the development and implementation of the Mexican Digital Government Strategy. Interviewees were asked about the characteristics of their projects, projects' cost and benefits, their perceptions of project success, collaboration, and networking. Documentation analysis was used to enrich the contextual description and triangulate findings from the interviews. However, the names used for prospective program managers are fictional.

2 The Collaboration approach described in this section has been described in the literature using terms such as governance (Janssen & Joha, 2006; Klijn & Koppenjan, 2000; Klijn, Koppenjan, & Termeer, 1995) or joined-up government (Bogdanor, 2005). Those literatures can help to better understand that e-Mexico initiative is an instance of a larger trend to collaborate in government to solve "wicked" problems. Moreover, these ideas can be used as a framework to analyze the Mexican experience. However, the authors preferred to use the term "value creation" because it was the term used by the project participants to describe their efforts.

APPENDIX. A BRIEF DESCRIPTION OF THE MAIN AGENCIES INVOLVED IN E-MEXICO

- **E-Mexico Coordination:** The e-Mexico Coordination is the office in the Ministry of Communications and Transportation in charge of implementing the main objectives of the e-Mexico program, which is considered as the national information society project. The 13 professional staff members employed in the Coordination work closely with representatives from the Ministries of Education, Health, Economy, and Public Administration to create content for the e-Mexico portal. They have received support and professional advice from INFOTEC. The Coordinator is perceived as the Mexican CIO by some international agencies.
- **President's Office for Innovation:** An office in charge of developing policy and programs to promote innovation in government. This office was in charge of ICT use in the Federal agencies and ministries in 2000, but this responsibility was given to the Digital Government and IT Unit in the Ministry of Public Administration. Currently, the office motivates innovation through documenting and recognizing best practices as well as promoting President Fox's Agenda for Good Government.
- **Digital Government and IT Unit:** Is the Unit in the Ministry of Public Administration promoting ICT use and development in federal government agencies. The Unit director is the Executive Secretary of the E-Government Interministerial Committee, and coordinates the development of information systems to improve government productivity, transparency, and services. The director is perceived as the Mexican CIO by some international agencies.
- **President's Internet System:** Is an office in charge of opening communication channels between the President's office and the citizens through Internet applications such as e-mail and the World Wide Web. They actively promote the use of Open Source Standards, develop Web services and components, and share these components with any agency that approaches to them.
- **Infotec:** INFOTEC is the technology center that serves the Government of Mexico and other organizations to foster the Information Society in Mexico through a program of applied research.
- **Ministry of Economy:** The Ministry of Economy is responsible for the e-economy pillar of e-Mexico. The ministry interpretation of its participation in e-Mexico consists of content creation and the promotion of the development of the IT industry in Mexico as an important element for economic development.
- **Ministry of Health:** The Ministry of Health works with the e-Mexico Coordination to create health-related content in collaboration with other health-related public agencies. They are also exploring the application of ICT to telemedicine, which would make possible for people in isolated communities to obtain better medical services.
- **Ministry of Education:** The Ministry of Education has collaborated in the deployment of the Digital Community Centers, and the development of educational materials for the e-Mexico portal, and others to be used only in schools.

This work was previously published in International Journal of Cases on Electronic Commerce, Vol. 3, Issue 2, edited by M. Khosrow-Pour, pp. 54-70, copyright 2007 by IGI Publishing, formerly known as Idea Group Publishing (an imprint of IGI Global).

Chapter LXXV
The Impact of the Internet on Political Activism: Evidence from Europe

Pippa Norris
Harvard University, USA

ABSTRACT

The core issue for this study concerns less the social than the political consequences of the rise of knowledge societies; in particular, the capacity of the Internet for strengthening democratic participation and civic engagement linking citizens and government. To consider these issues, Part I summarizes debates about the impact of the Internet on the public sphere. The main influence of this development, as it is theorized in a market model, will be determined by the "supply" and "demand" for electronic information and communications about government and politics. Demand, in turn, is assumed to be heavily dependent upon the social characteristics of Internet users and their prior political orientations. Given this understanding, the study predicts that the primary impact of knowledge societies in democratic societies will be upon facilitating cause-oriented and civic forms of political activism, thereby strengthening social movements and interest groups, more than upon conventional channels of political participation exemplified by voting, parties, and election campaigning. Part II summarizes the sources of survey data and the key measures of political activism used in this study, drawing upon the 19-nation European Social Survey, 2002. Part III examines the evidence for the relationship between use of the Internet and indicators of civic engagement. The conclusion in Part IV summarizes the results and considers the broader implications for governance and democracy.

INTRODUCTION

The rise of knowledge societies represents one of the most profound transformations that has occurred in recent decades. The diffusion of information and communication technologies (ICTs) promises to have major social consequences by expanding access to education and training, broadening channels of expression and social networks, as well as revolutionizing the nature of work and the economy. The primary impact of this development has been evident in affluent societies, but the Internet has also been widely regarded as an important instrument for social change in poorer nations around the globe (Franda, 2002; UN, 2002).

PART I: THEORIES OF THE IMPACT OF KNOWLEDGE SOCIETIES ON DEMOCRACY

There are multiple theories about how the growth of knowledge societies could potentially influence civic engagement in contemporary democracies. Four main perspectives can be identified in the literature.

The Internet as a Virtual Agora

The most positive view is held by cyber-optimists who emphasize the Panglossian possibilities of the Internet for the involvement of ordinary citizens in direct, deliberative, or "strong" democracy. Digital technologies are thought to hold promise as a mechanism facilitating alternative channels of civic engagement exemplified by political chat rooms, remote electronic voting in elections, referenda, plebiscites, and the mobilization of virtual communities, thereby revitalizing levels of mass participation in public affairs (Barber, 1998; Budge, 1996). This view was certainly popular as the Internet rapidly expanded in the United States during the mid-1990s and the radical potential of digital technologies for democracy continues to be expressed by enthusiasts today (Gilder, 2000; Rash, 1997; Rheingold, 1993; Schwartz, 1996).

Moreover, the general claim that the knowledge society will stimulate widespread citizen deliberation in affairs of state so that the Internet functions like a virtual Agora while attractive as a normative ideal, became less plausible once it was widely recognized by many observers that there are substantial disparities in who becomes involved in digital politics. Studies of politically-oriented discussion groups, bulletin boards, and online chat rooms have found that these largely fail as deliberative forums, instead serving as places to reinforce like-minded voices due to their "easy entrance, easy exit" characteristics (Davis, 1999; Davis & Owen, 1998; Wilhelm, 2001). The survey evidence from many countries indicates that those who take advantage of the opportunities for electronic civic engagement are often activists who were already most predisposed to participate via the traditional channels of political participation (Hill & Hughes, 1998; Selnow, 1998; Toulouse & Luke, 1998). The Internet is a medium of choice par excellence, so it seems improbable that political Web sites, chat rooms and online news will reach many citizens who are otherwise disengaged, apathetic, or uninterested, if they choose to spend their time and energies on multiple alternative sites devoted to everything from the stock market to games and music (Bonfadelli, 2002; Johnson & Kaye, 2003). In this regard, the Internet seems analogous to the segmented magazine market, where some subscribe to the *Atlantic Monthly* and the *Economist* and *Foreign Affairs*, but others pick *Golfing Weekly* or *Playboy*. Therefore, claims for the potential of the knowledge society to revitalize mass participation or strong democracies find little support from the available empirical studies.

The Knowledge Elite and Social Inequalities

As the Internet evolved during the last decade, a darker vision developed among cyber-pessimists who regard the knowledge society as a Pandora's Box reinforcing existing inequalities of power and wealth and generating deeper divisions between the information rich and poor. In this perspective, the global and social divides in Internet access mean that, far from encouraging mass participation, the knowledge society will disproportionately benefit the most affluent sectors in the developed world (Golding, 1996; Hayward, 1995; Murdock & Golding, 1989; Weber, Loumakis, & Bergman, 2003). For example, the first phase of the UN World Summit on the Information Society (WSIS) held in Geneva in December 2003 concluded that the Internet holds great prospect for development for billions of people around the globe, endorsing ambitious principles and action plans, and yet no agreement was reached about the transfer of financial and technological resources necessary to facilitate wider electronic access in poorer nations (ITU, 2003). Despite the great potential for technological innovations leading towards political change, observers suggest that in established democracies, traditional interest groups and governments have the capacity to reassert their control in the virtual political sphere, just as traditional multinational corporations have the ability to reestablish their predominance in the world of e-commerce (Hill & Hughes, 1998; McChesney, 1999; Selnow, 1998; Toulouse & Luke, 1998). In authoritarian regimes, as well, studies have found that access to publishing and disseminating information on the Internet, can be strictly restricted by governments, such as limitations imposed in Cuba, Saudi Arabia, and China (Boas, 2000; Drake, Kalathil, & Boas, 2000; Hill & Hughes, 1999; Kalathil & Boas, 2003).

Politics as Usual

The third perspective, which has become more commonly heard in recent years, is articulated by cyber-skeptics who argue that both of these visions are exaggerated. In this view, the potential of the knowledge society has failed so far to have a dramatic impact on the practical reality of "politics as usual," for good or ill, even in countries such as the United States at the forefront of digital technologies (Margolis & Resnick, 2000). This perspective stresses the embedded status quo and the difficulties of achieving radical change to political systems through technological mechanisms. For example, commentators suggest that during the 2000 American election campaign, George W. Bush and Al Gore used their Web pages essentially as glossy shop windows, fundraising tools, and campaign ads, rather than as interactive "bottom up" formats facilitating public comment and discussion (Foot & Schneider, 2002; Media Matrix, 2000). During the 2004 presidential election in the United States, the fundraising function also seems to have predominated in the campaign for Vermont Democratic Governor, Howard Dean, and the Kerry-Edwards Web site.

Elsewhere, content analysis of political party Web sites in countries as diverse as the United Kingdom, France, Mexico, and the Republic of Korea has found that the primary purpose of these Web sites has been the provision of standard information about party organizations and policies that were also widely available offline, providing more of the same rather than anything new, with still less interactive facilities.

> *Party presence on the Internet seems to represent largely an additional element to a party's repertoire of action along with more traditional communication forms rather than a transformation of the fundamental relationship between political parties and the public, as some earlier advocates of cyber-democracy hoped.* (Gibson, Nixon, & Ward, 2003, p. X)

Studies of the content of government department Web sites in many countries at the forefront of the move towards e-governance (e.g., the United States, Canada, and India) and surveys of users of these Web sites have also found that these Web sites are often primarily used for the dissemination of information and the provision of routine administrative services. The Internet thereby serves as an aid to good governance by increasing government transparency, efficiency, and customer-oriented service delivery, but it does not function as a radical medium facilitating citizen consultation, policy discussion, or other democratic inputs into the policymaking process (Allen, Jullet, & Roy, 2001; Chadwick & May, 2003; Fountain, 2001; Haque, 2002; Stowers, 1999; Thomas & Streib, 2003). In the skeptical view, technology is a plastic medium that flows into and adapts to pre-existing social molds and political functions.

The Political Market Model

The last theoretical perspective—the one developed in this study—can be characterized as the political market model. In this account, the impact of the knowledge society depends upon the interaction between the "top-down supply" of political information and communications made available via the Internet, e-mail, and the World Wide Web from political institutions, notably government departments, parliaments, political parties, the news media, interest groups, and social movements, and upon "demand" in the use of information and communications about politics among the online public.

This model suggests that, in turn, demand depends upon the social characteristics of the online population, especially the preponderance of younger, well-educated citizens who are commonly among the heaviest users of the Internet, and their prior political interests and propensities. The theory suggests that, given these assumptions, use of the Internet in the public sphere is most likely to strengthen and reinforce cause-oriented and civic-oriented dimensions of political activism, which are more popular among the well-educated younger generation, while having far less impact upon traditional channels of participation through voting, parties, and election campaigns (Norris 2001, 2002).

Therefore, rather than accepting that either everything will change as radical forms of direct democracy come to replace the traditional channels of representative governance (as optimists hope), that the digital divide will reinforce socio-economic disparities in politics (as pessimists predict), or alternatively that nothing will change as the digital world merely replicates "politics as usual" (as the skeptics suggest), the political market model suggests that it is more sensible to identify what particular types of democratic practices will probably be strengthened by the rise of the knowledge society, understanding that these developments remain a work in process.

PART II: CONCEPTUAL FRAMEWORK, EVIDENCE, & DATA

What evidence would allow us to examine these propositions, particularly testing the impact of the Internet upon political activism? To understand these issues, we need to recognize that involvement in public affairs can take many different forms, each associated with differing costs and benefits. This study compares the impact of frequency of use of the Internet on four main dimensions of activism: voting, campaign-oriented, cause-oriented, and civic-oriented. These are summarized into a 21-point "Political Activism Index" combining all dimensions[1]. The basic items used to develop this Index are listed in Table 1 and reported fully in Appendix A.

Voting in regular elections is one of the most ubiquitous forms of citizen-oriented participation, requiring some initiative and awareness for an informed choice but making fairly minimal demands of time, knowledge, and effort. Through the ballot box, voting exerts diffuse pressure over parties and elected officials, and the outcomes of elections affect all citizens. Participating at the ballot box is central to citizenship in representative democracy, but due to its relatively low costs, the act is atypical of other more demanding forms of participation. The Internet can be expected to encourage voting participation mainly by lowering some of the information hurdles to making an informed choice, although the provision of remote electronic voting through a variety of new technologies can be expected to have a more radical impact on turnout (Tolbert & McNeal, 2003).

Campaign-oriented forms of participation concern acts focused primarily on how people can influence parliament and government in representative democracy, mainly through political parties in British politics. Verba, Nie, and Kim (1978) focus on this aspect when they define political participation as "...those legal activities by private citizens that are more or less directly aimed at influencing the selection of governmental personnel and/or the actions they take." Work for parties or candidates, including party membership and volunteer work, election leafleting, financial

Table 1. Political activism in Europe, ESS-2002 (Source: European Social Survey, 2002 [ESS-19]. Pooled sample N. 31741 in 18 ESS nations, excluding Germany [where Internet use was not monitored])

Percentage that have...	Regular internet user (%)	Not regular user (%)	Activism Gap (%)	Sig
VOTING				
Reported voting in the last national election	28	26	+2	***
CAMPAIGN-ORIENTED				
Contacted politician	22	13	+9	***
Worn campaign badge	12	6	+6	***
Donated money to party	11	7	+4	***
Worked for party	6	4	+2	***
Party member	6	5	+1	***
CAUSE-ORIENTED				
Bought product for political reason	41	17	+24	***
Signed petition	35	16	+19	***
Boycotted product	25	11	+14	***
Demonstrated legally	10	5	+5	***
Protested illegally	2	1	+1	***
CIVIC-ORIENTED				
Member sports club	35	14	+21	***
Member trade union	33	17	+16	***
Member consumer group	25	11	+14	***
Member hobby group	20	10	+10	***
Member educational group	12	4	+8	***
Member professional group	14	6	+8	***
Member environmental group	9	4	+5	***
Member humanitarian group	9	4	+5	***
Member church group	15	11	+4	***
Member social club	11	10	+1	***
TOTAL 21-POINT ACTIVISM INDEX				
Mean index score	4.43	2.56	+1.87	***

*Note: For the specific items used in the construction of the Index, see the Technical Appendix. 'Regular internet user' is defined as reported personal use of the Internet, email or World Wide Web at least weekly. The 'activism gap' is measured as the percentage of regular Internet users minus the percentage of regular non-users who engage in this activity. A positive gap indicates that regular Internet users are more active than non-users. The total activism index counts participation in each form of activity as one and sums the 21-point scale. Significance tested by Chi-squares and by ANOVA. *** .001 ** .01 * .05 N/s Not significant.*

donations to parties or candidates, attending local party meetings, and get-out-the-vote drives, typifies this category. Parties serve multiple functions in representative democracies, notably simplifying and structuring electoral choices, organizing and mobilizing campaigns, aggregating disparate interests, channeling political debate, selecting candidates, structuring parliamentary divisions, acting as policy think tanks, and organizing government. Not only are parties one of the main conduits of political participation, they also serve to boost and strengthen electoral turnout. If mass party membership is under threat, as many indicators suggest, this could have serious implications for representative democracy (Mair & Biezen, 2001; Scarrow, 2001).

Campaigning and party work typically generate collective rather than individual benefits, but require greater initiative, time, and effort (and sometimes expenditure) than merely casting a ballot. The Internet can be expected to provide new opportunities for activism in parties and election campaigns (e.g., through downloading information, joining parties or donating funds, and participation in discussion groups hosted on party or candidate Web sites) (Gibson, Nixon, & Ward, 2003; Hague & Loader, 1999; Norris, 2001;). Experience of campaign-oriented activism is gauged in this study by a five-battery item, including whether people are members of a party and whether they have donated money to a party, worked for a party, contacted a politician, or worn a campaign badge during the previous 12 months.

Cause-oriented activities are focused primarily upon influencing specific issues and policies. These acts are exemplified by consumer politics (e.g., buying or boycotting certain products for political or ethical reasons), taking part in demonstrations and protests, and organizing or signing petitions. The distinction is not watertight; for example, political parties can organize mass demonstrations, and social movements often adopt mixed action strategies that combine traditional repertoires such as lobbying representatives, with a variety of alternative modes such as online networking, street protests, and consumer boycotts. Nevertheless, compared with campaign-oriented actions, the distinctive aspect of cause-oriented repertoires is that they are most commonly used to pursue specific issues and policy concerns among diverse targets, both within and also well beyond the electoral arena.

These acts seek to influence representative democracies within the nation-state through the conventional channels of contacting elected officials, ministers, civil servants, and government departments, but their target is often broader and more diffuse, possibly in the non-profit or private sectors, whether directed at shaping public opinion and lifestyles, publicizing certain issues through the news media, mobilizing a networked coalition with other groups or non-profit agencies, influencing the practices of international bodies such as the World Trade Organization or the United Nations, or impacting public policy in other countries. Experience of cause-oriented activism is measured in this study by a five-battery item, including whether people have signed a petition, bought or boycotted products for a political reason, demonstrated legally, or protested illegally during the previous 12 months.

Lastly and by contrast, **civic-oriented** activities involve membership and working together in voluntary associations, as well as collaborating with community groups to solve a local problem. The core claim of Toquevillian theories of social capital is that typical face-to-face deliberative activities and horizontal collaboration within voluntary organizations far removed from the political sphere (exemplified by trade unions, social clubs, and philanthropic groups) promote interpersonal trust, social tolerance, and cooperative behavior. In turn, these norms are regarded as cementing the bonds of social life and creating the foundation for building local communities, civil society, and democratic governance. In a win-win situation, participation in associational life is thought to generate individual rewards, such as career opportunities and personal support networks, as well as facilitating community goods by fostering the capacity of people to work together on local problems. Putnam suggests that civic organizations such as unions, churches, and community groups play a vital role in the production of social capital where they succeed in bridging divisive social cleavages, integrating people from diverse backgrounds and values, promoting "habits of the heart" such as tolerance, cooperation, and reciprocity, thereby contributing towards a dense, rich, and vibrant social infrastructure (Pharr & Putnam, 2000; Putnam, 1993, 1996, 2000, 2002). This dimension involves direct action within local communities (e.g., raising funds for a local hospital or school) where the precise dividing line between the social and political breaks down.

Trade unions and churches, in particular, which have long been regarded as central pillars of civic society in Europe, have traditionally served the function of drawing citizens into public life. For a variety of reasons, including the way that voluntary associations can strengthen social networks, foster leadership skills, heighten political awareness, create party linkages, and facilitate campaign work, people affiliated with church-based or union organizations can be expected to participate more fully in public life (Cassel, 1999; Radcliff & Davis, 2000). Access to the knowledge society can be expected to expand social networks and information, facilitating membership in civic associations and social groups, although the evidence as to whether the Internet strengthens or weakens social capital remains under debate (Bimber, 1998; Horrigan, Rainie, & Fox, 2001). Experience of civic activism is measured here by a 10-point scale summarizing membership in a series of different types of voluntary organizations and associations, including traditional sectors such as trade unions, church groups, and social clubs, as well as "new" social movements exemplified by groups concerned about the environment and humanitarian issues.

The summary 21-point political activism index, which provides an overview, is composed very simply by adding together experience of each of these different types of acts (each coded 0/1). It should be noted that in this conceptual framework, this study focuses upon political *activity*; we are concerned with *doing* politics rather than being attentive to public affairs or having psychological attitudes such as trust in parliament or political efficacy, which are thought to be conducive to civic engagement. The study, therefore, does not regard exposure or attention to mass communications, including following campaign events in newspapers or watching party political broadcasts during the election, as indicators of political activism per se. These factors may, indeed, plausibly contribute towards participation and thereby help explain this phenomenon as prior pre-conditions, but they are not, in themselves, channels that citizens can use for expressing political concerns or mobilizing group interests.

Survey Evidence & Data Sources

To establish the extent and significance of the role of the Internet on political activism, the primary source of evidence for this study is drawn from the 19-nation European Social Survey 2002 (ESS-19). This is a new, academically driven study designed to chart and explain the interaction between Europe's changing institutions and the attitudes, beliefs, and behavior patterns of its diverse populations[2]. The survey includes a wide range of items designed to monitor citizen involvement, including a battery of a dozen items that can be used to create a summary political activism scale, as well as multiple indicators of political interest, efficacy, trust, party allegiances, subjective well-being, family and friendship bonds, and a rich array of detailed socio-demographic data, including household composition, ethnicity, type of area, and occupational details. This survey provides recent evidence, and it also facilitates comparison among similar advanced industrialized European societies and democratic states. The size of the total pooled sample (with over 36,000 cases) also allows us to monitor differences among smaller European populations, such as ethnic minorities.

The survey currently includes four nations in Scandinavia (Norway, Sweden, Finland, and Denmark), six nations in Northern Europe (Britain, Germany, Luxembourg, Ireland, the Netherlands, and Switzerland), four from Mediterranean Europe (Greece, Spain, Italy, Portugal, and Israel), and four post-Communist societies in Central Europe (the Czech Republic, Hungary, Poland, and Slovenia). All these countries were classified by Freedom House in 2001-02 as fully "free" in their political rights and civil liberties, using the Gastil Index. Most can also be categorized as affluent post-industrial economies, with an average per capita GDP in 2002 ranging from $16,000 (in

Example 1.

"Now, using this card, how often do you use the internet, the World Wide Web or e-mail—whether at home or at work—for your personal use?"

No access at home or work	00 (41%)	}
Never use	01 (17%)	}
Less than once a month	02 (3%)	} Regular use
Once a month	03 (2%)	}
Several times a month	04 (4%)	}

Once a week	05 (5%)	}
Several times a week	06 (11%)	}
Every day	07 (16%)	}
(Don't know/No answer)		

Greece) to $30,000 (in Norway), although all of the post-Communist states except Slovenia fall below this level.

Internet Use

In some of these societies, the knowledge society has been widely diffused, with two-thirds or more of the public using the Internet at least occasionally. By contrast, in other societies, few of the public accesses the Internet. The survey monitored Internet use by the question in Example 1.

This is a limited measure that does not gauge what people do online or where they commonly seek information, nor does it distinguish among access to the Internet, email, or World Wide Web. These are only some forms of access to the knowledge society, and other electronic technologies may be equally important, such as text messaging; mobile or cell phones; or cable, satellite, and interactive television. In addition, people may also use the Internet at work, and the measure does not attempt to monitor the length of experience of using the Internet. Nevertheless, this item provides a standard measure of exposure to the Internet widely used in other studies, which gives a suitable benchmark for cross-national comparison.

The main cross-national contrasts that emerged on this item are illustrated in Figure 1, which compares a third of Europeans in the sample who report that they *regularly* use the Internet (defined here as personal use of the Internet at least weekly) in the ESS-19. The remaining two-thirds say they never used the Internet or used it far less regularly than weekly. As many other Eurobarometer surveys have regularly reported, sharp differences are evident in Internet access within Europe (Norris, 2001). In Scandinavia (notably Denmark, Sweden, and Norway), regular Internet use is widespread among the majority of the population. Many of the countries fall into the middle of the distribution where anywhere from one-fifth to one-half use the Internet at least weekly. By contrast, in some countries in Mediterranean and post-Communist Europe, less than a fifth of the public made regular use of this technology, notably in Greece, Hungary, Poland, and Spain, which were all at the bottom of the distribution.

Figure 1. The proportion of regular Internet users in Europe, ESS-2002

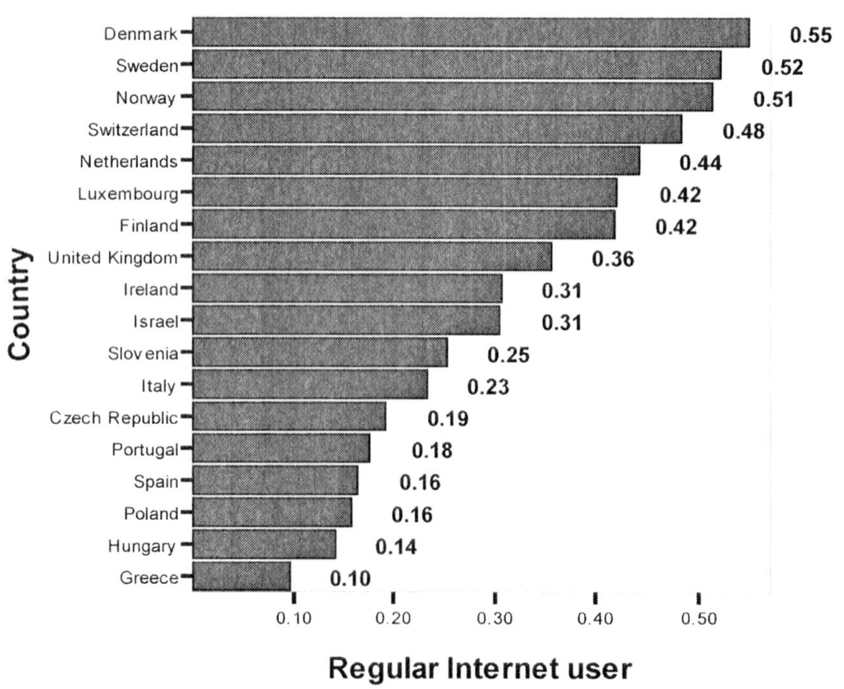

PART III: ANALYSIS & RESULTS

How do those Europeans who are and are not regular users of the Internet compare across the different types of political activism? We can first compare the overall patterns using the pooled ESS-19 sample without using any prior social or attitudinal controls, and then go on to consider the results of the multivariate analysis and differences among European nations. One important qualification to note is that in the analysis, we cannot establish the direction of causality in these models; with a single cross-sectional survey, it is impossible to disentangle satisfactorily whether use of the Internet facilitates and encourages political activism, or whether prior habits of political engagement lead towards continuing activism via electronic channels. To establish causality in any media effects, we really need either to analyze repeated panel surveys among the same respondents over successive years, or to examine experimental research designs, neither of which are available on a cross-national basis (Kent, Jennings, & Zeitner, 2003; Norris, 2000; Norris & Sanders, 2003). In the model, based on standard theories of political socialization, we assume that the cultural values and norms of behavior are acquired from formative experiences with family, school, and community in early youth. We theorize that these processes are likely to shape long-term and enduring political orientations and habitual norms of behavior, such as patterns of partisan identification, ideological values, and forms of activism. We assume that use of the Internet is a relatively recent and, therefore, short-term influence that will facilitate and reinforce the cognitive and attitudinal factors associated with habitual political activism (e.g., expanding people's awareness of election issues or party policies) but will not necessarily alter or transform broader patterns of civic engagement.

Given these assumptions, Table 1 shows a clear and consistent pattern: regular Internet users are significantly more politically active across all 21 indicators. The overall score on the mean Political Activism Index, which summarizes this pattern, was 4.43 for regular Internet users compared with 2.56 for others, a substantial and significant difference. Yet the size of the activism gap does vary among different types of engagement; it is relatively modest in reported voting turnout as well as across most of the campaign-oriented forms of activism, such as party membership, party volunteer work, and party donations. By contrast, the gap is substantial (in double digits) among many forms of cause-oriented activism, such as buying or boycotting products for political reasons and signing petitions, as well as in membership of certain types of civic organizations notably belonging to sports clubs, trade unions, consumer groups, and hobby groups.

To see whether this activism gap was an artifact of the way that regular Internet use was measured, Figure 2 illustrates the mean distribution of the political activism index across all categories of Internet use, ranging from no access at home or work to personal use of the Internet every day. The figure confirms that the overall scale of political activism rises sharply and steadily with each category of Internet use, more than doubling across the whole scale.

Moreover, if the patterns are analyzed by country, again similar results are evident in every society. As Figure 3 shows, political activism rises steadily with increasing Internet use in nearly all nations, and the only exceptions to this are Portugal and Poland where levels of technological diffusion remain very limited.

Figure 2. Internet use and the political activism index (Source: European Social Survey, 2002)

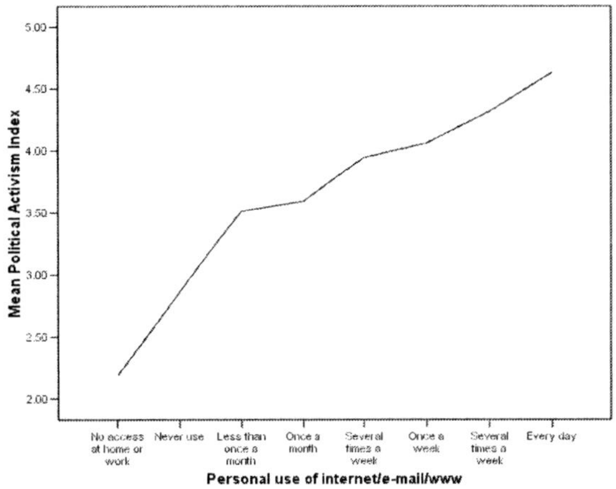

Figure 3. Internet use and the Political Activism Index by nation (Source: European Social Survey, 2002)

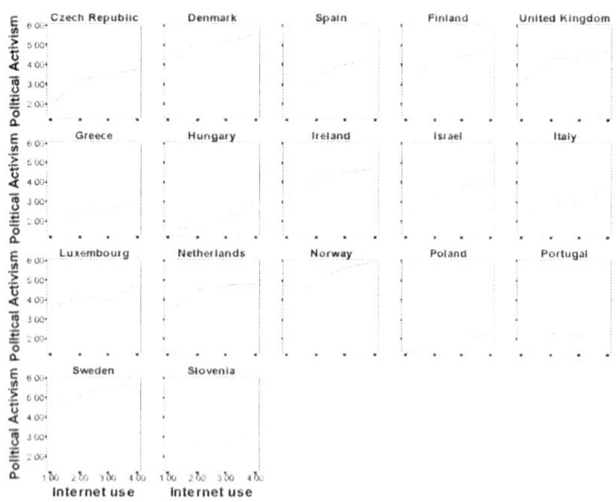

Despite this clear and important pattern, the theoretical framework in this study suggests that, given the characteristics of the online population, we should find systematic variations in engagement by the different types of political activism, and, indeed, this is confirmed by the data. Figure 4 illustrates the strong and significant linear relationship between use of the Internet and civic activism in a wide range of voluntary organizations and local associations (R=318***). The cause-oriented activism scale is also significantly associated with the frequency of using the Internet (R =.318***). Nevertheless, voting activism is relatively flat across levels of Internet use, and the correlation proves to be significant but negative in direction (R=-0.024**), while the campaign-oriented activism scale shows only a modest positive correlation (R=.136). The results suggest that any association between access to the Internet and political activism is heavily contingent upon the particular forms of participation that are under analysis.

Nevertheless, many factors may be influencing this process, including the prior social characteristics and cultural attitudes of Internet users. To examine these issues we need multivariate regression models. The main explanations of political activism can be categorized into the following four groups:

1. **Structural** explanations emphasizing the resources that facilitate civic engagement; notably, time, education, and income, which are closely associated with demographic groups and social status;
2. **Cultural** accounts focusing upon the motivational attitudes that draw people into public affairs, such as a sense of political efficacy, institutional confidence, and citizenship duty;
3. **Agency** explanations prioritizing the role of mobilizing organizations such as churches and unions, as well as the role of the news media and informal social networks, which bring people into public affairs. The use of the Internet can best be conceptualized in this model as a mobilizing agency;
4 **Historical** accounts suggesting that there could be a regional effect generated by traditions in each area; notably, the length of time that representative democracy has operated in Scandinavia, Western Europe, and the "third-wave" democracies in the Mediterranean region and post-Communist societies that only experienced free and fair elections from the early 1990s onward.

Given this framework, Table 2 first includes the standard demographic and socioeconomic variables that many studies have commonly found to influence participation, including belonging to an ethnic minority, educational qualifications, household income, social class, work status, total hours normally worked per week, marital and family status, and religiosity. These were entered into the model in this order before adding the cultural attitudes of frequency of political discussion, the importance of politics, social and political trust, internal and external political efficacy, a sense of civic duty, and interest in politics. The mobilizing agency variables were then entered, including social networks and attention to politics on television, radio, and newspapers. The use of the Internet was entered at the end of this category to see whether there was any residual impact associated with this technology net of all other factors. Lastly, the major European regions were added, coded as

Figure 4. Internet use and types of political activism (Source: European Social Survey, 2002 Pooled sample)

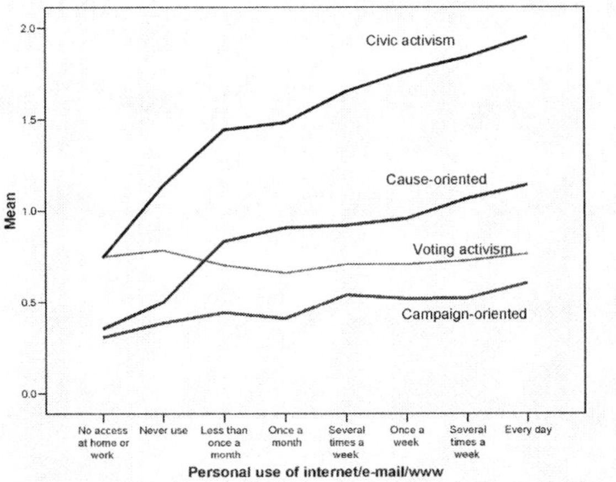

dummy variables, where the Nordic region was the default category for comparison.

The results in the pooled model confirm the significance of many of these factors upon the political activism scale. The only exceptions proved to belong to an ethnic minority, the amount of hours in the paid workforce, and the salience of politics, which all proved to be non-significantly related to participation, contrary to expectations. But after adding the complete battery of controls, use of the Internet continued to be significantly related to political activism, suggesting that this relationship is not simply explained away as a result of the prior social or attitudinal characteristics of those who are most prone to go online. The most

Table 2. The impact of Internet use on political activism, with controls (Source: European Social Survey, 2002 [ESS-19]. Pooled sample N. 31741 in 18 ESS nations, excluding Germany [where Internet use was not monitored])

	B	Std. Error	Beta	Sig.
(Constant)	-1.39	0.28		0.00
SOCIAL STRUCTURE				
Gender	-0.17	0.05	-0.03	0.00
Age (years)	0.02	0.00	0.13	0.00
Belong to ethnic minority	0.03	0.13	0.00	0.81
Educational qualifications	0.22	0.02	0.11	0.00
Income	0.07	0.01	0.06	0.00
Work status	0.38	0.06	0.06	0.00
Total hours per week in main job + O/T	0.00	0.00	0.00	0.88
Married	0.19	0.05	0.03	0.00
Have children at home	0.13	0.05	0.02	0.01
Importance of religion	0.12	0.05	0.02	0.01
CULTURAL ATTITUDES				
Discuss politics/current affairs, how often	-0.14	0.01	-0.09	0.00
Important in life: politics	0.01	0.01	0.01	0.54
Social trust	0.02	0.00	0.04	0.00
Trust in national political institutions	-0.02	0.01	-0.03	0.01
Trust in international institutions	-0.03	0.01	-0.04	0.00
Internal political efficacy	0.27	0.01	0.18	0.00
External political efficacy	0.12	0.01	0.08	0.00
Civic duty scale	0.04	0.00	0.11	0.00
How interested in politics	-0.34	0.04	-0.09	0.00

continued on following page

Table 2. continued

MOBILIZING AGENCIES				
How often socially meet with friends, relatives or colleagues	0.17	0.02	0.08	0.00
TV watching, news/ politics/current affairs on average weekday	-0.12	0.02	-0.05	0.00
Radio listening, news/ politics/current affairs on average weekday	0.03	0.01	0.02	0.06
Newspaper reading, politics/current affairs on average weekday	0.09	0.03	0.03	0.00
Personal use of internet/e-mail/www	0.10	0.01	0.10	0.00
REGION				
Northern Europe	-0.30	0.06	-0.05	0.00
Mediterranean Europe	-1.35	0.08	-0.16	0.00
Post-Communist Europe	-1.73	0.09	-0.23	0.00
Adjusted R2	.373			

Note: The models represent the result of ordinary least squares regression analysis where the total political activism index is the dependent variable. The index counts participation in each form of activity as one and sums the 21-point scale. The figures represent the unstandardized beta coefficient (B), the standard error (s.e.), the standardized beta coefficient (Beta), and the significance (sig). The default dummy regional variable was the Nordic region. All variables were checked to be free of problems of multi-collinearity by tolerance statistics. See Table1 for the items in each scale.

Table 3. The impact of Internet use on types of political activism, with controls (Source: European Social Survey, 2002. Pooled sample N. 31741 in 18 ESS nations, excluding Germany [where Internet use was not monitored])

Type of activism	B	Std. Error	Beta	Sig.	Adjusted R2
Voting	.005	.001	.034	.002	.145
Cause-oriented	.036	.004	.095	.000	.213
Campaign-oriented	.006	.004	.018	.102	.161
Civic-oriented	.042	.006	.073	.000	.308

Note: The models represent the result of ordinary least squares regression analysis on each form of activism as the dependent variables. For the full range of prior controls in the models (not reported here) see Table 2. The figures represent the unstandardized beta coefficient (B), the standard error (s.e.), the standardized beta coefficient (Beta), and the significance (sig).

important factors predicting activism (measured by the strength of the standardized regression coefficients) concern internal political efficacy (a feeling that the person could influence the political process), age, education, region, and civic duty. After these factors, use of the Internet proved the next strongest predictor of activism, which was more important than other indicators such as social and political trust or use of any of the news media. The overall model explained more than one-third of the variance in activism (R^2=.37).

Similar regression models were then run with identical controls to predict the four types of political activism under comparison, using the pooled sample. Without showing all the coefficients, the summary of the results in Table 3 shows that use of the Internet was significantly associated with voting, cause- and civic-oriented forms of activism, but not with campaign-oriented forms of activism. This confirms that, rather than claims about the effect of the knowledge society on activism, we do need to distinguish among the types of participation that generate different effects. The reason for these differences most probably lies in the residual effect of the typical social background and the political values of Internet users, notably the propensity of well-educated younger generations to predominate online, as noted in many studies of the well-known "digital divide" (Norris, 2001).

PART IV: CONCLUSION & DISCUSSION

The theory developed in this study considers the more pessimistic claims that the development of the Internet will serve to reinforce the voices of the powerful, the more skeptical arguments that it will merely reflect "politics as usual," and the more optimistic view that the knowledge society will transform governance as we know it and strengthen levels of mass political participation. The study hypothesizes that contemporary democracies are a market where the impact of the Internet depends in part upon the "supply" of political information and communications, primarily from political agencies, and also upon the "demand" for such information and communication from the mass public. In turn, the public's demand comes from the social and cultural profile of the online population reflecting long-standing patterns of civic engagement. As a result, use of the Internet is significantly related to overall patterns of political activism, even with multiple prior controls, but there are several distinct dimensions or channels of activism. The survey evidence analyzed in this study confirms that the rise of the knowledge society in Europe has indeed had the greatest positive consequences for politics by strengthening cause-oriented and civic-oriented activism, rather than by encouraging mass participation in campaigns and elections.

What are the broader implications of this pattern for democracy and for the future of electronic governance? We can speculate that the primary beneficiaries of this process will probably be political actors lacking traditional organizational resources that are useful in politics, such as those without a large-scale, fee-paying mass membership base, substantial financial assets, and paid full-time bureaucratic officials. This type of organization is exemplified by new social movements, transnational advocacy networks, alternative social movements, protest organizations, community activists and development workers, single-issue causes from all shades of the political spectrum, as well as minor parties. The knowledge society is not expected to drive these insurgent movements, but rather to facilitate their organization, mobilization, and expression (Keck & Sikkink, 1998). These organizations have the greatest incentives and the fewest constraints to using the knowledge society. If this perspective is correct, then the result of the rise of the Internet may be greater pressures on governments to respond to the demands of single-issue groups and more amorphous social networks. By contrast, established political parties and traditional interest groups can be expected to adapt far more slowly to the knowledge society, because they are capable of drawing upon alternative organizational and financial resources, including legal authority, full time paid officials, press officers, lobbyists, and grassroots fee-paying mass memberships. Yet these are the umbrella organizations, particularly parties, which are capable of aggregating diverse issues into broader programmatic platforms, encouraging compromise, deliberation, and bargaining among members and channeling demands on a more predictable basis into government. It remains to be seen how far these developments alter the channels of participation in representative democracy in Europe and elsewhere, but the consequences will probably provide government with greater opportunities to connect with citizens and to greater challenges in the inevitable pressures that arise from satisfying multiple fragmented zero-sum constituencies represented by single-issue politics.

REFERENCES

Allen, B.A., Juillet, L., Paquet, G., & Roy, J. (2001). E-governance & government on-line in Canada: Partnerships, people & prospects. *Government Information Quarterly, 18*(2), 93-104.

Barber, B. R. (1998). Three scenarios for the future of technology and strong democracy. *Political Science Quarterly,* I(4), 573-589.

Bimber, B. (1998). The Internet and political transformation: Populism, community and accelerated pluralism. *Polity XXXI,* (1), 133-160.

Bimber, B. (2001). Information and political engagement in America: The search for effects of information technology at the individual level. *Political Research Quarterly, 54*(1), 53-67.

Boas, T. C. (2000). The dictator's dilemma? The Internet and U.S. policy toward Cuba. *The Washington Quarterly, 23*(3), 57-67.

Bonfadelli, H. (2002). The Internet and knowledge gaps: A theoretical and empirical investigation. *European Journal of Communication, 17*(1), 65-84.

Budge, I. (1996). *The New Challenge of Direct Democracy.* Oxford: Polity Press.

Cassel, C.A. (1999). Voluntary associations, churches, and social participation theories of turnout. *Social Science Quarterly, 80*(3), 504-517.

Chadwick, A. & May, C. (2003). Interactions between states and citizens in the age of the Internet: "E-government" in the United States, Britain and the European Union. *Governance, 16*(2), 271-300.

David, R. (1999). *The Web of Politics.* Oxford: Oxford University Press.

Davis, R. & Owen, D. (1998). *New Media and American Politics.* New York: Oxford University Press.

Drake, W.J., Kalathil, S., & Boas, T. C. (2000, October). Dictatorships in the digital age: Some considerations on the Internet in China and Cuba. *iMP: The Magazine on Information Impacts.* Retrieved from: www.cisp.org/imp

Foot, K.A. & Schneider, S.M. (2002). Online action in campaign 2000: An exploratory analysis of the US political web sphere. *Journal of Broadcasting & Electronic Media, 46*(2), 222-244.

Fountain, J. E. (2001). *Building the Virtual State: Information Technology and Institutional Change.* Washington, DC: Brookings Institution Press.

Franda, M. (2002). *Launching Into Cyberspace: Internet Development and Politics in Five World Regions.* Boulder, CO: Lynne Rienner.

Gibson, R., Nixon, P., & Ward, S. (eds.). (2003). *Political Parties and the Internet: Net Gain?* London: Routledge.

Gilder, G. (2000). *Telecom: How Infinite Bandwidth Will Revolutionize Our World.* New York: Free Press.

Golding, P. (1996). World wide wedge: Division and contradiction in the global information infrastructure. *Monthly Review, 48*(3), 70-85.

Hague, B. N. & Loader, B. D. (eds.). (1999). *Digital Democracy: Discourse and Decision Making in the Information Age.* New York: Routledge.

Haque, M.S. (2002). E-governance in India: Its impacts on relations among citizens, politicians and public servants. *International Review of Administrative Sciences, 68*(2), 231-250.

Hayward, T. (1995). *Info-Rich, Info-Poor: Access and Exchange in the Global Information Society.* K.G. Saur.

Hill, K. A. & Hughes, J. E. (1998). *Cyberpolitics: Citizen Activism in the Age of the Internet.* Lanham, MD: Rowan & Littlefield.

Hill, K. & Hughes, J. E. (1999). Is the Internet an instrument of global democratization? *Democratization, 3,*29-43.

Horrigan, J., Rainie, L., & Fox, S. (2001). Online communities: Networks that nurture long-distance relationships and local ties. *Pew Internet & American Life Project.* Retrieved from: www.pew internet.org

ITU. (n.d.). Retrieved from: http://www.itu.int/wsis/

Johnson, T.J. & Kaye, B.K. (2003). Around the World Wide Web in 80 ways: How motives for going online are linked to Internet activities among politically interested Internet users. *Social Science Computer Review, 21*,(3), 304-325.

Kalathil, S. & Boas, T. C. (2003). *Open Networks Closed Regimes: The Impact of the Internet on Authoritarian Rule.* Washington, DC: Carnegie Endowment for International Peace.

Keck, M. E. & Sikkink, K. (1998). *Activists Beyond Borders: Advocacy Networks in International Politics*. Ithaca, NY: Cornell University Press.

Kent, J. M. & Zeitner, V. (2003). Internet use and civic engagement: A longitudinal analysis. *Public Opinion Quarterly, 67*(3), 311-334.

Mair, P. & van Biezen, I. (2001). Party membership in twenty European democracies 1980-2000. *Party Politics, 7*(1), 7-22.

Margolis, M. & Resnick, D. (2000). *Politics as Usual: The Cyberspace "Revolution."* Thousand Oaks, CA: Sage.

McChesney, R. W. (1999). *Rich Media, Poor Democracy.* IL: University of Illinois Press.

Media Matrix (2000, October). *Campaign 2000: Party politics on the World Wide Web.* Retrieved from: www.media metrix.com

Murdock, G. & Golding, P. (1989). Information poverty and political inequality: Citizenship in the age of privatised communications. *Journal of Communication, 39*, 180-195.

Norris, P. (2000). *A Virtuous Circle.* New York: Cambridge University Press.

Norris, P. (2001). *Digital Divide.* New York: Cambridge University Press.

Norris, P. (2002). *Democratic Phoenix: Reinventing Political Activism.* New York: Cambridge University Press.

Norris, P. (2003). The bridging and bonding role of online communities. In P. N. Howard & S. Jones (Eds.), *Society Online: The Internet in Context.* Thousand Oaks, CA: Sage.

Norris, P. & Sanders, D. (2003). Medium or message? *Political Communications.*

Pharr, S. & Putnam, R. (eds.). (2000). *Disaffected Democracies: What's Troubling the Trilateral Countries?* Princeton, NJ: Princeton University Press.

Putnam, R. D. (1993). *Making Democracy Work: Civic Traditions in Modern Italy.* Princeton, NJ: Princeton University Press.

Putnam, R. D. (1996). The strange disappearance of civic America. *The American prospect, 24.*

Putnam, R. D. (2000). *Bowling Alone: The Collapse and Revival of American Community.* New York: Simon and Schuster.

Putnam, R. D. (ed.). (2002). *Democracies in Flux.* Oxford: Oxford University Press.

Radcliff, B. & Davis, P. (2000). Labor organization and electoral participation in industrial democracies. *American Journal of Political Science, 44*(1), 132-141.

Rash, Jr., W. (1997). *Politics on the Net: Wiring the Political Process.* New York: W.H. Freeman.

Rheingold, H. (1993). *The Virtual Community: Homesteading on the Electronic Frontier.* Reading, MA: Addison Wesley.

Scarrow, S. (2001). Parties without members? In R. J. Dalton & M. Wattenberg (Eds.), *Parties Without Partisans*. New York: Oxford University Press.

Schwartz, E. (1996). *Netactivism: How Citizens Use the Internet.* Sebastapol, CA: Songline Studios.

Selnow, G.W. (1998). *Electronic Whistle-Stops: The Impact of the Internet on American Politics.* Westport, CT: Praeger.

Shah, D.V., Kwak, N., & Holbert, R.L. (2001). "Connecting" and "disconnecting" with civic life: Patterns of Internet use and the production of social capital. *Political Communication, 18*(2), 141-162.

Stowers, G.N.L. (1999). Becoming cyberactive: State and local governments on the World Wide Web. *Government Information Quarterly, 16*(2), 111-127.

Thomas, J.C. & Streib, G. (2003). The new face of government: Citizen-initiated contacts in the era of e-government. *Journal of Public Administration Research and Theory, 13*(1), 83-101.

Tolbert, C.J. & McNeal, R.S. (2003). Unraveling the effects of the Internet on political participation? *Political Research Quarterly, 56*(2), 175-185.

Toulouse, C. & Luke, T. W. (eds.). (1998). *The Politics of Cyberspace.* London: Routledge.

United Nations/American Society for Public Administration (2002). *Bench Marking e-Government: A Global Perspective.* New York: United Nations/DPEPA.

Verba, S., Nie, N., & Kim, J.-on (1978). *Participation and Political Equality: A Seven-Nation Comparison.* New York: Cambridge University Press.

Weber, L.M., Loumakis, A., & Bergman, J. (2003). Who participates and why? An analysis of citizens on the Internet and the mass public. *Social Science Computer Review, 21*(1), 26-42.

Wilhelm, A. (n.d.). *Democracy in the Digital Age: Challenges to Political Life in Cyberspace.* New York: Routledge.

ENDNOTES

1 Since the dimensions are theoretically defined and constructed, based on understanding the role of different forms of participation in representative democracy, the study did not use factor analysis to generate the classification or measurement.

2 For more details of the European Social Survey, including the questionnaire and methodology, see http://naticent02. uuhost. uk.uu.net/index.htm. Data for an initial nineteen countries, along with comprehensive documentation, is accessible at http://ess. nsd.uib.no. The survey is funded via the European Commission's 5th Framework Program, with supplementary funds from the European Science Foundation which also sponsored the development of the study over a number of years. I am most grateful to the European Commission and the ESF for their support for this project and to the work of the ESS Central Coordinating Team, led by Roger Jowell, for making this survey data available.

3 *"Personal use"* is defined by the ESS-2002 as private or recreational use that does not have to do with a person's work or occupation.

This work was previously published in International Journal of Electronic Government Research, Vol. 1, No. 1, edited by M. Khosrow-Pour, pp. 19-39, copyright 2005 by IGI Publishing, formerly known as Idea Group Publishing (an imprint of IGI Global).

Chapter LXXVI
Adoption and Implementation of IT in Developing Nations: Experiences from Two Public Sector Enterprises in India

Monideepa Tarafdar
University of Toledo, USA

Sanjiv D. Vaidya
Indian Institute of Management Calcutta, India

ABSTRACT

This case describes challenges in the adoption and implementation of IT in two public sector enterprises in the postal and distribution businesses respectively, in India. In spite of similarities in the scale of operations and the general cultural contexts, the IT adoption processes and outcomes of the two organizations were significantly different. While one failed to implement IT in its crucial processes, the other responded effectively to changes in external conditions by developing and using IT applications for critical functions. The case illustrates how differences in organizational factors such as top management commitment, unions, middle management participation, capabilities of IS professionals and specific aspects of organization culture resulted in such differences. The case is interesting and significant because it is representative of experiences of many government-aided organizations in India, which have undertaken IT modernization as a response to external changes and government mandates. The findings can also be generalized across similar organizations in other developing countries.

ORGANIZATIONAL BACKGROUND

Introduction

The adoption of IT in large public sector organizations poses some interesting challenges and issues. These are related to specific characteristics of these organizations with regard to their entrenched processes, culture, the role of bureaucracy, performance measurement criteria and decision-making processes (see for example, Caudle et al., 1991). This case describes challenges in the adoption and implementation of IT in two public sector enterprises in India. The enterprises were in the postal and distribution businesses respectively.

Public sector enterprises (PSEs), in the context of the Indian economy, are companies that are largely administered and supported by the government. They exist in different areas such as transportation, goods distribution, postal services, telecommunications, and other manufacturing and service sectors of the economy. There are different types of PSEs (Mathur et al., 1979). Some of them are statutory corporations established through legislative resolutions of the Parliament. The Parliament is the executive branch of the Government of India, similar to the House and the Senate in the United States. Many other PSEs are departmental agencies, functioning directly under a particular department of the government. Others are established as companies with limited liability under the Companies Act of India. A few PSEs, like those in the Railways sector, function exclusively under one ministry of the government.

The government plays an important role at the strategic level, in activities such as policy making and financial outlay. At the operational level, PSEs run directly by government departments are staffed through a cadre of bureaucrats and administrators. In PSEs that are established through legislative acts, professional managers and technical specialists manage the operations. These bureaucrats, administrators, professional managers and technical specialists are responsible for achieving annual objectives in terms of activities accomplished and budgetary goals. Policy implementation with respect to modernization and IT adoption is the responsibility of organizational employees, who have autonomy over operational details of the implementation process, within a broad framework specified by the government.

National Couriers Limited (NCL) was in the business of providing postal, courier and information transfer services to different parts of India. It functioned directly under a government department. The company also provided limited banking services such as money transfer, insurance and certificate of deposit services. It had about 90,000 employees working in offices in various states in the country. Eighty-five percent of the personnel of the company were unionized and were either unskilled or clerical level workers. The remaining were professionally trained administrators.

National Traders Limited (NTL) was a distributor of agricultural products, particularly food grains, to different parts of the country. It was created by a Parliament resolution. It provided services such as procurement of these products from producers, their storage and management in warehouses, and distribution to non-producing consumers through retail outlets. During the 1970s and 1980s, the organization had played a key role in encouraging farmers to increase their production, by providing them with an assured market and stable purchase prices. Subsequently, the major function of the company had been to collect part of the surplus agricultural produce, and suitably store and distribute it, so that it could be used during lean production seasons and in places where emergencies and natural calamities happened. The organization procured, distributed and transported about 22 million metric tons of produce, annually. Most of the purchasing centers were located in the northern part of the country. Consumers were located all across India and also in the islands off the southern part of the country. NTL had about 63,000 employees, 95% of whom were unionized.

Services & Processes: Brief Description

Both NCL and NTL were service organizations. The major processes of NCL were collection, sorting and delivery of articles. Articles were collected from more than half a million collection centers, sorted in 550 sorting offices and delivered through more than 100,000 delivery offices. Other processes included activities related to banking, money transfer and information transfer functions.

Some financial details about the operations of the company are provided in Table 1.

All these functions involved managing and processing significant amounts of information. In this context, the head of the operations of the Eastern Region observed:

"The sheer volume of information and articles that is required to be handled is tremendous."

Table 1. Background information for National Courier's Limited

	1992-93 million	1993-94 million	1994-95 million	1995-96 million	1996-97 million	1997-98 million	1998-99 million	1999-2000 million
Total Mail (No. of articles)	13400	13051	13607	13957	15096	15750	16790	17430
Money Transfer (number of transactions)	105	99	102	106	111	111	120	122
Money Transfer (Rs. mn)	29124	31825	33555	37872	41018	44654	47450	48790

Table 2. Procurement of food grains from different parts of the country

Year	PROCUREMENT OF FOOD GRAINS (in * 100,000 tonnes)	
	WHEAT (April—March)	RICE (October—September)
1999-2000	120	185
2000-2001	150	220
2001-2002	200	215
2002-2003	185	160
2003-2004	150	170
*(As on 27.02.2004)		

Table 3. Movement of food grains in different parts of the country

Year	**Movement of Food Grains (in Million Tonnes)**
1996-97	25
1997-98	20
1998-99	22
1999-2000	20
2000-2001	15
2001-2002	19.5
2002-2003	26.8
2003-2004 (up to Nov'03)	15.3

The major activities of NTL related to the distribution of agricultural produce. Relevant figures in this context are provided in Tables 2 and 3.

There were four critical activities for NTL, as described next.

1. *Purchase of agricultural produce from producers:* This was done through a network of purchase centers all over the country.
2. *Storage of the purchased produce in appropriate places and under appropriate environmental conditions:* NTL had a network of storage depots for this purpose.
3. *Interfacing and maintaining liaison with administrative authorities in different states:* This was required in order to plan for state-wise requirements of produce.
4. *Distribution planning and transportation of produce:* This function involved the transfer of produce from purchase centers to storage warehouses and then to the numerous distribution centers. It required access to good transport infrastructure, and liaising with professional transport agencies.

The overall processes of both organizations were therefore similar, in that they involved the transfer of physical goods and the accompanying information to and from different parts of the country. They also involved interfacing with government authorities at the state and national levels.

Organization Structure & Characteristics

The bureaucracy in India is typically the administrative arm of the central government and is largely responsible for turning legislation into policies and policies into practice. Bureaucrats therefore have a wide range of functions in many sectors of the economy, including the government departments. Their responsibilities can be broadly visualized in terms of two types of functions.

One, they are responsible for assisting in policy formulation in the different ministries and departments. They are also charged with the direct running of the day-to-day government functions like general administration, law enforcement, resources disbursement and tax collection. Two, they are also required to head government controlled PSEs in different industries such as utilities, postal services, nationalized banks, railways and public distribution systems for food grains. Both NCL and NTL, being public sector enterprises, were headed by a senior member of the administrative arm of the bureaucracy. They also had bureaucrats in different top management functions.

The operations of NCL were divided into four regions. Each region was headed by a Regional Office, with the Regional Manager as the executive head of the region. The Regional Manager was a member of senior management who supervised a team of middle management. Each region was further divided into districts, with a District Office supervising the operations of each district. The head of each District Office was a member of middle management. Members of junior management worked in the Regional and District Offices. There were about 200 districts and each district supervised the operations of a given number of collection centers, sorting offices and delivery centers, which were staffed by unionized employees and clerks. At the apex, there was one head office, from where the top management and company policymakers operated.

In a similar manner, NTL also carried out its operations through a network of administrative offices across the country. There was one central administrative office from where the top management functioned. The operations were divided into five zones and 17 regions. Each zone had a Zonal Administrative Office and each region had a Regional Administrative Office, supervised by a Zonal Manager and Regional Manager respectively. The regions were divided into a number of districts and each district was administered through a District Office, which managed the functions of a number of purchase centers and storage warehouses. There were 123 districts. There were 12,000 purchase centers and 1,700 depots and storage warehouses. Zonal Managers belonged to senior management cadre. Regional Managers and District Managers were middle managers. Junior managers also worked in all these offices. All employees in the management cadre were professional administrators. The company also had a number of clerical employees to carry out low-skilled functions in the different offices, purchase centers and warehouses.

The scale and scope of the operations of the company were very large. One of the senior managers in the company observed:

"The scale of operations is among the largest for any organization in the country. The amount of information required to be processed is tremendous."

Although the particulars of the organizational hierarchy such as specific office names and designations of managers were different, the broad organization structures of the two organizations were similar, as shown in Figure 1. There were five levels of hierarchy and the decision-making processes were largely centralized. The top management in the apex (central) office and senior management in the zonal and regional offices was responsible for overall policy setting and strategic planning. All new initiatives and programs were designed at the higher levels, and were subsequently communicated through orders and directives to the middle and lower levels. Implementation strategies were planned by the senior management in consultation with middle management and implemented by middle management. This kind of planning and implementation structure is often a feature of public sector enterprises. This is because public sector enterprises usually operate on a large scale and scope, and hence it is more efficient to decide on policy at the top and leave the implementation to the middle managers in the various regional offices. The role of middle managers in policy implementation is therefore crucial (Caudle et al., 1991). In India, the accountability of the public sector to the people of India only further enhances the justification for rigid bureaucratic procedures. Such procedures lead to this rather strict division of labor between the senior management and the middle management.

Traditionally, both organizations were similar in that they were large and centralized, and had historically functioned in stable economic and business environments. They had been largely supported by the government and had not seen any major changes in their business strategies or processes for the past 20 years. Between 1980 and 1987, the top management of both companies was indifferent towards the use of IT and there was no commitment on the part of the organizational leaders to deploy IT in any of the functions. Further, most employees did not have any knowledge or awareness about IT, and tended to associate technology with loss of jobs. This observation has also been recorded in other organizations in India during the 1970s and 1980s. During this time, the Indian economy was a closed one and most organizations did not have any exposure to the use of IT (Nidumolu et al., 1993; Tarafdar & Vaidya, 2002b; Wolcott & Goodman, 2003).

Figure 1. Decision hierarchy and organization structure at National Couriers Limited and National Traders Limited

Level One: Top Management at the Apex—Both NCL and NTL

Responsible for strategic planning and policy making, in consultation with senior management (Level Two)

↓

Level Two: Senior Management

Regional Managers—NCL
Zonal Managers—NTL

Responsible for aiding Top Management (Level One) in strategic planning and policy making
Responsible for deciding on implementation strategies, in consultation with middle management (Level Three)

↓

Level Three: Middle Management

Regional Managers and District Managers—NCL
District Managers—NTL

Responsible for aiding Senior Management (Level Two) in planning implementation strategies
Responsible for executing implementation strategies and directing Junior Management (Level Four) and unionized staff

↓

Level Four: Junior Management

Employees in the Zonal, Regional and District Offices—NCL
Employees in the Regional and District Offices—NTL

Responsible for carrying out instructions related to implementation as directed by Middle Management (Level

↓

Level Five: Unionized Staff

Employees in the Zonal, Regional and District Offices, and in the collection, sorting and delivery centers—NCL
Employees in the Regional and District Offices, and in the procurement centers and storage warehouses—NTL
Responsible for carrying out instructions related to implementation as directed by Middle Management (Level Three)

SETTING THE STAGE (1987-1991)

External Conditions

The government financially aided NCL and, to a large extent, decided the rates for its services. NCL catered to both urban and rural segments of the population. During this time, the rural and semi urban segments accounted for over 70% of the customer base, and the company was a monopoly in this segment. Entry barriers were high because a vast distribution network was required to handle the volumes and reach in order to operate on a national scale. In the urban retail and corporate segments, the first major changes in the environment came in the late '80s and early '90s when a number of private companies were set up which provided faster deliveries, although at much higher prices. Hence there was some competition in this category. However, these new competitors were too small to pose any threat to NCL on a nationwide basis. Even then, NCL did have an internal drive towards business innovation. It introduced special premium "Speed" services in 1987, which were faster and more expensive than their regular services. Corporate customers were interested in efficient and reliable service and accounted for a majority of the high value transactions through the premium services. According to a senior manager in the eastern region:

"The products and services prior to 1987 were standard. There were no innovations. However, after 1987, we could sense some of the then happening and some impending changes in the competitive environment. Hence, even though we were a monopoly in the rural retail segment, we introduced new services directed towards the urban corporate and retail segments."

NTL was financially aided by the government and many of the policies regarding purchase price, selling price, and distribution requirements were decided in consultation with the government and representatives of the producers. The company was required to interact with a number of external agencies such as distribution and transport service providers in order to carry out its functions. All interactions with these external organizations were through established procedures. For example, producers were given a fixed price for their produce, and customers also paid a fixed price. Similarly, transporters were selected on the basis of tenders. There had been no significant change in most of these processes over the years. Therefore, the external environment had remained stable. In case of calamities such as floods and drought however, the company faced tremendous pressures because produce had to be rushed to specific places at all costs. The regional manager of one of the regions observed that:

"Normally there are no pressures on us. We function in a regulated and financially supported environment. However in times of emergencies, we have to deliver at all costs."

Such instances however, were few and had occurred once in two or three years on an average. Moreover, in such times, NTL and other similar companies were given financial support from the government and also used their own slack resources. On the whole, NTL did not have any innate drive for business innovation. For example, it did not initiate efforts for introducing changes in its processes in a proactive manner. Its managers functioned within the parameters laid down by the government. The performance of the company was measured by the amount of produce purchased, the manner of quality control of stored produce and effectiveness of distribution. There was scope for performance slack because the company was financially supported by the government. In this context, one senior manager who had been with the company for 30 years observed:

"Everyone follows standard procedures. There is no inherent drive to change and improve."

Process Descriptions & Information Processing Requirements

The primary processes for NCL included the logistical activities of sorting and transferring articles. The company also carried out limited operations related to banking functions such as money transfers and money orders.

Information processing had to be carried out quickly because article delivery times depended largely on the speed with which articles could be sorted and transported. Organizational processes were standardized through the use of standard operating procedures. Procedures were laid down for collection, sorting, delivery, after-sales activity like enquiry handling, refund, lost articles or other specific customer complaints. Tasks were structured and routine and, the context in which information had to be processed was clear. The presence of bureaucratic procedures, along with inherently simple tasks, did not leave much room for decision support requirements in the day-to-day operations. Decision making followed predictable patterns. There were well-defined rules for communicating information. All official communication was in written format. Information required for decision making was mostly available.

A senior executive explained the situation in this manner:

"There are fixed procedures that we are trained to follow. All possible requirements can be anticipated because there is a limited set of options that customers can choose from."

Organizational processes for NTL included functions like packing, storing and handling of the produce. These were routine, standardized and well documented. There were written instructions and well-defined procedures for different activities. For instance, there were norms for storing bags in the warehouses, for deciding how many bags would be placed in a stack, how they would be stacked, how they would be issued for distribution and so on. There were specifications for the way in which warehouses were to be constructed. There were standards for preserving the produce in the warehouses according to the desired purity and quality levels. Information regarding relevant parameters such as humidity, temperature and cleanliness were clearly specified. All official communication was in standardized formats, formal and always recorded on paper.

One of the middle managers in a regional office in the eastern region said:

"All tasks are standardized and we have to follow standard operating procedures. There is no ambiguity."

As far as information processing was concerned, some aspects of the company's operations required information to be processed within a given period of time. For instance, all the purchasing activities had to be completed within two to four months from the time that the produce was plucked and harvested. Transport and logistics operations involved coordination of activities across many geographical regions, and the produce had to be distributed to specific areas within a very short time, in case of disasters. The manager of one of the districts in the eastern region said:

"There is a short span of two to three months within which we have to finish off all the purchase and storage activities. This is a time of great pressure for all of us."

Both organizations functioned in a stable environment and were financially supported by the government. This led to the possibility of having extensive bureaucratic procedures and well-defined processes. Thus, there was not much room for ambiguity and decision support. This is a common feature in public sector organizations, and has been found to influence the adoption of decision support aids in these organizations (Mohan et al., 1990). All policy decisions regarding the adoption of new innovations were taken by the top management team in consultation with representatives of the government and communicated clearly within the organization. However, there were some differences. NCL was widely regarded as one of the best public sector organizations in India, and within the broad framework of government-mandated policies, there was considerable scope for small-scale, local-level initiatives and innovations by its middle and junior managers. NTL, on the other hand, was more prone to functioning within the confines of government mandates, and there were not many opportunities for local innovation.

IT Adoption During This Period

Basic computerization was first introduced in both these organizations in the mid- to late-1980s. This period was also marked by commencement of similar initiatives in other public sector enterprises in India (such as nationalized banks). These initiatives were largely driven by policies of the central government. To begin with, both NCL and NTL went in for applications like payroll and financial accounting at their respective central administration offices. These were later extended to their different regional offices. Overall, the IT infrastructure during this time was quite elementary and did not have any significant impact on their critical operations.

Soon after, NCL took steps to introduce some additional IT applications as well. In 1989, money transfer pairing machines were first introduced in each zone. Hitherto, all the money transfer order slips originating in a particular region and bound for all other regions were collated separately and sent to each region. This was done by all the regions, so that a number of slips changed hands everyday between all the regions. With the introduction of the computerized pairing machines, instead of counting off individual slips for each region, each region's outgoing sum was simply netted off against the incoming sum. This was a spreadsheet application in which the total amount of money ordered for each zone was collated on a spreadsheet and paired and matched for each zone. Also in 1989, counter operations for article booking were computerized in the largest office in the two largest cities. Stand-alone PCs were given to the counter clerks at these offices. This significantly reduced the waiting time for the customer and rationalized queues at the counters. Although these applications were introduced in a limited manner, it was an important step for NCL in that it had proactively implemented some IT beyond the overall parameters suggested by the government. Although the monetary investment in IT during this period was small, it nevertheless set the stage for the implementation of IT in more critical processes, in subsequent years. Further, it also served as a pilot project for demonstration and learning purposes.

Impending Changes in the External Environment

Government policies form an important aspect of the external environment for public sector organizations. Changes in these policies have often been the cause of IT deployment in organizations in developing nations in general (Albadvi, 2002; Li et al., 2002; Molla & Licker, 2002) and in India in particular (Tarafdar & Vaidya, 2002a).

In 1991, the Government of India took a policy decision to liberalize the Indian economy. This decision resulted in an increase in external pressures for public sector undertakings in many industries including telecommunications, steel, banking and transportation, among others. The resulting changes in the business and economic environment had implications for adoption of IT in both NCL and NTL. There were also overall pressures for process re-engineering, modernization and human resource development.

CASE DESCRIPTION (1992-2000)

Changes in the External Environment

Economic liberalization in the early 1990s resulted in changes in the external and competitive environment for both organizations. Liberalization provided enormous opportunities for firms from developed economies to set up manufacturing, service or distributing units in India. This resulted in the entry of many of these companies in a number of Indian industries including banking, financial institutions and the manufacturing sector (see for example, Cavusgil et al., 2002; Joshi & Joshi, 1998; Tarafdar & Vaidya, 2002, 2003). Many of these companies had advanced IT-enabled processes. This created pressures for improved performance of processes among Indian organizations. There were also pressures from different customer segments for more flexibility and better service.

As far as NCL was concerned, private companies—from both India and outside—that provided courier and fax services entered the urban markets, and targeted the retail and corporate segments.

There was also an increase in the volume of business related mail. Some customer segments like businesses, government organizations and institutional bodies required faster delivery, even if it was at a higher cost. Thus, increasing competition gave rise to a need to segment customers on the basis of specific needs and provide customized service options. Therefore, a Business Development Cell was set up in 1996 to design and develop a market for value-added premium products for specific customer segments. New services were introduced for corporate customers, and the accent was on speed and reliability rather than on cost. Utility payment and e-mail services were also introduced.

That the organization perceived the pressures to be somewhat high can be gauged by the following statement, which appeared in the Annual Report of 1997-1998:

"... will spend 65% of its plan budget on the induction of technology with a view to improving and upgrading the quality of service...developing and providing new value added services and products. NCL will continue to look at the technology options so that the postal products and services can be re-oriented to the needs of the customers."

The second change as a result of economic liberalization was related to the role of the government. As mentioned before, the government can, through its policies and regulations, influence the adoption of IT (Nidumolu & Goodman, 1996; Rainey et al., 1976). Toward the later part of the eighties, the government laid down certain policies and mandates for adoption of IT in all major public sector enterprises in India, across different industries. Public sector banks, manufacturing units and service organizations embarked upon IT modernization programs. These organizations typically generated and processed huge volumes of transaction data due to their large scope of operations. Consequently, the most pressing requirements were for transaction processing systems.

Initiating & Implementing IT Adoption: Two Contrasting Approaches

Both NCL and NTL initiated a program for organization-wide computerization in response to the government's mandates.

According to Caudle et al. (1991), there are four major concerns that are required to be addressed for adoption and implementation of IT in public sector organizations. The two organizations addressed these four factors in different ways.

1. *Goals of IT Adoption & Identification of Information Requirements:* Market signals and profits guide companies in the private sector. In contrast, the public sector faces different goals, many of which are not necessarily related to financial performance. These could be related to efficiency and quality of customer service, scale of operations, the different kinds of customers served, social objectives and addressing political influences (Caudle et al., 1991). Thus, it is not always possible to directly link the adoption of IT with financial parameters, particularly for public sector enterprises. Hence, one of the ways to approach IT planning is to identify improvements that are required in concerned critical processes, and implement IT in the individual activities entailed in those processes. Identification of information requirements thus forms an important part of the planning for IT adoption and implementation in public sector organizations.

National Couriers Limited

Interviews with the head of the Eastern Region illustrated the process of identification of important information processing activities and requirements at NCL:

"We had already implemented computerized transaction processing systems in the payroll and financial accounting functions, starting in 1988. After the government mandates in 1991, we

identified three critical areas in order to focus our computerization efforts. The first was the handling of and sorting registered mail articles. This process was the key to speed, efficiency and customer satisfaction in our operations. The second was the transfer of information related to the status of mailed articles, money transfer and banking services. Information transfer processes formed our second largest area of operations after mail handling. The third focus for computerization was information exchange activities within our offices. These included sharing of files, data and other resources such as printers. Our computerization efforts during the period 1992-1999 were concentrated largely in these three areas."

Between 1992 and 1999, a number of new information technologies were introduced at NCL. In 1992, computerized mail handling and sorting was introduced in the two busiest centers in the country. This reduced the time required for sorting and directing articles by half. Computerized systems for article booking, tracking and delivery systems for select cities were introduced in 1997-98 in select cities (refer to Figure 2). This sped up the booking and delivery procedure, and enabled customers to keep track of their articles. A VSAT network consisting of 75 terminals was installed for this purpose. The articles would be booked with the help of a computerized system at the booking office, and the information would be transferred via a modem connection to the Central City sorting center, where the tracking system was installed. This center was connected through the VSAT network to other sorting centers. Customers could call up at the sorting center and find out the status of the booked articles. Computerized money transfer services were introduced in 1998. This was also done through the VSAT network. Individual offices were connected to the network through a leased line modem connection. This reduced the transit time of money orders from nearly a week to a few seconds. In 1997-1998, office operations were computerized and put on a WNT-based local area network. This enabled the sharing of files, data and other resources, and significantly enhanced the efficiency of office operations.

The approach used by NCL has been referred to as the "functional approach" to IT planning (Nidumolu & Goodman, 1996). Organizations that follow this approach believe adoption of IT is desirable because it can improve the timeliness of information flow and reduce process cycle times. NCL was able to respond effectively to the external conditions and government mandates through deployment of IT applications and infrastructure in many critical functions. The financial expenditure on IT between 1990 and 1999 was

Figure 2. Computerized booking, tracking & delivery system at national couriers limited

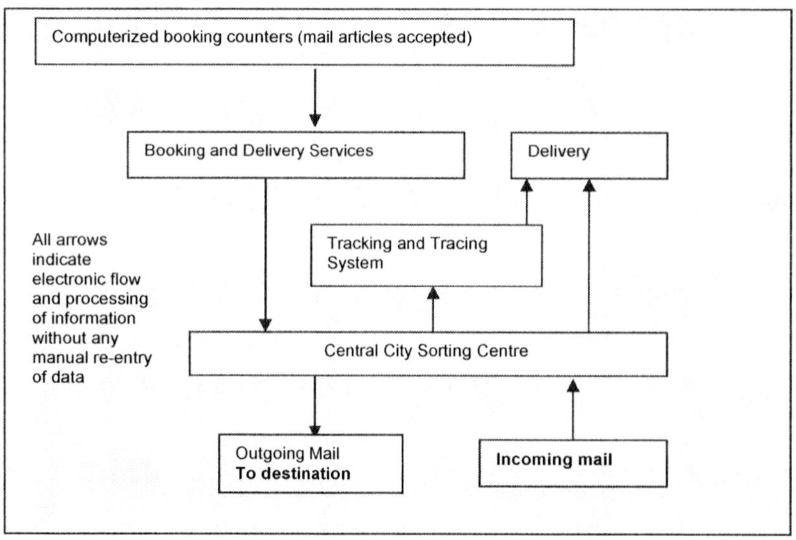

INR 1000 million[1], which was 75% of the total expenditure on modernization during this period and about 2.75% of the organization's revenues. This was relatively much higher than that during the previous 10 years.

According to the head of operations of the eastern region:

"For the first time, substantial budgets were being allocated annually, for the computerization process."

A senior manager in the eastern region further described the possible financial implications in the following way:

"The areas that we targeted for IT adoption covered 65% to 70% of our operations. So we expected to see significant cost savings in around 70% of our functions."

National Traders Limited

A member of the top management, who had been with the organization for more than 30 years, described the overall phenomenon of IT planning and adoption at NTL in the following manner:

"We tried to follow the general instructions from the government, in identifying potential areas of IT adoption. The first step in this regard was the computerization of all high volume transaction processes. We decided to begin by computerizing the payroll and financial accounting processes."

In the mid-1990s a UNIX mainframe system was installed at the central office. This was used in batch processing applications for calculation of accounts, reporting of produce inventory and stock positions, and payroll accounting. In the late 1990s, the mainframe system was converted to a PC-based LAN. An ORACLE-based client server system was installed and the mainframe data were transferred to this. The administrative offices in the different regions carried out the same functions at the regional level using PC-based dBase applications.

In 1998, NTL connected its central administrative office, five zonal offices and 17 regional offices through VSAT links. The district offices were connected to the respective regional offices through dial-up modem connections. At the time of the study, there were about 50 PCs at the central headquarters, four to five PCs in each zonal office, two in each regional office and one in each district office. The depots communicated with the district offices through postal mail and the districts communicated with the regional offices through modems. Forty percent of the data transferred between depots and district, regional and zonal offices related to the inventory and stock position. Forty percent related to financial information and 20% to payroll data. Stock and inventory data were sent in by the depots and district offices to the regional and zonal offices manually, or through leased line modem connections. The regional and zonal offices consolidated the data and then transferred them to the central administrative office through VSAT as well as on paper. Data from all the regional and zonal offices were again consolidated at the central office. Reports about stock positions and requirements were generated for senior managers at both the head office and the regions. The transfer of stock-related information took place on a weekly basis from the depots to the zones and subsequently to the headquarters. A central server housed the consolidated data from all the regions. All the communication links were backed up by traditional mail and fax systems. The IT infrastructure is shown in Figure 3.

The investment in IT acquisition, maintenance and training during the period between 1992 and 1999 was INR 35 million, which was less than 5% of the total capital expenditure during this period.

2. *Management of Bureaucracy and Paperwork:* The public sector produces a lot of paperwork that results in a proliferation of forms and paper (Caudle et al., 1991). All these records need to be computerized in an integrated manner during the process of computerization, in order to make electronic transfer of information possible between of-

fices and minimize manual re-entry of data. Hence it has been suggested (Mohan et al., 1990) that a central governing structure be set up. This structure should oversee the integration of IT management with records management and other information resource management areas.

For NCL, the different systems were designed such that seamless integration and flow of information between different functions was possible, in a limited manner, as shown in Figure 2. For instance, in the computerized booking and tracking system, article information generated at the time of booking was transferred using electronic means through intermediate stages, all the way to the central sorting centers. Similarly, office information related to administrative activities was shared electronically within each office. These capabilities were also planned to be extended to cover electronic transfer among different offices.

For NTL, information transferred from the depots and district offices was manually reentered at the regional offices prior to consolidation and transferred to the Head Office, as shown in Figure 3. At the Head Office also, information was partly reentered manually before the generation of management reports.

3. *Role of Top Management:* The top management plays a key role in deciding the thrust and direction of IT adoption in public sector organizations (Nidumolu & Goodman, 1996). This is because the planning and decision structure with respect to implementation of changes is usually centralized.

National Couriers Limited

At NCL, there was a change in the top management in 1991 as a new CEO joined the organization. The new top management team was favorably disposed towards IT adoption and took many proactive initiatives in this regard. NCL was a member of the Universal Postal Union, and hence information about the latest IT applications in similar organizations around the world was available to the top executives. It was the thinking, planning and drive of top management that led to the introduction of the early IT initiatives. A middle manager in the eastern region office described the new priorities of the top management in this manner:

"After 1991, a number of new thrusts towards IT adoption have been generated at the central office. Our new CEO is enthusiastic about the introduction of IT, and is aware of the possible areas of application. Seminars are often organized to educate and inform us about the use of IT in postal services worldwide."

All decisions regarding IT planning and deployment were centralized. However, the implementation of IT initiatives was decentralized. According to a member of the top management at the central office:

"We tell the regions what the overall plans are, regarding the purchasing of hardware, installation of software and the applications required to be used. Broad decisions regarding all IT applications, hardware and software are taken at the headquarters in consultation with the regions and communicated to the zones and regions. The zones and regions have the power to make their own implementation decisions and purchases within given financial limits."

National Traders Limited

At NTL, the top management was not, in principle, unfavorably oriented towards IT. They did realize the benefits that could accrue from the use of IT, in view of the size of the company and its scale of operations. However, they were not proactive about identifying areas where the company could benefit from IT. The senior managers and policy makers were typically professional administrators and bureaucrats, and the average age was more than 50 years. They did not have any knowledge of emerging IT applications and their use by similar companies around the world. Nor were they comfortable with the use of computers. They were content to depend on the government for direction and instructions on IT adoption.

One of the middle managers who had worked in the organization for the last 15 years said:

" ...If the government had not made certain suggestions, computerization might have come to NTL even later than the late 1980s."

Interviews with some of the senior managers revealed attitudes that varied from measured tolerance for IT, "*It seems to be useful, but it is not indispensable,*" to downright rejection, "*Computers are just expensive typewriters.*"

4. *Role of Middle Management in Driving IT Implementation:* There is evidence that middle managers play a very critical role in driving IT implementation and use in public sector organizations (Caudle et al., 1991). This is because these organizations are usually large, with multiple levels of decision hierarchy (Figure 1), and it is not possible for top management to oversee the details of the implementation processes. Further, middle managers have considerable bureaucratic power in the individual departments and units. Hence, while the top management is responsible for policy setting and strategic planning with respect to IT adoption, it is the middle managers who play the most crucial role in driving the implementation processes within different organizational units.

National Couriers Limited

The middle management influenced IT adoption at NCL in two ways.

First, they were actively involved in framing the specifics of IT adoption policies and driving implementation initiatives within their units. They used their collective organizational power to frame implementation schedules and timelines. They also developed programs for end-user training and education. This was a crucial aspect of the implementation process, given the large number of unskilled and unionized employees in the organization, who viewed IT as a potential threat to their jobs. In this context, one of the middle managers observed:

"We encouraged the clerical and low skilled employees to get familiar with the PC, and start out by just playing games. We hoped that once they became comfortable with the use of PCs, they would be able to appreciate the benefits of computerization. We also conducted education programs regarding the use of IT in organizations. Further we took steps to assure them that their jobs were safe. Throughout the entire computerization process, there was not a single day in which there was a loss of working hours because of union problems."

In this connection, studies in the domain of IT adoption suggest that IT acceptance and innovation at the grassroots levels in different end-user units are crucial to the adoption of IT by an organization (Agarwal & Prasad, 1998; Nambisan, 1999; Rockart, 1988; Vaidya, 1991). In many developing countries, IT is seen to be the cause of reduction in opportunities for employment, and there is a hostile attitude to IT adoption and acceptance, not only at the level of semi-skilled and unskilled employees, but also by middle management. This has been a crucial factor in the introduction and management of IT in developing countries (Jantavongso & Li, 2002; Tarafdar & Vaidya, 2003).

The middle management also played an effective role as IS professionals. While the overall head of the IS function was a member of the senior management, IS activities in each regional and district office were supervised by middle management. These managers were also responsible for IT implementation in the delivery and sorting centers. In other words, middle managers were the IS heads in their respective functional departments. They supervised teams of junior managers who were responsible for installing and maintaining the hardware and software. These junior and middle management members had received technical training and were hence capable of managing the technical aspects of project implementation and systems maintenance. This kind of an "indigenous" implementation strategy is often followed in public sectors. This is because in such organizations there are constraints on hiring and firing employees. Hence existing employees are retrained and reallocated to the newer functions (Nidumolu & Goodman, 1996). Thus there was no separate IS department in NCL. Members of middle and junior management were responsible for IT implementation.

The middle management IS professionals also played an important part as IT champions. The role of IT champions in driving IT adoption has been well documented (Beath, 1991). The middle managers in NCL were credible and commanded authority by virtue of their positions. They had a good working relationship with the top management as well as the unskilled and clerical workers in the company. They were powerful enough to influence decisions at the higher levels, and saw to it that the resources required were made available. Initially there was considerable resistance — especially from the unionized staff — but this was neutralized through the efforts of middle and junior managers. In fact, in many instances, some of the unionized staff subsequently became advocates of the IT-related changes, after having gone through the training processes. They became IT champions themselves and saw to it that strong resistance groups were convinced and neutralized.

Various studies have explored the role of IS professionals in influencing the adoption of IT. IS professionals have a positive impact on IT adoption in the organization when they are technically aware of the possibilities from IT, are competent at developing new IS and maintaining existing IS, and are capable of promptly solving end-user needs (Al-Khaldi et al., 1999; Dvorak et al., 1994; Swanson, 1994). At NCL, the IS professionals influenced IT implementation through their traditional organizational power as middle managers. They were able to effectively carry out project management and end-user training; they were also able to ensure that resources were available.

Table 4. Similarities and differences between NTL and NCL

	National Couriers Limited	National Traders Limited
Similarities		
Size	90,000	63,000
Overall Organization Structure	Multiple levels of hierarchy, centralized planning	Multiple levels of hierarchy, centralized planning
Public Sector Enterprises and the accompanying characteristics	Having functioned in stable business and economic environments.	Having functioned in stable business and economic environments.
	Historically supported by the government.	Historically supported by the government.
	Working under overall policy directives of the government.	Working under overall policy directives of the government.
	Subject to the IT adoption and modernization plans of the government.	Subject to the IT adoption and modernization plans of the government.
	Staffed by bureaucrats. Professional managers and technical specialists who were responsible for tactical and operational tasks.	Staffed by bureaucrats. Professional managers and technical specialists who were responsible for tactical and operational tasks.
Service Organizations	Postal Sector	Distribution Sector
Differences		
Goals of IT adoption	Based on systematic identification of critical processes (article handling and sorting, Information management of mailed articles, Information exchange within offices) and their computerization.	Followed general instructions from the government and did not attempt to identify critical processes. Computerization aimed at basic transaction processing, and not at critical processes.
	IT investment between 1990 and 1999 was INR 900 million, which was 70% of the total expenditure on modernization.	IT investment between 1992 and 1999 was INR 35 million, which was less 5% of the total expenditure on modernization

continued on following page

Table 4. continued

Management of paperwork	Different systems were designed so as to try to enable seamless integration and information transfer through electronic means. This was a consequence of an integrated approach to records management	In absence of an integrated approach to records management, information transferred from the depots to the district offices was re-entered manually before the generation of management reports.
Role of top management	Favorably disposed towards IT adoption. Kept abreast of the latest IT developments in similar organizations in other countries. Resources were allocated to new IT thrusts.	Not, in principle, favorably oriented towards IT. Not proactive about identifying areas that could potentially benefit from IT, beyond the obvious high transaction areas. Not comfortable with the use of computers and depended on the government for instruction and directions on IT adoption.
Role of middle management and the IS department	Actively involved in framing IT adoption policies and driving IT implementation efforts, schedules and timelines.	IS department was headed by a senior manager who reported to the head of the finance function. Junior level employees were responsible for data entry, data consolidation and report generation.
	Supervised IS activities in the regions and districts, and took on the role of IS professionals. Acted as IT champions, generated grassroots awareness and interest, and developed management and union buy-in for IT adoption efforts.	The IS head did not have any control over the implementation issues and schedules in the regional offices.
		Middle management was reluctant to use computers and depended on junior management to provide reports. They did not participate in or influence the IT adoption process in any way.
Extent of IT adoption	Basic computerization in conjunction with computerization in other public sector enterprises in India.	Basic computerization in conjunction with computerization in other public sector enterprises in India.
	Use of IT in transaction processing for payroll and accounting.	Use of IT in batch processing transactions and for reporting- for payroll, accounting and stock calculations. Information transfer between offices manually or through modems. In many cases information from one MIS report was re-entered manually at the next organizational level, because of incompatibility of technology and/or formats.
	Proactive IT adoption beyond the overall parameters suggested by the government such as pairing machines and computerization of counter operations.	
	Introduction of IT in key processes: Computerized mail handling and sorting, article tracking, money transfer. LANs within offices and a VSAT network connecting different offices.	
Current and future issues	Transition from Turnaround to Factory Mode, which would imply:	Transition from Support to Turnaround, which would imply:
	Extension of existing applications	Proactive identification of critical processes for IT implementation
	Broad based end-user training	IT education and awareness
	Budget driven IT planning processes	Driving mechanisms for development of successful IS which can be used as an "example" to generate interest and acceptance
		Change Management

This case therefore illustrates a new dimension of the role of IS professionals in driving IT adoption and considerably enhances similar preliminary findings by Caudle et al. (1991).

National Traders Limited

The Central IS department at NTL was headed by a senior manager who reported to the head of the finance function. He was somewhat aware of the possibilities of IT and had some limited ideas of its usefulness for the company. He supervised a team of 60 Central IS employees. Out of these 60 people, 10 had a diploma or some other professional training in different aspects of software development, and could develop applications on dBase, MS Access and ORACLE. About 30 people were data entry operators, whose tasks were to key in and consolidate the data from the zonal, regional and district offices. All these employees had received the requisite training and looked after various functions in the IS department. They worked in the central administrative headquarters, and were responsible for centralized consolidation and collation of data from the regions. They also designed and implemented training programs for data entry staff in the different regions. They looked after incremental modifications to the existing applications. Further, they managed third-party vendors who carried out maintenance of existing hardware and the development of new applications.

The IS departments in the zones and regions comprised junior-level employees who had been transferred from other departments after training. They had no formal education in computer hardware or software. They were responsible for entering and consolidating the data received from the districts and depots, and generating relevant reports for senior managers at the zonal offices. At the time of the study, about 200 such employees, mostly staff and junior managers, had been trained in various applications, and had later been shifted to dedicated IS functions. They themselves were reluctant to use computers. Third-party vendors carried out the maintenance work.

The IS manager was not powerful and senior enough to convince top management to make resources available for any IT initiative other than the most basic applications. He had no significant power to independently make important decisions relating to IT deployment. Moreover the IS professionals at the central office did not have any control over whether or not the regional heads would actually implement specific IT applications. The IS department had not met with much success in this regard and there had been stiff resistance in many cases. This greatly hindered the penetration of IT because regional heads had independent authority over IT implementation initiatives in their areas.

The chief of the central IS function said:

"The implementation and use of computers in the offices is completely decentralized. We cannot force anyone to start using computers. Ultimately the extent of IT use depends on the policies of the respective regions and zones."

There were more than 60,000 employees in the company, 85% of whom performed low skilled and clerical jobs. Similar to the situation at NCL initially, employees were not favorably biased towards IT, because they feared that they would lose their jobs. Hence they tried various ways to express their opinions in this regard. For example, very often, when reports were not made available on time to senior managers, subordinate junior employees would excuse themselves by saying that the computers were not working or the relevant officer in charge of taking the print-outs was not available. They would even suggest that such problems did not exist before computers were introduced. The reluctance of employees to use computers is exemplified by the fact that those who used them had to be given monetary incentives. Further, most of the middle mangers and even some of the senior managers in the regions were against the deployment of IT. There was limited penetration of IT into the user departments. Senior managers did not directly use computers. They would ask data entry operators to enter data and furnish printouts.

The similarities and differences between the two organizations have been described in Table 4.

CURRENT CHALLENGES & PROBLEMS (2000 & BEYOND)

In spite of similarities in their overall nature and scale of operations and historical and cultural contexts, the IT adoption processes and outcomes in the two companies were considerably different. While NTL failed to implement IT in its crucial processes, NCL was able to respond effectively to the external conditions and government mandates through organization-wide deployment of IT applications and infrastructure in many critical functions.

National Couriers Limited

The computerization process at NCL took place in two distinct phases. In the first phase, from 1987 to 1991, computerization was limited and driven by the requirements of high-volume transaction processing. During this period, the company used IT for very basic and rudimentary transaction processing operations. It was in the Support Mode (McFarlan et al., 1983) or Delayed Sector (Earl, 1989). These two modes are the first stages of IT adoption in organizations where IT is not fundamentally essential for the smooth running of operations of the company. It is used to accomplish nonessential and noncritical tasks, and the IS department functions as a back-room support department, with no participation in functions like strategic planning and implementation.

The second phase of computerization between 1992 and 2000 saw an acceleration of the computerization process. The acceleration was partly in response to government mandates and partly as a result of the enthusiasm of the new leadership about IT. During this period, NCL went through the Turnaround Stage (McFarlan et al., 1983). IT became increasingly crucial to the future development of the organization. There was a change in focus, as far as IT planning and implementation were concerned. New applications were developed and there was an increase in IT investment. At the time this study was conducted, different applications had been introduced in a limited number of offices, and covered about 40% of the operations of the company. The Annual Report of 1994-95 described the induction of computerization in this manner:

"... NCL has made a gradual and phased attempt to introduce information technology into the postal system, so as to provide better services to its customers ..."

The most important impact of IT had been to increase operational efficiencies, and IT was accorded a high priority by the top management. Hence the organization was well positioned to move to the next level of IT use, that is, the Factory Mode (McFarlan et al., 1983) or the Dependent Sector (Earl, 1989). This would include the extension of current applications to more offices and the development of more sophisticated applications. The challenge before NCL was therefore to transform from a Turnaround organization into a Factory organization. One of the most important aspects of the Factory Mode is to ensure that IT is delivered efficiently and reliably. This implies that resource requirements and budgets be correctly estimated (Earl, 1989). In this context, Mohan et al. (1990) suggest that since public sector organizations operate under fixed and often tight budgets, an inability to logically derive and clearly communicate IS budget requirements is a primary reason for these organizations not allocating adequate resources for IT adoption. A similar problem existed at NCL also, in that there were no budget-driven planning processes that could broaden the scope of the existing IT applications.

National Traders Limited

NTL was an interesting organization to study because it was large and there was significant potential for the use of IT. However, the organization did not use IT for any but the most basic functions. This was because there was a strong overall negative inclination towards IT adoption and use among the middle and junior management. For instance, none of the departmental heads at the head office or in the regional and zonal offices used computers for the latest available inventory positions. They would ask their secretaries for the relevant paper files or would simply ask their immediate subordinates over the phone.

One senior manager observed:

"Anyway, I have to ask for most of the information over the phone or through fax. So what is the use of the computer in tracking the movement of the stock?"

Lack of enthusiasm among managers in public sector enterprises for using IS has been documented by Mohan et al. (1990). The primary reasons for this are a low comfort level with the use of computers and a lack of awareness of applications relevant to the organization. Nidumolu and Goodman (1996) suggest that perceptions towards IT can change from unfavorable to favorable, as more projects are undertaken and more functions are computerized.

At the time this study was conducted, IT was used for routine administrative tasks, and not for any critical activities like logistics and distribution planning. Hence IT was not crucial to the achievement of the strategic objectives of the firm. Moreover, all electronic information was also stored in paper format. Transfer of information was both electronic and paper based. The challenge for NTL therefore was to move from the Support Mode to the Turnaround Mode (McFarlan et al., 1983), and increase the scope of existing IT applications. At the time of writing, they were pilot testing the use of a software for managing distribution and storage of food grains.

Change Management Issues

Change management has been suggested as an especially important issue in government organizations because of their entrenched processes (Caudle et al., 1991). In fact, the adoption of IT in the nationalized banks in India, which commenced in the mid-1980s, had been fraught with issues regarding acceptance of process changes and the fear of job losses due to automation. Employee unions, perceiving that their concerns had not been adequately addressed, had offered considerable resistance and had significantly slowed the process of IT adoption in the banks (Joshi & Joshi, 2002). Hence it is anticipated that change management issues would be crucial to the continued infusion and diffusion of IT at NTL and NCL.

The first aspect of change management had to do with overcoming resistance at different levels of the two organizations, especially at NTL. In a study of e-government initiatives in the Indian state of Kerala, Kumar (2003) reports that top management drive has been an important issue in driving IT adoption in various government departments and has facilitated the acceptance of IT at lower organizational levels. In this regard NCL had so far been able to manage differences between the various units and had been able to convince unions and clerical staff about the benefits of IT adoption, largely through the efforts of its middle and top management.

This process had been more difficult at NTL, given that the top and middle management themselves were not quite convinced about the usefulness of IT and that they had not proactively driven its adoption. As Joshi and Joshi (2002) have pointed out, it is relatively easier to work towards middle and lower management commitment after top management commitment has been secured.

It has been observed that supervisors may often be reluctant to adopt IT in their departments because of possible reductions in head count, which might lead to a decrease in their span of control. This may partially explain the reluctance of middle and junior management cadres to adopt IT, especially in NTL. The middle mangers were afraid of losing headcount in their departments as a result of the junior management receiving training and getting relocated to IT-based functions. Similarly, junior management was apprehensive about the reduction in the number of unionized employees, the resultant loss in their own power and possible backlash from the labor unions.

The second aspect of change management was that of managing the work environment during the change process. Studies by Amabile (1996) have suggested that the work environment often becomes negative in times of new technology implementation and significant business process changes. This is because the difficulties associated with adjusting to the changes often result in collective cynicism and confusion. Such conditions stifle creativity and motivation. This was observed in NTL, where the new IT was met with collective skepticism from all levels of the organization.

Public sector organizations are characterized by complex performance measurement criteria. The lack of a clearly defined bottomline in most cases leads to a focus on inputs and budgets, rather than on outputs and productivity measures. Economic liberalization in India has resulted in an emphasis on service quality, process efficiency and overall modernization in both the public and private sectors (Wolcott & Goodman, 2003). The challenges before NCL and NTL would be to use IT for enhancing their service quality, for increasing the efficiency of their operations and to appropriately manage their IT adoption processes. In absence of such an effort, both organizations would be burdened with high-cost operations and increasingly dissatisfied customers.

REFERENCES

Agarwal, R., & Prasad, J. (1998). The antecedents and consequents of user perceptions in information technology adoption. *Decision Support Systems, 22*(1), 15-29.

Al-Khaldi, M.A., & Wallace, R.S.O. (1999). The influence of attitudes on personal computer utilisation among knowledge workers: The case of Saudi Arabia. *Information and Management, 36*(4), 185-204.

Amabile, T., Conti, R., Coon, H., Lazenby, J., & Herron, M. (1996). Assessing the work environment for creativity. *Academy of Management Journal, 13*(5), 1154-1184.

Beath, C.M. (1991, Sept). Supporting the information technology champion. *MIS Quarterly, 15*(3), 155-371.

Caulde, S.R., Gorr, W.L., & Newcomer, K.E. (1991). Key information systems management issues for the public sector. *MIS Quarterly, 15*(2), 171-188.

Cavusgil, S.T., Ghauri, P.N., & Agarwal, M.R. (2002). *Doing Business in Emerging Markets: Entry and Negotiation Strategies.* CA: Sage Publications.

Dvorak, R., Dean, D., & Singer, M. (1994). Accelerating IT innovation. *The McKinsey Quarterly,* 123-135.

Earl, M.J. (1989). *Management Strategies for Information Technology.* London: Prentice Hall.

Jantavongso, S., & Li, K.Y.R. (2002, May). E-business in Thailand: Social and cultural issues. In M. Khosrow-Pour (Ed.), *Issues and Trends of IT Management in Contemporary Organizations. Proceedings of Information Resources Management Association Conference* (pp. 443-446).

Joshi, V.C., & Joshi, V.C. (2002). *Managing Indian Banks* (2nd ed.). CA: Sage Publications.

Khera, S.S. (1979). Public sector management. In B.C. Mathur, K. Diesh & C.C. Sekharan (Eds.), *Management in Government.* Publications Division, Ministry of Information and Broadcasting, Government of India.

Kumar, A. (2003). E-government and efficiency, accountability and transparency: ASEAN Executive Seminar on e-Government. *International Journal of Information Systems in Developing Countries, 12*(2), 1-15.

Lachman, R. (1985, Sept). Public and private sector differences: CEOs' perceptions of their role environments. *Academy of Management Journal, 28*(3), 671-679.

Li, Q., Zhang, X., Sun, C., & Wang, S. (2002, May). Strategies of securities electronic commerce in China: Implications of comparative analyses between China and other countries. In M. Khosrow-Pour (Ed.), *Issues and Trends of IT Management in Contemporary Organizations. Proceedings of the Information Resources Management Association Conference,* (pp. 1080-1083).

McFarlan, F.W., McKenney, J.L., & Pyburn, P. (1983). The information archipelago: Plotting a course. *Harvard Business Review, 61*(1), 145-156.

Mohan, L., Holstein, W.K., & Adams, R.B. (1990). EIS: It can work in the public sector. *MIS Quarterly, 14*(4), 435-448.

Molla, A., & Licker, P.S. (2002, May). PERM: A model of e-commerce adoption in developing countries. In M. Khosrow-Pour (Ed.), *Issues and trends in IT Management in Contemporary Organizations. Proceedings of the Information Resources Management Association Conference,* Seattle, WA (pp. 527-530).

Moynihan, T. (1990). What chief executives and senior managers want from their IT departments. *MIS Quarterly, 14*(1), 15-25.

Nambisan, S. (1999). Organisational mechanisms for enhancing user innovation in information technology. *MIS Quarterly, 23*(3), 365-395.

Nidumolu, S.R., & Goodman, S.E. (1993). Computing in India: An Asian elephant learning to dance. *Communications of the ACM, 36*(4).

Nidumolu., S.R., Goodman, S.E., Vogel, D.R., & Danowitz, A.K. (1996). Information technology for local administration support: The Governorates project in Egypt. *MIS Quarterly, 20*(2), 197-224.

Rainey, H.G., Backoff, R., & Levine, C. (1976). Comparing public and private organizations. *Public Administration Review, 36*(2), 233-244.

Rockart, J.F. (1988, Summer). The line takes the leadership: IS management in a wired society. *Sloan Management Review, 29*(4), 57-64.

Swanson, E.B. (1994). Information systems innovation in organizations. *Management Science, 40*(9), 1069-1091.

Tarafdar, M., & Vaidya, S.D. (2002). Evolution of the use of IT for e-business at century financial services: An analysis of internal and external facilitators and inhibitors. *Journal of IT Cases and Applications, 4*(4), 49-76.

Tarafdar, M., & Vaidya, S.D. (2003). Challenges in the adoption of information technology at Sunrise Industries: The case of an Indian firm. *Annals of Cases in Information Technology, 6,* 457-479.

Vaidya, S.D. (1991, Dec 26-29). End user computing: An Indian perspective. *Proceedings of the Indian Computing Congress* (pp. 533-541).

Wolcott, P., & Goodman, S. (2003). Global diffusion of the Internet in India: Is the elephant learning to dance? *Communications of the Association for Information Systems, 11,* 560-646.

ENDNOTE

[1] 45 INR (Indian Rupee) = 1 U.S. Dollar

This work was previously published in Journal of Cases on Information Technology, Vol. 7, No. 1, edited by M. Khosrow-Pour, pp. 111-135, copyright 2005 by IGI Publishing, formerly known as Idea Group Publishing (an imprint of IGI Global).

About the Editors

G. David Garson is full professor of public administration at North Carolina State University, where he teaches courses on American government, research methodology, computer applications, and geographic information systems. In 1995 he was recipient of the Donald Campbell Award from the Policy Studies Organization, American Political Science Association, for outstanding contributions to policy research methodology and in 1997 of the Aaron Wildavsky Book Award from the same organization. He is author of the *Guide to Writing Quantitative Papers, Theses, and Dissertations* (Dekker, 2001), editor of *Social Dimensions of Information Technology* (2000), *Information Technology and Computer Applications in Public Administration: Issues and Trends* (1999), and the *Handbook of Public Information Systems* (1999), and author of *Neural Network Analysis for Social Scientists* (1998), *Computer Technology and Social Issues* (1995), and is author, co-author, editor, or co-editor of 17 other books and author or co-author of more than 50 articles. For the last 20 years he has also served as editor of the *Social Science Computer Review* and is on the editorial board of four additional journals.

Mehdi Khosrow-Pour, DBA, is currently executive director of the Information Resources Management Association (IRMA). Previously, he served 20 years on the Faculty of The Pennsylvania State University as an associate professor of information systems. He has written or edited more than 20 books in information technology management and is also editor of the *Information Resources Management Journal, Journal of Cases on Information Technology, Journal of Electronic Commerce in Organizations*, and *International Journal of Cases on Electronic Commerce.*

About the Contributors

Esharenana E. Adomi had his university education at the University of Ibadan, Ibadan, and Delta State University, Abraka, both in Nigeria. He holds BEd, MEd, MLS, and PhD degrees. He lectures at the Department of Library and Information Science, Delta State University, Abraka, Nigeria. His research interests lie in Web and Internet technology and ICT development and applications in different settings.

Amalia Agathou is currently in the final year of her undergraduate studies in the Department of Information and Communication Systems Engineering of the University of the Aegean in Greece. Her research interests include computer security, data modeling, and databases.

Stephen K. Aikins received a PhD from the University of Nebraska at Omaha where he has taught graduate-level courses in public-sector information management. He is a certified public accountant (CPA) and a certified information systems auditor (CISA). Dr. Aikins has several years of experience working in various capacities in government and in the private sector. He has been a state revenue auditor, a municipal government auditor for a public accounting firm, a Medicare auditor for a federal government contractor, and an assistant vice president for a multinational bank. His research interests are electronic government, Internet-based citizen participation, electronic democracy, information security, public sector economics, public financial management and public budgeting.

Eugene J. Akers is the senior director for the Center for Advanced Technology in the University Outreach Program of Auburn University Montgomery. The purpose of the center is to extend the resources and expertise of Auburn University Montgomery (AUM) and Auburn University to individuals, organizations, the community, and the environment in a manner that enhances productivity and the quality of life for individuals in Alabama. The center provides consulting services, training programs, economic development endeavors, technological advancements, and community service. As the senior director, Dr. Akers is responsible for establishing the strategic direction of the center. Dr. Akers also is responsible for business development, contract management, and client relationships. Dr. Akers currently serves as an adjunct assistant professor in the Department of Information Systems and Decision Science and the Department of Political Science and Public Administration of Auburn Montgomery.

Micah Altman (PhD, California Institute of Technology, 1998) is an associate director of the Harvard-MIT Data Center, is archival director at the Henry R. Murray Research Archive, and is senior research scientist in the Institute for Quantitative Social Science at Harvard University. Dr. Altman has served as co-investigator in a number of research projects promoting the collection, sharing, citation, and preservation sharing of research data through the development of open-source software tools and methods. His extensively reviewed book, *Numerical Issues in Statistical Computing for the Social Scientist*, corrects common computational errors made across the range of social sciences. His more thab two dozen publications and four open source software packages span many disciplines in social and information sciences.

Andrea Baker is a PhD candidate of information studies at the College of Computing and Information and a graduate research assistant at the Center for Technology in Government, University at Albany, State University of New York. At the University at Albany and Siena College, she is also an adjunct professor at the Department of English. Baker is the co-author of a chapter in *The Internet Election: Perspectives on the Web in Campaign 2004* and several papers presented at conferences of prestigious professional associations such as the American Society for Information Science and Technology and the American Society for Public Administration. Her research interests include computer-mediated communication, the impact of new media on the press, open-source technology and community, and collaborative e-government.

David A. Bray is currently with the Goizueta Business School, Emory University. He will be a visiting fellow with Oxford University's Internet Institute in 2007. Bray's research focuses on bottom-up (i.e., grassroots) sociotechnological approaches for fostering interindividual knowledge exchanges. Before academia, he served as the IT chief for the Bioterrorism Preparedness and Response Program at the Centers for Disease Control where he led the technology response to 9/11, anthrax, WNV, SARS, and other major outbreaks.

Lia Bryant is deputy director for the Hawke Institute of Sustainable Societies, University of South Australia. She is also director of the Research Centre for Gender Studies and is a senior lecturer in the School of Social Work and Social Policy. Her research interests include gender and technologies, gender and sexuality, organizations, work, rurality, and space and place.

Anthony W. Buenger, Jr. (Lt. Col., USAF, retired), is a professor of systems management (Military Faculty) and information operations and assurance at the Information Resources Management College, National Defense University, Fort McNair, Washington, DC. Buenger received his bachelor's degree in electrical engineering from the University of Maryland in 1988. In 1992 he received an MA in space systems management from Webster University, Colorado. He is currently working on a PhD in business administration from Northcentral University, Arizona. He served his entire 21-year career in the communications, information technology, and information security fields.

Donna Canestraro brings more than 25 years of professional experience to her role as program manager at the Center for Technology in Government (CTG). Prior to joining CTG, Canestraro has worked with both public- and private-sector organizations including Unisys Corporation and General Electric. Her most recent position prior to CTG was as program manager with the Professional Development Program at the University at Albany's Nelson A. Rockefeller College of Public Affairs and Policy. Her current work focuses on the policy, management, and technology issues related to inter- and intra-organizational information integration. As project manager for the XML Testbed, she has orchestrated the development of the XML Testbed, as well as various conference presentations and academic papers about XML.

Elena Castro received an MS in mathematics from Universidad Complutense of Madrid in 1995. Since 1998 she has been working at the Advanced Databases Group in the Department of Computer Science, Universidad Carlos III of Madrid. Recently, she has obtained a PhD in information science from Universidad Carlos III of Madrid. She is currently teaching relational and object-oriented databases. Her research interests include database conceptual and logical modeling, advanced database CASE environments, and information and knowledge engineering.

Mirko Cesarini is currently working as professor's assistant with the Faculty of Statistical Science, University of Milan Bicocca. He is also affiliated with CRISP (Interuniversity Research Center on Public Utility Services for the Individual). His research focuses on information systems. He has published several papers in refereed journals, and in proceedings of international conferences. He earned a PhD in 2005 in computer engineering and a master's degree in the same field in 2001, both at the Politecnico di Milano, Milan, Italy.

Ioannis P. Chochliouros is a telecommunications electrical engineer who graduated from the Polytechnic School of the Aristotle University of Thessaloniki, Greece, holding also an MS and a PhD from the University Pierre et Marie Curie, Paris VI. He possesses extreme research and practical experience in a great variety of matters for modern electronic communications. He currently works as the head of the research programs section of the Hellenic Telecommunications Organization S.A. (OTE) in Greece, where he has been involved in different national, European, and international R&D projects and market-oriented activities, many of which have received international awards. He has published more than 80 distinct scientific and business papers and reports in the international literature (books, magazines, conferences, and workshops), especially for technical, business, and regulatory options arising from innovative e-infrastructures and e-services in a global converged environment. He is a member of several national and international scientific committees and fora. He also works as a university lecturer with the Faculty of Science and Technology, Departments of Telecommunication Science, Computer Science and Technology, University of Peloponnese, Greece.

Stergios P. Chochliouros is an independent consultant who is a specialist for environmental-related studies. He holds a PhD from the Department of Biology, University of Patras, Greece, and a university degree as an agriculturist. He has gained enormous experiences as an academic researcher and has been involved in various research activities, especially in options for the extended use and/or applicability of modern technologies. In particular, he has participated as an expert in many European research projects relevant to a variety of environmental studies. Moreover, he has gained significant experience both as an educator and advisor while being an author of several papers, studies, and reports.

Gabriel Puron Cid received a master's degree in public administration and policy at the Center for Research and Economics Teaching (CIDE) in Mexico. After the conclusion of this program, he contributed actively at the Ministry of Finance of the federal government in Mexico to design and implement budgeting for results. Today he is a doctoral student of public administration at the Rockefeller College of Public Affairs & Policy of the University at Albany with a specialization in information management and policy in the public sector. His research interests are information technology applications in public finance and budgeting, digital government, IT investment and failures in intergovernmental systems, and public management of information systems in governmental contexts.

David Cook is an associate professor in the Department of Information Systems and Decisions Sciences, College of Business and Public Administration at Old Dominion University. His educational and work experience is in the area of operations management. He graduated from the University of Kentucky with a PhD in production and operations management. Dr. Cook has published in such journals as *Production and Inventory Management, Human Systems Management, Production and Operations Management, The Journal of Computer Information Systems*, and the *e-Service Journal.* His research interests include quality management, service operations, and electronic commerce. He is a member of the Decision Sciences Institute and INFORMS.

James Costello serves as Webmaster and Web application developer at the Center for Technology in Government. Prior to joining CTG, Costello operated his own Web design and development company and worked for several private and public organizations, including KeyCorp, the Professional Development Program of Rockefeller College, Coopers & Lybrand, and the Office of Data Processing, Human Resources Administration, City of New York. Based on his experience at CTG, he developed a curriculum on the benefits and challenges of using XML for Web site content management, which he has presented to over 30 different NYS agencies. He and Derek Werthmuller were the two chief architects of the XML Toolkit (http://www.thexmltoolkit.org), a product of the XML Testbed.

Ron Craig is a professor of business in the operations and decision sciences area of the School of Business & Economics, Wilfrid Laurier University, Waterloo, Canada. His research interests cover small business and information systems. He has published several articles and cases in these areas.

Dolores Cuadra received an MS in mathematics from Universidad Complutense of Madrid in 1995. Since 1997, she has worked as an assistant lecturer at the Advanced Databases Group in the Department of Computer Science, Carlos III University of Madrid. In 2003 she obtained a PhD in computer science from Carlos III University of Madrid. She is currently teaching files organization, database design, and data models. Her research interests include data models, conceptual and logical modeling, and advanced database CASE environments. She has been working in the Department of Computer Science at Purdue University of West Lafayette (Indiana) for nearly a year, where she has applied her research in spatiotemporal databases.

Alex Dunayev worked at the St. John IT Department developing the National Events Management System (NEMS). This won a national award for excellence in the not-for-profit organizations category. While working at St. John, Dunayev was also finishing degrees at the University of Auckland. His BCom (Hons) dissertation, which also received an award, forms the basis for his chapter in this book. Dunayev is CEO of AQXI Creative Software at the University of Auckland's ICEHOUSE. He founded AQXI, largely staffed by other graduates from Auckland.

Antonina Durfee (Kloptchenko) is an assistant professor at Appalachian State University in Boone. She holds a PhD from Abo Akademi University. Her current research is in text mining, knowledge discovery, human issues in technology adoption, and seeking behavior. She published in *International Journal of Intelligent Systems in Accounting, Finance, and Management* and *International Journal of Digital Accounting Research.*

William D. "Denny" Eshee, Jr., attorney-at-law, is professor of business law at Mississippi State University. He received his Juris PhD degree from the University of Mississippi. He has been admitted to the Mississippi Bar Association, Federal Bar Association, Alabama Bar Association, United States Court of Military Appeals, and The United States Supreme Court. He has authored or co-authored four books, *Mississippi Small Claims Court: A Debt Collection Guide for Mississippi Businesses*, *The Mississippi Entrepreneur's Guide*, *The American Entrepreneur's Guide*, and *The Legal Environment of Business*, as well as a host of journal articles and other business publications.

Vesile Evrim is currently a PhD student in computer science at the University of Southern California, and a research assistant in the Semantic Information Representation Laboratory at USC. She has received BS and MS degrees in applied mathematics and computer science at the Eastern Mediterranean University in Cyprus and another MS degree in computer science from USC. Her current research focuses on trust-based information retrieval, search engines, recommender systems, and social networks.

Lixin Fu has been an assistant professor at the University of North Carolina at Greensboro since he joined the university in 2001. He has published more than a dozen papers in refereed journals and international conferences in the past 5 years. His main research areas include data warehousing, data mining, databases, and algorithms. Dr. Fu has obtained a PhD in computer and information sciences at the University of Florida in 2001. He earned a master's degree in electrical engineering at Georgia Institute of Technology in 1997. He is a member of IEEE, ACM, and Upsilon Pi Epsilon Honor Society.

Mariagrazia Fugini is an associate professor of computer engineering at Politecnico di Milano. Previously, she was an assistant professor at the Department of Industrial Automation, Faculty of Engineering, Università di Brescia (1983-1991), and an associate professor with the Department of Computer Science, University of Pavia. She has been a visiting professor at the University of Maryland (1985-1986), the Technical University of Vienna (1986-1991), and the University of Stuttgart. Her research interests are in information system security, information systems development, software reuse, information retrieval, cooperative information systems, and reengineering in public administrations. She has published several books, papers in refereed journals, and papers in proceedings of international conferences and symposia.

J. Ramon Gil-Garcia is an assistant professor in the Department of Public Administration at the Centro de Investigación y Docencia Económicas in Mexico City and a research fellow at the Center for Technology in Government, University at Albany, State University of New York. Dr. Gil-Garcia is the author or co-author of articles in numerous academic journals including *The International Public Management Journal, Government Information Quarterly, Journal of the American Society for Information Science and Technology, European Journal of Information Systems, Public Finance and Management*, and *Gestión y Política Pública*. His research interests include collaborative e-government, interorganizational information integration, adoption and implementation of emergent technologies, digital divide policies, public management, public policy evaluation, and multimethod research approaches.

Sheng-Uei Guan received an MS and PhD from the University of North Carolina at Chapel Hill. He is currently a professor and chair in intelligent systems in the School of Engineering and Design at Brunel University, UK. Professor Guan has worked in a prestigious R&D organization for several years, serving as a design engineer, project leader, and manager. After leaving the industry, he joined Yuan-Ze University in Taiwan for three and a half years. He served as deputy director for the Computing Center and the chairman for the Department of Information & Communication Technology. Later he joined the Electrical & Computer Engineering Department at National University of Singapore as an associate professor.

Shahidul Hassan is a doctoral student in public administration and policy at the University at Albany, State University of New York. His research interests are interorganizational collaboration and technology and work-practice transformation in government agencies.

Wen-Chen Hu received a PhD in computer science from the University of Florida, Gainesville, in 1998. He is currently an assistant professor in the Department of Computer Science at the University of North Dakota. Dr. Hu has been advising more than 50 graduate students and has published over 60 articles on refereed journals, conferences, books, and encyclopedias. His current research interests are in handheld computing, electronic and mobile commerce systems, Web technologies, and databases. He is a member of the IEEE Computer Society, ACM, and IRMA (Information Resources Management Association).

Xiaohua (Tony) Hu is currently an assistant professor at the College of Information Science and Technology, Drexel University, Philadelphia. He received a PhD (computer science) from the University of Regina, Canada (1995) and an MS (computer science) from Simon Fraser University, Canada (1992). His current research interests are biomedical literature data mining, bioinformatics, text mining, rough sets, information extraction, and information retrieval. He has published more than 100 peer-reviewed research papers in the above areas. He is the founding editor-in-chief of the *International Journal of Data Mining and Bioinformatics*.

Marijn Janssen is an assistant professor in the field of information systems at the Faculty of Technology, Policy, and Management, Delft University of Technology, The Netherlands. His research is focused on designing service architectures for public service networks. He received a PhD (2001) at Delft University of Technology in the field of management information systems and has been a consultant and information architect for the Ministry of Justice.

Anton Joha is a consultant at Morgan Chambers in The Netherlands and an affiliate of Delft University of Technology. His projects are mainly in the field of outsourcing and shared service centers. He holds an MS in management information systems from Delft University of Technology, The Netherlands.

Jimmie L. Joseph is an assistant professor in the Department of Information and Decision Sciences, College of Business, University of Texas at El Paso. He earned a BS in the triple majors of biology, computer science, and natural sciences from Indiana University of Pennsylvania, an MBA from the University of Pittsburgh's Joseph M. Katz Graduate School of Business, an MS in MoIS from the University of Pittsburgh's Joseph M. Katz Graduate School of Business, and a PhD in MIS from the University of

Pittsburgh's Joseph M. Katz Graduate School of Business. Dr. Joseph has published in such journals as the *Journal of Management Information Systems*, *Human Systems Management*, and the *International Journal of Electronic Business*. His research interests include human computer interaction, electronic commerce, and social impacts of information systems. He is a member of the Association for Information Systems and the Decision Sciences Institute.

Rhoda C. Joseph is an assistant professor of information systems and technology at The Pennsylvania State University – Harrisburg. She has earned her PhD in business with a specialization in information systems from the City University of New York (CUNY), and her MBA from Baruch College (CUNY). Dr. Joseph's research interests are in the area of technology nonadoption, e-government, and human factors in information systems.

Kalu N. Kalu is an associate professor of political science at Auburn University Montgomery. He is also a research fellow at The Macmillan Center for International and Area Studies, Yale University. His research emphasis is in the areas of institutional development and democratic theory, citizenship and administrative theory, civil-military relations, IT-leadership interface, national security and intelligence policy, e-government, and health care politics and policies. Dr. Kalu has published articles in the *Journal of Political and Military Sociology*, *Administrative Theory & Praxis*, *Public Administration Review*, *Administration & Society*, *International Review of Administrative Sciences*, *Social Science Computer Review*, *the Yale Political Quarterly*, and others. His book *Rentier Politics: State Power, Autarchy, and Political Conquest in Post-War Nigeria* is forthcoming.

Atreyi Kankanhalli is an assistant professor in the Department of Information Systems, School of Computing, National University of Singapore (NUS). She received a PhD in information systems from NUS. Dr. Kankanhalli's research interests include knowledge management, e-government, virtual teams, and information systems security. Her work has been published in journals such as *MIS Quarterly*, *Journal of the American Society for Information Science & Technology*, *Journal of Management Information Systems*, *International Journal of Human Computer Studies*, *Communications of the ACM*, *Decision Support Systems*, and *International Journal of Information Management*, and conferences including *ICIS*, *HICSS*, and *WITS*.

Dimitris K. Kardaras is an assistant professor in information systems management in the Department of Business Administration, Athens University of Economics and Business (AUEB), Greece. He holds a BS (Hons) in informatics and a BS (Hons) in management both from the Athens University of Economics and Business, and an MS in information systems engineering and PhD in information systems from the Department of Computation at the University of Manchester Institute of Science and Technology (UMIST), England. Dr Kardaras has participated in many research projects in IS and IT since 1990 and has been teaching in IS courses for over 12 years. He has published journal and conference papers in the areas of IS planning, fuzzy cognitive maps, IS modeling, and e-commerce.

David P. Kitlan is an instructor in information sciences and technology at The Pennsylvania State University – Harrisburg. He is a PhD candidate in the public administration program at The Pennsylvania State University – Harrisburg. Kitlan holds an MS in information systems, an MBA, and an MEng from The Pennsylvania State University, Harrisburg. Mr. Kitlan completed his undergraduate degree in mechanical engineering, also at The Pennsylvania State University. He has over 20 years of corporate and industry experience in engineering, manufacturing, management, marketing, consulting, six-sigma methods, training, and project management. Kitlan's research interests include areas of management, work teams, distance learning, e-government, data mining, information security, and the use of information systems in private, public, and nonprofit organizations.

Hsiang-Jui Kung is an assistant professor of information systems at Georgia Southern University. He received a PhD in management information systems from Rensselaer Polytechnic Institute in 1997. He joined Georgia Southern University full time in 2001. His research interests include systems analysis and design, database, e-business, IS education, and software evolution.

Giorgos Laskaridis holds a degree in informatics from the Department of Informatics, University of Athens, Greece, and is now a PhD candidate in the same department. As a research fellow, he has participated in several European and national R&D projects. His research interests are in the fields of electronic services, e-government, software engineering, and system analysis and design. He has published journal and conference publications in the area of e-services and e-government. He is currently advisor to the secretary general, general secretariat for information systems of the Hellenic Ministry of Economy and Finance.

Vincent Lasnik is currently an independent knowledge architect and instructional design consultant in Oregon. His professional experience includes 18 years beyond the PhD in cross-disciplinary technical and creative communications; instructional design and training; hybrid, blended, distance, and/or online learning; information design; interactive learning and multimedia production; research and development; and knowledge generation and dissemination. He holds a BA in history and psychology (Case Western Reserve University), an MA in humanities education, a PhD in instructional design and technology (both from the Ohio State University), and an MS in human factors in information design (Bentley College, McCallum Graduate School of Business).

Richard A. Leipold received a BA from Washington and Jefferson College in English literature, and an MA and PhD from the University of Pittsburgh in mathematics. After working as a computer engineer for Westinghouse Electric Corporation, he joined the Faculty of Waynesburg College. He is a professor of computer science and chair of the Department of Mathematics and Computer Science. He is a member of ACM, MAA, and Phi Beta Kappa. In addition to teaching, he directs a project to standardize training modules for digital forensics.

Gloria Liddell, attorney-at-law (presently inactive), is an assistant professor of business law at Mississippi State University. Dr. Liddell obtained a Juris doctorate degree from Howard University in Washington, DC. She was admitted to the bars of the District of Columbia and the states of Maryland, Florida, and Mississippi. Her experience includes practicing in the Division of Market Regulation at the headquarters of the Securities and Exchange Commission and the Federal Reserve Board. She has authored several publications on bankruptcy law and received numerous honors and awards from civic, nonprofit, and academic organizations.

Pearson Liddell, Jr., attorney-at-law, is an associate professor of business law at Mississippi State University. He obtained a Juris doctorate degree from Howard University, Washington, DC. He was admitted to the bars of Washington, DC, Maryland, Florida, and Mississippi, as well as admitted to practice before the federal courts, including the United States Supreme Court. Dr. Liddell is a coauthor of the textbook *The Legal Environment of Business*. He has published several articles on such diverse business law topics as taxation, bankruptcy, the Digital Millennium Copyright Act, and legal concepts of Internet marketing.

Chad Lin is a research fellow at Curtin University of Technology. Dr. Lin has conducted extensive research as in the areas of IS and IT investments evaluation and benefits realization, IS and IT outsourcing, electronic commerce, e-health, virtual teams, and strategic alliance. Dr. Lin has published more than 80 refereed journal articles (e.g., in *Information and Management*, *International Journal of Electronic Commerce*, *Information Technology and People*, *Industrial Management and Data Systems*, and *Journal of Research and Practice in IT*) and conference papers as well as book chapters. Dr. Lin has also served as a member of the editorial review boards for several prestigious international journals.

Luis Felipe Luna-Reyes is a professor of business at the Universidad de las Américas in México. He holds a PhD in information science from the University at Albany. Luna-Reyes is also a member of the Mexican National Research System. His research focuses on electronic government and on modeling collaboration processes in the development of information technologies across functional and organizational boundaries.

Xenia J. Mamakou is a PhD candidate in the Department of Business Administration, Athens University of Economics and Business, and her field of study is in the development of methodologies for Web site evaluation. She received an MS in business information technology from UMIST in 2003. She has published articles on privacy and is doing research on e-commerce, online privacy, management information systems, and so forth. She is working at the Business Informatics Laboratory of AUEB teaching lab courses on business informatics, Web design, and design and development of management information systems.

Konstantinos Markellos is an electrical and computer engineer and researcher in the Department of Computer Engineering and Informatics, University of Patras. He obtained a diploma from the Department of Electrical and Computer Engineering (1999) and an MS in hardware and software integrated systems (2003) from the Department of Computer Engineering and Informatics. Today, he is a PhD candidate in the latter department. His research interests lie in the area of Internet technologies and especially e-commerce and e-government, and he has published several research papers in national and international journals and conferences; he is coauthor of one book and three book chapters.

Penelope Markellou is a computer engineer and researcher in the Department of Computer Engineering and Informatics, University of Patras. She obtained a PhD in techniques and systems for knowledge management in the Web (2005) and an MS in usability models for e-commerce systems and applications (2000) from the above university. Her research interests focus on algorithms, and techniques and approaches for the design and development of usable e-applications including e-commerce, e-learning, e-government, and business intelligence. She has published several research papers in national and international journals and conferences and is co-author of two books and eight book chapters.

Paloma Martínez Fernández earned a degree in computer science from Universidad Politécnica of Madrid in 1992. Since 1992, she has been working at the Advanced Databases Group in the Department of Computer Science, Universidad Carlos III of Madrid. In 1998 she obtained a PhD in computer science from Universidad Politécnica of Madrid. She is currently teaching database design and advanced databases in the Department of Computer Science, Universidad Carlos III de Madrid. She has been working in several European and national research projects about natural language processing, information retrieval, advanced database technologies and software engineering.

Dennis McLeod is currently a professor of computer science at the University of Southern California (USC), and director of the Semantic Information Representation Laboratory at USC. He received PhD, MS, and BS degrees in computer science and electrical engineering from MIT. Dr. McLeod has published widely in the areas of data and knowledge base systems, federated databases, database models and design, and ontologies. His current research focuses on dynamic ontologies, user-customized information access, database semantic heterogeneity resolution and interoperation, personalized information management environments via cooperative immersipresence, information management environments for geoscience and homeland security information, crisis management decision support systems, and privacy and trust in information systems.

Kostas Metaxiotis is a lecturer in the National Technical University of Athens and senior advisor to the secretary for the information society in the Greek Ministry of Economy and Finance. He has wide experience in knowledge management, expert systems design and development, artificial intelligence, object-oriented knowledge modeling, inference mechanisms, and e-business. He has published more than 60 scientific papers in various journals, such as *Journal of Knowledge Management*, *Journal of Information and Knowledge Management*, *Knowledge Management & Practice*, *Journal of Intelligent Manufacturing*, *Applied Artificial Intelligence*, *Industrial Management & Data Systems*, *Journal of Computer Information Systems*, and so forth. He is a member of editorial boards of several leading journals in the field and is a member of the program committee at international conferences. Since 1996 he has been participating in various EC-funded projects within Tacis, Phare, MEDA, and IST Programmes as Senior ICT Consultant and Manager.

Mario Mezzanzanica is currently an associate professor with the Faculty of Statistical Science, University of Milano Bicocca. His research and professional interests focus on information technology management. He has been chairman of the scientific committee of CRISP (Interuniversity Research Center on Public Utility Services for the Individual) since July 2005. He has also been a member of the scientific committee of CEFRIEL at the ICT Center of Excellence for Research, Innovation, Education and Industrial Labs since March 2006. His scientific research activities focus on information systems, on which several research activities have been carried out and were published in scientific journals, books, and conference proceedings, both international and national. He was awarded a degree in electronic engineering from the Politecnico di Milano (1985).

Michael Middleton, PhD, is a senior lecturer in the School of Information Systems at Queensland University of Technology. His interests include information management, information use analysis and evaluation, and digital libraries. His publications include the books *Information Management* (published by Charles Sturt University Centre for Information Studies) and *Integrative Document and Content Management*, with Len Asprey (published by Idea Group). Middleton also has extensive experience as a consultant with investigations in information services areas including multicultural affairs, parliamentary services, library portals, and controlled vocabularies.

Melissa Moore (PhD, University of Connecticut) is an associate professor of marketing at Mississippi State University. She received her PhD from the University of Connecticut. Dr. Moore's research interests concentrate on understanding the development and maintenance of customer-firm relationships. Her research has appeared in the *Journal of Internet Law, Journal of Business Research, Transportation Journal, Journal of Consumer Psychology, Marketing Management Journal,* and the *American Journal of Agricultural Economics*, and has been presented at both domestic and international conference venues.

Robert S. Moore (PhD, University of Connecticut) is an associate professor of marketing at Mississippi State University. He has presented at numerous conferences and published his research in various outlets including *Journal of Internet Law, Journal of Advertising, Transportation Journal, Journal of Public Policy and Marketing, Journal of Services Marketing, Journal of End User Computing, Advances in Consumer Research, Marketing Management Journal, Journal for the Advancement of Marketing Education, Albany Law Journal of Science and Technology,* and *Seton Hall Legislative Review.* His research interests center upon consumer behavior in e-commerce settings.

Lourdes Moreno López received an MS in mathematics from Universidad Complutense of Madrid in 1999. She has been working with several IT companies, in R&D departments, working in matters about infometrics (information measurement) especially in Web channels. Since 2002, she has been working at the Advanced Databases Group in the Department of Computer Science, Universidad Carlos III of Madrid. She is a teacher in database design. She's currently developing her doctoral thesis and her research interests include design and accessibility in Web applications.

Krysnaia Nanini was awarded a degree in economics, management, and industrial engineering from the Politecnico di Milano, Milan, Italy, in 2005. She has published several papers in proceedings of international conferences.

Dale K. Nesbary serves as vice president and dean for academic affairs at Adrian College. He also holds an appointment as professor of political science. His past positions include being a member of the Oakland University Faculty, and he held administrative/research positions with the City of Boston, the National Conference of State Legislatures, and the Michigan Senate. His research interests include public-sector technology, state tax policy, and policing. He has published in a wide range of outlets, including *The Journal of Public Affairs Education, The Journal of Contemporary Criminology, Social Science Computer Review, The British Journal of Educational Technology, The International Journal of MS Care,* and *State Legislatures.*

Bruce Neubauer teaches in the public administration program in Government & International Affairs, University of South Florida. His areas include information systems, e-government, e-democracy, and the modeling and simulation of complex systems. His present research projects relate to the local provision of emergency medical services in the instance of a bird flu pandemic or similar event, and knowledge management among members of emergency response teams.

Donald F. Norris is the director of the Maryland Institute for Policy Analysis and Research and professor of public policy at the University of Maryland, Baltimore County. He is a specialist in urban politics, public management, and the application, management, and impacts of information technology, including e-government, in public organizations. Dr. Norris' works have been published in a number of scholarly journals. He holds a BS in history from the University of Memphis and both an MA and PhD in government from the University of Virginia.

Carlos Nunes Silva, PhD, is a professor auxiliar in the Department of Geography, University of Lisbon, Portugal. His research concerns local government, urban planning, e-planning, urban and metropolitan governance, and planning ethics.

Craig Orgeron currently serves as the enterprise architect for the Mississippi Department of Information Technology Services. Since being employed at the Mississippi Department of Information Technology Services, Orgeron has participated in numerous government information technology task forces and committees, such as the Digital Signature Committee, the Electronic Government Task Force, and the Governor's Commission on Digital Government, which led to the implementation of the Enterprise Electronic Government in Mississippi. He holds a BBA degree in MIS and a master's degree in public policy and administration from Mississippi State University. He is a certified public manager and a graduate of the Senator John C. Stennis State Executive Development Institute.

Angeliki Panayiotaki obtained a diploma in computer engineering and informatics from the University of Patras (1996) and an MS in advanced information systems from the University of Athens (2000). She is currently working as a researcher (PhD student) at the Computer Engineering and Informatics Department of the University of Patras and also at the General Secretariat for Information Systems of the Hellenic Ministry of Economy and Finance. Her research interests focus on personalization, Web mining, and interoperability techniques applied in the e-commerce, e-government, and e-health domains. She has published several research papers in international and national conferences.

Haralambos Papageorgiou is a professor of statistics in the Department of Mathematics, University of Athens, and is currently chairman of the Department of Mathematics. He has also served as a professor at the University of Kansas, and as a visiting professor at the Universities of Lille in France, Vienna in Austria, and City University of New York. His main research interests over the last 8 years are in the area of official statistics, in particular, in statistical metadata; statistical harmonization; and quality issues as well as data mining. He has authored more than 50 research articles published in International Statistical Journals and for more than 12 years he has participated in European research projects.

Eleutherios A. Papathanassiou is a professor in MIS and director of the Business Informatics Lab at the Department of Business Administration, Athens University of Economics and Business (AUEB),

Greece. He holds a BS (Hons) in mathematics from the University of Athens and a PhD in computer science from the University of St. Andrews, Scotland. He is scientific advisor to Greek companies and head of the center for distance learning (TeleEducation Centre) of the AUEB. He has published in the areas of IS modeling, e-commerce, and computer science.

Parviz Partow-Navid has been at CSU, LA, since 1983. He earned his MBA and PhD from the University of Texas at Austin. He is currently director of graduate programs for the College of Business. He has published in journals such as the *Computers and Operations Research, Journal of Systems Management, Journal of Information Technology Management*, and *Software Engineering*. Dr. Partow-Navid's interests are in decision support systems, intelligent systems, e-commerce, cybersecurity, and distance learning.

John Paynter was formerly a lecturer at the University of Auckland where he supervised over 30 postgraduate students, including Alex Dunayev. Paynter has also worked in government elections and for the national census. These assignments were to pursue his interest in democracy services and particularly in e-government. He is currently working on contracts to document and improve the processes around local government elections.

Gabrielle Peko is a lecturer in operations management within the Department of Information Systems and Operations Management, University of Auckland. She teaches process modeling, project management, and enterprise systems. Her research focus is on supply chain management and in this instance in the processes around government systems involving supply chains and how they may be mediated electronically.

Emery M. Petchauer is an instructor of education at Lincoln University, Pennsylvania, a historically black university. His research and writing surround hip-hop as an emerging worldview in formal and informal educational settings and its implications on teaching and learning. He is a former high school teacher who has contributed to local communities of hip-hop in San Diego, California and Norfolk, Virginia.

Iolanda Principe is a director with the South Australian Department of Health. She has extensive experience in management and continues to undertake research. Her research interests include social capital and the digital divide, social justice, information and communication technologies, and primary health care.

Imad Rahal is an assistant professor of computer science at the College of Saint Benedict & Saint John's University, Minnesota. He earned PhD and MS degrees in computer science from North Dakota State University (2005 and 2003, respectively). He graduated summa cum laude with a bachelor's degree from the Lebanese American University, Beirut. He was awarded a doctoral dissertation assistantship from the National Science Foundation. His research interests are largely in the broad areas of data mining, machine learning, databases, artificial intelligence, and bioinformatics. He is an active member of the ACM and ISCA professional societies.

Christopher G. Reddick is an assistant professor of public administration at the University of Texas at San Antonio. Dr. Reddick regularly teaches courses in information technology, public administration, and public-sector financial management. Dr. Reddick's research interests are in the tools and techniques that public managers can use to make their organizations efficient and effective. Some of his publications can be found in various public administration and information technology journals such as *Government Information Quarterly, Public Budgeting & Finance,* and the *Review of Public Personnel Administration.*

Jean-Philippe Rennard is a senior professor at Grenoble Graduate School of Business and head of the Department of Management and Technology. He received his PhD from the University Pierre Mendès France of Grenoble. An economist, he is specialized in industrial development. A computer scientist, he is deeply involved in biologically inspired computing. He now mainly works on the applications of biologically inspired computing to economics and management

Anne Rouse is an associate professor of IT and business strategy at the Deakin Business School, Deakin University, Melbourne, Australia. She has been researching outsourcing since 1997, and her doctoral thesis on outsourcing risks and benefits won the 2003 ACPHIS medal for best Australasian PhD thesis in information systems. Dr. Rouse conducted a longitudinal study into the Australian government's "whole of government" IT outsourcing initiative, which had to be abandoned after it became clear that it was not meeting government expectations.

Alfred P. Rovai is a professor of education at Regent University in Virginia and teaches research design, statistics, program evaluation, and assessment of student learning in a mostly online doctor-of-education program. Previously, he taught similar courses at Old Dominion University and instructional technology courses at UCLA in an online teaching program. He has written extensively on distance education and multicultural topics and recently coedited a book titled *Closing the African American Achievement Gap in Higher Education.*

Jeffrey Roy is an associate professor in the School of Public Administration at Dalhousie University in Halifax, Nova Scotia, Canada. He specializes in models of democratic and multistakeholder governance and electronic government reforms. He is also a member of the Organization for Economic Cooperation and Development's E-Government Network, associate editor of the *International Journal of E-Government Research,* featured columnist in *CIO Government Review* (a Canadian publication devoted to the nexus between technology and government), and author of a recent 2006 book *E-Government in Canada: Transformation for the Digital Age* (University of Ottawa Press).

Giovanni Maria Sacco is currently an associate professor of information systems and human-computer interaction with the Department of Informatics, University of Torino, Italy. He is the author of two U.S. patents (one is an international IBM patent), and has held positions in industry for over 25 years as the chief designer and engineer for information retrieval and content management systems. He has published several scientific papers on the most important international journals. In addition to dynamic taxonomies, his work on security with Dorothy Denning is one of the bases of the MIT Kerberos security architecture, and his work at IBM on buffer management and the invention of recursive hash join are fundamental results for high-performance database systems.

Rodrigo Sandoval-Almazán is an assistant professor in the Department of Business and Economics, Instituto Tecnológico de Estudios Superiores de Monterrey (ITESM) in Toluca City and a research fellow at the Center for Development of Information Technologies and Electronics of the ITESM. He has lectured on topics such as information systems for business, information systems strategy for business, political marketing strategy, electronic commerce development, political sciences foundations, the digital divide in emergent countries, policy analysis, organization theory, database applications, statistics, Web development, quantitative analysis and modeling, research methods, public administration theory, and local government management. His research interests include electronic government, information technologies and organizations, digital divide technology, online political marketing, new public management, and multimethod research approaches.

Yuan Sherng Tay received a BEng from the National University of Singapore. He is currently an MEng student at the National University of Singapore.

Giuseppe Sindoni is currently a national seconded export at Eurostat, Statistical Office of the European Commission, where he leads the Statistical Data and Metadata eXchange project. He has been a technologist at the Italian National Statistics Institute and assistant professor at Roma Tre University. He received a PhD in computer system engineering from La Sapienza University of Rome in 1999. He has published numerous research papers, and contributed a chapter to the book *Multidimensional Databases* and two entries to the *Encyclopaedia of Data Warehousing and Data mining*. He has co-authored a book on problem solving in economics with office automation tools.

Ludwig Slusky is a professor of information systems at California State University, Los Angeles. He has published in *Software Engineering, Information and Software Technology, Data Management, Idea Group Publishing*, and others. Dr. Slusky's latest research interests are in information security with emphasis on trustworthy health care networks and in capability maturity model integration (CMMI) with emphasis on software engineering. He is a certified computer information systems security professional (CISSP) and has completed a certified training at Carnegie Mellon Software Engineering Institute in the intermediate concepts of CMMI. His other professional interests are in database administration, systems development, e-commerce, and HIPAA.

Anastasia S. Spiliopoulou is a lawyer, LLM, and member of the Athens Bar Association. During the latest years, she had a major participation in matters related to telecommunications and broadcasting policy in Greece and abroad within the wider framework of the information society. She has been involved in current legal, research, and business activities as a specialist for e-commerce and e-businesses, electronic signatures, e-contracts and e-procurement, e-security and other modern information society applications. She has published more than 70 scientific and business papers in the international literature (books, magazines, conferences, and workshops), with specific emphasis given on regulatory, business, commercial, and social aspects. She has mainly focused her activities on recent aspects of the European regulatory policies and on their implications in the competitive development of the converged telecommunications market. She currently works as an OTE (Hellenic Telecommunications Organization S.A.) lawyer for the Department of Regulatory Issues of the General Directorate for Regulatory Affairs.

Larry Stillman, PhD, is a senior research fellow at the Centre for Community Networking Research, Monash University, Australia. His main interest is working with community-based organisations to better use technology for social and community change, as well as theoretical aspects of human-computer relationships. He is particularly interested in how we know what is valued by communities and people (usually government) who support community initiatives—they are not always the same thing. Other areas of interest include gender, culture, and their relationships with technology use. He is very active in international community informatics research networks.

Randy Stoecker is an associate professor in the Department of Rural Sociology, University of Wisconsin with a joint appointment at the University of Wisconsin – Extension Center for Community and Economic Development. He moderates and edits *COMM-ORG: The On-Line Conference on Community Organizing and Development* (http://comm-org.wisc.edu), conducts trainings, and speaks frequently on community organizing and development, participatory research and evaluation, and community information technology. Stoecker has written extensively on community organizing and development and community-based research, including the books *Defending Community* (Temple University Press, 1994) and *Research Methods for Community Change* (Sage Publications, 2005), and he co-authored the book *Community-Based Research in Higher Education* (Jossey-Bass, 2003).

Leonardo Tininini is currently a researcher at the CNR Institute of Systems Analysis and Computer Science and lecturer at the Campus Bio-medico University in Rome. He received a PhD in computer science engineering from La Sapienza University of Rome in 2000. He has published numerous scientific papers on statistical databases, aggregate data, query languages, and spatiotemporal databases, and has been referee for prestigious international conferences and journals. He also worked at the Italian National Institute of Statistics (ISTAT), mainly on the design and implementation of statistical dissemination systems on the Web.

Athanasios Tsakalidis obtained a diploma in mathematics from the University of Thessaloniki, Greece (1973), and a diploma in computer science (1981) and PhD (1983) from the University of Saarland, Saarbuecken, Germany. His is currently a full professor in the Department of Computer Engineering and Informatics, University of Patras, and R&D coordinator of the Research Academic Computer Technology Institute (RACTI). His research interests include data structures, graph algorithms, computational geometry, expert systems, medical informatics, databases, multimedia, information retrieval, and bioinformatics. He has published several research papers in national and international journals and conferences and is co-author of the *Handbook of Theoretical Computer Science* and other book chapters.

Hui-Lien Tung is an assistant professor of management information systems in the Division of Business at Paine College. Her teaching and research interests include database management, system analysis and design, and Web-based learning systems.

Theodoros Tzouramanis received a 5-year BEng (1996) in electrical and computer engineering and a PhD (2002) in informatics from the Aristotle University of Thessaloniki. Currently, his is lecturer at the Department of Information and Communication Systems Engineering, University of the Aegean. His research interests include access methods and query processing for databases, database security and privacy, and geographical information systems.

Maria Vardaki is the holder of a BS in mathematics, an MS in management, and a PhD in public administration. Her current research interests are in the area of official statistics and data mining and she is author of 20 research papers published in international journals, encyclopedias, and conferences in research areas like statistical metadata, modeling, quality issues and harmonization of time series data. Since 1996 she has participated in various European and national research projects.

Baoying Wang received a PhD in computer science from North Dakota State University. She received a master's degree from Minnesota State University, St. Cloud. She is currently an assistant professor in Waynesburg College, PA. Her research interests include data mining, data warehouse, bioinformatics, and high-performance computing. She serves as a reviewer and committee member of several internal conferences. She is a member of ACM, ISCA, and SIGMOD.

John Wang is a full professor at Montclair State University. Having received a scholarship award, he came to the U.S. and completed his PhD in operations research from Temple University in 1990. He has published over 100 refereed papers and four books. He has also developed several computer software programs based on his research findings. He is the editor of the *Encyclopedia of Data Warehousing and Mining* (1st and 2nd editions). Also, he is the editor in chief of both the *International Journal of Information Systems and Supply Chain Management* and the *International Journal of Information Systems in the Service Sector.*

Chee Wei Phang is currently a doctoral candidate in the Department of Information Systems, School of Computing, National University of Singapore (NUS). His research interests include e-government, e-participation, IT-induced organizational change, and IT innovation adoption. His work has been published or is forthcoming in *IEEE Transactions on Engineering Management, Communications of the ACM, and* top-tier information systems conferences, such as *International Conference on Information Systems* (ICIS), *International Federation for Information Processing* (IFIP) *WG8.2 Conference, European Conference on Information Systems* (ECIS), *Hawaii International Conference on System Sciences* (HICSS), and *Americas Conference on Information Systems* (AMCIS).

Derek Werthmuller has managed the Technology Solutions Laboratory and the Technology Services Unit at the Center for Technology in Government for over 10 years. Prior to joining CTG, Werthmuller spent 6 years at Siena College as a computer and network specialist. His accomplishments at Siena include establishing an Internet presence for the college, expanding the campus network, and designing a multilayer computer and network security system. Werthmuller is the co-author, along with Jim Costello, of the white paper *XML: A New Web Site Architecture* (September 2002), which detailed the CTG's migration to an XML-based Web site.

Anne Wiggins recently completed a PhD in the Department of Information Systems, London School of Economics and Political Science. She also holds an undergraduate degree from the University of Sydney and a master's degree from Birkbeck, University of London. As a consultant in the fields of ICTs and the Internet, she has worked with public and commercial organizations in Australia, the U.S., and the UK. Her research focuses on EU and UK SME (small- to medium-sized enterprise) e-business adoption and implementation.

David C. Wyld is the Robert Maurin professor of management at Southeastern Louisiana University where he directs the College of Business' Strategic e-Commerce/e-Government Initiative. He is a noted RFID speaker, consultant, and writer, being a frequent contributor to both academic and industry publications. He is a contributing editor to both *RFID News* and *Global Identification*. He is also the author of the recent research report *RFID: The Right Frequency for Government*, the most downloaded report in the history of the IBM Center for the Business of Government. In 2006, he was named a Rising Star in Government Information Technology by *Federal Computer Week*.

Feng Xu received a BS in electronic engineering from Lanzhou University. She is currently a PhD candidate in the Department of Electronic Engineering at Tsinghua University. In 2005, she worked as an intern in Microsoft Research Asia for more than 3 months. Her research interests include content-based image retrieval, automatic image annotation, and machine learning.

Yu-Jin Zhang (PhD, State University of Liège, Belgium) has been professor of image engineering at Tsinghua University, Beijing, China, since 1997. He has published 300 research papers and a dozen of books, including two monographs, *Image Segmentation* and *Content-Based Visual Information Retrieval* (Science Press), and two edited collections, *Advances in Image and Video Segmentation* and *Semantic-Based Visual Information Retrieval* (IRM Press). He is vice president of the China Society of Image and Graphics and the director of the academic committee of the society. He is deputy editor-in -chief of *Journal of Image and Graphics* and on the editorial board of several scientific journals.

Dan Zhu is an associate professor at the Iowa State University. She obtained a PhD from Carnegie Mellon University. Dr. Zhu's research has been published in the *Proceedings of National Academy of Sciences*, *Information System Research*, *Naval Research Logistics*, *Annals of Statistics*, *Annals of Operations Research*, and so forth. Her current research focuses on developing and applying intelligent and learning technologies to business and management.

Index

E

F

G